POLITICAL ISLAM IN SOUTHEAST ASIA

Political Islam in Southeast Asia

Gordon P. Means

Viva Books

New Delhi | Mumbai | Chennai | Kolkata | Bangalore | Hyderabad | Kochi | Guwahati

First Indian Edition 2011

VIVA BOOKS PRIVATE LIMITED

- 4737/23 Ansari Road, Daryaganj, New Delhi 110 002
  E-mail: vivadelhi@vivagroupindia.net, Tel. 42242200
- 76, Service Industries, Shirvane, Sector 1, Nerul, Navi Mumbai 400 706
  E-mail: vivamumbai@vivagroupindia.net, Tel. 27721273, 27721274
- Jamals Fazal Chambers, 26 Greams Road, Chennai 600 006
  E-mail: vivachennai@vivagroupindia.net, Tel. 28290304, 28294241
- B-103, Jindal Towers, 21/1A/3 Darga Road, Kolkata 700 017
  E-mail: vivakolkata@vivagroupindia.net, Tel. 22836381, 22816713
- 7, Sovereign Park Apartments, 56-58, K. R. Road, Basavanagudi, Bengaluru 560 004
  E-mail: vivabangalore@vivagroupindia.net, Tel. 26607409, 26607410
- 101-102 Mughal Marc Apartments, 3-4-637 to 641, Narayanguda, Hyderabad 500 029
  E-mail: vivahyderabad@vivagroupindia.net, Tel. 27564481, 27564482
- Beevi Towers, First Floor, SRM Road, Kaloor, Kochi 682 018, Kerala
  E-mail: vivakochi@vivagroupindia.net, Tel: 0484-2403055, 2403056
- 232, GNB Road, Beside UCO Bank, Silpukhuri, Guwahati 781 003
  E-mail: vivaguwahati@vivagroupindia.net, Tel: 0361-2666386

www.vivagroupindia.com

Published by arrangement with

Lynne Rienner Publishers, Inc.
1800 30th Street, Suite 314
Boulder, Colorado 80301
USA

ISBN : 978-81-309-1533-3

Published by Vinod Vasishtha for Viva Books Private Limited, 4737/23, Ansari Road, Daryaganj, New Delhi - 110 002. Printed and bound by Raj Press, R-3, Inderpuri, New Delhi - 110 012.

S0000 / S0810 / S0630

Contents

Part 2 The Struggles of Decolonization

Part 3 Islamic Resurgence

Part 5 Facing Hard Choices

Preface

Research for this study began before I was aware of the topic of political Islam. As a young graduate student in 1954 I visited Singapore and Malaya on a Ford Foundation Research Grant to study the politics of decolonization. In this period before the first elections, political parties were just being founded and aspiring leaders were cultivating their political constituencies. To get a feel for local politics, I attended Legislative Council sessions and quickly discovered that political leaders welcomed interviews and were generous with invitations to attend their political meetings. One of the first invitations came from Dato Onn bin Ja'afar, the founding president of the United Malays National Organization (UMNO). Over the next several months, I accompanied Dato Onn to various political meetings in southern Johor to hear his views of politics and to see him in action with constituents in Malay villages.

I soon learned that much of the political action was centered in Malaya's capital at Kuala Lumpur. On the advice of some UMNO members, I booked a room at the Government Rest House, across the street from the Selangor Cricket Club. Shortly after my arrival, I learned that Tunku Abdul Rahman was a regular guest in a room two doors down the hall from mine. At dinnertime, he usually had political aides at his table, and he often came into the lounge after dinner for coffee and welcomed an opportunity to talk politics. Invitations to attend political meetings began to fill my calendar. At the time, I had no idea that Tunku would become Malaya's first prime minister.

From these activities, it did not take long for me to notice that Malay political leaders could discuss and analyze political issues with a "rational calculus" perspective, but when they campaigned for support from constituents, communication shifted into a distinctively Islamic idiom. For Malay villagers, Islam epitomized their way of life and their identity. Leaders recognized that support from their constituents depended on their roles as leaders of the community of Muslims—the *umma.* These were my first encounters with "political Islam."

I returned to Malaya in 1962 funded by the US government as a Smith-Mundt Visiting Professor at the University of Malaya. I was expected to assist in the development of public policy studies and was appointed to the University Senate. At this time the Federation of Malaya was in the process of evaluating political options for the formation of the larger Federation of Malaysia. It was also a time when generous scholarships had dramatically increased the numbers of Malay students from rural areas enrolled at the university. Many changes had to be made by the university to accommodate their presence, their social practices, and their previous educational background. With increasing numbers, these students became politically active, demanding greater use of the Malay language and courses specially tailored for their needs. Malay students were mobilized and represented by the National Muslim Students Association, led by Anwar Ibrahim.[1] The actions of Malay university students became ever more politically charged, inspired by the *dakwah* movement dedicated to forging a resurgent Islamic political order. The University Senate became a focus of their proposals and demands, and I began to realize that "political Islam" was becoming the politics of the future.

Over the years, on numerous trips to Southeast Asia, I expanded my research interests to include political and policy implications of Islam in Indonesia, Thailand, and the Philippines. In 1974–1975, I headed a nine-person team that conducted survey research examining individual sociocultural beliefs and behavior at twenty-one rural villages and urban fringe settlements in Indonesia.[2] While that study did not focus exclusively on religious beliefs, some data were collected to identify the impact of religion on individual behavior and social change. From that experience, I gained a much more comprehensive appreciation of the impact of religion on individual behavior patterns, especially relating to the role of Islam in defining individual Muslim responses to issues of public policy. It became apparent that political Islam was a more formidable force at the grassroots level than had been assumed by most political commentators and policy analysts at that time.

From this experience with random sample survey research, it became clear that village beliefs are not monolithic and that Islam at the village level involves power, hierarchy, and a system of rewards and penalties. The village imam who leads the prayers and gives the sermon at the local mosque is the only local leader who has a regular, continuing, captive audience for his political views and his interpretations of Islam. An imam at a rural mosque will usually assume that his role is to admonish and instruct the faithful concerning their obligations to Islam. Part of his responsibility is to uphold morality by defining "virtue and vice" and by sanctioning community punishments for those who violate the prescriptions of Islam. Argument and debate over issues of morality, politics, or religion by ordinary villagers will not be sanctioned, even when factional differences at the village level become severe. Village politics may seem unified, but can be as conflictual and as convoluted as national politics.

When terrorists attacked the World Trade Center in New York and the Pentagon in Washington, DC, I was as shocked as most Americans. I knew that Islam had acquired greater militancy worldwide, and grievances against the West had escalated in recent years. But because Southeast Asian Islam is usually identified as being "moderate," it was even more shocking to learn that plans for the 9/11 attacks were approved at a conference of clandestine militant Islamic groups meeting in Malaysia. Because of my experiences working in Southeast Asia, I knew that issues of Islamic militancy were far more complicated than had been depicted in media reports—while the attackers, to justify their actions, had appropriated the symbols and ideology of Islam, that religious tradition should not be made into the "cause" for those attacks. I also realized that the 9/11 attacks would have a profound impact on the politics of Islam in Southeast Asia. From this assessment, I determined to engage in research to produce this book.

Fortunately for me, a number of former graduate students who studied under my direction had become leading scholars at research institutes in Southeast Asia. After making inquiries to colleagues from previous research projects, offers of support arrived from Southeast Asia. Over a period of three years, I became a visiting senior scholar, first at the Institute of Public Policy and Strategic Studies at the National University of Malaysia and, later, at the Institute of Defense and Strategic Studies at Nanyang Technological University in Singapore, where I was provided an office and a congenial work environment. My most recent affiliation was with the Institute of Southeast Asian Studies in Singapore, where a number of years earlier I had engaged in year-long research projects. In addition to the research facilities in Singapore and Malaysia, the Asian research collections at the University of Minnesota and the Southeast Asian Library Collection at Northern Illinois University have proven to be invaluable sources for this study.

—Gordon P. Means

Notes

1. The Malay name was Persatuan Kebangsaan Pelajar Islam Malaysia (PKPIM).
2. Gordon P. Means, "Exploring Individual Modernity in Sumatra," *Sojourn* 4, no. 2 (August 1989), 157–189.

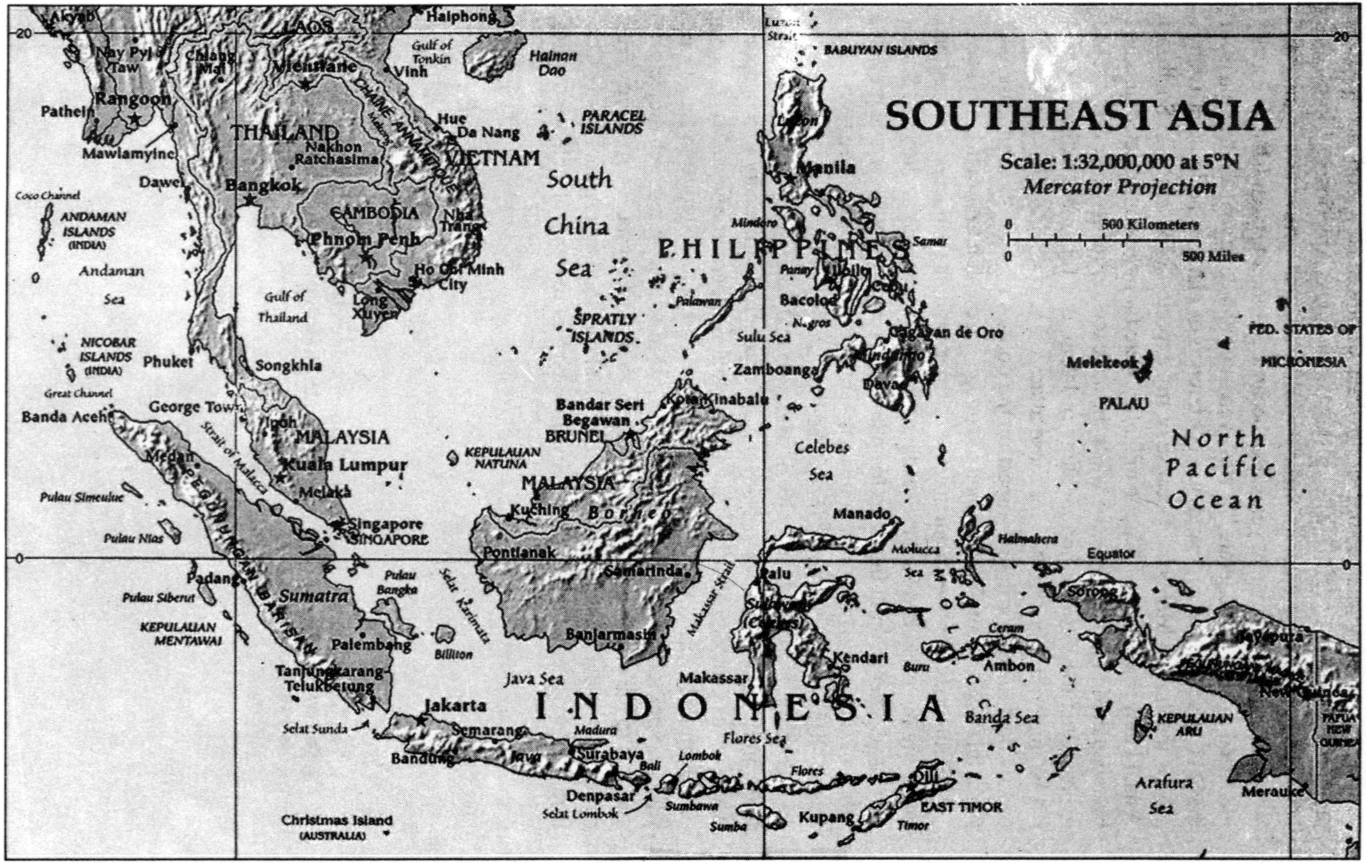

Map courtesy of University of Texas Libraries

1

Introduction

To understand the political ideology of contemporary Islamic polemics, it is essential for non-Muslim readers to learn about the origins and basic doctrines of Islam. This study begins by examining the historical accounts from an Islamic perspective of how the Prophet Muhammad received "revealed truth" directly from God, and how Muhammad forged the first community of believers. For orthodox Muslims, Islam's founding community is considered to be the ideal standard for emulation by subsequent generations of believers. The core doctrines of the faith assert that Islam is eternal, absolute, and immutable. Its principles are derived from God's commandments that define the ultimate rules of life for individual believers and for the proper organization of society and its political order. That "revealed truth" is preserved for eternity in its holy book, the Quran, while the laws, practices, and precedents of the first community have also been preserved in oral and recorded history, as the Hadith. Islam is not only a religion of the law, it is a religion that celebrates and idealizes its origins as a utopia that, for orthodox Muslims, becomes the basis for Islamic society and governance. For Islam, revelation, law, and history are fused into a comprehensive system of beliefs and commandments that define a moral and ethical political order.

Islam is a religion. It is also a political, social, cultural, and ideological force that commands the loyalty and defines the identity of over one billion people. The combination of all these elements is infused with a sacral meaning that intensifies Islam's impact and inhibits both analysis and public discussion of its content and its role. While Islam's theological doctrines assert its absolute and unchanging Truth, its believers must make that Truth meaningful and adapt their faith to the changing circumstances of their daily lives. While Islam's theological doctrines may claim absolute and eternal Truth, the practice of religion is a collaborative human endeavor—the ultimate form of the collective creation of a culture and of a civilization based on inspiration from religious ideals.

Southeast Asia is a uniquely important region for the study of the political culture of Islam. It is a region that includes a state with the largest population of Muslims in the world. It is a region having great cultural and ethnic diversity that gave to Islam adaptive mechanisms to incorporate that diversity within Muslim society. Southeast Asia is on the farthest perimeter of the Muslim world, where Islam evolved with different processes than happened at the Arab center of Islam. Even before the era of European colonialism, Arab traders developed commercial links with Southeast Asian producers to sustain the Arab economy by supplying Southeast Asian spices and Asian luxury goods to European markets. Because of these and many other factors, Southeast Asian Islam developed a relatively more cosmopolitan perspective than many other regions of the Muslim world.

After presenting an account of Islam's origins and core doctrines, this study examines the process by which Islam spread to Southeast Asia. Readers may be surprised to learn how quickly Islam spread across the southern regions of Southeast Asia and how much Islam became part of a way of life for the new converts. The account will reveal how and why local monarchs became among some of the first converts, and their subjects tended to accept Islam later from royal example and sponsorship. The Islamic principles of power derived from Allah were readily combined with the preexisting Hindu and Buddhist doctrines and rituals of divine kingship. Therefore, at the apex of the political order, Islam was a conservative and stabilizing set of principles for the existing power holders. At the peasant village level, Islam provided a link with royal authority and it also provided a basis for the ordering of peasant life and activities. At that level, Islam was combined with existing animist rites and social relations. Again, Islam was conservative and adaptable to the cycle of life events and the ideological perspectives of a localized peasant community.

In practice, as Islam gained converts, the newer converts to Islam did not always accept what had been previously deemed to be eternal, immutable, and absolute. And, if they did, the new converts created diversity through varying interpretations of the "revealed truth," and through the surviving practices of preexisting cultures and institutions. When Islam spread from its Arabic origins to new regions and to civilizations having different cultural, economic, and political systems, Islam became somewhat modified. This study explores the questions of how Islam evolved in the Southeast Asian setting to produce a pragmatic symbiosis between the stark ideals of Islam's religious doctrines and the rich cultural traditions of earlier religious beliefs and cultural practices. That adaptive process has continued throughout the history of Southeast Asian Islam and will very likely continue into the indefinite future, with increasing complexity and diversity. That process has also created fundamental divisions within Islam over theological doctrines, law, politics, and legitimacy.

For Southeast Asia, after the arrival of European explorers, European trading bases and then colonies began to be established. That colonial era lasted for almost five centuries. The Muslim regions of Southeast Asia came under the control of five different colonial powers—Portugal, Spain, the Netherlands, Great Britain, and the United States. Each colonial power devised separate policies and strategies to limit, control, or manage Islamic affairs. These colonial policies not only increased the diversity within Islam, but also generated grievances within Muslim communities that provided the motivation and popular support for some Islamic-based radical movements dedicated to challenging colonial rule. Although colonial authorities had sufficient power and resources to suppress these self-generating insurgent movements, the legacy of a radical, autonomous warrior-hero tradition became well-entrenched in popular epic accounts of Islamic history. When combined with Islamic doctrines of "jihad against the enemies of Islam," these warrior traditions could be easily revived in the postcolonial era, when ethnic or religious conflicts became severe.

The colonial era was a period of steady and dramatic changes. All colonial powers tolerated or promoted large-scale immigration from other regions of Asia. Immigrants from China and India came to the region in vast numbers, bringing with them their own religious traditions, social organizations, and economic skills and preferences. And finally, European colonial officials and military officers, combined with European planters, traders, professionals, and missionaries, constituted a dominant European strata that sustained the colonial system.

As will be demonstrated in subsequent chapters, each colonial power devised unique policies and strategies for its relations with Muslim communities. In the chapter covering the colonial era, the study focuses on the impact of colonial policies toward Islam to explore how those policies shaped Islamic politics in the postcolonial era. After centuries of colonial rule, the politics of Islam created distinctive institutions and a long legacy of grievances that Muslims expected to be addressed when colonial rule ended. The legacy of past colonial policies continues to define many of the key issues for Islamic politics in the region. In each state, the issues generally revolve around specific policies, but patterns of conflict can become quite similar.

The colonial era was a time when colonial officialdom ruled with authoritarian powers, even when colonial authorities consulted with advisory councils and were solicitous of the views of native rulers. When decolonization finally arrived, nationalist leaders inherited the existing practices and institutions of colonial authoritarianism, along with the central legislative institutions of democracy that were rapidly established by colonial authorities just before the transfer of power to independent national states. The postcolonial era in Southeast Asia began with an extended contest between democracy and authoritarianism. The debate over these issues continued to surface within most political factions and ideological divisions. Why that contest between democracy and authoritarian rule has never been fully resolved will be explored later in this volume.

After the former colonies gained their independence, the primary political divisions tended to pit the ideologies of secular nationalism against the more radical and revolutionary ideology of communism, with Islamic-based parties forming a less formidable third faction. After communism was defeated as an ideological force in the 1960s and 1970s, what had been a three-way ideological split in the arenas of politics among nationalism, communism, and political Islam now devolved into a two-way contest between secular nationalism and political Islam. As that contest became manifest, incumbent nationalist leaders, to gain legitimacy for their rule and support from Muslim constituents, became more pious and attempted to exercise greater control over Islamic institutions. This work will explore the questions of how and why governments became preoccupied with devising new policies and strategies to support and manage the institutions of Islam. Incumbent leaders also learned that measures to promote and control Islam by defining orthodoxy and limiting "deviant sects" produced results that intensified political conflicts. The exercise of government authority over Islam gave leaders more power and political support, but these policies also exposed leaders to intense criticism and accusations of abuse of power and raised issues of the denial of human rights. Most leaders realized that sacralized politics in a multicultural and multireligious setting could become an explosive mix that might degenerate into communal conflict.

The roles and significance of Islamic politics changed rather dramatically when Islamic resurgent movements, known as *dakwah,* became active during the late 1970s and early 1980s. This was a period when Malaysia, Indonesia, the Philippines, and Thailand all had strong semi-authoritarian leaders. Each of these leaders made concessions to the rising tide of Islamic protests and demands for increased representation of Islamic interests. This was a confusing period of turmoil during which Islamic-based parties became more active and militant. In response, incumbent leaders devised various policies and strategies to deflect, defeat, or co-opt the leadership of Islamic-based parties and radicalized Muslim youth mobilized by the dakwah movement. A major proportion of this study is devoted to accounts of various Islamic groups and sects that became part of the dakwah movement. Some of these groups were defeated and suppressed through government action. Other groups remained active in politics and by forming paramilitary forces that made their political impact through vigilante violence. Some dakwah supporters were co-opted into government and made their impact through their roles in administration and the policymaking processes of government. These case-study accounts trace the motives, activities, and consequences of each political group dedicated to implementing their version of an Islamic political agenda.

One section of this study is devoted to the massive campaign mounted by Saudi Arabia to propagate and promote the religious and doctrinal principles of Sunni Islam as practiced in Arabia. With billions of dollars of oil money, Saudi Arabia funded Islamic schools and universities and sponsored major programs of religious conversion to make new converts among Southeast Asian Muslims for a conservative and orthodox Arabic form of Islam. But what was conservative for Saudi Arabia became a radical message for Southeast Asian's moderate and eclectic Muslim communities. Segments of this study explore how the politics of the Middle East impacted the politics of Southeast Asia's Muslim communities. When the Soviet Union invaded Afghanistan, Saudi Arabia and the United States joined together to sponsor the anti-Soviet Afghan mujahideen, composed of volunteers recruited from across the Muslim world. Saudi money, combined with US money and weapons, armed these volunteers, who were trained and indoctrinated by Osama bin Laden and his associates. This segment of the work explains how Al Qaeda was formed, how its ideology developed, and how a much more radical and militant form of Islam emerged in the aftermath of the Afghan war.

The next significant cycle of politics in Southeast Asia was triggered by the Asian financial crisis that began in 1988 and continued for a period of about five years. During that cycle, the quasi-dictatorship of Suharto in Indonesia collapsed. The semi-authoritarian leadership of Malaysia ended with the resignation of Mahathir, and all the countries in Southeast Asia struggled to recover from the economic disaster created by inappropriate management of their economies. During the period of greatest distress caused by the financial crisis, a nearly spontaneous movement arose in both Indonesia and Malaysia that adopted the slogan Reformasi. Mobilized for mass public protests, this movement demanded democratic reforms. In Indonesia, those demands eventually resulted in constitutional changes that established for the first time genuine elections and effective limitations on unbridled executive power. In Malaysia, this movement elicited promises of democratic reforms that proved to be much less significant.

This period of recovery from the Asian financial crisis was also a time when those Southeast Asian Muslims who had volunteered for the Afghan mujahideen returned home with military training and heightened indoctrination to utilize jihadi tactics to "protect Islam" against real and imagined enemies. It was during this period that radical Islamist conspirators met secretly in Malaysia to plan the terrorist attacks in Aden and the 9/11 attacks in the United States. It was also a period when deadly terrorist bombings took place in Indonesia and the Philippines, and national police throughout the region uncovered the existence of various terrorist networks. With Al Qaeda becoming an active participant in the region, the politics of Islam in Southeast Asia had become much more volatile and threatening, producing a loss of foreign investment and a decrease in foreign tourism. Those events of conflict and militancy are too complicated to summarize here, but will be described in significant detail in later chapters.

The final era covered by this study (approximately 2005 to 2008) is a period when more pragmatic leaders acquired the reins of power in Indonesia,

Malaysia, the Philippines, and Thailand. Some of the most difficult policy issues remain to be resolved. These leaders are confronting the issues of Islamic militancy while also meeting demands and expectations for greater democracy. Many of the most critical issues can be posed as questions. The study identifies some of the most difficult and sensitive issues of politics, and raises the questions of how and when they may be resolved.

Will Islamic-based parties participate freely and openly in secular democratic institutions? Can human rights and individual freedoms coexist harmoniously with political Islam? Will the Islamic separatist movements in the southern Philippines and in southern Thailand be resolved through peace negotiations? Will globalization provide sufficient economic incentives for Muslim leaders to support reforms granting greater equality and tolerance for non-Muslim minorities? Will Islam as a political force become more pluralized and more willing to accept doctrinal diversity within its own ranks, including individual freedoms for nonconformist Muslims? Will democratic processes generate leaders committed to the politics of tolerance and pragmatic accommodations for cultural and religious diversity?

This study will not answer all these questions conclusively. The book will meet its purpose if it promotes an understanding of the complexities of the region and leads to open and civil dialogue concerning critical public policy issues. The work is based on an implicit faith that, over a longer time span, democracy, human rights, tolerance, and mutual respect across cultural and religious divides will gradually become established as the accepted consensus within the region. The future rests not with prediction but with the actions and commitments of Southeast Asian leaders and their constituent citizens. Even so, countries beyond the region, combined with international aid and humanitarian nongovernmental agencies, can accelerate and assist that process. When expatriate staff, visiting professionals, and casual visitors gain an empathetic understanding of the complexities of the cultural, religious, and political environments within the region, that partnership will become much more productive.

PART 1

The Early Years

2

Islamic Origins and Southeast Asian Adaptations

Islam, as a religious belief system, has a set of basic affirmations and principles that inherently define the relationship between an ideal Islamic political order and the community of believers, as well as defining the rights and obligations for resident nonbelievers. For pious and orthodox Muslims, these core characteristics of Islam provide an ideological framework for their political actions and their views of politics. To assess the appeal and ideology of politicized Islam that shapes the dilemmas facing Southeast Asia's current leaders, it is essential that we begin with a brief review of key characteristics and basic doctrines of Islam.

The Revelation

The beginning of Islam can be dated from 610 A.D. when Muhammad experienced the first of a series of revelations that later became the basis for the Quran, the holy scriptures of Islam. The divine revelations to Muhammad continued over a period of twenty-two years and were reported as coming directly from the Angel Gabriel, acting as the heavenly intermediary from God.[1] Muhammad was employed in Mecca to manage a trading enterprise owned by a widow named Khadija, whom he later married, and she became his first convert. Over the next twelve years, Muhammad gathered the support of a few converts, but also encountered opposition from the leaders of the powerful Quraysh clans of Mecca. Muhammad's doctrine of strict monotheism posed a threat to the local economy, because Mecca was a pilgrimage site for Arabs who worshiped a multitude of animist pagan deities. These pilgrims were attracted to a black meteorite stone known as the Kaabah.

Muhammad denounced the validity of animist deities, thereby challenging the activities of those who operated the pilgrimage business. Over time, the economically dominant Quraysh clans became overtly hostile to Muhammad and his small band of converts. To escape persecution in Mecca, Muhammad secured a promise of protection from the Arab leaders of Yathrib, a town now called Medina and located about 200 miles to the north of Mecca. On the night of July 16, 622, the small band of converts to Islam fled to Yathrib. Their migration from Mecca to Yathrib is known as Hijrah. The Muslim calendar marks that date as A.H. 1, identifying that event as the beginning of a new era with the formation of the first viable Muslim community of believers.[2]

In the new environment, the power and the religion of the refugees from Mecca began to flourish. Yathrib had been plagued by bitter feuds, and Muhammad used his political skills to resolve these disputes and consolidate his political power. Under his leadership, most of Yathrib's residents converted to Islam and accepted Muhammad's leadership. A few Arabs had previously converted to Judaism and remained as a significant minority. For them, Muhammad negotiated a charter that became known as the "Constitution of Medina" or Muhammad's "Charter." In that document, the rights and duties of all residents were defined and non-Muslims were granted protection and cultural autonomy so long as they preserved the unity of the community and acknowledged the primacy of Muhammad's political and military authority as the "Apostle of Allah." To assert the new basis of that authority, the city of Yathrib was renamed Medina (Medinat Rasul-Allah—the city of the Apostle of God).[3] Over the next five years, Muhammad worked to unify the clans of Medina and, with his expanded support base, he developed a formidable military force to wage a war of attrition against his critics and opponents in Mecca. By a combination of religious fervor, courage, stealth, and military prowess, Muhammad led his forces to victory over Mecca in 629, only seven years after he and his followers had fled from that city.

After the defeat of Mecca, the leader of Mecca's Quraysh clans, Abu Sufyan, surrendered and paid homage to Muhammad. In return Muhammad granted amnesty and gifts to Sufyan's followers, who also submitted to the authority of Muhammad and accepted the doctrines of Islam. Muhammad demanded the destruction of all idols and he restored the practice of pilgrimages to the Kaabah, with the proviso that, after four months, pagans and non-Muslims would no longer be allowed to visit the Kaabah for worship of pagan gods. By this move, he placated the concerns of his critics and incorporated an established religious practice of Arab animism into the structure of Islam, making the pilgrimage to Mecca a compulsory obligation for all Muslims at least once in a lifetime.[4]

From his new power base in Mecca, Muhammad began the process of expanding to other regions and gaining converts to the new religious doctrines he proclaimed. The period of Muhammad's rule of the first community of Muslim believers lasted for only one decade and ended with Muhammad's death from fever in 632 A.D.[5] Over subsequent centuries, many orthodox Muslims developed the doctrine that this ten-year period of rule by Muhammad established the ideal utopian political and social order ordained by Allah. What may seem to be ancient history has been viewed by some Muslims as the blueprint for the future.

From this early beginning, Muhammad's prophetic message and his leadership example established a number of principles that became enshrined as precedents for political authority in Islam. These included the idea that the community of Islam extends beyond tribe and ethnicity to include all those who willingly submit to the absolute and all-embracing law of God. Full citizenship in that community is based on each individual believer affirming Islam's core doctrines and membership within the community of Islam—the *umma.* Islam is viewed as a total system of life that fuses religion and political power. In combination, these principles convey to those in the political order a responsibility to enforce the religious obligations of Islam for professing Muslims and to incorporate Islamic ideals and values into public policy. These principles also provide the justification for different rules and a lesser legal status for resident non-Muslims, known as *dhimmi.*

The fusion of religious and political power in the ideal Muslim state means that there are compelling incentives for politicians to become preachers and for preachers to aspire to become politicians. For Islam, political rulers are impelled by the structure of the political order to demonstrate their piety as a visible component of their claim to legitimacy. To have a secular state, with politics divorced from religious authority, is deemed by Muslim conservatives to be a system that sanctions gross dereliction of duty by leaders who, by their acts of noncommitment, effectively reject or ignore Allah's laws of divine governance.

The Succession

At the time of Muhammad's death in 632 A.D., the Islamic community was overwhelmed by grief and anxiety over the future. The Quran provided no guidance on the selection of a ruler, and Muhammad had left no will, had no male offspring, and had not selected a successor. A small group of Muhammad's closest advisers agreed that Abu Bakr should lead the expanding community of Islam. Abu Bakr was Muhammad's father-in-law, his closest friend, and one of the earliest converts to Islam. Abu Bakr assumed the title Khalifa Rasul Allah (Successor of the Messenger of God) and reaffirmed the principles that political and religious leadership would be fused and would be based on Allah's word as revealed in the Quran and by Muhammad's example.[6] The precedent set by Abu Bakr's selection would prove troublesome. Neither principle nor process was clearly established for the selection of future leaders for the community of Islam.

As Islam expanded, the basis for its power also shifted. The first four caliphs after Muhammad—Abu Bakr, Umar, Uthman, and Ali—had direct links to Muhammad by family ties and had both administrative and military experience. Although the Quran commands Muslims to have unity with one another and not to engage in war or conflict with fellow Muslims, even during Muhammad's rule, political divisions were apparent. They became more endemic with time. The rapid expansion of the Islamic Empire created factional cleavages based on clan, region, and patronage linkages. The second caliph, Umar (634–644), favored the "Companions of the Prophet"—the *ansor* who had followed Muhammad to Medina. The third caliph, Uthman (644–656), favored the Quraysh aristocracy of Mecca and newer converts to Islam, including the powerful clan leaders of the pre-Islamic era. Eventually, these factional rivalries became more severe and developed into Islam's first civil war. This Arab civil war split the Muslim world between the Sunni Muslims and the Shia Muslims, a division within Islam that continues to the present day.[7]

The defeated party, identified as Shia, asserted that Ali had been entitled to become caliph at Muhammad's death, but Ali's rightful authority had been usurped by Abu Bakr, Umar, and Uthman. From the perspective of Shia Islam, the latter three caliphs were all illegitimate successors to the Prophet Muhammad. Espousing divergent interests and reflecting the perspectives of the newer converts to Islam from Persia (Iran) and other non-Arab converts to Islam from Zoroastrianism and other eastern religions, Shia Muslims established different doctrines for interpreting the Quran and developed a unique system of political authority under imams rather than caliphs.[8] Although Shia Muslims constitute about 15 percent of Muslims worldwide, they are virtually unrepresented in the populations of Southeast Asia. For this study, concentrated on Islam in Southeast Asia, we will not attempt to summarize the doctrines and political manifestations of Shia Islam.

By the time of Muhammad's death, the entire Arabian Peninsula had already come under Islamic rule. Twenty-nine years later, Islamic rule had been extended to Persia and parts of Afghanistan in the east, to the Tigris-Euphrates valley, to the lower Caucasus and eastern Turkey to the north, to Syria, Lebanon, and Palestine along the Eastern Mediterranean shores, and to Egypt, Libya, and Tripoli in the west. By 759, Arabs completed the conquest of most of Spain and Portugal. By 998, a series of invasions by Muslim armies mounted from Afghanistan began three centuries of Muslim rule over northern sections of the Indian subcontinent. These early Turkish dynasties ruling from Delhi and Agra were replaced in 1398 by Islamic-based Mogul dynasties that continued to rule the northern and eastern provinces of India until the advent of British rule in the nineteenth century.[9]

We need not review the tangled web of Islamic politics involving the multiple dynasties and empires that established Muslim rule over vast regions of Central Asia, South Asia, the Middle East, North Africa, the Balkans, the Iberian Peninsula of Spain and Portugal, and the Indian subcontinent. By these Islamic conquests and expansion to new regions of the world, Islam was becoming much more diversified, more cosmopolitan, and more pragmatic in the institutions formed to rule large empires having great wealth and with increased cultural diversity. Not only were Islamic political systems changing, but also their character and the qualities of Islamic political leadership. Over time, new elites gained greater administrative and technical skills and acquired more diverse cosmopolitan perspectives to provide dynamic leadership for complex emerging empires. In this medieval period, political leadership depended in part on recasting Muslim law to address changing realities.

Islamic Law

Despite the increasing political differences and the cultural diversity found within the expanded borders of Islam, there remained a commonality based on Islamic law. These features of Islamic law created patterns of uniformity across the great diversity of peoples and cultures that became part of the Muslim world. As a practical matter, the Quran proved to be an incomplete and enigmatic source for a legal, social, and economic system. The Quran reads more like poetry than law, and in content it tends to take the form of a sermon with powerful and repeated arguments to reinforce persuasion, but often without legal precision. Not all parts of the Quran appear to be entirely consistent. To complicate matters further, some verses of the Quran abrogated or modified earlier verses, and when the Quran was compiled after the Prophet's death, both "abrogating" and "abrogated" verses were included in the final text.[10]

The most important supplement to the text of the Quran is the Hadith—the reports of the Prophet's actions, decisions, and course of conduct as a spiritual and political leader of the umma. The practice and actions of Muhammad are known as Sunna, literally "the trodden path," which is considered authoritative rules for Muslim societies. The Hadith is based primarily on the accumulated orally transmitted accounts of Muhammad's actions and sayings during his rule. Because of different "transmitters" of oral traditions, disputes over authenticity resulted in divergent versions of Islamic doctrine and law. Gradually, four main schools of jurisprudence, based on the works of different juridical scholars, were accepted as "accredited" by Sunni Muslims. These four legal "schools," known as *madhhabs*, stress somewhat contradictory "traditions" and each became adopted as authoritative in different parts of the Muslim world.[11]

The Hanafite school follows the commentaries of Abu Hanifa, who lived in Kufah and Baghdad, and sanctions the use of analogy, consensus, and rational opinions. This school gained acceptance in the Ottoman Empire, parts of India, and throughout Central Asia. The Malakite school follows the commentaries of Malik ibn Anas. He lived in Medina and emphasized the traditions of Medina while rejecting "private opinion" and the use of analogy. The

Malakite school prevails in eastern Arabia, upper Egypt, and North Africa and was adopted during Muslim rule in Spain. The Shafi'i school follows the interpretations of al-Shafi'i, who taught in Baghdad and Cairo. He utilized the doctrine of community consensus and thus enhanced the roles of consultation and legislative authority derived from Islamic representational institutions. The Shafi'i school prevails for Sharia law in Palestine, lower Egypt, parts of eastern and western Africa, parts of India, as well as most of Southeast Asia.

The Hanbalite school is the smallest and most orthodox legal school, following the precepts of Ahmad ibn Hanbal, who lived in Baghdad. He rejected "private opinions," analogy, and consensus as a basis for the elaboration of "God's will." The Hanbalite doctrines were nearly extinguished by opposition of the Ottoman Empire, but the Wahhabi movement in the eighteenth century revived this legal system. When the Saudi tribe began the conquest of most of Arabia, they did so in league with the Wahhabis, and Hanbalite doctrines were adopted by Saudi Arabia as the basis for its theological doctrines and Sharia law.[12] For the past half century, Saudi Arabia has promoted the Wahhabi/Hanbalite version of Sharia law as part of its worldwide campaign to convert Muslims to its more rigid and stark version of Islam.

Because Islamic law is supposed to be derived directly from Allah, there was an assumption that it should be fixed and eternal. Yet, over time, with the emergence of different juridical schools, greater diversity of interpretations had become apparent. This diversity was attributed to independent interpretation or juristic reasoning—*ijtihad*. In the tenth century, a majority of Muslim jurists, but not all, came to a general consensus that the Sharia had become fully delineated and that therefore ijtihad was neither necessary nor appropriate and would no longer be accepted. This principle made Islamic law much more rigid, relying on strict and literal interpretations of the Quran and previous interpretations of law and doctrine.[13] Some modern and reformist Muslims have referred to this as "Closing the Gate of Knowledge," and they attribute many of the problems of Islam's adaptation to the modern world to that legal principle which closed off "knowledge based on reasoning."[14] While this principle of restricted interpretation had significant consequences for the development of Islamic law, in practice, there remained other techniques for adaptation of Islamic law to diverse cultures and political systems.

The Content of Islamic Law

At the center of the Sharia are the set of religious rituals and duties for Muslims that assert and reinforce their recognition of the omnipotence of God and their obligations to shape their actions to submit to God's will. Islam means to "submit or surrender to God," so the central rituals and obligations of Islam provide the occasions to reassert the central vows and obligations of the faith. These are called the "Five Pillars of Islam," and they establish the main rituals of Islam regarding prayer, almsgiving, fasting, and pilgrimage to Mecca. Some Muslims recognize a sixth pillar of Islam. That is known as *jihad*, which has been defined as "struggle for the faith." Depending on circumstances, jihad can be interpreted in many ways. For some, it has meant "holy war" to expand the borders of Islamic rule and subdue or convert non-Muslims. For others, it has meant waging war to repel an enemy of Islam. Or, some interpret jihad to be a call to personal struggle and redemption to perfect Islamic faith and justice. Even with the latter definition jihad is viewed as a communal duty rather than a matter of individual striving.[15]

In the matter of personal behavior and private law, the Sharia establishes a very elaborate and detailed set of rules. A Muslim is subject to dietary restrictions (no meat from pigs or from defiled animals and a prohibition of consumption of alcoholic liquors), rules of personal hygiene, rules for prayers and mosque attendance, rules governing fasting, rules of interpersonal conduct, rules for courtship, rules for marriage and responsibilities of family members (men may take up to four wives under certain restrictive conditions), rules governing sexual intercourse, rules of divorce, rights of women, laws of inheritance, and rules governing charitable and Islamic trusts (*waqf* and *bayt ul-mal*).

These aspects of private and personal Islamic law concern the state and become a matter of political concern and controversy primarily because, under Islamic rule, the state has a role in the interpretation and enforcement of these rules. Which rules require public enforcement and which should be left to persuasion and individual commitment can be a matter of dispute. An overcommitment to enforcement of all aspects of private Islamic law can overload the administrative and judicial system with police oversight and law enforcement responsibilities. Where Muslim law is relaxed, public responsibility for these personal and private aspects of Islamic duties are left largely to personal commitment or through private legal actions, such as in the matters of marriage, divorce, wills, and inheritance.

Sharia Commercial and Criminal Law

The desert Arabs lived primarily from the proceeds of commerce and the operations of the camel caravans that traversed wide swaths of the Arabian desert to link the great civilizations of Asia with populous regions of the Mediterranean and Europe. Even before the advent of Muhammad, a fairly comprehensive commercial law had evolved and most of these customary laws were incorporated into the Sharia commercial codes. The rules of Sharia commercial law are designed to prevent speculation and to assure that both the buyer and seller are fully informed of the product and terms of sale. To sell goods for a profit is both permitted and accepted as a normal commercial transaction. However, in the matter of monetary loans and financial transactions, the Quran forbids, as a deadly sin, the taking of "increment" or "rent" from credit and loans, known as *riba*. This doctrine is virtually identical to the medieval Christian doctrine that interest on loans, known as "usury," was a serious sin for Christians. For Muslims, riba continues to be prohibited by Sharia law. For Muslim jurists, riba, translated as "usury," was deemed to be a form of economic exploitation. As commonly interpreted, the rule on riba prohibits Muslims from acquiring interest on any investments or monetary instruments or from paying or collecting interest on loans and deferred commercial payments, such as mortgages, letters of credit, annuities, and some forms of insurance.

In matters of criminal justice, Sharia law appears to be most in conflict with Western legal concepts. Yet, there is an amazing similarity with much of Mosaic law as enunciated in the Bible's Old Testament books of Exodus and Deuteronomy. In both legal systems, there is a preoccupation with punishment for "false belief" and failure to honor the covenant with God. In both systems, fearsome and gruesome punishments await those who break marriage vows, violate property rights, fail to obey lawful authority, or give false witness. Many of the punishments are promised to be administered directly by God, but both systems also rely on severe physical punishments administered against transgressors by officials, by victims of crime, or by an enraged general public.[16] In both legal systems, there is a greater concern for values of community harmony than for the rights and freedoms of individuals.

In Muhammad's day, there was no criminal justice system of penitentiaries for long-term incarceration of criminals. Instead, laws provided for rapid justice involving primarily physical punishment that would be quick and easy to administer, severe enough to deter crime by others, and providing some form of involvement and compensation for the victims. Draconian punishments compensated for weak and ineffective police and judicial administration that was unable to apprehend most criminal activities. Furthermore, the high costs of incarceration were minimized and opportunities for legal appeals or parole were virtually eliminated.

The primary punishments of Sharia criminal law involve caning or flogging, stoning to death, crucifixion, execution by the sword, amputation of a limb or limbs, exile, and finally, imprisonment (see Table 2.1). The more serious crimes, known as *hadd* offenses, call for physical punishments because these crimes are deemed to violate the ethical public order and contravene the purposes of God. For hadd cases, the judiciary has no judicial discretion over the nature or magnitude of the punishment. For the less severe offenses, known as *ta'zir*, the judge (*kathi*) hearing the case has significant discretion over penalties and compensation to victims.

Sharia legal procedures are highly dependent on witness testimony and give much attention to the credibility of witnesses, who are certified before testifying, largely on the basis of their standing in the community. For the most serious crimes, four witnesses are required for conviction, and for lesser crimes, two witnesses are sufficient. The testimony of witnesses to criminal

Table 2.1 Examples of Sharia Criminal Punishments

Hadd crimes	
Adultery	100 lashes / death by stoning[a]
Willful murder	The victim's relatives can demand death, payment of blood money, or they may forgive the accused
False accusation of unlawful intercourse	80 lashes
Consumption of alcohol	80 lashes / 40 lashes[a]
Theft	Amputation of a hand
Sodomy and homosexual acts	Death by stoning or buried alive / 40 lashes[a]
Highway robbery without murder	Amputation of right hand and left foot
Highway robbery involving murder and theft	Crucifixion
Apostasy and blasphemy	Execution
Ta'zir crimes	
Perjury, usury, slander Petty penal offenses	Penalties are set by the judge, ranging from reprimand to death

Sources: David F. Forte, *Studies in Islamic Law* (Lanham, MD: Austin & Winfield, 1999), 78–193; Mir Wali Ullah, *Muslim Jurisprudence and the Quranic Law of Crimes,* 2nd rev. ed. (Lahore, Pakistan: Islamic Book Service, 1982), 137–167; 'Abdur Rahman I. Doi, *Shari'ah: The Islamic Law* (Kuala Lumpur: A. S. Noordeen, reprint of 1984, 1990), 219–269.

Note: a. Alternative penalties based on juridical schools.

acts must be identical and there is no opportunity for cross-examination of witnesses, either for the defense or the prosecution. Cross-examination of witnesses is the prerogative of the judge, usually before testimony is presented. The testimony of a woman is worth only half that of a man. Because of this cumbersome procedure, conviction is frequently difficult and the opportunity for the appearance of paid "witnesses" who present identical testimony is an ever-present issue. The outcome of Sharia criminal justice relies primarily on the capacity of the judge to discern deceptions in testimony. The ideal is not so much "equal justice for all" as it is to preserve the unity, harmony, and authority of the community.[17]

The Islamic Pattern of Governance

For the purposes of this study, the more important aspects of Sharia law are in the areas of public law governing the operation of the state, Islamic institutions, rules governing non-Muslims, public policy related to taxes and revenues, and rules of international relations. For untold centuries in the Middle East, the prevailing form of government was based on inherited kinship through tribe and clan. For Islam, submission to the articles of faith in the Quran became the sole factor and necessary condition for inclusion in the community of Islam—the umma. For that period, this was a revolutionary doctrine. This principle enabled diverse peoples and cultures to accept Islam and become full members of Islamic states, but it also made the state responsible for protecting, defending, and defining the faith. For Muhammad, his role as a religious leader was dependent on his role as a political leader. Politics depended on religion and religion depended on politics. With Muhammad's rule as the model, there could be no separation or division between mosque and state.[18]

Contemporary commentators on Sharia law refer to the concept of consultation as a restraint on unbridled political authority under Islam. Hadith reports provide evidence that Muhammad consulted with "Companions of the Prophet," but there was no fixed constitutional process for selection of representatives and no clear allocation of authority or functions for such a council. Neither the Quran nor the Sunna specifies what form consultation may take. Under Muhammad, such consultation came in the form of an advisory council, subject to the ultimate authority of the Prophet, both as to membership and its powers. The ambiguity for the role of consultation has enabled Muslim rulers to claim legitimacy for various forms of authoritarian and autocratic regimes. Muslim rulers have been able to cite Islamic legal precedents to justify their rule, so long as the public rituals of Islam are supported and the most distinctive aspects of Sharia law are acknowledged, even when they have not been enforced.

The "Medieval Synthesis"

When the first Islamic empires began to be formed, the caliphs discovered the difficulty and cost of attempting to apply Sharia law in matters of public law, penal law, taxation, and the laws of war and peace. Private law, family law, and matters of faith and ritual could be promoted and casually enforced, but Islamic judicial procedures were too cumbersome and inflexible, while some laws seemed irrational and difficult to administer. The difficulties of implementing the public aspects of Sharia law led to what has been called the "medieval synthesis"—the ideal goals were acknowledged, but pragmatic solutions were devised to address practical governance issues.[19] For example, Sharia courts continued with their rigid rules of procedure and evidence, but to resolve disputes and keep the peace, Muslim states in the Middle Ages often created a separate judicial system based on tribal or customary laws. This parallel judicial system was administered through complaint (*mazalim*) courts that operated with more simple procedures and reasonable rules of evidence that produced more balanced decisions based on equity, with results that were acceptable to the community at large. Typically, Muslim rule operated with a separate system of administrative mazalim courts that applied administrative regulations, known as *siyasa*, to enforce and administer many aspects of public security and justice that were otherwise covered by Sharia law. With this dual system of administrative justice, the Sharia courts often ended up primarily responsible for family law and not much more. Many disputes were settled by local police. In this way, law enforcement could take cognizance of local customs and reflect community values and sensitivities, but there was also the endemic problem of corruption and "purchased justice" (with bribes).

Most Muslim rulers in the medieval era developed common strategies for effective governance while avoiding some of the strict demands imposed by the Sharia ideal of the Muslim state. The Muslim ruler would usually gain the support of a few compliant ulama as coadjutors to legitimize the regime. They would be given stipends and official status on an Islamic council, often headed by a mufti. In cases of dispute over the interpretation or administration of Muslim law, the ruler could secure from his coadjutors a favorable decision in the form of a fatwa to provide an acceptable and authoritative decision on any issues of Islamic law. Under the Sharia theory of the state, the Muslim ruler has supreme power while being responsible exclusively to God. By his careful cultivation of and support from his religious coadjutors, a ruler could quite easily sustain an Islamic basis for the legitimacy of his rule.[20]

The compromises and adjustments made by Muslim rulers to the unyielding principles of Sharia law and the theological doctrines of Islam were worked out anew whenever Islam spread to new regions and cultures. What had been the previous rules of social organization and the basis of community norms could not be entirely ignored when new Islamic political systems became established, whether by conquest or through conversion. Each Muslim empire and dynasty had to work out these practical realities of rule based, in part, on the unique cultural, economic, and political environment of that particular region. During this process of adaptation, the stark ideals and rigid doctrines of Islam's origins usually became modified with complex innovations that often produced noncongruent manifestations. Religious and cultural innovations came to Islam from many sources, while its core rituals and the central messages of the Quran remained largely unchanged and unchallenged. To understand the unique qualities of Islam in Southeast Asia, we must now examine the pre-Islamic cultural characteristics of the Malay world.

Adat Law and the Malay Worldview

The pre-Islamic Malay and Indonesian world developed a system of law based on custom and traditions that had emerged over centuries into a fairly fixed system of laws, legal principles, and procedures. Rajas and local rulers had extraordinary powers and a mystique that sanctioned and even encouraged extremes of arbitrary exercise of prerogative authority. Despite the authoritarian patterns of traditional rule, no ruler could claim to alter or abrogate the traditional law, known as Adat, without undermining the legitimacy of his authority. The boundaries of states were not precisely fixed and the power of the ruler was supreme in his capital, but diminished with distance. Where rule was ineffective or legitimacy was undermined, peripheral areas could switch their allegiances and make tribute payments to another ruler. The options of shifting loyalties contributed to the rise and fall of political systems and provided for both political and economic competition between states for support from local communities for taxes, for labor levies to maintain public works, and as recruits for military forces. Thus, authoritarian monarchies faced the prospects of losing their population base if draconian measures alienated segments of their populace. The cultural and legal norms of society had to be respected and upheld if the royal authority was to be retained with popular support.

Central to the Malay worldview is the idea of *semangat*, which can be defined very briefly as "soul force" or as "soul substance," but which acquired more nuanced meanings in rituals and culture as an explanatory force pervading the universe. Semangat is the soul or "spirit of life" that is present in man and higher animals, but also is present in most plants, in houses, and in some valued minerals. Magic can be used to gain control of semangat, enabling ritual specialists, known as *bomoh, dukun,* or *pawang*, to perform secret rituals designed to manipulate the spirit world. These rituals were believed to heal sickness, to enable communication with the dead, and to invoke the life forces in food crops to enhance agricultural production. Some ritual specialists claimed powers to interpret the spirit world through hypnotic trances, allowing them to read omens, create love charms, and foresee the future. The need to control and interpret the spirit world affected nearly all aspects of life, especially at important, defining moments of the life cycle, such as birth, circumcision, marriage, building a new home, departing on a long trip, at death, and for burial. Communal feasts, known as *selamatan,* were usually celebrated for such events. These ritual feasts were usually conducted by mature women who served food to family and clan with ritual worship "offerings" to the spirits inhabiting the immediate vicinity. The line between "empowered clergy" and the "laity" did not exist since everyone was assumed to have some capacity to interact with the spirit world. Those who acquired the occult science of appropriate rituals could display an aura of charisma that appeared to be derived directly from the supernatural "spirit world."[21]

During the early history of Southeast Asia, numerous empires established political order based on rice cultivation and the control of coastal and riverine waterways. Utilizing small seagoing vessels, these states engaged in trade and had contacts both with India and China. Malay merchant seamen traveled as far as East Africa, while both Indian and Arab traders plied Southeast Asian waters well before the founding of Islam. In peninsular and insular Southeast Asia, dating from the first century B.C., a number of large, loosely organized empires emerged that were greatly influenced by Indian culture and religion, including both Hinduism and Indian Buddhism.[22] At ruling court circles, Hindu principles of divine kingship and Buddhist symbols of authority became a source for enhanced political rule. Indian cultural influences were less pronounced at village levels, but even so, some classic epics from Hindu literature and Indian cosmology became widely disseminated as part of popular culture. In a highly selective way, a number of these Indianized cultural elements became infused into the mores, arts, social organization, and the belief systems of the Malay/Indonesian world. These early contacts between India and the Southeast Asian states later paved the way for the introduction of Islam to Southeast Asia after that religion had became well established as part of the Indian landscape.

Islam Comes to Southeast Asia

During the fourteenth century, the demand in Europe for spices and Chinese luxury goods expanded rapidly. To meet that demand, Arab and Indian Muslim trading links into Southeast Asia steadily increased. About 1400, a prince named Parameswara from the Sumatran kingdom of Majapahit established the fortified trading port of Melaka at the narrowest part of the straits formed between Sumatra and the Malay Peninsula. Very quickly, Melaka's power grew, based on extracting duties from passing traders. Toward the end of his reign, Parameswara converted to Islam, and in doing so assumed the Islamic name Megat Iskandar Shah. His conversion marked the beginning of a period during which Islam rapidly expanded to other parts of Southeast Asia.[23]

Melaka established a system of favored treatment for Muslims both involving trade agreements and payment of transit duties. By these measures, Muslim traders discovered the advantages of a monopoly trading system. Southeast Asian rulers who converted to Islam gained privileged access to the lucrative spice trade system that extended to markets in China, India, and beyond Arabia to Europe. Local rulers were also attracted to Islam for a variety of other reasons. Malay society was hierarchical and organized under a monarch usually holding the Indian title of raja. Hindu and Buddhist concepts of kingship attributed magical powers and a divine sanction to that office. In the cosmic theology of the Malay world, the mystical powers of rulership, known as *daulat,* provided the ideology for royal legitimacy. The Islamic doctrine that a Muslim ruler was God's representative on earth and protector of the one true faith enhanced the power and authority of any ruler choosing to adopt Islam as a "state religion." Not only was Islam congruent with the idea of daulat, but it also enhanced that concept by imparting to the ruler divine sanction to establish God's ordained rule.[24]

Arab and Indian Muslim traders not only established contacts with the outside world, they had access to improved technology. Their ships and navigation skills were superior to those of local traders and they had better weapons, including muskets and more formidable cannons. They understood economics and operated with a degree of coordination and knowledge of market conditions to anticipate and calculate risk, both economic and political. By their actions and their foreign contacts, they exuded the aura of success and power, which was attributed to their superior knowledge and to God's beneficence.[25]

Some of the missionaries who came to Southeast Asia were Indian Muslims who had already been influenced by Indian philosophy and were thus better prepared to confront the religious and philosophical assumptions of Malay mystical beliefs that had been influenced by Hindu and Buddhist concepts. Through a process of acculturation, new converts were able to adapt the rituals and obligations of Islam to make them fairly congruent with traditional beliefs and social structures. The more stringent requirements of Islamic public law governing government, taxes, and criminal law were often ignored, just as they had been in Islam's medieval period and under Muslim rule in the Indian subcontinent. Islamic rules of social organization and property were not entirely ignored, but they were frequently modified to permit the continuation of existing practices regarding marriages, inheritance, and the status of women. In some places, such as the Minangkabau areas of Sumatra, the population adopted Islam while also retaining their earlier matrilineal social system. The spread of Islam was also facilitated by the religious tolerance that characterized Buddhist and Hindu cultural systems, as well as by the fact that Hinduism and Buddhism had not penetrated deeply into Malay/Indonesian culture, but had been instead primarily accepted as the basis for royal authority. When Islam became the preferred basis for the authority of the rulers, it was a relatively easy process for their subjects to convert to Islam with the sanction and support of those in power.[26] By this process, Islam came, not as a destabilizing process, but rather as an additional pillar of authority for the existing social and political order. For converts, this meant accepting new rituals and doctrines, without making a revolutionary break with the past.

Islam's "Southeast Asian Synthesis"

The version of Islam that came to Southeast Asia was Sunni, and the established system of juridical interpretation was Shafi'i. This combination is the most flexible and adaptable to non-Islamic or pre-Islamic cultural traditions. The Shafi'i school of jurisprudence gives weight to community consensus (*ijma*) and to the processes of community decisions, providing that core Islamic principles are not violated. That system of jurisprudence also sanctions the use of analogy and precedent in the interpretation of law. One of its most important principles is to understand the underlying "premises" (*illa*) of the Quran, rather than concentrating on overly legalistic literal interpretations that might be inappropriate for diverse circumstances and cultures.[27]

During the process of conversions to Islam, some of the missionaries who came to Southeast Asia were Sufi Muslims. Sufism began as an Arab Islamic movement in the eighth century and was considered by orthodox Muslims to be heresy, but it spread across the Muslim world, usually organized as Muslim fraternal brotherhoods that preached Sufi doctrines. Because Sufis searched for "new truths," they often incorporated local beliefs and religious ideas, grafting them on to the corpus of the Quran's doctrines. While most Muslims concentrate on the proper fulfillment of the obligations of Sharia law, Sufis focused instead on the quest for salvation through mystical experiences. Taking Muhammad as the ultimate example of one who gained salvation through a personal relationship with Allah, Sufis sought to replicate that experience as the ultimate goal for the true believer. Through careful study of the Quran, the Sufi seeks to obtain divine grace through thankfulness to God and thereby acquire an intimacy with God that will ultimately lead to "pure truth" (*haqq*). The term *Islam,* which means "submission to God," was interpreted by Sufis to mean the quest for "union with God" through direct mystical experiences that transcend the limitations of worldly existence. Each Sufi order developed its own rituals and devotional forms designed to achieve direct contact with God and thereby obtain sublime salvation.[28]

The Javanese philosophical tradition views the temporal world as essentially unreal, like the performance of Indonesian shadow puppets (*wayang*), with the puppeteer acting as an agent of eternal reality and ultimate truth. That tradition asserted the doctrine of "nonduality" of all being, between the temporal and the spiritual world. The reality within man is thus viewed as "nondifferent" from the divine, which is deemed to be not confined by space and time and thus indwelling or present in man, even if he may not be aware of it. Javanese religious texts taught nonduality as a Muslim doctrine, but it is clear that Islamic orthodoxy proceeded on contradictory assumptions. For orthodox Islam, the temporal world is real, corrupt, changeable, and transient, while God is pure, eternal, and transcendent—outside of and untouched by his own creation. By contrast, Javanese mystic doctrines view the temporal world as "unreal," but behind this temporal world lies the eternal reality of God, which is immanent in all creation. For the Sufi, the assumption is that Allah is everywhere and is in everything; he is concealed, unreachable, and without equal. When combined with the doctrine of nonduality, Javanese Sufis concluded that man and God share the same identity and "there is no difference between worshiper and worshiped" because the divinity of both are subject and object. The core Islamic profession of faith is: "There is no God but Allah and Muhammad is his Prophet." When combined with the nonduality principle, a few Javanese Sufis concluded that ultimately, "There is no God."[29]

The Sufi devotee utilized self-induced trance to achieve an ecstatic religious experience of the presence of God. The religious rituals of Sufism were designed to suppress the sense of self to achieve a oneness with God that was viewed as being everywhere throughout creation. In that state, the devotee was believed to acquire supernatural powers that could be transmitted to followers who were less able to achieve this ecstatic direct experience of God. The successful Sufi *wali* (saint) thus was often able to acquire a charisma that attracted a following of devotees. The doctrines and legal requirements of Sharia were of less importance for Sufis, because their direct experience of God was assumed to be more meaningful and valid than the elaborate rules and doctrines of orthodox Islam.

For the orthodox Muslims, Sufism was considered to be a deviant version of Islam that appeared to challenge the monotheist doctrines of Islam. Existing on the fringes of Islamic society, Sufis developed a tradition of resistance to state authority. Instead, they preached that a Mahdi would eventually come to overthrow state authority and create a truly Islamic society as the prelude to the final Judgment Day. With this "revolutionary" ethos, some Sufi practitioners developed a cult following based, in part, on Malay martial arts known as *silat.* The leader of a Sufi sect would often claim to confer "invulnerability" to his followers who were called upon to defend the faith against critics or the *kafir* (heathen unbelievers). The various schools of Sufi doctrine, known as *tarikat,* could range from an emphasis on otherworldly self-contemplation, to the formation of militant activism, often based on highly mobilized paramilitary units ready for mortal combat with real or imagined enemies of God.[30]

Because of the Sufi view of God as being immanent rather than transcendental, these doctrines could accommodate many of the assumptions of the traditional Malay/Indonesian worldview based on semangat. Sufis venerated walis, who were believed to have achieved union with God through miraculous feats or evidence of extreme piety. Holy places, known as *keramat,* were preserved as shrines where the souls of venerated religious figures from the past were believed to exist as centers of power. At these sites, devotees came to invoke intercession from the spirits of departed walis.[31] Sufi doctrines could be use to validate these mystical practices that perpetuated many of the pre-Islamic beliefs of the Malay world.

Popular Islam

Just because indigenous converts to Islam in Southeast Asia adapted Islam to their culture and their previous belief system does not mean that Islam had a very small impact on their lives, their social system, and their behavior. Islamic law, when added to Adat law, provided a more complete system of personal law, and it also provided enhanced legitimacy for the system of monarchical rule that predated the coming of Islam. Because the royal courts of Malay/Indonesian monarchies were most exposed to foreign Muslim traders and missionaries, these coastal trading centers were likely to be more orthodox in persuasion and in the application of Muslim law. The underpinnings of past beliefs and assumptions about motive forces in the universe revealed by the common surviving elements have remained within the culture and belief systems of the Malay/Indonesian world despite conversion to Islam. The folk religion of the interior peasant villages tended to reflect the perseverance of more traditional beliefs and customs. Yet, under the banner of Islam, links between the interior villages and the monarchy at the capital were greatly enhanced. The ruler was acknowledged as the head of the umma and at the apex of the system of moral authority.

The religious duties of Islam are very effective in creating a sense of community with precise obligations and clear boundaries. The requirement of daily prayers publicly performed makes visible the commitment to religious duties. At the Friday mosque service, the mass prayers performed with unison oral responses and prescribed prayer gestures and postures presents a moving sight providing visual indication of social and religious unity. Some villagers may have found the requirement of prayer five times a day at prescribed times to be difficult to perform, especially during the peak labor periods of rice planting and rice harvesting, or when engaged in offshore ocean fishing. The requirement of collective prayer, as an evidence of piety, became a hallmark of the status system in Malay peasant communities. The social benefits of prayer were greater when performed publicly.

Islamic doctrine was more egalitarian than the earlier Hindu doctrines based on ascriptive social status of birth and caste. In Islamic theory, all members of the umma are supposed to be socially equal. However, in practice, the Malay and Indonesian social systems were hierarchical and usually based on a system of patron-client linkages. This system has persisted despite the professions of the equality of believers within the umma, and some of the ceremonies and celebrations of Islam provide the opportunity for the reassertion and affirmation of patron-client obligations. At the end of the fasting month, the celebration of Hari Raya Puasa (in Java known as Rijaja) involves the customary practice of lower status clients visiting their patron superiors to beg for pardon and to pledge continued obeisance and support to their patron.[32]

While Islam did increase the sense of unity and mutual support within the community, it also increased the division between those who accepted Islam as "true believers" (*maumin*) and those who continued to practice various pre-Islamic rituals. Orthodox Muslims often castigated those Muslims who openly expressed belief in a mystical spirit world as "unbelievers" (kafir). These more orthodox Muslims tended to be centered in coastal and urban areas, while the more syncretic Muslims who practiced the more mystical forms of Islam tended to be located in rural villages and settlements farther from the more cosmopolitan centers of trade and commerce.

From a functional perspective, it is apparent that Islam was a very appropriate religiopolitical system for the organization of a peasant society. The central issues of authority, family, marriage, economic exchange, and death were all covered with a certitude that well suited a society based on rice production and fishing. Differences developed between principalities and regions, while at the village level Islam projected an image of unity and conformity. Each local mosque served a *mukim* (parish), which usually included one primary village.

The mosque and *surau* (prayer house) were usually built through local village effort, and local officials, who were supervised by a committee of village elders, staffed these facilities. Members of the mosque committee would be selected for their pious demeanor and their claims to Islamic knowledge. Because of its decentralized and local character, Islam generated unity and vitality at the village level, while also accommodating the diverse cultural panorama of Southeast Asia.

Islam preaches the doctrine that "there is only one Islam." At the local level, this was certainly a primary characteristic. However, within Southeast Asia as a whole, Islam developed many different and somewhat competing characteristics, and in comparison with Islam in other regions of the world, Southeast Asian Islam had both greater diversity and an enhanced capacity to tolerate and incorporate both cultural and theological diversity.[33] The tolerant and adaptive practices of Southeast Asian Islam also set the stage for the eventual emergence of political Islam. All these compromises between the practical realities of the social order and the stark ideals of Islam that led to the medieval synthesis were replicated in Southeast Asia with issues generated by the Southeast Asian synthesis. Muslim states and minority Muslim communities are still grappling with many of the same issues as their medieval ancestors. Can devout Muslims replicate the ideals and practices of Muhammad's first community in Medina in the contemporary world? If Sharia law has divine origins, how can it be implemented for Muslims and how should it apply to non-Muslims? Can the ideals of divine governance be made compatible with democratic institutions? What is the responsibility of the Muslim state to enforce orthodoxy and to punish apostasy? How much religious diversity can be tolerated within the community of Islam? In a Muslim political order, what are the rights of non-Muslims? A recurring theme in the politics of contemporary political Islam is the search for answers to the question: How can the ideals of Islam be implemented in practice and made into a guiding set of principles for the modern world?

These are some of the recurring and formidable issues that are especially difficult for Muslim leaders who are presently attempting to formulate new answers to old problems affecting their societies and their political systems. These are also the core issues and themes that will permeate the remaining chapters of this book.

Notes

1. Muslims are taught that the text of the Quran is exactly the same as what the Prophet Muhammad received as divinely revealed truth. The argument is made that the Quran could not have been composed or edited by him because he was illiterate and that the Quran also could not have been composed or edited by any human being because of its "unique, sublime and exalted quality." For a summary of the arguments in

support of the divine origin of the Quran, see Suzanne Haneef, *What Everyone Should Know About Islam and Muslims,* 14th ed. (Chicago: Kazi Publications, 1996), 28–39.

2. Ira M. Lapidus, *A History of Islamic Societies* (Cambridge: Cambridge University Press, 1988), 21–29; Fred McGraw Donner, *The Early Islamic Conquests* (Princeton, NJ: Princeton University Press, 1981), 51–53; John L. Esposito, *Islam: The Straight Path* (Oxford: Oxford University Press, 1988), 1–10. For a cultural evolutionary perspective on Islam see Patricia Crone and Michael Cook, *Hagarism: The Making of the Islamic World* (Cambridge: Cambridge University Press, 1977); Ibn Warraq (ed.), *The Quest for the Historical Muhammad* (Amherst, NY: Prometheus Books, 2000); Chase F. Robinson, *Islamic Historiography* (Cambridge: Cambridge University Press, 2003); Yehuda D. Nevo and Judith Koren, *Crossroads to Islam: The Origins of the Arab Religion and the Arab State* (Amherst, NY: Prometheus Books, 2003); Jonathan P. Berkey, *The Formation of Islam: Religion and Society in the Near East, 600–1800* (Cambridge: Cambridge University Press, 2003).

3. Muhammad's "Charter" is reproduced with commentary in Reuben Levy, *The Social Structure of Islam* (Cambridge: Cambridge University Press, 1957, reprinted 1962), 2–277. A substantially different translation of the Charter is reproduced in Bishiruddin Mahmud Ahmad, *The Life of Muhammad* (Rabwah, Pakistan: Tahrik-i-Jadid [1950]), 42–43. The terms of the Charter were a source of conflict when the Jews rejected Muhammad's claim to be a prophet and objected to his interpretations of Jewish sacred history. After 627, Muhammad accused the Jews of disloyalty and all Jews in Medina were either killed or expelled from the domains under Muhammad's jurisdiction. See Lapidus, *A History of Islamic Societies,* 28, 32.

4. Carl Brockelmann, translated by Joel Carmichael and Moshe Perlmann, *History of the Islamic Peoples* (London: Routledge & Kegan Paul, 1948, reprinted 1980), 1–36. For a detailed analysis of Muhammad's political skills, see McGraw Donner, *The Early Islamic Conquests*, 62–82.

5. Because the Islamic dating system is based on the lunar calendar with a shorter yearly cycle of 354 days, Muhammad's death is recorded as 11 A.H. by Islamic chronology.

6. Brockelmann, *History of the Islamic Peoples*, 45–53; Levy, *The Social Structure of Islam*, 276–279.

7. Lapidus, *A History of Islamic Societies*, 115–119; Esposito, *Islam: The Straight Path*, 40–54; Sydney Nettleton Fisher and William Ochsenwald, *The Middle East: A History* (New York: McGraw-Hill, 1990), 37–48, 93–97.

8. For an account of Shia Islam, see Berkey, *The Formation of Islam*, 130–140; Patricia Crone, *God's Rule: Government and Islam* (New York: Columbia University Press, 2004), 17–23, 70–86.

9. Beatrice Pitney Lamb, *India: A World in Transition* (New York: Frederick A. Praeger, 1963), 34–52; Percival Spear, *India: A Modern History* (Ann Arbor: University of Michigan Press, 1961), 102–159.

10. Levy, *The Social Structure of Islam*, 162–164.

11. The Muslim historian al-Bukhari is reported to have collected 600,000 Hadith reports and judged fewer than 8,000 to be authentic. Other Islamic jurists concluded that only 4,000 could be accepted as valid. Muhammad 'Ali, *The Religion of Islam: A Comprehensive Discussion of Its Sources, Principles and Practices* (Lahore, Pakistan: The Ahmadiyyah Anjuman Isha'at Islam, 1950), 76–77; Crone, *God's Rule,* 124–129.

12. Mohammed Hameedullah Khan, *The Schools of Islamic Jurisprudence* (New Delhi: Kitab Bhavan, 1991), 1–134; Ahmad Ibrahim, *Islamic Law in Malaya* (Singapore: Malaysian Sociological Research Institute, 1965), 10–39, 54–117; Levy, *The Social Structure of Islam*, 165–180.

13. Esposito, *Islam: The Straight Path,* 84–86; David F. Forte, *Studies in Islamic Law: Classical and Contemporary Application* (Lanham, MD: Austin & Winfield, 1999), 19–23.

14. Ozay Mehmet, *Islamic Identity and Development* (London: Routledge, 1990), 10–11, 60–61.

15. Carlo Caldarola (ed.), *Religions and Societies: Asia and the Middle East* (Berlin: Mouton Publishers, 1982), 10–11.

16. Some Muslim jurists argue that both Sharia law and Mosaic law originally came from God and that whenever Sharia law is silent or incomplete, Mosaic law still prevails to fill in any gaps in Sharia law. See, for example, Mir Wali Ullah, *Muslim Jurisprudence and the Quranic Law of Crimes* (Lahore, Pakistan: Islamic Book Service, 1982), 37–39, 143.

17. Abdulaziz Sachedina, "The Ideal and Real in Islamic Law," in R. S. Khare (ed.), *Perspectives on Islamic Law, Justice, and Society* (Lanham, MD: Rowman & Littlefield Publishers, 1999), 28–29.

18. Bernard G. Weiss, *The Spirit of Islamic Law* (Athens: University of Georgia Press, 1988), 145–149.

19. Daniel Pipes, *In the Path of God: Islam and Political Power* (New York: Basic Books, 1983), 48–69; Bassam Tibi, *Islam Between Culture and Politics* (Basingstoke: Palgrave; New York: Macmillan, 2005), 148–166.

20. Forte, *Studies in Islamic Law,* 22–25; Weiss, *The Spirit of Islamic Law,* 24–37; Pipes, *In the Path of God,* 57–63.

21. For a sample of research on Malay beliefs, see Kirk Michael Endicott, *An Analysis of Malay Magic* (Oxford: Clarendon Press, 1970), 13–95; Walter William Skeat, *Malay Magic: An Introduction to the Folklore and Popular Religion of the Malay Peninsula* (London: Macmillan, 1900); R. J. Wilkinson, *Malay Beliefs* (London: Luzac, 1906); R. O. Winstedt, *Shaman, Saiva and Sufi: A Study of the Evolution of Malay Magic* (London: Constable, 1925); Zainal Kling, "Magical Practices in a Rural Malay Community in Sarawak," in H. M. Dahlan (ed.), *The Nascent Malaysian Society: Developments, Trends and Problems* (Kuala Lumpur: Jabatan Antropologi dan Sociologi, Universiti Kebangsaan Malaysia, 1976), 71–97.

22. Michel Jacq-Hergoualc'h, *The Malay Peninsula: Crossroads of the Maritime Silk Road,* trans. by Victoria Hobson (Leiden: Brill, 2002), 74–105; D. G. E. Hall, *A History of South-East Asia,* 3rd ed. (New York: St. Martin's Press, 1970), 41–93.

23. Hall, *A History of South-East Asia,* 205–219; John F. Cady, *Southeast Asia: Its Historical Development* (New York: McGraw-Hill, 1964), 152–171.

24. Mark R. Woodward, *Islam in Java: Normative Piety and Mysticism in the Sultanate of Yogyakarta* (Tucson: University of Arizona Press, 1989), 53–60; Khoo Kay Kim, *Malay Society: Transformation and Democratisation* (Petaling Jaya, Malaysia: Pelandok Publications, 1991), 6–21.

25. Huub de Jonge and Nico Kapstein, *Arabs, Politics, Trade and Islam in Southeast Asia* (Leiden: KITLV Press, 2002), 1–10; Anthony Reid, *Charting the Shape of Early Modern Southeast Asia* (Cheng Mai, Thailand: Silkworm Books, 1999), 20–34.

26. C. A. O. Van Nieuwenhuijze, *Aspects of Islam in Post-Colonial Indonesia* (The Hague: W. van Hoeve, 1958), 10–40; M. C. Ricklefs, "Islamization in Java: An Overview and Some Philosophical Considerations," in Raphael Israeli and Anthony H. Johns (eds.), *Islam in Asia:* Vol. 2, *Southeast and East Asia* (Jerusalem: The Magnes Press, 1984), 11–23; Reuven Kahane, "Notes on the Unique Patterns of Indonesian Islam," in Israeli and Johns, *Islam in Asia,* 162–188.

27. Levy, *The Social Structure of Islam,* 177–180.

28. Brockelmann, *History of the Islamic Peoples,* 148–154.

29. Ricklefs, "Islamization in Java," 15–19; Woodward, *Islam in Java,* 60–78.

30. Geertz, *The Religion of Java,* 182–184; Endicott, *Analysis of Malay Magic,* 42–46; Lapidus, *A History of Islamic Societies,* 545–547.

31. Endicott, *Analysis of Malay Magic*, 90–95; Peter Riddell, *Islam and the Malay-Indonesian World* (London: Hurst, 2001), 168–204, 216–224.

32. Clifford Geertz, *The Religion of Java* (New York: Free Press of Glencoe, 1964), 379–381.

33. For an exploration of the capacity of Southeast Asian Islam to accommodate various cultural traditions, see Gustav E. von Grunebaum, (ed.), *Unity and Variety in Muslim Civilization* (Chicago: University of Chicago Press, 1955), especially the article by G. W. J. Drewes, "Indonesia, Mysticism and Activism."

3

Islam Under Colonial Rule

The penetration of Islam into Southeast Asia began about two centuries before the beginning of the colonial era. For most Muslim areas of Southeast Asia, Islam had barely taken hold and the processes of adapting to a Muslim way of life were still being worked out when European powers arrived. Thus, for many Muslims, the process of adaptation to Islam occurred nearly simultaneously with the challenges of confrontation with European powers and the gradual extension of colonial rule over their societies. Over a period of nearly five centuries, four European powers—Portugal, Spain, the Netherlands, and Great Britain—established colonial control over regions with significant Muslim populations. At the beginning of the twentieth century, the United States also became a colonial power within the region. Each of these colonial powers pursued unique policies toward Islam that later shaped the trajectory of political Islam. This chapter will briefly explore the political legacies of the colonial era for Islamic-based politics.

Portugal's Impact on Islam

Both Portugal and Spain had experienced more than seven centuries of Arab Islamic rule that finally came to an end in 1492 with the Christian conquest of Granada.[1] During that long period of exposure to Islam, Portuguese and Spanish leaders had become familiar with the Muslim trading system based on monopoly control of high-valued products, primarily spices, silk, and ceramics transported from China and Southeast Asia. Over time, the Muslim trading system created financial problems for European states, because payments depended primarily on gold. During the earlier period of Muslim rule, Portuguese ship traders acted as middlemen, distributing goods from Muslim sources to retail traders in northern Europe. After Islamic rule ended in Iberia, both Portugal and Spain were determined to break the economic system of Islam and to do so as part of their Reconquista wars against Muslim rule.

Despite Portugal's small size and relative poverty, it had the advantage of having a formidable naval fleet that was built with excellent maritime technology. Portuguese ships could sail closer to the wind, were larger and sturdier, and their guns had better range and accuracy than any ships available to Muslim powers. With royal support, in 1487 Bartholomew Diaz rounded the southern tip of Africa. In 1509 a formidable Portuguese fleet confronted and defeated a combined Turkish, Egyptian, and Gujerati fleet off Diu at the entrance to the Gulf of Cambay. That year the Portuguese captured Goa, on the Indian west coast, to make that port the center of Portuguese power in Asia.[2] A small fleet of ships also continued to Melaka but returned without some Portuguese sailors who were taken hostage by the local raja. Two years later, the Portuguese assembled a fleet of eighteen ships and about 1,400 men to lay siege to Melaka. The Portuguese captured that city in 1511 and proceeded to build a fortified city in anticipation of counterattacks.[3]

Melaka became the center of the Portuguese system of trade and political intervention into Southeast Asia. From this base, the Portuguese established a "factory-fort" system designed to sustain a monopoly mercantilist system of trade. To do so, the Portuguese had to destroy the Muslim trading system that had flourished for several centuries. To secure their lines of communication, Portugal established bases at Socotra, near the mouth of the Persian Gulf; at Goa, on the Indian west coast; at Colombo, in Ceylon; at Melaka, on the Malay Peninsula; and at Tidore and Amboina, in the Moluccas. Later, Portugal also acquired enclaves on Timor Island, east of Java and at Macao on the China coast.

The coercive tactics of the Portuguese were fairly successful in controlling the sea lanes, but their actions created deep resentments among those traders who had operated and supplied the Muslim trading system. Portuguese efforts to convert native peoples to Christianity were met with determined resistance. The Jesuit missionary, Francis Xavier, who later was made a saint, came to Melaka to start mission work. Almost no natives were converted to Christianity at Melaka, surrounded as it was by Malay Muslim supporters of the earlier sultanate. Francis Xavier continued on to Amboina and northern Halmahera and despite great efforts had very little success in converting any natives to Christianity. Eventually, he departed for Macao and Japan, where his missionary endeavors proved to be more successful.[4]

Because of limited resources to maintain this multibase system of "factory forts," the Portuguese established a policy of prohibiting their officers and men from bringing wives from Europe. Instead, they organized a system of securing native women as wives or mistresses for those men recruited for service abroad. At each Portuguese base, a small Catholic Eurasian community did form, and their heirs have mostly survived to the present day because of religious and social barriers that kept them apart from the local populations. By this process, the Portugal shaped the human geography of the region in a small but significant way.

With their trade links to India and Arabia severed, Muslim traders gave increased attention to local trade links within Southeast Asia. Aceh, at the northern tip of Sumatra, became a new center for Malay trading vessels. Because the Sunda Straits between Java and Sumatra was relatively unguarded, the nearby state of Bantam also flourished as an Islamic center of commercial activity. Further to the east, the small sultanate of Brunei became another major port for Muslim traders to use as a base of operations. In each of these three port cities, Aceh, Bantam, and Brunei, Islam became a powerful unifying force that inspired Muslims to resist the forceful interventions of the European traders and the expansion of colonial regimes. The grievances of Muslim traders were translated into an intense commitment to Islam—a commitment that has persisted in these areas to the present day.

In response to Portuguese monopoly restrictions, some Malay and Indonesian seafaring communities perfected tactics of "smuggling and piracy." They improved their sailing ships by copying Portuguese shipbuilding technology. With crafts of smaller draft and size, they could elude Portuguese surveillance especially while engaged in coastal and interisland trade. Among the most famous of the Malay seafarers were the Bugis, who originated in Sulawesi but established settlements on islands south of Malaya. From those sites, they combined trade and Islamic politics while also engaging in part-time smuggling and piracy as a means to avoid the stranglehold of rules imposed by colonial authorities.[5] For some Bugis, living "beyond the law" has become a way of life that persists to the present day.

The Spanish Conquest of the Philippines

The Portuguese system of trade with Southeast Asia was first challenged by its larger Iberian neighbor, Spain. Having had a similar experience with centuries of Muslim rule, Spain actively sponsored voyages of discovery and eagerly challenged Islam wherever it was confronted. After Ferdinand Magellan's expedition in 1521 crossed the Pacific and confirmed that the world was round, Spain sought access to trade with China and Japan and to the spice trade.

Prior to the arrival of the Spaniards, the population of these islands consisted of aboriginal tribes, known as Igorots, that inhabited the interior jungles of the main islands. Immigrants from the Malaysian world and perhaps from Melanesia formed other settlements, known as *barangays*, named after their sailing vessels that enabled them to establish their pioneer settlements. These scattered "boat communities" engaged in rice cultivation and fishing and they practiced animism, sharing a Malay worldview that existed prior to the advent of Islam. With no overarching political organization and divided by numerous languages, these coastal settlements were vulnerable to, or ready for, colonial rule, depending on one's interpretation of subsequent events.

When the Spaniards arrived in the Philippines, two powerful Islamic principalities were already well established. The sultanate of Sulu had been founded in the mid-fifteenth century, and the Magindanau Confederation was formed half a century later on the southern shores of the Island of Mindanao. The remainder of the Philippine Islands had not yet been converted to Islam, although a few scattered settlements farther north had become Muslim or had acknowledged vassalage relations with Brunei. The first four Spanish expeditions to establish a colonial base in the Philippines foundered, but finally the fifth, under Miguel de Legazpi, was better prepared and proceeded to make Manila its capital. To accomplish that objective, the Spanish forces in 1571 defeated the warriors of a local barangay leader named Raja Sulaiman, who died in the battle along with 300 of his supporters. Within two years Spaniards gained control of most of Luzon and systematically extended their authority over most of the Philippine Islands.

Unlike the Portuguese, the Spanish authorities determined to establish a colonial system with complete control over native populations and lands supported by an active state-sponsored program of conversion to Christianity. Spain had both the financial and human resources to accomplish its objectives and also had experiences with colonial rule in Mexico and the Caribbean to guide their endeavor. Indeed, the administration and support for Spanish activities in the Philippines came from Mexico rather than directly from Spain. The conquest of the Philippines was accomplished by about 300 Spanish soldiers, and during the period of Spanish rule, the size of the armed forces never exceeded 600 Spanish soldiers, who were supplemented by native auxiliaries. From the start, responsibility for organizing native society and for the success of the colony depended upon the work of Catholic missionaries. Because anticipated trade with China and Japan never proved to be profitable, over time resources for civil administration dwindled and the responsibilities of Catholic missionary orders were greatly expanded. All the regions of the Philippines, except for the Muslim sultanates of Sulu and Magindanau, were divided into five regions and allotted exclusively to each designated Catholic monastic missionary order. The Spanish missionary enterprise started with about 140 Catholic missionary priests in 1591. Their number remained below 400 through the eighteenth century and reached 1,962 by 1876.[6]

The missionaries from the Catholic orders went to live among the people in the barangay villages where they built churches, schools, introduced agricultural technology, and built what became the cities of the Philippines. They organized and built roads and other public works, as well as operating hospitals and orphanages. They also founded universities, the first being the University of Santo Tomas, founded in 1611, to make it the oldest university in Asia. The missionaries utilized Spanish as the language of instruction, government, and commerce, to make it the lingua franca across the many native languages of the Philippines. Aspects of Catholic ritual, doctrine, and practice enabled Filipinos to retain much of their folklore and some of the features of their Malay folk religion and worldview to facilitate their conversion to Christianity. These included elaborate Catholic rituals, the veneration of saints, and Catholic doctrines of afterlife. Considering the small number of Spanish missionary priests and the size and diversity of the population, these Catholic missionary orders generated an amazing transformation of Philippine society, its economy, and its governance. By the beginning of the nineteenth century, these changes eventually created the conditions for the rise of Philippine nationalism.

Relations Between Spanish Rule and the Moros

For understandable reasons, the transformation and benefits derived from Spanish rule and Catholic missions did not extend to the Muslims. The Spanish referred to Muslims as "Moros," based on their previous experience with the Moors of Morocco. The Moros, who vigorously resisted Spanish authority and the proselytizing activities of Catholic priests, matched Spanish animosity for the Moros with their own contempt for the kafir. Spanish rule gradually broke the prior trade and political links between Moro communities and the powerful Muslim sultanate of Brunei. Moros viewed Spanish rule as threatening their very existence by blocking access to regions where they had previously acquired wealth through vassalage, trade, and raids. The Sulu Sultanate had its center on the Island of Jolo and exercised authority over all the Sulu island chain as well as the southern half of the Island of Palawan and the northeast coast of the Island of Borneo. Magindanau was another Muslim state led by petty chiefs, who had unified to form a confederation on central Mindanao during the seventeenth century. Sulu converted to Islam about 1450, followed by Magindanau about 1480. Because these states were on the farthest periphery of the Muslim world, their incorporation into a Muslim way of life was incomplete. Very few Muslims in these states knew much about the Quran, and the obligations of Muslims were largely ignored. Prescribed prayers, dietary restrictions, and Sharia laws were viewed as optional, and very few mosques were built for religious functions. Yet, under the threat of extinction or subjugation, the Moros developed an intense conservatism in religious, political, and social matters, with Islam as the symbol of their identity and the basis for their grievances.

With the Spanish conquest of the northern Philippine Islands blocking their trade, the Moros shifted to their other specialty—raiding. The native craft of the Moros were small in comparison to European vessels, but they could sail well and could be paddled at good speed to overtake becalmed ships or suddenly attack settlements. Enterprising Moros would recruit volunteers for a raiding party that operated with a fleet of vessels that ranged to vulnerable settlements on the Philippine Islands and along the coasts of Borneo, Thailand, and even Sumatra. Some of the raiding squadrons consisted of up to sixty vessels and 3,000 warriors. On some raids, as many as 1,000 captives were taken. The captured bounty would be sold at local markets, while captured victims were sold as slaves or held for ransom.

The conflicts between Spanish authorities and Moros continued for almost 300 years with various ups and downs in intensity and costs. For more than two centuries, Spanish expeditions were unable to subdue Sulu or Magindanau, and from both states Moro raids on Philippine settlements continued on a regular basis. Gradually, Spain began to deter raiding after it established a fort at Zamboanga in 1635 and later became more effective after Spain purchased four British gunboats in 1843. Despite the nominal recognition of Spanish sovereignty by these two Muslim sultanates, Spain never had the capacity or ability to bring these regions under effective administration. Most Muslim-majority regions remained under de facto Moro autonomy until after the US occupation of the Philippines.[7]

The US Conquest of the Philippines

Despite the earlier successes of Spanish rule in the northern islands, Spanish authorities were forced to confront rebellions that were largely based on local grievances and were relatively easy to subdue. However, in the late nineteenth century a sense of Philippine nationalism began to emerge. In 1896, the Spanish authorities uncovered a Philippine nationalist revolutionary movement, known as Katipunan, which Spain answered with a policy of terror. That revolution culminated with the execution in 1896 of fifty-seven prominent Filipinos, including the moderate nationalist, Jose Rizal.[8] The Katipunan rebellion continued for two years, and finally in 1898 Spanish authorities offered a negotiated truce with the Katipunan guerrillas to terminate their revolt. Indemnities were paid to the insurgents and their leader, Emilio Aguinaldo, went into exile in Singapore.

In that same year, the United States and Spain became embroiled in a dispute, focused primarily on Cuba, that rapidly escalated into the Spanish-American War. A US naval squadron was in Hong Kong when war broke out, and it received orders to attack the Spanish fleet in Manila Bay. In the ensuing battle, Spain's fleet was totally destroyed. Commodore George Dewey, commander of the US fleet, sent a naval vessel to return Aguinaldo to the Philippines. What the United States wanted from Aguinaldo was support from Filipino nationalists to fight against Spanish ground forces and to effect their surrender. However, when Aguinaldo arrived in the Philippines, he was willing to help defeat the Spanish regime, but also demanded US recognition of Philippine independence. US authorities were willing to discuss the first objective, but not the second. President William McKinley and his cabinet reflected an assertive cycle in US foreign policy, and the United States was concerned that a weak or inexperienced Philippine government would invite foreign interventions from aggressive European powers looking for new colonial opportunities in Asia. US leaders seemed oblivious to grassroot currents in Philippine politics and assumed that concessions to Philippine nationalist objectives were unnecessary.

Five days after landing in the Philippines, Aguinaldo issued a "Declaration of Independence" for the Philippines. By July 1898, a nationalist revolutionary government was formed at an assembly in Malolos, during which the nationalists adopted a constitution modeled on that of the United States. When President McKinley announced his decision for military occupation of the Philippines and promised a policy of "benevolent assimilation," a clash between the US forces and the nationalists became inevitable. Over the next two years, more than 4,200 US troops battled Filipino forces, which sustained more than 16,000 killed in action. Civilian casualties were even higher because of famine and plague. The capture of Aguinaldo in December 1899 and the surrender of the last Filipino general in May 1902 marked the end of formal hostilities, although some residual resistance continued until 1907. For most of the Philippines, US military rule ended and civilian administration began in 1901, but for Muslim areas, military rule continued until 1913.[9]

In the southern Philippines, the sultan of Sulu and his chiefs signed an agreement in 1898 with US authorities to suppress piracy, control firearms, and maintain the peace in return for emoluments and autonomy related to Islam. In 1904, this agreement was abrogated by the US authorities who accused the chiefs of lack of cooperation in maintaining peace and order. The US army encountered open resistance from Muslim guerrilla fighters as well as passive resistance from many Muslims who resisted what they viewed as kafir rule. The number of Muslims killed in armed resistance to US military operations in Mindanao between 1903 and 1945 has been estimated to be between 15,000 and 20,000.[10] During some operations, US soldiers met mass resistance of civilians who chose death rather than submission. In one incident, 600 men, women, and children were killed on the slopes of the volcano Bud Dajo on Jolo Island, and on another occasion 300 perished on Mount Bagsak, also on Jolo.

In 1911, US authorities decided to incorporate all Moro areas into the Philippines. The first stage involved military pacification to eliminate or neutralize all armed resistance. By 1913, military pacification had been completed, with the next stage involving a transmigration program to move settlers to Mindanao from the northern islands. The legal principle that the government held title to all unoccupied land enabled the government to offer land titles to non-Muslim Filipinos willing to move. By 1917, 15,000 new settlers had been resettled on Mindanao, and by 1934, their number had increased to 34,000. By 1939, 1,000 settlers a month were arriving to claim lands in areas that had been claimed as boundaries of the Muslim sultanates. During World

War II, when Japan occupied the Philippines, migration into Moro areas ceased, but when US rule was restored following Japan's surrender, transmigration policies resumed. By 1975, out of a total population of 9.7 million, about 6 million were estimated to be Christian immigrants.[11] These transmigration operations involved land-grabbing and questionable land transactions that led to great distress among Muslims who believed that Christian immigrants were encroaching upon and stealing their traditional lands. These disputes involved numerous armed confrontations, with both Christian and Muslim communities forming self-defense private militias dedicated to violence against their rivals.

While policies of integration, assimilation, and "modernization" reflected US social policies, they were implemented without reference to demands for autonomy by Muslims who aspired to national independence. From the Moro perspective, Muslims had previously formed independent political entities that could claim rights of nationhood four centuries earlier. Instead, they were now forcefully incorporated, largely by the military forces of the United States, into a social and political system that was not only alien to their religious and political culture, but also hostile to it. After Philippine independence, the policies of incorporation and subjugation of the Moro areas continued, with policies of induced immigration of Christian Filipinos to Moro areas, designed to ensure that Christian majorities would counterbalance Muslim aspirations for independence. The legacy of these policies created lasting and bitter animosities among Moros, most of whom refused to acknowledge the legitimacy of Philippine institutions or to participate in the political and social life of that country.

Building the Dutch Empire in Indonesia

After Spain, the next colonial power to establish a colonial regime in Southeast Asia was the Netherlands. By the latter half of the sixteenth century, the Netherlands had survived a half-century of Spanish rule during which many thousands of Dutch citizens were subjected to the Inquisition and sentenced to death for their Protestant beliefs. When Spain attempted to invade England from the Netherlands, the British decisively defeated the Spanish Armada in 1588, and that victory gave the Dutch their independence from Spain. It also left both Spain and Portugal severely weakened and on the verge of bankruptcy.[12] With the balance of power shifting in Europe, the Netherlands was able to challenge both Portugal and Spain in Southeast Asia.

The Dutch were a nation of seafaring merchants, with commercial skills that were more advanced, at that time, than any others worldwide. To ensure success, in 1602, six Dutch chambers of commerce united seventy-six trading companies to form the Dutch East India Company (Vereenigde Oost-Indische Compagnie—VOC). The Dutch Parliament issued a charter to the VOC to act with sovereign authority to make it the instrument of Dutch colonial power.[13]

When the Dutch first arrived in force to Southeast Asia, they captured the Portuguese enclave of Ambon in 1605 and by 1623 had decisively asserted Dutch supremacy in the Moluccas. Meanwhile, they explored for an appropriate base in Southeast Asia for their operations. Eventually, they gained approval from a local chief to build a factory at a virtually unused river port in East Java called Jakatra. In a later dispute over that agreement, the Dutch, in 1619, conquered the Jakatran Kingdom. The town was renamed Batavia to make it the center for Dutch authority in its East Indies possessions.[14] With Dutch supremacy firmly established in the Moluccas and Java, the Dutch faced no rivals of comparable power. The Portuguese remained at Melaka and Timor, while Spain was fully occupied in the Philippines. To eliminate the residual Portuguese presence, the Dutch organized an assault on Melaka. Their attack began with a blockade in 1633, and intensified into siege by 1640. The next year, the Portuguese defenders at Melaka finally surrendered.

During the seventeenth century, the Dutch established a monopoly system of trade. Contracts were made with local rulers for the supply of valued products, especially spices. To address the issues of security and stability, the Dutch intervened to stop internecine conflicts in their region and began bringing the states of Java into their orbit of control. This system of rule required the use of Dutch troops to support treaty-bound rulers and periodic involvement in wars and conflicts with "rebel" factions and recalcitrant rulers. By 1772, the VOC had extended some form of control over all of Java.[15]

Although most of the Dutch were Calvinist Christians, most of them were not militant in their religious commitments. They had experienced the appalling brutality of the Spanish Inquisition; principles of religious liberty were strongly supported in the Netherlands, and sympathy for the victims of the Inquisition extended to both Jews and Muslims. Later, these attitudes helped to shape Dutch policies. For the VOC directors, the religion of the rulers was of little importance, so long as the terms of contract agreements were met and incidences of piracy or hostile actions were kept under control. Some native states benefited from the system and were allies, while others were excluded and became the objects of surveillance and police actions. Many native rulers were willing to make agreements with the Dutch by sharing in the profits of trade and being supported by Dutch forces to protect their claims to rulership. However, a few rulers resisted the rules of the mercantilist system, and those who opposed Dutch rule often utilized Islam as an ideological basis for their actions. Early opposition to the Dutch presence came from the state of Bantam, with its capital in West Java and its primary domains in South Sumatra. The Dutch first intervened in 1683 to support a rival Bantam court clique in a palace revolt, and a century later Bantam was converted to a Dutch protectorate.[16]

During the Napoleonic Wars, France occupied the Netherlands in 1795 and appointed a French governor general for the East Indies. However, a Dutch government in exile was formed to resist that occupation, and they authorized

England to expel French officials from the East Indies and to act as a trustee until Dutch authority could be restored. Accordingly, in 1811 British troops seized Batavia, forcing the surrender of French forces. The British government appointed Stamford Raffles as lieutenant governor of Java, and under his rule, the monopoly system of trade was ended and other reforms were instituted based on liberal principles of open economic competition.[17] When Dutch administration returned in 1816, the Netherlands and England agreed in 1824 to redefine their respective spheres in Southeast Asia.[18] The Dutch also decided to establish full control over all the islands of Indonesia within the Dutch sphere as defined by that treaty. It took two wars with staunchly Muslim native states before that process of incorporation was completed in 1898.

Islamist Opposition to Dutch Rule

The first war involved Minangkabau lands in central Sumatra. In 1803, some pilgrims went to Mecca for the haj and became converted to the Hambali version of Islamic orthodoxy. On their return, they began a campaign, as the Padri movement, to enforce Islamic orthodoxy and challenge the authority of Minangkabau rulers. A civil war ensued between Islamist reformers and Minangkabau rulers and chiefs. The insurgents killed the entire Minangkabau royal house in 1809, and fugitive chiefs appealed for Dutch intervention. Dutch-led forces began operations in 1823 with skirmishes that continued until 1838, after which most of the Padri leaders had been captured, tried, and either executed or sent to exile. In response to this uprising, the Dutch instituted some reforms relating to taxes and local grievances, and thereafter Dutch officials were careful to select chiefs who opposed the radical Padri movement doctrines.[19]

The second and more costly colonial war involved the state of Aceh. Because Aceh became the first state in Southeast Asia to convert to Islam in the thirteenth century, it enjoyed a special status throughout the region. The Acehnese were proud of their piety and their Islamic faith and fiercely defended their autonomy. For several centuries, the Dutch were careful not to challenge the Acehnese directly. However, by the nineteenth century, the strategic balance in Southeast Asia shifted when the British established their two bases at Penang in 1786 and at Singapore in 1819. Competition between Dutch, British, and US traders for access to Aceh's market destabilized Aceh's political scene, which was dominated by powerful territorial chiefs called *uleebalangs*. Increased profits from production of pepper and from piracy raids gave these chiefs the capacity and incentive to defy the authority of the sultan of Aceh. To stabilize the region, the Dutch decided to extend colonial administration to Aceh. To secure a protectorate agreement from the sultan, they sent a force of 3,000 troops to Aceh in 1873. Instead of agreeing to Dutch demands, the sultan's forces mounted fierce resistance that killed General Johan Köhler, who was commanding the Dutch forces. When the sultan's stockade could not be stormed, the Dutch retreated with their troops to their ships and returned to their bases. The next year, Dutch officers returned with 14,500 troops equipped with cavalry and artillery. This was the beginning of a conflict that lasted for over thirty years.

When the Dutch forces arrived, they took the capital at Aceh Besar and expected the regional chiefs (uleebalangs) to come to sue for peace after a period of persuasion and the effects of a Dutch blockade. Over the next several years, Dutch military tactics vacillated between waiting behind fortified positions around Aceh Besar and making offensive forays to exert control over Aceh's central valley and its two coasts. However, because of divisions among the uleebalangs, unified action for either peace or war was not possible. In this vacuum, new leaders emerged to mobilize the Acehnese peasantry to resist Dutch colonial rule. When the first Dutch expedition attacked Aceh, some ulama proclaimed jihad for Muslims to resist Dutch demands. When a second expedition arrived, the ulama had mobilized mass support for a jihad to resist Dutch forces. The leader of that resistance was Tuengku Chik di Tiro, who acted as the military commander during Sultan Daud's preteen regentship. After several years, the war had been so radicalized that peace was virtually impossible for both sides. The Dutch could attack at will with devastating consequences, but ulama-led guerrilla forces were able to mount ambush attacks that decimated Dutch forces, creating low morale and defections from their ranks. In January 1891, Tuengku Chik di Tiro was killed, but his descendants and others from the ulama-led resistance continued to mount episodic attacks against Dutch authority.[20]

Eventually, the Dutch authorities began looking for a resolution to the seemingly endless stalemate. They turned for advice to a Dutch Islamic scholar, Christiaan Snouck Hurgronje, who was professor of Islamic law at Leiden University. After eight months of research in Aceh, he submitted his report in May 1892. Because of intense Acehnese hatred of the East Indies government, he recognized that force was needed and identified the ulama as the war party that inspired and incited resistance. He proposed ending negotiations with the sultan's family to restore the sultanate and ending the relentless pursuit of ulama leaders. Instead, he opted to restore the role of the uleebalangs, provided that they swore full loyalty to the government. He proposed greater efforts to conciliate a sullen but passive majority, including welfare measures for peasant farmers and strict rules to avoid military operations that harmed local communities. Initially, this report on Aceh was not well received, but eventually most of its recommendations were implemented. Gradually, the Dutch defeated or captured most of the militant ulama, and in 1903 Sultan Daud finally surrendered to the East Indies government. However, some descendants of Tuengku Chik di Tiro continued scattered guerrilla activities until 1913.[21]

Although Aceh was finally integrated into the Dutch colonial system, the Aceh War created a legacy of bitterness and religious militancy that has continued to the present. Thousands of peasants learned the strategies and tactics of guerrilla warfare and became attuned to an ethos of violence. These experiences were easily revived in the postindependence era when contentious issues and high-value resources, such as oil, increased the stakes of politics.

Islam and Society in the Indies

The interaction between Islam and Dutch colonial rule created important fissures and social divisions within Indonesian society. Even as early as the VOC period, the Dutch believed that the key to their power depended upon retaining the loyalty of Indonesia's royal houses and their indigenous aristocracy. As the Dutch built up a structure of treaties and agreements with the sultans, Dutch rule became ever more dependent upon the aristocratic stratum of society, called *priyayi,* meaning "a person of rank." In the Netherlands East Indies colonial system, the native ruler was paid an emolument to support the functions of the throne. The ruler was given the title regent and expected to represent his subjects in consultation with Dutch authorities. In traditional Malay and Javanese society, authority is hierarchical and based on a code of etiquette according to rank. Because the East Indies government exercised ultimate power, what remained for the regents were the rituals of government and responsibility for the application of Adat law and Islamic affairs. Thus, at a time when their real power was greatly diminished, the regents became more responsible for the enforcement of Islamic law and doctrine.

Many of the priyayi were employed as lower-level civil servants, under the supervision of Dutch officers. Over time, many of the priyayi acquired Dutch education, often in private schools, and they became comfortable in two cultures—native aristocratic and Dutch colonial. As they became Westernized, they could no longer act as devout leaders of the umma.[22] During the nineteenth century, peasants were required to devote one-fifth of the land area for the cultivation of an assigned cash crop, which was collected in kind by the government in lieu of taxes. Known as the Culture System, it had the effect of escalating demands on peasant agricultural producers for unpaid labor. That system lasted from 1831 to 1870, but its economic and social impact extended much longer.[23] Because the Dutch expected the priyayi to organize and mobilize compulsory peasant labor, the priyayi were paid with generous monetary and status rewards, and they could easily acquire even more through various forms of corruption. This system bound traditional rulers and Indonesian aristocrats into the structure of colonial production, but these practices also eroded popular respect of ordinary Indonesians for their rulers and the priyayi.

Islamic doctrine provides for a Muslim ruler to act as the vice-regent of God and the protector of Islam. Under colonial rule, Muslim monarchs continued to exercise that authority, aided by a small bureaucracy of ulama and Sharia court officials. The kathi courts administered Islamic family law, inheritance, Islamic taxes, pilgrimage, and Islamic religious foundations. The Dutch administrative system applied Islamic law only to professing Muslims and to relations between Muslims. For these jurisdictions, Sharia law was combined with Adat law to produce a very conservative legal system. Most native rulers and the priyayi culturally represented the Javanese Great Tradition, with their courtly manners and their participation in Hindu, Buddhist, and animist rituals that were openly displayed. Consequently, their interpretations and practices of Islam tolerated wide diversity in Islamic beliefs and rituals. For orthodox Muslims, most native rulers and their priyayi represented a "watered down" version of Islam, if not outright examples of heresy.

At the other, lower end of the Javanese class structure were fairly autonomous peasant societies that represented the Little Tradition of the same cultural mix. Peasants with this perspective believed that they were good Muslims who were also committed to Adat law and to the selamatan ceremonies that sustained their mystical view of a spirit world. Orthodox Muslims referred to these peasants as *abangan*, by which they meant "nonreligious or unbelieving people." Those who lived in these rural village societies accepted that term to mean "brotherhood, or kinship," viewing themselves as a community of believers committed both to Islam and the traditional rituals and beliefs of their forefathers. For the abangan, many of the obligations and practices of Islam were viewed as worthy displays of piety, but they interpreted Islamic obligations to be a matter of individual choice, rather than for compulsory enforcement through community sanctions.

The third major cultural-religious division within Indonesian Islam came to be called *santri*. This term is applied to orthodox Muslims who pray five times a day, who strictly observe Islamic food restrictions and the fasting month of Ramadan, and who faithfully study and consult the Quran. The santri were usually products of the many Islamic schools, called *madrasahs,* often established by Arab teachers or by Indonesians who had made the haj pilgrimage to Mecca and studied Islam in the Middle East. Students at these privately run Islamic schools usually dressed in Arab-style white, flowing garments as a means of displaying and asserting their Islamic piety. Because Islam came to Indonesia through the port cities, the santri became more numerous in urban areas and among merchant and seafaring communities. Because the santri valued religious and cultural links with Saudi Arabia, it was relatively easy for any Arab immigrant to gain respected status within the santri community. If an Arab claimed the title Syed, denoting a direct descendant of the Prophet Muhammad, his leadership in the santri community was greatly enhanced. The infusion of both Arab and Indian Muslims into leadership roles within Indonesian society on the basis of their Arab origin, their orthodoxy, and their displays of piety made them natural protagonists against the older traditional Indonesian priyayi gentry class.[24]

The triad division between priyayi, abangan, and santri is present throughout Indonesia but is less pronounced in the outer islands.[25] Other religious traditions can also be found in Indonesia, with a more complex mix often present in these peripheral areas. Classical medieval Hinduism survived in Bali, where the indigenous population is almost entirely Hindu. The highlands of central Sumatra, populated by the various Batak tribes, were entirely animist, but during the colonial era many Bataks were converted to Christianity by the Rhenish Lutheran Mission, the Methodists, or by Catholic missionaries. Among the Torajas of Sulawesi, Christian missions generated widespread conversions from animism to Christianity. Finally, the immigrant communities that came to Indonesia all brought their native religions with them. The Chinese practice a mixture of Taoism and Buddhism. South Indian immigrants have been mostly Hindu. In the colonial setting, some immigrants converted to Islam, but a greater number from immigrant communities converted to Christianity.

Despite the conflicts between colonial authorities and Islamic-based movements in Aceh, Minangkabau, and Bantam, for most areas of the Dutch East Indies, colonial rule was extended with a minimum of conflict and with very little disruption to the indigenous structures of authority. Dutch authorities did not consider Islam to pose a direct threat to the colonial political order, but they were aware that Islam could be used for political purposes that could destabilize and threaten the colonial political order. For that reason, they were eager to make accommodations for Islam that would bring both the native rulers and their Islamic coadjutors into the political structure of the colonial system. A carefully crafted system of mutual accommodation and support emerged between colonial authorities and native elites who derived their power from colonial authority and their status from Islam. The Dutch accorded official recognition to Islam, and public funds were allocated for the construction of mosques and the support of mosque officials. Practicing Muslims were protected against proselytizing activities of non-Muslim missionaries. Islamic courts were established, but their jurisdiction was severely limited and their powers of enforcement depended on the confirming actions of secular courts. The Dutch supervised the codification of some aspects of Sharia law but combined it with Adat law to make a unique and conflictive amalgam.

This combination of legal systems was specifically designed to take "radicalism" out of Islamic movements by stressing autonomous Adat communities.[26] Thus, formal and institutional Islam was given a very conservative and stabilizing role deemed to be appropriate for peasant society, but Sharia law was deemed to be not relevant or appropriate for matters of public law, commercial and contract law, tort, or criminal law. By their actions, the colonial authorities helped to preserve the medieval and ritualistic qualities of Islam at the same time that its formal legal structures and its salience for practicing Muslims was also being diminished. For the Dutch, their policy toward Islam was designed to keep Muslim peasants engaged in their traditional patterns of life, protected from the destabilizing impact of the modern world in matters of economics, politics, and ideologies.[27] In many ways, Islam, as shaped by colonial rule, helped to encapsulate a peasant-based society to preserve its identity boundaries and basic ritual forms. That encapsulation tended to insulate peasant society from the rapid social and intellectual changes imparted by the globalized economy of the colonial order.

British Rule in Malaya and the Straits Settlements

After the defeat of the Spanish Armada, the opportunities for direct trade with China and the Spice Islands attracted both British and Dutch traders. In 1600, the British formed the East India Company to promote trade with Asia. For over two decades, the British followed Dutch traders to Southeast Asia, but conflicts over facilities and monopolies soon led to open warfare. In 1623, the Dutch expelled all British traders from Amboina and the Moluccas.[28] Thereafter, the British East India Company concentrated on trade with India. It would be a century and a half later before the British attempted a return to Southeast Asia.

The first British base on the Indian subcontinent was obtained at Madras in 1639, followed by Bombay in 1688 and Calcutta in 1691.[29] Protected by impressive forts, these three ports became bastions for the extension of Company control over much of the Indian subcontinent during the eighteenth and nineteenth centuries. When the French, operating from Mauritius and Pondicherry, began challenging British supremacy in India, Company officials became anxious to find an all-weather port to support naval patrols in the Bay of Bengal and to service ships engaged in their China trade. To address this issue, in 1786 the East India Company authorized Francis Light to negotiate with the sultan of Kedah to establish a base at the Island of Penang. Kedah was a vassal state of Siam and the sultan wanted protection both from Siam and from neighboring states. That agreement established terms for a lease by the British at Penang in return for a promise of protection.[30]

The British return to Southeast Asia came just as the Napoleonic Wars were creating havoc in Europe. As mentioned earlier, after France invaded the Netherlands, Britain acted as trustee over Dutch colonies on behalf of the Netherlands' exile government. Stamford Raffles was appointed lieutenant governor of Java during the years of that trusteeship, which extended from 1811 to 1816. After his term in Java expired, Raffles returned to the region in 1819 to explore for a new British base. He discovered that the Malay state of Johor was embroiled in a succession dispute, and one claimant agreed to cede the Island of Singapore to Britain in return for a nominal payment and British recognition of his claim to the Johor throne.[31] In 1824, the Dutch agreed to cede Melaka to the British in exchange for the British enclave of Bencoolen on Sumatra's west coast. Penang, Singapore, and Melaka became three British colonies, administered together and called the Straits Settlements. Because they were acquired for strategic purposes to protect shipping, British officers expressed no interest in the affairs of adjacent Malay states, which they viewed as unruly areas where anarchy flourished.[32] British intentions were soon tested by events that forced their hand.

By the 1830s, Chinese immigrants began flocking to the tin fields of Selangor and Perak, bringing with them their Chinese secret societies that were organized into paramilitary formations. The rivalries between Chinese secret societies were mirrored by rivalries between Malay court factions. Soon, one Malay-Chinese coalition confronted a rival Malay-Chinese coalition over control of the tin fields. Known as the Larut Wars, vicious battles between rival factions lasted from 1861 through 1873. When violence spilled over to the Straits Settlements, the governor of Penang, Sir Andrew Clarke, summoned key Chinese secret society leaders and Malay chiefs of Perak to a meeting on Pangkor Island in 1874 to settle their dispute. Under the terms of that agreement, the Sultan Abdullah of Perak agreed to accept a British officer, to be called Resident, "whose advice must be asked and acted upon in all questions other than those touching Malay Religion and custom."[33] The leaders of the Chinese factions also signed a bond promising to disarm and to keep the peace. This treaty established the basis for the Resident System, whereby British officers defined policy, supervised the collection of taxes, and became responsible for government administration.

The first Resident appointed to the state of Perak was J. W. W. Birch, who went to Perak by himself without any police escort. Birch reflected the reformist zeal of Benthamite liberals, who were calling on British officers to initiate reforms of native societies. He was especially eager to end slavery, extortion, blackmailing, and the feudal dues that were collected by local chiefs as protection money from whomever they could. What some of the chiefs viewed as "old customs," Birch viewed as the violation of the rule of law. In November 1874, assassins hired by a cabal of Malay chiefs murdered Birch. Very quickly British authorities ordered an expedition of troops to hunt down the murderers. Three Malay chiefs were hanged and Abdullah and other co-conspirators were banished to the Seychelles. An official inquiry into the events concluded that Birch had acted "injudiciously" with regard to Malay customs and that he should not have interfered with the "feudal taxation system" until after allowances had been fixed to compensate the Malay chiefs for their losses.[34]

This decision regarding relations with Malay states was influenced by the British experience in India during the Sepoy Mutiny of 1857. In the postmortem to that mutiny, British authorities concluded that social and religious reforms had come at too fast a pace, without adequate measures to ameliorate their effects on native society. They also concluded that it was dangerous to tamper with religious affairs and "proclaimed a policy of justice, benevolence and religious toleration," enjoining colonial officials to "abstain from all interference with the religious belief or worship of subjects."[35]

After the Pangkor Engagement with Perak and restoration of order in that state, similar treaties were signed with all other Malay sultans transferring rights of protection to Britain and providing for British officers to assume primary responsibility for civil administration. The sultan of Johor signed the last treaty in 1914 providing for his state to become part of the Resident System, with British officers providing "advice" and exercising "indirect rule."[36]

Malaysian Islam Codified, Protected, and Marginalized

Under the Resident System, British officers were extremely sensitive to Malay concerns and were willing to acknowledge Islam as a central pillar of authority for Malay society. Although Islamic law and doctrine acknowledge no distinction between religious and secular authority, the British made a clear distinction between civil authority and "Malay religion and custom." Civil authority became the responsibility of British officers, while Islam and Malay custom became the preserve of the sultans. English common law, as modified by statutes passed by legislative councils in each state, were established as the supreme law of the land. Gradually Islamic law was codified according to the Shafi'i school of jurisprudence into statutes for each state. By this process, the scope of Islamic law was reduced primarily to Islamic personal law and religious obligations of Muslims with other Muslims. Thus, marriage, divorce, family law, Islamic institutions, inheritance, bequests and Islamic trusts, the collection of *zakat* (charity) taxes, and the responsibility of Islamic officials were all deemed to be within the jurisdiction of Islamic courts.[37]

For Muslims, the structure of administration was more elaborate and the symbols of Islam were more prominent, because each Malay state was deemed to be Islamic, and Islamic institutions were directly supported by the state. At the apex of the authority structure of Islam was the Malay ruler, acting as the vice-regent of Allah. In most Malay states, the highest Islamic official was the mufti, who acted as chief justice for the Islamic court system and was responsible for interpreting Muslim law and doctrine. The most important power of the mufti involved the issuing of fatwas, which are legally binding rulings interpreting Muslim law, defining orthodoxy, or for an enforcement order of an Islamic edict. In states with no mufti, fatwas were issued by a fatwa committee or a Sharia committee.[38]

Judicial administration of Islamic affairs rested with a separate court system known as Sharia courts or kathi courts. The following are typical criminal offenses that were included in Islamic statutes and enforced by Malaya's Sharia courts:

- failure to attend Friday prayers at the mosque
- consumption of intoxicating liquor
- consumption of food, drink, or tobacco during daylight hours during the month of Ramadan

- willful disobedience by a Muslim woman of an order lawfully given by her Muslim husband
- a Muslim male found in suspicious proximity with any woman, other than a woman he is forbidden to marry because of consanguinity, is guilty of *khalwat*[39]
- sexual intercourse between a husband and wife in a manner forbidden by Islam
- teaching any doctrine of Islam without written permission of the Malay ruler of the state
- propagating any religious doctrine other than Islam or teaching false doctrines among persons professing Islam
- printing or distributing books or documents repugnant to Islamic law and doctrine
- use of passages from the Quran or sacred words in public entertainment
- contempt of any Islamic authorities or officials in the state or of the law of Islam or its tenets[40]

Although Islam was the official state religion in the Malay states and Islamic institutions were supported with state funds, Islam remained in the backwash of economic, social, and political activities during the colonial era. The Sharia courts had a narrow jurisdiction, applying only to Muslims and in civil cases; they were limited to disputes of very small sums; and in criminal cases, the maximum penalty that could be applied was a fine, usually less than M$50.[41] Nearly all the political, criminal, and commercial provisions of traditional Sharia law were placed beyond the jurisdiction of Malaya's Sharia courts. What was preserved and propagated in both law and theological doctrine was a very conservative form of Islam that was mixed with Adat law, and British authorities assumed this combination reflected the values, practices, and needs of a peasant-based society.

Because the Straits Settlements were crown colonies directly under the authority of the British government, Islam was not the official religion in Penang, Melaka, and Singapore. Therefore, Islam was not protected in those crown colonies, but Sharia law was still applied to Muslims in matters relating to family law, just as Chinese family law, Hindu family law, and Christian family law applied to each community of faith. The Church of England was the nominal established church in those colonies, but all faiths were given full freedom to practice and preach among any community in the Straits Settlements. Because of possible Malay reactions that might affect the Malay states, British administrators discouraged, but did not prohibit, Christian missions from working among the Malays in the Straits Settlements. Otherwise, in these three British colonies there was a fairly equal degree of religious liberty for all faiths.

Colonial "Trusteeship" and Malay Special Privileges

British officers took very seriously the legal fiction of British rule on behalf of the Malay rulers and their subjects. The power structure of Malay society from regional chiefs to the sultan of each state was not only preserved and supported with titles and government emoluments, but it was also utilized to represent Malay interests very effectively in policymaking. In effect, the tables were turned. The sultans had become advisers to the British administrators on how best to placate and ameliorate Malay concerns that emerged as the country was opened up to large numbers of foreign immigrants and to foreign investments in resource-extractive enterprises, such as tin mining and rubber plantations. To meet the demands that were generated through the traditional hierarchical power structures of Malay society, the colonial authorities instituted a set of policies to give special advantages and protections to Malays.

To reflect the Malay character of government, the British established a preferential system for recruiting Malays into government service. The top administrative positions of government were held by the Malayan Civil Service (MCS), which was staffed entirely by Europeans, mostly British, recruited on the basis of exams that were based on British university degree requirements. Below the MCS was the Malay Administrative Service (MAS), recruited exclusively from those legally defined as Malay. Most positions in the MAS were filled by the Malay aristocracy. In 1905, the government opened the Malay Residential School at Kuala Kangsar, later renamed the Malay College. In 1920, the English College was established at Johor Bahru. At both these institutions the students were Malays from aristocratic families who received support from the government for their education. These schools educated a small stratum of Malay elites who later were employed and gained leadership experience in the Malay Administrative Service.

For the ordinary nonaristocratic Malays, the government also established a free and compulsory vernacular education system, beginning about 1896. Only the Malays received free public education at government expense. All other communities had access to government-aided schools that also collected school fees for student enrollment. The vernacular Malay schools suffered from a shortage of teachers, but gradually most areas of Malay settlement were served by schools teaching in Malay based on Romanized script (*rumi*) rather than Arabic *jawi* script. In Malay schools, poorly trained teachers used rote teaching techniques of mass student unison repetition of instructional materials. The curriculum consisted of instruction in Islamic rituals and principles, transmission of Malay cultural values, plus some rudimentary instruction in reading, health, and practical skills for peasant farmers and fishermen. These schools terminated at the primary level in the fourth year and provided no access to further education. The majority of students in Malay vernacular schools dropped out after the third year. These schools helped to reinforce commitment to Islam and

Malay culture, but they did little to raise aspirations of Malay peasants or enhance educational skills beyond rudimentary literacy.[42]

Government policies provided two other areas of "special protection" for Malays. Large areas of land where Malays were settled and where peasant agriculture prevailed were designated as Malay Reservations. In these areas, the traditional Malay system of land ownership was acknowledged in law, and only Malays could own or buy land in these specified areas. In the matter of certain trades or businesses, permits or licenses were reserved for Malays on a quota system. Both of these measures were designed to assure that Malay society would not become disadvantaged by the competition posed by the immigrant communities to Malaya. Because of the superimposed definition of Malay and Muslim, these rights depended upon the continued affirmation of Islam as well as the linguistic and cultural inheritance of Malay identity. A Malay who would abandon Islam, even without conversion to another faith, would lose all claims to Malay "special privileges," and if he owned title to land in a Malay Reservation, in law, he would also lose title to that land.

British policies toward the Malays and the Malay rulers received the wholehearted support of Malays in nearly all walks of life. The Malay lifestyle and culture at the peasant level were protected from the vicissitude and challenges posed by modern competitive economic enterprise and the urban style of life. Malays were protected in their religion and secure in the life cycle of peasant activities. Islam was an integrative force providing meaning and structure to the repetitive cycle of rice cultivation and the fishing seasons. The nature of Islam was benign and tolerant of the residual pre-Islamic elements in Malay culture and beliefs. Colonial rule had established peace, ending the precolonial cycles of violence and political instability that plagued precolonial Malay politics and culture. In the prewar years, Malay women were not secluded or veiled, although they would wear a light head scarf when they engaged in religious or ceremonial activities. Malay women were well represented as petty merchants in village market selling. They worked long hours in the padi fields during planting and harvest cycle, because it was believed that the rice would grow better and the flavor of the rice would be superior when women did the planting and harvesting of the crop. Many of the restrictive injunctions of Islam about dress codes and restrictive rules limiting the roles of women were ignored in Malay society, because Adat rules gave women substantial property rights and sanctioned an egalitarian role for women in traditional Malay society and family life.

Malay royalty and aristocracy enjoyed the financial and status benefits from colonial rule. The sultans had large and lavish palaces, polo stables, and multiple garages to house their collections of Rolls Royce cars and sport vehicles. Most Malay sultans and some princes owned villas in England, where they would spend a month or more each year, basking in the status and pomp that the British lavished on "native rulers" who were part of the British Empire. Rulers and their titled elite usually sent their sons to English schools, either in Malaya or to boarding schools in England. Upon graduation, they often continued at English universities, usually pursuing, at a leisurely pace, a degree in law, political economy, or officer training at a police or military academy. These were all benefits that Malays of aristocratic rank assumed were inherently theirs by virtue of their status in Malay society. Who could complain about that and why would Malays criticize colonial policies that provided those benefits that Malay leaders sought and defended?

In many ways the colonial system enabled Malay society to exist in an idyllic form, protected and isolated by policies that had been formulated in consultation with traditional Malay elites. These protective policies were designed to perpetuate peasant traditions based on Islamic norms against the economic and cultural challenges posed by immigrant communities and by Western norms and values that were being transmitted by colonial rule. The cumulative consequence of these pro-Malay policies was to create a virtual encapsulation of most Malays into self-contained communities that were isolated from the pressures and demands of modern life that were yet to become manifest.

At the time, British colonial power seemed to be projected into the indefinite future, and colonial policy based on the primacy of Malay political institutions seemed to be a formula for both economic development of the country and the cultural survival of the Malays. Very few people had the insight to anticipate a different future and even fewer were willing to challenge those assumptions.[43] Dramatic and unforeseen forces would soon challenge the colonial system as well as the assumed primacy of traditional forms of Malay power, culture, and religion.

The Legacy of Colonial Rule for Southeast Asian Islam

The first colonial power in Southeast Asia established a pattern of hostility toward Islam that had long-term consequences for the region. The Portuguese suppressed and fractured the Muslim trading system, but did not eliminate those who operated that system. Instead, those traders sought refuge in Muslim sanctuaries, which became "enclaves of Islamic militancy" where Islam flourished as a political opposition to the extensions of rule and power by European colonial powers. At these enclaves, Islamic militancy was cultivated, honored, and passed on from generation to generation as a legacy of community heroism. The Portuguese did not create these enclaves of militancy, but their policies induced Malay seafaring traders to mobilize around Islamic principles to protect their culture and their resources by fostering militancy. These "enclaves of Islamic militancy" formed at Aceh, Bantam (West Java), South Sulawesi, Brunei, and the southern Philippines. At these enclaves, Islam became an ideology of resistance to subjugation by colonial authorities, and in the postcolonial era, traditions of political militancy were revived in defense of autonomy, independence, and Islamic orthodoxy.

Spanish colonial rule created the only Christian majority state in East and South Asia, and in doing so, it also created the enduring hostility of the Muslims in the southern Philippines. That religious and cultural divide became more intensified by the United States when it suppressed the low-level insurgency of the Moros and as a "solution" promoted the settlement of Philippine Christians into regions that Muslims claimed as their traditional lands. By changing the demographic landscape of the Southern Philippines, the option of Moro independence was effectively blocked. Yet, without addressing Muslim concerns, the net result produced an accumulation of grievances and hostility that would sustain insurgency into an indefinite future.

Dutch rule in the East Indies produced three and a half centuries of relative peace and developed the economic potential of the region to produce products for world markets. But, it did so by policies that diverted large profits to the Netherlands. The Dutch were tolerant and supportive of Islam, so long as Muslims did not invoke Islam to generate opposition to Dutch rule. The Dutch encountered opposition when they attempted to extend authority over "enclaves of Islamic militancy" that had formed earlier in response to the Portuguese destruction of the Muslim trading system. Dutch authorities made virtually no effort to prepare natives to acquire education and representation in colonial governing institutions. After the Japanese occupation, the Dutch campaign to regain control of Indonesia by military force merely added to the chaos and the destruction of the economic infrastructure that had been built up by previous years of Dutch rule. Whatever benefits that Dutch rule had brought to the Indies became wasted and despised by the new leaders of Indonesia.

The British established generally favorable relations with Muslim communities in Malaya by asserting the privileged status of Malays in the colonial system and by cultivating and respecting the symbolic status of Malay rulers. They also promised to preserve "the Malay way of life," which was a short-term benefit to the Malays, but a long-term impediment. Islam was a crucial part of "the Malay way of life," so it was also preserved in its Southeast Asian syncretic forms. When the era of decolonization came after World War II, in comparison to the other immigrant communities, the Malays were least prepared to assume a leadership position and gain equitable economic benefits from independence. The so-called Malay dilemma became the product of the policy consensus worked out between colonial authorities and Malay rulers in the nineteenth century. The legacy of that era continues to plague policymakers in the twenty-first century.

Notes

1. Ira M. Lapidus, *A History of Islamic Societies* (Cambridge: Cambridge University Press, 1988), 378–389.

2. John F. Cady, *Southeast Asia: Its Historical Development* (New York: McGraw-Hill, 1964), 172–176.

3. Nicholas Tarling, *Southeast Asia: A Modern History* (South Melbourne: Oxford University Press, 2001), 21–25; Cady, *Southeast Asia,* 174–183; D. G. E. Hall, *A History of South-East Asia* (London: Macmillan, 1955), 197–203; D. J. M. Tate, *The Making of Modern South-East Asia*, Vol. 1, *The European Conquest,* rev. ed. (Kuala Lumpur: Oxford University Press, 1977), 42–45, 49.

4. Cady, *Southeast Asia,* 179–186; Hall, *A History of South-East Asia,* 201–203.

5. Nicholas Tarling, *Piracy and Politics in the Malay World* (Singapore: Donald Moore, 1963).

6. Edward J. McCarthy, *Spanish Beginnings in the Philippines* (Washington, DC: The Catholic University of America Press, 1943), 15–94; Tate, *Modern South-East Asia,* Vol. 1, 332–345; Frederic H. Chaffee, *Area Handbook for the Philippines* (Washington, DC: US Government Printing Office, 1969), 47–87, 119–131; Hall, *A History of South-East Asia,* 248–255.

7. Tate, *Modern South-East Asia,* Vol. 1, 346–353, 359–363.

8. H. W. Brands, *Bound to Empire: The United States and the Philippines* (New York: Oxford University Press, 1992), 39–59; Cady, *Southeast Asia*, 461–465.

9. Tate, *Modern South-East Asia*, Vol. 1, 369–383; Cady, *Southeast Asia*, 466–467.

10. Peter Chalk, "Militant Islamic Extremism in the Southern Philippines," in Jason F. Isaacson and Colin Rubenstein (eds.), *Islam in Asia: Changing Political Realities* (New Brunswick, NJ: Transaction Publishers, 2002), 214, citing B. R. Rodil, *The Minoritization of the Indigenous Communities of Mindanao and Sulu* (Quezon, Negros, Philippines: Alternate Forum for Research in Mindanao, 1994), 49.

11. Tate, *Modern South-East Asia*, Vol. 1, 379; D. J. M. Tate, *The Making of Modern South-East Asia,* Vol. 2, *The Western Impact, Economic and Social Change* (Kuala Lumpur: Oxford University Press, 1979), 451–452; Isaacson and Rubenstein, *Islam in Asia*, 187–188.

12. Ferdinand Schevill, *History of Europe* (New York: Harcourt, Brace, 1947), 174–177, 185–194; Goldwin Smith, *A History of England* (Chicago: Charles Scribner's Sons, 1949), 254–259.

13. J. J. van Klaveren, *The Dutch Colonial System in the East Indies* (Rotterdam: Drukkerij Benedictus, 1953), 36; Holden Furber, *Rival Empires of Trade in the Orient, 1600–1800* (Minneapolis: University of Minnesota Press, 1976), 186–191.

14. Tate, *Modern South-East Asia,* Vol. 2, 47–57; Klaveren, *The Dutch Colonial System*, 39–43.

15. Hall, *A History of South-East Asia,* 266–277.

16. Tate, *Modern South-East Asia,* Vol. 1, 63–70.

17. Bernard H. M. Vlekke, *Nusantara: A History of Indonesia* (The Hague: W. van Hoeve, 1959), 259–283.

18. Under the terms of the Anglo-Dutch Treaty of 1824, the British transferred their settlement of Benkulen on Sumatra's west coast to the Dutch, and the Dutch transferred Melaka and Ceylon to the British. The British "sphere of influence" included the Malay Peninsula and to the east and north of the equator, while the Dutch sphere included Sumatra and to the east and south of the equator. Anthony Reid, *The Contest for North Sumatra: Atjeh, the Netherlands and Britain 1858–1898* (Kuala Lumpur: Oxford University Press, 1969), 10–14; W. G. Maxwell and W. S. Gibson (eds.), *Treaties and Engagements Affecting the Malay States and Borneo* (London: Jay Truscott and Son, 1924), 8–16.

19. M. C. Ricklefs, *A History of Modern Indonesia Since c. 1200,* 3rd ed. (Stanford: Stanford University Press, 2001), 184–189; Tate, *Modern South-East Asia,* Vol. 1, 152–156.

20. Tate, *Modern South-East Asia,* 222–231; Reid, *The Contest for North Sumatra,* 91–112, 250–256.

21. Tate, *Modern South-East Asia,* Vol. 1, 231–236; Reid, *The Contest for North Sumatra,* 270–283; Vlekke, *Nusantara,* 317–328; Tim Kell, *The Roots of Acehnese Rebellion* (Ithaca, NY: Cornell Modern Indonesia Project, 1995), 7–8.

22. Clifford Geertz, *The Religion of Java* (New York: Free Press of Glencoe, 1960, 1964), 234–260.

23. Tate, *Modern South-East Asia,* Vol. 2, 34–110.

24. Geertz, *The Religion of Java,* 16–111, 177–198, 227–260; Robert W. Hefner, *Civil Islam: Muslims and Democratization in Indonesia* (Princeton, NJ: Princeton University Press, 2000), 82–89.

25. Because most abangan do not believe they are outside the pale of Islam, and most santri assume that the abangan are targets for conversion to "the eternal truth of Islam," there is a natural blurring of these divisions that has occurred over the years. Instead of viewing these terms as precisely differentiated categories, it is more appropriate to utilize these terms as a bipolar typology. At one end of the scale, respondents can be ranked on the basis of Islamic orthodoxy; at the other end, they can be ranked on their syncretic adaptation of pre-Islamic practices and beliefs. For a criticism of Clifford Geertz's use of these categories, see Zifirdaus Adnan, "Islamic Religion: Yes, Islamic (Political) Ideology: No! Islam and the State in Indonesia," in Arief Budiman (ed.), *State and Civil Society in Indonesia,* (Clayton, UK: Monash Papers on Southeast Asia, No. 22, 1990), 441–477.

26. M. B. Hooker, *Indonesian Islam: Social Change Through Contemporary Fatawa* (Honolulu: University of Hawaii Press, 2003), 12–14. For an analysis of the Dutch colonial policy, beginning in 1925, to control Islamic "fanaticism" by emphasizing Adat law administered through village headmen rather than by ulama, see Harry J. Benda, *The Crescent and the Rising Sun: Indonesian Islam Under the Japanese Occupation, 1942–1945* (The Hague: W. van Hoeve, 1958), 61–99.

27. W. F. Wertheim, *Indonesian Society in Transition: A Study of Social Change,* 2nd rev. ed. (The Hague: W. van Hoeve, 1959), 300–303.

28. Furber, *Rival Empires of Trade*, 191–201; William Foster, *England's Quest for Eastern Trade* (London: Hakluyt Society, 1933).

29. Stanley Wolpert, *A New History of India* (New York: Oxford University Press, 1993), 143–148.

30. Hall, *A History of South-East Asia,* 489–501.

31. Ibid., 497–511; Tate, *Modern South-East Asia,* Vol. 1, 119–121; Charles Burton Buckley, *An Anecdotal History of Old Times in Singapore* (Singapore: Fraser & Neave, 1902, reprinted Kuala Lumpur: University of Malaya Press, 1965), 26–61.

32. Richard O. Winstedt, *Malaya and Its History,* 3rd ed. (London: Hutchinson's University Library, 1953), 63.

33. C. Northcote Parkinson, *British Intervention in Malaya, 1867–1877* (Singapore: University of Malaya Press, 1960), 125–142. Pages 323–325 contain the complete text of the Pangkor Engagement of 1874.

34. Winstedt, *Malaya and Its History,* 67–68; Barbara Watson Andaya and Leonard Y. Andaya, *A History of Malyasia,* 2nd ed. (Honolulu: University of Hawaii Press, 2001), 160–167.

35. R. C. Majumdar, H. C. Raychaudhuri, and Kalikinkar Datta, *An Advanced History of India*, 2nd ed. (London: Macmillan, 1953), 782.

36. Windstedt, *Malaya and Its History,* 76; Andaya and Andaya, *A History of Malyasia,* 167–184; Hall, *A History of South-East Asia,* 554–567; Frank Swettenham, *British Malaya*, 3rd rev. ed. (London: George Allen & Unwin, 1948), 245–271.

37. M. B. Hooker, *The Personal Laws of Malaysia* (Kuala Lumpur: Oxford University Press, 1976), 19–61. It should be noted that similar legislation governing marriages and family law was drafted for religious communities, including Buddhism, Taoism, Hinduism, Sikhism, and Christianity, as well as those who elected to have nonreligious civil marriages.

38. For a more complete account of Muslim law enactments in Malaya, see Gordon P. Means, "Malaysia: Islam in a Pluralistic Society," in Carlo Caldarola (ed.), *Religion and Societies: Asia and the Middle East* (Berlin: Mouton Publishers, 1982), 494.

39. Under this offense, any premarriage unchaperoned dating or nonpublic social interaction between a man and a woman who are not married to each other and not related by blood ties is viewed as a form of moral turpitude. In the early years, khalwat rules were applied only to men, but in the late 1930s these rules were applied to Muslim men and women. However, Muslim men faced no such restrictions in relations with non-Muslim females.

40. These examples of Islamic offenses are taken from the following state statutes: Johore—*Council of Religion Enactment, 1949*, No. 2 of 1949; Kedah—*Administration of Muslim Law Enactment, 1962*, No. 9 of 1962; Malacca—*Administration of Muslim Law Enactment, 1959*, No. 1 of 1959; Negri Sembilan—*Council of Muslim Religion Enactment, 1957*, No. 1 of 1957; Pahang—*Administration of Muslim Law Enactment, 1956*, No. 5 of 1956; Penang—*Administration of Muslim Law Enactment, 1959*, No. 3 of 1959; Selangor—*Administration of Muslim Law Enactment, 1952*, No. 3 of 1952; Trengganu—*The Administration of Islamic Law Enactment, 1955 (1375)*, No. 4 of 1955.

41. Mohamed Khalil bin Hussein, "The Department of Religious Affairs, Perak," academic exercise, Malay Studies Department, University of Malaya, Singapore, 1958; Moshe Yegar, *Islam and Islamic Institutions in British Malaya: Policies and Implementation* (Jerusalem: The Magnes Press, 1979), 5–93, 119–186.

42. Tham Seong Chee, *Malays and Modernization* (Singapore: Singapore University Press, 1977), 94–99; Chai Hon-Chan, *The Development of British Malaya, 1896–1909,* 2nd ed. (Kuala Lumpur: Oxford University Press, 1967), 247–252; Khoo Kay Kim, *Malay Society: Transformation and Democratisation* (Petaling Jaya, Malaysia: Pelanduk Publications, 1991), 185–194; William R. Roff, *The Origins of Malay Nationalism* (New Haven: Yale University Press, 1967), 100–113.

43. Rupert Emerson exposed incongruities and long-term liabilities of British colonial rule in his book: *Malaysia: A Study in Direct and Indirect Rule* (New York: Macmillan, 1937).

PART 2

The Struggles of Decolonization

4

Indonesia: Independence Without Consensus

During most of colonial rule, Dutch officers and compliant native rulers who understood the realities of colonial political power monopolized politics. During the first four decades of the twentieth century, that monopoly began to be challenged by aspiring leaders of constituencies that had grievances or concerns of cultural survival. The process of political mobilization was inchoate and usually began with a narrow agenda, but gradually expanded from cultural and religious issues to more comprehensive political agendas. The levels of political mobilization remained very low until after 1941. A brief survey of early organizations and their primary constituencies will illustrate how the political mobilization of one cultural constituency tended to induce rival constituencies to do the same. It becomes an issue of arbitrary definition whether these early groups should be called "parties" and whether they can be classified as "nationalist" during the early manifestations of political activity outside the closed circles of power.

In 1908, three students founded Budi Utomo (High Endeavor) to promote the idealism of Javanese Islam as represented by the priyayi strata of lower-level Javanese government officials and intellectuals. In 1911, Sarekat Islam was founded in the aftermath of anti-Chinese riots, initially reflecting primarily the interests of Indonesian petty traders, richer peasants, and urban ulama who generally adhered to more traditional orthodox santri interpretations of Islam. In 1912 Muhammadiyah was founded to promote a "modernist" form of santri Islam with cosmopolitan influences from both Arabia and Egypt. It gained support from better-educated Indonesian intellectuals, professionals, and civil servants. In 1926, rural-based ulama and teachers at rural Islamic schools founded Nahdlatul Ulama to represent the interests of abangan Muslims. Their leaders were mostly rural ulama and members were primarily peasant agriculturalists from Java and southern Sumatra.[1]

In 1914, the Indies Social Democratic Association became the first Marxist ideological party. It was founded by a Dutch citizen, H. Hendrik Sneevliet, and was reorganized in 1920 as the Indonesian Communist Party (PKI). In 1926–1927, the PKI led a revolutionary uprising among peasants in West Java and West Sumatra, but that revolt was decisively suppressed by Dutch authorities, and 1,300 accused PKI members were imprisoned in New Guinea and elsewhere. This defeat ended the PKI as a political force until its revival in the postcolonial era.[2]

In 1927, students in Bandung founded the Indonesian Nationalist Party (PNI), with Sukarno as its leader. His flowery language and charismatic personality rapidly attracted supporters with his call for Indonesian independence. His message of noncooperation and defiance prompted the Dutch to arrest him in 1929, with a sentence of two years in prison. In 1933, he was imprisoned again until 1942. Following Sukarno's arrest, the remaining PNI members voluntarily "dissolved" and most of its members joined a new organization called Partindo that avoided agitational politics and promised cooperation with Dutch authorities.[3]

By these measures, popular political activities remained primarily clandestine and most Indonesians remained passive and quiescent until the outbreak of war.

The Japanese Interregnum

For Southeast Asia, Japan's sudden invasion and occupation of the region had the effect of suspending all indigenous demands for political reform and decolonization. Never before had a single power established its rule over the entire region. Beginning with the December 7, 1941, surprise attack on the US fleet at Pearl Harbor, the Japanese conquest of Southeast Asia proceeded rapidly and efficiently. From bases in Indochina, Japanese forces landed near Pattani in Thailand and proceeded south through Malaya to capture Singapore on February 15, 1942. Another invasion force landed on Luzon and by January 3, 1942, the Japanese had captured Manila. The surviving US forces in the Philippines fled to Corregidor Island and eventually surrendered on May 6, 1942. The Japanese conquest of the Dutch East Indies was completed on March 9, 1942. By June, Japanese forces invading through Thailand had captured all of Burma.[4]

The Japanese were not as well prepared to administer such large and diverse areas as they had been to conquer Southeast Asian colonies from weakened colonial powers. The Japanese assumed complete control with plans to pursue two competing objectives. They expected to win widespread popular support from the population for their defeat of colonialism. They were also determined to seize control of strategic resources, such as tin, rubber, oil, and rice production to sustain the Japanese war machine. The latter objective was given priority over the former, but in their planning, both objectives were assumed to be complementary. To gain popular support, they expected to establish rapport with the common citizenry through a combination of anticolonial propaganda and support for the religions of their new subjects. For Indonesia, this meant a pro-Islamic policy enlisted to support Japanese rule. Shortly after their arrival, Japanese authorities announced the formation of an organization to prepare for the unification of the Islamic community. The two largest Muslim organizations were Nahdlatul Ulama and Muhammadiyah, each with significantly different Islamic constituencies. Leaders of both organizations were unwilling to give up control over their schools and welfare networks, forcing the Japanese to convert their proposed unification of Muslims into a loose ineffective umbrella grouping. In 1943, the Japanese made a second attempt to create a unified Muslim organization under their control. With various inducements, both Muhammadiyah and Nahdlatul Ulama finally agreed to join a single mass Islamic organization, called Masjumi, but they did so without merging.[5] By then, most Muslim leaders had become suspicious of Japanese motives.

The failure of Japan's pro-Islamic policy came partly because of serious rice shortages. To address this issue, the Japanese demanded that Indonesian peasants make compulsory deliveries of rice to support the war effort.[6] Early in their rule, the Japanese conscripted from the lower classes some 300,000 persons into "Labor Battalions" called Romushas. Most of these laborers were sent to Thailand for construction of the Burma-Siam railway to provide a supply link to Japanese forces in Burma. Smaller contingents worked on Japanese military projects in New Guinea (Irian Jaya) and northern Moluccas (Sulawesi and Halmahera). Their labor conditions were so harsh, brutal, and unhealthy that fewer than 70,000 Romushas survived their service as slave laborers. While the burdens and hardships of the war were shared by all sectors of Indonesian society, those burdens rested most onerously on peasants and the lower classes.[7]

The Japanese military commanders were initially skeptical about cooperation from Indonesian nationalist leaders, whom they viewed as having too little public support, of being too eager to seek political power, and therefore likely to create complications for Japanese rule. Even so, to provide a semblance of legitimacy for their rule, the Japanese established a central advisory committee, and nominated Sukarno to chair that body. The advisory bodies that the Japanese established had virtually no power without Japanese approval, yet Sukarno used his symbolic authority to build a constituency of support that became greater as the war progressed.

Although nationalist activists had been forced into a form of "self-exile" by Japanese restrictions on political activities, deteriorating conditions in Indonesia and Japanese losses in the war prompted the Japanese to change their policies. In 1943, after Japanese reverses in the Pacific and Allied incursions into northern Burma, the Japanese granted nominal independence to Burma and the Philippines in an attempt to gain popular support from populations under their control. Indonesia was not offered nominal independence, but instead they formed Pusat Tenaga Rakjat (Putera), which was intended to be a mass organization that could mobilize support for Japan's war effort. Sukarno and Mohammad Hatta, who had been founding members of the PNI, were selected by the Japanese to head Putera. That organization was promised limited autonomy and later the Japanese made a vague promise of eventual independence for Java and other nonspecified areas.

In combination with Putera, the Japanese also authorized a special volunteer Muslim military force known as Peta that was headed by an Indonesian politician but organized under Japanese command. This force was armed and trained by the Japanese army, and it expanded to a force of about 120,000 Indonesian volunteers and draftees. Apparently, the Japanese expected Peta to become a Muslim counterforce to the secular nationalists in Putera, but after the defeat of Japan, these two bodies were able to combine to lead the Indonesian nationalist movement.[8]

Indonesia's Independence Struggle

On August 17, 1945, two days after Japan's surrender, Sukarno declared Indonesian independence and shortly thereafter formed a provisional republic that he headed as president with Hatta as vice president.[9] When Dutch and British troops arrived to take the surrender of the Japanese forces, conflicts erupted between Indonesian and Dutch forces. The Dutch expected to be able to reestablish their colonial authority by supporting Indonesian leaders who favored close links between Indonesia and the Netherlands. Between September 1945 and December 1949, Indonesia became a battlefield in a power struggle over who would lead what kind of government for all areas formerly ruled by the Netherlands. On one side were the nationalists, led by Sukarno and Mohammad Hatta, who had issued the proclamation of Indonesian independence and who were leading a revolutionary struggle to expel the returning Dutch forces. On the other side were Dutch-backed governments that were being established in the outer islands by Dutch colonial officials backed by their military forces. Over this period of four years, the Dutch and the Indonesian Republic, led by Sukarno, alternately fought and negotiated for a final settlement. Before a peace agreement could be signed, the new Indonesian Republic had to demonstrate wide popular support and defeat a Communist rebellion in Java in 1948.

In the immediate aftermath of Japan's surrender, Indonesia entered a period of chaos and conflict characterized by roving military and militia units linked to newly formed political parties, all competing for power and for very limited resources. In this environment, two Communist leaders emerged as key players in the contest for political supremacy. Tan Malaka had been arrested in

1922, and after his release from prison, he fled to Moscow where he became a Comintern agent. He later lost his job because of "deviations," by opposing Comintern strategy for violent revolution. Instead, he favored joining with other political groups to share power and then "from within" seizing complete power in a Communist coup. Musso was another former PKI organizer who fled from the East Indies to Moscow to become a Comintern agent. In 1947, the reorganized Comintern, now called Cominform, pronounced the Zdhanov Doctrine, promising Soviet support for Communist-led "wars of national liberation" in former colonies of European powers. In August 1948, Musso returned to Indonesia to begin implementing the Cominform's tactics of revolution. These two Communist leaders, pursuing different strategies, attempted to seize power from the nationalist coalition headed by Sukarno and Hatta.

Following his secret strategy, Tan Malaka joined the Indonesian nationalist government, and played a Machiavellian role, pitting one faction against another and espousing more radical policies than Sukarno and Hatta were prepared to accept. He founded Partai Rakyat Djelata (Common Peoples Party), recruiting radical youth, unemployed discharged soldiers, and former PKI members. The Indonesian political scene was chaotic, since elections did not determine power, but representation within the government was based on assumed popular support. Therefore, parties organized demonstrations as a tactic to display and demand representation in government councils.[10] Nearly all parties also cultivated relations with military, paramilitary, and police units to maximize their power. In this environment, Tan Malaka expected to create a crisis that would dislodge Sukarno and Hatta from power. However, when Tan Malaka openly challenged Sukarno and Hatta to resign in March 1946, Sukarno, supported by the cabinet, had Tan Malaka arrested. At the last moment, several key "fence sitters" had thrown their support to Sukarno to save the nationalist government.

Meanwhile, under Musso's leadership the Indonesian Communist Party was revived and began mobilization of paramilitary units in anticipation of fomenting a proletarian revolution. Sensing an increasing threat from a revived PKI under Musso's leadership, Sukarno released from prison Tan Malaka, who quickly mobilized his followers in a renamed Partai Murba (Proletarian Party) to confront and undermine the PKI. When skirmishes broke out between the two Communist factions over the control of Maduin, in Java, Musso decided to announce the start of the "proletarian revolution." The PKI militia forces began attacking orthodox Muslims who were condemned as "capitalists, landowners," and government supporters. Quickly, the main units of the Indonesian Army intervened and recaptured Maduin, and within a few weeks about 35,000 persons were arrested, many from the PKI's paramilitary formations. During those operations, the army killed Musso and many other PKI leaders.[11] Although Tan Malaka had opposed the PKI, he had also alienated the top command in the Indonesian Army. Under Major General Abdul Haris Nasution's leadership, the army pursued Tan Malaka, who was arrested and put to death in March 1949, by the same division that had earlier promised him political support.[12]

These events revealed Sukarno's political skills and established a pattern of army intervention in Indonesian politics that became more apparent over time. For the second time in Indonesian history, a Communist revolution had been crushed. And, Sukarno gained increased legitimacy for his leadership of Indonesia in its continuing contest with the Netherlands.

The Nationalist Victory

With the return of its forces to Indonesia in early 1946, Dutch policy was designed to reestablish its authority over Indonesia by creating a decentralized government that would be independent but also willing to protect Dutch interests. The Dutch were unwilling to recognize the Republic of Indonesia that had been formed by those who were accused by the Dutch of being "Japanese collaborators." The Indonesian nationalists, in response, accused those who supported Dutch-backed regimes as "colonial collaborators." By the end of 1946, the Dutch had regained control of north-central and much of southern Sumatra, most of Kalimantan (Indonesian Borneo), the region of Java around Batavia (later renamed Jakarta), and many of the "outer islands." In December 1948, Dutch airborne troops occupied Jogjakarta and were able to capture Sukarno, Hatta, and other nationalist leaders. They also captured most major towns in Java and Sumatra. This offensive proved to be a military success, but it became a political disaster for the Dutch.

The United States had been hesitant to support the nationalist cause so long as a Communist threat to the Republican Government seemed imminent. The defeats of both rival Communist movements not only strengthened the Republican Government but also increased its international stature. Together, the United States and the UN Security Council became directly involved in efforts to end the fighting and resolve the disputes through negotiations. Under intense international pressure, the Dutch released Sukarno and Hatta in July 1949 and began negotiations for a final agreement. Finally, a draft agreement was formulated at a Round Table Conference at The Hague in November and the Indonesian Parliament ratified that agreement. Under its terms, the Dutch agreed to transfer full sovereignty to a federal republic composed of the Republic of Indonesia, consisting of Java and Sumatra, and including fifteen constituent states that had been created by the Dutch in the outer islands. Sukarno was made president with reduced powers under a parliamentary system, and Sutan Sjahrir became prime minister of the Republic of the United States of Indonesia.[13]

Many Indonesian nationalist leaders did not consider their new federal constitution to be legitimate, but with the Dutch agreeing to withdraw, and facing political reality, parliamentary democracy with a federal system of divided powers was reluctantly seen by most Indonesian leaders as an acceptable settlement.[14] However, one constitutional provision gave the cabinet power to enact emergency laws without the approval of Parliament. One year later, after invoking emergency powers, Sukarno dissolved the federal system and replaced the negotiated federal constitution with another constitution providing for a unitary state, a presidential system, and a unicameral legislature to be directly elected by popular vote. The first general elections were scheduled for 1951 but not held until 1955. Without elections, seats in Parliament were allocated on the basis of claimed membership. This system rewarded parties that could organize mass demonstrations of "street power."[15]

Indonesian Islam Divided

Before Indonesian independence, a preparatory committee had prepared a draft set of principles for the Indonesian constitution. An Islamic group drafted what came to be known as the "Jakarta Charter," which proposed that Sharia law should be enforced for all Muslims and that the president of Indonesia should be a Muslim.[16] This issue generated more controversy than all other issues relating to the new constitution. Sukarno did not want to alienate non-Muslims, especially when he anticipated the impending struggle with the Netherlands over a postwar regime. Therefore, he asked Muslim-based parties to make concessions and proposed the phrase: "the state should be based on Belief in the One and Only God" and that Muslims have an obligation to conform to Islamic law. After heated debate, the phrase was changed to "the Indonesian State is founded on Belief in God."[17] This statement was combined with four other principles to create what was called Pancasila (Five Principles), which became the ideological foundation for the new state. These five principles were: Ketuhanan (Belief in God); Kebangsaan (National Consciousness); Perikemanusiaan (Humanism); Keadilan Sosial (Social Justice); and Demokrasi (Sovereignty of the People). These principles were designed to be inclusive of all religions and political ideologies. They also allowed delegates to agree to disagree. While the nationalist struggle was being fought, issues of religion remained in the background. When Indonesian independence became assured, Muslim-based parties became more militant and openly critical of Pancasila, attacking it as justifying secular government, which, they argued, was a violation of Islamic principles.

When the first Provisional Assembly met in March 1951, the largest party was Masjumi with 49 seats, followed by the nationalists (PNI) with 36 seats, out of a total of 232. The large number of seats held by other parties and independents made a stable majority coalition impossible. For the first parliamentary elections in September 1955, the four main Islamic parties were expected to win an overwhelming majority of the seats. Although there was no census data on religious affiliation, estimates of Muslims in the total population varied from over 80 percent to 95 percent. After the votes were counted, the four largest Islamic parties had won only 43.5 percent of the vote, with only two of those Muslim parties being committed to an Islamist agenda. Because of political differences between Masjumi and Nahdlatul Ulama, those two parties tended to reduce the political impact of Islam. Consequently, political support within Parliament became divided between three fairly equal factions: Islamic, Communist, and Nationalist (see Table 4.1). The chaotic instability in Parliament, combined with weak public consensus on issues of legitimacy, later provided the opportunity and justification for Sukarno to institute his system of authoritarian rule under the guise of "Guided Democracy."

Table 4.1 Summary of 1955 Indonesian Parliamentary Elections

Party	Percentage of Vote	Number of Seats Won
Partai Nationalist Indonesia	22.3	57
Masjumi	20.9	57
Nahdlatul Ulama	18.4	45
Partai Komunis Indonesia	16.4	39
Twenty-four other parties	22.0	59

Source: Herbert Feith, *Indonesian Elections of 1955* (Ithaca, NY: Cornell University Press, 1957), 58–59.

Darul Islam Movements

At several regions in Indonesia, where militant Islam had previously flourished, local firebrands launched separatist movements, rejecting the authority of the "secular" national government and claiming to establish a genuine Islamic form of government. These movements adopted the label Darul Islam (Abode of Peace) to identify their religio-political orientation. From 1945 to 1959, three primary Darul Islam movements formed in West Java, South Sulawesi, and Aceh.[18]

In West Java, the leader of Darul Islam was S. M. Kartosuwirjo, who had been active in Serikat Islam in the 1930s and had risen through the ranks to become its vice president. Later, after he was expelled from the party, he founded an Islamic *pesantren* school, which became a center for religious instruction and paramilitary training. When Japan surrendered, his paramilitary trainees were able to acquire weapons from surrendering Japanese units. Backed by his paramilitary force, called "The Army of Islam," he refused to accept the Renville Agreement cease-fire with Dutch forces. However, instead of fighting against the Dutch, his forces clashed with the Siliwangi Division of the Indonesian Army. Only then did he proclaim the Islamic State of Darul Islam. The manifesto for Darul Islam objected to the secular provisions of Indonesia's constitution, and Indonesian authorities offered reconciliation, but those overtures were rebuffed. Between 1949 and 1962, Darul Islam waged a full-scale guerrilla war in West Java, recruiting fighters who lived off the land through forced extractions of food crops and protection money from local residents. By 1954, the Indonesian Army had defeated most of the guerrilla units, and in April 1962, they captured Kartosuwirjo, who was tried and convicted of treason. Sukarno rejected his appeal for a reprieve and he was executed.[19]

In South Sulawesi, another Darul Islam movement evolved around a paramilitary guerrilla group led by Kahar Muzakkar, a Buginese. During the Japanese occupation, he had moved to Java, where he organized Sulawesi migrants. At the war's end, he and many of his followers moved back to Sulawesi, where they formed a movement to claim autonomy for Sulawesi. Because of their opposition to Dutch plans for regional authorities in a federal system, anti-Republic forces, led by the Dutch freebooter, Captain Raymond Westerling, attacked Muzakkar's guerrilla bands. The atrocities committed by Westerling's revenge policies merely added to the ranks of Muzakkar's guerrillas. Sensing a common purpose, negotiations opened between Muzakkar and the Indonesian Army (TNI) for incorporation of his guerrillas into the army. Muzakkar demanded that all his forces should be accepted into the Indonesian Army and that they should remain a separate unit under his command. Muzakkar was given the rank of lieutenant colonel, but when he asserted his demand that he remain in command of his forces as a separate unit within the army, this was rejected. Rather than accept the terms offered, on July 5, 1950, Muzakkar led his forces out of Makassar (now called Ujung Pandang) and into the jungles of South Sulawesi. Apparently, Muzakkar expected to become the regional warlord of South Sulawesi, and when that was denied, he preferred to assert Sulawesi autonomy against the claims of national authorities in Jakarta.

In the early days of the guerrilla struggle, Muzakkar successfully cultivated the support of Buginese and Makassarese, but the Torajas in Central Sulawesi, who are Christian, rejected any affiliation with his cause. In August 1953, Muzakkar proclaimed Darul Islam and issued a manifesto called the Makalua Charter that stated an Islamist agenda, followed by a declaration authorizing forced collection of money and resources from the local population. By 1960, the Indonesian Army had eliminated most Darul Islam forces. Finally, in February 1965, Muzakkar was trapped and killed near the village of Lawali in Southeast Sulawesi.[20]

Aceh became the third area where a significant Darul Islam movement emerged. During the Dutch-Aceh War of 1873–1903, political conflicts between the ulama and the uleebalang chiefs had become exacerbated, partly as a result of Dutch policy favoring the chiefs. After that war, the Dutch appointed about 100 uleebalangs (regional chiefs) as agents of the colonial administration, and gave them local power, status, and privileges, including access to Dutch education for their children. The traditional ulama viewed uleebalangs as Dutch collaborators and apostate Muslims.[21] In 1939, activist ulama, led by Daud Beureueh, formed Persatuan Ulama Seluruh Aceh (PUSA, All-Aceh Ulama Association) to challenge the uleebalang, and indirectly to mobilize opposition to Dutch rule. When the Japanese occupation began, the political tables were turned. The Japanese supported the ulama and permitted PUSA to form paramilitary units led by ulama and organized as Angkatan Pemuda Indonesia (API, Brigade of Indonesian Youth). API brigades were provided with Japanese arms, and some Japanese officers provided training for API forces. After Japan surrendered, the Dutch made no effort to reoccupy Aceh, which enabled API forces to stage a revolution in Aceh from December 1945 to February 1946. Most uleebalang and their families were massacred, and Daud Beureueh was unilaterally installed as governor of Aceh. Whether it was a nationalist anticolonial revolution, a religious revolution establishing an Islamic state, or a class revolution of the dispossessed depends on what analytical perspectives one prefers to employ.

Aceh's newly installed regime requested from the Indonesian Republic recognition for Aceh's status as a de facto autonomous province. Instead, the central government decided to create a single province of North Sumatra, composed of Aceh, Tapanuli, and East Sumatra, and appointed a military commander as governor for all of North Sumatra. Fearing military security operations, Daud Beureueh and his associates retreated to the interior highlands and on September 21, 1953, declared Aceh's independence and ruled as Darul Islam.[22]

After extended negotiations, the Indonesian government agreed to make Aceh a separate province of Indonesia and appointed Ali Hasjmy as governor backed by the Indonesian Army. Daud Beureueh with his Darul Islam guerrilla forces defied the Aceh government installed by Jakarta. Finally, in May 1959, a new agreement was signed with the Darul Islam leaders providing for Aceh to have autonomy in Islamic affairs, Adat law, and education. With this agreement, Darul Islam troops surrendered their arms, and Daud Beureueh retired on a government pension as an ex-governor.[23] While this agreement appeared to resolve the status of Aceh, disputes over autonomy and Islam would later return to generate new cycles of violence.

From Federalism to Guided Democracy

During its first years, the new Republican Government struggled to establish order and stability throughout Indonesia. The government faced daunting problems of economic development with very limited resources, while factional divisions in Parliament impeded decisionmaking. The result was near-paralysis for any government action. Sukarno sensed the frustrations and disillusionment of the public and decided to break the stalemate with a dramatic move. At a series of mass rallies, he ridiculed Western democracy as promoting conflict and oppression by majority rule. Instead, he proposed what he called Guided Democracy, which would operate on the basis of "deliberation and consensus," which was part of the Indonesian "way of life." Finally, in August 1959, to reform the political system, he dissolved Parliament and restored the Constitution of 1945 by presidential decree. That earlier constitution drafted by the nationalists had provided for a unitary system with a strong president exercising powers independent of the legislature. Although he had no legal authority to revoke the existing constitution or to establish another, he proceeded as though his acts were legal and his few critics were ignored. Thereafter, nearly all legislation was enacted by presidential decree without reference to the People's Deliberative Assembly. By guile and fiat, he acquired extraordinary powers that enabled him to become the unchallenged leader of Indonesia.[24]

Sukarno's new system of Guided Democracy was supposed to operate with "deliberation and consensus." Parties continued to exist, and advisory councils, consisting of party and functional representatives, were created, but Sukarno selected most representatives from a list nominated by the parties or by functional organizations. In a sense, it became a system of selecting advisers to represent national diversity, and when consensus was not forthcoming, Sukarno was free to create "consensus" by decree or public announcement. In many ways it worked like the colonial system of advisory councils that had been established by the Dutch. Sukarno's skill consisted in keeping a balance between four main political blocs: the army, the Communists, the combined Muslim parties, and the Nationalists. All Muslim parties were forced to join in one bloc, while the Nationalists were combined with the small Catholic and Protestant parties in another. The object of this "managed representation" system was to reduce the impact of radical or extremist elements in politics and reward those who were willing to cooperate with Sukarno in support of "middle ground" compromise solutions to public policy issues. Among the more radical groups that were effectively excluded from the councils of government were Islamists, as represented by Masjumi, which Sukarno banned in 1960.[25]

Sukarno's Guided Democracy continued from 1959 to 1965, and it was characterized by flamboyant public rhetoric, with the creation of many slogans and political acronyms, supposedly setting forth government goals. These slogans became the shibboleths that were substitutes for political discourse on public policy. It also was a time when public resources were diverted to construction of colossal monuments, massive statues, and a national sports stadium, all to symbolize Indonesian nationalism. Meanwhile, public infrastructure had become eroded due to years of lack of maintenance and repair, the economy collapsed due to runaway inflation and an increase of public debt covered by printing of paper money, and the public services were undermined by low wages and endemic corruption. Sukarno rejected advice from economic advisers and became more interested in the symbols and rituals of politics than in managing economic affairs. His style of leadership was characterized as Keraton (palace) politics, in reference to traditional roles of Javanese sultans.

Eventually public discontent and competition between political factions could no longer be balanced and manipulated by Sukarno's facile rhetoric, and he lost his legitimacy as founder of Indonesian independence.

The "Gestapu Coup"

By 1965, the PKI had rebuilt its membership, partly by recruiting Sukarno's followers when the PNI collapsed. The PKI controlled a cadre corps of about 300,000, and its party membership approached two million. It had also organized a large following of peasants in a front organization called Indonesian Peasant Front (BTI), which gained support from about 5.7 million peasants by promises of land redistribution from properties seized from Dutch firms and from absentee land owners. The PKI had also organized labor unions into a front (called SOBSI). The BTI and SOBSI together claimed a membership of about ten million members. In 1958, the Indonesian government seized all Dutch properties, including plantations, properties, mines, oil facilities, and factories. Both the army and the PKI competed for control of assets seized from Dutch firms. In this contest, both the army and the PKI attempted to shift the political balance to gain those assets. When the PKI sought government approval for a scheme to acquire weapons and training for its paramilitary militia called Pemuda Rakjat (Young Citizens), the stakes in the contest were dramatically escalated.

Behind the scenes, rumors of plots led some leaders to believe that the Indonesian Army was about to stage a coup against Sukarno. One faction, including some PKI youth leaders and others, decided to preempt that possibility by decisive action. On September 30, 1965, several squads of Pemuda Rakjat members attempted to assassinate the top generals of the Indonesian Army in their homes at night. Six of the highest-ranking generals were murdered, but Defense Minister Nasution and General Suharto escaped and were able to mobilize the army to regain control of Jakarta. Then the army began a systematic campaign to hunt down both the PKI members and their supporters in front organizations. General Suharto accused the PKI of attempting to stage a coup against Sukarno, which event was identified by the acronym Gestapu.[26] Communist Party Chairman D. N. Aidit was captured and killed near Solo in Java, and most high-ranking leaders of the party met a similar fate.

Angered by the allegations against the PKI, various organizations volunteered to take "direct action" against accused supporters of the coup. Nahdlatul Ulama's youth wing, called Ansor, and PNI militia initiated a jihad against accused supporters of the PKI. In urban areas, Chinese and Christian minorities were assaulted, on the assumption that the PKI had secret support from the People's Republic of China and that Islam was under attack.[27] In central and northern Sumatra, similar gangs of urban unemployed youth also formed to loot and attack Christian communities and those accused of being PKI supporters. Because the Communist-front peasant organization BTI had recruited millions of members, rural peasants became the target of these well-armed mobs. While many peasants had been recruited to BTI by promises of free land, they were not Communists. In the period from mid-November of 1965 to mid-January 1966, various jihad mobs systematically slaughtered vast numbers of peasants, as well as Chinese, Christians, and Balinese Hindus. During the period, the army and the police often encouraged or supported vigilante groups with weapons and provided information on suspects. In some areas, the police provided armed gangs with lists of people who had been "removed from public protection," thus assuring that attackers could be rewarded by the proceeds of loot.[28] The cycle of slaughter continued for over two months, with most law enforcement being suspended, thus revealing official acquiescence and passive complicity in the slaughter. The estimates of the numbers killed vary between 80,000 and 1,500,000, with 250,000 to 500,000 being widely quoted figures.[29] If the numbers of those arrested and imprisoned are added to the estimates of those killed, the figure is in excess of 2,000,000.

The impact of this "time of killing" created a permanent scar across the Muslim community of Indonesia. People hesitate to talk about these events for fear of reprisals or out of guilt from their complicity or knowing friends who were implicated. Imagine how many thousands of Muslims were involved in the mass killings and how such experiences have shaped their attitudes toward violence and the use of deadly force to punish alleged apostasy. On the other side, peasants who survived that holocaust acquired a mortal fear of those who militantly preach the santri version of Islam. In the aftermath of those events, some abangan quietly abandoned Islam and a few survivors even decided to become Christian, both as protest and as a means of protection.

Following the Gestapu events, Sukarno remained as president, even though he was suspected of being involved with political intrigues that culminated with the attacks by the PKI's assassination squads. After the army had eliminated the PKI as a political force, Suharto gradually reduced Sukarno's maneuver room, and by March 1966, Suharto gave an ultimatum demanding increased authority for the army. In March 1967, Indonesia's Provisional Peoples Consultative Assembly convened to give General Suharto full powers as acting president, while Sukarno was stripped of his title "President for Life" and assigned a symbolic role. A year later, Sukarno was retired and placed under virtual house arrest. The transition from Sukarno to Suharto was accomplished by incremental stages over a two-year period.[30] A new era in Indonesian politics was about to begin with a new emphasis on order and national unity.

Notes

1. Sarekat Islam initially formed as Sarekat Dagang Islam but adopted the shorter name in 1912. Bernard H. M. Vlekke, *Nusantara: A History of Indonesia,* rev. ed. (The

Hague and Bandung: W. van Hoeve, 1959), 347–363; Howard M. Federspiel, *Islam and Ideology in the Emerging Indonesian State: The Persatuan Islam (PERSIS), 1923 to 1957* (Leiden: Brill, 2001), 84–92; Peter G. Riddel, *Islam and the Malay-Indonesian World: Transmission and Responses* (Honolulu: University of Hawaii Press, 2001), 207–322. Muhammadiyah was founded by Ahmad Dahlan who was influenced by the political writings of Jamal al-Din al-Afghani and Muhammad 'Abduh. For the theological antecedents of Muhammadiyah, see Giora Eliraz, *Islam in Indonesia: Modernism, Radicalism, and the Middle East Dimension* (Brighton, UK: Sussex Academic Press, 2004), 4–24.

2. M. C. Ricklefs, *A History of Modern Indonesia Since c. 1200*, 3rd ed. (Stanford: Stanford University Press, 2001), 216–226; Justus M. van der Kroef, *The Communist Party of Indonesia* (Vancouver: University of British Columbia, 1965), 3–21; David Joel Steinberg (ed.), *In Search of Southeast Asia*, rev. ed. (Honolulu: University of Hawaii Press, 1987), 292–311.

3. Bernard Dahm, *History of Indonesia in the Twentieth Century* (London: Praeger Publishers, 1971), 66–70; Frederica M. Bunge, *Indonesia: A Country Study* (Washington, DC: American University Foreign Area Studies, 1983), 30–39.

4. Young Hum Kim, *East Asia's Turbulent Century* (New York: Appleton-Century-Crofts, 1966), 107–109; D. G. E. Hall, *A History of South-East Asia*, 3rd ed. (New York: St. Martin's Press, 1970), 815–818; Harry J. Benda, "The Beginnings of the Japanese Occupation of Java," in Harry J. Benda, *Continuity and Change in Southeast Asia* (New Haven: Yale University Southeast Asia Studies, 1972), 64–65; J. M. Pluvier, *South-East Asia from Colonialism to Independence* (Kuala Lumpur: Oxford University Press, 1974), 163–281.

5. Pluvier, *South-East Asia from Colonialism to Independence,* 220–222, 250–254.

6. Kurasawa-Inomata Aiko, "Rice Shortage and Transportation," in Peter Post and Elly Touwen-Bouwsma (eds.), *Japan, Indonesia and the War: Myths and Realities* (Leiden: LITLV Press, 1997), 111–133.

7. Dahm, *History of Indonesia,* 82–95; Harry J. Benda, *The Crescent and the Rising Sun* (The Hague: V. van Hoeve, 1958), 120–149. Ricklefs, *A History of Modern Indonesia Since c. 1200*, 247–252.

8. Putera was an acronym for Pusat Tenaga Rakjat (Center of People's Power) and Peta was an acronym for Tentara Pembala Tanah Ayer (Army for the Defense of the Fatherland). Pluvier, *South-East Asia,* 217–222, 240–241.

9. In Sukarno's declaration of independence, Indonesia was defined as including all the former Dutch East Indies, plus Malaya, Singapore, and the British-protected states of Sarawak, North Borneo, and Brunei. Indonesia began with this grand vision, known as "Greater Indonesia," that the entire Malay/Indonesian world should unify into one national entity.

10. The ruling body that substituted for a parliament was a temporary committee called Komité Nasional Indonesia Pusat (KNIP). S. Tas refers to the republic as "a community of agitation" because of its incapacity to evaluate political support through elections. S. Tas, *Indonesia: The Underdeveloped Freedom* (Indianapolis, IN: Pegasus, 1974), 195.

11. Malcolm Kennedy, *A History of Communism in East Asia* (New York: Frederick A. Praeger, 1956), 463–467; Leslie Palmier, *Communists in Indonesia* (London: Weidenfeld & Nicolson, 1973), 127–137; Kroef, *The Communist Party of Indonesia*, 30–43.

12. Kennedy, *A History of Communism,* 456–465; Palmier, *Communists in Indonesia*, 115–126, 139–142.

13. Pluvier, *South-East Asia,* 21–24, 427–430, 434–441, 475–490; John F. Cady, *The History of Post-War Southeast Asia* (Athens: Ohio University Press, 1974), 46–50.

14. George McTurnin Kahin, *Nationalism and Revolution in Indonesia* (Ithaca: Cornell University Press, 1952); Bernhard Dahm, *Sukarno and the Struggle for Independence,* translated from German by Mary Somers Heidhues (Ithaca, NY: Cornell University Press, 1969); A. J. S. Reid, *Indonesian National Revolution, 1945–50* (Hawthorn, Vic. Australia: Longman, 1974); Tas, *Indonesia: The Underdeveloped Freedom,* 170–205.

15. Dahm, *History of Indonesia,* 143–160.

16. For the key provisions of the Jakarta Charter, see M. B. Hooker, *Indonesian Islam: Social Change Through Contemporary Fatawa* (Honolulu: University of Hawaii Press, 2003), 17.

17. B. J. Boland, *The Struggle of Islam in Modern Indonesia* [Verhandelingen Van Het Koninklijk Instituut Voor Taal-, Land- En Volkenkunde, Vol. 59] (The Hague: Martinus Nijhoff, 1971), 15–39; E. Saifuddin Anshari, *The Jakarta Charter 1945: The Struggle for an Islamic Constitution in Indonesia* (Kuala Lumpur: Muslim Youth Movement of Malaysia, 1979), 11–18; Julia D. Howell, "Indonesia: Searching for Consensus," in Carlo Caldarola (ed.), *Religion and Societies: Asia and the Middle East* (Berlin: Mouton Publishers, 1982), 520–524.

18. A fourth Darul Islam movement formed in South Kalimantan under the leadership of Ibnu Hajar from 1951 to 1963. This movement arose from a guerrilla force that had been formed to fight the Dutch, and after independence when officials from Jakarta arrived, the guerrillas sought to be incorporated into the Indonesian Army. Altogether, 16,000 former guerrillas entered the army, but about 6,000 guerrillas remained in the jungle led by Ibnu Hajar. Known by the acronym KRIYT, they proclaimed themselves Darul Islam and made efforts to enforce Islamic law in areas that they controlled. The Indonesian Army pursued and eliminated many guerrillas, forcing Ibnu Hajar and his men to surrender. In March 1965, Ibnu Hajar was sentenced to death at a special military court. See C. Van Dijk, *Rebellion Under the Banner of Islam: The Darul Islam in Indonesia* (The Hague: Martinus Nijhoff, 1981), 218–268.

19. Ibid., 69–154; Boland, *The Struggle of Islam,* 54–62.

20. Van Dijk, *Rebellion,* 155–217; Boland, *The Struggle of Islam,* 62–68.

21. Anthony Reid, *The Blood of the People: Revolution and the End of Traditional Rule in Northern Sumatra* (Kuala Lumpur: Oxford University Press, 1979), 7–37.

22. Nararuddin Sjamsuddin, *The Republican Revolt: A Study of the Acehnese Rebellion* (Singapore: Institute of Southeast Asian Studies, 1985), 1–122; Clive J. Christie, *A Modern History of Southeast Asia: Decolonization, Nationalism and Separatism* (London: I. B. Tauris Publishers, 1996), 140–156.

23. Boland, *The Struggle of Islam,* 68–75; Sjamjsuddin, *The Republican Revolt,* 254–331.

24. S. Takdir Alisjahbana, *Indonesia: Social and Cultural Revolution* (Kuala Lumpur: Oxford University Press, 1966), 137–177.

25. Carlien Patricia Woodcroft-Lee, "From Morocco to Merauke," in Raphael Israeli and Anthony H. Johns (eds.), *Islam in Asia,* Vol. 2, *Southeast and East Asia* (Jerusalem: Magnes Press, Jerusalem University; Boulder, CO: Westview Press, 1984), 80–90.

26. In Indonesian it was called Gerakan September Tiga Puloh, which was shortened to the acronym Gestapu and means "September 30th Movement." Because the PKI was not mobilized and was not prepared for the aftermath, there remains substantial doubt about the official account of the "coup plot." Harold Crouch, *The Army and Politics in Indonesia,* rev. ed. (Ithaca, NY: Cornell University Press, 1988), 107–118.

27. In Indonesia, the Chinese often live in urban shop-house ghettos that provide a degree of security during periods of ethnic violence that periodically erupt when political tensions are high.

28. From personal accounts to the author by Indonesians who were employed in government service at that time.

29. Boland, *The Struggle of Islam,* 135–156; Arnold C. Brackman, *The Communist Collapse in Indonesia* (New York: W. W. Norton, 1969); Crouch, *The Army and Politics*; John Hughes, *Indonesian Upheaval* (New York: David McKay, 1967); John Hughes, *The End of Sukarno* (London: Angus & Robertson, 1968); Brian May, *The Indonesian Tragedy* (London: Routledge and Kegan Paul, 1978); Oey Hong Lee, "Sukarno and the Pseudo Coup of 1965," *Journal of Southeast Asian Studies* 7, no. 1 (March 1976). A moving account of the Gestapu killings, based on personal interviews, is presented in the book by Theodore Friend, *Indonesian Destinies* (Cambridge, MA: Belknap Press of Harvard University Press, 2003), 100–125.

30. Crouch, *The Army and Politics,* 197–220; Ricklefs, *A History of Indonesia,* 342–358; Justice M. van der Kroef, *Indonesia After Sukarno* (Vancouver: University of British Columbia Press, 1971), 1–44.

5

Malaysia: Challenged by Ethnicity

During the colonial era, the British built a system of "indirect rule" by support of Malay sultans and a promise to the Malays that their way of life would be preserved. Part of that policy also depended on colonial protection and support for Islam. At the same time, the British were also committed to nineteenth-century liberal principles of free trade and relatively free immigration. Free trade brought commerce and economic development, while free immigration permitted the growth of immigrant communities from China and India. Chinese had been attracted to Malaya prior to the coming of Europeans to Southeast Asia, but the largest influx arrived after British rule became well established. The Chinese initially became involved in trade, commerce, and tin mining, but later they engaged in rubber production, market agriculture, and a full range of urban occupations. The Indians were initially recruited to provide police services and to build and operate the railways, but their roles expanded to a wide range of urban occupations. Both the Chinese and Indian communities tended to move into the more modern and developed sectors of the economy, while the Malays remained largely insulated in their traditional rural peasant economy and social system. By the 1930s, in the Malay states, the Malays constituted about half of the population, the Chinese about one-third, and the Indians about one-sixth of the population. Despite their meager economic power based largely on a peasant economy, and their limited exposure to education in comparison with the other ethnic communities, the Malays, nonetheless, considered the country to be their exclusive birthright. In anticipation of decolonization, the Malays expected to reclaim the political power they had previously exercised before the colonial system had become established. Much of the politics of the immediate postwar era involved efforts by Malay leaders to resolve the dilemma created by the disjunction between Malay capabilities and their political aspirations.

Malay Nationalism and the Japanese Occupation

Malay nationalism first emerged, not in Malaya, but in Singapore, where the Chinese constituted about 75 percent of the population, and Malays composed about 8 percent of the population. As a small minority, Malays competed against immigrant communities and they were exposed to European economic power and culture in pervasive forms. In the 1920s, Malays in Singapore began debating, through the vernacular Malay press, religio-political issues concerning Islam. One view, known as Kaum Tua (Old Faction), represented the conservative doctrines of the court-centered Muslim hierarchy in Malaya. The other, known as Kaum Muda (New Faction), reflected the pan-Islamic revivalist ideology emanating from Egypt and the Al-Manar Circle, named after the journal *Al-Manar* where these doctrines were espoused. This movement was often identified as "modernist Islam," attempting to combine some vision of pan-Islamic unity with fundamentalist interpretations of the Quran. A few Malays in Singapore were attracted to this ideology. In 1937, Ibrahim Yaacob and Ishak bin Haji Mohammad founded Kesatuan Melayu Muda (Union of Malay Youth), which became the first Malay organization seeking to expel the British, perhaps by force. They proposed to form a union between Malaya and the yet to be formed Indonesia that would bring Malays and Indonesians under the combined banner of Islam. This proposal for uniting Malaya with Indonesia was called Indonesia Raya (Greater Indonesia). Sukarno later endorsed that objective, but established Malay royalty and political leaders viewed Indonesia Raya as a near-treasonous doctrine.[1]

The 1941 Japanese assault on Malaya and the Straits Settlements totally reshaped the political landscape. Prior to their invasion, the Japanese had made plans to remove Malay elites from power and replace them with Malays who were known to be anticolonial and anti-British. They were aware of radical Malay organizations that were seeking to use Islam to resist colonialism. They believed that radical Malays would welcome Japan's leadership of an Asian anticolonial movement. Immediately after their conquest, the Japanese recruited Kesatuan Melayu Muda leaders, but soon discovered that organization had few supporters and could not assist with administration of the country.[2] Out of necessity and political prudence, the Japanese were forced to respect the political authority of the Malay monarchs who remained popular and respected among most Malays. The Malayan Police Force already employed large numbers of Malays and the Malayan Administrative Service was staffed entirely by Malays as junior officers, who could continue to provide essential government services after senior British administrative officers were arrested and sent to internment prison.

By 1943, the Japanese abandoned all semblance of a pro-Islamic agenda for Malaya and Singapore. Instead, they attempted to generate Malay hostility against the Chinese, who were viewed as enemies of Japan. While Japanese rule produced great hardship, its consequences for the Malays were more benign than for other communities. After more than a decade of fighting in China, Japanese troops were hardened to brutal force and atrocities against all Chinese. During the 1930s, Japanese brutalities against civilians in China had been reported in gruesome detail and had evoked both sympathy and financial support from the overseas Chinese. Consequently, when Japanese forces captured Malaya and Singapore, they treated all Chinese as hostile enemies, subjecting them to extremely harsh conditions, including mass summary executions, and forced donations of money and gold to support the Japanese war machine.[3]

Just prior to the British surrender to the Japanese, the British had sponsored the formation of an anti-Japanese underground called the Malayan Peoples Anti-Japanese Army (MPAJA). Most of the recruits were Chinese, and the leadership came from the previously outlawed Malayan Communist Party. During the occupation, those guerrillas operated from the Malayan jungles to harass Japanese forces and to attack Malay police and officials working with Japanese authorities. Although these guerrilla attacks did little to impede Japan's war effort, those operations invited Japanese retaliatory measures against noncombatant Chinese. Japan's extremely arbitrary and oppressive measures in turn induced a flow of young Chinese recruits to the MPAJA.

Japan's differential treatment of the Malays and the Chinese intensified interethnic hostility and distrust between these two communities. The Chinese viewed many Malays as collaborators with a brutal and repressive regime. By contrast, the activities of the MPAJA guerrillas made Malays aware that immigrant communities posed a security threat, a political threat, and an economic threat to Malay society. These alternate perceptions of each community by the other became part of their collective memory to shape the nature of ethnic politics in the postwar era. Although the Japanese, during their interregnum, had greatly increased interethnic hostilities in Malaya and Singapore, their rule had also preserved the political stature of traditional Malay elites, who were fundamentally conservative Malay nationalists. These Malay leaders had the advantage of continuity in their leadership of Malay society, and as the war ended, they expected to acquire sovereign powers in an independent nation.

British Postwar Policies

After the surrender of Japan, most of the population greeted the return of the British with a sigh of relief and welcomed the efforts to rebuild a war-ravaged country. During the war, the British had made preliminary plans for their eventual return to Malaya and Singapore. Shortly after their return, Harold MacMichael, representing the Crown, secured from each Malay ruler an agreement to transfer "full power and jurisdiction" to Britain to initiate constitutional reforms. In January 1946, the British government released a white paper establishing outlines of Malaya's new constitution. Most residents of

Malaya and Singapore were to acquire citizenship and franchise rights. The separate Malay states were to be abolished and joined with Penang and Melaka to be replaced by a unitary government called the Malayan Union. Singapore was to be retained as a crown colony with its future to be decided later. On April 1, 1946, the British government, by an Order in Council, promulgated the Malayan Union Constitution, despite the unanimous objections of the Malay rulers.[4]

The formation of the Malayan Union became the catalyst for mass Malay mobilization and an upsurge of Malay nationalism. All the Malay rulers boycotted the installation of the new governor, Edward Gent, and almost overnight the United Malays National Organization (UMNO) was founded to lead mass Malay protest rallies. Utilizing the existing power structure of Malay society, from the sultans down to village headman, UMNO emerged as a mass organization having several hundred thousand members within several months. UMNO leaders argued that Malays were losing their "birthright" by ending Malay "special rights," by eliminating the Malay states, and by allowing alien residents to qualify for citizenship. For the Malays, the British proposals were too democratic, independence appeared to be coming too soon, and Malays were losing their special status as the original founders of the country. Malay leaders realized that ordinary rural Malays could not compete economically with immigrant communities and feared they might lose preeminent political power as well.

Because of the mass Malay boycotts, the British governor finally agreed to consider constitutional changes to meet the objections of Malay leaders. Eventually, a new constitution was drafted and approved that established a federal system, preserved the Malay states and the roles of the sultans, and established stringent qualifications for citizenship by immigrants. In addition, Malays regained their "special rights" relating to land tenure, preferential recruitment for Malays in the public service, and preferential support to Malays for education, and Islam was restored as the official state religion.[5] The mass boycotts by Malays ended and Malay leaders were generally reassured that they would retain political supremacy when Malaya gained its independence.

The Communist Insurrection

While the negotiations were under way with Malay leaders over the new constitution and over issues of the conditions for gaining independence, a new challenge emerged to complicate the process of decolonization. In July 1948, the Malayan Communist Party (MCP) launched its revolutionary struggle against British imperialism. The party had led the guerrilla resistance against the Japanese, and it assumed that it could seize power by doing the same against British rule. The Communists were outspoken in their opposition to the Federation of Malaya, with its pro-Malay policies and its Malay leaders who were being groomed to lead the country when independence was to be finally achieved. Although the MCP claimed to represent workers and peasants of all ethnic groups, it failed to gain any popular Malay support. Instead, the MCP capitalized on Chinese grievances in its appeals for support and recruits. It gained the support of some rural Chinese squatters who lacked land titles, and some Chinese labor unions and Chinese students in Chinese media schools were also attracted to the party by Communist ideology. In effect, the MCP reflected the radical Chinese version of ethnic politics.

After years of experimenting with a policy mix of social programs and aggressive military tactics against the guerrillas, the government gradually isolated the guerrillas from their supporters to gain full control of all areas of Malaya. The number of MCP guerrillas reached a peak in 1951 at about 8,000 armed fighters. From 1948 to 1960, the MCP waged a costly and deadly guerrilla war, with lesser harassing incidents continuing until 1989. In that year, the leaders of the Malayan Communist Party finally signed a peace agreement with both Malaysia and Thailand that provided for the cessation of hostilities and granted limited amnesty for the few remaining guerrillas, allowing them to depart to China or settle in Thailand.[6]

Ethnic Political Mobilization

Even before the start of the Communist insurrection, a majority of the Chinese had avoided affiliation with the Malayan Communist Party, and most Chinese were distressed when Communist leaders decided to begin a revolutionary struggle against the British and the newly formed Federation of Malaya. To many Chinese, a Communist revolution seemed dangerous and foolhardy, especially after the British had already announced their intention to transfer full sovereignty to an independent and democratic government of Malaya. Partly because of complacency, it took some time for non-Communist Chinese to organize for political action. In February 1948, eight months after the Malayan Communist Party launched its revolutionary struggle, the Malayan Chinese Association (MCA) was launched, led by Tan Cheng-lock, a prewar leader affiliated with the Chinese Chambers of Commerce. The MCA began by sponsoring charitable lotteries and used the money to fund welfare workers in rural Chinese villages, dispensing a system of "welfare patronage."[7] At the same time, the MCA gradually built up a political organization that had the capacity to represent the Chinese and to deliver a substantial bloc of votes when elections were introduced. That party has remained a primary representative of Chinese interests and a key player in Malaysian politics ever since.

While the controversy over the Malayan Union had triggered the formation of UMNO, the subsequent controversies over the formation of its successor, the Federation of Malaya, also provided incentives for the political mobilization of other non-Malay communities that rejected their classification as immigrants. To assert their claims in Malaya's politics, each community created at least one political party to represent their interests and concerns. In the 1920s and 1930s, separate ethnic associations had formed to represent their communities in advisory councils that were part of the British system of colonial rule. The Indians had been represented by the Malayan Indian Association, and after the war, it was revived and renamed the Malayan Indian Congress in 1946. The Ceylonese formed the Ceylon Federation, and Eurasians operated through the Eurasian Union.[8]

As the Communist threat subsided, aspiring political leaders began to pressure British authorities to fulfill their promise of independence for Malaya. British colonial authorities were concerned about the increasing political tensions between ethnic communities and were extremely hesitant to accelerate the transfer of authority to an independent Malaya when ethnic tensions were high. To address that issue, the British persuaded the first leader of UMNO, Dato Onn bin Ja'afar, to leave that organization and form a noncommunal Independence of Malaya Party that could become a suitable recipient of independence representing a multiethnic Malayan electorate. When the first democratic elections were held in 1951 for municipal councils in Penang and Kuala Lumpur, it appeared likely that the noncommunal Independence of Malaya Party would emerge victorious. To compete with that party, the new leader of UMNO, Tunku Abdul Rahman, forged an agreement with the Malayan Chinese Association to create a unified slate and avoid competition between the two allied parties. This combined multiethnic party was called the UMNO-MCA Alliance. When it won those municipal elections, their simple election strategy was expanded to include the Malayan Indian Congress (MIC). Later, in the first federal elections in 1955, the expanded UMNO-MCA-MIC Alliance won an overwhelming victory, capturing all but one seat in the Federal Legislative Council.

Independence: Preserving Malay Hegemony

Shortly after the government was installed, Tunku Abdul Rahman and his Alliance associates began negotiations with Britain for the constitutional provisions that led to full independence for the Federation of Malaya on August 31, 1957. During those negotiations, difficult ethnic issues arose that almost split the Alliance, but eventually compromises were worked out by stressing a multicultural Malayan nationalism based on agreements between the leaders of the three parties representing Malaysia's largest ethnic communities.[9]

In 1963, the Federation of Malaya was expanded to incorporate Singapore and the Borneo territories of Sabah (formerly North Borneo) and Sarawak into the Federation of Malaysia. Both Indonesia and the Philippines objected to the new federation and used various tactics to thwart the new union.[10] Despite their opposition, the newly expanded Malaysia came into existence on September 16, 1963. In the political calculus for creating the larger federation, Malaysia's leaders expected that the indigenous tribal populations of the two new states of Sabah and Sarawak would offset Singapore with its 83 percent Chinese and Indian population. That would assure that "Malays and other indigenous people" would constitute the largest ethnic category, representing about 47 percent of the total population in the Federation of Malaysia. With special arrangements to give Malays more political power, Malays were assured of their continued political supremacy.

After Malaysia was formed, Singapore's governing party, the People's Action Party (PAP), led by Lee Kuan-yew, began a campaign to promote multiculturalism, indirectly challenging the assumptions of Malay preferences and Malay domination of the political system. As the campaign heated up over the role of Singapore, street violence and riots developed in Singapore, promoted by some second-level UMNO leaders. Malaysia's prime minister, Tunku Abdul Rahman, concluded that the only way out of the crisis was to expel Singapore from Malaysia. Amid great secrecy, Parliament was convened and two hours later, on August 9, 1965, Singapore was expelled from Malaysia.[11] This decisive act to exclude Singapore shifted the political balance to assure once more that Malays would continue to be the dominant electoral majority within Malaysia.

In the early years of Malayan independence, the Islamist vision of politics was promoted by Persatuan Aislam Sa-Melayu, popularly known as PAS or Partai Islam.[12] PAS was founded in 1948, and after Burhanuddin Al-Helmy became its leader in 1956, its membership began to expand. PAS objected to the communal compromises that the Alliance made with non-Malay parties and stressed the principle that "Malaya belongs to the Malays." It campaigned for enforcement of Islamic principles and supported the application of Sharia law in matters relating to criminal, public, and commercial law.[13]

At the polls, PAS was less effective than its vote totals might indicate, since its electoral support came from constituencies with high concentrations of Malay voters. In the first federal election in 1955, only one PAS candidate was elected to become the sole opposition to the Alliance majority. In subsequent elections, PAS representation in Parliament varied from highs of thirteen seats to lows of five from 1959 to 1982. Despite its minority position, the ruling Alliance government viewed PAS as its most formidable and dangerous opponent because it threatened to win sufficient Malay support to undermine the basis for UMNO's political power, which depended on its capacity to gain massive support from Malay voters.

In the first two decades after Malayan independence, nationalist themes and issues dominated the political agenda. The issues were complicated by ethnicity and the competing claims of alternative perceptions of how a multi-ethnic society could be accommodated within nationalist institutions. The Islamist vision of politics was generally viewed as too radical and too divisive by those who acquired leadership positions in the early years of nation-building. The first prime minister, Tunku Abdul Rahman, was proud of his Muslim heritage, but he viewed Islam as a matter of personal faith rather than providing a blueprint for public policy or a faith to be propagated by government to convert non-Muslims. As prime minister, he sponsored the Muslim Welfare Society, known as PERKIM, but also insisted that Islam be tolerant in its doctrines and sensitive to the views and interests of non-Muslims who were also citizens of the country.[14] Under his leadership, a secular nationalist idiom prevailed in Malayan politics.

Malaysia's Ethnic Crisis and the New Economic Policy

In 1969 Malaysia held national elections. PAS challenged the governing Alliance Party for making too many concessions to the non-Malay partner parties in the Alliance—the MCA and the MIC. On the other flank, the Democratic Action Party (DAP), representing Chinese constituents, challenged the Alliance coalition for ignoring non-Malay citizens of Malaysia, and it renewed the call made earlier by Singapore's leader, Lee Kuan-yew, for a "Malaysian Malaysia" where all citizens would be treated equally and equitably.

Under assault from both sides on the ethnic/religious divide, the Alliance tried to chart a middle political course. When the election results came in, the Alliance gained less than half the votes, but retained power in Parliament with 66 out of a total of 103 seats. At the state level, the Alliance lost control of three states, Penang, Perak and Terengganu, while in Selangor there was a deadlock between the Alliance and the combined opposition. The surprising results triggered massive ethnic rioting with rural Malays coming into urban centers in the belief that Malay political hegemony was being challenged. These events were called "The May 13th Crisis." The severity of the rioting produced a high death toll and enormous property damage. This crisis prompted the government to declare a national emergency. The Constitution and Parliament were suspended, and a National Operations Council (NOC) headed by Deputy Prime Minister Abdul Razak assumed full powers. Representation on the NOC included seven Malays, one Chinese, and one Indian.[15]

Emergency rule by the NOC continued for one year and nine months. During this period a strategy was devised to reduce ethnic conflict by incorporating new principles into the constitution that would remove certain issues from political contestation. The argument was made that when Malaya gained independence there was agreement on a national compact produced by leaders of all ethnic communities through interethnic bargaining. This compact provided the basis for ethnic harmony and collaboration in political affairs. After the May 13th riots, under Emergency Rule, Abdul Razak was selected by the NOC as prime minister. The decision was made that before democratic institutions could be restored, constitutional changes were required to enshrine certain principles as nonnegotiable and to remove "sensitive issues" from political debate.[16] To that end, the government formulated a "national ideology" called Rukunegara that called for all citizens to be sensitive to the views and concerns of other communities and to be tolerant and respectful of religious diversity, while also upholding the "legitimate interests" and privileges of other communities.[17]

As part of the recovery strategy, the government amended the Constitution "to remove sensitive issues from the realm of public discussions so as to allow the smooth functioning of parliamentary democracy and to redress the racial imbalance in certain sectors of the nation's life and thereby promote national unity."[18] Amendments to the Sedition Act limited freedom of speech and press, defining as a criminal offense any discussion or questioning of the powers and status of the Malay rulers, citizenship rights of non-Malays, Malay special rights and privileges, the status of Islam, and the status of Malay as the sole national language. The Sedition Act applied to members of Parliament, suspending their parliamentary immunities if they spoke about "sensitive issues." By constitutional amendments, the Malay Conference of Rulers was made guarantor of a package of "inalienable Malay and indigenous rights." When Parliament was finally reconvened on February 23, 1971, it was required to pass these amendments as a condition for ending Emergency Rule. In this way, authoritarian powers were combined with democratic institutions, with the critical balance being held by the prime minister through his extraordinary prerogative executive powers.[19]

Besides the measures to limit the issues of political contestation, the government's recovery strategy also involved a massive program to raise the economic position of the Malays through "affirmative action" programs designed to promote their participation in the modern and advanced sectors of the economy. The assertion of Malay supremacy in politics made such a program for economic redistribution of economic benefits possible through political means. The argument was made that the violence of the May 13th riots was the result of the "relative deprivation" of Malays in comparison to non-Malays, and to avoid further ethnic violence, economic disparities based on ethnicity had to be addressed with radical policies.

The blueprint for these policies was formulated by the NOC during Emergency Rule, but the more-detailed policies were incorporated into the Second Malaysia Plan and submitted to Parliament in July 1971. Called the New Economic Policy (NEP), it proposed to reduce poverty for all Malaysians, but also to restructure "Malaysian society to correct economic imbalance, so as to reduce and eventually eliminate the identification of race with economic function."[20] The stated goal was to improve the economic position of the Malays so that they would be equitably represented in all sectors of the economy and at all levels of professional achievement, wealth, and ownership of assets and share capital. The NEP established the target of 30 percent of Malay and indigenous ownership of share capital and participation in all industrial and commercial activities by 1990. To attain its goals, the NEP established a new system of "special rights" for Bumiputra, which included Malays and indigenous people into a single category.[21] These affirmative action rights for Bumiputra included high quotas for university admission and full financial support for higher education, high quotas for employment in the public and private sectors of the economy, a reduced price system for the purchase of housing and for stock investment purchases, and accelerated promotion to management and professional positions after employment in public and private enterprises. To promote a rapid increase in Malay ownership and control of the economy, the government created Bumiputra trust agencies to purchase share capital to gain control of corporations that were later to be transferred to Malay ownership and control. All these programs were designed to provide Malays with privileged access to education, to promote Malay employment in the professions and in management positions, and to secure substantial Malay ownership of and employment in all sectors of the economy.[22]

During the regimes of prime ministers Abdul Razak and Hussein Onn, from 1970 to 1981, the government gave very high priority to implementing new programs and strategies to achieve the objectives of the NEP. The government had the advantage of a healthy economy, stimulated by the rapid growth of petroleum production and the fourfold increase in world oil prices imposed by OPEC in 1974. With its large increase in revenues, the government bought controlling stock in many foreign corporations and founded new corporations to operate as Bumiputra enterprises providing employment and management experience for Malays. Frequently, these government-funded enterprises were placed under the management control of a senior politician, who used political connections to secure contracts or other advantages for the enterprise that he managed. In 1975, the Malayan Chinese Association founded a holding company, Multi-Purpose Holdings, for private Chinese to invest in a large portfolio of enterprises. The number of corporations under its control expanded rapidly to provide the MCA with an independent source of funding and patronage. Shortly thereafter, the Malaysian Indian Congress launched its funding arm, Maika Holdings, and later UMNO did the same by founding, Fleet Holdings and the Renong Group. The corporate empire under the management and control of UMNO grew rapidly with government assistance into a portfolio worth many billions of Malaysian ringgit. With a web of interlinking stock ownership managed by politicians in each of the three major incumbent parties, it became increasingly easy to create new wealth and new rewards for partisan advantage. Increasingly, party activities became focused on the benefits and patronage that came from its responsibilities for managing its corporate empire. Political disputes over these issues and the benefits derived from corporate-based patronage came to be known as "money politics."[23] These overlapping responsibilities between political power and economic control over a partisan-owned corporate empire were justified as being necessary for the success of the NEP policies. With fused responsibilities for public leadership and partisan business empires, distinctions were virtually impossible to be made between legitimate political decisions and "conflicts of interest" by senior leaders in violations of their public trust.

Prior to the May 13th Crisis, Malays were preoccupied with political unity, which was deemed essential to meet what they viewed as the challenge to their supremacy from the immigrant communities. After these events, with Malay power decisively reasserted, Malays began to express more openly their political differences and divisions. As ethnic issues subsided, the issues over the political role of Islam became more intense. While there was no sudden crisis or dramatic incident to bring Islam to the forefront of politics, there was a long gradual period of increasing Malay mobilization pitting a secular Malay nationalist agenda against more radical Islamist perspectives of politics.

Student Activism and Dakwah

Starting about 1970, Malaysia experienced an upsurge of interest and debate about how Islam could be revitalized and coordinated with movements and trends occurring in the broader Islamic world. This movement became known as *dakwah* or *da'wah* depending on whether a Malaysian or Arabic spelling was used. The term means "summons" or "call" and refers to Islamic missionary endeavors to recall lapsed Muslims to renew their faith and to make new converts to Islam. Such calls for religious renewal and revival had been made throughout the colonial era in rather muted form by Arab immigrants to Malaya and Singapore and by some Muslims who returned from the haj pilgrimage with commitments to Islamic piety.[24]

Part of the appeal of the Islamic resurgence came from the experience of 1969 when militant Malays went on a rampage against non-Malays, primarily Chinese and Indians, when they believed that Malay political primacy was being challenged. The moral virtue of Islam was contrasted with the evil, corrupting, and crass world of the kafir—the life and culture of nonbelievers. From that perspective, nearly all intruding influences were depicted as a challenge to the Malay way of life. Dakwah activists made the argument that Malays must make a more intense commitment to Islam in order to defend their faith and culture.

The dakwah movement gained its largest following among Muslim university students. During the post-1970 years, the New Economic Policy generated a social and economic transformation in Malay society created by the government programs designed to bring Malays into the more modern sectors of the economy. When the government rapidly expanded universities and technical colleges and provided generous student bursaries to all Malays who could meet minimum entrance requirements, this produced a tremendous influx of Malay students to higher educational institutions. Many of these students were from rural peasant villages and many were the products of mediocre-quality Malay vernacular schools. In the new urban environment, these students came into direct contact with an alien urban culture where non-Malays dominated and where the contrasts between rural village poverty and urban centers of wealth were beyond their comprehension. So much of the urban lifestyle and values seemed to conflict with their Islamic values. Many of these rural Malay students experienced severe culture shock when exposed to secular values; women's fashions; the liberated roles of women; Western images projected through movies, television, and advertising; and the apparent "immorality" of non-Muslims regarding Western dating practices and courtship. Some Malays feared ritual contamination by interacting with non-Muslims who consumed liquor or food that did not meet Muslim standards of being halal.

Shortly after they arrived on campus, the rural Malay students were confronted by the pressures of academic performance where the instruction was in Malay, the teachers were largely non-Malay, and the reading assignments were often in English. The contrast between the Malay worldview as interpreted through the Islamic teachings of rural-based ulama and the rigorous rational scientific perspective of modern and secular education based on a Western curriculum proved to be particularly disturbing to many of these students. In addition to the problem of social and political adjustment, these Malay students had to overcome their poorer educational background and found it difficult to accept new ideas and theories that challenged some of the dogmas and perspectives that were part of the ethos of rural Islam. Unable to compete with the achievement ethic of students from the immigrant communities, some Malay students opted instead to seek promotion and status through becoming "defenders of the faith." Initially most Malays chose as their majors Malay Studies or Islamic Studies, fearing the competition from non-Malay students. Eventually the government established Malay quotas for nearly all university subjects and provided remedial classes and offered other inducements. Gradually, more Malays were persuaded to opt for scientific and professional degree courses that would prepare them for modern and technical occupations as envisaged by the NEP for a racially balanced economy.

During this period of maximum social and psychological stress for the new wave of Malay students, the dakwah movement began to gain a mass following on campuses. The largest and most influential Malaysian dakwah organization was Angkatan Belia Islam Malaysia (Islamic Youth League of Malaysia, ABIM). It was founded in 1971 through the efforts of the Faculty of Islamic Studies at Universiti Kebangsaan Malaysia. Siddiq Fadil became the first president, and in 1974, Anwar Ibrahim succeeded him. Under Anwar's leadership, ABIM recruited Muslim students from all Malaysian universities and technical colleges. After students graduated, their membership in ABIM continued, providing a network of supporters in government and private sectors of the economy. ABIM's membership also extended to many Malays who had studied abroad in Europe or the United States on fully funded Malaysian government scholarships.[25]

In the pre-1969 era, Malay students' demands had focused on the conversion to the Malay language as the medium of instruction in all institutions of higher education. By 1970, that objective had been achieved. ABIM selected for its next campaign the issues of Malay poverty in rural areas. In December 1974, ABIM organized large student demonstrations based on allegations that Malay peasants in the Baling area of Kedah were starving because of poverty due to depressed rubber prices. When students assembled for large protest demonstrations, federal police arrived and arrested about 1,100 students. Anwar Ibrahim was among those arrested under the preventive detention provisions of the Internal Security Act.[26]

Following these demonstrations, the government passed new legislation in 1975 that ended university autonomy and prohibited political meetings, political activities, or demonstrations at all colleges and universities.[27] Although further student demonstrations were effectively suppressed, student membership in ABIM continued to expand. Under the banner of Islam, most issues of politics were openly discussed, with students claiming Islamic principles as justification for their actions. When Anwar Ibrahim emerged from detention two years later, in 1976, his image as a fearless leader enhanced his political stature and contributed to ABIM's membership growth to about 35,000 by 1980.[28]

ABIM's political and religious message extended far beyond campus boundaries. It published a journal, *Risalah* (Treatise), as well as many other pamphlets and tracts. These stressed the development of a sense of Muslim identity based on "spiritual rehabilitation," usually in contrast with "Western secular materialism," which was condemned as the source of most immorality and cultural degradation. The literature stressed the necessity for commitment and conformity with "true Islam," with the argument that Islamic principles needed to be incorporated into all disciplines of study at the university level. In speeches, Anwar asserted that Islam does not condone racism in any form, and attributed racial conflicts to colonialism and "Western nationalism." Instead, Anwar, in his student days, stressed the sharp distinction between the true Muslim and the unbeliever, what is known as the *kafir-mengkafir* divide. Anwar, and others in the dakwah movement, gave religious explanations for conflicts that others defined as ethnic or cultural conflicts. The idea of the universalism of Islam and the Unity of God (*tawhid*) provided the argument against ethnic or racial discrimination and in opposition to nationalism, but these ideals would only prevail for Muslims after a genuine Islamic regime had been established.

Like other dakwah groups, ABIM stressed the importance of Islamic identity markers for the true believer. These preferred visual markers included

Arab-style robes for men, and for women, required dress with a shoulder-length head cloak (called a *tudong* or *telekung*), which frames the face and covers all the hair. A more complete covering called a *burka* or *jilbab* involves Arab-style black flowing robes or dress for women covering parts of the face, except for eyes, and totally covering the body including arms and legs. Additional Islamic "identity markers" for ABIM and the other dakwah groups involved strict observance of Islamic dietary rules, included avoiding any public eating places where non-Muslim food was served, and open and public displays of praying five times a day at the prescribed intervals. In addition, ABIM stressed the ideals of the Islamic State, without providing details or a timetable for its implementation. It advocated policies to restrict Western "pop culture" characterized as "decadent," and it criticized the government for tolerating horse racing, gambling, and the consumption of liquor. Despite its advocacy of cultural controls to protect Islamic values, ABIM did endorse the concept of a Muslim version of fundamental human rights and was especially critical of violations to freedom sanctioned by the Internal Security Act, the Printing and Presses Publication Act, and the University and University Colleges Act. Although ABIM did not support any political party, it became a persistent critic of the Malaysian government on most public issues and was generally more sympathetic to the political agenda of Partai Islam. Because of its widespread support among university-educated Malay youth, ABIM posed a more serious long-term threat to the Alliance and its successor, the Barisan Nasional, than its membership totals would otherwise indicate.[29]

In our next two chapters we will explore how Indonesia and Malaysia each responded with different strategies to the rising salience of Islamic-based politics in its many diverse manifestations.

Notes

1. William R. Roff, *The Origins of Malay Nationalism* (New Haven: Yale University Press, 1967), chapters 3, 4, 6, and 7; Radin Soenarno, "Malay Nationalism, 1900–1945," *Journal of Southeast Asian History* 1, no. 1 (March 1960), 9–15.

2. Gordon P. Means, *Malaysian Politics*, 2nd rev. ed. (London: Hodder and Stoughton, 1976), 21–23, 90–93; Khoo Kay Kim, *Malay Society: Transformation and Democratisation* (Petaling Jaya, Malaysia: Pelandok Publications, 1991), 243–279.

3. For an account of the close collaboration between Malay political elites and British colonial officials who were genuinely pro-Malay in policy and sentiment, see Robert Heussler, *British Rule in Malaya: 1942–1957* (Singapore: Heinemann Asia, 1985), 187–221. For other accounts of Japanese rule in Southeast Asia, see Paul H. Kratoska, *Malaya and Singapore During the Japanese Occupation* (Singapore: Singapore University Press, 1995); Alfred W. McCoy (ed.), *Southeast Asia Under Japanese Occupation* (New Haven: Yale University Southeast Asian Studies, 1980); Chin Kee Onn, *Malaya Upside Down,* 3rd ed. (Singapore: Federal Publications, 1976).

4. James de V. Allen, *The Malayan Union* (New Haven: Yale University Press, 1967); Albert Lau, *The Malayan Union Controversy, 1942–1948* (Singapore: Oxford University Press, 1991).

5. James P. Ongkili, *Nation-Building in Malaysia, 1946–1974* (Singapore: Oxford University Press, 1985), 38–74; Gordon P. Means, "Ethnic Preference Policies in Malaysia," in Neil Nevitte and Charles H. Kennedy (eds.), *Ethnic Preference and Public Policy in Developing States* (Boulder, CO: Lynne Rienner Publishers, 1986), 95–118.

6. Anthony Short, *The Communist Insurrection in Malaya, 1948–1960* (New York: Crane Russak, 1975); Richard Stubbs, *Hearts and Minds in Guerrilla Warfare: The Malayan Emergency, 1948–1960* (Singapore: Oxford University Press, 1989), 201–264; Gordon P. Means, "Malaysia in 1989: Forging a Plan for the Future," in *Southeast Asian Affairs, 1990* (Singapore: Institute of Southeast Asian Studies, 1990), 183–203. For an account of the insurrection by the leader of the Malayan Communist Party, see Chin Peng, *My Side of the Story* (Singapore: Media Masters, 2003).

7. Means, *Malaysian Politics*, 120–127.

8. Usha Mahajani, *The Role of Indian Minorities in Burma and Malaya* (Bombay: Vora, 1960), 121–128.

9. Ongkili, *Nation-Building in Malaysia*, 105–136; Means, *Malaysian Politics*, 153–192.

10. Means, *Malaysian Politics*, 292–332.

11. Albert Lau, *A Moment of Anguish: Singapore in Malaysia and the Politics of Disengagement* (Singapore: Times Academic Press, 1998).

12. The party later changed its name to Partai Islam Se-Malaya, but retained the PAS abbreviation.

13. N. J. Funston, *Malay Politics in Malaysia: A Study of the United Malays National Organisation and Party Islam* (Kuala Lumpur: Heinmann Educational Books, 1980), 118–120, 135–161; Means, *Malaysian Politics*, 226–232; Gordon P. Means, *Malaysian Politics: The Second Generation* (Singapore: Oxford University Press, 1991), 123–131.

14. After his retirement Tunku Abdul Rahman wrote a column in *The Star* newspaper. His articles were later published in the book: Tunku Abdul Rahman, *Contemporary Issues in Malaysian Politics* (Petaling Jaya, Malaysia: Pelanduk Publications, 1984). His views on Islam are presented in pages 239–341.

15. John Slimming, *Malaysia: Death of a Democracy* (London: John Murray, 1969), 29–48.

16. Goh Cheng Teik, *The May Thirteenth Incident and Democracy in Malaysia* (Kuala Lumpur: Oxford University Press, 1971); William Shaw, *Tun Razak: His Life and Times* (Kuala Lumpur: Longman Malaysia, 1976), 212–231.

17. Government of Malaysia, *Rukunegara* (Kuala Lumpur: Jabatan Chetak Kerajaan, 1970).

18. Government of Malaysia, *Towards National Harmony* (Kuala Lumpur: Jabatan Chetak Kerajaan, 1971), 2.

19. Gordon P. Means, "Soft Authoritarianism in Malaysia and Singapore," in Larry Diamond and Marc F. Plattner (eds.), *Democracy in East Asia* (Baltimore: Johns Hopkins University Press, 1998), 96–110.

20. Government of Malaysia, *The Second Malaysia Plan. 1971–1975* (Kuala Lumpur: Jabatan Chetak Kerajaan, 1971), 1.

21. The category Bumiputra in 1980 comprised about 93 percent Malays, defined by ethnicity and Islam, and 7 percent "other indigenous," most of whom were non-Muslim tribal people from Sabah and Sarawak.

22. R. S. Milne and Diane K. Mauzy, *Malaysian Politics Under Mahathir* (London and New York: Routledge, 1999), 50–79; Gordon P. Means, "Ethnic Preference Policies in Malaysia," 93–111.

23. Edmund Terence Gomez, *Political Business: Corporate Involvement of Malaysian Political Parties* (Townsville, Australia: Centre for South-East Asian Studies, James Cook University, 1994), 1–47. For Bruce Gale's account of corruption arising from mixing politics and business in the "Patrimonial State," see *Politics and Public Enterprise in Malaysia* (Singapore: Eastern Universities Press, 1981), 175–204.

24. For samples of theological discourse, see Peter G. Riddell, *Islam and the Malay-Indonesian World: Transmission and Responses* (Honolulu: University of Hawaii Press, 2001), 101–204.

25. Kamarulnizam Abdullah, *The Politics of Islam in Contemporary Malaysia* (Bangi: Penerbit Universiti Malaysia, 2002), 83–97.

26. *Straits Times,* December 8, 1974, 1; *New Straits Times*, January 1, 1975, 1.

27. Government of Malaysia, *The Universities and Colleges Act of 1975.*

28. J. Victor Morais, *Anwar Ibrahim: Resolute in Leadership* (Kuala Lumpur: Arenabuku, 1983), 2–7; Judith Nagata, *The Reflowering of Malaysian Islam: Modern Religious Radicals and Their Roots* (Vancouver: University of British Columbia Press, 1984), 87–91.

29. Chandra Muzaffar, *Islamic Resurgence in Malaysia* (Petaling Jaya, Malaysia: Penerbit Fajar Bakti, 1987), 13–55; Nagata, *The Reflowering,* 87–105.

PART 3
Islamic Resurgence

6

Indonesia Under Suharto

In the wake of the political crisis of the 1965 September 30th Movement (popularly known as the Gestapu Coup), Lieutenant-General Suharto gradually outmaneuvered President Sukarno and effectively replaced him as acting president of Indonesia by March 1966. During this transition period, Suharto and the army's high command made a strategic alliance with the largest Muslim political party, Nahdlatul Ulama (Awakening of Islamic Scholars). Both the army and Nahdlatul Ulama were militantly anti-Communist and were united in their determination to purge all Communists, as well as their supporters and sympathizers, from the Indonesian political scene.[1] Popularly known as NU, that party represented the ulama and *kiai* (teachers) at pesantren located primarily in small towns across Java and southern Sumatra. Influenced by traditional Javanese cultural perspectives, the NU ulama assumed that they should exercise religious and moral leadership over the rural peasantry who practiced the abangan versions of Islam. Therefore, much of the antagonism between the NU and the Communists involved their political competition for the loyalty and leadership of the same peasant constituency.

Once General Suharto and the army gained control of Jakarta, the purge of Communists began. Vigilante groups were formed (with tacit or overt army and police support) mostly from urban Muslim youth and from the floating urban street population. The NU youth wing, Ansor, was well represented in these vigilante formations, which also included recruits from other organizations to keep their identities concealed. In November 1965, the Muhammadiyah issued a fatwa calling for the "extermination" of PKI members, calling such action an "obligatory religious act."[2] The cultural and religious differences between the attackers and the victims were very small, except when Chinese also came under attack, supposedly for their "Communist inclinations or sympathies." In North Sumatra, some of the attacks were perpetrated on Christian communities, especially in Batak areas where Christianity had taken deep roots. In those regions, the core cultural differences were also slight, but the symbolic aspects of Christian versus Muslim conflicts provided some, but not all, of the motivations for the attacks. The viciousness and methodical nature of the slaughter raise many unresolved issues about the values and motivations of the attackers that might explain such behavior, let alone provide self-justification to those who perpetrated the terror and mass slaughter.[3]

Suharto's Rise to Power and Leadership Style

Suharto was born in 1921 in a peasant village near Jogjakarta, Java. Since his parents separated shortly after his birth, during his early years, he was passed around to various family members who raised him amidst severe poverty. For a while, he attended an Islamic school run by Muhammadiyah. After several efforts to find a job, he joined the Royal Netherlands Indies Army shortly before the Japanese invasion. With the arrival of the Japanese, he joined the Japanese-sponsored militia known as Peta, and when the war ended, Suharto joined the nationalist revolution against the Dutch, serving in the Diponegoro Division. After the nationalist victory, he rapidly rose to the rank of colonel as commanding officer of that division, and during his service with that division, became engaged in putting down a regional revolt in Sulawesi in 1950 and in suppressing the Darul Islam revolt in Central Java from 1950–1957. Later, in 1960, he was placed in command of the Strategic Reserve Command (Kostrad), which he commanded until 1965.

Although Suharto had received mediocre and minimal formal schooling, his years in the army had taught him about the practical politics of personal loyalties and patronage. In its early days, the Indonesian Army relied heavily on external sources of income from army-sponsored businesses and from various illegal operations such as smuggling. During this period, many army commanders, including Suharto, developed ties with important business leaders to provide supplies for their units and to generate other income on the side. With the assistance of several close advisers, Suharto became adept at managing financial resources from questionable or quasi-illegal sources. The money was placed in nontaxable charitable foundations called *yayasans* that he controlled and used to fund the Deponegoro regiment he commanded. For Suharto, the army was a realpolitik lesson in the exercise of power, both military and economic.[4]

The experiences of Suharto fighting for the nationalist cause and suppressing Islamic-inspired rebellions undoubtedly gave him an abiding concern for preserving national unity and created a profound distrust of both Communists and Muslim radicals. At the time of the Gestapu Coup, Suharto was relatively unknown, but his occupation of the strategic position of commander of the elite, rapid-reaction force Kostrad enabled him to act decisively to mobilize the resources of the army and to restore order in the wake of the crisis created by the attempted coup. Within half a year, Suharto had acquired effective power to enable him to begin the creation of a new political system that he called "The New Order."

The New Order

Suharto acquired leadership of a poorly managed authoritarian state apparatus that was virtually bankrupt and an economy with massive debt and uncontrolled inflation. His predecessor, Sukarno, had ruled by authoritarian decree, balancing factional domestic alignments and exhibiting a charismatic image with nationalist demagogic rhetoric directed primarily against the Dutch but also against the "imperialism" of the West. Sukarno revealed little interest, and even less ability, in managing Indonesia's economy. In 1965, the annual inflation rate in Indonesia was more than 500 percent, government expenditures were 300 percent more than its revenues, and the national debt was 524 percent of its total annual exports. The poverty level in Java was 61 percent of the population, while in the remainder of Indonesia it was 52 percent.[5] With this dismal record, Suharto's rule and the New Order would become the beneficiary of accumulated failed policies. Whatever policies and institutions that were to be established to address current problems would be measured against the very low benchmark of the previous regime.

With his power firmly established, Suharto was able to co-opt many of the key Indonesian elites into a new power structure that was built around an ideology of controlling conflict and generating a consensus around the ideals of stability and economic development. The primary objective was to make politics replicate the hierarchy, harmony, and mutual support that are supposedly exemplified in Indonesian families and in well-run village societies. Although Sukarno's Guided Democracy was not mentioned, the ideals of Sukarno's previous political system, based on mutual support and a nonconflictual process of *musjawarat dan mufakat* (deliberation and consensus), were also incorporated into the ideals for the New Order. The practical objective was to devise a new political system that would create national unity and stability by disenfranchising the extremes of the political spectrum and that would enable representatives of the centrist segments of society to confer legitimacy on the new regime.[6]

To provide a core basis of support for the government, the Indonesian Army was assigned the dual function of protecting the nation and participating in the processes of government and administration. This was called *dwifungsi*, meaning "dual function." To institutionalize that dual function, army officers were given cabinet posts in the government and in various administrative positions. In addition, the army was awarded seats in the Indonesian Parliament and on various other bodies through its membership in the political organization Golkar, which represented the government in Parliament and in other bodies.[7]

To accomplish the objectives of the New Order, Suharto's government determined to reorganize the party system. In place of the ten legally recognized parties during Sukarno's rule,[8] political activity under the New Order was limited to two authorized parties that existing parties were ordered to join. The United Development Party (Partai Persatuan Pembangunan, PPP) incorporated four Muslim-based parties. The Indonesian Democratic Party (Partai Demokrasi Indonesia, PDI) incorporated previously existing nationalist, socialist, and Christian parties into a single entity. The Communist Party of Indonesia had been thoroughly defeated, but to prevent its revival, the PKI was banned and Communist or Marxist-Leninist writings and teachings were proscribed, with violators facing very serious penalties.[9]

The organization providing direct support for the government, Golkar, was defined as a "functional group" and was not subject to the restrictions placed on "political parties." During election time, Golkar would post a slate of candidates and mount a well-orchestrated campaign for public support. All civil servants, all the military, and everyone employed by state-owned enterprises were incorporated as members of Golkar. As "government employees" under the New Order, they were bound by what was called the "mono-loyalty policy." They could not join any political party and all these employees were required to work for and vote for Golkar or they would lose their jobs.[10] Thus the Golkar membership included not only its active party workers, but also 5.1 million civil servants, 4.1 million in government departments and state-owned enterprises, and Indonesian military personnel numbering more than 270,000 members. This enormous voting bloc gave Golkar a tremendous boost at the polls and provided a continuous body of political workers who applied political leverage on all levels of the political system. Government workers and civil servants controlled the allocation of government services and infrastructure investments to reward or penalize communities according to the level of their electoral political support. Local leaders and their constituents soon realized that voting for either of the two authorized "opposition" parties would have detrimental and costly consequences regarding government services. While Golkar continued its activities throughout the year, parties were prevented from any campaigning except just prior to elections and they were required to disband their organization at the local level between elections. This election system was designed to ensure overwhelming electoral majorities for Golkar.

Indonesia's representative body at the national level, the People's Representative Assembly (Dewan Perwakilan Rakyat, DPR), operated as Parliament, with nominal legislative powers including investigation and the right to question and censure government. The DPR had 460 members of whom 360 were directly elected, 75 were reserved for the army and were selected by the president, and 25 were selected by provincial assemblies. Under Golkar's leadership, the DPR met for only a few days each year and passed very little legislation, thus leaving most laws to be based on presidential decrees and executive orders.[11] All bills passed by the DPR were subsequently sent to the president for assent or veto, which when exercised could not be overruled and the vetoed legislation could not be resubmitted in the same session.

A second body, the People's Consultative Assembly (Majelis Permusyawaratan Rakyat, MPR), acted as an electoral college to elect a president and vice president, to define broad guidelines of state policy, and to draft or amend the Constitution. The MPR consisted of all 460 members of the DPR plus 460 additional representatives appointed by the government. Suharto's control of the MPR was assured through his wide-reaching appointment powers, which enabled him to select about 70 to 85 percent of MPR members. From 1966 to 1997, the MPR met for two or three days every five years to perform its primary function—to elect the president of Indonesia. It is easy to understand how Suharto was elected by acclamation seven times without having to campaign against any challenger. The "consensus and unanimity" ideal of the New Order was best exemplified in the managed process of election for the president of Indonesia.[12]

A weak and ineffective legislature and a court system that was often corrupt and easily manipulated by the power of the executive to appoint and reassign judges enabled the concentration of powers in the president. The president's powers of appointment to cabinet posts, diplomatic posts, high administrative positions, and the higher commands of the army gave Suharto the capacity to build an enormous patronage network that rewarded supporters and sidelined critics. As political support depended on the distribution of patronage, the resources needed to support the patronage system increased, and so too did the level of corruption. To be part of the patronage system provided inside advantage on access to government contracts, to favored treatment by the bureaucracy, and through "skimming" of profits from government

Table 6.1 Indonesia DPR Election Results, 1971–1997 (percentage of total votes cast)

Election Year	Golkar	PPP (Muslim)	PDI (Democratic)
1971[a]	62.8	27.1	10.1
1977	62.1	29.3	8.6
1982	64.2	28.0	7.9
1987	73.2	16.0	10.9
1992	68.1	17.0	14.9
1997	74.3	22.6	3.0

Sources: Hal Hill (ed.), *Indonesia's New Order: The Dynamics of Socio-economic Transformation* (Honolulu: University of Hawaii Press, 1994), 12; Damien Kingsbury, *The Politics of Indonesia*, 3rd ed. (South Melbourne, Australia: Oxford University Press, 2005), 58.

Note: a. The PPP and PDI percentage of votes cast in 1971 are based on the total vote for the parties that were later merged in 1972–1973 into these two groupings.

projects, foreign assistance, and funding by the World Bank and the International Monetary Fund (IMF).

The nationalization of Dutch-owned industries and trading companies by Sukarno in 1957 had created a large sector of the Indonesian economy that was owned and operated by the state. These enterprises remained under state control in the Suharto era and became an enormous source of patronage. In addition, many sectors of the economy were protected by tariffs and by the granting of monopoly licenses, both for import and export of commodities. The enormous profits that could be made in these protected sectors provided the incentives for the exchange of wealth for favorable political and administrative decisions. At the center of the patronage system was the family of Suharto—his wife, his six children and their spouses, plus various in-laws and cousins. The network of patronage extended far beyond the Suharto family to include a large contingent of Chinese business leaders, many key officers in the military, and favored political supporters.[13] When patronage becomes a primary basis for generating political support, there are never sufficient resources to please all those who will actively profess their loyalty in return for the enormous material benefits that can be derived from proximity to political power.[14]

Development Strategies

In the early days of the New Order, there was widespread public support for the new government and its policies. The violence and the mass killings of 1965 had created an overwhelming desire for public order. The Indonesian Army's sanctioning of and complicity in those killings was carefully concealed from public view, so that the onus for the violence and turmoil was placed on the Communist Party of Indonesia. Therefore, the new government under Suharto, with the backing of the army, was able to project an image of supporting peace, order, and economic development.

During the early years of the New Order, the Indonesian economy grew at the rate of 7 to 8 percent per year, a figure that was in dramatic contrast to the dismal economic performance of the Sukarno era.[15] This new economic vitality could be attributed to two primary factors. First, the world oil crisis of the 1970s pushed up the price of crude oil from US$3 a barrel in 1972 to US$30 in 1980. As a major oil producer, Indonesia gained a tremendous bonanza of revenue that was used for infrastructure development programs and the expansion of the bureaucracy to provide more government services. Second, the government reversed previous policies that had discouraged foreign investments. Instead, Bappenas (the National Planning Board) drafted a set of pragmatic economic policies designed to encourage foreign investment, establish fiscal discipline, and promote export-led industrialization. The leading role for economic growth was allocated to the private sector, which was expected to promote diversification and reduced reliance on oil exports. In combination, these policies brought in enormous levels of foreign investments, especially from Japan and from the more dynamic newly industrializing countries (NICs) of Asia—China, South Korea, Taiwan, and Hong Kong. US and European investments were also forthcoming, but at a much lesser level than investments from Asian countries.[16]

Two other areas of accomplishments during the New Order era need to be briefly mentioned to indicate both its achievements and liabilities. One of Suharto's greatest achievements, in his view, was the New Order policy related to agriculture. Perhaps that pride reflected his early life in a poor rural village and working in the padi fields.[17] When Suharto came to power, Indonesia was importing more rice than any other country. These rice imports consumed 20 to 25 percent of the country's export earnings, creating a serious balance of payments problem for the economy.[18] In 1974, the government initiated a package of reforms designed to achieve rice self-sufficiency within a decade. The policy included land reform, subsidized fertilizer, low-interest credit, development of high-yield disease-resistant rice, rural technical support, and improved marketing and storage facilities.[19] During the early 1960s, rice yields in Java were 1.7 tons per hectare. From 1988 to 1990, the yields had increased to 3.2 tons per hectare. During the same period, the poverty category in Java of "very poor" had been reduced from 61 percent to 10 percent.[20]

Another area of high priority involved Indonesia's rapid population growth. In 1962, Indonesia's fertility rate was among the highest in the world at 4.3 percent. An interlocking cluster of programs was devised to address this problem, including health services, education, reproductive rights information, family planning, and subsidized contraceptive services. Gradually the fertility rate was reduced about 40 percent, and the annual population growth rate was reduced from 2.3 percent for 1971–1980 to 1.7 percent for 1990–2000. Even so, Indonesia's population continued to increase at an alarming rate, challenging the capacity of the economy to produce jobs and improved standards of living for all its citizens.[21]

In some other areas, government policies were moderately successful and making some progress in addressing long-standing social and economic issues. Altogether these achievements created what some scholars have referred to as "performance legitimacy."[22] With an increasing gross national product (GNP), the regime accused critics of being antinational for failure to support consensus politics. The heavy reliance on performance legitimacy provided the camouflage to mask the excesses of authoritarian rule and the waste and corruption of the patronage system.

Islam Under the New Order

In the aftermath of the Gestapu Coup, the tacit alliance between Nahdlatul Ulama and the Indonesian Army produced a split in the NU leadership between those committed to Sukarno and those supporting Suharto. As Sukarno's power waned, the pro-Suharto faction in the NU leadership expected to be given an influential role in the new regime. Yet, as the regime evolved, Suharto sidelined all Islamic parties, including Nahdlatul Ulama, and subjected all political activity to stringent state control.[23] Rather than incorporating Muslim political leaders into the government, in 1971, Suharto authorized the formation of a new Islamic party, Partai Muslimin Indonesia (Parmusi) under the leadership of a government nominee, Djaelani Naro. Partai Masyumi, which had been banned by Sukarno in 1960, appealed for reinstatement, but that was denied and all former Masyumi leaders were banned from political activity.[24] Because of Suharto's heavy hand in the formation of Parmusi, that party failed to attract much support in the 1971 elections. What Suharto had accomplished was the fracturing of the Islamic vote among three Islamic parties, with the Nahdlatul Ulama gaining only 18 percent and Parmusi only 5.3 percent of the vote.[25] The victory of Golkar had already been assured by the nature of the election rules.

With its new "mandate," the government began a massive campaign to stress Pancasila, the national ideology (*asas tunggal*), as the basis for consensus and national unity. All political parties were required to declare their adherence to Pancasila. The opposition of Muslim leaders tended to focus on issues related to the forced acceptance of Pancasila, which they interpreted to prevent public demands for an Islamic State including implementation of Sharia law. For orthodox Muslims, the Pancasila doctrine was viewed as a betrayal of Islam. With the four Islamic-based parties forced to dissolve and join the new United Development Party (PPP) and the non-Islamic, nationalist, and Christian parties also forced to join the Indonesian Democratic Party, the internal divisions within these forced unions further weakened their political clout. To assure the regime their political support, both these parties were infiltrated by government agents to monitor their political activities.

In 1973, another issue raised the ire of conservative Muslim groups. The government introduced a marriage reform law designed to prevent parents arranging a marriage of their daughters before the onset of puberty. The new reform legislation also provided for limitations to a husband's rights to divorce and to take multiple wives. The proposed reforms also sanctioned the appointment of some women judges to Islamic courts. Conservative Islamic organizations mounted strong opposition to this bill because, they argued, it contravened Sharia law. To dramatize their opposition to the proposed bill, Nahdlatul Ulama led a walkout from Parliament. Eventually, critics of the proposed legislation gained a partial victory when the bill was altered to address some of their criticisms. Eventually the Marriage Law passed in 1974; it retained some reform provisions but provided for Islamic religious courts to have only an advisory role in interpreting Sharia law. Civil courts retained ultimate judicial authority over the Marriage Law, and its administration was assigned to the civil bureaucracy.[26]

Because Islamic institutions posed a potential challenge to state authority, Suharto devised a system providing for an Islamic council to act on religious matters. Founded in 1975, the Majelis Ulama Indonesia (MUI) became a central body to govern Islamic affairs. Its membership came from ulama appointed to local Islamic councils. The MUI received funding from the government and was treated as an advisory body under the authority of the Department of Religion. The MUI was granted authority to issue fatwas that were not legally binding unless they were followed by authorizing legislation or an executive order. One of the early fatwas issued by MUI in 1980 declared the Ahmadiyah community to be a heretical sect. That fatwa accused the founder of Ahmadiyah, Mirza Ghulam Ahmad, of claiming to have received a revelation directly from God, which contravened the Islamic doctrine that the Prophet Muhammad received the "last and final revelation from God." That fatwa effectively convicted all Ahmadis of *murtad,* but they were not condemned to death according to Sharia criminal punishments for apostasy. Instead, the fatwa prohibited Ahmadis from disseminating their ideas and religious doctrines in Indonesia and warned Muslims not to be misled by their "false doctrines."[27] The fatwa remained without legal sanction, and government authorities did not enforce the fatwa. Instead, authorities continued to permit Ahmadis to immigrate to Indonesia. Before the MUI issued that fatwa, the Indonesian government had already issued a charter in 1980 allowing Ahmadis to build their own mosques and to teach Ahmadiyah doctrines to their own members. Years later, when Suharto was no longer president, this MUI fatwa convicting Ahmadis of murtad would become a matter of national debate over the future direction of Islam. While Suharto remained in power, however, issues of protecting and enforcing Islamic orthodoxy versus religious freedom were obfuscated by deft administrative sleight of hand.

Although the Muslim-based parties acted as the primary opposition to Suharto's rule during the New Order era, the government made efforts to court Muslim support by generous grants to mosques and Islamic schools. At the same time, political leaders of Muslim parties and organizations were not appointed to important cabinet positions and were treated as though they represented antinational and antimodern sectors of society. For Suharto, the ideals of national unity, the economic development of the country, and the transition to a modern economy were far more important than esoteric and divisive arguments about the religious orthodoxy of Islam and the implementation of Sharia laws.[28]

In 1973, Suharto forced all Muslim parties to unify within the PPP; however, this action did not create unity, but rather generated factional splits. The Muhammadiyah wing believed that their strict Islamic ideals should not be compromised, and therefore they were essentially denied access to the councils of government and to the patronage that was available to those who supported the government. By contrast, the Nahdlatul Ulama were much more accommodating to Suharto's rule, believing that incremental benefits to their community were more important than making strident demands for politically unobtainable ideals. They openly accepted and defended the principles of Pancasila; they accepted and welcomed positions on government bodies and in administration; and they collaborated with non-Muslim parties and leaders on various public issues. NU's leader, Abdurrahman Wahid, believed that if the state became responsible for defining and enforcing Islamic principles and law, then serious political divisions would be created that would wreak havoc between santri Muslims and abangan Muslims, as well as impinging on the rights of non-Muslims. Abdurrahman argued that state control of Islam would result in the violation of the freedom of conscience and religion for many of its citizens. For awhile the leadership echelons of the party agonized over alternative strategies and objectives. Finally, in 1983, Abdurrahman organized meetings with his party to define the basis for NU's participation within the government. The main formulation read: "Islam is pluralistic and because of this, implementation of Islamic teachings should be pluralistic, and this is in accordance with the tradition of NU."[29]

Although Nahdlatul Ulama held more government posts and was more influential with the government than other Islamic parties and organizations, it chafed at restrictions that were placed on it within the "unified" United Development Party. In the 1982 elections, the PPP gained 28 percent of the vote, while Golkar's majority remained remarkably steady at 64.2 percent. By 1983, after continued frustration with the election process, Abdurrahman concluded that Nahdlatul Ulama should completely withdraw from politics to give it more freedom to cultivate support from its constituency through religious and social service activities. The party adopted that policy, effectively terminating its status as a political party and ending its participation in the PPP. Defining itself as "a religious and cultural organization," the NU was able to generate wider public support, and it acquired greater freedom to discuss issues that affected its primary constituency. Without the restraints that came from official patronage, the legitimacy of the NU increased and so too did its following. By supporting Pancasila and its pluralist ideology, NU also gained some endorsement from government authorities that assumed NU would no longer be a political force.[30]

Nahdlatul Ulama's withdrawal from overt politics severely weakened the voice of orthodox and pious Islam in Parliament and left the Muhammadiyah as the sole official voice for an orthodox Islamic perspective on public issues. The weakened position of Islam in politics created increased frustration among the supporters of orthodox and political Islam, which led to increasing militancy among some orthodox Muslims who were willing to take their grievances to the street in public displays of power and popular discontent. In this environment, the mosques were often transformed into the centers for mobilization of the power of disaffected Muslims.

The Islamic Revival and Alienation

During the 1970s, Muslims experienced the beginnings of the dakwah movement that stressed the importance of strict conformity with Sharia law and emphasis on Islamic piety through dress, public prayer, and social pressure on religious commitments. While this had been a recurring theme in Islam, this movement was accelerated by increased contacts of Southeast Asian Muslims with the Middle East and increasing numbers of Arabs migrating to Southeast Asia to assume leadership roles in Muslim communities. During the New Order, pious and devout Muslims, especially those following the santri orientation, had accumulated grievances and were becoming more politicized. Their alienation prompted them to consider more radical tactics to achieve their objectives. Reports circulated in 1977 that a secret militant paramilitary Islamic unit had been formed, known as Komando Jihad (Holy Warriors), that was committed to fight for an Islamic state and to protect Islamic interests. Later, in March 1981, an Islamic radical group led by Imran bin Zein engineered the hijacking of a Garuda DC9 airliner taking off from Palembang and diverted it to Bangkok. The highjackers demanded the release of eighty religious extremists in Indonesian jails. In response, the Indonesian military provided an elite commando force that stormed the plane, killing all five hijackers.[31]

This early example of terrorism prompted increasing government efforts to limit the political activities of Muslim groups; Suharto's New Order government gave closer scrutiny to activists and agitators who were attempting to mobilize political support around the banner of Islam. At the same time, leaders of Islamist groups made strident demands for all Muslims to conform to Sharia law and that Islamic orthodoxy be openly observed. They called for enforcement of mosque attendance, public reservation of special time and place for prayers five times a day at prescribed times, and conformity to Islamic dress rules, especially for Muslim women. To counter these demands of fundamentalist Muslims, the government renewed its requirement that all organizations must assert their acceptance of the principles of Pancasila. In addition, the government banned women students from wearing extra-long skirts and the complete face-covering veils (jilbab) for being in violation of school uniform regulations. A storm of protest was generated by orthodox Muslim imams, who, during sermons and in speeches, accused the authorities of being opposed to the Muslim way of life. With fiery language and strident rhetoric, these preachers depicted pious Muslims as victims of an oppressive secular and anti-Muslim government.

When tensions mounted in the Jakarta suburb of Tanjung Priok, the authorities sent some soldiers to investigate potential political activities at the mosque, and they removed some offensive political posters. In retaliation, a bystander set a soldier's motorcycle on fire, whereupon four people were arrested for arson. By nightfall a crowd of about 1,500 people armed with crude weapons arrived at the local police station demanding the release of those arrested. Their demand was rejected and the crowd refused to disperse. As the crowd became more unruly, the police fired into the threatening crowd, triggering serious rioting directed against Chinese businesses, police, and military units that were called in to suppress the violence. When military reinforcements arrived, excessive force was used to apprehend rioters. Later, government authorities reported about 40 killed during the riots, but observers subsequently claimed that the death toll may have been more than 1,000. Islamist critics of the regime claimed that those killed were quickly carried away and buried in mass graves at secret locations. In the aftermath of the riots, the Tanjung Priok killings became, for many Muslims, a symbol of the government's repressive policies toward the political demands of orthodox Islam. The political imams, who had earlier radicalized their Muslim followers, now conferred martyr status on those Muslims killed by the military during the riots.[32] The Tanjong Priok events generated high levels of anger and militancy among orthodox Muslims in opposition to the policies and tactics of the New Order regime. That crisis was a harbinger of more serious conflicts yet to come.

Suharto Discovers Piety Politics

In the early days of the New Order, the government exercised overt coercion against critics and built much of its support base through the development of its patronage network. Responsibility for keeping track of and thwarting any potential opposition was assigned to the agency known by the acronym Bakin.[33] This organization was formed in 1967 as a clandestine arm of the military and it operated essentially beyond the purview of the law as a form of secret police. The targets of its surveillance and harassment tactics were political parties, dissidents, the Chinese community, and the remnants of those believed to have Communist sympathies or links to Communist regimes abroad. In 1974, General Benny Murdani was appointed head of Bakin, and in 1983 he was also appointed commander-in-chief of Indonesia's armed forces and the operational commander of Kopkamtib,[34] the special security corps of the Indonesian Army. Over the years, many of the operations of Bakin and Kopkamtib were directed at Muslim political parties and organizations that had been excluded from the councils of government. General Murdani became a symbol of their resentments, especially because of his mixed Javanese-Eurasian origin and his Catholic identity. While commander-in-chief of the army, he tended to promote non-Muslims to the higher ranks and slowed the promotion of officers who displayed Islamic piety. Taking a cue from Suharto, General Murdani could justify his appointments as part of the secular nationalist agenda proclaimed by Pancasila. To Muslims, this was evidence of blatant discrimination. Over time, these resentments tended to create a division within the Indonesian armed forces that came to be characterized as an Islamic "green faction" and a nationalist "red and white faction."[35]

As one of the inner circle of advisers to Suharto, General Murdani assumed that he could discuss sensitive issues that were the basis for unrest and widespread public criticisms of the Suharto government. The regime's critics had become increasingly incensed over the operation of the patronage system, especially the enormous wealth that was being diverted to Suharto's immediate family.[36] As an example, in 1988 it became common knowledge that Suharto's daughter Tutut (Siti Hardiyanti Rukmana) and his son Tommy (Hutomo Mandala Putra) had acted as agents for foreign companies bidding for contracts to deliver minesweepers for the Indonesian Navy, and they had received large commissions for securing those contracts. Murdani raised this issue in his reporting to Suharto. The full extent of what he communicated to President Suharto in 1988 is not known. Some years later, in an interview with Adam Schwarz, Murdani is quoted as saying: "I told my staff that the president's children should be treated like any other businessmen, and not be given favorable treatment. I told Suharto I had done this. He just smiled and I interpreted this as his approval."[37]

Suharto believed that his family and children had as much right to be in business as any other Indonesians, and he argued that their success in business acted as a counter to the dominant role of the Chinese in business affairs. What some viewed as nepotism, Suharto argued was merely "affirmative action" in support of *pribumi* entrepreneurs. General Murdani soon learned that any hint of criticism of Suharto's family affairs was not received with thanks. In 1988, Murdani was removed as army commander-in-chief and given the less critical post of defense minister. Then in 1993, he was removed from the cabinet, and a large cohort of officers at the rank of colonel or above who had been associated with Murdani were retired or sidelined.

In retrospect, it appears that Suharto believed that he could deal with criticisms within the ranks of the military and also reclaim support from the Muslim constituency by a shift of tactics. With rather contorted logic, he assumed that new overtures to the Islamic constituency would generate a new base of support for his regime and that his critics, both vocal and silent, would learn the high cost of criticism of the business dealings of his family members.[38] Suharto's decision to shift political course was based on more than just a response to reports of public criticism of the favoritism awarded to his family members. He could also deflect some of the criticism of his regime to the heavy-handed tactics of General Murdani to suppress dissent.[39]

To initiate his strategic realignment, in December 1990, Suharto announced the formation of an organization called the Indonesian Association of Muslim Intellectuals (ICMI).[40] This organization was described as a forum for moderate educated Muslims to act as a Muslim-based policy "think tank."[41] Suharto selected B. J. Habibie, the minister of research and technology, to head the ICMI. Membership was by invitation approved by Suharto, but it did include some prominent Muslims who had previously been opposed to the government. The initial announcement that the ICMI was being formed received a positive response from most Muslim leaders, many of whom expected a Muslim-based political agenda to follow.[42]

Soon after the ICMI began operations, division within its ranks became apparent. In his analysis, Schwarz identified four primary factions: technocrats, led by Habibie, who were primarily university professors and business leaders; moderate Muslims, led by Nurcholish Majid, who were concerned with making Islam a positive social force to improve the economic conditions of poor Muslims; nongovernment "modernist" and "neomodernist" Muslims, led by Amien Rais, who favored democratic norms; and a fourth faction espousing radical Islamist doctrines and affiliated with Dewan Dakwah Islamiyah Indonesia (Indonesian Council for Islamic Preaching, DDII).[43] To promote the ICMI agenda and generate support for an Islamic approach to public policy, the ICMI launched its own newspaper, *Republika.*

The largest Muslim organization in Indonesia, Nahdlatul Ulama, was not represented in the ICMI because its leader, Abdurrahman Wahid, believed that the organization would espouse essentially fundamentalist Islamic views and that it would promote the *salafiya* ideal of an Islamic State. Abdurrahman was also extremely suspicious of the ICMI as a dangerous and undemocratic organization. When the ICMI was being formed, he issued a public warning to Suharto stating that ICMI would become dominated by Islamists and that his strategy was courting disaster. When Suharto proceeded with his decision to found the ICMI, Abdurrahman formed his own elite think tank in 1991—the Democracy Forum—which also produced policy papers and reports to rebut ICMI proposals and to critique the policies of Suharto.[44]

At the founding sessions of the ICMI, Habibie gave a boost to Suharto's Islamic credentials by reporting allegedly confidential statements from Suharto about his long-standing commitment to the Muslim faith and his willingness "to struggle for the Muslim cause." Later, in June 1991, Suharto went on the haj pilgrimage to Mecca with his family and a large coterie of loyal supporters. The press gave this trip extensive coverage, which led some observers to speculate that this was the beginning of Suharto's 1993 campaign for reelection as president. The public received an unmistakable message that the earlier New Order rules designed to separate religion from politics had now been effectively reversed.[45]

As part of the effort to recruit Muslim support, in late 1991, Suharto approved the formation of an Islamic bank based on the prescriptions of Sharia law, whicn prohibits usury involving fixed interest on loans.[46] Government money was allocated for Bank Muamalat Indonesia, promising interest-free loans to Muslims in accordance with Sharia rules on banking and commercial transactions.[47] Government subsidies were also increased for mosques, Islamic madrasah and pesantren schools, and for Muslims going on the haj pilgrimage to Mecca.

For Muslim leaders who were nominated to membership in the ICMI, their initial enthusiasm for their new role soon waned. When Suharto chose his cabinet and made other appointments to government posts, the ICMI members were virtually ignored and, apart from Habibie, no ICMI members gained cabinet positions. Even so, the organization did have an important symbolic impact on government affairs. Government officials at public functions openly displayed the outward manifestations of Islamic piety. The most important command posts in the army were thereafter assigned to the green faction, which became a mainstay of support for Suharto's regime in its latter years.[48]

With such a formidable array of leaders of Indonesian Muslim organizations on the ICMI, many members expected significant policy proposals would be generated by their deliberations. While the ICMI met regularly and debated substantive topics, important divisions were never resolved. The leader of the second-largest Islamic organization (Muhammadiyah), Amien Rais, became a prominent member of the Council of Experts in 1999 and a member of the editorial board of the ICMI magazine *Ummat.* When he made outspoken statements on public issues, he was removed as chairman of the council and asked to resign from the ICMI, which he promptly did.[49] Members of the ICMI gradually realized that their organization could not become a venue for political action. Instead, Suharto was determined to make it into a vehicle for generating political support for the New Order regime but was not willing to concede any power-sharing role to the ICMI. The political role of the ICMI only came in later years when the New Order regime was ending and the political contest developed over who was to be elected to succeed Suharto as president. At that juncture, the ICMI became the primary organization supporting the candidacy of Habibie.

Suharto's 1998 Reelection

Although Suharto's New Order regime had effective control of electoral mechanisms, that did not prevent erosion of legitimacy for his system of rule. By 1997, a managed election cycle was about to begin. General elections were scheduled for May 1997, with the presidential election to follow in March 1998. In the general elections to Parliament, Golkar won a decisive majority, capturing 74.5 percent of the votes, and in the presidential election ten months later on March 10, 1998, Suharto was reelected with unanimous acclamation by the People's Consultative Assembly for a seventh term. Despite the overwhelming confirmation of support from the body charged with electing the president, Suharto's legitimacy was seriously compromised. His public support had been slowly eroding over a number of years, but the collapse of his legitimacy occurred both suddenly and dramatically, largely because of his manipulation and control of political institutions. While it is not within the scope of this study to explain the intricacies of the tangled web of Indonesian politics, it will be useful to highlight a few of the key events from 1996 to 1998 that precipitated Suharto's fall from power two months after his unanimous reelection.

One of the two permitted political parties during the New Order was the PDI. That party comprised many nationalists who had been associated with Sukarno, as well as Christians and secular nationalists. For the elections in 1987 and 1992, Suryadi led the PDI. He was reform minded and mounted a campaign in 1992 that called for political changes, utilizing the slogan "Status Quo, No!, Changes, Yes." As a result, Suryadi lost the support of the government, which arranged, behind the scenes, for his removal as PDI leader.[50] Earlier, in 1986, the PDI had recruited into the party the eldest daughter of Sukarno, Megawati Sukarnoputri, who had become an effective campaigner for the party. When Suryadi was removed from party leadership by the actions of government agents within the party, she became a candidate and was elected PDI leader in 1993. Instead of becoming a passive and compliant follower, Megawati was outspoken and fearless and attracted wide popular support. For Suharto, Megawati appeared to be his nemesis, likely to seek retribution for the way he had removed her father from power twenty-eight years earlier.

Confronted with this dilemma, Suharto decided that it would be preferable to arrange to restore Suryadi to the leadership of the PDI. To accomplish this task, a covert campaign was mobilized to collect signatures calling for a special PDI congress. To implement the change of leadership, the government ordered the PDI to hold a special congress in Medan for June 1996. Megawati, as PDI chairman, was not even informed, and she and her supporters refused to attend what they viewed as an "illegal rump" meeting. The PDI congress sessions in Medan went smoothly, attended mostly by military delegates, PDI dissidents, and the supporters of Suryadi. Following instructions from a faction led by armed forces commander General Faisal Tanjung, Suryadi was elected party leader once again. The government immediately recognized Suryadi as PDI leader.

Meanwhile, Megawati and her followers were barricaded in the PDI headquarters in central Jakarta. Crowds assembled each day to hear free speech forums openly critical of the government's crude manipulation of political parties. Student and disaffected groups became energized by Megawati's fearless candor. Finally, Suharto ordered the military to suppress the protests and expel Megawati's supporters from the PDI headquarters. The Jakarta army command recruited 200 thugs and street toughs called *preman,* added 100 military personnel in plain clothes, and trained them for the assault on PDI headquarters. Armed with sharpened staves and dressed with PDI shirts, they stormed the PDI headquarters in the middle of the night on July 27, 1996. Two pro-Megawati PDI defenders were killed and 181 injured. The next morning, a crowd of 10,000 appeared to protest the assault by surging against police and army lines. Later in the day, rioting broke out in Jakarta. Although Megawati and her supporters had been removed from the PDI headquarters, in the eyes of the protesters, many of them university students, Megawati had become their "Mega"-hero, and among students she became popularly known as "Mega-Bintang" (Superstar). What had been planned to appear as an internal matter within the PDI had instead been exposed by the heavy-handed intervention of the government acting through the military with its crude and devious tactics.[51]

The plan to expel Megawati from PDI leadership was fully implemented as intended. What was not expected or anticipated was the mobilization of student protests around her cause, which she and her followers highlighted with the simple slogans: Reformasi and Democrasi. From the beginning of the New Order, student demonstrations had been a recurring problem for the regime. In the early days, student protests were often triggered by rising prices in food and basic commodities, but increasingly the protesters turned to issues of corruption and political favoritism. In 1978, the Campus Normalization Law was passed, which provided stiff penalties for students' political activities at university campuses. This law had effectively quelled student protests. The Megawati PDI expulsion operations, however, exposed the government's role and further tarnished its legitimacy. These events re-energized university students to engage in a continuing cycle of slogan-driven protests.

With the approach of general elections in May 1997, the government's potential critics had been effectively isolated or sidelined. Megawati was removed from active legal politics. Amien Rais had been removed from ICMI, while Abdurrahman Wahid was pressured to support Golkar, which he did reluctantly, explaining that he did not want all the Islamic vote to go to the Muhammadiyah Islamic extremists in the PPP who were agitating for implementing the salafiya version of an Islamic State. Although Nahdlatul Ulama was officially a "nonparty" after it withdrew from politics, its leaders feared the rising demands of santri Islamists in the PPP as a challenge to abangan Islam. Therefore, NU chose to support Golkar, with its promise of defending Pancasila, as the lesser of two evils. Because of the effective techniques of political control exercised by Suharto over the party system, and NU's support for the regime, it was no surprise that the 1997 general elections returned Golkar with its largest majority ever at 74.5 percent.[52]

The Evolving Crisis of Confidence

In the period between the general elections and the presidential elections of March 1998, a period of ten months, Indonesia experienced a major economic crisis. The world economy was affected by an economic decline and many of the more vigorous East Asian economies suffered from depressed markets and overextension of dollar-denominated credit. The Thai currency plunged in value and then the slowdown hit South Korea, forcing both countries to seek IMF assistance. The Indonesian rupiah dropped in value in July. Government measures to meet the crisis proved ineffective. By August, the rupiah was spiraling out of control, dropping in value from about Rp2,500 to the US dollar in June, to Rp5,500 in October and reaching Rp14,500 in January 1998.[53] As the exchange rate plummeted, large numbers of bank depositors withdrew their funds, sending money abroad and forcing many banks into bankruptcy. The overextension of credit from foreign sources had left the corporate sector with enormous debt, estimated at between US$45 billion and US$140 billion. These debts could not be repaid with the devalued rupiah. Capital flight accelerated the rupiah's collapse at the same time that prices of imports and basic commodities, including food, skyrocketed. The economic collapse forced many industrial plants to close or severely restrict their production. With a major portion of the industrial workforce being laid off, unemployment reached record levels. By 1998, the estimate of the total numbers of Indonesians living in poverty had risen from 11.3 percent to 48 percent, based on a poverty line at US$0.45 per capita per day.[54] The economic crisis may have started at the top, but it quickly spread to the lowest ranks of society.

As the economic crisis escalated, both the World Bank and the IMF offered assistance and advice. During the first round of negotiations in October 1997, the IMF proposed a rescue package of US$43 billion spread over three years. This package was contingent on a series of structural reforms, including ending import and market monopolies, rebalancing the national budget, ending wasteful subsidies, and imposing tight fiscal and monetary policies. Before those reforms could be implemented, the crisis had become worse, in part because investors had little confidence that the reforms would be implemented and doubted that, if implemented, the reforms were sufficient to remedy the root causes of the economic malady. In January 1998, the IMF returned with a second rescue package, and shortly after Suharto's reelection as president in March, the IMF negotiated once again a third agreement in April 1998. All these agreements were focused on structural and financial reforms, which were either being sidestepped or implemented very slowly and haphazardly. All these signals were being closely watched in the world's financial markets, so that lack of confidence on the economic front was being mirrored by domestic lack of confidence on the political front.

The economic crisis exposed the corruption and the economic drain imposed on the economy by the patronage and crony system of favoritism, subsidies to inefficient and wasteful enterprises, monopoly schemes, and commission payoff to Suharto's cronies. The most favored beneficiaries of the system were Suharto's children and their kin. In Indonesia, the prevailing system of "crony capitalism" was popularly referred to as KKN—*korupsi, kolusi,* and *nepotisme.*[55]

While the economic crisis had many causes, the intertwined strands of unbridled political power, combined with corrupt and mismanaged economic power, severely inhibited the capacity of the Suharto government to address issues of reform and recovery in a coherent and consistent manner. What the IMF proposed was for political and economic reform from within and from the apex of the political and economic order. The remedies may or may not have been appropriate or adequate, but the responsibility for implementation was misallocated to Suharto and therefore doomed to failure. The IMF proposals were equivalent to giving advice for a brain-tumor patient to perform self-administered surgery.

As the economic crisis increased economic hardship throughout the society, the intensity and frequency of student demonstrations also increased. Defenders of the regime accused the Chinese and Christians of creating the economic crisis, while the green faction of the army joined with some militant Islamic groups to attack Chinese and Christian minorities. Regime defenders in the army organized and paid preman to trigger riots against these communities. In addition, some elements of the army's special forces, known as "The Rose Team," under the command of General Prabowo Subianto, Suharto's son-in-law, engineered a series of kidnappings of twenty-three student leaders associated with the prodemocracy agitations.[56] Later investigations revealed that some army funds were also diverted by green officers to an Islamist paramilitary organization known as Laskar Jihad, which became involved in attacks on Christian communities in Maluku in 1998. This organization was probably also involved in a series of mysterious murders of abangan Muslims in eastern Java who practice the mystical animist version of Islam known as Kebatinan. For orthodox Muslims, this offshoot of Islam is viewed as apostasy. The scapegoat tactic against non-Muslim communities created a wave of violence across Indonesia that resulted in the burning of some 500 churches, the destruction of much private property, and the killing of many thousands of victims.[57] For many participants in this political struggle, there were grave risks, high casualties, and devastating property losses.

During this period of political turmoil and escalating economic crisis, key Muslim constituencies were divided in their responses and support. Abdurrahman and the Nahdlatul Ulama were in a cautious intermediate "nonpolitical" stance, but many of their supporters were easily motivated to join anti-Chinese demonstrations. The Muhammadiyah were also in a political holding pattern, but their leader, Amien Rais, increasingly became identified with the Reformasi movement and eventually joined in a coalition with Megawati called Democracy Forum. However, some of the second-level Muhammadiyah leaders remained in the ICMI, and many of the rank-and-file Muhammadiyah were greatly disturbed by the radical stance represented by university student demonstrations. Some Muhammadiyah members were swayed by the anti-Christian and anti-Chinese rhetoric that was being generated by Suharto's defenders as the political and economic crisis escalated.

When the People's Consultative Assembly convened in March 1998 for presidential elections, it did so amidst massive student demonstrations calling for a "reform agenda." Suharto gave his required speech to the MPR defending his government and outlining policy principles for the next five years. In replies to his speech, there were some mild criticisms from PDI and PPP members, but when it came time to vote for president, the assembly elected Suharto by acclamation and with a standing ovation. The following day, Habibie was elected vice president. The demands and concerns of the student demonstrators had been completely ignored, despite their massive presence in the streets outside the Parliament building.

Suharto's Departure

Three days after his reelection, Suharto announced his new cabinet. Nine cabinet members were army officers, very few had previous governmental experience, and most were close associates of Suharto. Many of the cabinet had been the principal beneficiaries of the monopoly, subsidy, and concession system that the IMF was attempting to abolish. Included in the cabinet was Suharto's daughter, Tutut, and Bob Hasan, the timber baron who had acquired enormous wealth under the timber monopoly system. Members of the previous cabinet who had favored cooperation with the IMF were all dropped.

The announcement of the new cabinet triggered waves of protest, led by students but joined also by opposition parties and prominent Indonesians in other walks of life. The press labeled his selections the Crony Cabinet. Since negotiations were still ongoing with the IMF, the message interpreted by the press and financial markets was clear: Under Suharto's leadership, Indonesia was not willing to accept any reforms demanded by the IMF but was seeking and willing to accept its bailout money.

From mid-March to mid-May the cycle of student demonstrations intensified over the corruption issue and over the increasingly desperate economic situation caused by the rupiah collapse as well as the decisions to remove subsidies on basic commodities—rice, cooking oil, gasoline, and diesel fuel. The student movement sought to blame Indonesia's political and economic plight on Suharto and his "cronies." These demonstrations often turned into riots, and the riots usually became anti-Chinese rampages with looting and massive destruction of property and many deaths. Defenders of the regime responded to student activism with more threatening countertactics. Key student activists were identified, targeted, and abducted by disguised military squads in civilian attire. The abducted were imprisoned at secret locations and subjected to aggressive interrogation and torture for periods of up to two months, and then released after being given warnings that they would be killed if they told anyone about their experiences. Regime defenders resorted to the tactic of hiring preman to incite rioting at student-led demonstrations, attempting to deflect popular anger to the Chinese and minority Christian communities.[58]

In the contest between the student activists versus regime defenders, the climax came during a demonstration at Trisaki University on May 12. Three days earlier, Suharto had left Indonesia to attend the G-15 summit of developing countries being held in Cairo, Egypt. Because Parliament (DPR) was meeting for the first time on its own initiative to consider reforms, the students decided to organize a mass march to Parliament. Trisaki University is a private institution, with high tuition rates. Many of its students came from the elite families of Indonesia in the civil service, military, Parliament, and leading businesses. Not noted for their radicalism, the presence of Trisaki students in the protest movement was an indication of the changed political environment. On their way to Parliament, some two miles away, the student march was blocked by troops. After an extended standoff, the students moved to alternate routes. The military responded with baton-wielding charges followed by arrests. Eventually, rubber bullets and tear gas were used, and finally, from a distance of about 100 yards, disguised sharpshooters fired live ammunition that killed four students.

The killings of Trisaki University students created shock among Indonesia's political elite, but those events were overshadowed by the waves of violence that swept over Jakarta for a period of over four days following those killings. Politically enraged mobs in Jakarta attacked and burned about 6,000 buildings, including shop-houses, stores, businesses, and banks. The Chinese community suffered the greatest losses of life and property, but the properties of the Suharto family and favored cronies were also ravaged. Hired preman gangs and Pancasila Youth made unprovoked attacks against the Chinese and their property. These attacks were organized by supporters of the green faction under the command of General Prabowo Sianto. The students and their allies also engaged in violence, directing their ire against the properties of the Suharto family and its cronies. When the rioting turned from burning properties to looting, all political lines became blurred as valuable goods became accessible for the destitute, the vengeful, and "grab and run" artists. Rioting also spread to Medan, Solo, and Palembang. If they were able to elude hostile crowds, Chinese by the thousands flooded into airports to flee the country. Altogether, in Jakarta 1,218 people were killed and the property damages were estimated to be US$500 million. The value of the rupiah plunged to Rp17,000/US$1 from its July 1997 value of Rp2,500/US$1.

When Suharto returned from Cairo on May 15, the severity of the crisis was apparent to all. The ranks of Indonesian politicians calling for Suharto's resignation read like a who's who of Indonesia's elite. Suharto promised to form a new "reform cabinet," but this only triggered more mass demonstrations across Indonesia. He invited forty-five persons to join his proposed new cabinet, but forty-two of those invited refused to serve. Finally, on May 21, 1998, with all other options blocked, Suharto resigned, handing power over to his vice president, B. J. Habibie.[59] Suharto's resignation marked a dramatic turning point in Indonesian history. It was the beginning of a new era of political strife and open political contestation, during which time Indonesians searched for a new political system based on democracy and the ideals of the Reformasi movement. In order to evaluate the evolving political role of Islam in the region, we will now consider parallel developments in Indonesia's Muslim-majority neighbor—Malaysia.

Notes

1. Andre Feillard, "Traditionalist Islam in Indonesia's New Order: The Awkward Relationship," in Greg Barton and Greg Fealy (eds.), *Nahdlatul Ulama, Traditional Islam and Modernity in Indonesia* (Melbourne: Monash Asia Institute, 1996), 42–67.

2. Robert W. Hefner, *Civil Islam: Muslims and Democratization in Indonesia* (Princeton, NJ: Princeton University Press, 2000), 108, citing B. H. Boland, *The Struggle of Islam in Modern Indonesia* (The Hague: Verhandelingen van Het Koninklijk Instituut voor Taal-, Land-, en Volkenkunde No. 59, rev. 2nd ed. 1982), 146.

3. For a retrospective account by an Indonesian scholar of the excesses and injustices perpetrated during the post–September 30 purges and mass murders, see Ariel Heryanto, *State Terrorism and Political Identity in Indonesia: Fatally Belonging* (London: Routledge, 2006), especially 1–61.

4. Adam Schwarz, *A Nation in Waiting: Indonesia's Search for Stability*, 2nd ed. (St. Leonards, Australia: Allen & Unwin, 2000), 26–28; Michael R. J. Vatikiotis, *Indonesian Politics Under Suharto: The Rise and Fall of the New Order,* 3rd ed. (London: Routledge, 1998), 7–18.

5. Hal Hill, "The Economy," in Hal Hill (ed.), *Indonesia's New Order: The Dynamics of Socio-economic Transformation* (Honolulu: University of Hawaii Press, 1994), 54–59.

6. For a sample of the writings of Suharto and some of his supporters explaining the ideological foundations for the New Order, see David Bourchier and Vedi R. Hadiz (eds.), *Indonesian Politics and Society: A Reader* (London: RoutledgeCurzon, 2003), 27–55.

7. For an exposition on dwifungsi, see Ali Moertopo, "The Dual Function of the Armed Forces," in ibid.

8. During Sukarno's rule, the ten legal parties were organized under three groupings: the Nationalist Group included four parties; the Religious Group included three Muslim parties and two Christian parties; and the Communist Party of Indonesia (PKI) constituted the sole party in the Communist Group. All parties were required to subscribe to Pancasila as the national ideology, but they interpreted it rather differently without penalty.

9. Most party leaders opposed this new election law, but under coercive pressure from Suharto's government, the Parliament (DPR) finally passed the law in October 1969. See Harold A. Crouch, *The Army and Politics in Indonesia,* rev. ed. (Ithaca: Cornell University Press, 1988), 245–272.

10. Kevin O'Rourke, *Reformasi: The Struggle for Power in Post-Soeharto Indonesia* (Crows Nest, Australia: Allen & Unwin, 2002), 200.

11. Greg Fealy, "Parties and Parliament: Serving Whose Interests?" in Grayson Lloyd and Shannon Smith (eds.), *Indonesia Today: Challenges of History* (Singapore: Institute of Southeast Asian Studies, 2001), 104–109.

12. Fredrica M. Bunge (ed.), *Indonesia: A Country Study*, 3rd ed. (Washington, DC: American University Foreign Area Studies, 1983), 183–184; Jamie Mackie and Andrew MacIntyre, "Politics," in Hill, *Indonesia's New Order,* 1–53; Vatikiotis, *Indonesian Politics Under Suharto,* 3–5; Schwarz, *A Nation in Waiting,* 37–40.

13. For an account of the culture of corruption during the New Order, see Schwarz, *A Nation in Waiting,* 133–161. That account reveals that the US Central Intelligence Agency estimated Suharto's personal wealth at US$15 billion in 1989 and the combined wealth of the Suharto family as being twice that amount. In the mid-1990s, the CIA estimated Suharto family assets at US$2–3 billion. Vatikiotis, *Indonesian Politics Under Suharto,* 50.

14. Adrian Vickers, "The New Order: Keeping Up Appearances," in Lloyd and Smith, *Indonesia Today,* 72–84.

15. Between 1980 and 1991, the Indonesian economy averaged an annual rate of real gross domestic product growth of 5.6 percent. World Bank, *World Development Report,* 11 vols. (New York: Oxford University Press, 1981–1992).

16. Tan Kong Yam, Toh Mun Heng, and Linda Low, "ASEAN and Pacific Economic Cooperation," *ASEAN Economic Bulletin* 8, no. 3 (1992), 317–319.

17. Vatikiotis, *Indonesian Politics Under Suharto,* 7–10.

18. John W. Henderson et al. (eds.), *Area Handbook for Indonesia* (Washington, DC: American University, Foreign Area Studies, 1970), 384.

19. Gordon P. Means, *The Rural Sector and Human Resource Development in Indonesia* (Toronto: Joint Centre on Modern East Asia, Canada and the Pacific, Working Paper No. 39, 1985).

20. Hill, "The Economy," 57.

21. In 1960 Indonesia's population was 96 million; in 1990 it was 184 million; and by 2000 it was 219 million. UN Development Programme, *Human Development Report, 1991* (New York: Oxford University Press, 1991), 161; Terence H. Hull and Gavin W. Jones, "Demographic Perspectives, Fertility Decline in the New Order Period: The Evolution of Population Policy 1965–90," in Hill, *Indonesia's New Order,* 123–145.

22. R. William Liddle, "Soeharto's Indonesia: Personal Rule and Political Institutions," *Pacific Affairs* 58, no. 1 (Spring 1985), 69–90.

23. Barton and Fealy, *Nahdlatul Ulama,* xix–xx.

24. After the rejection of the request for reinstatement, some of the Masyumi leaders became affiliated with the Muslim Students Association (Himpunan Mahasiswa Indonesia), while others became active in the Indonesian Dakwah Council (Dewan Dakwah Islamiyah Indonesia), which helped to generate the Islamic resurgence movement of the 1970s and 1980s. Hefner, *Civil Islam,* 97–109.

25. John F. Cady, *The History of Post-War Southeast Asia: Independence Problems* (Athens, OH: Ohio University Press, 1974), 634–637; Jamie Mackie and Andrew MacIntyre, "Politics," in Hill, *Indonesia's New Order,* 10–13, 31–32; Schwarz, *A Nation in Waiting,* 30–31. For the percentage of vote and parliamentary seats held by parties from 1955 to 1982, see Bunge, *Indonesia,* Table 15, 294.

26. For Islamic criticisms of the Marriage Law, see Hamka, "The Shocking Draft Bill on Marriage," in Bourchier and Hadiz, *Indonesian Politics*, 85–88. For the legal aspects of the Marriage Law and the role of the Religious Courts see M. B. Hooker, *Indonesian Islam: Social Change Through Contemporary Fatawa* (Crows Nest, Australia: Allen & Unwin, 2003), 17–25, 74–80. On the issues of marriage and gender relations, see Susan Blackburn, "Gender Relations in Indonesia: What Women Want," in Lloyd and Smith, *Indonesia Today,* 270–282.

27. For an account of the fatwa accusing the Ahmadiyah of murtad, see M. B. Hooker, *Indonesian Islam: Social Change Through Contemporary Fatawa* (Honolulu: University of Hawaii Press, 2003), 70–71.

28. For example, see Soeharto, "Muslims Who Fail to Understand," and Soeharto, "Pancasila, the Legacy of Our Ancestors," in Bourchier and Hadiz, *Indonesian Politics,* 99–109.

29. Greg Barton, *Abdurrahman Wahid: Muslim Democrat, Indonesian President* (Honolulu: University of Hawaii Press, 2002), 135–138; Hefner, *Civil Islam,* 99–106; Schwarz, *A Nation in Waiting,* 32, 36–37.

30. Barton, *Abdurrahman Wahid,* 147–155; Martin van Bruinessen, "Indonesia's Ulama and Politics: Caught Between Legitimizing the Status Quo and Searching for Alternatives," *Prisma—The Indonesian Indicator* (Jakarta) 49 (1990), 52–69.

31. Born in West Sumatra, Imran began forming a revolutionary group about 1979. Within a month of the hijacking, Imran and his close associates were arrested, and after trials they were sentenced to death. Ken Conboy, *The Second Front: Inside Asia's Most Dangerous Terrorist Network* (Jakarta: Equinox Publishing, 2006), 19–23.

32. Kees Van Dijk, *A Country in Despair: Indonesia Between 1997 and 2000* (Leiden: KITLV Press, 2001), 222–224 In June 2000, Indonesia's National Human Rights Commission made an investigation of the Tanjung Priok riots and concluded that both protesters and soldiers were responsible for the death toll, with only 33 killed and 55 injured. That commission concluded that security forces killed only 26 people during the riots. This report created a new storm of protest among critics who expected the investigation to confirm a death toll in the hundreds and to expose abuse of power by security forces. Damien Kingsbury, *The Politics of Indonesia,* 3rd ed. (South Melbourne, Australia: Oxford University Press), 90–91.

33. Bakin is an acronym for Badan Koordinasi Intelijen Negara (State Intelligence Coordinating Body).

34. Kopkamtib is the acronym for Komando Operasi Pemulihan Keamanan dan Ketertiban (Command for the Restoration of Security and Order).

35. Kingsbury, *The Politics of Indonesia,* 97–102; Richard Robinson, "Indonesia: Tensions in State and Regime," in Kevin Hewson, Richard Robinson, and Garry Rodan (eds.), *Southeast Asia in the 1990s: Authoritarianism, Democracy and Capitalism* (St. Leonards, Australia: Allen & Unwin, 1993), 41–74.

36. For an account of the role of Suharto's children at the apex of the patronage system, see Schwarz, *A Nation in Waiting,* 133–161; Jeffrey Winters, *Power in Motion: Capital Mobility and the Indonesian State* (Ithaca, NY: Cornell University Press, 1996).

37. Schwarz, *A Nation in Waiting,* 333.

38. Vatikiotis, *Indonesian Politics Under Suharto,* 82–91; Schwarz, *A Nation in Waiting,* 333–337.

39. O'Rourke, *Reformasi,* 18–19.

40. The Indonesian title is Ikatan Cendekiawan Muslimin Indonesia.

41. The ICMI was supposed to act as a counterbalance to the Centre for Strategic and International Studies, which had acquired the reputation of being dominated by Christian intellectuals.

42. Bourchier and Hadiz, *Indonesian Politics,* xiv–xv, 16–17, 185–187, 226–230.

43. Schwarz, *A Nation in Waiting,* 176–185; Hefner, *Civil Islam,* 125–143.

44. Stefan Eklöf, *Indonesian Politics in Crisis: The Long Fall of Suharto, 1996–98* (Copenhagen: Nordic Institute of Asian Studies, 1999), 18–22; O'Rourke, *Reformasi,* 18–21. For an account of the founding and operations of Democracy Forum, see Mohammad As Hikam, "Non-Governmental Organizations and the Empowerment

of Civil Society," in Richard W. Baker, et al. (eds.), *Indonesia: The Challenge of Change* (Singapore: Institute of Southeast Asian Studies, 1999), 224–227.

45. Vatikiotis, *Indonesian Politics Under Suharto,* 132–137.

46. The Quran outlaws "interest," which it views as usury (riba), which is condemned as a form of economic exploitation and a very serious sin for both the lender and the borrower. However, Sharia law does permit "trading and profits from business investments" and also permits rents and leases. The difference between "interest" and "profit" is a matter of definitional legerdemain. Elaborate rules are employed to claim that commercial and financial transactions are confined to the one permitted category while claiming no compromise with the other. Historically, Islamic jurists and religious leaders have always found ways to circumvent riba by concealing it or combining it with these other permitted business transactions. In the modern era, an Islamic system of banking operates like a venture capital company. Investors receive a share of the profits (or losses) based on the size of their investment and the profitability of how the bank invests and manages its portfolio of assets. Usually depositors get about the same return as regular banks, but with less protection and without the deposit insurance that is common for regular banks. When depositors open accounts in the bank, there can be no promise of a fixed return on deposits. Borrowers can obtain interest-free loans, but various "charges" can be assessed and the loans may be of relatively short duration with relatively high penalties for late repayments. Or the loans can be secured by mortgages on land or property, with the values adjusted to account for interest equivalent. Or the loans to individuals can be partially subsidized, either through bank profits or through government subsidies. Most Islamic banks operate with a higher percentage of nonperforming loans than regular Western-style banks, and this can affect the profitability of the bank. The object of these rules is to have about the same returns and charges as Western-style banks but to do so while avoiding the Islamic definition of riba. For traditional Islamic banking and credit practices, see Maxime Rodinson, *Islam and Capitalism* (London: Penguin, 1973). For Islamic credit and loan transactions in colonial Malaya, see Jomo Kwame Sundaram, *A Question of Class: Capital, the State and Uneven Development in Malaya* (Singapore: Oxford University Press, 1986), 48–51.

47. Schwarz, *A Nation in Waiting,* 188–189. The NU leader, Abdurrahman Wahid, who refused to join ICMI, was very critical of the formation of this Islamic-style bank, which he said was based on an outdated tenet of Islamic scripture, and argued that such a bank was vulnerable to abuse.

48. Among the key figures of the "Greens" was General Feisal Tanjung, who was appointed commander-in-chief of the army in May 1993; Suharto's son-in-law, Prabowo Subianto, who commanded the elite unit Kopassus; and General R. Hartono, who was appointed army chief of staff in February 1995. These three military leaders headed the army's green faction and, along with B. J. Habibie, were noted for their intense personal loyalty to Suharto. Eklöf, *Indonesian Politics,* 20–22.

49. Van Dijk, *A Country in Despair,* 56–60.

50. Ibid., 5–7; Schwarz, *A Nation in Waiting,* 264–269. The government's ability to intervene in PDI internal affairs came through the number of military and government agents who had joined the party and were able to sway the votes through their numbers and their capacity to intimidate other members.

51. O'Rourke, *Reformasi,* 9–15; Eklöf, *Indonesian Politics,* 82.

52. Eklöf, *Indonesian Politics,* 76; Barton, *Abdurrahman Wahid,* 221–224.

53. Ignatius Tri Handoyo, "The Political Dimensions of the Indonesian Economic Crisis," in Abdul Rahman Embong and Jürgen Rudolph (eds.), *Southeast Asia into the Twenty First Century: Crisis and Beyond* (Bangi, Selangor: Penerbit Universiti Kebangsaan Malaysia, 2000), 150–153.

54. Eklöf, *Indonesian Politics,* 106–120. The estimates on poverty levels are citing publications by the International Labour Organisation's Jakarta office for 1998 and the Indonesian Biro Pusat Statistik for 1997. For two balanced accounts of the Indonesian economic and political crisis of 1997–1999, see Van Dijk, *A Country in Despair,* 51–135, and O'Rourke, *Reformasi,* 22–152.

55. Van Dijk, *A Country in Despair,* 115.

56. Investigations conducted after the fall of Suharto revealed that the "kidnap squads" and the preman "rent-a-riot" units were organized by Lieutenant General Prabowo Subianto, commander of the army's elite force Kostrad (Army Strategic Reserve), who was appointed to that command by Suharto and who is also Suharto's son-in-law. Van Dijk, *A Country in Despair,* 147–160; Eklöf, *Indonesian Politics,* 154–158.

57. O'Rourke, *Reformasi,* 69–70, 79–81, 163–165; Eklöf, *Indonesian Politics,* 50–54.

58. O'Rourke, *Reformasi,* 106–108.

59. Van Dijk, *A Country in Despair,* 187–208; O'Rourke, *Reformasi,* 88–135; Schwarz, *A Nation in Waiting,* 354–366; Eklöf, *Indonesian Politics,* 175–219.

7

Malaysia Under Mahathir

Malaysia's first three prime ministers following independence all embodied the core values of Malay nationalist perspectives on political issues. These included the principle that the Malays were the legitimate "original inhabitants" of the country, who deserve a special status to ensure a government led by Malays with Malay rights and culture effectively protected. Most Malays expected their leaders to utilize political power to create government policies that would dramatically raise their economic status in comparison to that of the immigrant communities. These core values were incorporated into the legal status of Bumiputra that became the basis for the system of indigenous rights for Malays and native peoples.

The first prime minister, Tunku Abdul Rahman, embodied the Malay nationalist perspective in its quintessential form. As a prince of the Kedah royal family, he commanded the stature derived from traditional Malay aristocracy. His congenial temperament and low-key demeanor appealed to traditional Malay attitudes toward authority and facilitated amicable relations with the non-Malay constituents. During his term in office, he not only effectively met the challenge of the Communist insurrection but also defined the terms of Malaysian independence by negotiating the terms of the Constitution to ensure Malay political supremacy. His downfall came when that supremacy was challenged by election results that triggered the ethnic riots of May 13, 1969. While government policies were addressing those issues, the pace of change under Tunku Abdul Rahman's leadership did not match the elevated expectations of most Malays.

Tun Abdul Razak became Malaysia's second prime minister, not by a vote of Parliament, but by virtue of heading the National Operations Council under Emergency Rule. He had been deputy prime minister and minister of defense at the time of the May 13th riots, so he was well positioned to assume the leadership of the government under provisions of the Emergency Ordinance.[1] In a move to consolidate Malay support for his government, Abdul Razak brought back into UMNO some of the more radical Malay nationalists who had been expelled from the party for violation of party discipline during the era of Tunku Abdul Rahman. Among those who were "absolved" of previous indiscretions were Musa Hitam, former UMNO executive secretary, and Mahathir bin Mohamad, who had led an underground campaign against Tunku Abdul Rahman during the race riots and crisis of 1969. In the Razak cabinet, Musa Hitam was appointed minister for primary industries and Mahathir was named minister of education. A decade later, these two men would change Malaysia's political scene.

During Abdul Razak's tenure as prime minister, he initiated the New Economic Policy and many other programs designed to raise the economic position of the Malays in all sectors of the economy. In comparison to his predecessor, Abdul Razak had a much greater sense of urgency to bring Malays into the mainstream of a rapidly modernizing and dynamic economy. His policies were designed to transform Malay society from its rural peasant base into a society based on urban professional and industrial manufacturing employment, and to do so with the active intervention of government programs. Amendments to the Constitution entrenched Malay special rights; under the Sedition Ordinance, questioning Malay rights, or mentioning the status of Islam and other "sensitive issues" were defined as seditious offenses, which could not be discussed in public. Like Tunku Abdul Rahman, Abdul Razak was essentially a Malay nationalist, but with more drive, greater intensity, and a willingness to use coercive measures to suppress dissent in order to meet the elevated expectations and demands of his Malay constituents.[2]

Abdul Razak's term in office as prime minister was cut short by his sudden death from leukemia at the age of fifty-four in January 1976. Without adequate preparation for his successor, the deputy prime minister, Hussein Onn, automatically became Malaysia's third prime minister. He was the son of UMNO's founding leader, Dato Onn bin Ja'afar, who had left the party at the beckoning of the British to found the ill-fated Independence of Malaya Party. Hussein Onn returned to UMNO in 1969 but never developed a solid base of delegate support within UMNO. Consequently, few party members expected him to remain as prime minister for long. Despite his apparently fragile political base, Hussein Onn remained Malaysia's leader for five and a half years. During his tenure, he remained committed to the secular Malay nationalist agenda. Hussein Onn gradually gained the confidence and respect of his Malay constituents and would have remained in office if his health had permitted. Even before he became prime minister, he had suffered a heart attack, and when he became ill once again in 1981, he decided to retire, transferring power to his deputy prime minister.[3]

The New Regime

Malaysia's new prime minister was Mahathir bin Mohamad. His road to power had been circuitous and his reputation was controversial. In 1969, Mahathir, joined by Musa Hitam, had campaigned against Tunku Abdul Rahman by authoring a privately circulated letter accusing the latter of responsibility for the May 13th race riots and the deaths of those "who sacrificed their lives" by "giving the Chinese what they demand" and thus provoking Malay riots against "infidels."[4] In response to those criticisms, Tunku Abdul Rahman accused Mahathir and Musa Hitam of being Malay "ultras" who were unwilling to accept the outcome of interethnic bargaining within the Alliance. At the Tunku's initiative, both Mahathir and Musa Hitam were accused of violating party discipline and were expelled from UMNO. While Musa Hitam pursued a master's degree at Sussex University in England, Mahathir used his "political retirement" to write *The Malay Dilemma.*[5] Because of its criticisms of incumbent Malay leaders and its polemical tone, the book was banned in Malaysia but was available in Singapore and circulated clandestinely fairly widely in Malaysia as a consequence.

In *The Malay Dilemma,* Mahathir gives explanations for the inferior position of the Malays, which were attributed to a variety of factors, including: genetic "inbreeding," Malay cultural norms that stress "politeness" rather than competition and achievement, an abundant environment that "allowed the weakest and least diligent to live in comparative comfort and to procreate," the inability of Malays to gain access to and compete in modern higher education, a persistent pattern of colonial and Chinese discrimination against Malays, and laws and institutions that primarily served the interests of colonial rulers and immigrant communities. To overcome these limitations, he claimed that Malays are the original "definitive people" of the country who have prior rights above all other citizens and therefore deserve guarantees of "special rights." He also called upon Malays to be prepared to assert their hegemonic authority within government and politics, derived in part from their rights as "definitive people" of Malaysia.[6]

In this book Mahathir says very little about Islam. He describes how Islam brought important changes to the Malay way of life through increased literacy, but, in his view, Islam became mingled with animism, "which resulted in the development of a permanent barrier against further changes in religion."[7] The main focus of the book concentrates on the angst and anxieties of ardent Malay nationalists concerning their future. As such, the book became a virtual political manifesto for Mahathir during his political exile, preparing the way for his return to active politics.

The first years of the Mahathir administration were focused on the implementation of the basic policies formulated in the post-1969 crisis era designed to raise the economic position of the Malays and to bring more Malays into the modern sectors of the economy. The New Economic Policy and the Rukunegara ideology were forged by the two previous regimes. Mahathir promised no major changes in policy orientation. Instead, he promised effective administration with more haste and less waste. Shortly after taking office, the number of detainees held under the Internal Security Act was substantially reduced, and the ban on Mahathir's book, *The Malay Dilemma*, was lifted. At the same time, the government submitted to Parliament the Societies Act (Amendment) Bill 1981, which passed, giving the government increased power to control and deregister public interest groups, professional associations, and nongovernmental organizations (NGOs). These amendments to the Societies Act were combined with a wide array of other emergency and security laws, giving evidence that the government would not tolerate strident criticism or protest demonstrations concerning public policy issues. Despite his early hints of tolerance for political debate, the Mahathir administration expanded its powers to silence critics and to suspend or override basic human rights.[8]

The NEP established as its goals the elimination of poverty for all Malaysians and the restructuring of society "to reduce and eventually eliminate the identification of race with economic function."[9] In short, it proposed to accelerate programs to raise the economic position of the Malays and held out the promise that Malays would acquire ownership of 30 percent of Malaysian share capital by 1990. While this policy had been formulated during Abdul Razak's administration, by the time Mahathir became prime minister, it became clear these NEP goals were unlikely to be met by the target date. To address that issue, Mahathir accelerated the programs for ethnic redistribution and restructuring. They included a vast system of Bumiputra quotas for admission to higher educational institutions and for employment, both in government and in the private sector. Sales of share capital on the stock market and sales of new homes in the real estate market were also covered by Bumiputra quotas. Stocks and housing could not be sold to non-Bumiputra except in proportion to the sales previously made to Bumiputra. That created a two-price system for both stocks and housing, which meant that Bumiputra could buy stock on credit and sell it almost immediately on the nonregulated resale market and make a substantial profit with no risk and large financial returns. The accumulation of wealth by Malays was quite easy for those who already had wealth. To promote Malay ownership of the economy, the government also formed and generously funded Bumiputra trust corporations that provided employment and business experience to Malays. These Bumiputra corporations acted as a holding company on behalf of the Malays with the tacit assumption that these "trust" corporations would eventually divest their shares to Malay owners. Government investments in Bumiputra corporations were counted as a component of Bumiputra-share market quota requirements. Within a few years, these corporations acquired ownership and control of a substantial number of well-established foreign corporations through stock market purchases. In combination, these programs were designed to create a Malay professional, entrepreneurial and business class within the span of a decade or two. The goals of the NEP called for a Herculean effort by the government as the primary agent for forging the new society.

During the first two years of Mahathir's leadership of the country, the acceleration of the New Economic Policies was producing steady results. Large numbers of Malays, many from rural peasant origins, were finishing university degrees and were entering professional and business jobs, and these new graduates anticipated accelerated promotion to the higher management levels within a few short years of service. The economy was buoyant, which sustained the financial resources of the government to fund a multitude of programs that provided both jobs and higher education for Malays. The expanding job market provided improved employment opportunities for Malays in the newer and dynamic sectors of the economy. It may seem surprising, but the very success of the NEP programs also created the basis for a growing political opposition.

Mahathir's Islamic Gambit

By the time Mahathir became prime minister, the dakwah movement had generated a mass following, particularly among university students. When Mahathir returned from his political exile, he was first given responsibility for the Ministry of Education. With that responsibility, his first task was to complete the conversion of higher educational institutions to utilize Malay as the medium of instruction. At the same time, under the NEP, university education was dramatically expanded with fully funded bursaries offered to all qualified Malay students. The influx of large numbers of Malay students into universities and colleges provided a receptive constituency for ABIM with its brand of militant Islamic rhetoric that challenged more traditional patterns of Malay authority. Mahathir had to address the issues raised by Islamic students who were recipients and beneficiaries of generous government bursaries and foreign study fellowships.[10] When ABIM began mobilizing mass student demonstrations, Mahathir moved decisively, utilizing a large police contingent to arrest thousands of student demonstrators, including Anwar Ibrahim, then leader of ABIM.

During this period of student militancy, Mahathir must have given much thought to the political and social implications of the dakwah movement. This movement was capturing the imagination and the support of a generation of Malays who were being prepared to assume leadership roles in all professions and in the political leadership of the country. Despite government policies designed to prepare them for these roles, this cohort of Malay students was being infused with radical doctrines that challenged the leadership and the policies devised to effect the transformation of Malaysia's economy and social system.

As the primary beneficiaries of such policies, Mahathir viewed radical Malay students as being both unruly and ungrateful. Instead of Islam being used to undermine those goals, could Islam be mobilized to become a motivational force to effect a transformation to a modern and just future? This must have been the question that Mahathir began to ponder, even before he became prime minister.

Eight years later, in 1982, Mahathir faced his first general election as prime minister. His multiethnic Barisan Nasional coalition faced an antigovernment coalition comprising Partai Islam, various dakwah groups, and the primarily Chinese-based Democratic Action Party. Shortly after he had become prime minister, Mahathir indicated that he viewed Islam as a powerful source of motivation and identity for Malays, and he revealed that UMNO would take up the gauntlet thrown down by Partai Islam to defend and promote Islam. In his interview nine months before the election, Mahathir gave no indication of any specific reform agenda for the administration of Islamic affairs.[11]

Later, only three weeks before the 1982 elections, Mahathir picked up the Islamic gauntlet in a most dramatic fashion. He persuaded ABIM's president, Anwar Ibrahim, to stand for election as an UMNO candidate and to join his government to promote issues of Islamic reform.[12] With this move, Mahathir prevented a possible link-up between the highly energized ABIM constituency and Partai Islam, which was the most-feared possible opposition coalition because that combination could have expanded Partai Islam's core Malay constituency. Instead, with Anwar Ibrahim on the Barisan Nasional ticket, the elections of 1982 assured Malay support for UMNO and stressed Islamic issues as had never been done before.

During the election campaigning, Mahathir promised that the government would establish an International Islamic University, and an Islamic bank that would operate without riba—the payment of interest on banking transactions, as prohibited under Sharia law. In addition, Mahathir pledged to "review" the need for the Societies (Amendment) Act of 1981, which had generated such opposition from ABIM in the preceding year.[13] Beyond that, the campaign revealed an increasing emphasis on establishing UMNO's Islamic credentials as the party of the Malays. The 1982 election results renewed the government's mandate with a slight increase in the number of parliamentary seats and in its percentage of the popular vote. In that election, Anwar Ibrahim contested and won a seat in Parliament from a district in Penang where his father had previously served as an UMNO member of Parliament from 1959 to 1964.[14] His decisive electoral victory was rewarded by Mahathir, who appointed him deputy minister of the Islamic religious affairs section in the Prime Minister's Department.[15] Within a few short months, Anwar contested for the leadership of UMNO Youth and, with Mahathir's support, he defeated the incumbent, Suhaimi Kamaruddin. As the new UMNO Youth president he also became ex officio one of the five vice presidents of UMNO. His rapid rise to positions of power made him one of the most visible public figures in Malaysian politics.[16]

The recruitment of Anwar Ibrahim into the government split the ranks of ABIM, with one faction considering his departure to be political treason, and the other welcoming the opportunity to gain access to power in order to change policies from within the structures of government. Many of Anwar's critics, who remained in ABIM, later joined Partai Islam, which reflected their critical views of government policies and their fundamentalist perspectives of Islam. When Anwar joined the high councils of government, he was able to bring several hundred of his ABIM supporters into UMNO and secure government employment for them. Over the years, with these former ABIM members as a core constituency, Anwar cultivated the allegiance of a growing band of well-organized supporters who became an identifiable faction in UMNO, in Barisan Nasional councils, and in government agencies.

In the early days of Mahathir's administration, Anwar projected an image of a leader on the move, seeking to build a modern dynamic economy that would be increasingly based on industrialization and producing for world markets. For Mahathir, the new emphasis on Islam was expected to generate social and political changes to enable Malays to adapt to the demands of an industrialized, highly productive economy. He also viewed Islam as a means to create "Muslim/Malay unity" to ensure Malay support for UMNO and to retain Malay hegemony within the political system. Mahathir expressed his views in his 1982 address to the UMNO General Assembly:

> UMNO has preserved and upheld Islam in Malaysia. UMNO has ruled justly and brought about development, and many other things. These are the results of UMNO's struggle. But I repeat, UMNO's struggle has not ended. Today we face the biggest struggle—the struggle to change the attitude of the Malays in line with the requirements of Islam in this modern age. . . . UMNO's task now is to enhance Islamic practices and ensure that the Malay community truly adheres to Islamic teachings. . . . Naturally this cause is far bigger than the previous struggles of UMNO. Of course it is not easy to succeed. But UMNO must pursue it, whatever the obstacles, for this is our real cause.[17]

The new priority for Islam entailed a greater effort to make existing policies conform with Islamic principles. Because Anwar Ibrahim worked as deputy minister within the Prime Minister's Department, it is not possible to determine how many of these initiatives can be attributed to Anwar Ibrahim and how many to Mahathir. At this stage in their careers, both appeared to be working in a mutually supportive interaction with agreement on objectives. Under the Constitution of Malaysia, responsibility for the administration of Islamic affairs was assigned to state governments, except for federal territories, where the federal government had exclusive jurisdiction.[18] The issue of whether state powers over Islam were exclusive or shared remained ambiguous. However, federal powers could easily override state actions because states, with their limited tax base, were so reliant on federal funds. The federal government rapidly expanded its Islamic support services to gain preeminent control over Islamic affairs, despite the constitutional provisions assigning responsibility for Islamic affairs to state governments and to the Malay rulers.

Before Mahathir became prime minister, the federal government had founded the National Council for Islamic Affairs (Pusat Islam) that was administered by the Department of Religion (Jabatan Agama) placed under the Prime Minister's Department. While the Pusat Islam had representatives from all the states, the initiatives for unified action came primarily from the Prime Minister's Department. By 1970, nearly all state governments had revised their Islamic laws to provide for more vigorous enforcement of Sharia law with increased penalties for violations in matters of personal behavior and public deportment.[19] As the federal government assumed a preeminent role in Islamic affairs, the issues of promoting Islamic values and defining the obligations and content of Islam became a matter of higher priority for federal authorities. Under Mahathir's direction, the federal bureaucracy charged with administering Islamic affairs expanded rapidly. By 1982, 100 ulama were working within the Prime Minister's Department, mostly within Pusat Islam. Within the Ministry of Education, 715 ulama were employed to prepare materials on Islam and to teach courses on Islam in Malaysia's public schools.[20] Within the Prime Minister's Department, the Department of Religion was reorganized and renamed the Department for the Advancement of Islam (Jabatan Kemajuan Agama Islam Malaysia, better known as JAKIM). That body formulated policy on Islam and prepared drafts of laws that were sent to the states for enactment.[21]

Under the Islamization initiatives of Mahathir and Anwar Ibrahim, new federal laws were passed prohibiting Muslims from entering any gambling establishments. The largest center for gambling was at Genting Highlands casino at Cameron Highlands. Muslims were permitted to own shares and receive profits from casinos, but they were prohibited from participation in gambling activities as customers. Consumption of alcohol was banned at all government functions and government-owned facilities, including universities, government rest houses, and community centers. Importation of all fresh pork to Malaysia was prohibited, although non-Muslims could import live pigs, mostly from Thailand, for non-Muslim consumption. Other fresh meat, mostly beef and mutton, could be imported, but it had to be certified as halal, meaning that it had to conform to Islamic requirements concerning the method of butchering. Fresh meat could only be imported from slaughterhouses that employed a Malaysian imam duly authorized to provide halal certifications. All hotels catering to government servants or catering for government functions were prohibited from serving any pork or any *haram* (forbidden) foods to any customer. The list of haram foods was expanded to include processed foods such as mayonnaise, ketchup, chocolates, jams, and gelatins, on the argument that they may include pork lard or be processed in kitchens where pork products are also processed. The requirements for halal certification generated specialized production facilities to produce processed foods for Muslim countries, especially in Australia, New Zealand, Eastern Europe, and the former Soviet Union.

Throughout Malaysia, new mosques and prayer houses were constructed in nearly every Malay village or settlement. In many villages, this created a dispute between the defenders of the older-style mosque with its adjoining graveyard and those who attended the new concrete, more-imposing mosque that operated with a government-supplied imam. For peasant villagers, emotional historical ties to the older mosque were often difficult to abandon. Yet, in time, for most villages, these issues subsided, and the new mosque, a symbol of government largesse, became the center for the religious life events of the community.

At the national level, television stations sponsored Quran reading contests with large and increasing prizes that attracted contestants from other Muslim countries as well as Malaysia. Regular television programming was suspended five times a day at specified prayer times, to be replaced by visual prayer scenes and with readings from the Quran. Industries and workplaces across the country were required to provide prayer locations and permit Muslims to pray at the assigned prayer times. At government offices and universities, both work and classes were halted for Muslim prayers. Television stations gave greatly increased coverage to Islamic events, including conferences, mass meetings, and lectures on the knowledge and motivations that commitment to Islam entails. The themes of such sessions can be summarized: "When Muslims try harder, they are able to out-achieve non-Muslims in all walks of life."

As promised during the 1982 election campaign, the government passed legislation authorizing an Islamic bank that became operational the following year. Capital funds for Bank Islam Malaysia were derived from state religious departments, the Pilgrim's Fund Management Board, and Perkim, the moderate dakwah organization that had been sponsored by Malaysia's first prime minister, Tunku Abdul Rahman. The bank offered riba-free loans by treating those loans as "equity participation," so that an equivalent of interest was paid, but the payment was classified as "profit" rather than riba.

Mahathir's pledge to establish an international Islamic university was implemented by July 1983 when the International Islamic University of Malaysia (IIUM) opened its doors. At its founding it was at a site adjoining the campus of the University of Malaya, but it later moved to its own campus in Kuala Lumpur. The university was jointly sponsored by the Organization of the Islamic Conference, with a Board of Governors having representatives from eight sponsoring Islamic governments. Initial funding came from the government of Malaysia, supplemented by substantial contributions from the government of Saudi Arabia. Students from any country could enroll, and they need not be Muslim, provided that they accepted "Islamic philosophy as a basis [for learning]." Instruction was in English and Arabic, but not in Malay (Bahasa Malaysia). The well-known Islamic scholar and former head of the Islamic Center in Washington, DC, Muhammad Abdul Rauf, was appointed rector, and Anwar Ibrahim became president of IIUM. From this position, Anwar was able to create many jobs at the university for his ABIM supporters. A large proportion of the faculty was recruited from Arab states in the Middle East. The curriculum of the university was modeled after Egypt's Al-Azhar University. The university's mission statement established its basic objective: "To revive and revitalize the Islamic concepts and traditions of learning, which regard the quest of knowledge as an act of worship and the spirit of science as emanating from the holy Quran." Accordingly, its curriculum was designed to impart an "Islamic perspective" to all academic subjects, starting with the assumption that Revealed Truth takes precedence over human knowledge. Reflecting this perspective, a subdivision of the university was called Kulliyyah (College) of Islamic Revealed Knowledge and Human Sciences. By 2004, the IIUM expanded to four campuses: three in the Kuala Lumpur area and one campus at Kuantan, Pahang. By 2005, IIUM had expanded to over 15,000 students. The central campus houses the International Institute of Islamic Thought and Civilization (ISTAC). This institute was founded in 1987 by Syed Muhammad Naquib al-Attas. The director of that institute at its inception was Anwar Ibrahim. ISTAC became IIUM's postgraduate institution, offering advanced degrees in subjects related to Islam.[22]

Defining Islamic Orthodoxy

By assuming increased responsibility for Islamic affairs, the federal authorities began a program to standardize Muslim practices and doctrines. One of the first issues concerned the method for determination of the end of the fasting month of Ramadan and the start of the most important celebration on the Muslim calendar—the feast day of Hari Raya Aidilfitri. Some states selected the date by visual sighting of the moon, and others utilized astronomical calculation. When Mahathir announced that the day would be fixed by astronomical calculation for all states, the sultan of Johor challenged his authority to make such a pronouncement for the entire country.[23] Mahathir exercised his executive power to enforce his decision, without reference to the constitutionally defined powers of Malay rulers over matters related to Islam.[24]

As the federal government took more responsibility for Islam, it became actively involved in defining "deviant sects" and censoring Islamic publications if they propagated "false doctrines deviating from true Islam." When government authorities tried to limit the activities of Islamic sects accused of propagating "false doctrines," serious conflicts ensued. To improve the federal government's capacity to deal with the issues of controlling religious activities and defining Islamic orthodoxy, the government passed constitutional amendments and statutory revisions to the penal and criminal procedure code that gave the federal government absolute rights to interpret Islamic precepts, tenets, and Sharia law. Anyone who created "disharmony, disunity, or feelings of enmity, hatred or ill-will" among Muslims faced the prospect of criminal prosecution.[25] By these acts, primary responsibility for the control of Islamic organizations and the definition of Islamic orthodoxy was effectively transferred from the Malay rulers and the state governments to the federal government and the prime minister.

At the federal level, JAKIM became responsible for the enforcement of Islamic orthodoxy. In 1999, the director-general of JAKIM reported that 195 books and leaflets in the Malay language and 80 in English had been banned for content that was "contrary to Islam." JAKIM also identified 94 versions of "deviant teachings" that were being propagated in Malaysia. Of particular concern were Shia doctrines and teachings.[26] Instead of permitting a wide latitude of beliefs and doctrines reflecting the diversity of Islam, the government followed the often-repeated doctrine that "there is only one Islam" and proceeded to assert what constituted that "one Islam," with the explicit conclusion that all other beliefs were "deviant."

Before Mahathir became prime minister, Partai Islam had been a member of the ruling Barisan Nasional coalition from 1973 to 1977. By 1981 the contest between UMNO and Partai Islam had resumed once more, and Mahathir's Islamization policies had intensified those peasant conflicts, with both parties competing for the support of rural Malays. By the time of the 1982 election campaign, that contest had become even more contentious. Partai Islam leaders accused UMNO members of being kafir because they failed to uphold "true Islam" by their collaboration with non-Muslims and by their failure to establish "an Islamic Republic." Hadi Awang, vice president of Partai Islam, even admonished "true believers" not to pay government taxes and promised that those who opposed UMNO would be rewarded in death as martyrs. This conflict over the definition of Islamic orthodoxy became known as the kafir-mengkafir (infidel-disbelief) dispute. In response, Mahathir accused Partai Islam of "splitting the umma" and obstructing government efforts to improve the economic and social condition of the Malays.[27]

In 1980, a Muslim Cambodian refugee named Mohamed Nasir Ismail came to Malaysia and began to attract a following among Malay peasants by exhibiting "spirit possession" during self-induced trances. He later claimed to be a Mahdi (savior) and became popularly known as Imam Mahdi. Malaysian religious authorities charged him with "false teachings" and "false beliefs" and warned that failure to desist would result in trial in a Kadi's court. Rather than submit to the demands of the police officers, he conferred "invulnerability" on his followers and organized an attack on the nearby police station at Batu Pahat. During that assault, eight of the attackers were killed, twenty-three were injured, and Imam Mahdi was among the deceased.[28]

In 1985, federal authorities moved against another "deviant sect." Its leader was Ibrahim Mahmud, who had been a member of ABIM in his student days and was associated with Anwar Ibrahim during the university student demonstrations of 1974. Later he traveled to Egypt to attend Al-Azhar University and may have received some support from Colonel Muammar Gadhafi's regime. After his return to his home in Kedah, Ibrahim founded a *pondok* at Memali, attracting a following by espousing radical Islamist ideology. In 1978 and 1982, he became PAS candidate at the state level but lost on both occasions. Because of his teachings and his earlier experiences, he became known as Ibrahim Libya. To his supporters he promised the heavenly rewards of martyrdom for those who might die in a fight against infidels in the government. When his followers began preparing for militant action by collecting weapons, authorities issued a warrant for the arrest of Ibrahim Libya and five of his associates. Rather than comply with that warrant, Ibrahim barricaded himself at Memali, defended by about 400 supporters. A standoff continued for over a year but ended in November 1985, when a 200-man unit of the Federal Police Reserve, equipped with armored cars and heavy weapons, arrived to arrest Ibrahim Libya. Armed villagers repulsed the arriving police unit, and a five-hour battle ensued, resulting in the death of 14 defenders and 4 police. Ibrahim Libya was among the dead. After the battle, 160 defenders were arrested, including 37 men who, the police reported, were wanted as suspects of various other crimes.[29] After police operations concluded, sympathizers moved all but one of the dead defenders to another village for burial services attended by Partai Islam's vice president, Hadi Awang, who issued a fatwa pronouncing that those who opposed the government with jihad had earned *mati syahid* (a martyr's death).[30] In Parliament, opposition parties raised the issue of excessive force used to apprehend the accused. The government answered those criticisms by accusing Partai Islam of covert support for the deviant acts of Ibrahim Mahmud's supporters, including jihad tactics in defiance of lawful authority.

Another much less publicized event in 1986 prompted the federal government to intervene once again to define the boundaries of Islamic orthodoxy. In this case, the issue involved the publication of a book written in Malay by Kassim Ahmad entitled *Hadith—A Re-evaluation*.[31] Kassim Ahmad had been chairman of the small, left-oriented Partai Sosialis Rakyat Malaysia (PSRM, Socialist Workers Party of Malaysia), and from 1967 to 1981, he had been detained under the Internal Security Act. After his release, he joined UMNO, where he gained respect as an Islamic scholar. In this book, he argues that the Hadith, which became the basis for Sharia law, had been created by ulama a century or more after the Prophet Muhammad's death to maintain their power. Therefore, he concluded that the Hadith was not "revealed" and their reports by themselves were not valid sources for Islamic law. For this reason, he concluded Sharia law should be opened to social reform through ijtihad (individual interpretation). He explained that his book was addressed to the "30 percent of Muslims who were modern, liberal and pragmatic in outlook and were committed to social reform."[32] This book generated controversy between liberal and conservative Malay intellectuals, and did so largely though short summaries and commentaries appearing in the local press. ABIM invited Kassim Ahmad to present his views in a five-hour closed session with ulama, during which he defended his research and his views. The book was bitterly attacked by Partai Islam and various Muslim organizations, including members of the state religious councils, who called for the book to be banned. Finally, Mahathir, acting on a recommendation of the Religious Affairs Division in the Prime Minister's Department, issued an order banning the book from sale and made possession of the book a criminal offense.[33] With this action, government religious authorities defined the acceptable ideological and theological boundaries of Islam on both the radical-traditional flank and the liberal-pragmatic flank.

■ The Case Against Darul Arqam

One of the most troublesome issues for government authorities responsible for oversight of Islamic activities involved the dakwah group known as Darul Arqam. This group began as a relatively small movement that withdrew into its own fairly remote peasant-style, self-contained community that practiced strict adherence to an Islamic code and developed a home-based economy to produce food products that were certified as halal. Its leader, Ashaari Mohammad, studied Sufism while quite young, joined ABIM for awhile, but eventually in 1975 gathered his own following to build their first community at Sungai Pencala about 20 kilometers north of Kuala Lumpur. As a charismatic firebrand preacher of a Sufi-messianic message, he recruited an expanding following for Darul Arqam. Within a few years, the number of Darul Arqam settlements in Malaysia increased to forty, with a membership of 7,000. Many of those who joined were from peasant origins, but it also attracted support from middle-class urban Malays, including those employed in government service. By 1994, Darul Arqam claimed to have established branches in sixteen countries outside of Malaysia, with a total membership of about 12,000, and with "sympathizers" numbering 200,000.[34] Darul Arqam produced four newspapers, fifteen monthly magazines, and operated 257 schools with an enrollment of 9,541. These schools were not registered and only included Islamic religious education in their curriculum. Darul Arqam's total assets of businesses, schools, and retail outlets in 1994 were estimated to be worth about RM300 million (US$120 million).[35]

Within the Muslim community, opinions differed over whether government authorities were more worried about the rapid recruitment of followers or the religious doctrines that were being propagated by Darul Arqam. Perhaps a combination of both factors prompted the government to take notice and ultimately to act. In 1988, Malaysia's National Fatwa Council proscribed Ashaari

Mohammad's book *Aurad Muhammadiah,* and in 1994 it issued a fatwa against Darul Arqam, citing the organization as "deviant and deviationist." This decision came after Ashaari had accused Pusat Islam of being more concerned with preventing "false doctrines" than in "the propagation of true ones."[36]

The government's case against Ashaari was based partly on his book *Aurad Muhammadiah,* which was an account of a nineteenth-century Sufi mystic, Sheikh Muhammad, whose doctrines formed the basis of Darul Arqam's religious teachings. There had been two earlier accounts of his life, and the reports of his miraculous exploits and religious powers expanded with each new publication. In the last version by Ashaari, Sheikh Muhammad is described as receiving his teaching directly from the Prophet Muhammad while he was at the Kaabah in Mecca. According to Ashaari's account, Sheikh Muhammad did not die but only disappeared and will return as an Imam Mahdi to become Khalifah Rasulullah (God's representative on Earth). Beyond the text of the book, Ashaari also claimed in sermons that he communicated with the long-departed Sheikh Muhammad, that he could guarantee forgiveness of sins to Darul Arqam members, and that he could accurately predict doomsday. He also claimed he could invoke magical powers against those who opposed him. In Malaysia, Sufi practitioners had made many similar claims for their beliefs but had not been prosecuted. Because these Sufi beliefs violated Sunni doctrines now defined as "orthodox," the government charged Ashaari with propagating false beliefs and alleged that Darul Arqam had formed a 313-man secret Army of Badar (also called Tentera Al-Mahdi) that was preparing to stage a coup in Malaysia. Mahathir stated that the movement was dangerous to the society and likened it to the David Koresh sect in Texas.

The fatwa against Darul Arqam and the banning of Ashaari's book forced Ashaari to flee to Thailand. At Malaysia's request, he was arrested by Thai authorities and returned to Malaysia. Finally, in September 1994, eighteen Darul Arqam leaders were detained under the Internal Security Act. Ashaari was not formally arrested but was restricted to his house under virtual arrest and held incommunicado to all except for immediate members of his family. The commune settlements were closed and all former members were prohibited from "intermingling" to revive the organization. However, outside Malaysia, Darul Arqam survived, including a large contingent of followers who moved to Singapore to build and operate an impressive center in the area of Geylang known as the Malay Village. Ashaari blamed Anwar Ibrahim for the repressive measures taken against Darul Arqam and predicted that Anwar would suffer a political downfall as the price he would pay for his role in these events.[37]

Anwar's Ascent

To explore Anwar Ibrahim's role as the leader and spokesman for the Islamization policy of the government, we must return to the period in 1982 when

Anwar Ibrahim and his ABIM cohorts were co-opted into government service. With his admission into government service, there was a dramatic increase in activities and government services to make Malaysia appropriately Islamic. These changes reinforced the unstated assumption that the government was designed to serve the Muslim population as its first priority while also providing services for non-Muslim citizens as a practical and secondary objective. Understandably, non-Muslims became worried about the implications of these developments and wondered where Islamization would lead and when a "balance point" would be reached when non-Muslims would receive proportionate benefits for what they believed to be their legitimate contributions to the nation.

The rapid pace of Islamization became a factor in Anwar Ibrahim's rise to his ever more significant postings in government and in UMNO. After Anwar won the position as president of UMNO Youth, in 1988 he was elected as one of UMNO's vice presidents. In 1993, he contested the position of deputy president of UMNO and won that post by acclamation when the incumbent, Ghafar Baba, withdrew without contest. For his government posts, Anwar served as deputy for Islamic affairs in the Prime Minister's Department for one year. In 1983, he was appointed minister of youth culture and sport, and in 1984 became minister of agriculture for two years, followed by his appointment as minister of education, which he held for five years. Finally, in 1991, he became minister of finance and in 1993 he also became deputy prime minister while retaining the finance portfolio.[38]

Anwar's meteoric rise in the political scene had been facilitated by the active sponsorship of Mahathir and accelerated by Anwar's ambition and charisma. The relationship between these two was both supportive and conflictive. Each showed mutual respect and admiration for the other, but there was also tension between the two because they did not always interpret politics in the same way. Both leaders had strong egos, making it difficult for Anwar to sustain an appropriate demeanor of deference as a subordinate. Their mutual support for each other was particularly notable in the earlier years of their collaboration. Even then, there were differences in outlook, strategy, and ideals that became more pronounced with time.

When Mahathir became prime minister, he inherited the New Economic Policies that had been formulated under Prime Minister Abdul Razak, and these he fully endorsed, accelerating their implementation. Although not all the goals were achieved, and some aspects of the policies were adjusted over its twenty-year life span, the NEP had dramatically changed the political and economic landscape when its target time had expired. In 1991, Mahathir announced a New Development Policy (NDP) as part of a ten-year Second Outline Perspective Plan, for the period from 1991 to 2000. In effect, the NDP continued most of the NEP programs of ethnic restructuring, but with fewer guarantees to Malays and greater concern for overall economic growth objectives. This new policy also anticipated an expansion of the private sector through increased privatization of services and transfer of government-held assets to the private sector. These policy adjustments of the NDP made no mention of "ethnic preferences," so there was a general impression created that economic liberalization would follow with greater cultural liberalization and diversity.[39]

Shortly after the NDP had been announced, Mahathir delivered a speech to the Malaysian Business Council that he entitled "Vision 2020."[40] In this address, he stated that the ultimate objective was for Malaysia to become a "fully developed country by the year 2020" creating a society with social justice, a high quality of life, intercommunal tolerance, and national pride. To achieve these goals, the economy would need to expand and the population would require "a mental revolution and a cultural transformation." The economic changes envisaged a growth rate of about 7 percent per year to increase Malaysia's gross domestic product (GDP) from RM115 billion (US$46 billion) in 1990 to RM920 billion (US$368 billion) in 2020. With annual population growth projected at about 2.5 percent, he envisioned per capita income to rise from RM6,180 to RM26,100 (US$2,472 to US$10,440) over the thirty-year span from 1990 to 2020.[41] Innovation, invention, and knowledge would drive the new economy, with the private sector being the primary engine to generate export-led economic growth. Knowledge- and technology-intensive industries would become the most dynamic sector of the economy. It would be "an economy driven by brainpower, skills and diligence, in possession of a wealth of information, with the knowledge of what to do and how to do it."[42] It may or may not be significant, but Islam as a source of societal values or as a motivator for the achievement-oriented workforce was not mentioned once in Mahathir's vision of Malaysia's future.

In 1996, when he was both minister of finance and deputy prime minister, Anwar Ibrahim published a book, *The Asian Renaissance,*[43] which outlined his vision of the future for both Malaysia and for Asia as a whole. In substance and in tone, it was far removed from the polemics of his student days as leader of ABIM. Instead of treating Islam as an exclusive and self-contained community facing a kafir world bent on undermining or corrupting its moral fiber, he explored common elements in all the civilizations and religions to focus on characteristics that made for civilized society. In the chapter on "Islam in Southeast Asia," he argued that Islam demands "a balanced emphasis on material and spiritual well-being" with material progress and economic development being insufficient to achieve the cultural potential of an "Asian Renaissance." Citing current academic-based expositions on civil society, he articulated a message of reform in refined and polished English, obviously aimed at educated Malaysian elites and a foreign readership. The book's message could be taken in two ways: as a statement of ideals that were being vigorously pursued by the administration that he was a part of, or as a statement of unachieved goals that he would bring to fruition when, as commonly expected, he became prime minister of Malaysia. The alternative interpretations were left for each individual reader to interpret for himself.

Two Visions, One Leadership

Consumed by the desire to make Malaysia the most modern and technologically advanced country of the Muslim world, Mahathir encouraged his economic advisers to produce economic development plans with maximal targets for growth and included many prestigious projects that utilized cutting-edge technology for their successful implementation. Some of the projects were chosen for their "spinoff" effect into other sectors of the economy. Other projects had a substantial psychological and ego component to demonstrate to Malaysians and the world that Malaysia was at the forefront of technological advancement and was becoming a major player in the global economy. With Malaysia's fairly rapid economic growth and low inflation rate during Mahathir's years at the helm,[44] this buoyant and optimistic attitude about Malaysia's economic future spread to the private sector, which also assumed that the economy would zoom to higher and higher levels with only slight adjustments and few risks. This outlook was incorporated into Mahathir's Vision 2020 and was widely accepted by the private sector as the blueprint for the future.

Part of the reason for this rapid economic expansion was to generate new economic opportunities for Bumiputra—the indigenous Malay population—as part of the economic restructuring goals of the New Economic Policy. With government sponsorship, Bumiputra entrepreneurs gained concessionary loans, favorable licenses, employment quotas, and a host of other programs designed to create a new middle- and upper-class strata in Malay society. The privatization of the NDP became the primary mechanism for the government to transfer government-generated industries and assets to entrepreneurs politically linked to the government at favorable prices and terms. A large proportion of those "privatization" transfers went to Malays having political affiliations with UMNO. In addition, the main political parties within the ruling Barisan Nasional coalition all established party-owned holding companies to own and manage large investment portfolios.[45] These holding companies operated by political parties invested in the corporate sector and utilized the political power of their party leaders to gain government concessions and contracts and to promote the economic interests and protect the corporate investments of that political party. In this environment, many of the most successful private sector corporations became dependent on their political linkages with government to gain privileged access to lucrative government contracts and to market shares. The opportunities for making enormous profit were especially evident in the awarding of contracts for the many mega-projects that were initiated during the Mahathir administration.

Inexperienced Bumiputra managers who were recruited and promoted without open competition often headed both party-owned and government-owned corporate bodies. With few controls over lax administration and imprudent investments of easily obtained credit, a culture of inefficiency and reliance on government bailouts affected many enterprises that exploited political linkages and Bumiputra privileges. One economist summarizes the vulnerability of the Malaysian economy prior to the Asian financial crisis with the following assessment: "The main cause of vulnerability originated from the Malaysian government's affirmative action in correcting racial economic imbalances and promotion of Malay capitalists."[46]

By 1997, all countries in Southeast Asia had balance-of-trade deficits with large foreign debts denominated in US or other foreign currencies. The first symptom of financial crisis began in Thailand in July 1997 when the Thai government lost US$20 billion in a futile effort to maintain the value of the Thai baht, which had come under heavy selling pressure. Rapidly, international markets reacted by a loss of confidence in Asia's newly industrializing countries that had been previously described as "tiger economies." As domestic currencies lost their value, their foreign debt could not be repaid, and this created a "stampede effect" of currency depreciation, sale of stock shares, and capital flight. While Malaysia was better situated than most of the other Asian NICs, the Malaysian ringgit was vulnerable, losing more than one-third of its value, and the Malaysian stock market lost about US$175 billion in slightly over one year.

At the time, Anwar Ibrahim was finance minister, and in combination with Bank Negara Malaysia, he was responsible for the overall management of the economy and for government financial transactions. At first, Anwar initiated some reforms to strengthen corporate governance, tighten credit, and cut government spending by 18 percent. However, the large and growing numbers of nonperforming loans and other deteriorating indicators of the economy forced the government to open negotiations with the International Monetary Fund. The conditional terms established by the IMF for its large loans were difficult to accept. The IMF proposed opening the markets to more vigorous competition, initiating foreclosure and bankruptcy proceedings against failed and nonperforming banks and corporations, ending uneconomic "mega-projects," and imposing strict measures to deter corruption and end the patronage system that created market distortions favoring politically connected enterprises.[47]

On these issues, Anwar and Mahathir began to disagree. Anwar was willing to attempt an "IMF lite" version of the recovery package and was willing to consider more liberalized market reforms as a means of recovery. As the crisis unfolded, Mahathir blamed "currency traders" and named the international financier George Soros as part of a "Zionist conspiracy to undermine Muslim progress in Malaysia." Mahathir favored the idea of "currency controls" to check the flight of capital from Malaysia. He viewed the IMF prescription for an open-market solution as a strategy to defeat and demolish much of what he had worked so hard to construct over his political lifetime. Under his leadership, Malaysia was acquiring an emerging Malay capitalist class, and a political and economic system that generated economic growth, with Malays assuming leading roles in all sectors of the economy. For Mahathir, if the government acted as an active partner with these favored enterprises, that was to his credit, not something that demanded reforms.

As these subtle differences between Malaysia's two highest leaders became more apparent, the allies and supporters of each leader began making moves and seeing conspiracies in the actions of the other faction. When the foreign press took up the cause of Anwar as the champion of "reform," the suspicions and animosities of the Mahathir camp became heightened. Mahathir concluded that it was time to take dramatic action.[48] In December 1997, he appointed his longtime political ally, Daim Zainuddin, as special functions minister to head a newly created National Economic Action Council to deal with the financial crisis, thus effectively limiting Anwar's powers. At the UMNO General Assembly in June 1998, the struggle for power between Anwar and Mahathir became more apparent and much more personal.[49] All the delegates could discern and interpret the meanings of the muted ambiguity of earlier accusations and thinly veiled threats by those on each side of the widening divide. If there were any doubts about the intensity of the conflict, they were soon dispelled when arriving delegates were offered for sale a book known as *50 Dalil*.[50]

This book repeated and expanded on an anonymous poison-pen letter that had circulated the year before accusing Anwar of corruption, adultery, unnatural and homosexual sex, and complicity to murder. During the General Assembly sessions, an associate of Anwar delivered a rousing speech against nepotism, cronyism, and corruption, calling for implementation of social justice. These were themes that Anwar had previously expressed in speeches and interviews, but in more muted form. Behind his smiles and professions of loyalty and support for Mahathir, most delegates interpreted the speech as a tactic to secure Assembly support to force or persuade Mahathir to resign. In response, Mahathir smiled when he accepted Anwar's assurances of loyalty. Both leaders were adept practitioners of the creative art of hypocrisy.

Finally, on August 29, Mahathir began playing his trump cards. The governor and the deputy governor of Bank Negara resigned over policy differences with Mahathir. Two days later, Malaysia imposed capital controls, pegging the Malaysian ringgit at RM3.80 to US$1. All ringgit deposits outside the country were made illegal tender, but Malaysian holders of outside deposits had one month to repatriate their holdings. Nonresidents wishing to convert Malaysian ringgit to foreign currency had to deposit funds in an authorized account and could not convert those funds to foreign currency until after one year.[51] These measures effectively terminated convertibility of currency and further direct foreign investments to Malaysia. This stabilized the economic situation over the short run, but it did not stabilize the political situation.

The day after the imposition of currency controls, Mahathir dismissed Anwar as finance minister, and two days later, on September 4, 1998, Anwar was expelled from UMNO amid allegations that he might be charged with sexual misconduct and other crimes.[52] The allegations of personal misconduct against Anwar riveted the attention of the entire country and led to the near spontaneous countermovement that took the name Reformasi—inspired in part by the movement that had toppled Suharto in Indonesia some four months previously. It had become a bare knuckle fight to the finish.

Reformasi, Semburit, and the 1999 Elections

For almost three weeks after his dismissal from the cabinet and from UMNO, Anwar was free to tour the country, during which time he addressed mass rallies giving his side of the story and issuing a call for Reformasi to end "corruption, cronyism, and nepotism." His campaign reached a climax on September 20, the day Queen Elizabeth II arrived in Kuala Lumpur to close the Sixteenth Commonwealth Games. While Queen Elizabeth was at the National Stadium, Anwar and about 15,000 of his supporters congregated at the National Mosque. At that rally, Anwar denied the charges being leveled against him and issued the call for Mahathir to resign. Later that evening, Anwar was arrested and charged with nine counts of corruption and for committing "unnatural acts of sex" (sodomy) with four men.[53]

What followed were two trials. The first trial lasted almost six months, beginning on November 2, 1998, and ending on April 14, 1999. While the first trial had combined corruption and sodomy charges, part way through the trial, the sodomy charges were withdrawn after the prosecution realized that witnesses had presented conflicting testimony and the trial was likely to end with a "not guilty" judgment. The corruption charges were almost entirely concerned with alleged acts by Anwar designed to impede the criminal investigations of the sodomy charges. This first trial ended with a verdict of guilty on all counts, with Anwar sentenced to six years of imprisonment from the date of conviction. That criminal conviction automatically disqualified him from elective office until five years after serving his sentence. Partly because of unfavorable public reaction to this sentence, a second set of charges was leveled against Anwar at a second trial beginning in June 1999. That trial involved renewed charges accusing him of sodomy. The second trial was suspended during the 1999 election campaign, because the judge claimed he "had a bad back." At the conclusion of the second trial, Anwar was convicted once again and sentenced to a further nine years of imprisonment. The combined sentences from the two trials added up to fifteen years imprisonment and had the effect of removing him from seeking elective political office for twenty years, which was 2019, the year before the Vision 2020 date! With a reduced sentence for good behavior, his release date would then be April 14, 2009.[54] The two trials took place amid mass protests by Anwar's supporters, joined by many thousands of others who were distressed by the turn of events. The trials had produced a number of surprising and bizarre twists. Testimony revealed that corroborating witnesses' confessions had been extracted under extreme duress. Some witnesses changed their testimony and the inspector general of police admitted that he assaulted Anwar Ibrahim while in police custody. When the prosecution dropped the accusations of sodomy and sexual misconduct during the first trial, the defense was not permitted to answer the earlier testimony and charges that had already been presented. There were openly expressed doubts about the independence of the court, and Anwar's supporters alleged that higher authorities had instigated "political conspiracies" to silence or to poison Anwar while he was in prison.[55]

For his defense against the charges, Anwar mounted a near-revolutionary rhetoric against "cronyism, corruption, and nepotism" to energize his supporters and encourage their continuing mass protests. He claimed that he was a victim of a "conspiracy at the highest levels," and his lawyers followed this defense strategy. As a result, his defense did not effectively address issues of his illegal acts. As the trial proceeded, the presiding judge became ever more determined to limit Anwar's political accusations against an unnamed Mahathir. As the trial dragged on, the public became more aware of the excesses of an authoritarian system, and most Malaysians were appalled at the lurid accounts of sexual encounters that became part of daily news reports. Many Malaysians, who are rather prudish, were shocked that such matters should become part of the public discourse.

At the conclusion of the two trials, both Anwar and Mahathir had suffered a loss of respect and public support. The judicial proceedings were tarnished by the highly politicized nature of the trials and the attempts by each side to destroy the cloak of moral rectitude of the other. Without going into the tangled web of accusations and legal moves,[56] what emerged from the trials was a cloud of ambiguity. The public, in following the reports of the trials, could pick and choose whom to believe and make congruent assessments of evidence and likely motives. Convincing and irrefutable truth was not a byproduct of the trial process.

Traditional Malay attitudes have always been tolerant of and slightly amused by homosexuals and transvestites, who have tended to congregate in self-defined urban settlements or villages. Traditionally, Malays have also given their rulers and political leaders wider latitude for transgressions of sexual mores, perhaps on the assumption that such behavior was a prerogative of high office. The mores of traditional Malay society and the strict code of the Sharia represented contradictory extremes of popular attitudes on this issue. Large numbers of Malaysians viewed Anwar's sentence as unduly severe, even if he was guilty, but his sentence was less fatal than what Sharia law prescribes (see Table 2.1).[57]

Because of the political nature of Anwar's criminal trials, most political activities surrounding the 1999 elections revolved around that trial. Shortly after Anwar was arrested, his wife, Wan Azizah Ismail, founded a new party, Partai Keadilan Nasional (National Justice Party) in April 1999. Although elections had not been called, everyone realized that there would be general elections sometime before the end of 2000. Therefore, negotiations began in earnest to build an opposition coalition to challenge the ruling Barisan Nasional (BN) coalition. After extended discussions four parties formed what was eventually called Barisan Alternatif (Alternative Front, BA). That coalition included Partai Islam (PAS), Democratic Action Party (DAP), Partai Keadilan Nasional (PKN), and Partai Rakyat Malaysia (Malaysian People's Party). All these parties had somewhat different objectives and clientele, but what provided the common denominator was their opposition to the Barisan Nasional and the leadership of Mahathir. Within the opposition, most activists were Anwar supporters, and Malays constituted a majority support base, but the coalition crossed ethnic and religious lines. PAS came closest to supporting an Islamist ideology. Many Keadilan supporters were liberal Muslims, some of whom had lost their jobs by being politically affiliated with Anwar's patronage entourage. Many Christians and non-Muslim NGO activists joined BN because they were seeking a non-communal forum for political action. The DAP represented its Chinese constituents and supported Chinese cultural issues and the protection of workers' rights. Because of extremes within the BA coalition, concessions were required. Partai Islam agreed to remain silent about its proposals to create an Islamic state and its commitment to implement Sharia law, and the DAP agreed not to criticize Malay special rights as well as ethnic preference quotas and privileges associated with the NEP.[58] After prolonged negotiations, the Barisan Alternatif produced a joint manifesto[59] and allocated seats to its constituent parties according to estimates of likely support in each electoral district.

The formal election campaign was restricted to nine days following the receipt of nominations. In its campaign, the BA invoked populist themes that were expressed with the slogans demanding "justice" and an end to "corruption, cronyism, and nepotism."[60] The BA also announced that Anwar Ibrahim was their candidate for prime minister once "justice was restored" through a promised "fair judicial inquiry" for him. Mahathir went on a pilgrimage to Mecca before the election, and in the prelude to the election campaign he castigated Anwar for having committed sodomy. He explained that he had personally interviewed the witnesses against Anwar before the charges were laid, and he claimed that there was no doubt of Anwar's guilt and that he was unfit for leadership of a Muslim country. Mahathir also accused the opposition of telling lies (*fitnah*), a serious offense in Sharia law. The Barisan Nasional candidates argued that failure to return a BN majority would likely lead to riots and disorder, especially against the Chinese. The Barisan Alternatif stressed the gross injustice of the trials and the harsh police repression of "peaceful demonstrations."

During the campaign, both sides exhibited lack of candor, with each side picking the most extreme symbolic issues to exaggerate and distort. The bitterness and vitriol on both sides made this the most contentious and ugliest campaign of personal defamation in Malaysian political history. It was also the first time that a credible multiethnic opposition coalition had been formed to contest Malaysia's Barisan Nasional system of ethnic power sharing.[61]

The election results reveal that the votes of Malay constituencies were split almost evenly between UMNO, as represented by the Barisan Nasional ticket, and the Barisan Alternatif. The substantial decline of Malay votes for the ruling coalition alarmed the ranks of incumbent Malay leaders. Malay voter support for the Barisan Nasional declined more than 9 percent, while Chinese voters shifted slightly to the Barisan Nasional, partially compensating for the loss of Malay support. The DAP, representing Chinese constituencies, gained slightly, from seven to ten seats, while Keadilan won five parliamentary seats and four state seats.[62] While the percentage shift of votes cast from the previous election was only about 9 percent, its impact on representation was greater because of single-member electoral districts. Partai Islam posted the biggest gains by increasing its representation in Parliament from eight seats to twenty-seven.

The shift of power at the federal level was also reflected in the state-level elections. In the state legislatures, Barisan Nasional representation dropped from 350 to 281. The most dramatic shift occurred in Terengganu, where the Barisan Nasional was ousted from power to be replaced by Partai Islam, winning twenty-eight out of thirty-two state seats and all of Terengganu's federal seats. PAS gained a more substantial political base in a state with significant revenues derived from offshore oil production.[63] Measured in terms of representation in Parliament and in state legislative assemblies, Partai Islam emerged as the big winner.

Table 7.1 Election Results in Dewan Rakyat, Malaysia, 1990–1999

	Government			Opposition			
Election Year	Number of Seats	Percentage of Seats	Percentage of Votes	Number of Seats	Percentage of Seats	Percentage of Votes	Total in House
1990	127	70.55	53.4	53	29.45	46.6	180
1995	162	84.83	65.2	30	15.62	34.8	192
1999	148	76.68	56.5	45	23.32	43.5	193

Source: Zakaria Haji Ahmad, "The 1999 General Elections: A Preliminary Overview," *Trends in Southeast Asia* 1 (January 2000), 8.

Because the Barisan Alternatif was such a diverse coalition, unified primarily by opposition to Mahathir, it was difficult to discern a clear mandate from this election. The government had retained a two-thirds majority, deemed sufficient to amend the Constitution at will. The opposition was larger, but essentially leaderless, and it remained divided on most crucial issues. The primary impact of the election was a warning to the Barisan Nasional that it needed to build up its support at the grassroots level, especially among Malays. This became Mahathir's most pressing issue as he reconstituted his government following the 1999 elections.

The "Islamic State" Issue

As soon as the election concluded, Partai Islam restated its goal of establishing an Islamic State and promised to establish Sharia law, including the imposition of *hudud* punishments for criminal acts. Partai Islam argued that Islamic law would be the ultimate answer to eliminate social and political evils and to restore a true Islamic social and political order for Malaysia. In Kelantan it passed a Sharia criminal law, including the draconian hudud penalties, and it called for the adoption of Sharia apostasy laws to provide for the penalty of death. Because the Malaysian Constitution assigns criminal law exclusively to the federal government, when these Sharia-based criminal statutes were passed, government authorities immediately challenged them as unconstitutional. Even so, the political impact remained.[64]

Partai Islam's unilateral reversion to Islamist ideology created serious tensions within the Barisan Alternatif coalition. The DAP gave notice that it would leave the BA if Partai Islam did not modify its goal of setting up a theocratic state. When no conciliatory response was received, the DAP on September 22, 2001, quit the coalition, effectively ending the Barisan Alternatif as a functioning coalition. A month later, Keadilan virtually collapsed, and Wan Azizah, who acted as its leader while her husband was in prison, announced that she was retiring from active politics. Three other resignations, Chandra Muzaffar, Marina Yusof, and Zainur Zakaria, further decimated the ranks of that party. The BA coalition did hold together long enough to field a candidate for a state by-election in November 1999, which was its last electoral victory before its final demise. Keadilan continued to organize protests over Anwar Ibrahim's continuing imprisonment, but arrests of protesters by police produced dwindling numbers of volunteers for such futile exercises.[65]

The postelection Islamist ideological campaign of Partai Islam that contributed to the breakup of Barisan Alternatif also had an impact on Barisan Nasional, which mounted its own Islamic-based counter campaign. In April 2000, the Prime Minister's Department urged states to adopt a "Restoration of Faith Bill," drafted by JAKIM. This bill provided that those convicted of "deviation from Islam" were to be detained at a "faith rehabilitation center" where they would receive instruction to renew their faith in officially defined "true Islam." The legislation provided no time limit for detention of apostates, and no provisions for those who insisted on renouncing their commitment to Islam, or for "deviationists" who continued to subscribe to deviations from Islam. The bill also provided stiff penalties for anyone attempting to change the *aqidah* (belief) of a Muslim. A big controversy arose over whether the bill contravened Article 11 of the Malaysian Constitution guaranteeing freedom of religion for "every person." In the midst of the controversy, twenty-nine Muslims presented a petition to the Human Rights Commission[66] protesting the Restoration of Faith Bill. A few weeks later the federal government announced that the draft legislation would be withdrawn for further study.[67]

Rebuffed by negative public reaction to its apostasy proposals, the government adopted a new strategy for competition with Partai Islam. In 2002, at a special *muzakarah* (consultation) with religious leaders, academics, and activists representing nearly all religious faiths, a government spokesman made the announcement that "Malaysia has fulfilled the requirements of an Islamic State." This announcement was followed by the circulation of a booklet in Malay published by the Ministry of Information[68] that argued that Malaysia had met all the conditions of an Islamic State. The booklet cited the Hadith jurists Abu Yaala of the Hanbali school and al-Mawardi from the Shafi'i school defining the conditions for an Islamic State. The primary text of al-Mawardi, on the duties of an Islamic ruler, was written prior to 1058 A.D. On the basis of that booklet, Prime Minister Mahathir and his deputy, Abdullah Badawi, proudly affirmed that Malaysia had indeed attained the status of an Islamic State.

What followed was a storm of controversy and criticism. The MCA and Gerakan held large closed-door forums for critics, including the Malaysian Consultative Council of Buddhism, Christianity, Hinduism, and Sikhism (MCCBCHS), as well as liberal Muslims and many others without religious affiliation. The arguments appeared in the press but were more actively continued through uncensored websites such as *Malaysiakini.* What proved to be particularly controversial were the provisions of "orthodox" Sharia law based on al-Mawardi's text that denied *dhimmis* (non-Muslims) civil, political, and equal legal rights, and subjected them to extra taxes *(jizya).* Al-Mawardi's version of Sharia law also restricts religious activities of non-Muslims and excludes them from various occupations. The cited text confines women to inferior and subordinate roles, which provisions elicited severe criticism from Sisters in Islam, a liberal Islamic organization that defends the rights of Muslim women.[69]

At the height of the "Islamic State" controversy, the Ministry of Information withdrew the booklet from public circulation. Defenders of the government's pronouncement argued that the dispute was essentially semantic and did not change the legal rights of citizens. Rather than argue that issue, the government announced instead that it would follow a policy of "absorption of Islamic values" without explaining precisely what that would entail.

The End of an Era

During the entire period of political turmoil following Mahathir's expulsion of Anwar Ibrahim from government service and from UMNO, some of Anwar's closest political allies were arrested and pressure was applied to his supporters to renounce him or face dismissal. By mid-1999, about four hundred of his sympathizers lost their jobs and were expelled from UMNO. Others retained their jobs and membership by switching sides. Mahathir was slow to select a new deputy prime minister, preferring to leave the position open. In January 1999, perhaps in anticipation of the 1999 election, Mahathir selected Abdullah Badawi to fill that position, although Badawi had been part of a rival coalition that challenged Mahathir many years earlier in 1987.[70] He gradually returned to the UMNO fold and became a respected and effective member of the government for many years. As a leading critic of Anwar, Badawi's loyalty to Mahathir was no longer in doubt.

By 2002, Malaysia's economy began to revive, creating political speculation on the question of when Mahathir would retire. Since he avoided any hint of his intentions, many assumed that he would remain in power for a long time. His deputy prime minister and apparent heir, Badawi, had promised to remain loyal until Mahathir decided to retire. At the UMNO General Assembly in June 2002, Mahathir, appearing on live television, made the surprise announcement that he would retire, but senior UMNO officials who had not been consulted interrupted him. After a quickly arranged closed meeting, Mahathir agreed to remain in office for an undisclosed period. Three days later, the UMNO secretary-general announced that Mahathir would retire in October 2003, after which Badawi would succeed him to become Malaysia's prime minister and president of UMNO. This arrangement left a sixteen-month transition before the Mahathir era finally came to a close.[71]

In recognition of Mahathir's achievements and stature in the Muslim world, Malaysia hosted the annual meeting of the Organization of the Islamic Conference (OIC). In his last major speech as prime minister, delivered at the OIC plenary session, Mahathir called for Muslim unity to build up a military and economic capacity to defeat the Jewish people who have acquired the capacity to "rule the world by proxy." Although other leaders did not echo his call for dramatic action, Mahathir's distress over the Palestinian situation and the US-led invasion of Iraq did resonate with many of the delegates.[72] Mahathir left office highly regarded in the Muslim world but also exhibiting frustration that many of his objectives remained unfulfilled.

On October 31, 2003, Mahathir retired. By that act, power was transferred to his nominated successor, Abdullah Ahmad Badawi, in a peaceful and constitutional manner, thus ending an era of twenty-two years.

Notes

1. The "Emergency" was justified in law by Article 150 of the Malaysian Federal Constitution and by the Emergency (Public Order and Crime Prevention) Ordinance of 1948, which was originally promulgated by the British to meet the challenge of the Communist rebellion. See Harold Crouch, *Government and Society in Malaysia* (Ithaca: Cornell University Press, 1996), 77–95; "Laws of Malaysia, Federal Constitution (Reprint), Incorporating All Amendments up to 31 January 2002," *Malayan Law Journal* (2002), 130–133.

2. William Shaw, *Tun Razak, His Life and Times* (Kuala Lumpur: Longman Malaysia, 1976), 202–249.

3. Gordon P. Means, *Malaysian Politics: The Second Generation* (Singapore: Oxford University Press, 1991), 54–81.

4. Karl von Vorys, *Democracy Without Consensus: Communalism and Political Stability in Malaysia* (Princeton: Princeton University Press, 1975), 372–374.

5. After Abdul Razak became prime minister, he arranged in 1971 and 1972 for Musa Hitam and Mahathir to return to full membership in UMNO. Mahathir was appointed minister of education and later served as minister of trade and industry while Musa Hitam was elected deputy chairman of UMNO Youth and later appointed as deputy minister of trade and industry. Bruce Gale, *Musa Hitam: A Political Biography* (Petaling Jaya, Malaysia: Eastern Universities Press, 1982), 18–47; R. S. Milne and Diane K. Mauzy, *Malaysian Politics Under Mahathir* (London: Routledge, 1999), 23–28; J. Victor Morais, *Mahathir: A Profile in Courage* (Petaling Jaya, Malaysia: Eastern Universities Press, 1982), 27, 56–62.

6. Mahathir bin Mohamad, *The Malay Dilemma* (Singapore: Asia Pacific Press, 1970).

7. Ibid., 23. For a critical analysis of *The Malay Dilemma*, see Khoo Boo Teik, *Paradoxes of Mahathirism: An Intellectual Biography of Mahathir Mohamad* (Kuala Lumpur: Oxford University Press, 1995), 24.

8. For an assessment of human rights issues, see Aliran, *Issues of the Mahathir Years* (Penang, Malaysia: Aliran, 1988), 1–143; Lim Kit Siang, *Human Rights in Malaysia* (Petaling Jaya, Malaysia: DAP Human Rights Committee, n.d. [1986]); Milne and Mauzy, *Malaysian Politics Under Mahathir,* 103–121.

9. Government of Malaysia, *Second Malaysia Plan, 1971–1975* (Kuala Lumpur: Government Printing Office, 1971).

10. Between 1969 and 1980, Malaysian government investments in higher education increased from RM25.8 million to RM350.8 million, and the number of universities was increased from one to six. Expenditure per student per year had been raised from RM3,700 to RM12,900. By 1982, there were 23,000 students studying in universities and higher-degree institutions in Malaysia, with 68,000 university students studying abroad, about 65 percent of whom were Malays on the Malaysian government's fully funded educational foreign fellowships. See Yip Yat Hoong, "The Cost of University Education in Malaysia," manuscript, Institute of Advanced Studies, University of Malaya, 1982, 6–14.

11. *Asiaweek*, March 27, 1981, 30–35. As part of the policy to promote Malay as the national language, the Alliance coalition changed its name to Barisan Nasional in the mid-1970s.

12. *New Straits Times,* March 29, 1982, 1. Mahathir was persuaded to consider recruiting Anwar Ibrahim to UMNO by Ismail Faruki, professor of Islamic studies at Temple University. Professor Faruki's message to Mahathir stated that collaboration with the "Islamic Movement" would give new vitality to Malaysia. To Anwar, he argued that by joining the government Anwar could "effect change from within" the existing power structure. See John Hilley, *Malaysia: Mahathirism, Hegemony and the New Opposition* (London: Zed Books, 2001), 94–95.

13. Diane K. Mauzy, "The 1982 General Elections in Malaysia: A Mandate for Change?" *Asian Survey* 23, no. 4 (April 1983), 497–517, also reproduced in Bruce Gale, *Readings in Malaysian Politics* (Petaling Jaya, Malaysia: Pelanduk Publications, 1986), 3–23.

14. From 1978 to 1982, the incumbent Barisan Nasional increased its parliamentary seats from 130 to 132, while the seats held by Partai Islam remained at 5. Harold Crouch, *Malaysia's 1982 General Elections* (Singapore: Institute of Southeast Asian Studies, 1982), 58–62; John Funston, *Political Careers of Mahathir Mohamad and Anwar Ibrahim: Parallel, Intersecting and Conflicting* (Bangi, Malaysia: Institute of Malaysian and International Studies, Universiti Kebangsaan Malaysia, 1998), 19.

15. Diane K. Mauzy and R. S. Milne, "The Mahathir Administration: Discipline Through Islam," *Pacific Affairs* 56, no. 4 (Winter 1983–1984), reproduced in Gale, *Readings in Malaysian Politics*, 90–92.

16. Khoo Boo Teik, *Beyond Mahathir: Malaysian Politics and Its Discontents* (London: Zed Books, 2003), 88–91.

17. Mauzy and Milne, "The Mahathir Administration," 97.

18. *Laws of Malaysia, Federal Constitution,* Ninth Schedule, List II (Malaysia: Commissioner of Law Revision, 2002), 186.

19. Ahmad Ibrahim, *Islamic Law in Malaya* (Singapore: Malaysian Sociological Research Institute, 1965); Moshe Yegar, *Islam and Islamic Institutions in British Malaya: Policies and Implementation* (Jerusalem: The Magnes Press, Hebrew University, 1979); Gordon P. Means, "Malaysia: Islam in a Pluralistic Society," in Carlo Caldarola (ed.), *Religion and Societies: Asia and the Middle East* (Berlin: Mouton Publishers, 1982), 475–493.

20. Farish A. Noor, "Blood, Sweat and *Jihad*: The Radicalization of the Political Discourse of the Pan-Malaysian Islamic Party (PAS) from 1982 Onwards," *Contemporary Southeast Asia* 25, no. 2 (August 2003), 206, citing Shanti Nair, *Islam in Malaysian Foreign Policy* (London and Singapore: Routledge and ISEAS, 1997), 112.

21. Patricia A. Martinez, "The Islamic State or the State of Islam in Malaysia," *Contemporary Southeast Asia* 23, no. 3 (December 2001), 474–478.

22. Khoo, *Paradoxes of Mahathirism,* 174–181; Kamarulnizam Abdullah, *The Politics of Islam in Contemporary Malaysia* (Bangi: Penerbit Universiti Kebangsaan Malaysia, 2003), 94; *Far Eastern Economic Review,* May 31, 1984, 52–54. Consult www.iiu.edu.my.

23. *Far Eastern Economic Review,* September 15, 1983, 16.

24. For an account of the constitutional crisis over the rulers' powers, see Milne and Mauzy, *Malaysian Politics Under Mahathir,* 30–39.

25. *New Straits Times,* August 31, 1984, 1–2, 16; September 1, 1984, 1–2; September 2, 1984, 14; *Far Eastern Economic Review,* January 13, 1983, 9–10.

26. Patricia Martinez, "Mahathir, Islam, and the New Malay Dilemma," in Ho Khai Leong and James Chin (eds.), *Mahathir's Administration: Performance and Crisis in Governance* (Singapore: Times Editions, 2003), 238.

27. Abdullah, *The Politics of Islam,* 192–196.

28. Means, *Malaysian Politics: The Second Generation,* 71; *New Straits Times,* October 22, 1980, 1; *New Straits Times,* October 23, 1980, 1. For an examination of Malay peasant poverty, see James C. Scott, *Weapons of the Weak: Everyday Forms of Peasant Resistance* (New Haven, CT: Yale University Press, 1985).

29. *New Straits Times,* November 21, 1985, 1 and 2; Government of Malaysia, *The Memali Incident,* Parliamentary Paper, No. 21 of 1986 (Kuala Lumpur: Jabatan Percetakan Negara, 1986); *Far Eastern Economic Review,* December 5, 1985, 28–29.

30. *New Sunday Times,* December 8, 1985, 2; *New Straits Times,* December 12, 1985, 1; December 14, 1985, 1 and 2; December 19, 1985, 1. In interviews, some years later, Partai Islam officials claimed that Abdul Hadi Awang's message had been misinterpreted and that no fatwa had been issued. Abdullah, *The Politics of Islam,* 198–199.

31. Kassim Ahmad, *Hadis: Satu Penilaian Semula* (Petaling Jaya, Malaysia: Media Intelek, 1986).

32. Means, *Malaysian Politics: The Second Generation,* 129.

33. *New Straits Times,* July 17, 1986, 24; *Far Eastern Economic Review,* July 17, 1986, 24–26.

34. Abdullah, *The Politics of Islam,* 100–110; Ahmad Fauzi Abdul Hamid, "Political Dimensions of Religious Conflict in Malaysia: State Response to an Islamic Movement," *Indonesia and the Malay World* 28, no. 80 (2000), 43.

35. Abdullah, *The Politics of Islam,* 99–107.

36. Hamid, "Political Dimensions," 38–41.

37. Abdullah, *The Politics of Islam,* 166–177; Hamid, "Political Dimensions," 41–55.

38. Funston, *Political Careers,* 27.

39. Mohamad Nor Abdul Ghani, et al. (eds.), *Malaysia Incorporated and Privatization: Towards National Unity* (Petaling Jaya, Malaysia: Pelanduk Publications, 1984); In-Won Hwang, *Personalized Politics: The Malaysian State Under Mahathir* (Singapore: Institute of Southeast Asian Studies, 2003), 246.

40. Mahathir bin Mohamad, *Vision 2020* (Kuala Lumpur: Published for the Malaysian Business Council by Institute for Strategic and International Studies, 1991). In Malay, this statement came to be known as Wawasan 2020.

41. Claudia Derichs, "Competing Politicians, Competing Visions: Mahathir Mohamad's *Wawasan 2020* and Anwar Ibrahim's *Asian Renaissance,*" in Leong and Chin, *Mahathir's Administration,* 191–192.

42. Mahathir, *Vision 2020,* 9.

43. Anwar Ibrahim, *The Asian Renaissance* (Singapore: Times Books International, 1996).

44. From 1989 to 1996, Malaysia's real GDP growth remained above 8 percent for the entire period. See World Bank, *World Development Report,* 7 vols. (New York: Oxford University Press, 1990–1997).

45. Edmund Terence Gomez, "Governance, Affirmative Action and Enterprise Development: Ownership and Control of Corporate Malaysia," in Edmund Terence Gomez (ed.), *The State of Malaysia: Ethnicity, Equity and Reform* (London: RoutledgeCurzon, 2004), 157–183.

46. Ng Beoy Kui, "Vulnerability and Party Capitalism: Malaysia's Encounter with the 1997 Financial Crisis," in Leong and Chin, *Mahathir's Administration,* 180, 161–187.

47. Gerald Tan, *ASEAN Economic Development and Cooperation,* 2nd ed. (Singapore: Times Academic Press, 2000), 209–222.

48. Khoo, *Beyond Mahathir,* 71–98; Hwang, *Personalized Politics,* 276–296.

49. Hwang, *Personalized Politics*, 297–305.

50. Khalid Jafri, *50 Dalil Mengapa Anwar Tida Boleh Jadi PM* [50 Reasons Why Anwar Cannot Become Prime Minister], as cited in Ian Stewart, *The Mahathir Legacy: A Nation Divided, A Region at Risk* (Singapore: Talisman Publishing, 2003), 65.

51. Prema-Chandra Athukorala, "Swimming Against the Tide: Crisis Management in Malaysia," in H. W. Arndt and Hal Hill (eds.), *Southeast Asia's Economic Crisis: Origins, Lessons and the Way Forward* (Singapore: Institute of Southeast Asian Studies, 1999), 28–40; Khoo, *Beyond Mahathir,* 47–56.

52. Ranjit Gill, *Anwar Ibrahim: Mahathir's Dilemma* (Singapore: Epic Management Services, 1998), 11–34.

53. Ibid., 63–65; Stewart, *The Mahathir Legacy,* 104–118.

54. Amnesty International Press Release, May 9, 2004, available from www.amnesty.org.

55. For an account of the trial and the public demonstrations in support of Anwar, see Raja Petra Kamarudin, *The Reformasi Trial* ([Shah Alam, Malaysia]: Raja Petra Kamarudin, 2001); Sabri Zain, *Face Off* (Singapore: BigO Books, 2000). For an evaluation of the trials, see *Amnesty International Report 2000—Malaysia,* and *Amnesty International Report 2001—Malaysia,* www.amnesty.org. Also see Amnesty International report numbers ASA 28/002/1999 and ASA 28/009/2000.

56. For an account of the trial and its political ramifications, see Stewart, *The Mahathir Legacy,* 104–237.

57. For an account of Malay attitudes toward this issue based on interviews during the period of Anwar's trial, see Michael G. Peletz, *Islamic Modern: Religious Courts and Cultural Politics in Malaysia* (Princeton, NJ: Princeton University Press, 2002), 239–275.

58. In August 1999, eleven Chinese organizations drafted a document, known by its Chinese acronym as *Suqui.* It asked the Malaysian government to move toward "universal goals" and to abolish the ethnic quota systems for the economy and education and replace them with a "means-tested sliding-scale." Lee Hock Guan, "Malay Dominance and Opposition Politics in Malaysia," in *Southeast Asian Affairs 2002* (Singapore: Institute of Southeast Asian Studies, 2002), 177–195.

59. *Towards a Just Malaysia,* www.malaysia.net/dap/ba-ind.htm, as cited in Khoo Boo Teik, *Beyond Mahathir,* 132.

60. Ibid., 112–115.

61. John Funston, "Malaysia's Tenth Elections: Status Quo, *Reformasi* or Islamization?" *Contemporary Southeast Asia* 22, no. 1 (April 2000), 23–48.

62. Hwang, *Personalized Politics,* 325; Zakaria Haji Ahmad, "The 1999 General Elections: A Preliminary Overview," *Trends in Southeast Asia* 1 (January 2000), 1–11.

63. Hilley, *Malaysia,* 260–264.

64. Maznah Mohamad, "Malaysia in 2002: Bracing for a Post-Mahathir Future," in *Southeast Asian Affairs 2003* (Singapore: Institute of Southeast Asian Studies, 2003), 160–161.

65. Khoo Boo Teik, *Beyond Mahathir,* 154–159; Stewart, *The Mahathir Legacy,* 96–200; K. S. Nathan, "Malaysia: 11 September and the Politics of Incumbency," in *Southeast Asian Affairs 2002* (Singapore: Institute of Southeast Asian Studies, 2002), 163–165; Lee Hock Guan, "Malay Dominance and Opposition Politics," 177–189.

66. In 2000, the Malaysian government established a National Human Rights Commission, known as Suhakam. Headed by Musa Hitam, a former deputy prime minister, Suhakam held hearings on alleged human rights violations. Musa Hitam charted a cautious but fairly independent role for that commission. Khoo Boo Teik, *Beyond Mahathir,* 162. See also Amanda Whiting, "Situating Suhakam: Human Rights Debates

and Malaysia's National Human Rights Commission," *Stanford Journal of International Law* 39, no. 1 (Winter 2003), 59–98.

67. Martinez, "The Islamic State," 482.

68. Dato' Wan Zahidi Wan Teh, *Malaysia adalah Sebuah Negara Islam* [Malaysia is an Islamic Nation]. The book cites the "Twelve Distinct Duties of an Islamic Government" from al-Mawardi's text, *Al-ahkam as-sultaniyya*, and compares those requirements with Malaysia's political and legal system. English translations with quotations and a summary of Teh's book are reproduced in Christian Federation of Malaysia, *Malaysia as an Islamic State: An Analysis* (CFM, January 2002).

69. Martinez, "The Islamic State," 490–503; Christian Federation of Malaysia, *Malaysia as an Islamic State,* 9–15.

70. Hilley, *Malaysia,* 108–111; Hwang, *Personalized Politics,* 306–311. Abdullah Badawi had been a supporter of Tunku Razaleigh's "Team B" faction in UMNO, which challenged the leadership of Mahathir at the UMNO General Assembly in April 1987 and led to the formation of a rival party, Semangat '46, which lasted until 1996. Milne and Mauzy, *Malaysian Politics Under Mahathir,* 39–46; Means, *Malaysian Politics: The Second Generation,* 199–243.

71. Khoo Boo Teik, *Beyond Mahathir,* 167–169.

72. Michael Vatikiotis, "One Angry Man," *Far Eastern Economic Review* (October 30, 2003), 18–22.

8

Southeast Asia and Global Jihad

Although Islam came to Southeast Asia indirectly through connections with South Asia, contacts with Mecca and the centers of Islamic learning in Arabia were sustained from the fifteenth century to the present with varying degrees of intensity and impact. The obligation of Islam that every Muslim must perform the haj pilgrimage to Mecca at least once in a lifetime was a difficult challenge that few Southeast Asian Muslims could afford a century ago. By the time of steam navigation, the flow of pilgrims from Southeast Asia became increasingly significant.[1]

Pilgrims, Piety, and Politics

The obligation for Muslims to perform the haj produced a continuous industry in Mecca to accommodate and serve the flow of pilgrims from across the Muslim world. The profits derived from the pilgrimage industry provided the primary source of income for this region until 1930, when the discovery of oil dramatically changed the economy of the Gulf states. Whoever controlled Mecca not only gained the profits from the haj industry but also was able to propagate Islamic doctrines to vast numbers of pilgrims from across the Muslim world. Until 1919, Sharif Husayn, the leader of the Hashimite lineage, was the emir of Mecca. In 1919, after World War I, Ibn Saud of the Saudi lineage defeated the forces of Sharif Husayn, gaining complete control of Mecca as well as unifying most of the Arabian Peninsula under his authority. Because the Saudis subscribed to the Hanbali school of jurisprudence as interpreted by ‘Abd al-Wahhab, these doctrines were defended and propagated from Mecca after the Saudi conquest. The uncompromising, fundamentalist Islamic doctrines, known as Wahhabism, were conservative within Saudi Arabia, but they were radical when applied to the social structures of Southeast Asia. In later years, Wahhabism became a source for many of the doctrines propagated in Southeast Asia by the dakwah movements of the 1970s and 1980s.

With Mecca as the ideological center of Islam, the Arabs claimed a special role in protecting and preserving Islamic holy places as well as transmitting the traditions and Sunni version of Islam. For that reason, Islamic doctrines tended to reflect the political environment and issues that most directly affected the Arabs. While the complex issues of Middle East politics fall beyond the scope of this work, it is important to mention a few events that shaped Arab political aspirations and ultimately generated some of the main political doctrines of political Islam.

At the turn of the century, the Ottoman Empire had been slowly disintegrating with the rise of nationalism that challenged the Islamic basis for rule. When World War I broke out, it quickly spread from Europe to the Middle East. Because of Turkish fear of Russia, Turkey joined the Triple Alliance of Germany, Austria, and Italy. The mobilization of Turkish and German forces that captured Baghdad and advanced toward Palestine prompted the British to appeal for Arab support against Turkey. The High Commissioner of Egypt, Sir Henry McMahon, and Sharif Hussein Ali of Mecca exchanged a series of letters in 1916 that promised the Arabs that their aspirations for independence would be addressed in postwar settlements for the Middle East. Later, in response to pressure from Zionists in England, the British Cabinet approved the Balfour Declaration of 1917, which also promised the Jews of the Diaspora that the British protectorate of Palestine would become a "home for the Jewish people." Because of the concerns of Britain's wartime allies, other secret agreements were made with France and Russia to allocate concessions and spheres of influence to those powers in postwar settlements for the Middle East. While these various promises and agreements to different political constituencies did not seem totally incompatible at the time, they became increasingly difficult to implement, especially in Palestine, as Jewish immigrants expanded existing Jewish communities that had lived in Palestine for centuries. Soon political attitudes hardened, creating cycles of violence between Jews and Palestinian Arabs that made resolution of their differences ever more intractable. Without going into the details of these conflicts, it is significant that Southeast Asian Muslims followed these issues with concern and primordial empathy.

During the war, the Arabs of the Hejaz under the leadership of Sharif Husayn revolted against Ottoman rule in 1916, and Arabs in Syria and Mesopotamia (later called Iraq) formed anti-Ottoman secret societies to resist Ottoman rule. After decisive victories in Palestine by British forces in 1918, the Turks were defeated and an armistice ended the Ottoman Empire and provided for a temporary Allied occupation of Constantinople. The postwar political configuration was not finally defined until 1923. Under the newly created League of Nations, a Mandate System was established creating provisionally recognized "independent nations," but these newly configured "nations" were placed under the supervisory authority of Mandatory Powers. The latter were charged with an obligation to report to the League on preparations and progress for eventual full independence. Under this trusteeship system, Great Britain acquired the Mandates for Palestine, Transjordan, and Iraq, while France acquired the Mandates for Syria and Lebanon. This system reflected the military configuration of Allied powers, but it virtually ignored the aspirations of the region's diverse populations.[2] The creation of multiple Arab states under the control of Mandatory Powers, and the promise to Jews of the world that they could immigrate to Palestine, created in the Middle East the conditions for a prolonged and escalating antipathy against European colonial authority.

In the turmoil of the postwar period, a secular government in Turkey under Mustafa Kemal Ataturk came to power and deposed Sultan Mehmed VI in 1922. Two years later, the Turkish republican government abolished the caliphate in March 1924. This action greatly distressed Sunni Muslims in the Middle East, India, and Southeast Asia. Sunni Muslims had looked to the caliph for leadership and guidance on religious issues. Without that institution, the Muslim world would witness greater diversity of doctrines and sects, and the symbols of unity among Sunni Muslims were more difficult to maintain.

The Rise of Islamist Ideology

In the period between World War I and World War II, most Middle Eastern politics involved various manifestations of Arab and Turkish nationalism based on prevailing Western ideologies. These included liberalism, socialism, and communism, along with other hybrid ideologies. At the same time, a countermovement began that stressed Islam as the only appropriate basis for government and society. The leading organization committed to an Islamic agenda was the Muslim Brotherhood (el-Ikhwan el-Muslimin), which was founded about 1928 in Egypt by Hasan al-Banna. With fiery rhetoric, he exhorted his followers to accept the Quran, Hadith, and Sharia law as "divine revelation" and the only basis for rule in Muslim societies. Combining a populist appeal with fundamentalist Islamist doctrines, he summarized the Brotherhood's core message with the slogan "The Quran is our Constitution." Appealing to Muslim xenophobia, he promised to rid Egypt of all foreigners and non-Muslims and to establish the primacy of a "Muslim system" of rule after an Islamic revolution that would replace the secular government of Egypt under the "foreign" monarchy of King Farouk. To achieve their objectives, the Brotherhood instigated political assassinations of critics and political leaders who opposed their agenda. In 1948, they assassinated Egypt's Prime Minister Mahmud al-Nuqrashi. In retaliation, a member of King Farouk's "Iron Guard" killed Hasan al-Banna.[3] After a failed attempt by the Muslim Brotherhood to assassinate Colonel Abdul Nasser in 1952, mass arrests and police repression forced many of its leaders to seek asylum in Saudi Arabia. From their Saudi base they propagated their ideology and promoted political alliances with other Islamist organizations across the Muslim world. Over the years, the Muslim Brotherhood built a network of similar radical Islamist organizations inspired by their tactics and ideology.[4]

In the post–World War II era, the three best-known theorist-publicists for Islamist ideology were Sayyid Qutb, Maulana Maududi, and Ayatollah Khomeini. Sayyid Qutb was an Egyptian who became the primary ideologist for the Muslim Brotherhood and was executed in 1963 during Nasser's purge of the Muslim Brotherhood. Maulana Maududi lived in British India and later Pakistan as a journalist who wrote political and religious commentary promoting a political struggle to forge an Islamic State. Ayatollah Khomeini led the revolution that overthrew Shah Mohammad Reza, ending Iran's Pahlavi Dynasty and establishing himself as the leader of the Islamic Republic of Iran.[5] A brief summary of their ideas will provide a sample of the doctrines being transmitted from the Middle East to Southeast Asia by subsidized literature available through mosques and Islamic bookstores.

Sayyid Qutb began with the proposition that the first responsibility of a Muslim ruler is to dispense justice. To do that, the ruler must observe complete obedience to Sharia law. If that law is not observed, the orders of the ruler are "contrary to the will of Allah," and Muslims cannot give obedience to anyone who disobeys the Creator. Rulers should take advice from the Muslim community on matters that pertain to "worldly affairs," but not on matters that pertain to observance of the law.[6] Qutb was opposed to nationalism for being against Allah's will because it divided the umma and fragmented "the land of Islam" (dar ul-Islam). All modern political systems that attribute sovereignty to the people were condemned for being in violation of Islam, since sovereignty (*hakimiya*) is vested in God alone. Qutb condemned all contemporary politics, especially of incumbent rulers of Arab states, as the rule of *jahiliyya*—the state of ignorance and barbarism that prevailed in the pre-Islamic era before the Prophet Muhammad received Allah's "Final Revelation." For Qutb, the consequence of jahiliyya is *takfir*—which is a state of impiety requiring a revolution by the Community of the Faithful against unrighteous and impious leaders. Much of Qutb's invective was directed against "secular governments," with the obvious but unstated conclusion that all devout Muslims have an obligation to reject obedience to their "illegitimate rulers" who rule with the evils and falsehood of jahiliyya. From these assumptions, Qutb's followers concluded that Muslims have a God-commanded obligation to engage in jihad to battle against Westernization and return their societies and governments to the "straight path of Islam."[7]

Writing during the same period as Qutb, but for a South Asian audience, Maududi was primarily concerned with founding an ideal Muslim state. Both Qutb and Maududi revived the early medieval theories of Islamic governance based on the Quran, Hadith, and the unique Islamic creation myths that describe how God revealed his laws to Adam and Eve.[8] Maududi asserted that all legislation, social organization, and personal behavior must conform to the Quran, which is free from human error and is based on Allah's commands. Any deviations from the interpretations of "enlightened Islam" by state authorities disqualify the regime from being an Islamic State. Maududi does recognize a place for consultation through a *shura* (advisory council) and a republican form of government with elections, but he would restrict elective office to a circle of pious and practicing Muslims. Maududi's commentaries on Islam addressed current issues related to politics. During the 1920s and 1930s, he opposed nationalism for being counter to Islam and argued against the creation of Pakistan on the grounds that the Muslim League was incapable of producing an Islamic State. Instead, he favored the mobilization of Muslims to implement Islamization throughout the Indian subcontinent. He also expected Muslims to convert their faith into a jihad of political struggle against all political leaders who have "usurped" Allah's sovereignty.[9] This was essentially a call for an anticolonial struggle against British rule in India.

In 1941 Maududi founded his own political party, Jamaat-i-Islami, and after India and Pakistan gained independence in 1947, Maududi accepted the reality of Pakistan's existence but opposed its rulers and Pakistan's constitutional system. He demanded that the Ahmadis be declared "non-Muslim," and when government refused to accede to this demand, his Jamaat supporters engaged in riots, killing many thousands of Ahmadis and looting their property.[10] For his role in the riots, Maududi was jailed from 1948 to 1950 on charges of sedition. After his release, he resumed his leadership of Jamaat-i-Islami.[11] The party was organized with an authoritarian, clandestine structure with Maududi as the unchallengeable "emir." Despite the popularity of its Islamist rhetoric, the party never gained a mass following in Pakistan.[12] In later years, Maulana Maududi's doctrines gained a much wider audience when exported abroad through books and religious tracts as part of the dakwah movements of the 1980s.

Ruhollah Khomeini was born in 1902 to a family of Shia religious scholars. He gained a theological education at Iran's Islamic center at Qom and upon graduation became an instructor of Islamic studies. When the shah of Iran began programs to secularize and "modernize" Iran, Khomeini became a persistent critic of the shah's regime. When the shah initiated measures to undermine the role and power of the Shia ulama establishment, Khomeini gathered their support and the support of bazaar traders, who were suffering from an economic recession and unemployment. Khomeini accused the shah of selling the country to the United States for Iran's oil. He argued that the shah's policies had ignored Islamic law and undermined the role of the ulama, who were harassed and arrested through the actions of "spies of the Jews and Zionists" and by their agents in Iran, the Baha'is. After many encounters with the shah's secret police—the Savak—Khomeini was exiled in 1964, and spent the next thirteen years at the Shia shrine at Najaf, in Iraq. In 1978, under pressure from the shah's regime, Iraq expelled Khomeini, who moved to the outskirts of Paris, where he continued his insurrectionary campaign against the shah. In February 1979, Khomeini returned to Tehran, just as the shah's regime was collapsing in the throes of an Islamic revolution, guided and inspired by Khomeini's leadership and revolutionary doctrines.

When Ayatollah Khomeini was in exile, he organized a political offensive against Reza Shah's programs of Westernization and secularization. He castigated the shah for his dictatorial powers and the violations of human rights, the lack of democracy, and the failure to abide by the rule of law. After Khomeini came to power, the issues of human rights, rule of law, and democracy were sacrificed to the calculus of creating a system of absolute power for Khomeini, who claimed to be the vice-regent of God. Khomeini's views on the characteristics of Islamic government were presented in a series of lectures in 1969 in Najaf when he was in exile. These lectures were later published as a book entitled *Velayat-e Faqih.*[13]

In this book, Khomeini begins by condemning monarchy for being alien to Islam. The proper political order for a Muslim state should be based on the first Islamic community governed by the Prophet Muhammad in the seventh century. For Khomeini, this model of an Islamic state is a practical and realizable form of government that can be instituted with the support of pious, believing Muslims who are committed to the ideals of Islam. To do so requires the assertion of the political role of the ulama, who are heirs to the mantle of authority transmitted from Allah to the Prophet Muhammad. The supreme leader in an Islamic state must be an expert in Islamic law and must be a Faqih (Islamic jurist), who will act as the vice-regent of Allah in the enforcement of divine laws. So long as power is exercised by wicked governments and governors who are "traitorous, wicked, cruel, and tyrannical," Muslims, who are true to their faith, must devote their energies to overthrow such "false governments." Faithful Muslims should create a parallel system of authority by supporting Islamic leaders who are dedicated to the ideals of the Islamic revolution.[14]

It should be obvious from the above summaries that the core political doctrines of Qutb, Maududi, and Khomeini are remarkably similar. They are committed to the salafiya doctrine that Islamic societies should return to the practices and political forms of "the ancestors"—to emulate the political system of the first Muslim community under Muhammad's rule. As such, these doctrines are *extremely conservative*, having ideals that suggest a society of minimal technology and based on personal bonds of loyalty reinforced by uniform beliefs with unchallenged leaders enforcing "God's law." On the other hand, these doctrines are *extremely radical*, because they espouse a total revolution against contemporary regimes and an unyielding challenge to the primary characteristics of modern society with its socioeconomic, political, and cultural diversity; its high levels of education; and its emphasis on technology.

The apparent contradictions between Islamist conservatism and its radicalism come about because the Islamist ideals have never been fully attained in the history of Islam, and the evolving nature of the modern world makes these goals ever more remote and unattainable. The doctrines propagated by these archetypal writers provide rationalizations for jihad as the solution for any contentious political issues.

Islamist Doctrines Toward Religious Minorities

Another common theme in the writings of these three writers is their sanctions for vigilante violence against non-Muslim minorities living within the borders of their state. Qutb railed against Coptic Christians who held a significant number of positions in government, higher education, and business. Their higher educational and economic status made them natural targets of envy, while Qutb's Islamist doctrines were utilized to justify the organized violence directed against both the Coptic Christians and domestic Jews.[15] Two offshoots of the Muslim Brotherhood, Tazim al-Jihad and Gamaat Islamiya, organized attacks on the Copts but also were involved in the assassination of prominent Muslim intellectuals who were accused of apostasy for their "secular" beliefs that refuted Qutb's Islamist doctrines.[16]

In a similar manner, Maududi sanctioned vigilante mob violence against the Ahmadis, who claimed to be Muslims but who were accused by Sunnis of being heretics. The leader and founder of the Ahmadiya movement, Mirza Ghulam Ahmad, did accept the Quran as the source of superior revelations, but he also claimed to be a prophet who had received other direct revelations from Allah and claimed to be the promised Messiah of Islam. That movement became a messianic offshoot from Sunni Islam and represented an attempt to revitalize Islam with a series of revelations by Ghulam Ahmad that modified Islamic doctrines, stressing nonviolent and nonretaliatory responses to physical violence. In 1953, Maududi organized a campaign against Ahmadis by recruiting 55,000 volunteers to engage in mob action to force Pakistan's leaders to ban Ahmadis from government employment and to punish Ahmadis for "Islam betrayed."[17]

Under persistent pressure from Islamic parties, Pakistan passed laws in 1974 declaring Ahmadis to be "non-Muslim." In 1958, Sharia law was given constitutional status. In 1984 and 1986, blasphemy laws were passed that defined Ahmadi religious practices as blasphemy and imposed a penalty of three years' imprisonment for any participation in such practices. The Ahmadiya community constitutes about ten million members, many of whom were highly educated and employed in government service or in professional occupations. Ahmadis were forced from their jobs in the public service and persistently subjected to vigilante attacks. This persecution, both by law and by mob violence, continues to the present day.[18]

Like Qutb and Maududi, Ayatollah Khomeini also identified a domestic enemy as a pariah community to be a scapegoat target for attack and condemnation. For Khomeini, the Baha'i was his community of abomination. The religious faith of the Baha'is originated as an offshoot of Shia Islam. The founder was Sayyid 'Ali Muhammad who assumed the title of Bab (Gate) and, in 1844, declared that he was the "returned twelfth imam," who was, through prophecy, anticipated by the Shias. In that capacity, he claimed to have acquired divine inspiration to reveal a new holy book that abrogated and revised some precepts of the Quran. For these refutations to orthodox Shiite doctrine, the Bab was arrested, tried, and executed by a firing squad in 1850. The surviving community of thousands continued with new leaders and gradually developed a more complete theology. Baha'i doctrines assume that God's revelation is progressive and without end and that all the major religions of the world represent partial aspects of God's Truth.

Without a clergy, the Baha'i community is governed by freely elected representatives. Baha'is preach pacifism, equality of the sexes, freedom of the individual to investigate truth, and a call for the creation of an international order based on world federalism to bring about the unity of mankind. Because they reject the Islamic doctrine that Muhammad was the last and final prophet, Shiite clergy view the Baha'i faith as a dangerous heresy. At the time of the Islamic revolution, the Baha'is constituted a religious community of about 300,000 in Iran.[19]

Because of their eclectic theology and their high valuation for modern secular-based education, the Baha'is had moved into the professions and educational institutions and were well represented in the modern sectors of the economy. Even before the Islamic revolution, when Khomeini was in exile in Paris, he announced that there would be no religious freedom for Baha'is. When Khomeini was installed as Velayat-e Faqih of the Islamic Republic of Iran, he revealed by his actions what he had in mind. The new Constitution proclaimed Shia Islam as the state religion and recognized Judaism, Christianity, and Zorastrianism as "permitted religions," but the Baha'is were unmentioned and had the status of unprotected infidels. In the fall of 1978, about 200 of the most prominent Baha'i leaders were arrested and summarily executed while thousands of other Baha'is were arrested and tortured.[20] Community properties were confiscated and all Baha'is in government and nationalized industries were fired and lost their pensions. Baha'i places of worship were demolished and Baha'is were denied the right to attend any institutions of higher learning. Baha'i lawyers were not allowed to practice law. Because of their status as unprotected infidels, in cases where a Muslim murders a Baha'i, the court has ruled, on the basis of a Khomeini pronouncement, that capital punishment and damages do not apply and the accused in such cases should be acquitted. In 1993, the Supreme Revolutionary Cultural Council prepared a document outlining policy toward the Baha'i community that was endorsed by

Khomeini. This document was entitled, "A Blueprint for the Destruction of a Religious Community." The theme of this policy was to deny Baha'is access to any influential or lucrative jobs and to prevent Baha'is from acquiring higher education or technical training. In 1999, the General Prosecutor announced that any membership in Baha'i institutions was a crime. To justify these measures, the Baha'i were accused of being a political movement, rather than a religion, and were accused of being agents of the CIA, Zionists, and/or the Russians.

Because of the laws prohibiting Baha'i from enrolling in university-level courses, the Baha'i organized private courses in homes for teaching Baha'i students in regular nonreligious subjects. In 1998, government agents raided 500 Baha'i homes, seized books, teaching materials, and laboratory equipment and arrested suspected teachers. The Iranian authorities ordered the teachers to sign a pledge that they would no longer teach any subjects privately, but all those arrested refused to sign such a pledge. While these various legal restrictions on the Baha'i remain in force, there has been a slight relaxation of enforcement in the years after 1998. While the Baha'i community has survived over twenty years of persistent repression, about 30,000 Baha'is have been able to emigrate abroad. With fairly high rates of reproduction, the number of remaining Baha'is in Iran in the year 2000 has been estimated to be about 400,000.[21]

Saudi Foreign Assistance Programs

The doctrines and political views of the three Islamic ideologues, summarized in the preceding section, represented a small faction of radical Islamist commentaries. For Southeast Asia, these ideas had to be imported and supported domestically to produce the anticipated and predicted Islamic revolution that was being espoused in Islamist polemics. To do so, there needed to be a sponsor or patron, and, wittingly or unwittingly, that patron became Saudi Arabia.

Over the span of half a century, the Kingdom of Saudi Arabia was transformed from one of the world's poorest nations to one of the richest countries in the world.[22] This wealth came at a time of increasing instability in the Middle East. The victory of the Islamic revolution in Iran led by Khomeini in February 1979 challenged all regimes in the Muslim world with its revolutionary rhetoric, its militant anti-American policies, and its example of how to establish an Islamic State. The radical version of Shia Islam was openly challenging the claims of conservative Wahhabi Sunni Islam for primacy of place and status due to its trusteeship of the holy places of Medina and Mecca. The Shiite establishment linked to Khomeini actively championed the Palestinian cause by funding and sponsoring Hezbollah and Islamic Jihad to radicalize Lebanon's Shiite community in a guerrilla war against both Israel and Lebanese moderates. Both these organizations became active participants in Palestine's Intifada campaign against Israel, which began in late 1987. During this period, Muslims in Algeria, Sudan, Pakistan, and Muslim immigrant communities in Europe were all becoming more radicalized.[23]

To meet the challenge of radicalized Islam from Iran, Saudi Arabia greatly expanded its program of foreign assistance to Muslim countries in a bid to promote the Wahhabi form of Islam and to project Saudi leadership throughout the Muslim world. Tremendous amounts of money were expended on building mosques, Islamic centers, colleges and universities, and Islamic schools (madrasahs) and sponsoring world conferences on Islam on issues of current salience. This projection of Saudi financial power extended to Africa, South Asia, Southeast Asia, Europe, Australia, and the United States. After the Soviet invasion of Afghanistan in December of 1979, Saudi Arabia, with the support of the United States, poured millions of dollars into support for Afghan refugees and for the expansion of radical Deobandi-operated madrasahs that were allied with Maududi's Jamaat-i-Islami party.[24] In 1947, when Pakistan was founded, there were only 137 madrasahs in the country. By 2004, there were 20,000 madrasahs in Pakistan, most of them built or financially supported by Saudi money, and nearly all of them teaching only Islamic subjects in a curriculum that indoctrinated students into radical Islamist ideology. The students were taught that Muslims had an obligation to be willing to make the jihad sacrifice for Islam. A large number of the Taliban's mujahideen, who mounted attacks against the Soviet invasion of Afghanistan, were recruited from the Deobandi madrasahs in Pakistan.[25]

The Saudis were also generous with their money in Southeast Asia and eager to promote their version of Wahhabi Islam. Much of the Saudi financial assistance for the propagation of Wahhabi doctrines abroad was funneled through the Jeddah-based World Muslim League. The International Islamic University Malaysia and its affiliated International Institute of Islamic Thought and Civilization, both founded in 1983, were generously funded by Saudi Arabia. Thousands of book titles and pamphlets on Islam printed in Saudi Arabia were distributed through a web of Islamic bookstores in Southeast Asia at subsidized, cut-rate prices or offered free through mosques. Not only were Wahhabi doctrines widely disseminated, but the literature that helped to drive the Dakwah movements in Malaysia and Indonesia also included the works of Maulana Maududi, Sayyid Qutb, Maryam Jameelah, and many other polemicists for the Islamist cause. These works were available in vernacular languages as well as English. Besides the theme of the coming Islamic revolution, this literature attacked "Westernization, Zionism, and US imperialism."[26] There was also a concerted effort to denounce "Western science and knowledge," accusing both the natural and social sciences of "Orientalism" by their failure to acknowledge the validity of the "revealed truth" of the Quran. Some of the literature mounted strident rejection of "Western" natural sciences, especially concerning theories of the evolution of species, and challenged the validity of psychology, biology, and archaeology. For the social sciences, invective was addressed against the alleged cultural bias of Western knowledge and its false assumption that Western values are universal. Any historiography that raises questions about the validity of the accounts in the Quran or Bible of Adam and Eve as the origin of humankind has generated impassioned refutation and a demand for censorship of the offending sources.[27]

The effect of the Saudi-sponsored campaign to promote a Wahhabi version of Sunni Islam was to create a division between "liberal Islam" and "literal Islam," with the latter more identified with Saudi perspectives that imparted much more exclusivist and radical perspectives on Islamic politics.[28] In both Indonesia and Malaysia, the propagation of radical Islamist doctrines was associated with a few madrasahs. According to Indonesian government data for 2002, there were 37,362 madrasahs in the country, with a total enrollment of 5.6 million students. Most of these schools were operated privately. Only a small number of these madrasahs became centers for radical Islamist activities and recruiting grounds for jihadi forms of direct-action politics. Yet, with such a large student population, it takes only a few centers of radical madrasahs to create political havoc within the country at large. Some of these more radical madrasahs are openly Wahhabi-inspired.[29] Whether these more radical madrasahs received direct funding from Saudi Arabia has not been revealed, but even if such funds were not provided, the influence of Saudi religious authority and the political message of Wahhabi doctrines are unmistakable.

Those who promoted Wahhabi Islam often claimed that Wahhabi doctrines were conservative and modernist, representing the future version of Islam. Whatever their intention, the Saudi monarchy discovered that some of the main themes of Wahhabi doctrine could be utilized by Saudi critics to support revolutionary and terrorist activities within Saudi Arabia to challenge their rule. These same doctrines and their supporting institutions were also utilized by some terrorist activists in other regions of the Islamic world, including Southeast Asia, to enable them to operate with substantial and sustaining local support.[30]

Afghanistan: The Proving Ground for Jihad

Up through the 1970s, radical Islamic groups had sprung up in all areas of Southeast Asia having significant clusters of Muslims. Most of these militant Islamist groups were inspired and motivated by radical Islamist doctrines emanating from the Middle East or Pakistan, but there was very little mutual support and coordination between them in their exercise of violence and coercive operations. The homegrown characteristic of radical Islamist groups in Southeast Asia began to change as a result of political developments in Afghanistan from 1978 to 2001.

Afghanistan was and remains severely divided by ethnic, tribal, religious, and linguistic differences and by recurring conflicts and foreign invasions. Despite its poverty and underdeveloped status, Afghanistan was making strides to modernize and improve its infrastructure in the post–World War II period. King Mohammad Zahir, who had limited powers because of regional chiefs, headed its political system. Afghanistan's leaders experimented with parliamentary democratic institutions from 1949 to 1952 and from 1963 to 1973, but that experiment ended in a coup led by Muhammad Daoud who deposed the king in 1973. Five years later, Daoud was overthrown in another coup resulting in his death and the death of thirty members of his family.

What followed was a long period of instability. The new ruling junta split into two factions, and the new prime minister Hafizullah Amin faced opposition from about twelve different rebel groups, calling themselves mujahideen and led by local warlords. In the fighting that ensued, about half of the recruits in the Afghan Army either defected to the mujahideen or deserted by crossing into Pakistan or returning to their home villages. Within half a year, the spreading insurrection had driven more than 400,000 refugees into Pakistan and another 60,000 Afghans fled into Iran. Out of desperation, Prime Minister Hafizullah Amin asked for Soviet military assistance in the form of helicopter gunships, improved weapons, and military advisers. Later, as the situation deteriorated even further, he requested direct Soviet assistance to fight rebels in regions adjoining Pakistan.

The Soviet Union was clearly disturbed by the rise of militant Islamic guerrilla movements on its southern borders and decided that it had to intervene. On December 24, 1979, the Soviet Union launched its invasion of Afghanistan with an initial force of 8,000 Soviet troops. Three days later, Amin and many of his supporters were killed, after which Babrak Karmal became prime minister, backed by Soviet troops. Within a few months, the number of Soviet troops in Afghanistan had risen to 50,000.[31]

Alarmed by the extension of Soviet power into Afghanistan, the United States led a three-way Washington-Islamabad-Riyadh alliance to aid the Afghan guerrillas that were resisting the Soviet-backed Afghan government in Kabul. The Afghan rebels had been badly divided, but the Soviet invasion provided the catalyst for the formation of a seven-party Islamic Alliance of Afghan Mujahideen (IAAM), which became the prime recipient of assistance from the US-Saudi-Pakistan coalition of unofficial donors. The United States provided funding, advanced weapons training, military equipment, and supplies, distributed through its Central Intelligence Agency (CIA). Pakistan's Inter-Services Intelligence Directorate (ISI) provided bases, training, and support services. Saudi Arabia, acting through its intelligence services, the Istikhabarat, created a large number of "religious charities" and "humanitarian assistance organizations" that transferred hundreds of millions of dollars from Saudi and Muslim communities to fund the Afghan mujahideen and to provide minimal support for the Afghan refugee population in Pakistan. Saudi Arabia also sponsored the recruitment and support of volunteers who came from across the Muslim world to fight the Soviet forces supporting the Republic of Afghanistan.[32]

To fulfill Saudi commitments to the Afghan resistance, Saudi Prince Turki al-Feisal, who headed the Saudi intelligence services, asked Osama bin Laden to recruit volunteers for the anti-Soviet jihad.[33] Rather than tour the Muslim world to promote recruiting operations, in January 1980, Osama moved to Peshawar on the Pakistan frontier to establish "guest houses" and training facilities for volunteers to the mujahideen. With the arrival of new recruits, Osama organized a 17,000-man Arab Brigade, and spent some of his own fortune to purchase supplies and weapons.

The United States aided the Afghan resistance by providing weapons, technical training, and financial support. When Soviet forces began using helicopter gunships to attack mujahideen forces, the United States provided Blowpipe and Stinger shoulder-fired anti-aircraft missiles to the mujahideen, who downed sixty helicopters with these new weapons in the first year of use. In addition, the United States supplied heavy equipment and technical assistance to construct an enormous underground complex of tunnels to house a fully operational military base near Khost, close to the Pakistan border. Other similar complexes of caves were constructed at strategic locations to provide mujahideen forces with bases protected against aerial assault.[34] By 1989, the overall cost of the nine-year Afghan war totaled for its three foreign sponsors more than US$5 billion per year.[35] A large portion of those funds was transferred to Osama bin Laden's Arab Brigade.

Al Qaeda: Origins and Support Network

Shortly after Osama bin Laden arrived in Peshawar in 1980, he became closely associated with Abdullah Azzam and Ayman Muhammad Rabi' al-Zawahiri, who enabled Osama to build his network and shape his ideology and strategy. Azzam was a member of the Jordanian Muslim Brotherhood who had earned a doctorate in Islamic jurisprudence at Al-Azhar University in Cairo. From there he went to King Abdulaziz University in Jeddah but was expelled in 1979 for his militant Islamic activism, after which he secured a position at the International Islamic University in Islamabad, Pakistan. With his command of Islamic theological discourse, Azzam formulated the polemical arguments for militant jihad as an obligation for all able-bodied Muslims to volunteer in the fight against the Soviets. In 1984, Azzam and Osama bin Laden jointly founded the Afghan Service Bureau (Maktab al Khidmat lil-Mujahidin al-Arab, MaK) to recruit, indoctrinate, and train the many thousands of recruits who were coming through Pakistan to participate in the Afghan jihad.[36] By 1988 and 1989, differences between the two began to emerge. At issue were control over training bases and management of the large financial assets coming in from donors. Another issue in dispute was whether the mujahideen should launch a global jihad to fight for all "oppressed Muslims." Osama supported the view of globalized jihad, while Azzam did not wish to challenge jahiliyya regimes, such as Egypt or Saudi Arabia, that were actively supporting the mujahideen effort in Afghanistan.

The conflict and power struggle between Osama and Azzam came to an abrupt end when Azzam and his two sons were killed by a remote-controlled bomb on November 24, 1989, while they were driving to a mosque in Peshawar. Osama extolled Azzam and never criticized him in public, but subsequent interrogations of captured Al Qaeda members revealed that Osama had personally ordered the killing of Azzam because Osama suspected that Azzam had collaborated with the CIA. With Azzam out of the picture, Osama bin Laden became undisputed emir of MaK.[37]

The assassination of Azzam marked a turning point in the rise to power of Osama bin Laden and a shift in his political alliance with a new associate—Ayman al-Zawahiri who was was born in 1951 into an established and well-respected Egyptian family. At a young age, he joined the Muslim Brotherhood and was arrested by the police. After his release, he attended Cairo University, where he completed a master's degree in surgery. Two years later, following the assassination of President Anwar Sadat of Egypt on October 6, 1981, Zawahiri was arrested again, along with hundreds of others, and was charged and convicted of being an accomplice to those who perpetrated the assassination. After three years in an Egyptian prison where he was subjected to interrogation and torture, he was released. Two years later, in 1984, Zawahiri proceeded to Peshawar, Pakistan, where he worked with the Red Crescent Society treating wounded mujahideen. In that capacity, he met Osama bin Laden and the two formed a lasting alliance. When Zawahiri arrived in Pakistan, he may have come with a contingent of Egyptian asylum-seekers, since he became the leader of a group called the Egyptian Islamic Jihad that later engineered the bombing that killed Azzam.

Although Ayman al-Zawahiri became Osama bin Laden's close political ally, he also retained his leadership of Egyptian Islamic Jihad. What Zawahiri brought to Osama bin Laden's leadership echelon was exceptional organizational talent, a skill at writing polemical tracts from a radical Islamist perspective, and a capacity to appeal to educated Muslims who harbored resentments or grievances against the West, particularly the United States. In his writings, he projected a vision of a global struggle between Islam and the West, both in economic and political realms. Even before Zawahiri had joined Osama bin Laden's inner circle, the concept of Al Qaeda—"The Base"—had been formulated. It began as little more than a set of computer files of intelligence information on mujahideen recruits from around the world who had been trained and indoctrinated at the facilities operated by MaK. Over time, Al Qaeda was transformed into an intertwined cluster of terrorist cells, a network of business enterprises and money-laundering schemes, a network of affiliated "humanitarian" and welfare organizations, and a source of ideological propaganda disseminated to Muslims throughout the world. While Ayman al-Zawahiri was not solely responsible for all these activities, his coordination of these enterprises reflected his vision of a global organization capable of mobilizing and linking existing radical Islamist groups. The objective was to create a mass political movement that could act for and defend the interests of Muslims all over the world. This idealized vision became the motivating impetus for Al Qaeda.[38]

Al Qaeda's Sudan Interlude and the Second Afghan Campaign

After nine years of war with the Afghan mujahideen and the loss of 14,500 soldiers, the Soviet Union was eager to find a way out of Afghanistan. Peace talks sponsored by the UN finally led to an agreement between the Soviet Union, the Afghanistan Republic, and Pakistan in April 1988 for a cessation of hostilities. The last Soviet troops withdrew from Afghanistan in February 1989. As part of that agreement, US and Saudi subsidies ended for the Afghan mujahideen. Osama bin Laden returned to Saudi Arabia, where he was greeted as a hero. Even so, he was embittered by the termination of funding from Saudi sources for his mujahideen operations. He asked for and received an audience before King Fahd and his advisers to plead the case for continued funding for the Afghan mujahideen. King Fahd rejected his request, since that was counter to agreements with the Soviet Union for withdrawal of their forces from Afghanistan. Outspoken in his criticism of the monarchy, Osama rapidly fell from favor with the Saudi establishment and had to consider exile.[39]

About this time, on June 30, 1989, a coup had installed an Islamist regime in Sudan headed by Hassan al-Beshir and inspired by Sheikh Hassan al-Turabi as the organizer of the coup d'état. After receiving the sponsorship and asylum guarantees from al-Turabi, in December 1991, Osama bin Laden moved to Khartoum with a contingent of Afghan Arabs who became his personal guard. From this location, Osama formed trade and construction companies that also were used as fronts to purchase arms and promote terrorist movements. His experience in Afghanistan and the rejection by the Saudi monarchy of his plea for continued support had re-ignited his commitment to global jihad against what he considered Islam's enemies.

Meanwhile, Osama's close associate, Ayman al-Zawahiri, also left Afghanistan, perhaps for Denmark and Switzerland, where he lived incognito. By 1991, he was back in Egypt, where he published a tract called *The Bitter Harvest*, condemning the Muslim Brotherhood and justifying worldwide jihad. In 1992, fearing detection and capture by the police, Zawahiri fled to Sudan to join Osama, and by 1998 he formally incorporated his Egyptian Islamic Jihad into Al Qaeda.[40] The two most formidable global jihadists had joined forces once again.

In its new exile sanctuary, Osama and his Al Qaeda organization were revived. Besides building and operating twenty-three terrorist training camps and sponsoring terrorist groups abroad, Al Qaeda also infiltrated key ministries of the Sudanese government. From Sudan, Al Qaeda organized the first bombing of the World Trade Center on February 26, 1993, which led to six deaths but did not destroy the building. In October 1993, Al Qaeda was suspected of involvement in the Mogadishu attack on US Marines engaged in a peacekeeping mission to Somalia. The Saudis must have monitored Osama's activities, because they deprived him of Saudi citizenship in February 1994. Two years later, Al Qaeda agents mounted separate attempts to assassinate US president Bill Clinton, Philippine president Fidel Marcos, and Egyptian president Hosni Mubarak. All three assassination attempts failed, but each left a trail of evidence pointing to Al Qaeda.[41] As a consequence of these persistent attacks, Egypt, Saudi Arabia, and the United States pressured Sudan to arrest and extradite Osama bin Laden to the United States or to Saudi Arabia. Anticipating possible arrest, in May 1996, Osama quickly decided to flee by air to Jalalabad, Pakistan, with about 100 Afghan Arab fighters as part of his entourage. Within a year, he moved his operations to the cave complex of Tora Bora in Afghanistan.[42]

In the seven years since Osama bin Laden had last been in Afghanistan, the earlier mujahideen had split into warring rival factions, with the main contingent calling themselves Taliban—meaning "seekers of knowledge" or "students." This name reflected the influence of a large contingent of recruits from the Deoband madrasahs in Pakistan, where many of the Afghan refugees attended school and where they had received both radical religious instruction in Wahabbi doctrines and military training in weaponry and jihad tactics. The Deoband madrasahs were receiving generous funding from Saudi Arabia, which also provided significant funding for the Taliban. Although Pakistan expressed neutrality in Afghan affairs, its ISI had close links with the Taliban, providing them with weapons and financial support. When Osama returned to the scene, the Taliban were in the process of laying siege to the last vestiges of the Republic of Afghanistan centered on Kabul. With a militia force of about 25,000, heavily aided by supplies and manpower from Pakistan, the Taliban captured Kabul on September 27, 1996. Shortly, thereafter, an agreement was reached between the Taliban leader, Mullah Muhammad Omar and Osama bin Laden. The Taliban provided sanctuary for Al Qaeda and Osama made a *bay'a* pledge recognizing the absolute authority of Mullah Omar as "Commander of the Faithful." As part of the agreement, Osama promised to remain discreet about his opposition to the Saudi regime, which, at the time, was providing generous funding to the Taliban.[43] After its victory over the Republic of Afghanistan, the Taliban gained diplomatic recognition from only three countries: Saudi Arabia, Pakistan, and the United Arab Emirates.

Following its capture of Kabul, the Taliban mounted a campaign to capture all of Afghanistan. By 1997, the Taliban had extended its authority over almost 85 percent of Afghanistan, with the opposition confined to the Northern Alliance occupying northeastern Afghanistan. Al Qaeda formed a guerrilla unit of 1,500 to 2,000 Arab fighters organized as Brigade 055, which was integrated into the Taliban forces as an elite unit.[44] Between August 1996 and February 1998, four fatwas were issued by Al Qaeda endorsing suicide bombing and proclaiming that all Muslims have "a duty to kill Americans and their allies in any country wherever possible" in order to save the "lands of Islam" from occupation by the "Crusader-Zionist alliance."[45]

Al Qaeda followed up these pronouncements by engineering a series of dramatic bombings of US targets. On August 7, 1998, the US embassies in Nairobi, Kenya, and Dar as Salaam, in Tanzania, became targets of near simultaneous bombs that killed 227 people, 12 of them Americans. On October 12, 2000, two suicide bombers detonated a small skiff laden with high explosives next to the USS *Cole* in Aden harbor, killing 17 sailors and nearly sinking that high-technology warship. Finally, on September 11, 2001, the coordinated hijacking of four long-range commercial airliners, which were turned into flying bombs, succeeded in destroying the twin towers of the World Trade Center in New York and demolishing a sector of the Pentagon. The fourth plane headed to an unknown target, but crashed in Pennsylvania after a failed attempt by some passengers to retake control of the aircraft from the hijackers.[46]

These dramatic terrorist events were all widely covered in press accounts throughout the world and have been described and analyzed in great detail in many books. Rather than recount these events and the responses that they elicited, what is of greater relevance for this study is the extension of Al Qaeda's reach into Southeast Asia. From its newly revived operational base in Afghanistan, Al Qaeda began implementing its ambitious plans for worldwide jihad.

Al Qaeda's Southeast Asian Operations

From the location of its training bases and the pattern of its pre-9/11 terrorist attacks, Al Qaeda appeared to be but one of many Middle East–based terrorist organizations. That impresson provided useful cover for its involvement with Southeast Asia and helps to explain why many political leaders in Southeast Asia were so slow to acknowledge its presence in their region. All Southeast Asian countries with substantial Muslim populations have large, unprotected, porous borders that facilitate an active trade in smuggling, including goods, contraband, weapons, and people. The political turmoil in the region in the wake of the 1998 financial crisis generated widespread discontent and grievances that could be exploited for jihadi operations. Activist agents could operate with little risk of detection by concealment within Muslim populations, relying on the hospitality that is traditionally extended by one Muslim to another. Finally, the Muslim banking sector in Southeast Asia was very poorly regulated and when combined with the traditional *hawala* system of money lending and black-market currency traders, the transfer of money from anonymous foreign sources was easily accomplished without elaborate money-laundering schemes. All these factors created a favorable environment for concealing the terrorist operations of militant Islam.[47]

In all of Muslim Southeast Asia, privately supported Islamic schools—pesantren and madrasahs—operate beyond effective government control or supervision. During the first Afghan War against the Soviet intervention, many of these schools had become recruiting centers to secure volunteers for the Afghan mujahideen. When these volunteers returned from Afghanistan, some of these schools were turned into centers for the propagation of radical Islamist doctrines and as recruiting centers for radical Islamist organizations that were founded in the years after 1987. Some idea of the size of this potential constituency can be gleaned from the number and the student population of these Islamic schools. In Malaysia's state of Kelantan in 2001, there were 92 madrasahs with a student population of 40,000. Fewer Islamic schools operated in other Malaysian states, but statistics on their number are not available. In Indonesia, 37,362 madrasahs were in operation in 2001, with 81 percent being privately run and funded. These privately run Indonesian madrasahs served a student population of about 5.6 million. In the Philippines, 1,565 privately operated madrasahs served an undisclosed number of students.[48]

About 1984, Osama bin Laden established the first training camps for mujahideen recruits who came from across the Muslim world to participate in the war against the Soviet presence in Afghanistan. Altogether, some 35,000 recruits from thirty-five different countries joined the mujahideen in the years from 1982 to 1992. How many attended and were trained at about forty military camps first sponsored by MaK and later by Al Qaeda is a matter of much speculation. Western intelligence agencies have produced various estimates ranging from 10,000 to 110,000 recruits between the years 1989 and October 2001.[49] While the number of volunteers recruited into Al Qaeda was much smaller, perhaps numbering about 3,000 in the years from 1988 to 1993, Al Qaeda collected information on committed recruits who joined the Afghan mujahideen. After the anti-Soviet campaign ended in 1989, most mujahideen volunteers returned to their home communities, where they could be contacted and recruited once again for Al Qaeda's post-1993 jihadi agenda. In the years from 1993 to 2002, Al Qaeda is estimated to have expanded its membership to between 5,000 and 12,000, with branches in some sixty countries. From fragmentary evidence, it appears that more than 1,000 recruits from Southeast Asia attended MaK and Al Qaeda training camps before joining the Afghan mujahideen. In addition, between 600 and 800 foreign students who enrolled at Deobandi-run madrasahs in Pakistan came from Southeast Asia. Because of visa-free transit between Muslim-majority countries, immigration records could not be used by security services to track the movements of Al Qaeda volunteers or Deobandi students.

When Al Qaeda began to extend its reach into Southeast Asia about 1990, it did so with utmost secrecy and with the appropriate cover of business, educational, or humanitarian welfare activities. Whatever might have been the precise number of cells and the size of Al Qaeda its membership operating in Southeast Asia can never be known. As part of its strategy to become allied with and infiltrate existing radical Islamist organizations, Al Qaeda, in 1998, established the World Islamic Front for Jihad Against Crusaders and Jews at the same time that Zawahiri merged his Egyptian Islamic Jihad into the Al Qaeda structure.[50] In the Southeast Asian setting, the organizational tactic of operating through a network of local and regional Islamist organizations allowed Al Qaeda to retain a very low visible profile to avoid heightened surveillance from police and government security agencies.[51]

Jemaah Islamiyah

In 1971, two Islamic *ustaz*, Abu Bakar Ba'asyir and Abdullah Sungkar, opened a madrasah boarding school in the village of Ngruki, just east of Surakarta (Solo), Java, entitled Al Mukmin (The Faithful). Both founders were born in Indonesia to Arabs of Yemeni origin, and both considered themselves following in the ideological footsteps of the founder of Darul Islam—S. M. Kartosuwirjo. At Al Mukmin, the literalist doctrines of salafiya Wahhabism were taught, with an emphasis on the complete implementation of Sharia law and establishment of uncompromised Muslim rule through jihad against non-Muslims.[52] To further their cause, Ba'asyir and Sungkar began recruiting previous members of Darul Islam. By 1971, this assembly of reconstituted survivors of earlier radical Islamist causes adopted the name Komando Jihad and the Al Mukmin madrasah became its key recruiting center. The purpose of the organization was to initiate a revolutionary struggle to establish an Islamic State for all of Islamic Southeast Asia.[53]

In 1978, the Al Mukmin madrasah began operating a pirate radio station to propagate radical doctrines calling for jihad against non-Muslims and "misguided or insincere" Muslims. After some robberies and murders were traced to Komando Jihad members, Suharto ordered the arrest of Sungkar and Ba'asyir, and Komando Jihad was banned. Both men were imprisoned and after four years were finally brought to trial and convicted. They were sentenced to nine years imprisonment, but on appeal, their sentence was reduced to four years and they were released in 1982 for time served. Fearing re-arrest, both men fled to Malaysia in 1985, where they established another pesantren located in Johor. By then, the Afghan War was well under way, and with heightened sympathies of Muslims for the plight of victims of that war, they generated a flow of recruits for the Afghan mujahideen. With ample financial support from Arab-based Islamic "charities" and from Al Qaeda, Ba'asyir established a second pesantren on the outskirts of the city of Johor Bahru. From these locations, they continued to build a network of supporters, including returning veterans from the Afghan mujahideen.

In the early 1990s, Abdullah Sungkar traveled to Afghanistan to visit and encourage the growing number of students who arrived at the reestablished jihad training camps operated in Afghanistan by Al Qaeda within the sanctuary provided by the Taliban. While in Afghanistan, Sungkar met Osama bin Laden and other senior Al Qaeda leaders. At that meeting, he made a bay'a pledge of allegiance to Osama, which act may have marked the origins of Jemaah Islamiyah (JI). In return, Jemaah Islamiyah received regular funds from Al Qaeda sources.

The membership of Jemaah Islamiyah was composed of ideologically committed recruits who were organized into clandestine *fiah* (cells). These converts were highly trained to carry out assault and bombing operations and were instructed to remain in clandestine "sleeper cells" that could be called upon for heroic acts of jihad at some later date. Each fiah was grouped under a superior lieutenant who commanded a *mantiqi* (division) that had responsibility for JI operations in a defined region. Jemaah Islamiyah allocated its resources to four operational regions: (1) Malaysia, South Thailand, and Singapore; (2) Java and Sumatra; (3) the Philippines, Brunei, East Malaysia, Kalimantan, Sulawesi, and Maluku; and (4) Papua and Australia. It established active cells in all these regions with the distribution of funding and coordination of operations assigned to Abu Bakar Ba'asyir as emir at the apex of this command structure. To serve the operational training requirements of these four divisions, JI established a training camp in Negri Sembilan, Malaysia, and sent some of its recruits to Al Qaeda bases in Afghanistan or to training camps in Mindanao operated by the Moro Islamic Liberation Front.[54]

Jemaah Islamiyah's stated ultimate objective was the creation of a single Islamic regional state to embrace all Muslim-majority areas of Southeast Asia. Its more immediate goals, however, were to challenge and overthrow the "jahiliyya regimes" in Malaysia and Indonesia. The political turmoil that accompanied the fall of Suharto in May of 1998 opened a window of opportunity for Jemaah Islamiyah just at the time when its network of agents and cells had become well established. Political restrictions were relaxed in Indonesia at that time, and radical Islamic politics gained an aura of respectability and acceptance as part of the Reformasi movement.[55] In 1999, Indonesia offered amnesty for religious dissidents who had been exiled during the New Order era. Sungkar, who suffered from a heart condition, was eager to return to Indonesia. With some trepidation, both Ba'asyir and Sungkar moved back to their Al Mukmin pesantren in Ngruki village near Surakarta, Java. Upon their return, they became actively engaged in establishing collaborating links with other radical Islamist groups that had become energized by the political turmoil of Suharto's departure. On October 23, shortly after his arrival in Indonesia, Sungkar died in Bogor from heart failure. His death left Ba'asyir at the ideological center of the Jemaah Islamiyah movement. Leaders of JI met in Solo the following month to elect Ba'asyir as the new emir to act as the spiritual leader of the movement.[56]

In the post-Suharto political environment, Jemaah Islamiyah's political activities could be separated from its revolutionary jihadi agenda. The former could be pursued openly while the latter remained concealed and clandestine. In 2000, Ba'asyir founded the Mujahideen Council of Indonesia (Majelis Mujahidin Indonesia, MMI), which was self-proclaimed as a "civil society" NGO "committed to implementing Sharia law through a democratic process." The MMI was designed to serve as an overarching coordinating body to unite militant Islamist groups for political action. At the same time, its links with radical or subversive organizations were vigorously denied, and accusations to the contrary were attributed to conspiracy theories emanating from "foreign intelligence" sources. The fact that the MMI board was composed almost entirely of radical Islamists, some of whom had earlier been convicted of terrorist or subversive activities, should have attracted the attention of Indonesian security and police authorities. Apparently, this never happened until the Bali bombing attack on October 12, 2002. The MMI recruited about 100 small radical Islamist groups under its umbrella structure and openly operated some thirty branches throughout Indonesia. Although its political activities were publicized, it was careful not to keep membership lists, so its supporters could not be traced. It also became the recipient of substantial sums of money from Arab-based charities and "humanitarian" organizations, such as the Islamic International Relief Organization, Al Haramain, and the World Assembly of Muslim Youth.[57]

Southeast Asian Responses to 9/11

The events of September 11, 2001, created a cataclysmic change in the politics of the United States and produced dramatic political tremors and aftershocks in Southeast Asia. Images were beamed around the world of the burning and collapse of the twin towers of the World Trade Center and the Pentagon. What had been designed as a coordinated attack by four hijacked passenger jets was partially thwarted when the fourth jet crashed in Pennsylvania. Even so, that single coordinated attack produced the most catastrophic damage of any single attack on the United States in its history. The final death toll was believed to be 3,025 people, and the economic fiscal impact just for New York City during the first year after the attack was calculated to be a financial loss of from $82.8 billion to $94.8 billion.[58]

Public reactions in Southeast Asia to the 9/11 events generated rather diverse responses. At the official level, all the governments in the area expressed shock and dismay over these attacks and promised cooperation with the United States to address the threat of terrorism. None of the statements of condolences from Southeast Asian governments made any acknowledgment that the events of 9/11 were linked in any way with organizations or activities originating in Southeast Asia. For Malaysia and Indonesia, the public debate turned on the question of whether the United States was partially responsible for "inciting" terrorist attacks because of its Middle East policies, its "unilateralism," and its indifference when Muslims become the victims of oppression. Some radical Muslims attributed the attack on the World Trade Center to be organized by the Israeli Secret Service and the CIA as a tactic to assure US support for Israel.[59] In a more muted response, Prime Minister Mahathir gave a speech on terrorism two months after the 9/11 attacks. In that speech he argued that the campaign of the United States to eliminate terrorism would ultimately fail unless the "causes of terrorism were removed." He argued that "the principal cause is the Palestine issue. Israelis believe they have a historical claim to the land of Palestine." He made no mention of Osama bin Laden's earlier speech threatening all Americans. Instead, he accused the United States of being ultimately responsible for the failure of peace in the Middle East and the denial of legitimate Arab and Muslim aspirations for Palestine.[60] Although Prime Minister Mahathir made no public commitment to the US "war on terror," Malaysia had previously taken firm measures to arrest and detain members of radical Muslim groups who threatened internal security within Malaysia. Noted for his blunt and outspoken views, Mahathir combined public criticism of US policies in the Middle East with a determination to eliminate any radical terrorist cells in Malaysia, whether they were homegrown or sponsored from abroad. Mahathir also utilized the 9/11 crisis to adroitly undermine and isolate Malaysia's domestic Islamist opposition, represented by PAS leaders, whom he depicted as dangerous and irresponsible extremists.[61]

When the United States began its military campaign in Afghanistan against the Taliban regime and its Al Qaeda cohorts, anti-US protests escalated both in Malaysia and Indonesia. PAS called for a jihad against the United States, and PAS president Ustaz Fadzil Noor called for a total boycott of US goods and services as well as for Malaysia to send troops to Afghanistan to resist the US attack on the Taliban. In support of these demands, PAS organized a large demonstration in front of the US Embassy in Kuala Lumpur with signs proclaiming "destroy the American kafirs and Jews."[62] The Ulama Association of Malaysia also issued a fatwa condemning the war against the Afghan Taliban regime and forbidding Malaysian Muslims from cooperating with the United States. Prime Minister Mahathir also opposed any US intervention in Afghanistan. He argued: "If the Americans are really waging a war against terrorism, why don't they attack Israel, who are terrorists against the Palestinians?"[63]

At the rhetorical level, Malaysian authorities were outspoken in their criticism of the US war on terrorism. Yet, when it came to action, Malaysia was effective and committed to apprehending identified terrorists and their supporters, but to do so as an exclusive Malaysian operation, untainted by any overt identification with US policies. Malaysia and the United States did agree to establish collaborative ties, including the implementation of an integrated system of sharing intelligence information on the activities and presence of known and suspected terrorist operators. Malaysian citizens were warned against volunteering to go to Afghanistan. The government imposed visa restrictions on visitors from Afghanistan, Iran, and Iraq. In November 2001, Malaysia announced the implementation of antiterrorism legislation. In October, Malaysian government funding for Malaysia's 2,160 private Islamic schools was terminated because two-thirds of those schools were accused of propagating Islamic extremism. A year later, in December 2002, Mahathir announced a plan to "end extremism" by controlling the curriculum of private Islamic madrasah schools with the objective of gradually integrating these schools and their 15,000 students into the public system of national schools.[64] In its campaign against members of identified terrorist organizations, by January 2003, Malaysian authorities had arrested a total of about seventy suspects under the Internal Security Act, which provides for detention without recourse to trial. Although Mahathir's forthright criticisms of US policy continued, he also authorized collaborative arrangements with the United States to prevent militant groups sponsoring or planning terrorism from operating within Malaysian borders.[65]

In comparison to Malaysia, Indonesia's responses to the challenge of terrorism evolved with a markedly contrasting scenario. Megawati Sukarnoputri became president of Indonesia only six weeks before 9/11 and had been invited to Washington to meet President George W. Bush before the 9/11 terrorist attack changed the political landscape. Her visit continued on schedule, with talks that began on September 19 and concluded with an agreement for Indonesia to support the campaign against terrorism and the United States to provide an aid package and other benefits to Indonesia totaling $630 million.[66] Upon her return to Indonesia, she was confronted by anti-American demonstrations and criticism from radicalized Muslims that she had "sold out to Islam's enemy." Some of the opposition to Indonesia's commitment to cooperate with the United States in its "war on terrorism" was orchestrated by Indonesia's vice president, Hamzah Haz, leader of Indonesia's largest Muslim party, PPP, and a long-time political rival to Megawati. Unlike some Muslim radicals who attributed the 9/11 attacks to the CIA, Hamzah Haz considered the attacks to be justified and he believed they might help the United States "atone for its sins."[67]

Another prominent and vocal critic of Indonesian cooperation with the United States was Din Syamsuddin, secretary-general of Indonesia's Council of Ulamas (Majelis Ulama Indonesia) and vice president of Muhammadiyah. Under his leadership, MUI issued a declaration to Muslims of the world to wage jihad against the United States, just as Megawati was returning from the United States. Din Syamsuddin attracted much public attention for his fiery sermons calling for jihad against the United States and his speeches castigating President Bush.[68] When US military operations in Afghanistan began, the Indonesian government issued a statement expressing concern, noting that the United States had stated its intentions were to apprehend terrorists and not as an act of hostility against Islam. The statement called for the United States to minimize civilian casualties, asked for UN involvement, and warned Indonesians not to express their concerns by actions contrary to the law. The next day, the Islamic Defenders Front (FPI) sponsored large anti-American protests in front of Parliament. Police dispersed the protesters with a show of force that produced injuries on both sides. Following these events, the anti-American rhetoric by prominent politicians became more muted, with greater public concern expressed about the cost to Indonesia of actions that would further damage the Indonesian economy and drive away needed foreign investment. The leaders of the two largest Islamic parties, Nahdlatul Ulama and Muhammadiyah, both rejected calls for jihad, but these more moderate responses to the war on terrorism were overshadowed by the focus of domestic media on the actions and statements of anti-American activists.[69] The relative silence of moderate Muslim voices contributed to the political uncertainty that undermined Indonesia's slow economic recovery from the depths of the 1999 political crisis.

Leading a fragmented and unstable coalition, President Megawati became cautious and timid in pursuing suspected terrorists. She expressed criticism of US operations in Afghanistan, and that criticism intensified when the United States initiated its "regime change" operations in Iraq in April 2003.[70] With anti-US passions at a high level and with an upsurge of support for militant Islamic groups, Megawati was unwilling to take decisive action to check the activities of various groups engaged in domestic vigilante operations, such as Laskar Jihad, Laskar Pembala Islam, and Gerakan Pemuda Islam. Even after the devastating bombing in Bali on October 12, 2002, that killed more than 200 people and wounded 300 others, President Megawati was hesitant to take action against militant Islamic organizations because of fears of a potential Islamic backlash. Instead, she chose to let the police and courts deal with the perpetrators through the regular proceedings of civil justice.[71]

The Jihad Militias: Riding the Aftermath of East Timor

Events in East Timor during 1998 and 1999 generated within Indonesia increasing Muslim antipathy against non-Muslims and intense criticism of Western powers. Opposition to Australia and the United States became especially virulent for their support for East Timor independence following the outcome of the East Timor plebiscite that produced a decisive majority for the independence option. Most Indonesians believed these matters were within the domestic jurisdiction of Indonesia. Public attitudes in Indonesia became further intensified when international organizations intervened and after Australia, New Zealand, and the United States provided material and military support to the East Timor independence movement. A very brief summary of that conflict will provide some perspective on the political environment in Indonesia that generated the impetus for the formation of jihadi militia units claiming to be protecting Islam against the threats from international and domestic kafir forces.

In 1975 Indonesia invaded the Portuguese colony of East Timor and incorporated it into Indonesia as its twenty-seventh province. What followed was a long and protracted struggle with East Timorese nationalists who supported a small guerrilla force led by Xanana Gusmo dedicated to creating an independent East Timor state. During this struggle, the Indonesian Armed Forces imposed years of oppression, torture, and massacres against any supporters of East Timorese independence. Although Gusmo was eventually captured and put in prison, periodic nonviolent protests continued to be staged by independence supporters. An extremely brutal massacre of unarmed demonstrators in November 1991 attracted international attention and condemnations that were followed by an investigation conducted by the UN Commission on Human Rights. Eventually, international pressure on Indonesia built up to such a level that President Habibie agreed to permit a plebiscite in East Timor on the issue of independence. Habibie may have assumed that the large number of non-Timorese Indonesian transmigrants who had been induced to settle in East Timor would tip the plebiscite balance to support continued Indonesian rule.

The referendum on independence was held in December 1999, closely monitored by international observers. Despite massive coercive intimidation of East Timorese voters from pro-Indonesian paramilitary units supported and armed by the Indonesian Armed Forces, when the vote was counted, the referendum supporting East Timor independence passed by 78.5 percent of the votes. In retaliation, the Indonesian Armed Forces and their paramilitary preman thugs staged a long campaign of brutality. Together these forces initiated a scorched-earth campaign, killing some 7,000 civilians, burning towns and villages, and organizing the forced displacement of one-third of the East Timorese population across the border to West Timor where Timorese refugees were interned in camps and held as virtual political hostages. Although the international community was rather slow to respond, eventually dramatic action on the part of the UN, followed by the presence of an international peacekeeping force led by Australia and New Zealand, gradually restored order. These international forces enabled an independent East Timor government to be formed, which began the rebuilding of the newly independent country.[72]

Because the East Timorese are largely Christian and were inspired by the moral leadership of the Catholic Church, the successful campaign for the independence of East Timor, despite overwhelming odds, generated in Indonesia a backlash of hostility against Indonesian Christians, especially among Indonesia's radicalized nationalists and Islamist elements. These events in Timor were viewed as a serious defeat for Indonesia, especially in Java. In that political climate, the "green faction" of the Indonesian Army, combined with its affiliated preman gangs that had ravaged East Timor during that conflict, now gained increased public support. This new political-military alliance combined ultranationalism with an Islamist ideology to justify extreme measures to suppress any separatist movements and to intimidate domestic critics and ethnic or religious minorities.

These same East Timor events also emboldened Indonesian Christians living in areas where they constituted local majorities. Fearful of their treatment within Indonesia, some Christians began to contemplate a political campaign for independence and to consider how they might defend themselves against the ruthless tactics of preman gangs tacitly or openly supported by green faction army units against non-Muslim minorities. The largest Christian-majority enclaves in Indonesia are in the eastern islands known in the West as the Moluccas, and now called by Indonesians Maluku. Some Maluku Christians began discussing the prospects for an independent Christian Republic in some part of Maluku before the East Timor referendum had been held. The large influx of Muslim transmigrants from other areas of Indonesia had increased ethnic and religious tensions. A pamphlet that called upon Christians to rise against Muslims was circulated in November 1999 among Muslims in Ternate, probably by provocateurs. In response, Muslims in Ternate went on a rampage of killing and burning that caused between 10,000 and 20,000 Christians and Indonesians of Chinese origins to flee to the predominantly Christian-majority city of Manado at the northern tip of Sulawesi. With the flare-up of ethnic conflict, the Christian communities rapidly organized a poorly equipped paramilitary force that was associated with a political movement called the Moluccas Sovereignty Front (FKM). These violent clashes provided an opportunity for the small number of Islamic radicals who preached jihad to mobilize supporters and transform their militant rhetoric into action.

In the late 1990s, just as the Maluku violence began to erupt, Jemaah Islamiyah issued a strident message calling for the formation of jihadi units capable of defending Islam. One of those who responded to this message was Jafar Umar Thalib, who had studied in Pakistan and later volunteered for the Afghan mujahideen to serve from 1987 to 1989. After his return to Java, he established a pesantren on the outskirts of Yogyakarta. In January 2000, he founded Laskar Jihad as a paramilitary organization that rapidly grew in numbers to a force of about 3,000 fighters. They trained at a private camp near Bogor that was secretly supported by units of the Indonesian Army. Within two months after its creation, Laskar Jihad fighters went to Maluku to join the attacks against Indonesian Christian communities in that province.

Another of JI's affiliated organizations was called Laskar Mujahideen. It was founded in January 2000 and led by Abu Jabril, who was later identified as a key Al Qaeda operative who distributed substantial sums of money from Middle Eastern charities to other radical Islamic groups. Laskar Mujahideen recruited from the Al Mukmin Ngruki network and was able to field a force of about 500 fighters for guerrilla warfare and assassination attacks against Christian clergy in Poso and Maluku. In June 2001, after Malaysian authorities arrested Jabril, Laskar Mujahideen went underground and may have been disbanded.[73]

In South Sulawesi during the late 1990s, a group called the Committee for the Enforcement of Islamic Law (KPSI) was formed to promote special autonomy for that province and called for the full implementation of Sharia law and a government under the direct control of an unelected Council of Ulamas. The KPSI had about 3,000 members who were organized for "eight fields of struggle," including a paramilitary formation called Laskar Jundullah, led by Agus Dwikarna who was also vice-chair of KPSI. Laskar Jundullah recruited primarily from South Sulawesi, but it also received recruits from Jemaah Islamiyah who joined to get military training. While the number of recruits in Laskar Jundullah was relatively small, they were actively engaged in the extended violence in Maluku and Sulawesi.[74]

When the conflict first erupted in the Maluku province, an offshoot of Laskar Jundullah known as the Action Committee for Crisis Response (Kompak) sent a video team to "document Christian attacks on Muslims."[75] They returned with graphic scenes of violence purporting to be "evidence" of Christians attacking Muslims. Primed with this video, Laskar Jihad organized a massive rally in January 2000 in Yogyakarta, followed by another in Jakarta attended by tens of thousands. Speakers at these rallies issued public declarations that Maluku Christians were *kafir harbi* (belligerent infidels), thus invoking an obligation for Muslims "to wage jihad unto death" against these mortal enemies, the Christian conspirators. At the Jakarta rally, Amien Rais of the PPP and Indonesian vice president Hamzah Haz both endorsed the call for jihad in Sulawesi and Maluku. The allegations of unprovoked attacks against Muslims, combined with claims that Christians were receiving foreign money and arms from abroad, gained wide public support in Indonesia for the Laskar Jihad campaign. The power of this message tended to paralyze political moderates and discredit pluralism. Although the government pledged that the Laskar Jihad militia would be prevented from traveling to Maluku, 3,000 of their well-armed militia proceeded unhindered to Maluku, traveling by commercial ferry from Surabaya. This militia had been secretly trained and armed by Kostrad (Army Strategic Command), which at the time was headed by the former Suharto cabinet member and noted "green-faction" Islamist leader General Djadja Suparman. The weapons for Laskar Jihad were transported separately and were picked up by the militia upon arrival in Maluku.[76] With later reinforcements, their number increased to about 5,000 in the Maluku region. At that time, Indonesian president Abdurrahman Wahid was politically vulnerable and was unwilling to intervene to stop the killings, despite his earlier, often-repeated public pronouncements about "tolerance and pluralism."[77]

The high levels of violence and widespread arson directed against Christian communities in Maluku produced a flood of refugees, many of whom fled to the neighboring province of Sulawesi. It did not take long before Laskar Jihad extended its campaign to that province, which also had significant numbers of Christian communities among the Torajas and the Menadonese. During the height of its Sulawesi operations, Laskar Jihad fielded a force of 7,000, while the local police and army in combination comprised a force of only 2,000 for all of Sulawesi.

The operations of Laskar Jihad, Laskar Mujahideen, and Laskar Jundullah in Maluku and Sulawesi continued for more than three years. Their rampages of arson, assassinations, and open battles were interrupted from time to time by cease-fires and the efforts of intermediaries to broker peace agreements. Such agreements were short-lived and quickly degenerated into renewed conflicts largely instigated by Laskar Jihad and their affiliated allies. In Sulawesi, some estimates placed the death toll on both sides at 2,000, and the District Social Welfare Agency in 2000, before the conflict had concluded, reported the number of displaced persons at 110,227.[78] In some areas of Maluku, there was almost complete ethnic cleansing of Christians in an effort to change the ethnic and religious balance. However, in most Christian-majority areas, both in Maluku and Sulawesi, the Christians were generally able to sustain the boundaries of their segregated enclaves, despite their losses. In the Maluku province, these clashes are estimated to have claimed more than 9,000 lives, with the largest casualties sustained by resident Christian communities.

During the later stages of the Maluku-Sulawesi strife, this pattern of ethnic and religious conflicts also spread to Kalimantan, with some Laskar Jihad units becoming involved there in a less-decisive manner. In the Kalimantan conflicts, the issues not only involved religion but also the incursion of recent Indonesian transmigrants from Java coming into conflict with indigenous tribal peoples over land, trade, and political control. In Central Kalimantan the conflicts were between Dayaks and Madurese, which pitted Muslims against animists and involved the local commanders of the Indonesian Army who apparently expected to exploit the conflicts to enhance their political power in Jakarta during the turmoil of the Wahid presidency. In Central Kalimantan, aid workers reported an estimated death toll of more than 2,000 and a refugee population of more than 50,000.[79] Similar estimates are unavailable for West Kalimantan.

During its many operations in Indonesia's outer islands, Laskar Jihad enjoyed the sympathetic support of a large segment of Indonesian society and of the green faction of the Indonesian Army, right up to its senior command. With this level of public support, Laskar Jihad received both direct donations from Muslim donors and an untold amount of support from Muslim "charities" as well as from Jemaah Islamiyah. From the Indonesian Army, Laskar Jihad received weapons, logistical support, and more than US$9.3 million that had been embezzled from the Indonesian Army by officers sympathetic to the Laskar Jihad cause.[80] This direct, but covert support provides an explanation of why the local police so often stood by without any intervention to protect victims and deter attackers. With the collapse of civil authority, Laskar Jihad fighters and their allies went on a rampage of burning churches and property and attacking those who fled or who organized resistance.

In its heyday, Laskar Jihad had about 10,000 members and maintained more than seventy branches throughout Indonesia. Their jihadi operations in Maluku and Sulawesi generated much publicity and increased the number of their recruits. Government efforts to bring about a cease-fire and a reconciliation between Muslims and Christians in eastern Indonesia somewhat impeded their ethnic-cleansing agenda. When the Bali bombing of October 12, 2002, killed 202 people, most of whom were Australian tourists, the political climate changed abruptly. Four days later, Laskar Jihad's leader, Jafar Umar Thalib, announced that Laskar Jihad was disbanding and its militia forces were being retired from active operations. Eventually, in January 2003, Thalib was charged with incitement to violence in the Maluku conflict, but in the ensuing trial he was acquitted of all charges. Because only 300 Laskar Jihad fighters returned from Maluku and Sulawesi, representing only a fraction of the total number sent to those locations, much speculation persisted concerning the identity and activities of those who did not return. Had they become fully demobilized to normal civilian life, or were they merely lying low as organized jihadi "sleeper cells"?[81]

Malaysia's Islamic Militants

The upsurge of militant Islam that flourished in Indonesia during the turmoil of the post-Suharto era can also be detected in Malaysia, but within a more stable and restraining environment. Malaysia did experience some political turmoil in the wake of the financial crisis of 1998 and the controversies surrounding the dismissal from government of Anwar Ibrahim and his subsequent trial, conviction, and imprisonment. The stability of the Malaysian regime was challenged but never fractured. For the jihadi militants, Malaysia was a land of opportunity but not where militants could enjoy tacit government sponsorship or a safe sanctuary. What Malaysia had to offer the Al Qaeda network was its climate of politicized Islam within a Muslim-majority population, its visa-free immigration to citizens of Islamic countries, its excellent worldwide communication linkages, and its advanced banking system that included a well-developed sector of Islamic banks. In the 1950s, Communist revolutionaries hid in tropical jungles to stage attacks. In the early years of the twenty-first century, Islamic revolutionaries discovered how to hide among populations with similar ethnographic and demographic characteristics to mobilize support and to provide cover for their activities.

Between 1979 and 1989, hundreds of Malaysian Muslims traveled to Pakistan to volunteer for the Afghan mujahideen or to enroll in Deoband madrasahs. In 1995, one of the returning Afghan veterans, Zainon Ismail, founded Kumpulan Mujahideen Malaysia (Malaysian Mujahideen Group, KMM), which recruited returning Afghan veterans and others committed to its radical doctrines. At the time that KMM was founded, it was portrayed as a stand-alone grouping of Afghan veterans sharing similar experiences. Later evidence revealed that Abu Bakar Ba'asyir of Jemaah Islamiyah was a sponsor and probably a prime mover at its founding.[82] Attending the first meeting of KMM were representatives from Laskar Jundullah (Philippines), Darul Islam (Indonesia), Free Aceh Movement (GAM, Indonesia), Republik Islam Aceh (Indonesia), the Moro Islamic Liberation Front (Philippines), the Rohingya Solidarity Organization (Myanmar), the Arakan Rohingya Nationalist Organization (Myanmar), and the Pattani United Liberation Organization (Thailand).[83] This gathering of Southeast Asian Islamists indicates the extent of the political links being formed and provides some idea of the anticipated theaters of action for their operations. About 1999, the leadership of KMM passed to Nik Adil Nik Aziz, the son of Nik Aziz Nik Mat, who was the Murshid'ul Am (Spiritual Leader) of Partai Islam and the chief minister of Kelantan. Although Partai Islam never endorsed Kumpulan Mujahideen Malaysia, the overlapping membership of KMM with some PAS members induced speculation about their collaborative links.

From 1998 through 2002, a number of radical Islamist organizations developed a network of coordination, allocating shared responsibilities, including maintenance of common training camp facilities. KMM was part of that network, but a relatively minor player, since its membership was estimated to be only sixty-eight. KMM sent some recruits to training camps in Mindanao, and other recruits joined Laskar Jihad units during operations in Kalimantan.

On January 5, 2000, radical Islamist organizations held a general conference in Kuala Lumpur. Kumpulan Mujahideen Malaysia and Jemaah Islamiyah acted as hosts, with sessions organized like the annual meeting of a trade association. This meeting was attended by many of the figures who later became famous for their involvement with the 9/11 terrorist attacks on the United States. Included in that list were Khalid al-Midhar and Nawaq al-Hazmi, who were part of the hijacking crew; Zakarias Moussaoui, the alleged twentieth hijacker, who was arrested in Minneapolis after he took flying lessons but declined lessons on how to land a plane; Ramzi bin al-Shibh, who had attempted to join the 9/11 hijackers but was denied entrance to the United States by Immigration officials; and Riduan Hambali, the operational chief of Jemaah Islamiyah. At the time of these meetings, Malaysian authorities were suspicious of what might be transpiring and secretly photographed those attending. They preferred to wait and track suspects, hoping later to identify their associates. Only after the completion of their terrorist operations, and the arrest of many key suspects, did the authorities learn what had transpired at this conference. Among the plans that were finalized by the delegates was the suicide bombing of the USS *Cole* in Aden, the 9/11 attacks on the World Trade Center and the Pentagon, and the plans to bomb US navy ships at Singapore and the US Embassy in Singapore.[84]

Evidence of Al Qaeda's presence in Southeast Asia had been carefully concealed prior to 9/11. After that event, systematic police work and shared intelligence between the United States and the countries of Southeast Asia gradually uncovered evidence that Al Qaeda and its radical jihadi affiliates had built an effective support network in a politically fertile environment. An important component of that environment included the regions of Southeast Asia where Muslims had formed insurrectionary movements demanding independence from rule by non-Muslim majorities or from centralized authoritarian rulers. Although not all separatist movements in the region were defined by an Islamist ideology, globalized radical Islamist organizations viewed these separatist movements as actual or potential allies that could further their agenda. This is the topic of the next three chapters.

Notes

1. Fred R. von der Mehden, *Two Worlds of Islam: Interaction Between Southeast Asia and the Middle East* (Gainesville: University of Florida Press, 1993), 21–25.

2. William Yale, *The Near East: A Modern History* (Ann Arbor: University of Michigan Press, 1958), 236–261, 271–276; Sydney Nettleton Fisher and William Ochsenwald, *The Middle East: A History* (New York: McGraw-Hill, 1990), 392–401; George Lenczowski, *The Middle East in World Affairs*, 2nd ed. (Ithaca: Cornell University Press, 1957), 84–113.

3. Don Peretz, *The Middle East Today*, 4th ed. (New York: Praeger Publishers, 1983), 224–226.

4. Gilles Kepel, *Jihad: The Trail of Political Islam,* trans. by Anthony F. Roberts (Cambridge: Harvard University Press, 2002), 48–52; Emmanuel Sivan, *Radical Islam: Medieval Theology and Modern Politics,* enlarged ed. (New Haven: Yale University Press, 1990), 1–129.

5. Shaul Bakhash, *The Reign of the Ayatollahs: Iran and the Islamic Revolution* (New York: Basic Books, 1984), 9–18, 38–40, 240–250.

6. Nissim Rejwan, *The Many Faces of Islam: Perspectives on a Resurgent Civilization* (Gainesville: University of Florida Press, 2000), 189–197, citing Nissim Rejwan, *Arabs Face the Modern World: Religious, Cultural and Political Responses to the West* (Gainesville: University of Florida Press, 1998), 71–73; Sayed Kotb, *Social Justice in Islam*, trans. by John B. Hardie (Washington, DC: American Council of Learned Societies, 1953), 93–96.

7. Kepel, *Jihad,* 25–32; Rafiq Zakaria, *The Struggle Within Islam: The Conflict Between Religion and Politics* (London: Penguin Books, 1989), 184–192.

8. For an account of how the Islamic creation myth shaped concepts of government, see Patricia Cone, *God's Rule: Government and Islam* (New York: Columbia University Press, 2004), 3–16.

9. Zakaria, *The Struggle Within Islam,* 433, citing Sayed Raiz Ahmad, *Maulana Maududi and the Islamic State* (Lahore: 1976), 116.

10. For Maududi's role in the campaign to banish Ahmadis from positions of authority and the constitutional struggle over Islam in Pakistani politics, see Keith Callard, *Pakistan: A Political Study* (London: George Allen & Unwin, 1958), 194–231.

11. Richard S. Wheeler, *The Politics of Pakistan: A Constitutional Quest* (Ithaca: Cornell University Press, 1970), 227–228, 252–255.

12. Zakaria, *The Struggle Within Islam,* 228–240.

13. Bakhash, *The Reign of the Ayatollahs*, 38–44, citing Imam Khomeini, *Velayat-e Faqih: Hakumat-e Eslami* [The Vice-Regency of the Jurist: Islamic Government] (Tehran: 1357 [1978]).

14. Mohammad Mohaddessin, *Islamic Fundamentalism: The New Global Threat* (Washington, DC: Seven Locks Press, 1993), 19–25.

15. In 1948, the Jewish community in Egypt numbered about 200,000, and by 1979 only a few hundred Jews remained in Egypt. Peretz, *The Middle East Today,* 155, 253–254.

16. Kepel, *Jihad,* 276–298.

17. Callard, *Pakistan,* 206–222.

18. Amjad Mahmood Khan, "Persecution of the Ahmadiyya Community in Pakistan: An Analysis Under International Law," *Harvard Human Rights Journal* 16 (Spring 2003), 217–245.

19. See Juan Cole, "The Baha'is of Iran," *History Today* 40, no. 3 (March 1990), 24–34; reproduced at www.sullivan-county.com/id3/bahai_iran.htm.

20. These executions of Baha'i leaders came before the main reign of terror against critics of the Khomeini regime. On June 20, 1981, about half a million residents of Tehran protested against the return of despotism. Khomeini ordered Revolutionary Guards to open fire on the demonstrators. Many of the demonstrators were killed, but what followed was even more severe. Mass arrests were followed by mass executions before firing squads, with about 100,000 dissidents executed over the next few years. Mohaddessin, *Islamic Fundamentalism,* 21 and 97.

21. Firuz Kazemzadeh, "The Baha'is in Iran: Twenty Years of Repression," *Social Research*, New School for Social Research (Summer, 2000), reproduced at www.findarticles.com.

22. In Saudi Arabia, sustained production of oil began in 1938. From that date, oil royalties from the Standard Oil Company of California and subsequent concession holders provided the Saudi regime with a steadily rising income. What began as a few million dollars per year rapidly rose to many billions of dollars in the period of three decades. After the Arab-Israeli War of 1973, to put economic pressure on Western countries supporting Israel, the Saudis led an oil embargo imposed by the Organization of Petroleum Exporting Countries (OPEC), which lasted five months and produced a fourfold increase in the price of crude oil to US$11.65 per barrel. After that date, the Saudi government was awash with money and found it difficult to spend it all on domestic projects. By 1984, Saudi annual revenues rose to $43 billion. This surplus provided the resources for a program of aggressive foreign investment to promote the Wahhabi version of Islam in the Muslim world. See Ian J. Bickerton and Carla L. Klausner, *A Concise History of the Arab-Israeli Conflict* (Englewood Cliffs, NJ: Prentice Hall, 1991), 180–181; Fisher and Ochsenwald, *The Middle East,* 550–557.

23. Kepel, *Jihad,* 61–134, 150–158.

24. The Deobandi movement began in the Delhi region of India in the late nineteenth century. It is a Sunni-based form of Islam that follows some Sufi practices, and it is a dedicated opponent of Shia Islam. It acquired a very strong missionary commitment to make ordinary people into pious Muslims. With Saudi financial support, the number of Deoband madrasahs rapidly increased, and the product of those schools became the

basis for the Taliban of Afghanistan. The alliance between the Deobandis and the Wahhabis helped to shape the political environment that was so effectively exploited in the 1990s by Osama bin Laden and the Al Qaeda movement. For an excellent account of the Deoband movement and its evolution as a political force, see Barbara Metcalf, "'Traditionalist' Islamic Activism: Deoband, Tablighis, and Talibs," in *After Sept. 11,* online collection, Social Science Research Council, available at www.ssrc.org/sept11/essays.

25. Owais Tohid, "Pakistan, US Take on *Madrassahs,*" *Christian Science Monitor*, August 24, 2004, 1 and 4.

26. For an exploration of the impact on Southeast Asia of Maududi and other Islamist writers as part of the Dakwah movements of the 1970s and 1980s, see M. Kamal Hassan, "The Influence of Mawdudi's Thought on Muslims in Southeast Asia: A Brief Survey," *The Muslim World* 93, nos. 3 and 4 (July/October 2003), 429–464.

27. Isma'il R. al-Faruqi became an ardent supporter of the project to develop a separate system of "Islamic knowledge" that was designed to become the basis for all university instruction in Malaysia. He was a Palestinian who was appointed professor of Islamic studies at Temple University and later came as a visiting professor to the University of Malaya in the 1970s and 1980s, during which time he became the ideological mentor of Anwar Ibrahim and an adviser to ABIM. Although he called himself a "modernist," al-Faruqi espoused Salafist doctrine that avoided challenging any literalist interpretations of the Quran and the Sunna, and he opposed any liberalized interpretations of Sharia rules regarding the status and role of women in Islam. He later became an active participant in the founding of the International Islamic University Malaysia and was reported to have persuaded Prime Minister Mahathir to recruit Anwar Ibrahim into UMNO and the Malaysian government in 1982. For an account of the ideas of al-Faruqi and of Syed M. N. Al-Attas, who together became champions of "de-Westernization of knowledge," see Georg Stauth, *Politics and Cultures of Islamization in Southeast Asia: Indonesia and Malaysia in the Nineteen-Nineties* (New Brunswick, NJ: Transaction Publishers, 2002), 199–238. For al-Faruqi's views on the role of women in Islam, see Gordon P. Means, "Women's Rights and Public Policy in Islam: Report of a Conference," *Asian Survey* 27, no. 3 (March 1987), 346–350.

28. Barry Desker, "Islam and Society in Southeast Asia after 9-11," *IDSS Commentaries,* 14/2002, Institute of Defence and Strategic Studies (Singapore: Nanyang Technological University, September 2002), 1–4, www.idss.edu.sg/Perspectives/research.

29. Leonard C. Sebastian, "Getting to the Root of Islamic Radicalism in Indonesia," *Perspectives* (Singapore: Institute of Defence and Strategic Studies and Nanyang Technological University, 2002), 1–4.

30. The amount of money that Saudi Arabia has spent to promote its version of Islam is difficult to estimate. The Saudi government does not provide the World Bank with financial data on its revenues, expenditures, or its budget. Some donations to Islamic institutions are announced publicly and many others are not. Despite these difficulties, the author Reza F. Safa estimated that the Saudi government spent $87 billion between 1973 and 1997 on a worldwide campaign to promote Wahhabism. This included constructing and maintaining 1,500 mosques, 202 colleges, 210 Islamic centers, and 2,000 schools in non-Islamic countries, mostly in the United States and Europe. It appears probable that more than half of the total sum was spent in Islamic countries, especially South Asia and Southeast Asia. Even if this estimate of total expenditures has been grossly exaggerated, it is apparent that the Saudi investment to promote its version of Islamic orthodoxy in Southeast Asia has been far greater than has been reported in the popular press. Reza F. Safa, *Inside Islam: Exposing and Reaching the World of Islam* (Washington, DC: Strang Communications, 1997), as cited in www.jfednepa.org/mark%20silverberg/wahhabi.htm.

31. Louis Dupree, *Afghanistan* (Princeton, NJ: Princeton University Press, 1980), 494–658, 753–778; Dilip Hiro, *War Without End: The Rise of Islamist Terrorism and the Global Response,* rev. ed. (London: Routledge, 2002), 202–209; *Encyclopaedia Britannica 2003*, CD version, "History/Afghanistan Since 1973," n.p.

32. Hiro, *War Without End,* 89–90, 209–215.

33. Osama bin Laden was born in Riyadh on July 30, 1957, the seventeenth son of fifty-two children fathered by Muhammad bin Laden, one of the wealthiest men in Saudi Arabia. Osama attended King Abdulaziz University, where he took courses in Islamic studies under the guidance of Muhammad Qutb, the brother of the famous Sayyid Qutb, who was noted for being the ideologue of the Muslim Brotherhood. Osama left the university after three years and never completed his degree. Osama's father, Muhammad bin Laden, owned and controlled a business empire of enormous wealth, the Saudi Binladen Group. In 1968, Muhammad bin Laden died in a helicopter crash and Osama inherited a large estate estimated by various sources to be worth from US$25 million to US$500 million. With prudent investments and skillful management, the wealth of Osama continued to increase over the years. Rohan Gunaratna, *Inside Al Qaeda: Global Network of Terror* (New York: Columbia University Press, 2002), 16–53; Roland Jacquard, *In the Name of Osama bin Laden: Global Terrorism & the Bin Laden Brotherhood* (Durham, NC: Duke University Press, 2002), 11–19; Peter L. Bergen, *Holy War, Inc.: Inside the Secret World of Osama bin Laden* (New York: The Free Press, 2001), 41–62.

34. Hiro, *War Without End,* 218–221.

35. Loretta Napoleoni, *Modern Jihad: Tracing the Dollars Behind the Terror Networks* (London: Pluto Press, 2003), 79–85.

36. Jason Burke, *Al-Qaeda: Casting a Shadow of Terror* (London: I. B. Tauris, 2003), 68–72.

37. Gunaratna, *Inside Al Qaeda,* 20–25.

38. Ibid., 25–27; "Who Is Ayman al-Zawahri?" msnbc.msn.com/id/4555901/; "Ayman al-Zawahri," newsvote.bbc.co.uk/mpapps/; "Ayman al-Zawahri," www.cbc.ca/.

39. Burke, *Al-Qaeda,* 124–129.

40. Several years earlier, in 1995, a failed attempt to assassinate Egyptian president Hosni Mubarak and the 1997 massacre of foreign tourists at Luxor were traced to Egyptian Islamic Jihad, which al-Zawahiri headed. In 1999, Ayman al-Zawahiri was sentenced to death in absentia by an Egyptian court for the Luxor massacre and for other activities traced to Egyptian Islamic Jihad. "Who Is Ayman al-Zawahri?" msnbc.msn.com/id/4555901/; "Ayman al-Zawahri," newsvote.bbc.co.uk/mpapps/pagetools/.

41. Gunaratna, *Inside Al Qaeda,* 37–38.

42. Jacquard, *In the Name of Osama bin Laden,* 27–36; Gunaratna, *Inside Al Qaeda,* 156–159; Hiro, *War Without End,* 245–249. Shortly after Osama left for Sudan, in September 1996, an enormous truck bomb was exploded in front of the Khobar Towers that was home to 3,000 US Air Force personnel in Dhahran, Saudi Arabia. The blast killed 19 and wounded 500 people. Al Qaeda was suspected as the perpetrator of the Khobar Towers blast, although eventually a New York federal jury charged that bombing to the Iranian-backed Hezbollah. However, because of the Al Qaeda–Hezbollah strategic partnership that had been forged earlier, there may have been an Al Qaeda link that was not detected. Saudi Arabia was uncooperative in the investigations following that bombing and refused to allow the Federal Bureau of Investigation to interrogate the eleven suspects who were charged in the federal indictment and were in custody in Saudi prisons at that time. Bruce Maxwell (ed.), *Terrorism: A Documentary History* (Washington, DC: CQ Press, 2003), 220–224.

43. Hiro, *War Without End,* 253–254; Jacquard, *In the Name of Osama bin Laden,* 38–39.

44. Gunaratna, *Inside Al Qaeda,* 58–60.

45. Ibid., 42–51; Hiro, *War Without End,* 259–264.

46. Hiro, *War Without End*, 267–269, 290–291, 300–372.

47. Zachary Abuza, *Militant Islam in Southeast Asia: Crucible of Terror* (Boulder: Lynne Rienner, 2003), 20–22; Zachary Abuza, "Funding Terrorism in Southeast Asia: The Financial Network of Al Qaeda and Jemaah Islamiyah," *NBR Analysis* 14, no. 5 (December 2003), 39–50; Napoleoni, *Modern Jihad,* 123–127.

48. Abuza, *Militant Islam,* 11–17; Leslie Lopez, "Islamic Schools Flourish in Malaysia," *Asian Wall Street Journal,* October 23, 2001; Michael Richardson, "Asians Taking a Closer Look at Islamic Schools," *International Herald Tribune,* February 12, 2002.

49. Gunaratna, *Inside Al Qaeda,* 8–9.

50. Hiro, *War Without End,* 108–109.

51. Abuza, *Militant Islam,* 4–10.

52. Ibid., 127.

53. When President Suharto first learned about the existence of Komando Jihad, shortly after its formation, his top intelligence officer, Ali Murtopo, made overtures to explore the possibility that it could become an anticommunist irregular strike force and recruit voter support from radical Muslims for Golkar during the 1977 elections. When Komando Jihad failed to respond to those overtures, it was considered a security threat that was confirmed when it assassinated a judge and engaged in other criminal activities. Finally, government authorities arrested 185 Komando Jihad members. To secure the release of their detained members, Komando Jihad staged several retaliatory incidents, including the hijacking of a Garuda Airlines commercial DC-9 jet that was forced to land in Bangkok with a full load of passengers. The hijackers expected to exchange passengers for the freedom of their jailed comrades, but instead an Indonesian commando unit stormed the plane, killing all five hijackers. Ken Conboy, *The Second Front: Inside Asia's Most Dangerous Terrorist Network* (Jakarta: Equinox Publishing, 2006), 1–23.

54. Abuza, *Militant Islam,* 132–135.

55. To assess the new opportunities for radical Islamist operations, Osama bin Laden was reported by CNN on July 9, 2002, to have sent two of his inner circle, Ayman al-Zawahiri and Mohammad Atef, to Aceh and Maluku in June 2000. They were supposedly met by Umar Faruq, who had extensive contacts with radical groups in the region and was later identified as a key Al Qaeda agent for Southeast Asia. The visit of these two Al Qaeda leaders was alleged to have established the plan for Al Qaeda's operations in Southeast Asia. See Abuza, *Militant Islam,* 144–145. After Umar Faruq was arrested in June 2002, under interrogation, he admitted that he had traveled to Aceh with a colleague from Sulawesi, but denied ever meeting al-Zawahiri or Atef in Aceh or Maluku. Whether the latter two ever visited Indonesia remains unconfirmed. Conboy, *The Second Front,* 101–105, including 101n.

56. Conboy, *The Second Front,* 83–84. After the first Bali bombing, Ba'asyir was arrested as a suspect in that operation. At his trial, Ba'asyir vehemently denied that he had been elected or selected as "emir" or held any formal position within Jemaat Islamiyah.

57. Abuza, *Militant Islam*, 140–145; Abuza, "Funding Terrorism in Southeast Asia," 22–33; Greg Barton, *Indonesia's Struggle: Jemaah Islamiyah and the Soul of Islam* (Sydney: University of New South Wales Press, 2004), 44–62.

58. Maxwell, *Terrorism: A Documentary History,* 351–352; William C. Thompson, "One Year Later, The Fiscal Impact of 9/11 on New York City," Report of the Comptroller of the City of New York, September 4, 2002, www.comptroller.nyc.gov/bureaus/bud/reports /impact-9-11-year-later.pdf. The total economic impact on the United States as a whole was far greater, involving also the damages from the attack on the Pentagon, the plane that crashed in Pennsylvania, economic losses sustained by the airline industry, and the negative impact on the stock market and the national economy.

59. Rizal Sukma, "Indonesia's Islams and September 11: Reactions and Prospects," in Andrew Tan and Kumar Ramakrishna (eds.), *The New Terrorism: Anatomy, Trends and Counter-Strategies* (Singapore: Eastern Universities Press, 2002), 178–181. A nearly identical conspiracy theory attributing the 9/11 terrorist attack to the CIA and the Israeli Secret Service circulated within Muslim circles in the United States shortly after the 9/11 attacks.

60. Mahathir bin Mohamad, *Terrorism and the Real Issues* (Subang Jaya, Malaysia: Pelanduk Publications, 2003), 29–40; Bergen, *Holy War,* 221.

61. K. S. Nathan, "Counter Terror Cooperation in a Complex Security Environment," in Kumar Ramakrishna and See Seng Tan (eds.), *After Bali: The Threat of Terrorism in Southeast Asia* (Singapore: Institute of Defence and Strategic Studies, Nanyang Technological University, 2003), 246–253; Abuza, *Militant Islam,* 212–220.

62. Farish A. Noor, "Globalization, Resistance and the Discursive Politics of Terror, Post–September 11," in Tan and Ramakrishna, *The New Terrorism,* 166–170.

63. Ibid., 166, citing "US Embassy Under Guard, PAS Labels Americans 'War Criminals,'" available at www.malaysiakini.com, October 8, 2001. See Ian Stewart, *The Mahathir Legacy: A Nation Divided, a Region at Risk* (Singapore: Talisman, 2004), 231.

64. S. Jayasankaran, "Malaysia: A Plan to End Extremism," *Far Eastern Economic Review* 165 (December 26, 2002–January 2, 2003), 12–16.

65. Abuza, *Militant Islam,* 212–220; Tan and Ramakrishna, *The New Terrorism,* 164–172; John Burton, "Malaysia's Mahathir Wins US Support for Crackdown," *The Financial Times* (London), May 2, 2002, download from sk@listserv.malaysia.net.

66. "This Week," *Far Eastern Economic Review*, October 4, 2001, 14; Dewi Fortuna Anwar, "Megawati's Search for an Effective Foreign Policy," in Hadi Soesastro, Anthony L. Smith, and Han Mui Ling (eds.), *Governance in Indonesia: Challenges Facing the Megawati Presidency* (Singapore: Institute of Southeast Asian Studies, 2003), 83–85.

67. Leonard C. Sebastian, "Indonesian State Responses to September 11, the Bali Bombings and the War in Iraq: Sowing the Seeds for an Accommodationist Islamic Framework?" *Cambridge Review of International Affairs* 16, no. 3 (October 2003), 6–9.

68. Sadanand Dhume, "Indonesia: The New Mainstream," *Far Eastern Economic Review*, January 8, 2003, 46–49; Sukma, "Indonesia's Islams and September 11," 183–184. Later, after the Bali bombings in October 2002, Din Syamsuddin became an outspoken defender of Abu Ba'asyir after the latter was convicted as an accomplice in the Bali bombings and was eventually identified by apprehended terrorists as the "spiritual leader" of Jemaah Islamiyah.

69. Sukma, "Indonesia's Islams and September 11," 178–190.

70. Angel M. Rabasa, *Political Islam in Southeast Asia: Moderates, Radicals and Terrorists* (New York: Oxford University Press, 2003), 32–34; Abuza, *Militant Islam,* 190–194, 199–201.

71. Dan Murphy, "Indonesia, Terror's Latest Front," *The Christian Science Monitor*, October 15, 2002, 1 and 9; Andrew Tan, "The New Terrorism: Implications and Strategies," in Tan and Ramakrishna, *The New Terrorism,* 233–245; Anthony L. Smith,

"The Bali Bombing and Responses to International Terrorism," in Soesastro, Smith, and Han Mui Ling, *Governance in Indonesia,* 305–322.

72. Kevin O'Rourke, *Reformasi: The Struggle for Power in Post-Suharto Indonesia* (Crows Nest, Australia: Allen & Unwin, 2002), 256–280. For the earlier period of conflict between Indonesia and the supporters of independence for East Timor leading up to the referendum for independence, see Adam Schwarz, *A Nation in Waiting: Indonesia's Search for Stability,* 2nd ed. (St. Leonards, NSW, Australia: Allen & Unwin, 2000), 194–229. The East Timor conflict is only peripherally relevant to the themes of the present study. More detailed accounts of that conflict may be found in the following sources: Irena Cristalis, *Bitter Dawn: East Timor, a People's Story* (London: Zed Books, 2002); Richard Tantor, Mark Sheldon, and Stephen R. Shalom (eds.), *Bitter Sweet Flowers: East Timor, Indonesia, and the World Community* (Lanham, MD: Rowman & Littlefield Publishers, 2001); Amnesty International, *Indonesia and East Timor* (London: Amnesty International Publications, 2000), at www.amnesty.org; Human Rights Watch Asia, "The Violence in Ambon," *A Human Rights Watch Report* 11, no. 1 (March 1999).

73. Abu Jabril was an alias name taken by Mohammad Iqbal Abdurrahman. After Malaysian authorities arrested Jabril, he was deported to Indonesia, where he was tried and acquitted of immigration offenses and released in October 2004. International Crisis Group, *How the Jemaah Islamiyah Terrorist Network Operates,* Asia Report No. 43 (December 11, 2002), Jakarta/Brussels, 1–40; Zachary Abuza, "Out of the Woodwork: Islamist Militants in Aceh," *Terrorism Monitor* 3, no. 2 (January 27, 2005), 1–4, www.jamestown.org.

74. Abuza, *Militant Islam,* 69–72, 148–152; Jennifer Donohoe, "Opponents of Islamic Law: Diverse Responses to Proponents of Islamic Law Indicate Democracy Is Healthy in South Sulawesi," *Inside Indonesia,* July–September 2004, 1–3, www.insideindonesia.org/edit79/p7-8_donohoe.html; International Crisis Group, *Weakening Indonesia's Mujahidin Networks: Lessons from Maluku and Poso,* Asia Report No. 103 (October 13, 2005), Jakarta/Brussels. An earlier Laskar Jundullah was formed in Makassar, and it sent a contingent of fifty jihadi fighters to Ambon in February 1999. This earlier militia using the Laskar Jundullah moniker was later upstaged by the larger Laskar Jundullah led by Agus Dwikarna.

75. The full title of the committee was Komite Penanggulangan Krisis, but Kompak also used the name Forum Kommunikasi in reference to its information and propaganda campaign.

76. Kostrad established a base near Bogor for training Laskar Jihad and secretly transferred US$20 million from its financial resources to support Laskar Jihad. At the time, the links between Kostrad and Jemaah Islamiyah were well concealed. International Crisis Group, *Indonesia Backgrounder: Jihad in Central Sulawesi,* Asia Report No. 74 (February 3, 2004), Jakarta/Brussels; Theodore Friend, *Indonesian Destinies* (Cambridge, MA: The Belnap Press of Harvard University Press, 2003), 480–488.

77. Michael Davis, "Laskar Jihad and the Political Position of Conservative Islam in Indonesia," *Contemporary Southeast Asia* 24, no. 1 (April 2002), 12–23; Human Rights Watch, "The Violence in Ambon," *A Human Rights Watch Report* 11, no. 1 (March 1999); Art Moore, "Christians Terrorized in Muslim Indonesia," *WorldNetDaily*, December 8, 2001, 1–5, www.worldnetdaily.com/news/article/article.asp?ARTICLE_ID=25599; International Crisis Group, "The Search for Peace in Maluku," (Jakarta/Brussels: Asia Report, No. 31, February 8, 2002), 1–27; International Crisis Group, *How the Jemaah Islamiyah Terrorist Network Operates,* 1–40.

78. Human Rights Watch Asia, "Indonesia Breakdown: Four Years of Communal Violence in Central Sulawesi," *A Human Rights Watch Report* 14, no. 9 (December

2002); Zachary Abuza, "Muslims, Politics, and Violence in Indonesia: An Emerging Jihadist-Islamist Nexus?" *NBR Analysis* 15, no. 3 (September 2004), 5–55.

79. Davis, "Laskar Jihad," 24–32; O'Rourke, *Reformasi,* 234–237, 394–397.

80. For several years, Laskar Jihad was able to conceal its sources of support, but after 2002, when significant numbers of Islamist radicals were arrested and interrogated, the patterns of support that had been suspected, but not proven, were later confirmed by the testimony from those in detention. For an account of the embezzlement of Indonesian Army funds, see www.cdi.org/terrorism/laskar.cfm.

81. Abuza, *Militant Islam,* 70–73.

82. Jemaah Islamiyah actively promoted the founding of KMM as an ancillary paramilitary unit to augment JI's more clandestine operations. When JI shifted its main base of operations to Indonesia, it sponsored Islamic Jihad in Indonesia as an affiliated organization.

83. Kumar Ramakrishna, "US Strategy in Southeast Asia: Counter-Terrorist or Counter-Terrorism?" in Ramakrishna and Tan, *After Bali,* 311–312.

84. Farish A. Noor, "Blood, Sweat and *Jihad*: The Radicalization of the Political Discourse of the Pan-Malaysian Islamic Party (PAS) from 1982 Onwards," *Contemporary Southeast Asia* 25, no. 2 (August 2003), 222–224; Abuza, *Militant Islam,* 101–115, 124–125; Gunaratna, *Inside Al Qaeda,* 174–203.

PART 4
Separatism and Rebellion

9

Moro Separatism in the Philippines

Three major separatist movements in Southeast Asia all have their origins in events and struggles that began over two centuries ago, but they have been perpetuated by current circumstances and recent memories. The major separatist conflicts are centered around the Muslim settlements of the southern Philippines; the Malays living in southern provinces of Thailand; and regional ethno-religious nationalists in Aceh, the northernmost region of Sumatra in Indonesia. Two other regions of less intense conflict involve Muslim enclaves in Cambodia and Muslim settlements along the Arakan coast of Myanmar (Burma). This study will focus only on the three that have proven to be the most long-lasting struggles—Moro Separatism, Pattani Separatism, and Aceh Separatism. Each of these separatist movements is covered in a single chapter.

Patterns of Philippine Politics

Prior to World War II, the United States promised the Philippines independence in 1932, to be fulfilled after a ten-year period of tutelage. Limited moves toward self-government were initiated, but the Japanese attack and World War II intervened. When the war was over, the Philippines finally gained independence on July 4, 1946, but only after the Philippine Parliament agreed to conditions that assured a strong link with the United States. The terms of independence provided for trade concessions and lease agreements that enabled the United States to retain control of more than 200 military bases. With this degree of economic and military presence, the United States became both a partner and a protagonist in many of the issues of Philippine politics in the post-independence era.

Like Malaysia and Indonesia, Philippine politics in the early postcolonial era reflected a three-way contest between nationalists, Communists, and Islamists, but the configuration of these ideological divisions in the Philippines produced very different patterns of politics from its Southeast Asian neighbors. In the Philippines, the nationalists were the dominant political force, but they were divided into competing factions of patronage hierarchies tied to leaders of wealthy land-owning families. The Communists and a cluster of affiliated left-wing groups became the de facto opposition that played both a legal-constitutional role, and one that also was heavily committed to a revolutionary strategy. The Islamists represented the Muslim-majority areas of the southern islands of the Philippines—Mindanao, the Sulu Archipelago, and Palawan. The influx of Christian settlers to the south rapidly increased after 1913, especially to Mindanao. Eventually, Muslims no longer constituted majorities in many areas previously ruled and dominated by Muslims.

According to the Philippine government statistics, Muslims in 1990 constituted about 4.6 percent of the total population of the country.[1] In the southern provinces of Mindanao, Sulu, and Palawan, out of a total population of 14.7 million, the Muslim Moros comprised 17.5 percent, Lumads (indigenous animist tribals) were 5.3 percent, and Christian Filipinos were a dominant majority of 70 percent.[2] These demographic changes had been induced by a century of transmigration of non-Muslims to the southern islands, creating an enormous obstacle to those Muslims who supported the cause of independence from the Philippines or proposed annexation into a neighboring Muslim-majority state.

Within the political landscape of the Philippines, the Communists were never eliminated, as happened in both Malaysia and Indonesia. Instead, they retained the support of a significant constituency in Philippine politics. Their leaders played a dual game of seeking access to power through electoral representation, while they promoted their goal of revolutionary overthrow of the government. In response to the Communist challenge, the Philippine government followed vacillating policies of confronting Communists through military and police suppression, offers of amnesty, and cease-fire agreements that inevitably broke down. The inability to secure a peace agreement produced cycles of violence, talks, negotiations, and a return to violence. Because Philippine Muslim separatists also pursued revolutionary tactics against the Philippine government, the operations and strategies of the other insurrectionary movement influenced both Communists and Islamists.

The New People's Army

With some support from the Comintern, a Moscow-trained labor leader, Cristanto Evangelista, founded the Philippine Communist Party (PKP) in 1930. The party recruited some labor leaders and intellectuals, but its activities were cut short in 1932 when its leaders were imprisoned. After these leaders were released in 1936, the party merged with the Socialist Party, seeking to conceal its identity. Following the Japanese invasion of the Philippines in 1941, the PKP in 1942 formed a "People's Army" to fight against Japan as a self-proclaimed ally of the United States. The guerrilla force, called Huk,[3] was led by Luis Taruc and operated with a force of several thousand men, primarily in the remote regions of Central Luzon. When the war ended, the Huks were not recognized by the United States as anti-Japanese guerrillas and received none of the back pay accorded to those guerrilla forces sponsored by the US Army. In 1945, Taruc and five other Huk candidates ran for election to Congress on an Alliance ticket and won seats to Congress. After the election, the Huk candidates were disqualified by the Philippine Election Commission for utilizing "terrorist tactics" and denied seats in Congress. Frustrated by their encounter with electoral politics, the Huk leaders in June 1946 decided to reconstitute their wartime guerrilla force and prepare for a "revolutionary struggle."[4]

Under the leadership of Taruc, the PKP gained a peasant following, but internal factional conflicts split the leadership at the same time that government counterinsurgency operations produced casualties and defections among Huk forces. During an internal power struggle in 1954, Taruc was expelled from the party, and fearing for his life, he surrendered to the government. A more militant faction survived, and in 1964 new leaders revived the party, now called the Communist Party of the Philippines (CPP). Jose Maria Sison, a former college teacher, became its new leader and was fully committed to the revolutionary doctrines of Marx, Lenin, and Mao Zedong. In 1969, the CPP formed its own guerrilla force, the New People's Army (NPA), to be the primary instrument for implementing its revolutionary doctrines. In its early days, the CPP and the NPA were relatively insignificant revolutionary organizations posing only a moderate security problem, but not threatening the Philippine regime. When Ferdinand Marcos was elected president in 1965, he instituted a campaign to induce NPA recruits to surrender, combined with intensified military operations against NPA guerrilla forces. He also promised a land reform program that would enable landless peasants to become property owners. As the security situation deteriorated, he introduced martial law in 1972 that suspended democratic institutions. With the escalation of violence, the regime became more dependent on local landowners. Consequently, promises of land reform were watered down and soon forgotten, which induced many landless peasants to volunteer for the New People's Army. With increased repression, the NPA capitalized on escalating grievances among peasants and a loss of legitimacy, which enabled the NPA to recruit a substantial support base, especially in remote rural areas among underemployed youth.

In November 1977, government forces captured Sison along with twenty out of twenty-six CPP Central Committee members. Despite their capture, the CPP/NPA recovered and formulated a "United Front" strategy calling for political alliances with "progressive forces," including the Moro separatist movement and various disgruntled leftist groups who were opposed to the Marcos regime. This attempt to forge an opposition alliance of radical opponents of the government proved to be a failure because of the rigid ideologies of the competing opposition factions. The new CPP leaders were unyielding in their commitment to Marxism; the Moro separatists would not compromise their goals and their radical Islamic ideology; and, opposition groups with Catholic and Protestant affiliations were hostile and fearful of both Marxists and Islamists. The doctrinal divisions of ideology and religion were too rigid and impermeable to facilitate a viable Communist-led opposition to the Marcos regime.[5]

The legitimacy of the Marcos regime rapidly eroded following the 1983 assassination of Marcos's political rival and critic, Benigno Aquino, who was killed just as he returned from exile abroad. The killers were never identified. Fragmentary and circumstantial evidence convinced the general public that the killing of Benigno Aquino had received sanction from the highest echelon of political authority. Three years later, in February 1986, Benigno's widow, Corazon Aquino, contested the presidential election against the physically ailing Marcos. The blatant fraud associated with that election further undermined the regime's legitimacy. After the voting, independent poll watchers reported that Aquino had won, while the Election Commission, dominated by Marcos appointees, reported a Marcos victory. For four days, mass protests in support of Corazon Aquino produced what came to be called "The Revolution of People Power." Orchestrated in part by the head of the Catholic Church in the Philippines, Cardinal Sin, it was later joined by General Fidel Ramos, leading a faction of the Philippine Army. The mass demonstrations and the defection of key political leaders led to the rapid departure of Marcos and the installation of Corazon Aquino as president of the Philippines on February 26, 1986. Those dramatic and fateful events need not be recounted here.[6] What is relevant to our present topic was the change of policy that President Aquino developed for addressing the Communist threat posed by the New People's Army.

Peace Talks with the CPP

During her election campaign, Corazon Aquino had proposed a cease-fire with the NPA and the legalization of the CPP, provided that they became nonviolent and participated in politics through legal electoral processes. Shortly after her inauguration, cease-fire negotiations began both with the NPA and the Moro National Liberation Front (MNLF; more on that issue later). Within the higher echelons of the Philippine Army there was open opposition to these moves, but she persevered in her determination to pursue a new policy. When no representatives of the army were selected for the negotiating team, Secretary of Defense Juan Ponce Enrile made moves to sabotage the peace talks. A coup plot was initiated by some officers in the army, and when the plot was discovered, President Aquino issued an arrest warrant against Enrile and replaced him with his deputy, General Rafael Ileto.[7]

While the talks with the NPA continued, the armed struggle also continued, during which time government forces arrested the NPA commander, Rodolfo Salas. Eventually, on November 27, 1986, a cease-fire agreement was signed between the government and the NPA and its "open" political arm, the National Democratic Front. To facilitate negotiations, in 1987 Corazon Aquino released from detention CPP founder Jose Sison and NPA commander Dante Buscayno. At the peace talks, the government offered amnesty for "political crimes" but not for murder and theft, while the NPA demanded "civil liberties, land reform, Moro self-determination," and "free public education," along with amnesty for all detained NPA forces. Agreement on these issues was not forthcoming by the date of February 7, 1987, when the cease-fire expired.

While the peace negotiations had failed, they had also created dissent within the ranks of the NPA. Many of the NPA guerrillas were exhausted by persistent harassment by government forces and were tired of the harsh conditions in remote jungle hideouts. Although the CPP/NPA had been organized around ideological conformity with Marxist doctrines, its cadres were vulnerable to government policies that combined coercion, discussion, and piecemeal offers of rewards for surrender and defection.[8] Even though the party central command had not signed a peace agreement, the offers of surrender and amnesty remained open for individuals who chose to surrender and had no record of atrocities. After the collapse of the peace talks, the successful transition of former NPA members to civilian life provided incentives for further defections.[9]

Aquino's successor, General Fidel V. Ramos, continued the "coercion-discussion-reward strategy" during his term of office from 1992 to 1998. While the Communist insurgency was not defeated, its base was significantly eroded. With increased security and continued efforts to promote defections, the NPA faced gradually dwindling public support, even among destitute peasants who were most affected by the costs of conflict. In the early 1980s, the NPA was estimated to have a military force of between 15,000 and 25,000; by 2004, its numbers were estimated to have dwindled to 8,700 full-time fighters. The conflict between the government forces and the NPA had cost the lives of 43,000 killed in the years between 1969 and 2002.[10]

As the NPA adopted a more defensive strategy, it gave higher priority to preventing defections from its ranks by utilizing assassination squads, called "sparrow units," to kill NPA defectors and by taking other draconian measures, including mass executions, to root out suspected government "spies and infiltrators" within its own ranks. The most spectacular assassination was carried out on January 23, 2003, against Romulo Kintanar, the former head of the New People's Army. Kintanar had been captured in 1991 but freed on bail the next year as part of a peace campaign. After his release, Kintanar became employed in a government department while also advising the government in negotiations with the NPA. For these acts, a CPP "People's Court" was convened, apparently in 1993, and secretly sentenced Kintanar to death for "counterrevolutionary activities," which sentence was carried out ten years later. The number of CPP/NPA members and former members who have been executed in bloody purges is estimated to be from several hundred to two thousand.[11]

When Secretary of State Colin Powell visited the Philippines in August 2002, he announced that the three components of the Philippine Communist Party (CPP/NPA/NDF) were all placed on the list of "foreign terrorist groups" and that their financial assets were frozen. The CPP leader, Jose Sison, was particularly concerned that his political asylum status in the Netherlands could be revoked and he might be turned over to the United States as a "foreign terrorist." While the Netherlands did not revoke his asylum status, this issue put increased pressure on the CPP/NPA to resume peace negotiations with the Philippine government.[12]

By the mid-1990s, the Communist Party and its New People's Army were no longer a serious threat to the political stability of the Philippines. Even so, their presence and continued survival complicated the issues of how the Philippine government responded to Islamic separatist movements within its borders. During its insurgency of over three decades, the NPA never admitted that it had formed an alliance with Islamic separatists. Instead, both parties developed a tacit acknowledgment that the political successes of one aided the other. Years later, a spokesman for the Moro Islamic Liberation Front (MILF) revealed that the NPA and the MILF had agreed to a tactical alliance respecting each party's exclusive areas of operations. Philippine National Police determined that the CPP/NPA, MNLF, and MILF came to a three-way agreement that the CPP/NPA would support ceding the entire region of Mindanao, Palawan, and the Sulu Archipelago to the two Moro-based organizations, while the NPA secured its arms from abroad by relying on Moro smuggling capabilities.[13]

In 2003, Philippine authorities engaged once again in peace talks with the CPP. The Philippine government offered a final peace accord that included most of the political demands of the CPP, on the condition that the CPP permanently cease hostilities, renounce violence, and operate under the Philippine Constitution for the conduct of its political activities. The NPA would be required to disarm and their members would be integrated into mainstream society. Although this final peace accord was not accepted by the CPP/NPA, the government's spokesman Ignacio Bunye reported that "the path to peace is always open."[14]

By February 2003, peace talks resumed once again between the Philippine government and the CPP/NPA, both in Oslo and in Utrecht, Netherlands, this time being hosted by Norway as a "third-party facilitator." At the top of the agenda, the CPP demanded that the Philippine government secure from the United States and from the European Union the removal of the National Democratic Front from their terrorist lists. The cycle of "fight and talk" had resumed once again for both the government of the Republic of the Philippines (GRP) and the CPP/NPA without any clear resolution to the low-level but persistent and continuing conflict. For Islamic separatists, the example of the NPA's campaign against the Philippine government and the experience of its tactical strategies were both an inspiration and a guide for similar political and military tactics.

Moro Nationalism—MNLF

The rigors of World War II and the Japanese occupation of the Philippines had muted but not extinguished the view of most Muslims within the borders of the Philippines that they were culturally and religiously a distinct people who could justifiably claim their rights to self-determination. When World War II ended, the United States returned to the Philippines as the colonial power and proceeded to make arrangements to grant Philippine independence without making special consideration for the concerns and accumulated grievances of Filipino Muslims. Identified by their Spanish name, the Moros' leaders made demands for separate Islamic laws and an Islamic educational system. The newly installed nationalist leaders of the Philippines rejected those demands. Furthermore, the new Philippine government continued the previous US policy of supporting a massive influx of non-Muslim settlers to lands that Moros believed to be their traditional domain. These new settlers generated bitter conflicts that developed into highly mobilized violent contests between Muslims and Christians.[15]

For centuries the Moros had trading and political links with Muslim communities beyond the boundaries of the Philippines. These political links inspired some Moros to contemplate options of political realignments that would reunite them with their religious compatriots who were part of Brunei's tributary system. During the colonial era, Brunei's dependencies became British North Borneo. When Malaysia was formed in 1963, North Borneo was renamed and incorporated into Malaysia as the state of Sabah. At the same time, the Philippines also claimed title to Sabah, based on ancient claims of the sultan of Sulu. Settlement of that claim was raised at the Manila Conference in 1963 among Malaysia, the Philippines, and Indonesia, but that dispute was never resolved.[16] In 1967, Tun Mustapha bin Harun became the elected chief minister of Sabah. He was a Sulut who had emigrated from Sulu to Sabah to become a founding leader of the Sabah National Organization, representing Muslim communities of Sabah. Once in power, Tun Mustapha gave both overt and covert support for the Moro liberation movement. With strong links to the Moro leaders in the southern Philippines, Tun Mustapha established secret guerrilla training camps in Sabah to promote the Moro separatist cause. These activities prompted an official complaint from the Philippine government, accusing Sabah authorities of permitting guerrilla training bases in Sabah and facilitating the transshipments of arms, money, and supplies to support Moro insurgents. The Malaysian government replied that such charges were "unsupportable."[17]

By 1969, several Moro separatist organizations began operations with significant foreign assistance. One was called the Mindanao Independence Movement (MIM), and another was called the Union of Islamic Forces and Organizations. Both these groups sent recruits to training camps in Sabah and Perak. Nur Misuari, a former student at the University of the Philippines, was one of ninety Moro military trainees at the first class that received training from Malaysian instructors at the Pangkor Camp in Perak. With the approval of his classmates and the support from foreign sponsors, Nur Misuari founded the Moro National Liberation Front in 1971.[18] Under his leadership, this organization rapidly gained recognition and financial assistance from Muslim states, including Malaysia, Indonesia, Libya, Saudi Arabia, and others. As the political power of the MNLF became evident, leaders of MIM decided to merge with the MNLF to further the Moro separatist cause.[19]

Increasing tensions between Muslim and Christian communities in the southern Philippines prompted many religiously defined communities to form paramilitary "self-defense" forces. Muslims called their paramilitary units "Barracudas" and referred to non-Muslim paramilitary units as Ilagas (rats). The non-Muslim private paramilitary forces received support and armaments from the Philippine military, while the Moro paramilitary received theirs from their foreign sponsors. Moros traditionally were noted for carrying firearms as a means of personal defense. For generations, Moros had well-developed smuggling and contraband connections, especially with Sabah, where local officials with Moro sympathies enabled gun runners to ply their wares. In Mindanao, serious clashes between these rival Muslim and Christian paramilitary groups began in 1968, often followed by atrocities that fueled continuing retaliatory conflicts.

This episodic violence escalated sharply in 1973 when the military wing of the MNLF, known as the Bangsa Moro Army (BMA), launched a military campaign to establish an independent Moro Republic in the southern Philippines. The BMA offensive brought ten towns under their control and temporarily occupied Jolo, the capital of Sulu. To crush the rebellion, the Philippine Army launched massive operations, often with brutal and devastating impacts upon civilian populations. While the army repulsed most attacks, both sides sustained high casualty rates. Between 1973 and 1976, the conflict had produced a death toll of over 100,000 with a refugee total of 500,000.[20]

By 1974, it became apparent that the struggle in the southern Philippines had reached a virtual stalemate. The foreign sponsors of the MNLF as well as the Philippine government realized that a political settlement was essential to limit the carnage on both sides. In Malaysia, Tun Mustapha was removed as chief minister of Sabah, which effectively restricted the use of Sabah as a "rear base" for MNLF operations. The Organization of the Islamic Conference (OIC) offered to supervise a cease-fire, and some Muslim states offered "good offices" to promote a political settlement. Eventually, both the MNLF and the

Philippine government agreed to negotiations that began in Jeddah in January and concluded in Tripoli, Libya, in December 1976. What came to be called the Tripoli Agreement provided for a cease-fire, with the MNLF, headed by Nur Misuari, agreeing to terms providing for the MNLF to lay down its arms, in return for recognition by the Philippine government. Thirteen provinces in the southern Philippines were to become a Muslim autonomous region, with the terms of autonomy to be determined later in consultation with MNLF leaders.[21]

During the Tripoli Agreement negotiations, serious divisions developed among the MNLF leadership over the terms offered by the Philippines. The opposition faction, led by Salamat Hashim, summarily announced the "takeover" of the MNLF. An internal coup never materialized, but the dissident faction broke away to form the Moro Islamic Liberation Front. Back in the southern Philippines, in a shuffle of loyalties over succession, a majority of guerrilla fighters opted to align with the MILF so that the original MNLF was not able to deliver the "peace" that it had promised by the terms of the Tripoli Agreement.

Because of the ambiguity of the agreement and lack of trust between the parties, neither side fully honored that agreement. The Philippine government made significant concessions to Muslims on education and culture, but sought to manage those concessions. At the same time, President Marcos undermined the promise for "autonomy" by authorizing plebiscites in the thirteen designated provinces, which process allowed non-Muslim majorities to "opt out" of the regional autonomy scheme.[22] The talks intended to create agreement for implementing the Tripoli Agreement finally broke down in 1987. Marcos then proceeded in 1990 to impose his version of an Autonomous Region of Muslim Mindanao (ARMM) staffed with compliant Muslims who were given limited powers and a moderate budget for development projects.

In frustration and disappointment with the Tripoli Agreement, Nur Misuari went abroad to solicit assistance from Islamic governments and organizations. In Iran, he gained the support of the Ayatollah Khomeini, who imposed an Iranian oil embargo on the Philippines in 1979 for its failure to implement the Tripoli Agreement.[23] In the southern Philippines, the military conflict resumed between the Philippine Army and various guerrilla groups—the BMA, the MILF, and the CCP/NPA—all involved in skirmishes for control of turf. During the years from 1976 to 1986, these conflicts appeared to have become a stalemate. However, during that period, the MILF gathered recruits and acquired from abroad more lethal weapons in preparation for a renewed rebellion for Moro independence.

The overthrow of the Marcos regime and the victory of Corazon Aquino in the People Power revolution of 1986 provided an opportunity to reevaluate the Moro issue from a new political perspective. President Aquino was eager to bring the Moro insurgency to a peaceful conclusion. In 1986, she met Misuari in Jolo, but those talks quickly stalled over the terms of autonomy and its territorial scope. A year later, her brother-in-law, Butz Aquino, acting as her emissary, met in Jeddah with Misauri under the auspices of the Organization of the Islamic Conference. Together they reached an agreement, known as the Jeddah Accord, whereby the MNLF renounced its goal of Moro independence and accepted autonomy for thirteen provinces "subject to democratic processes." Following this agreement, the Philippine Congress passed a law authorizing the ARMM, which provided for plebiscites in the thirteen identified provinces. When only four provinces voted for inclusion in the ARMM, the MNLF condemned both the process and the result. Nur Misuari had expected to head a thirteen-province regional government but was now offered a watered-down version of only four provinces plus the city of Marani in the heart of the former Maguindanao Sultanate.

New negotiations began in 1992 under President Fidel Ramos and concluded in 1996, with interventions and "good offices" provided by Libya, Indonesia, and the OIC. Finally, in March 1996, the MNLF and the government of the Philippines signed a peace agreement that established arrangements for a four-province ARMM and the integration of MNLF forces into the armed forces of the Philippines. Altogether, 5,070 MNLF fighters laid down their arms, and 2,200 were integrated into the Philippine Army or the Police. About 600 of those were formed into a Special Regional Security Force that was placed under the authority of the ARMM governor. When the ensuing ARMM elections were held, Misuari was elected governor without opposition.[24]

Besides being governor of ARMM, Nur Misuari was also chairman of the Southern Philippines Council for Peace and Development (SPCPD). This organization was funded by the Philippine government to support economic and social development projects for the autonomous region. In addition, Misuari solicited donations from Muslim organizations and governments abroad to support SPCPD projects. Within a year, large sums of money flowed through both agencies headed by Misuari. The Philippine government provided P43 billion (US$1.65 billion) to ARMM over five years, while the UN Multi-Donor Assistance Program provided P8.3 billion (US$319 million) for SPCPD projects.[25]

By 2001, many of Misuari's associates became disenchanted with his management of funds, arbitrary leadership style, patronage, and corrupt practices. They accused him of pocketing funds from poverty alleviation programs and spending P20 million (US$770,000) for his costly foreign travels.[26] On April 29 the MNLF Executive Council met and voted to make him chair emeritus, thereby removing his power base as governor of ARMM and as chair of SPCPD. Philippine president Gloria Macapagal-Arroyo supported this action and then reconstituted the SPCPD and appointed a new chairman, the secretary-general of MNLF, Muslimin G. Sema. To select a new ARMM governor, a special election was called, and Misuari refused to run, contending that his dismissal and the special election were both illegal. When the election votes were counted, Farouk Hussin emerged the victor.

Angered by his loss of power, Misuari mobilized about 600 ARMM fighters still under his command to attack four Philippine military installations in Jolo. In the initial attack, 118 civilians were captured and taken hostage. When faced with a formidable Philippine Army retaliatory force, Misuari and six of his closest associates fled to Malaysia. When he had been there previously, he was honored as a hero of the Moro struggle. This time, however, Malaysian authorities detained him and eventually extradited him to the Philippines where he was then charged with rebellion, sedition, and corruption. While in detention and awaiting trial in the Philippines, Misuari unsuccessfully ran for governor of Sulu against the former vice governor of ARMM, Benjamin Loong.[27] Despite this setback, Misuari, while in detention, announced he would eventually make a political comeback. ARMM and SPCPD continued to function with newly elected MNLF leaders who were more willing to cooperate with the Philippine government.

Philippine Islamist Alternative—MILF

When the Moro National Liberation Front split into two factions in 1976, at the time of the signing of the Tripoli Agreement, the breakaway faction founded the Moro Islamic Liberation Front. Led by Salamat Hashim, the MILF refused to compromise on the issue of demanding complete independence for Moroland based on the thirteen provinces originally identified in the Tripoli Agreement. While ideological differences were important, other issues help to explain the fracture. The MNLF reflected distinctive ethnic, tribal, clan, and regional divisions within Moro society. These group identities derived from the autonomous sultanates and *dato* fiefdoms of traditional society. Nur Misuari, leader of the MNLF, came from the Tausig group, who live concentrated on Jolo Island and the Sulu Archipelago. Misuari's international support came primarily from Malaysia and Libya. Salamat Hashim gained his domestic support from Maguindanaon, Iranun, and Maranaw Moros, and his international support came from Egypt and Saudi Arabia. Nur Misuari attended the University of the Philippines, gaining a degree in political science, while Salamat Hashim attended Al-Azhar University in Cairo where he gained a degree in *aqidah* (Islamic faith) in 1967. In his own "bio-data," he cites Sayyid Qutb and Maulana Maududi as the two most important Muslim thinkers who shaped his political and religious viewpoints.[28]

Differences between these two leaders over strategy reflected the strategic calculations of their respective constituencies. The Moro regions represented by Salamat Hashim included vast tracts of remote jungle forests, swampy bog lands, and imposing volcanic mountains on the large Island of Mindanao. The guerrilla fighters within this region were far more confident of their capacity to resist and survive the anti-insurgency operations of the Philippine Army. The MNLF guerrilla forces on the Sulu Archipelago, represented by Nur Misuari, were far more exposed to anti-insurgency operations and were thus more eager to accept a peace treaty that was a compromise, giving partial rewards and benefits rather than complete independence.

Once the MILF became established as an autonomous organization, it systematically expanded its military wing, named the Bangsamoro Islamic Armed Forces (BIAF). The central areas controlled by the BIAF included the central regions of Mindanao in the provinces of Lanao del Norte, Lanao del Sur, North Cotabato, and Maguindanao. Smaller contingents of the BIAF operated in Zamboanga del Norte and Zamboango del Sur. The BIAF established a number of training bases beyond effective control of the Philippine Armed Forces. Initially its main base, called Camp Bushra, was located near Lake Lano. Eventually, another base, named Camp Abu Bakar, was built in a remote region of Maguindanao. Many other lesser bases were built, providing ample facilities for training and sanctuary.

During the 1980s, the MILF engaged in skirmishes with the Philippine Army and with militia groups formed by non-Muslim immigrant communities.[29] When the Marcos government began to falter after the assassination of Benigno Aquino, the membership of the MILF rapidly expanded to 50,000 and the BIAF became more aggressive with direct assaults against military targets. In 1997, the Philippine government began negotiations with the MILF, but an initial agreement only provided for a cease-fire, with the MILF pledging not to provide sanctuary or assistance to criminals. While that agreement did not last long, its provisions were reconfirmed periodically after repeated incidents of conflict.

During the presidency of Joseph Estrada, from June 1998 to January 2001, peace talks continued between the Philippine government and the MILF, but without any progress on substantive issues. In February 2000, a ferry was bombed off Ozamis City, killing thirty-nine passengers. The bombing suspects were traced to an MILF camp, and the attack was in violation of an existing cease-fire agreement. This discovery provided justification for President Estrada to declare an "all-out war" on the MILF insurgents. The Armed Forces of the Philippines (AFP) began a major campaign against the MILF in May, which operations ended on July 9, 2000, with the capture of the MILF headquarters at Camp Abu Bakar. That facility included a complex of 20,000 hectares, complete with training barracks and an arms factory that produced rocket-propelled grenade launchers. Before the base was captured, the MILF forces dispersed to about sixty-five lesser camps in regions under its control.[30] Within a short time, the MILF had moved its primary training operations to Camp Jabal Quba, located on the slopes of the volcano Mount Kararao. By 2002, the MILF built another headquarters complex known as the "Buliok Complex" with an extensive set of military facilities and a large Islamic center, located in Cotabato Province in a remote area near the border with Maguindanao. When a cease-fire between the AFP and the MILF broke down, the

Philippine forces mounted a major attack on the Buliok Complex in February 2003, which ended with the capture of that base. This time the Philippine military established a permanent presence at that location.[31] While the Philippine Army captured that MILF base, its operations failed to significantly deplete MILF forces that retreated to other more remote bases. In 2001, the Philippine National Police estimated that the BIAF numbered between 8,000 and 11,000 fighters.[32] At the time, Philippine authorities were not aware of the international linkages that MILF leaders had successfully established with Al Qaeda and its web of collaborating terrorist groups.

MILF's Al Qaeda Links

Four years after its founding, the MILF addressed the issue of how to respond to the December 1979 Soviet invasion of Afghanistan. Muslims throughout the world were asked to volunteer for the Afghanistan mujahideen, which were being generously funded by their Saudi and US sponsors. Responding to this appeal, the MILF sent about 700 recruits to join the Afghanistan mujahideen. The MILF gave priority to recruiting mid-level ranks so that they could acquire military training and battle experience.[33] About 1987, this cohort of trained, ideologically indoctrinated, and battle-experienced fighters began returning to the Philippines. For the MILF this was a period when their leaders were in the process of building up their military capabilities to mount a major military campaign for the independence of Moroland. Libya provided money and weapons to the MILF until about 1995, after which date it became involved as a "neutral third party" in the peace talks between the MILF and the Philippine government.[34] A year later, Osama bin Laden returned to Afghanistan to open his second Afghan campaign and began renewing contacts with veterans of his first campaign.

In 1988, Osama bin Laden selected his brother-in-law, Muhammed Jamal Khalifa, to establish a network of businesses and organizations to recruit mujahideen and to solicit and manage funds earmarked to support the jihad campaign envisioned by Al Qaeda. Khalifa founded or controlled a cluster of trading and travel companies, as well as heading several Islamic charities. Operating together, these organizations laundered money and provided cover for the disbursement of funds to favored political groups and Islamic terrorist organizations. Many of the funds came from Saudi sources through the Islamic International Relief Organization (IIRO), which supported mosques and Islamic schools, but also surreptitiously funded the Al Qaeda network. To facilitate these activities, Khalifa became the president and chairman of the board of the Philippine branch of the IIRO. With large sums of money available from that source and from Al Qaeda, Khalifa established Al-Maktum University in Zamboanga, which became an institutional base for the promotion of the radical Al Qaeda ideology among the Moros. Al Qaeda provided the money, the

MILF provided training bases, while Libya provided weapons and supplies. The main MILF camp Abu Bakar became the key training base used by Al Qaeda and other militant organizations, including the Abu Sayyaf Group, the Raja Solaiman Movement, Jemaah Islamiyah, Kumpulan Mujahideen Malaysia, and Laskar Jundullah.[35]

Abu Sayyaf: The Radical Residual

In the early 1980s, both the MNLF and the MILF actively recruited Philippine Muslims to join the Afghan mujahideen. Among the 700 recruits from the Philippines who received military training in Afghanistan were two brothers, Abdurajak Janjalani and Khaddafy Janjalani. While training at the camp near Kost, they attracted the attention of Osama bin Laden, who commanded that facility. After the Soviet withdrawal from Afghanistan, the two Janjalani brothers became active within the MNLF, seeking to infuse the jihadi ethos into that organization, which was then committed to a passive guerrilla strategy and to peace negotiations. In 1991, probably after receiving communications from Osama bin Laden, who was then in Sudan, Abdurajak Janjalani made a return visit to Peshawar, where he met Ramzi Yousef, and with the encouragement of the latter, Janjalani agreed to form a group directly affiliated with Al Qaeda. They selected the name Abu Sayyaf and agreed that this group would train jihadi fighters to mount attacks against identified "enemies of Islam." As part of this agreement, Abu Sayyaf received an initial payment of US$6 million from Al Qaeda plus US$80,000 from the IIRO financier, Khalifa. Abu Sayyaf also received a large shipment of weapons from various foreign sources. With this newly acquired support, Abdurajak Janjalani cut his ties with the MNLF and moved Abu Sayyaf into a loose alliance with the MILF, while retaining its operational independence.

With its coffers full, Abu Sayyaf was able to construct a training base in a remote section of Basilan Island. In the latter part of 1993, Ramzi Yousef arrived in the Philippines from Pakistan to teach bomb-making and terrorist tactics to Abu Sayyaf recruits.[36] Several other "experts" and jihadi specialists were sent by Osama bin Laden to jump-start the Abu Sayyaf operation. Even before the arrival of Ramzi Yousef, Abu Sayyaf had begun a campaign of utilizing bombs indiscriminately placed to maximize the terror effect. In its first major attack in 1991, a bomb was set off in Zamboanga where the ship MV *Doulos* was operating as a floating Christian bookstore. Two foreign women were killed in that attack. When Ramzi Yousef began his operations, the pace of the bombing attacks intensified and high-value targets were selected. Some of the early targets were a Wendy's hamburger café and a movie house. Pope John Paul II and President Bill Clinton were both targeted for assassination, but those operations were thwarted. From 1991 to 2000, Abu Sayyaf staged 378 terrorist acts, kidnapped 640 people, and killed 288 civilians.[37]

Ramzi Yousef devised the most ambitious Abu Sayyaf operation, Oplan Bojinka. It was a scheme so brazen and ambitious that it went well beyond the bounds of what security agencies at that time considered their worst-case scenario. The plan involved the coordination of some fifteen or twenty cell members, who were to plant bombs on eleven US jetliners that flew across the Pacific, and to do so with such precision that the bombs would all detonate simultaneously. This was to be achieved by having members of the attack team board flights departing from one Asian city and stopping at another Asian city before continuing on a trans-Pacific flight. The team members were to depart with a trans-Pacific flight ticket, place a hidden bomb in the aircraft cabin during the first leg and then depart from the flight before it continued on its trans-Pacific leg. If this plan were successful, it would have destroyed eleven planes, producing a death toll of about 4,000 persons. This elaborate terrorist attack was supposedly to secure the release from prison of Sheikh Omar Abdel Rahman, the "blind cleric," who had been convicted for his role in the 1993 bombing of the World Trade Center. How the destruction of the eleven aircraft would lead to his release from a US prison remained unclear.

In a preliminary test for this plan, a Philippines Airlines flight was bombed in December 1994, killing a Japanese businessman. The plane did not disintegrate and was able to make an emergency landing. If the explosive charge had been larger, the result would have been very different. The next stage in the operation involved the manufacture of bombs. Abdul Hakim Murad, an expert bomb-maker, arrived at Ramzi Yousef's apartment in Manila to help with the bomb production. While they were mixing chemicals a fire broke out, producing poisonous gas. They fled the apartment, and when firemen arrived they found chemicals, bomb-making equipment, and manuals for the manufacture of bombs. They also found Ramzi Yousef's laptop computer containing details of Oplan Bojinka. When Murad returned to the apartment to collect the computer, Philippine police arrested him. Yousef fled to Pakistan, was arrested a month later, and was extradited to the United States. Both men faced trial in New York, during which Murad's testimony helped to convict Yousef, who was found guilty of masterminding both Oplan Bojinka and the 1993 New York World Trade Center bombing. Yousef and Murad were sentenced to life imprisonment for their terrorist acts.[38]

In 1998, the leader of the Abu Sayyaf Group (ASG), Abdurajak Janjalani, was killed in a skirmish with police at the village of Lamitan on Basilan Island. The ASG may have split into several factions because of disputes over succession and to avoid police detection. The capture in 2003 of Ghalib Andang, otherwise known as Commander Robot, who was a factional ASG leader, may have enabled Khaddafy Janjalani to become undisputed leader of the ASG. After the notoriety created by Ramzi Yousef's terrorist activities, the focus of ASG appeared to shift to acts of assassination, kidnapping for ransom, and random bombing incidents. For two or three years, the ASG focused on urban-based terrorism, perhaps on the assumption that targets of opportunity could readily be identified and operatives could be concealed amidst urban poverty population centers. The new strategy may also have been induced by the capture of a key ASG base in Basilan in June 1994 by the Philippine Army.

As financial support from foreign sources dwindled, Abu Sayyaf increasingly relied on hostage-taking for ransom, bombing, extortion, and trade in drugs and contraband. The targets for hostage-taking were Christian missionaries, Filipino Christians, businessmen, and US tourists. Quite often, during kidnapping operations some hostages were beheaded, both for political reasons and to intensify the pressure for ransom payment. After some incidents of hostage-taking, Libya, Malaysia, Germany, or France paid the demanded ransom for hostage releases. In one attack, the ASG seized the town of Apil in Mindanao; 57 people were killed and the town was set afire. In another operation in 2000, the ASG raided the Malaysian tourist resort of Sipidan, with 21 hostages taken, 3 persons killed, and Libya paid US$15 million to US$20 million ransom to ASG. A similar raid in 2001 on the beach resort of Dos Palmas on Palawan Island netted 20 tourists taken hostage, with 4 killed, 3 of whom were beheaded. The most audacious ASG bombing attack in 2004 involved a bombing that sunk *SuperFerry 14* shortly after it left from Manila on its way to Davao. That bombing produced a death toll of 116, with 300 others injured, to make it the second most deadly terrorist attack in Asia, exceeded only by the Bali bombing of October 12, 2002.[39]

In 2006, the Philippine Army mounted special operations against Abu Sayyaf fighters in Jolo and on Basilan Island. By January 2007, these operations had killed 300 Abu Sayyaf and Jemaah Islamiyah members, including the two top leaders of Abu Sayyaf, Khaddafy Janjalani and Abu Solaiman, who organized the *SuperFerry 14* bombing.[40] Most of the surviving Abu Sayyaf members escaped the dragnet operations by seeking refuge with MILF units in areas covered by their cease-fire agreements.

Raja Solaiman Movement

In the postwar period, poverty levels and unemployment in the Philippines remained at high levels, and these conditions provided incentives for large numbers of Filipinos to seek employment abroad. In the early days, the emigration tended to flow to Canada, the United States, and Malaysia. During the early 1970s, the Middle Eastern labor markets opened up, with Saudi Arabia becoming the largest employer of Filipino workers. Filipino men were recruited primarily as unskilled laborers, and women as domestic servants or nurses. The Saudi government established a set of well-funded institutions to convert non-Muslim migrant workers to Islam. After extended exposure to the Saudi dakwah campaign and to the doctrines of Wahhabi Islam, a small number of Filipino guest workers were persuaded to become Muslims and join the Balik-Islam (return to Islam) movement. Members refer to themselves as "reverts" rather than "converts," based on the argument that Islam was the original religion of the Philippines and that their ancestors had become Christian through forcible conversion by the Spanish conquest.

Reflecting this ideological perspective of "diverted destiny" enforced by colonial rule, one of the more dedicated Balik-Islam activists was Ahmad Santos. At his birth in 1971, he was named Hilarion Santos and was raised in a strict Catholic family, but he converted to Islam in 1993, at which time he changed his first name to Ahmad. Later, he became a leader of an Islamic dakwah group, and in 2001, with Abu Sayaaf support, he and some of his followers went to the MILF's Camp Bushra in Mindanao for guerrilla training. While at that camp in January 2002, he was persuaded to form the Raja Solaiman Movement (RSM).[41] The name commemorates the memory of the Muslim barangay chief who, in precolonial days, ruled in the locality of Manila and who was killed, along with 300 of his warriors, leading a futile battle in 1571 against the extension of Spanish rule.

The Raja Solaiman Movement became an offshoot of the Abu Sayaaf Group, with the objective of recruiting ex-Christians to become jihadi volunteers who would blend into the non-Muslim Filipino landscape in order to carry on an epic struggle against the kafir world. At its founding, the RSM was given US$200,000 by Khaddafy Janjalani, then head of ASG, with instructions to convert Filipino Christians and then recruit them for terrorist training at ASG or MILF camps. The RSM also received regular contributions of Saudi Arabian money delivered through various Muslim charities. Under the leadership of Ahmad Santos, the RSM operated from the suburbs of Manila and in northern Tarlac province on Luzon, recruiting Balik-Islam converts for guerrilla training activities. The political and ideological affinity between ASG and RSM was reinforced by multiple marriage links between the leaders of both organizations.[42]

RSM operatives became key players in many of the operations staged by Abu Sayyaf. Santos was identified as a participant in the Sipidan Island raid during which twenty-one tourists were kidnapped in 2000. After the bombing and sinking of *SuperFerry 14* on February 27, 2004, the police detained Redondo Dellosa who had openly boasted of his role in the ferry bombing. Police interrogation revealed that Dellosa was an RSM recruit who had received bomb-making training in 2002 at the Jemaah Islamiyah's Camp Medina in Mindanao. One year after the ferry bombing, RSM operatives set off three nearly simultaneous bombs in Manila's financial district, Davao City, and General Santos City, killing eleven and wounding fifty-three persons.[43]

Strategy and Tactics in "Peace Process" Negotiations

The first peace talks between the Philippine government and the MILF began in 1997 with a series of cease-fire agreements that were periodically broken both by guerrilla attacks and by military counterinsurgency measures, only to be followed by a resumed cease-fire agreement and further negotiations. When issues of a possible "political settlement" were discussed, the MILF was unyielding in demanding an East Timor–type plebiscite of Moros to sanction independence and demanded also that Moro "ancestral domains" be recognized to define boundaries for a Moro homeland territory. The MILF delegation argued that this would be the only solution to the "Moro problem." During these negotiations, the MILF gave high priority to having its main camps identified as cease-fire areas that established de facto sovereignty and created the semblance of legitimacy through "incrementality and irreversibility." When attacked by superior government forces, the guerrillas followed the strategy of "retreat, regroup, and return." As soon as government forces concluded their military forays into remote jungle areas where MILF guerrillas trained, the dispersed guerrillas rapidly reorganized to resume their insurgent operations. The MILF leaders believed that by their sustained actions they could eventually demonstrate that anti-insurgency operations would prove to be too costly and too counterproductive to be sustained.

The Philippine strategic plan was not made public until 2000 in a document entitled *National Peace and Development Plan*. It called for a long-term strategy addressing rebellions through coordinated security operations combined with development programs. In summary, the plan envisioned four phases: "clear, hold, consolidate, and develop." "Clear" involved destroying rebel bases. "Hold" involved maintaining a security presence in the area. "Consolidate" involved an integrated defense system while promoting civil "counter-organizations." "Develop" involved promoting economic growth and productivity through provisions of social services and through government and private investments.[44] Subsequent events revealed that this plan also included "peace negotiations" as part of this overall strategy.

The Philippine strategy approved cease-fire agreements with the MILF as a way to hold them accountable for activities within those boundaries. The strategy depended on a strong presence of the Philippine Army in MILF operational areas, ready and able to respond to overt cease-fire violations and "criminal activities" with powerful countermeasures. The early talks produced no agreements on substantive issues related to a final political settlement. Even so, both parties pursued a "talk and fight" strategy, on the assumption that over time their political objectives would be advanced.

The 9/11 terrorist attacks on New York and Washington, DC, in 2001 had an immediate impact on the peace process and on the counterinsurgency operations of the Philippine government. Shortly after September 11, President Gloria Macapagal-Arroyo announced that the Philippines would assist the United States and work with the UN to implement Resolution 1368, calling for a worldwide campaign against terrorism.[45] By November, the United States and the Philippines negotiated an agreement for the presence of US troops to train Philippine forces in counterterrorism operations. The initial deployment involved 1,300 US troops, and by February 2003, the number had increased to an estimated 3,000 troops, including 1,000 Marines. As part of the security collaboration, the United States provided a package of military assistance, direct financial aid, and trade benefits worth several billion dollars.[46]

When US troops arrived, they began training with Philippine military units and became involved with active joint operations in pursuit of the forces of Abu Sayyaf that had been identified by the United States as "a terrorist group." The Philippine government requested that the United States refrain from putting the MILF on its foreign terrorist list, primarily because the Philippines and the MILF were actively engaged in "peace talks" that had been under way before 9/11. Philippine officials argued that overly aggressive action against the MILF would jeopardize those negotiations. Even so, the active presence of US troops engaged in field operations put increased pressure on the MILF to avoid staging overt terrorist incidents or collaborating with organizations appearing on the terrorist list.[47]

The technical and military assistance package of the United States increased the security capabilities of the Philippine government. Not only was more equipment and better training available to the Philippine Army, but the military aid package enabled the Philippine Congress to authorize a 30 percent increase in the size of the Philippine Army, which provided support for about forty new army battalions. The anti-insurgency capabilities of the Philippines were also enhanced by a package of nonmilitary components. These included more-effective monitoring and interdiction of guerrilla supply routes, the freezing of assets of Islamic charities, and increasing control of the hawala system of banking that had been exploited to fund radical guerrilla operations. After 2002, US Special Operations Forces began monitoring suspected terrorist movements via surveillance by unmanned aerial vehicles and electronic intercepts.

In January 2001, when Vice President Gloria Macapagal-Arroyo became president of the Philippines, she was determined to restart peace talks with the Moro Islamic Liberation Front following President Estrada's "all-out war" against MILF insurgents that failed to end the insurgency. The resumption of peace talks between the GRP and the MILF began in Tripoli and concluded on June 22, 2001, with an agreement on guidelines for further talks. Malaysia was selected as the "host and official facilitator" of future negotiations concerned with security, rehabilitation, and ancestral domains. Malaysia acted as host for formal sessions that usually were held in Malaysia.[48] Malaysia's role as host and third-party facilitator expanded dramatically in 2004 after a series of cease-fire violations and peace-talk breakdowns. Both the GRP and the MILF agreed to the formation of an International Monitoring Team (IMT) composed of forty-six Malaysians, ten Bruneians, and four Libyans. The IMT was charged with monitoring cessation of hostility activities and progress on development agreements, with periodic reports to GRP-MILF peace panels on violations and actions that should be taken. The IMT began on-site monitoring on October 10, 2004.[49]

Over time, Malaysia's role in the peace process gradually shifted from conciliation to mediation. As a Muslim state that recognized and supported a political and cultural role for Islam, it was viewed by the MILF as a defender and advocate of Muslim rights and privileges. At the same time, Malaysia, as a member of the Association of Southeast Asian Nations (ASEAN), expressed a respect for the territorial integrity of the Philippines and had a proven record of combating militant Islamic radicalism within its own borders. Malaysia's policymakers were concerned about political instability in Southeast Asia and were fearful that major conflicts in Mindanao would trigger a large influx of refugees to Sabah and create security concerns about gun-running, piracy, and kidnapping. Malaysia had already experienced the devastating effects of Abu Sayyaf's raid on Sipidan Island when twenty-one tourists were taken hostage, three of whom were killed, and a large ransom was paid for the release of the survivors.[50] While Malaysia's leaders were sensitive to the grievances of Muslims in the Philippines, they were also committed to a just solution to the Moro insurgency that would preserve the territorial integrity of the Philippines.

The Evolution of Revolution

The enhanced security capabilities of the Philippine military and police, combined with more comprehensive antiterrorist policies, produced a significant attrition of support and recruits for insurgent and terrorist groups in the Philippines. With US support, the counterinsurgency operations targeted Abu Sayyaf as the prime listed terrorist organization. Generous rewards of up to US$5 million were offered to the public by the United States for information leading to the capture of Abu Sayyaf members and their supporters. The combination of military sweeps and reward incentives produced escalating numbers of arrests of highly ranked ASG members. By 2004, Abu Sayyaf operatives began moving from hiding in "safe houses" located in urban slums back to jungle hideouts, this time in the areas of Mindanao controlled by the MILF. The Abu Sayyaf leaders sought to take advantage of the GRP-MILF cease-fire to secure a safe sanctuary removed from the threats of citizen disclosures induced by reward money.[51] The antiterrorist tactics of the Philippine Army and Police also forced other jihadi groups to change tactics and seek the more remote sanctuaries of the MILF's cease-fire zones.

Although the MILF was not the prime target of the anti-insurgency operations, the Philippine security cordon around MILF cease-fire areas increased the logistical problems of maintaining the large forces under their command. The MILF's armed units of the BIAF were estimated to constitute a force of between 8,000 and 45,000 fighters.[52] Whatever the figure, the BIAF was of sufficient size that it faced serious problems of supply and financial support.

Effective interdiction by Philippine authorities of the MILF supply chain forced the BIAF to intensify its reliance on "revolutionary taxes," extortion, drug trafficking, and recruiting workers for overseas employment through a system of kickbacks from Middle East employers. These actions of participation in an "underground economy" created a dilemma for the MILF. Their representatives at the peace talks wished to project a public image of a peaceful organization capable of commanding wide public support. It was on the basis of this image and the projected expectation of an impending political settlement that the Philippine government persuaded the United States not to place the MILF onto its sanction list of terrorist organizations. Yet, the continuing incidents of terrorist tactics by BIAF units and the revelations that the MILF continued to maintain close ties with the Abu Sayyaf Group and Jemaah Islamiyah, both linked to Al Qaeda, undermined that public image. When terrorist incidents occurred, the spokesman for the MILF would usually attribute the atrocities and attacks to "lost commands" or "rogue units," rather than accepting MILF responsibility for those incidents. The commitment of the MILF to cease-fire agreements appeared to be ambiguous or insincere. Was it pursuing a "fight with deniability" campaign? Or had it become so decentralized that individual units were allowed to engage in "local initiatives" to secure funding and replenish supplies through coercive extractions and terrorist acts? The tactics used by "rogue" factions included bombings, assassinations of MILF defectors, and capturing of civilian hostages for ransom.[53]

At the peace talks in 2002, the GRP and MILF announced that they "agreed to the isolation and interdiction of all criminal syndicates and kidnap-for-ransom groups, including the so-called 'lost commands' operating in Mindanao."[54] In effect, this agreement attempted to make a distinction between "peace-seekers" and "terrorist criminals." The Philippine government assumed that the terms of this agreement authorized unilateral Philippine responses to any violent criminal acts or any use of rebel bases for training or harboring any persons affiliated with foreign terrorist organizations (FTOs) as identified by the United States and the UN. The MILF maintained that any such security action required a collaborative response through the joint Coordinating Committee for the Cessation of Hostilities (CCCH) that had been formed by both parties under the terms of earlier cease-fire agreements.[55] These differences of treaty interpretation became highlighted after several serious criminal apprehension incidents.

In August 2004, the Philippine Army raided the lair of a kidnap-for-ransom group known as the Pentagon Gang. During that operation, seventeen Pentagon Gang men were killed, including its leader. Later the same year, the military staged another raid on a kidnap-for-ransom group named Abu Sofia. That raid also killed a number of gang members including its leader, Bedis Binago. His brother, Abdul Rahman Binago, commanded the MILF's 105th Base Command. To avenge his brother's death, Binago led 200 MILF fighters in a surprise assault that overran two AFP cantonments. The Philippine military responded with a robust counterassault that lasted several days. News accounts reported the death of fifty MILF fighters, seven AFP soldiers, and over twenty civilians. The MILF chief negotiator at the peace talks attributed that attack to *rido*, the long-established Moro custom of settling family feuds by retaliatory vendetta. The MILF spokesman reported that Binago's attack was "not authorized" and promised "to investigate" the incident.

At the next peace-talk meetings in April 2005, the government turned over a list of fifty-three terrorist suspects, and the MILF negotiators agreed "to locate and arrest" those on the list. MILF spokesman Eid Kabalu also stated that "the MILF will arrest one of its commanders if found to be shielding those on the list."[56] One year later, in October 2005, the MILF announced that the 105th Base Command had been "deactivated" and two of its subcommanders had been "suspended." However, Commander A. R. Binago continued to command the loyalty of his fighters, and very little changed on the ground, but the MILF no longer assumed responsibility for their actions.[57] Despite their earlier promises to arrest "criminals and terrorists," by July 2006, the MILF had not turned over any terrorist suspect to Philippine authorities, while MILF training for jihadi recruits continued at remote locations, albeit at a reduced pace.[58]

The death of MILF chairman Salamat Hashim on July 13, 2003, appeared to have altered the political dynamics within the MILF. The announcement of his death was delayed for two weeks, following which Al-Haj Murad Ebrahim was reported to be the new chairman.[59] Most observers believed that Murad was more pragmatic than his predecessor and that he would be more willing to strike a peace deal to give MILF leaders substantial power in regions it controlled while preserving Philippine sovereignty. Yet, Murad's accession to leadership also exposed political divisions within the MILF. The decentralized nature of the MILF had allowed some MILF factions to retain links with Al Qaeda and other radical groups. In January 2003, two Al Qaeda agents involved with its financial operations were arrested and their interrogation revealed that Al Qaeda had provided financial support for the radical MILF faction to undermine peace talks by staging attacks on the Philippine Army.[60]

By 2005, the increased success of Philippine security operations had driven militant groups to seek sanctuary in remote areas of MILF's cease-fire zones. Some guerrillas became virtual freelance jihadis, who moved from one group to another based on personal contacts and shifting loyalties. The periodic security operations of the AFP tended to drive Islamist organizations into mutual support networks. An informal alliance began to emerge between Abu Sayyaf, the Raja Solaiman Movement, Jemaah Islamiyah, Mujahideen Kompak, Laskar Jundullah, and "renegade" factions of the MILF. In addition, some militants from the New People's Army migrated to the RSM to increase their pool of recruits. Based on police records and the testimony of captured terrorists, the number of foreign jihadi trainees at camps in Mindanao "easily exceeded 200" in the years from 2001 to mid-2005.[61] This complex interlinking of diverse militant groups produced severe complications for the GRP-MILF peace process. These political and factional rivalries effectively split the MILF into the "central command" and "renegade" or "lost command" units.

Despite continued frictions, both sides were eager to keep the peace process moving toward an eventual agreement. Murad and his leadership faction were eager to cash in on the rewards of an agreement that would transfer a large area of Mindanao to their authority. Peace-talk discussions had included issues of ceding control over the mineral and natural resources of the area to a newly created Muslim political entity. During the extended cease-fire agreements from 2001 to 2007, many of these top MILF leaders had moved their families to the cities and placed their children in state schools. Over the years, a sense of war weariness had undermined the militancy and zeal of the older generation of MILF leaders. The deterioration of weapons and aging ammunition stocks had gradually reduced the military capacity of the MILF forces. Even so, there remained within the MILF a formidable autonomous and militant faction committed to an unyielding campaign for Moro independence.[62]

The Ampatuan Incident

The politics within the MILF was partly shaped by the example of the MNLF and its 1996 agreement to operate within the political system of the Autonomous Region of Muslim Mindanao. At that time, some disgruntled MNLF members defected to the MILF to carry on the fight against Philippine rule. In addition, some MNLF fighters who had been demobilized after the 1996 peace agreement later reconstituted a militant, rearmed faction of the MNLF to control territory and extract further concessions. Yet, there was also a countermigration of MILF members who defected to the MNLF in order to return to civilian life and benefit from development projects sponsored by ARMM and supported by the Philippine government and foreign aid donors.

One such defector from the MILF was Andal Ampatuan who was a Datu of the Ampatuan clan that had traditionally ruled the municipality (regional subdivision) of Ampatuan. Capitalizing on his traditional status, he won election as mayor of Shariff Aguak, continuing in office for three terms. In 2001, he ran for governor of Maguindanao, defeating incumbent governor Zacaria Candao, who had close ties with the MILF. Governor Ampatuan rapidly developed a powerful province-wide political machine based on patronage and the loyalty network of the Ampatuan clan. He recruited ex-guerrillas and unemployed youth for the Civilian Volunteer Organization (CVO) that performed "social and political work." The CVOs became a political militia that was supposedly staffed by unarmed civilians, but when coercive force was needed, these units could rapidly be armed with weapons from concealed arms stashes. In addition, each district maintained an armed militia known as the Citizens

Armed Forces Geographical Units (CAFGU) to act as "home guard" units under the authority of mayors of municipalities.[63]

Governor Andal Ampatuan cultivated close relations with the Philippine Army's Sixth Infantry Division and skillfully established political alliances with other clan leaders as well as with Christian power holders. Because most of the revenues for the province and for ARMM came from the national government, the Ampatuan political machine became closely affiliated with President Gloria Macapagal-Arroyo's party, the ruling Lakas-Christian Muslim Democrats. The proven vote-getting capacity of the Ampatuan political machine was used to maximize its political clout at the national level. Within three years after his election as governor of Maguindanao, Andal Ampatuan had helped to elect four of his sons and a large number of his clan members as mayors of municipalities and as barangay council members in Maguindanao. In August 2005, his son, Zaldy Ampatuan, was elected governor of the Autonomous Region of Muslim Mindanao.

When Andal Ampatuan first became governor of Maguindanao, he retained his earlier contacts with the MILF, providing food supplies and tolerating several camps that were built by the "renegade" 105th Base Command within the borders of Ampatuan. At some point, a serious dispute erupted between the leaders of that MILF unit and the Ampatuan political machine. The dispute probably involved local control of land and the collection of "revolutionary taxes" by the 105th Base Command.[64] Rising political tensions in Maguindanao became manifest in 2002 when Governor Ampatuan and his son, the mayor of Datu Piang, Saudie Ampatuan, were ambushed while traveling in a motor convoy. Two bodyguards were killed in that attack but both Andal and Saudie survived without injury. Later that year, Saudie Ampatuan was assassinated by a bomb attack that killed thirteen and injured twelve others.[65] Governor Andal Ampatuan became the target of a third failed assassination attempt and later survived a fourth bombing on June 23, 2006, when a remotely triggered bomb exploded as his motorcade passed through Shariff Aguak. Seven people were killed, including two of the governor's relatives.

Director General A. C. Lomibao of the Philippine National Police immediately flew to Shariff Aguak to oversee the criminal investigation, which revealed that the bomb was made from 81-millimeter mortar shells and C-4 explosives. Police intelligence revealed that two Indonesian instructors had recently conducted bomb-making courses at the nearby MILF camp. Based on other collected evidence, General Lomibao issued four warrants for arrest of suspects, including the MILF's 105th base commander Jamil Ombra Kato and brigade commander Sajid Pakiladato. The ARMM chief of police was instructed to serve the arrest warrants.[66] Backed by a sizable contingent of CVO and CAFGU forces, the police chief attempted to serve the arrest warrants at nearby Camp Omar. The approaching party encountered deadly fire from the forces of the 105th Base Command.[67]

The next day, the Philippine Army's Sixth Infantry Division arrived to rescue the retreating and embattled local militia forces. The army employed several tanks and armored personnel carriers and used a barrage of 105-millimeter howitzers to cover CAFGU and CVO withdrawals.[68] Over the next week, fighting engulfed a large area comprising thirteen villages that were burned and involved the flight of over 22,000 refugees. After eight days of conflict and scores of casualties on both sides, the Malaysian-led IMT negotiated a cease-fire to separate the combatants. The issue of serving warrants of arrest on bombing suspects was turned over for future action to the joint GRP-MILF Coordinating Committee on the Cessation of Hostilities. Those warrants were never served, and the accused suspects never faced criminal prosecution.[69]

An Elusive Peace Process

Before the outbreak of the miniwar between MILF's "renegades" versus the militia forces of the Ampatuan clan, the Philippine government and the "regular" MILF, led by Murad, had been making significant progress toward a final peace agreement. Despite numerous breakdowns in the peace process, both parties repeated their determination to proceed with the formulation of a final peace treaty. In 2001, the negotiations had produced an agreement on security arrangements. In 2002, another agreement addressed humanitarian, rehabilitation, and development issues. In 2005, the two parties made further progress by signing a statement on April 20 of "points of agreement" on the issue of "ancestral domains" for Mindanao and other areas claimed by the MILF as their ancestral homeland. A further expansion of points of agreement on ancestral domains was signed on September 16, 2005, with a further elaboration agreed to at the February 2006 peace talks. Those agreements did not define the territory for a new Bangsamoro Juridical Entity and avoided issues of governance and rights of indigenous and non-Muslim communities.[70]

The extended discussions over a new political entity for Moros attracted the attention of the indigenous peoples known as Lumuds. In 1997, the Philippine government had passed the Indigenous Peoples Rights Act, which promised special development policies and a degree of autonomy for identified indigenous peoples.[71] In Mindanao, the Lumuds constitute about twenty-three ethno-linguistic tribes comprising about 1 million people, most of whom live in settlements located in interior regions. In 2001, sixty-seven representatives of twenty Lumud tribes met in Davao City to formulate "The Lumud Agenda for Peace in Mindanao." That document recounts how Lumud ancestral territories were taken without compensation, and how hostile combatants built camps and encroached on Lumud ancestral lands, killing many Lumuds and causing much destruction of livestock and property. That document ended with a demand for Lumud participation in the "peace process" among the GPR, the Moro insurgents, and the CPP/NPA.[72] Similar meetings in 2005 and

2006 of Lumud representatives produced a "unified position" paper declaring strong opposition to inclusion of any Lumud settlements in ancestral domains or ancestral lands in the Bangsamoro homeland. The MILF sent spokesmen to reassure the Lumuds that their rights would be respected, but no Lumud leaders were willing to accept any agreement that placed Lumud ancestral lands within an expanded Bangsamoro Autonomous Region.[73]

One year after agreeing on the general principle of "ancestral domains," formal peace talks began in Malaysia on September 5, 2006, to work out details of its boundaries. The Philippine government's proposal offered to expand the Autonomous Region of Muslim Mindanao by adding 613 villages that were identified as having Muslim majorities. The expanded region would be incorporated as the Bangsamoro Juridical Entity (BJE), and it would acquire greater fiscal autonomy than the ARMM and gain a share of profits from natural resources, including minerals and petroleum. The MILF representatives countered with demands for 1,000 additional villages, contiguous boundaries between settlements, and complete control over natural resources. After three days of negotiations, the talks ended with an indefinite postponement of further talks.[74]

Prior to those negotiations, the capacity of the Philippine government to take bold initiatives had been seriously weakened by the results of the 2004 election. President Arroyo had narrowly won reelection for a six-year term with only 40 percent of the vote, facing allegations of fraud in the election count, and with a Congress controlled by a coalition of anti-establishment parties. President Arroyo had to defeat two impeachment campaigns sponsored by opposition parties, and in February 2006, she declared a State of Emergency after alleging the discovery of a coup d'état plot involving "rightist military adventurers." President Arroyo lifted the Emergency Decree after eleven days, but her political vulnerability remained. Philippine commentators observed that any peace agreement that was dependent on a constitutional amendment faced an insurmountable political hurdle. Domestic political considerations had limited the risk-taking capacity of the Philippine government.[75]

For the Moro Islamic Liberation Front, the political constraints had also narrowed. The escalating conflicts involving renegade MILF forces had exposed political divisions within the MILF. It became apparent that no peace treaty could satisfy all MILF factions. Even the regular MILF spokesman stated they would not surrender their weapons or disband their fighting forces after a peace treaty was signed.[76] The Ampatuan miniwar with the renegade MILF 105th Base Command revealed that MILF leaders would not automatically inherit power in any new Bangsamoro Juridical Entity because other tradition-based Moro leaders and those affiliated with the MNLF were politically well entrenched. Even for MILF "moderates," the rewards of a potential peace settlement had become devalued.

The military successes of the Philippine military against Abu Sayyaf during December 2006 and January 2007 significantly altered the political environment for further peace talks. While some key leaders of Abu Sayyaf had been killed and many of its fighters had been captured, many others escaped to find refuge in MILF cease-fire zones. In retreat, these fighters became virtual freelance jihadis, still committed to their cause, but concealing their previous identity. Probably lacking funds, they needed to recoup their losses. On June 10, 2007, in Zamboanga, an Italian priest, Giancarlo Bossi, was kidnapped. Several weeks later, authorities received a report that he was held at a village in Basilan that was in MILF territory. A small patrol of fourteen Philippine Marines was ordered to investigate the area. On their return from their patrol, 400 or more insurgents ambushed the Marines. All members of the patrol were killed, and ten were found decapitated.[77] A week later, Father Bossi was released by his captors and Philippine officials insisted no ransom was paid. The MILF admitted its forces staged the ambush but denied they carried out the decapitations.[78]

The Philippine-MILF peace talks were scheduled to resume in August 2007 in Malaysia, but this kidnapping and ambush further complicated the issues to be resolved. Some members of the Philippine Parliament, responding to the ambush of the Marines, called for a review on whether the government should continue to pursue peace talks with the MILF.[79] When the peace talks finally resumed in November 2007, the MILF wanted to add 600 to 1,000 non-contiguous Muslim areas to the Bangsamoro Juridical Entity. The Philippine team reported that under the Philippine Constitution natural resources are "under the full control" of the Philippine state. The MILF accused the government of reneging on consensus points previously agreed to and later refused to attend peace talks scheduled for December 15–17 in Malaysia. The leader of the Philippine delegation, Jesus Dureza, stated that the government was considering amending the Philippine Constitution to establish a Bangsamoro federal state in Mindanao. Meanwhile, the Moro National Liberation Front warned that any peace accord between the GRP and the MILF would violate the 1996 agreement between GRP and the MNLF establishing the existing ARMM.[80] With no agreement on these conflicting demands, the Mindanao peace process reached a stalemate, with each side blaming the other for the impasse.

Because of the stalemate on the peace talks, the Malaysian government announced on May 10, 2008, that it would withdraw from the IMT when its mandate expired in August 2008. Whether that action would terminate the IMT was uncertain, but whatever may develop regarding the role of international monitors, there will still be plenty of pressure to continue the peace process.[81] The problem is not the lack of a desire for peace in the southern Philippines among the key constituents. Instead, the obstacles to peace arise from the competing claims of multiple constituencies that have vital stakes in the outcome of the peace process, and the low capacity of the leaders of those constituencies to deliver and enforce whatever agreement may emerge from negotiations.

Some form of final agreement may be produced at peace talks, but the process will be halting and laborious. If a final agreement is signed, it is likely to have some of the following ingredients: an expanded Bangsamoro entity with contiguous borders and operating within the Philippine constitutional system; increased autonomy for the region with shared control over natural resources; a set of guarantees to protect Christians and Lumuds within those borders; an agreement to demobilize MILF forces combined with assured employment options for MILF veterans; a large and assured commitment of development funds from Philippine sources, foreign donor governments, and from NGOs; and the establishment of an effective system of accountability to check endemic, rampant corruption, theft, and waste.

Even if a peace agreement were to be signed, most political observers predict that the radical faction of the MILF will not approve any agreement that fails to provide for full independence for an expanded Moroland. If that happens, a militant insurgency will continue and the Philippines will remain vulnerable to a costly prolonged struggle. Any insurgency led by a small number of Moro Muslims will continue to attract support from foreign and domestic Islamist groups, including groups constituting a resilient Al Qaeda–linked network.[82]

Notes

1. A defender of the Muslim political cause claims that Muslims constituted 7 percent of the Philippine population. Cesar Adib Majul, *The Contemporary Muslim Movement in the Philippines* (Berkeley, CA: Mizan Press, 1985), 10–14.

2. Fererico V. Magdalena, "The Peace Process in Mindanao: Problems and Prospects," in *Southeast Asian Affairs 1997* (Singapore: Institute of Southeast Asian Studies, 1997), 245–248. Other sources indicate that Muslims constitute about 27 percent of the population in Mindanao, Sulu, and Palawan. Paul H. Nitze School of Advanced International Studies, *Political Islam in Southeast Asia, Conference Report* (Washington, DC: Johns Hopkins University, March 25, 2003), 3.

3. The Filipino name of the guerrilla force was Hukbo ng Bayan Laban sa Hapon (People's Army Against Japan), and it adopted the shortened name Hukbalahap. This was the military arm of the Communist Party of the Philippines (PKP, Partindo Komunistang Pilipanas). In 1964 this force was renamed Hukbong Mapagpalaya ng Balayan (People's Liberation Army), while retaining the same abbreviated name.

4. David Wurfel, *Filipino Politics: Development and Decay* (Ithaca: Cornell University Press, 1988), 223–225; Benedict Kerkvliet, *The Huk Rebellion: A Study of Peasant Revolt in the Philippines* (Berkeley: University of California Press, 1977); Eduardo Lachica, *The Huks: Philippine Agrarian Society in Revolt* (New York: Praeger, 1971); Stephen Rosskamm Shalom, *The United States and the Philippines: A Study of Neocolonialism* (Philadelphia: Institute for the Study of Human Issues, 1981), 26–32, 52–59.

5. Wurfel, *Filipino Politics*, 165–176, 226–232.

6. Amy Blitz, *The Contested State: American Foreign Policy and Regime Change in the Philippines* (Lanham, MD: Rowman & Littlefield Publishers, 2000), 157–191; Wurfel, *Filipino Politics*, 289–309.

7. Wurfel, *Filipino Politics*, 311–318.

8. Patricio N. Abinales, "State Building, Communist Insurgency and Cacique Politics in the Philippines," in Paul B. Rich and Richard Stubbs (eds.), *The Counter-Insurgent State: Guerrilla Warfare and State Building in the Twentieth Century* (New York: St. Martin's Press, 1997), 26–49.

9. Wurfel, *Filipino Politics*, 310–320. During the elections of 1987, the former founder of the New People's Army, Dante Buscayno, who had been captured in 1976, but released in 1987, became a candidate for a far-left party. While he did not win a seat to the House of Representatives, three other "reformed" Communists were able to do so. Eight years later, a former member of the CPP "high command," Gregorio Honasan, who had also returned to civil life and had renounced his connections with the party, was elected to the Philippine Senate, thus making a complete transition from a "rebel" to a member of the Philippine establishment.

10. Wurfel, *Filipino Politics,* 321–324; Mely Caballero-Anthony, "The Winds of Change in the Philippines: Wither the Strong Republic?" in *Southeast Asian Affairs 2003* (Singapore: Institute of Southeast Asian Studies, 2003), 220; Paul A. Rodell, "The Philippines: Playing Out Long Conflicts," in *Southeast Asian Affairs 2004* (Singapore: Institute of Southeast Asian Studies, 2004), 199; Wolfgang Bethge, "Jose Maria Sison—The Co-founder of the CPP and NPA—in the Dead End," home.arcor.de/be/bethge/sisoneng.htm.

11. "On the Human Rights Violations of the CPP/NPA," www.philso.nl/L NPA-HRVs.htm. Jose Sison, who had been released from detention in 1987 after nine years in jail, fled to the Netherlands, where he claimed political asylum. From his base in Utrecht, he attempted to reclaim ideological leadership of the CPP, operating with a few associates as a "Politburo Out." "Politburo In," operating in the Philippines, was headed by Benito Tiamzon. Many years earlier, Sison and Kintanar had clashed over party politics. From his Netherlands sanctuary, Sison continued with an ideological battle against Kintanar. See Nathan Gilbert Quimpo, "Why Kintanar Was Killed—The Real Story," *Philippines Daily Enquirer*, January 28, 2003, www.philsol.nl/A03a/Kintanar-Quimpo-jan03.htm; Pierre Rousset, "The Post-1992 CPP Assassination Policy in the Philippines," www.philsol.nl. For Jose Sison's account of the peace negotiations and the years of struggle by the CPP, see Jose Maria Sison, *US Terrorism and War in the Philippines* (Breda, Netherlands: Uitgeverij Papieren Tijger, 2003).

12. Caballero-Anthony, "The Winds of Change in the Philippines," 220–223.

13. Interview of MILF spokesman, Eid Kabalu, by ABC–Asia Pacific, July 8, 2003, as cited in C. S. Kuppuswamy, "The Moro Islamic Liberation Front Imbroglio," South Asia Analysis Group, Paper No. 765, August 18, 2003, p. 3; Zachary Abuza, *Militant Islam in Southeast Asia: The Crucible of Terror* (Boulder, CO: Lynne Rienner Publishers, 2003), 41; Karl B. Kaufman and Ma. Theresa Torres, "NPA Raider's Arms Came from MILF," *Manila Times,* January 14, 2004, www.manilatimes.net.

14. Ma. Theresa Torres and Joshua Dancel, "Gov't Offers Cease-Fire as a Way to Restart Talks," *Manila Times*, January 28, 2003, www.manilatimes.net/national/2003/jan/28/top_stories/2003.

15. For an elaboration of Moro concerns and grievances, see Majul, *The Contemporary Muslim Movement in the Philippines*, 10–38.

16. For the basis of the Philippine claim to Sabah, see Gordon P. Means, *Malaysian Politics*, 2nd ed. (London: Hodder and Stoughton, 1976), 314–318.

17. Bruce Ross-Larson, *The Politics of Federalism: Syed Kechik in East Malaysia* (Singapore: Times Printers, 1976), 145–149. For an explanation of the ethnic cultural divisions of Sabah society, see Allen R. Maxwell, "The Origins of the Brunei Kadayan in Ethnohistorical Perspective," in Robert L. Winzeler (ed.), *Indigenous Peoples and the State: Politics, Land, and Ethnicity in the Malayan Peninsula and Borneo* (New Haven, CT: Yale Southeast Asia Studies, Monograph 46, 1997), 135–158.

18. International Crisis Group, *Southern Philippines Backgrounder: Terrorism and the Peace Process*: ICG Asia Report No. 80 (July 13, 2004), Singapore/Brussels, 3–4; Wurfel, *Filipino Politics*, 158; Moshe Yegar, *Between Integration and Secession: The Muslim Communities of the Southern Philippines, Southern Thailand, and Western Burma/Myanmar* (Lanham, MD: Lexington Books, 2002), 267–274.

19. Majul, *The Contemporary Muslim Movement*, 45–65; Andrew Tan, "The Indigenous Roots of Conflict in Southeast Asia: The Case of Mindanao," in Kumar Ramakrishna and See Seng Tan (eds.), *After Bali: The Threat of Terrorism in Southeast Asia* (Singapore: Institute of Defence and Strategic Studies, 2003), 97–100.

20. Wurfel, *Filipino Politics*, 155–161; Tan, "Indigenous Roots," 100–101, citing Temario C. Revera, "Armed Challenges to the Philippines Government: Protracted War or Political Settlement," in *Southeast Asian Affairs 1994* (Singapore: Institute of Southeast Asian Studies, 1994), 260; Christos Iacovou, "From MNLF to Abu Sayyaf: The Radicalization of Islam in the Philippines," 2, www.ict.org.il/articles/articledet.cfm?articleid=116; Bryan Leifer, "Terrorist Organizations in Southeast Asia: Islamic Nationalism," 3, www.ict.org.il/articles/articledet.cfm?articleid=518.

21. Majul, *The Contemporary Muslim Movement,* App. 3, 120–128.

22. Wurfel, *Filipino Politics*, 159-165.

23. Iacovou, "From MNLF," 3, citing Cesar A. Majul, "The Iranian Revolution and the Muslims in the Philippines," in John L. Esposito (ed.), *The Iranian Revolution: Its Global Impact* (Miami: Florida International University Press, 1990), 262–263.

24. Magdalena, "The Peace Process in Mindanao," 245–259; Paul A. Rodell, "The Philippines: Gloria *in Excelsis*," in *Southeast Asian Affairs 2002* (Singapore: Institute of Southeast Asian Studies, 2002), 230–233; "Moro National Liberation Front (MNLF)," at www.globalsecurity.org; Abuza, *Militant Islam,* 41–43. The provinces covered by this 1996 agreement were Tawi-Tawi, Sulu, Lanao del Sur, and Maguindano. Since the armed forces of the MNLF (BMA) were estimated to be about 15,000 in 1990, and only 5,070 of the fighters laid down their arms, a large contingent did not surrender. Many MNLF militia members merely switched loyalties to the more militant MILF, while some became aligned with Abu Sayyaf. For an account of Misuari's mismanagement and the disillusionment of a majority of his followers, see Marites Dañguilan Vitug and Glenda M. Gloria, *Under the Crescent Moon: Rebellion in Mindanao* (Quezon City, Philippines: Ateneo Center for Social Policy and Public Affairs, 2000), 264–301.

25. Eleanor Dictaan-Bang-ao, "The Question of Peace in Mindanao, Southern Philippines," in Chandra K. Roy, Victoria Tauli-Corpuz, and Amanda Romero-Medina (eds.), *Beyond the Silencing of the Guns* (Bagio City, Philippines: Tebtebba Foundation, 2004), 158.

26. Later investigations revealed that Misuari had diverted P42 million to purchase high-powered weapons for his MNLF supporters. Ann Bernadette S. Corvera, "Nur Misuari: Has the 'Good Warrior's' Long Struggle Come to a Disgraceful End?" *The Star*, January 16, 2002, also at www.seasite.niu.edu/Tagalog/Modules/Modules.

27. Rodell, "The Philippines," 230–233; Abuza, *Militant Islam,* 41–45; Julmunir I. Jannaral, "Nur Misuari Running for Governor in Sulu," *The Manila Times,* March 1, 2004, also at www.manilatimes.net/national/2004/mar/01/.

28. Sheikh Abu Zahir, "The Moro Jihad: Continuous Struggle of Islamic Independence in Southern Philippines," interview with Sheikh Salamat Hashim, in *Nida'ul Islam*, April-May, 1998, reproduced at www.islam.org.au.

29. For an account of the politics of the MILF during the 1980s and 1990s, see Vitug and Gloria, *Under the Crescent Moon,* 106–189.

30. Kuppuswamy, "The Moro Islamic Liberation Front Imbroglio," 2–3.

31. International Crisis Group, *Southern Philippines Backgrounder,* 5–8, 15–17. The Buliok Complex was built at a very small settlement named Pagalungan.

32. Angel Rabasa and Peter Chalk, *Indonesia's Transformation and the Stability of Southeast Asia* (Santa Monica, CA: The Rand Corporation, 2001), 87–88.

33. Abuza, *Militant Islam,* 90.

34. To protect its credibility in those peace talks, Libya avoided transferring funds to the MILF after 1995 even though it may have retained political links with the MILF. When Libyan agents were indicted for bombing Pan Am Flight 103 over Scotland in 1998, the United States accused Libya of sponsoring terrorism abroad as a key component of its foreign policy. See US Department of State, *Patterns of Global Terrorism: 1991*, Appendix C, "Libya's Continuing Responsibility for Terrorism," at www.ict.org.il/documents/documentdet.cfm?docid=2.

35. Abuza, *Militant Islam,* 95–103.

36. Ramzi Yousef was the ringleader and mastermind of the first World Trade Center bombing in New York on February 26, 1993. Within hours of that bombing, he flew from New York to Pakistan, where he stayed in "safe houses" operated by Osama bin Laden. While there, he hatched a plot to kill then-president Benazir Bhutto, which failed. Later that same year, Ramzi Yousef was sent to Manila, apparently by Osama bin Laden, along with two colleagues, Khalid Shaikh Mohammed and Abdul Hakim Murad, to provide bomb-making expertise and indoctrination to train the recruits to the newly founded Abu Sayyaf Group. See en.wikipedia.org/wiki/Ramzi_Yousef.

37. Rommel C. Banlaoi, "The Abu Sayyaf Group: From Mere Banditry to Genuine Terrorism," in Daljit Singh and Lorraine Carlos Salazar (eds.), *Southeast Asian Affairs 2006* (Singapore: Institute of Southeast Asian Studies, 2006), 249.

38. Abuza, *Militant Islam,* 99–110; "Bomber's 240-year Sentence," BBC News, April 3, 1998, news.bbc.co.uk/1/hi/world/Americas/73746.stm; "Ramzi Yousef," en.wikipedia.org/wiki/Ramzi_Yousef; "Abdul Hakim Murad," en.wikipedia.org/wiki/Abdul_Hakim_Murad. As of 2007, Ramzi Yousef remained incarcerated at a Supermax prison in Colorado, where he shared a cell with the Unabomber, Theodore Kaczynski. An uncle of Ramzi Yousef, Khalid Shaikh Mohammed, had traveled to the Philippines in 1994 to work with Ramzi Yousef on Oplan Bojinka. At the time of the fire in Ramzi Yousef's apartment, Khalid Shaikh Mohammed escaped initially to Qatar. He moved about to a number of countries before ending up once again in Afghanistan affiliated with Al Qaeda. After the September 11, 2001, terrorist attack on the New York World Trade Center and the Pentagon, the United States accused Khalid Shaikh Mohammed of being "the principal architect of the 9/11 attacks," which information was derived, in part, from Ramzi Yousef's computer outline for Oplan Bojinka. On March 1, 2003, a joint raid staged by the Pakistani Inter-Services Intelligence and the US Federal Bureau of Investigation arrested Khalid Shaikh Mohammed in Rawalpindi, Pakistan. See *The Final 9/11 Commission Report,* Chapter 5, www.gpoaccess.gov/911/index.html; "Khaled Sheikh Mohammed," en.wikipedia.org/wiki/Khaled_Sheikh_Mohammed.

39. Simon Elegant, "Mindanao's Biggest Boss: Al-Haj Murad Ebrahim of the M.I.L.F.," *Time Asia* 164, no. 9 (August 30, 2004); Simon Elegant, "The Return of Abu Sayyaf: The Philippine Group That Was Once Known for Brutal Kidnapping Has Graduated to Genuine Terror," *Time Asia* (August 30, 2004), time.com/time /asia/magazine/

printout/; "Abu Sayyaf Planted Bomb in 'Superferry,' Says GMA," manilatimes .net/national/ 2004/oct/12/yehey/top_stories/. The active membership of Abu Sayyaf peaked at 1,269 in 2000 and declined substantially by the end of 2005. For a summary report on Abu Sayyaf's ideology and terrorist incidents, see Banlaoi, "The Abu Sayyaf Group," 247–262.

40. "Abu Sayyaf Leader Janjalani Dead," *WorldPress,* January 20, 2007, 1–6, mikeinmanila.worldpress.com/2007/01/20/.

41. By June 2004, there were 940,000 Filipinos working in Saudi Arabia, of which 200,000 were employed at the oil complex at Al-Khobar. At that time, a total of about 1.5 million Filipinos were employed as migrant workers in Middle East countries. See Migrante International, "Filipino Soldiers and Civilians in Iraq, Saudi Arabia Are Targets of 'Terrorists,'" cq.indymedia.org/news/2004/06/737.php; International Crisis Group, *Philippines Terrorism: The Role of Militant Islamic Converts,* Asia Report, No. 110 (December 19, 2005), Jakarta/Brussels, 4–8.

42. International Crisis Group, *Philippines Terrorism,* 6–8.

43. Ibid., 16–18; Ahmad Santos and seven other RSM members were arrested at a hideout in Zamboanga City on October 25, 2005. They came to trial in November, with one of the eight turning state's witness to provide details on their activities and on their sources of foreign funding. See "Suspected Terrorist Seeks to Tell on Comrades," *Sun Star, Manila*, November 12, 2005, sunstar.com.ph/Santos%20trial.htm; Al Jacinto, "3 Terror Suspects Nabbed in Zambo," *Sun Star, Zamboanga,* December 21, 2005, sunstar .com.ph.

44. Fermin D. Adriano, "Elusive Peace in Mindanao," *The Manila Times,* February 28, 2003, www.manilatimes.net/national/2003/feb/28/opinion.

45. United Nations Resolution 1368 called on every UN member "to combat all forms of terrorism in accordance with its Charter responsibilities . . . and bring perpetrators to justice." This resolution was passed unanimously. Security Council Meeting, 4370, Press Release SC/7143, December 9, 2001, www.un.org/News/Press/docs/ SC7143.doc.htm.

46. For an account of US-Philippine relations from 2001 to 2004, see Sheldon W. Simon, "Philippines Withdraws from Iraq and JI Strikes Again," *Comparative Connections,* 3rd Quarter 2004, Pacific Forum CSIS, 1–9, csis.org/pacfor/cc/0403Qus_ asean.htm.

47. Abuza, *Militant Islam,* 203–208; Daljit Singh, "ASEAN Counter-Terror Strategies and Cooperation: How Effective?" in Ramakrishna and Tan, *After Bali,* 207–209; Congressional Research Service, "Abu Sayyaf: Target of Philippine—U.S. Anti-terrorism Cooperation," *Report for Congress,* January 24, 2007, 1–19.

48. The framework for the resumption of peace talks was established by the Tripoli Peace Agreement of 2001. See Benedicto Bacani, *The Mindanao Peace Talks: Another Opportunity to Resolve the Moro Conflict in the Philippines,* Special Report (Washington, DC: United States Institute of Peace, January 2005), 1–12.

49. Ayesah Abubakar, "Keeping the Peace: The International Monitoring Team (IMT) Mission in Mindanao," *Moro Voice*, August 14, 2005, 1–6, www.bangsamoro .com/mv_monitor%20MILF%20peace.htm.

50. Soliman M. Santos Jr., "Malaysia's Role in the Peace Process Has Yet to Reach Its Full Potential," *Newsbreak* 6, no. 1 (January 2–16, 2006), 1–3.

51. International Crisis Group, *Southern Philippines Backgrounder*, 21–26; "17 Abu Sayyaf Members to Die for Kidnapping, Murder Cases," *The Manila Times*, August 14, 2004, manilatimes.net/national/2004/aug/14/yehey /top_stories/; Bong Garcia Jr., "Wanted Abu Involved in Dos Palmas Raid Falls," *Minda News*, January 7, 2005, mindanews.com/2005/01/07nws-abu.html; Manuel R. Baliao, "Cops Nab 2 Abu

Sayyaf Bombers in S. Kudarat," *The Manila Times*, January 23, 2005, manilatimes .net/national/2005/jan/23/yehey/prov/200501; "U.S. Rewards Program—Philippines: Deterring Terrorism and Saving Lives," *Asia-Pacific Defense Forum,* Winter 2006–2007, forum.apan-info.net /2007-07.

52. In 1998, the MILF commander, Al-Haj Murad Ebrahim, claimed to lead a "pool of over 120,000 fighters," while the Philippine military at the time estimated the MILF forces to be between 8,000 and 10,000 guerrillas. Anthony Davis, "Rebels Without a Pause," *AsiaWeek*, April 3, 1998, 1–4, www.pathfinder.com/asiaweek/98/0403/isl.html.

53. Abuza, *Militant Islam,* 99–110, 208–210; Caballero-Anthony, "The Winds of Change in the Philippines, 218–221; Rizal G. Buendia, "The GRP-MILF Peace Talks: Quo Vadis?" in *Southeast Asian Affairs 2004* (Singapore: Institute of Southeast Asian Studies, 2004), 211–221.

54. "Joint Communiqué Between the Government of the Republic of the Philippines and the Moro Islamic Liberation Front," May 6, 2002, Cyberjaya [Malaysia], reproduced in: International Crisis Group, *Southern Philippines Backgrounder,* Appendix D, 33. In December 2004 a more formal mechanism for cooperation between the GRP and the MILF became activated with the formation of the Ad Hoc Joint Action Group (AHJAG).

55. Dana R. Dillon, "Southeast Asia and the Brotherhood of Terrorism," *The Heritage Foundation,* Lecture 860, December 20, 2004, 1–7, www.heritage.org/Research/AsiaandthePacific /hl860.cfm; Ayesah Abubakar, "Keeping the Peace," 2–4.

56. The list of terrorist suspects included names of key members of Abu Sayyaf and Jemaah Islamiyah. Agence France-Press, "MILF to Hunt Down Islamic Militants in Mindanao," May 30, 2005, news.inq7.net/top/index.php?index=1&story_id=38637. On the list were thirty-one Indonesians, twenty-one Filipinos, and one Malaysian. International Crisis Group, *Philippines Terrorism,* 14n.

57. "The RP-MILF Peace Talks," *The Manila Times,* August 17, 2004, www.manilatimes.net/OPINION; BBC News, "Philippine Army in Southern Clash," news.bbc.co.uk/1/hi/world/asia-pacific/4160719.stm; Reuters: "Philippine Army Says Foreigners Still Train Rebels," January 17, 2005, www.alertnet.org/thenews/newsdesk/MAN231832.htm; "MILF to Probe Maguindano Raid," *Philippine Daily Enquirer*, January 13, 2005, www.INQ7.net; Jeffrey B. Maitem, "MILF Says AFP Violating Truce but Palace Says Military Strike Won't Affect Talks," *Minda News,* January 30, 2005, mindanews.com/2005/01/30nws-truce.html.

58. Zachary Abuza, "MILF's Stalled Peace Process and Its Impact on Terrorism in Southeast Asia," *Terrorism Monitor* 4, no. 14 (July 13, 2006), 8–10, www.jamestown.org.

59. The death of Salamat Hashim triggered a power struggle within the MILF. Hashim's previously anointed successor did not become the new leader. Instead, Al-Haj Murad Ebrahim became the new chairman, probably because Murad commanded the largest MILF contingent of about 5,000 men. International Crisis Group, *Southern Philippines Backgrounder,* 9–12.

60. "AFP: Factions of MILF Get Funds from Al Qaeda," *The Manila Times,* January 2, 2003, www.manilatimes.net/METRO.

61. The Jemaah Islamiyah cell in the southern Philippines operated under the name Wakalah Hudiebiah. The leader of that cell, Mustaquim, was arrested in Malaysia in June 2004, after which the cell was headed by a man named Usman. "Philippine Army Says Foreigners Still Train Rebels," Reuters, at www.alertnet.org/thenews/newsdesk/MAN231832.htm; International Crisis Group, *Philippines Terrorism,* 8–12.

62. For an analysis of the internal politics within the MILF, see Zachary Abuza, "Crunchtime for the Mindanao Peace Process?" Philippine Facilitation Project, US In-

stitute of Peace, February 8, 2005, 2–6, www.usip.org; Zachary Abuza, "MILF's Stalled Peace Process," 8–10.

63. The CAFGUs operate at the local level and also recruited former MNLF fighters. The CAFGU,s replaced an earlier Civilian Home Defense Force that was designed to provide counterinsurgency forces at village levels.

64. Peter Kreuzer, *Political Clans and Violence in the Southern Philippines,* Peace Research Institute Frankfurt, Report No. 71 (2005), 16–20. For an investigative report on voting irregularities and the election tactics of the Ampatuan political machine, see Carolyn Arguillas, "Cheating Fields," *NEWSBREAK* 6, no. 3 (March 13, 2006), 1–5, partners.inq7/newsbreak/special/index.php?story_id=45415.

65. "13 Die in Philippines Bombing," *CBS News,* December 24, 2003, 1–2, www .cbsnews.com/stories/2003/02/11/world/main540152.shtml.

66. "2 MILF Commanders Sought for Maguindanao Explosions," PNP News Release No. 06-0621, June 27, 2006, www.pnp.gov.ph/press/content/news/2006/jun/ 2milfcom. Romie A. Avengelista, "MILF Tagged in Blasts," *Manila Standard Today,* June 28, 2006, www.manilastandardtoday.com/?page=regions04_june28_2006; "Police Hunt 2 MILF Commanders for Maguindanao Blast," *Manila Times,* June 28, 2006, 1–2, www.manilatimes.net/national/2006 /june/28/yehey/top_stories/. The 105th Base Command was the same unit that had been reported by the MILF spokesman to have been "deactivated" one year earlier, in the aftermath of Binago's assault on Philippine Army bases.

67. Carolyn O. Arguillas, "Rebels vs. Politicians," *NEWSBREAK,* August 29, 2006, 1–6, newsbreak.com.ph/newsbreak/story.asp?ID=633.

68. "AFP Sends Tanks to Fighting in Maguindanao," *Luwaran,* July 4, 2006, 1–3, www.luwaran.com/modules.php?name=News&file=article&sid=225; Al Jacinto, "Clashes Between MILF, Militia Intensify; 21 Dead," *The Manila Times*, July 1, 2006, 1–3, www.manilatimes.net/national/2006/july/01/yehey/top_stories/.

69. Jhong Dela Cruz, "Eroding Peace in Mindanao," *Luwaran,* July 10, 2006, www.luwaran.com/modules.php?name=Content&pa=showpage; Mindanao Peoples Caucus, "MPC, Mantay Ceasefire Appeal for Support to IDPs and Ceasefire," *Peace in MindaNow,* July 13, 2006, 1, www.mindanaopeaceweavers.org; Carolyn Arguillas, "Maguindanao Standoff Ends with 3-Day 'No Movement' Agreement," *Minda News*, July 7, 2006, 1–3; Carolyn Arguillas, "Buffer Zones Set Up to Prevent CVO-MILF Clashes in Maguindanao," *Minda News*, July 10, 2006, 1–2, mindanews.com/index.

70. Abubakar, "Keeping the Peace," 1–6, www.bangsamoro.com/mv_monitor% 20MILF%20 peace.htm. For a balanced account of the remaining issues as of January 2005, see Benedicto Bacani, *The Mindanao Peace Talks,* 1–12; "A Breakthrough in Negotiations," *The Christian Science Monitor,* February 8, 2006, 7, reporting on a supplementary agreement between the government of the Philippines and the MILF on "ancestral domains."

71. The Indigenous Peoples Rights Act (RA 8731) acknowledged Lumud identities and promised them some form of autonomy and cultural rights. A National Commission of Indigenous Peoples was created to represent their interests, and seventy-one indigenous peoples' areas were identified for development projects, but what form of autonomy or self-determination would be provided for Lumuds was left for later negotiations. See National Commission of Indigenous Peoples, www.ncip.gov.ph/resources/ ancestral.php.

72. Dictaan-Bang-oa, "The Question of Peace in Mindanao," 153–182.

73. Carolyn O. Arguillas, "Lumud Groups Oppose Inclusion in 'Bangsamoro Homeland,'" *Minda News*, July 30, 2006, 1–4, mindanews.com/index.php?option=com_ content&task.

74. Al Jacinto, "Moro Rebels Reject Government's Offer of Limited Autonomy," *Sun Star,* September 10, 2006, 1–4, www.sunstar.com.ph/static/net/2006/09/10/; Zachary Abuza, "Peace Talks Resume as Cease-Fire Comes Under Strain in the Philippines," *Terrorism Focus* 3, no. 34 (September 6, 2006), 1–2, jamestown.org/terrorism/article.php?articleid=2370118; "Talks Between Philippine Government, Muslim Rebels Stall over Territorial Issue," *Asia-Pacific Daily Report,* Center of Excellence, Crisis Reports, September 7, 2006, 1–2, pdmin.coe-dmha.org/apdr/index/; Carolyn O. Arguillas, "GPR-MILF Talks: Impasse Not Broken," *MindaNews,* September 9, 2006, 1, mindanews.com/index2.php?option=com_content&do_pdf=1&id =842.

75. Jim Gomez, "RP Peace Negotiator Says MILF Making Unacceptable Demands," Associated Press, September 14, 2006, 1–2, newsinfo.inq7.net/breakingnews/nation/.

76. As part of the GRP-MNLF Peace Agreement of 1996, the government agreed to integrate MNLF members into the Philippine armed forces and the police. Ultimately, 1,500 MNLF fighters were assigned to regular Philippine units, rather than in units under their former guerrilla commanders. The failure to allow separate Muslim units in the police and AFP was viewed by MILF spokesmen as a violation of the terms of the 1996 Peace Agreement. Rene Q. Bas, "Special Report: GRP-MNLF Agreement, 10 Years After the Government-MNLF 'Final' Peace Agreement Was Signed, the Dark Prospect Remains of an RP Without Mindanao," *The Sunday Times* (Manila), September 3, 2006, 1–4, www.manilatimes.net/national/2006/sept/03/yehey/top_stories/.

77. "14 Marines Killed in Basilan Clash," *Inquirer,* July 11, 2007, 1–3, services.inquirer.net/print.php?article_id=57990; "14 Philippines Troops Killed in Clash with Rebels," *MSNBC,* July 11, 2007, 1–3, www.msnbc.com/id/19703829/.

78. "Italy Priest Freed in Philippines," *BBC News,* July 20, 2007, 1–3, news.bbd.co.uk/2/hi/asia-pacific/6907639.stm.

79. "MILF Ease Up on Claims for Peace Talks," *Philippines Today*, July 15, 2007, 1–2, www. philippinestoday.net/index.php?module=article&view=449; Komfie Manalo, "Philippines to Rethink Peace Talks with Muslim Rebels," *AHN Global News,* July 12, 2007, 1, www.allheadlinesnews.com/articles/7007888507.

80. Agence France-Presse, "RP, MILF Peace Talks Hit New Snag," December 16, 2007, newsinfo.inquirer.net/breakingnews/nation/view_article.php?article_id=107163; Wadi, "The Mindanao Peace Process: An Untimely Stalemate," www.opinionasia.org/article/print/406; "Fragile Peace in Southern Philippines, *Jane's Country Risk News,* January 24, 2008, www.janes.com/news/security/jiaa/jiaa080124_1_n.shtml.

81. International Crisis Group, *The Philippines: Counter-Insurgency vs. Counter-Terrorism in Mindanao,* Asia Report No. 152 (May 14, 2008), Jakarta/Brussels, 1–26.

82. Kit Collier and Malcolm Cook, "The Philippines' Sanctuaries of Terror," *Webdiary,* August 18, 2006, webdiary.com.au/cms/?q=node/1448.

10

Pattani Malay Separatism in Thailand

Thailand, like the Philippines, has confronted a separatist movement from a Muslim minority that is concentrated in its southern provinces. Within Thailand as a whole, the religious affiliation of the population is 94.2 percent Buddhist and 4.6 percent Muslim. A majority of the Muslims live in the five most southern provinces, and in those provinces Muslims constitute 55.6 percent of the population. (See Table 10.1.)

The Malay Muslim communities of southern Thailand have a common identity shaped by a long history and a cumulative sense of grievance that they were separated from their ethnic and religious kin who are today across the border in Malaysia. Some Muslims have accepted the reality of living as a minority within Thailand, while others have strenuously resisted all efforts to integrate them into the social and political system of Thailand. The strongest supporters of separatism have been those communities that regularly speak Malay and have an intense commitment to Islam. To examine the core issues of Malay politics in Thailand, it is essential to trace, in broad strokes, the events that led to the southern provinces being incorporated into Thailand.

During the eleventh century, the Thais, as an ethnic and linguistic group, began a steady migration from Yunnan, in southern China, to the areas that today make up Thailand. By the thirteenth century, several Thai kingdoms were formed and competed for power, but in 1350 one state, centered at Ayuthia, emerged as the dominant power in control of the Menam Chao Phraya basin.[1] That state became known by its official name, Siam. Following the pattern of other powerful states in that era, Siam extended its power to other lesser states on its periphery through a system of tributary relations. Less powerful states acknowledged the more powerful imperial state by giving tribute. In return, the imperial state gave trading rights and offered protection and assistance to the tributary state against external threats. When the imperial state was powerful, the tributary system expanded. When it was weaker, its

Table 10.1 Population, Religion, and Language Group in Five Provinces of Southern Thailand, 2000 Census

Province	Total	Muslim	Percentage Muslim	Malay Speaking	Percentage Malay Speaking
Narathiwat	662,400	543,168	82.0	532,569	80.4
Pattani	596,000	480,972	80.7	456,536	76.6
Songkla	1,255,700	291,322	23.2	57,762	4.6
Satun	247,900	168,076	67.8	24,542	9.9
Yala	415,500	286,279	68.9	274,645	66.1
Total	3,177,500	1,776,241	55.9	1,346,054	42.4

Source: National Statistical Office, Thailand, *Population and Housing Census 2000,* www.nso.go.th/pop2000.

Note: Population totals are rounded to hundreds.

tributary dependencies became more autonomous, or were subdued by another regional imperial state.

By the middle of the fourteenth century, the Siamese state had extended its tributary system down the Kra Isthmus to Pattani and to the northern Malay states. During the fifteenth century, Pattani and other northern Malay states converted to Islam and that became the basis for their social and political system. These Malay states that were loosely linked to the Siamese tributary system included Pattani, Perlis, Kedah, Terengganu, and Kelantan. By the eighteenth century, this system was challenged when the British gained control of Penang in 1786. From that base, British power and influence competed with Siam for supremacy of the region. After a series of disputes between Britain and Siam, they finally signed a treaty in 1909 that established a fixed border between their "protected territories."[2] The former Siamese tributary states of Terengganu, Kelantan, Kedah, and Perlis were incorporated into British Malaya, while Pattani and Satun were acknowledged to be a part of Siam. That border remains today the border between Malaysia and Thailand.

During the earlier tributary relationship, these Malay states operated with considerable autonomy, provided that the tributary state gave symbolic recognition of Siamese supremacy. If open rebellion appeared imminent, the Siamese would usually respond with a punitive expedition. Three such rebellions broke out in Pattani in 1789, 1791, and 1808, which actions prompted the Siamese to divide Pattani into seven districts and impose a Siamese governor to oversee the recalcitrant raja and lesser Malay chiefs appointed by the Siamese to administer the newly created districts. The Siamese direct intervention over Pattani was one of the reasons that Siamese sovereignty could be claimed in 1909 when the new state boundary was being defined. That boundary treaty divided the Malays—as defined by ethnicity, culture, and Islam—into two political entities. Malays living on the southern side of the border were subjects of Malay rulers subservient to British rule. Malays living on the northern side of the border also had Malay rulers, but those rulers operated under increasing direct rule by Siamese authorities.

From 1851 to 1868, King Mongkut ruled Siam, followed by King Chulalongkorn who ruled from 1868 to 1910. Both these rulers had been exposed to some Western education and both initiated programs of liberal reforms. These reforms concentrated on developing a modern system of administration, improving educational standards based on a Westernized secular curriculum, the development of a modern military, and the promotion of a nationalist ideology based on Buddhist principles. By these measures, the Siamese government improved its capacity to extend its authority over local communities and became much more effective in imposing uniform policies designed to create the conditions for national unification. The Malays of southern Siam did not share these policy objectives. Instead, they questioned the value of secular education, and they viewed the Siamese state, with its Buddhist ideological underpinnings, to be in direct contradiction to the tenets of Islam.

The issue of autonomy for Malay rule in Siam initially focused on the role and powers of the sultan of Pattani, Raja Abdul Kadar Qamaruddin. King Chulalongkorn was determined to generate induced modernization combined with an increasing sense of Siamese nationalism. The central government established a centralized administration to oversee and control the actions and authority of Malay rulers and chiefs. The Pattani raja refused to agree to these changes, whereupon he was deposed and imprisoned in 1901. Two years later, he was released from detention and went into exile in Kelantan, where he became a symbol of resistance to Siamese rule. Under the new system of direct rule, most Sharia and Adat laws were replaced by royal ordinances administered by a centralized administration controlled from Bangkok. Sharia law continued to apply for Muslims, but only in the matters of family law and property inheritance. The earlier division of Pattani into seven districts was reapportioned to four provinces that were placed under the direct authority of a Siamese governor.

The policies of the Siamese government were designed to promote integration of minorities through promotion of Siamese nationalism, through compulsory education in public schools staffed by Buddhist Thai teachers, and by government development programs administered by "culturally sensitive" bureaucrats. The common Malay response was to avoid sending their children to public schools and to minimize contact with government officials. For example, in 1937, only 20 percent of Pattani Malay school-age children enrolled in schools, and most of those only completed two years of schooling. Malay opposition to the education law was expressed by organized protests against paying taxes, and in 1923 by the formation of the first Malay armed resistance movement. Siamese authorities forcibly suppressed both actions. Some of the rules relating to education were later relaxed, but their overall objective of promoting "integration" remained the same.[3] Not all Pattani Malays responded to these policies in the same way. Some did attend public schools and some were employed in government service or the military. Over time, a significant number of Pattani Malays learned the Thai language, becoming a bit more integrated and more cosmopolitan in outlook. These Muslims adapted more readily to Siam's economic and cultural environment and more of them attended public schools. These "secular" Muslims tend to be concentrated in the province of Satun.

In 1932 a military-backed bloodless coup brought an end to Siam's system of absolute monarchy. Following a short period involving a struggle for power, Siam entered a ten-year period of rule by the military-backed faction of General Phibul Songgram. Under his rule, government policy reflected xenophobia against Chinese minorities and the assertion of Thai dominance in politics and national affairs. Persons of Thai descent were given priority in recruitment and promotion in the civil service, and national patriotism was equated with Buddhism. The school curriculum was brought under stricter controls and made to project the preeminent position of the Thais as the defining majority. In 1939, the country was renamed Thailand, reflecting this ethnic component, rather than Siam, which referred to a geographic region rather than an ethnic cultural identity. The Chinese, Khmer, Malay, Laotian, and hill tribal peoples were all targeted for exclusion from the political system, and they were pressured to accept the privileged position of the Thai-Buddhist culture of the dominant majority. There was virtually no acknowledgment of Islam as a legitimate component of a national cultural mosaic. Laws were passed to enforce standard dress codes that limited traditional Malay dress styles and prohibited the chewing of betel nut in public places.[4] Muslims who worked in government service were required to adopt Thai names. These policies failed to generate loyalties or legitimacy among Malays for a political system so completely dominated by Thais.

In 1939 and 1940, events in Europe were shifting the power balance in Asia. The fall of France and the Netherlands in June 1940 exposed French Indo-China and the Netherlands East Indies as vulnerable undefended colonies. Shortly thereafter, Japan signed a treaty of friendship with Phibul Songgram's government in Thailand. Phibul recognized that Japan was a powerful imperial force prepared to advance into Southeast Asia while Britain faced a struggle of survival in Europe and the United States was hesitant to become involved in a major war. When the Japanese attacked Pearl Harbor on December 7, 1941, an ultimatum was issued to Thailand to join Japan as an ally or face invasion. Thailand chose to become an ally of Japan. On December 8, Japanese forces made a massive surprise landing on the beaches of Pattani and Songkla, and proceeded directly to mount their attack on Malaya and Singapore. By February 15, 1942, Singapore fell to the Japanese, and by March 9, organized resistance to the Japanese invasion ended in the Netherlands East Indies. The Japanese used Thailand as a base to invade British Burma and began the construction of the

Thailand-Burma "death railway" for the transport of supplies to Japanese forces on that front.[5] As a reward for Thailand's cooperation with the Japanese, the Malay states of Kelantan, Terengganu, Kedah, and Perlis were transferred by Japan to Thai sovereignty, thus reuniting the Malays of Thailand with the northern states of Malaya, but now under Thai rule. This short interlude of Thailand's wartime administration of the northern Malay states permitted renewed links between the exiled Pattani court circle in Kelantan with their supporters in the four southern provinces of Thailand.[6]

After the last raja of Pattani, Abdul Kadar Qamaruddin, chose exile in Kelantan, he openly supported the cause of Pattani secession from Thailand. When Abdul Kadar died in 1933, his second son, Tunku Mahmud Mayhiddin, took up that cause with determination and passion. Before the outbreak of World War II, Tunku Mayhiddin joined the British-led Kelantan Volunteer Force. When the Japanese invaded Malaya, Tunku Mayhiddin escaped to India along with some retreating British forces, and from that base he made secret contacts with Kelantan and Pattani Malays who were opposed to the combination of Thai-Japanese rule. The Malay underground that Tunku Mayhiddin helped to organize also made contact with the British Army's "stay-behind" guerrilla unit known as Force 136 that operated from secret locations in Malaya's jungle highlands. Together, Force 136 and the Mayhiddin guerrillas mounted some minor operations against the Japanese. When the war ended, Tunku Mayhiddin asserted that during the war promises were made by British officers that the former Pattani sultanate would be annexed to Malaya in a postwar settlement, as a reward for Pattani Malay support for the Allied war effort. The exact nature of those promises, and by whose authority they were made, was never revealed. Regardless of their validity, those reputed promises energized the postwar politics of Thailand's four southern provinces.

Before Japan's surrender, the military-backed, pro-Japanese Thai government of Phibun Songgram dissolved in July 1944 and was replaced by a government led by the civilian politician Pridi Phanomyong, who had led the Seri Thai (Free Thai) pro-Allied underground. The change of government in Thailand reflected the views of Thai elites that an Allied victory was imminent. When the war ended, both the British and the Americans did not want to undermine that government, or create political instability in the region. The support and cooperation of Thailand for postwar reconstruction became much more important than the issue of ceding the four southern Thai provinces to Malaya.[7]

The Pattani Malay Secession Movement

Without British support for the incorporation of the four former Pattani sultanate districts into Malaya, Tunku Mayhiddin and a coterie of Pattani exiles initiated a campaign to garner international support for annexation of those provinces into Malaya. An organization called the Pattani People's Movement (PPM) was formed in 1946, headed by Haji Sulong bin Abdul Kadir, chairman of Majelis Ugama Islam, who sponsored a petition demanding a form of Islamic rule by Muslims to be implemented in southern Thailand. That petition gained a quarter million signatures and fingerprints. In response, the Thai government promised some concessions in matters of culture and education, but the PPM was not in a conciliatory demeanor. Instead, a series of protests and riots turned into violent clashes by armed groups against Thai police. These incidents signaled the beginning of a separatist rebellion.[8] Between 1946 and 1969, a series of militant or revolutionary organizations were founded, backed by paramilitary units. These organizations competed against each other for support and tended to exaggerate their membership and the capabilities of their armed auxiliaries.

The Pattani People's Movement was founded in 1946 by Haji Sulong, as an offshoot of a Kelantan organization named GAMPAR (Gabungan Melayu Pattani Raya, Association of the Malays of Greater Pattani). GAMPAR had been formed earlier to represent the expatriate Pattani nobility, and Tunku Mayhiddin played a leading, but concealed, role in that organization. In 1947, the National Liberation Front of Pattani (NLFP, Barisan Nasional Pembabasan Petani) was founded by Tunku Yala Naser, the grandson of the last Pattani ruler, Raja Abdul Kadar Qamaruddin. The NLFP gained some support from Partai Islam in Malaysia, and by the early 1950s the NLFP commanded an armed contingent of some 200–300 fighters. By the late 1960s, the NLFP collapsed or merged with other groups. In March 1963, the Barisan Revolusi Nasional (BRN, National Revolutionary Front) was founded by Haji Abdul Karim. It claimed to be fighting for a pan-Islamic state in Southeast Asia, and in its early days it gained support from Sukarno's government. It may have collapsed for a few years, but was revived again in 1984 and continued with a relatively low political profile over the next decade. The Pattani United Liberation Organization (PULO, Pertubohan Persatuan Pembibasan Pattani) became the largest and most formidable secessionist organization. Tunku Bira Kotanila, who was a member of the Pattani nobility, founded PULO in 1967. Under his leadership, PULO made contact with leaders of the Arab world, gaining open support from the World Muslim Congress and semi-concealed support from a number of officials in Malaysia. During the 1980s, PULO claimed a membership of 20,000 Pattani Malays and a fighting force of about 600 fighters. It maintained a training base for guerrilla fighters in Syria, and Thai authorities claimed that it also operated a similar base in Kelantan.[9]

The Gerakan Mujahideen Islami Pattani (GMIP) was founded in 1993 but remained fairly insignificant until about 1995 when a number of Afghan veterans revived the organization. In its early days, much of its energy was devoted to criminal activities, including sale of weapons to Philippine and Aceh insurgents, kidnapping, extortion, and contract killings. After a purge of some of its leaders in 1999, the GMIP leaders established contacts with Jemaah Islamiyah and the Malaysian radical group called Kumpulan Mujahideen Malaysia, but the nature of its relationship to those two organizations is a matter of some dispute. By 2002, GMIP had become much more militant, utilizing tactics of direct attacks against Thai authorities.[10]

In the early 1970s, the Thai government initiated various programs to win the goodwill of the Malay community. Government funds were allocated for the construction of mosques, including the majestic Great Mosque in Pattani. Existing mosques also received funds for maintenance and repair. Radio and television programs in the Malay language catered to the Malay community. Assistance was provided to Muslims for the haj pilgrimage to Mecca. Prince of Songkla University with two campuses, one in Songkla and the other in Pattani, established a Department of Islamic Studies in 1967, and all departments were instructed to concentrate their research on the Muslim communities of southern Thailand. Special university scholarships were provided to qualified Malays who were citizens of Thailand. Government authorities discovered that many of the private pondok schools in southern Thailand were propagating Islamic radicalism and providing recruits for separatist organizations. These schools were difficult to monitor because they were usually founded by an ustaz who commanded respect as a religious leader. In the 1950s, over 500 pondok schools were in operation in the four southern Thai provinces. When Marshal Sarit Thanarat became premier, he decided to bring these pondok schools under government supervision and to reform their curriculum to meet national educational standards. By 1971, all pondok schools were required to register or close. Those schools that registered and had over forty students received government financial assistance, plus schoolbooks prepared by the Ministry of Education and scholarships for needy students. The curriculum included general subjects taught in the Thai language by non-Muslim teachers. Islamic religious instruction continued to be taught by Malay instructors. The pondoks competed with tuition-free government-operated general schools for all students. Between 1971 and 1991, the number of pondok schools declined from 537 to 189. By 1991, there were 1,218 public "general schools" operating in the four southern provinces, with an enrollment of 202,972 Muslim students, while the combined pondok school enrollment had declined to 22,423 Muslim students.[11] For hardline separatists, the increasing numbers of Malay students in secular schools posed a serious threat to the separatist cause by undermining the unity of the umma and challenging the political ideology of Islam.

The secular-based education available from public schools improved employment opportunities for Pattani Malays, but unemployment levels for Malays remained much higher than for ethnic Thais. With the slow demise of pondok schools, an increasing number of Pattani Malays went abroad to study in the Middle East, Pakistan, India, or Malaysia. Many madrasahs and centers of Islamic learning in those countries provided generous scholarships to Thai

Muslims, funded in part by Saudi money or by various Islamic charities. By 2004, about 2,500 graduates from Middle Eastern institutions had returned to southern Thailand.[12] When they returned to Thailand, the Thai government did not recognize their degrees, and opportunities for employment of madrasah graduates in the private sector were virtually nonexistent. With few other options, many of these returnees joined separatist organizations, both for employment and for the fulfillment of their ideological convictions.

The First Peace Agreement

In 1987, during the premiership of General Prem Tinsulanonda, peace talks were held between the government of Thailand and the Pattani United Liberation Organization. These talks concluded with a peace agreement that provided for PULO to end its armed insurrection, for Thailand to grant greater autonomy to the Malays in cultural and religious matters, and for an amnesty to be granted to all PULO members and their paramilitary forces. The Thailand government promised a substantial increase of development funds to Muslim communities. Pursuant with this agreement, most of the PULO's 20,000 members and fighters gave up their arms and returned to civilian life. Other militant Islamic groups were not covered by this agreement. Even so, because PULO was the largest and most formidable insurrectionary group, this agreement appeared to mark a watershed that was expected to usher in a period of peace and reconciliation.

In the 1990s up through 2003, southern Thailand gave the impression of being a sleepy, out-of-the-way place where tourists congregated around lush beach resorts, and Malay peasants cultivated padi fields or went ocean fishing with time-honored routines and technology that had remained unchanged for generations. Below this tourist-poster façade, however, there were significant changes that were reshaping the economy and the politics of the region. In response to the more relaxed political atmosphere, the government scaled down its military presence as well as dismantling its intelligence apparatus, which had been created to monitor separatist and insurrectionary activities. These tasks became the responsibility of the local police.

During 1989, Muslims from Thailand who had answered the earlier call to participate in the anti-Soviet jihad began returning from Afghanistan. These returnees came with military training, battle experience, and a more radical view of politics. The relatively peaceful political climate in southern Thailand in the 1990s provided new opportunities for those who had become exposed to Islamic radicalism and committed to a separatist agenda. At the time, Thailand had become the central marketplace in Southeast Asia for weapons. The borders were porous, with vast stretches of unprotected shorelines. Its immigration services were notoriously lax for foreign visitors, and its money-laundering industry made it an ideal location for the sale and purchase of military equipment and weapons. After the Vietnam War, vast quantities of light arms, mostly of Russian and Chinese origin, were imported illegally into Thailand for sale by middlemen, who re-exported the arms to guerrillas and insurgents in Southeast Asia and beyond. The Thai police were notoriously corrupt, and many of them acquired a stake in the success of the arms trade because payoffs from arms dealers and buyers provided a lucrative supplement to their meager regular income. Agents for guerrilla groups came from the southern Philippines, Sulawesi, Aceh, the Tamil Tigers in Sri Lanka, and multiple insurgent groups in Myanmar and northwest India. This arms trade was usually combined with the illegal drug trade, the smuggling of contraband, and transport of illegal immigrants. Insurgent groups often used profits from the sale of Burmese heroin and the transport of illegal immigrants to fund their purchase of weapons. These activities created a climate of lawlessness in southern Thailand.[13]

From 2002 to 2004, Thailand's tourist industry had attracted yearly about 10 million tourists, generating about US$7.6 billion of revenue each year. A majority of the tourists came to the beach resorts of southern Thailand at Phuket, Krabi, or Kor Samui. Because of the high revenues involved, Prime Minister Shaksin Shinawatra was careful not to frighten tourists with reports of terrorists or of political unrest. In addition, Malaysia was also sensitive about the sympathies in Malaysia for the Pattani separatist movement. The two northern Malay states of Kelantan and Terengganu had become strongholds of support for Malaysia's most formidable opposition group, Partai Islam, which supported the Pattani separatist cause. Therefore, when separatist groups engaged in cross-border operations to smuggle arms, drugs, or people, both Thai and Malaysian authorities, for domestic political reasons, preferred to have them called "bandits" or "smugglers," than to use the term "terrorists."

The Separatist Revival

The decade and a half of relative peace in southern Thailand was a time when separatist organizations regrouped and prepared for a new push to gain irredentist objectives. Some old organizations were revived while new organizations were founded to carry the separatist banner. Following the 1987 peace agreement between the Thai government and PULO, most PULO leaders remained in exile in Malaysia, Europe, or the Middle East, leaving a political void in southern Thailand. Eventually, other PULO members, led by Abdul Rahman Bazo, founded New PULO in 1997 to resume the struggle for Pattani independence. In 2005 New PULO held a three-day "reunification congress" in Damascus, attended by forty PULO leaders from Thailand, Europe, and the Middle East. The Barisan Revolusi Nasional split into three wings: BRN-Kongress, BRN-Uran, and BRN-Coordinate. BRN-K was the more moderate wing, while BRN-C became the best organized and most militant of the secessionist groups, dedicated to a violent struggle to create an independent Pattani state. A coterie of Afghan-trained veterans provided leadership for the BRN-C, and its support came from a network of mosques and radical pondok schools that trained recruits for its paramilitary units. By 2005, its core membership was estimated to be about 1,000, organized into secret cells that were formed in an estimated 70 percent of the Malay villages of southern Thailand. BRN-C leaders claimed a potential support base of 200,000 to 300,000 people. A split off from BRN-C, known as Runda Kumpulan Kecil (RKK), became a strike force for some of the most brutal attacks and ambushes against police, teachers, and Buddhist monks during 2005 and 2006. Key members of RKK are known to have gone to Indonesia for training in guerrilla tactics. The Thai police identified Rorhing Ahsong as its leader and estimated that it operated with a force of about 500 fighters.[14] Bersatu (Unity) claimed to be an umbrella group of all separatist organizations. That group operated from Malaysia and was led by Wan Abdul Kadir Che Man, who was a faculty member at the University of Malaya. Bersatu claimed to have communication links with all separatist groups and to represent them to the Organization of the Islamic Conference.[15]

During the late 1990s, the government of Thailand relaxed policies toward Muslim communities, which enabled many Islamic schools in southern Thailand to renew their propagation of radical Islamist doctrines. By the end of 2004, over 300 pondoks were unregistered, and about 30 ustaz, operating unregistered schools, were actively preaching radical Islamist doctrine combined with military-style training that prepared students for participation in assault operations.[16] Although the number of students attending these schools was relatively small, the graduates from these schools provided the core recruit base for remobilizing insurgent forces. In 1998, the Thai government permitted the formation of Yala Islamic College, which was funded by Saudi Arabia's Islamic Development Bank and the International Islamic Relief Organization.[17] The college started with 200 foreign and local students and by 2005 had expanded to a student body of 1,300. Both Thai and foreign sources report that by 2003 Yala Islamic College had become the ideological center of radical Islam for southern Thailand.[18] Perhaps as a counter to the influence of this Wahhabi-based institution, Prime Minister Thaksin Shinawatra promised $700 million in government funds to open a second Islamic university in Narathiwat after 2006.[19]

These concessions to the Muslim community in matters of education and cultural policies had little effect on the rising tide of Muslim discontent, represented by a steady increase of violent incidents beginning about 1999. In February 2000, the Thai military mounted large operations against New PULO and killed its military commander, Saarli Taloh-Meyhaw.[20] The deputy leader of BRN was arrested two months later. Following these clashes, there were a series of attacks on government schools, on government-operated clinics, and on police stations. In 2001, about fifty police and soldiers were killed in various incidents at police checkpoints, and several bombs were set off in public places. In the immediate aftermath of the 9/11 attacks on the World Trade Center, there was a further increase in the tempo of ambushes against Thai police and anti-insurgency actions by the Thai military.[21]

Al Qaeda and Jemaah Islamiyah Connections

From December 2001 to April 2002, both Malaysia and Singapore arrested over forty admitted or accused Jemaah Islamiyah members who were identified as suspects in planned bombings and terrorist attacks in both countries.[22] These arrests triggered a rapid departure by other JI members from Singapore and Malaysia to southern Thailand. The operational leader of Jemaah Islamiyah was Riduan Isamuddin, more commonly known as Hambali. He hid in Thailand, using it as a safe haven for directing JI operations throughout Southeast Asia. From this location, Hambali planned a series of bombings ordered by Al Qaeda as a response to the US attacks on the Taliban regime in Afghanistan. Hambali called two meetings of regional JI operatives to implement the Bali bombing of October 12, 2002, which killed 202 people. A year later, Hambali authorized the Marriott Hotel bombing in Jakarta of August 5, 2003, that killed 12 people and injured 147. Seven days after the Marriott bombing, Hambali was arrested in Ayutthaya, Thailand, in a joint operation by the CIA and Thai authorities. Hambali was turned over to the United States for custody, and his interrogation provided an extensive picture of Jemaah Islamiyah operations. The Thai police also arrested another senior JI member, Arifin bin Ali, and discovered evidence of plots to bomb foreign embassies and tourist sites in Thailand.[23]

Despite these arrests in Thailand, Thai government authorities continued to insist that there were no terrorists in Thailand. Instead, government spokesmen attributed the escalating violence in the south to criminals and drug traffickers. From February to April 2003, the Thaksin government initiated what it called a "war on drugs," involving extensive military and police operations. A blacklist of about 42,000 suspects was compiled and an unknown number of people on that list were arrested and interrogated. Many of the detained were arrested and "disappeared," apparently killed by extrajudicial executions. At the time, Thai authorities reported casualties of 2,275 deaths, including 107 suspected Muslim militants. Human rights groups criticized the government for use of excessive lethal force and violations of basic human rights.[24] While drug smuggling was a problem in Thailand, independent observers reported that the "war on drugs" had been used as a cover to conduct extralegal "anti-terrorist" operations.

The Return to Insurgency

For southern Thailand, the year 2004 was marked by an unprecedented increase in insurgent violence. Whether this was the product of a new strategy devised by Al Qaeda and JI leadership or merely inspired by their example is a matter of some dispute. Indeed, the size of JI membership in southern Thailand, their capability, and their roles have also been disputed. In mid-2004, some analysts estimated the membership of Jemaah Islamiyah in southern Thailand to be as high as 10,000,[25] while other commentators claimed that there was no evidence that Al Qaeda or JI were active in the area.[26] Between 1999 and 2003, a significant number of Thai Muslim students went to Bandung, Indonesia, where they enrolled in radical madrasahs and gained paramilitary training. A few of these students went for combat training at MILF camps in Mindanao.[27] Indian intelligence sources reported that a significant number of Muslims from southern Thailand had traveled to Bangladesh to enroll in madrasahs where terrorist strategy, tactics, and weapons training were being taught. These jihadi training centers were operated by Harkat-ul-Jihad-al-Islami (HUJI), which also had established a chain of contacts and safe houses in Myanmar linking Bangladesh with southern Thailand. This chain of contacts was referred to by Indian intelligence sources as the "OBL (Osama bin Laden) Trail." With this transit system, a flow of trained recruits returned to Thailand to join the southern insurgents. In addition, flows of funds, possibly from Saudi sources, were transmitted to Thailand's southern insurgents.[28]

On January 4, 2004, insurgents in Thailand mounted highly coordinated attacks, successfully storming a regional army depot in Narathiwat, killing four Thai soldiers and capturing a cache of over 300 assault weapons and some machine guns. The insurgents also mounted nearly simultaneous assaults on twenty-one government-operated schools that were torched with incendiary devices, and a number of police posts were attacked. During these combined attacks, a total of 113 people were killed. Immediately following this major attack on the military base, Prime Minister Thaksin Shinawatra imposed martial law on January 5, 2004, for three of the southern provinces: Narathiwat, Yala, and Pattani. An additional 3,000 Thai troops were sent to the region, raising the total of Royal Thai Army troops in the region to 12,000. Both the police and the army commands were reorganized to deal with the new commitment by the Thailand government to confront and defeat Muslim insurgents.[29]

Over the next two years, the patterns and pace of insurgent violence intensified with deadly effects. The tactics and nature of these attacks shifted over time. Previously, militants had clashed with troops in jungle highland areas, with relatively little violence spilling into settled communities and urban areas. After the attacks of January 4, 2004, the insurgents shifted from guerrilla tactics to urban warfare, based on small independent cells that were difficult to detect and to guard against. Besides setting off bombs and staging periodic larger-scale attacks, they resorted to targeted assassinations. These attacks on both Muslim and non-Muslim civilians were often coordinated with the destruction of rubber plantations and other productive facilities owned and operated by non-Muslims. The usual assassination tactic involved two-member squads using motorcycles for a quick shooting, followed by a rapid escape. Police records reveal that Muslims constituted over half of the assassinations of non-security personnel, many of whom were killed by militants, who accused them of *munafik* (being un-Muslim hypocrites), by cooperating with Thai authorities or participating in government-sponsored programs. The militants also relied on assassinations to enforce their predatory system of "taxes" imposed on both Muslim and non-Muslim communities. These tactics targeted moderates and "fence-sitters" among the Thai Muslim community and induced ethnic cleansing by forcing Thai Buddhists to seek refuge outside the southern states. The terror campaign paralyzed the local economy by diminishing the tourist trade, by forcing the closure of public markets, and by increasing the costs of security for all business enterprises. To counter these tactics, clandestine squads, presumably formed by members of Thai security services, targeted suspected militants for extrajudicial execution.[30]

On April 28, 2004, insurgents mounted a coordinated assault against a village police post, but the authorities had been forewarned and repulsed the attacks by killing 108 of the attackers while sustaining the deaths of 5 defending police and soldiers. From the insurgent force, 32 took shelter in the famed Krue Se Mosque near the town of Pattani. None of the militants were willing to surrender, and after a siege of six hours, the Thai military mounted an assault that killed 16 militants and captured 16 others alive. Most of the attackers were poorly armed young Thai Muslims, many of them members of a local football team. Seven foreigners, believed to be from Indonesia, were among the dead. The Pattani Muslim community became greatly distressed at what they believed to be a deliberate massacre of Muslim youth and a violation of the sanctity of their historic mosque.[31]

Following the incident at the Krue Se Mosque, police attempted to question the leader and staff of an Islamic boarding school. On October 25, 2004, a large crowd of more than 2,000 demonstrated outside a police station at Tak Bai, in Narathiwat province, demanding the immediate release of six detainees. As the crowd became more hostile, the police used tear gas, but the demonstrators did not disperse. The police responded by firing into the crowd, which killed six of the rioters. Eventually, the police subdued and arrested nearly 1,300 protesters, who had their hands tied behind their backs and were loaded on top of each other into trucks. After a trip of 120 kilometers to the Inkayut Military Camp, 78 of the arrested demonstrators had died from suffocation or renal failure. This tragedy generated widespread demands for an investigation of human rights abuses and criminal proceedings against responsible Thai authorities.[32]

Under pressure from multiple sources, Prime Minister Thaksin eventually agreed to establish two commissions, one to investigate the Krue Se Mosque siege and one to investigate the Tak Bai incident. The former commission concluded that the security forces had employed excessive force disproportionate to the threat at the mosque. The commission for the Tak Bai incident concluded that officials responsible for transport were "guilty of dereliction of duty" for the manner of transportation provided for arrested demonstrators. Before the two commissions reported their findings, three Thai generals were accused of mismanaging the situation at Tak Bai and removed from their posts, but they were not subject to further disciplinary action.[33] Prime Minister Thaksin refused to bring court-martial charges against the responsible officers, and his failure to do so generated intense criticism from Thai Muslim leaders and human rights organizations.[34]

Elections and Thaksin's Southern Strategy

On December 26, 2004, a massive tsunami hit the western coast of southern Thailand. More than 5,300 people were killed, many of them at the Phuket tourist resort. Prime Minister Thaksin moved very rapidly to mobilize relief efforts and to offer generous financial assistance to the survivors. This disaster did not change the political contest between the government of Thailand and the Islamic insurgents, but the effectiveness of the government in managing the disaster relief gave Thaksin a big boost in popular support that carried over to the national elections for the House of Representatives held on February 6, 2005.[35] In those elections, Prime Minister Thaksin's Thai Rak Thai Party gained 60.7 percent of the total vote cast, winning a landslide victory capturing 377 seats out of a total number of 500 seats in the House of Representatives.[36] These results gave Prime Minister Thaksin an unprecedented commanding majority to provide the basis for a very strong government.

Prime Minister Thaksin's electoral victory came when new evidence revealed that insurgents were preparing for further escalation of hostilities. In February 2005, the Thai-language press reported that Thai intelligence had uncovered a separatist plan to establish an independent state to include Yala, Pattani, and Narathiwat plus three districts of Songkla and two districts in Satun, with Betong as the proposed capital. The plan anticipated an eighty-day struggle during which a great number of people would be killed and high-level Thai government officers would be seized as hostages. That campaign was predicted to generate foreign support that would lead to a UN-supervised plebiscite, as had happened in East Timor.[37]

Although Thaksin's Thai Rak Thai Party lost all eleven seats in the south during the 2005 elections, Thaksin announced his policy regarding the insurgency would not change. Yet, very shortly thereafter, he devised new counterinsurgency plans to reward villages that cooperated with authorities. Each of the 1,580 villages in the south was to be ranked for their degree of cooperation with authorities, categorized as red, yellow, or green. Villages were designated as "red" if more than half of the residents were judged to be sympathetic to the insurgents. Thaksin established a fund of over US$500 million to be distributed, with red villages getting nothing and green villages getting the largest rewards.[38]

Thaksin's revised strategy also involved a comprehensive system of interrogation and detention of persons identified as supporters of insurgent organizations. Partly to address the earlier criticisms of martial law, on July 19, 2005, he ended martial law, but in its place invoked an Emergency Decree that transferred emergency powers to civilian officials, with the prime minister having ultimate authority. Under these new rules, soldiers were required to obtain the consent of a police officer and a civilian district official before applying to a court for an arrest warrant. A suspect could still be held for thirty days without charge, and "authorized officers" were protected by impunity for their actions.[39]

Under the new plan, police prepared a list of names of persons wanted for interrogation. Those wanted persons who refused summons were liable to imprisonment for up to two years and a fine of US$1,000 (B40,000). Members of separatist groups were informed that they could clear their names if they entered a voluntary rehabilitation program. Summoned individuals were denied access to legal counsel and rights of habeas corpus. Those persons who reported to authorities were interviewed, fingerprinted, had DNA samples taken, and were required to stay at an army base for one week for instruction and "reeducation." After interrogation, those who reported voluntarily feared being targeted by insurgents as informers.[40] Because the tactic of compulsory interrogation from a blacklist had previously been used in 2003 to combat drug dealers and smugglers, public knowledge of brutalities and extrajudicial killings of that campaign generated high levels of anxiety among Thailand's Muslims. By June 2004, authorities reported that 200 members of separatist organizations had "surrendered," and by October 2005, a new list of summoned persons was issued containing 4,000 names.[41]

Another part of Thaksin's revised strategy involved a dramatic expansion of volunteer self-defense groups. Dating from the 1950s, when Communist guerrillas operated in the southern border regions, some villages formed a Volunteer Defense Corps, known as Or Sor, supported by the Thai Interior Ministry. When the separatist insurgency began anew, the number of these units rapidly expanded to 2,187 villages by 2007. Their membership was recruited locally. Volunteers were given forty-five days of military training and received US$145–$255 monthly. The Thai Army in collaboration with the Department of Provincial Administration sponsored another protection corps called Chor Ror Bor for villages, and Or Ror Mor for towns. By November 2005, these self-defense militia operated in 1,580 villages. Each volunteer in a militia unit received three to ten days of military training and was expected to serve each month for ten days of guard duty as a volunteer without regular pay. Each thirty-member unit received fifteen shotguns, to be shared among volunteers for guard duty and manning checkpoints. These self-defense forces were established primarily in Buddhist villages but were also formed in some mixed villages. Muslims who volunteered for the village defense corps faced increased risks of assassination by insurgent death squads. While the village defense corps slightly increased village security, these units provided haphazard protection and sometimes engaged in "privatized" violence when ethnic tensions mounted within a village community.

In 1981, the Thai Army established a paramilitary force designed for combat operations. Commonly known as Rangers (Thahan Phran), this force was recruited for fighting ability. Rangers were initially formed to fight against Communist guerrillas and they were revived as a counterinsurgency fighting force in 2002. By October 2007, 7,560 Rangers were organized into seven regiments. Recruits to Ranger units received forty-five days of training, and a monthly salary of about US$300. Because Rangers were assigned combat duty, they recruited fearless young men eager for action. About 60 percent of Rangers were Thai-speaking Buddhists, and 15 to 30 percent were Muslim, mostly those who did not speak Malay. Often, recruiting focused on Muslim families who had suffered fatalities from insurgent death squads. Some Muslim recruits joined the Rangers with a personal motive to avenge the death of a father or a close relative.

The operations of these paramilitary forces were far from satisfactory. The village self-defense forces operated with minimal training and poor weapons, performing mostly static defense duty. These units provided no effective defense against the hit-and-run tactics of insurgent forces. When insurgents mounted attacks, Rangers were frequently sent as first responders, and they were ill equipped to distinguish between insurgent fighters and the civilian population. Rangers acquired a reputation for brutality, atrocities, and lack of concern for human rights, creating a legacy of fear and hatred among many Muslim villagers. Radical Islamist imams and insurgent leaders exploited these fears to generate a steady supply of new recruits for their campaign of violence and terror.[42]

After two years of the renewed insurgency, the conflict had become a continuing disaster with enormous costs for all persons living in the southern provinces. By 2005, Thai Malay peasant incomes had fallen to one-third of their previous levels, while urban incomes had also diminished substantially.[43] The economic costs of the conflict were devastating, but the human costs were even greater. As recounted earlier, beginning in January 2004, insurgent tactics gave high priority to the disruption and destruction of the public school system. For the militants, the public schools were viewed as an assault on Malay and Islamic culture, because most instruction was in the Thai language and the curriculum was secular rather than Islamic. Even so, a majority of Thai Malays chose to send their children to public secular schools where the curriculum prepared them for employment in higher-income business, technical, and professional jobs. Perhaps because of the choice made by a majority of Thai Muslims, the government schools became prime targets for insurgent attacks. Schools were burned, and teachers, principals, and officials in the Department of Education were assassinated. Both Muslim and Buddhist parents were warned by insurgents not to send their children to government schools. Hundreds of schools were closed because of arson attacks or because of fears for the safety of children and their parents. Between January 2004 and November 2005, more than 80 teachers and 70 employees of the Department of Education had been killed. More than 1,000 teachers had transferred out of the southern region, and more than 3,700 teachers applied for transfers to schools in other provinces. During 2004, separatists executed more than 500 local officials, and over 100 Muslims had "gone missing," including some who were victims of extrajudicial killing by state agents.[44]

Thai security authorities concluded that a network of radical Islamic schools supported the insurgency by indoctrinating and training students for guerrilla operations. The Thai military intelligence claimed that over 400 "red" villages were under the effective control of the insurgents. Thai police mounted raids on a number of Islamic schools and collected evidence of guerrilla training, including the capture of Al Qaeda training videos. Some pondok schools were closed, and some Muslim teachers were charged with treason for organizing terrorist attacks.

Thailand's Political Crisis

During the regime of Prime Minister Thaksin, government policies followed a populist agenda that favored the urban and rural poor. A series of programs provided direct payments and generous loans to rural villages, plus free healthcare services available to all, enabling Thaksin to cultivate a massive rural-based voting bloc that gave his Thai Rak Thai party (TRT) a decisive parliamentary majority. Empowered by his electoral mandate, and armed with added emergency powers, Thaksin acquired unprecedented prerogative powers. He established a massive patronage system to reward supporters, and he utilized extralegal tactics to undermine the Constitutional Court, the National Counter-Corruption Commission, the State Audit Commission, and the National Election Commission. Members of these commissions were threatened with lawsuits, and when they resigned, Thaksin appointed his party loyalists. Cloaked with the ritual trappings of democracy, the Thaksin regime became increasingly authoritarian and arbitrary.[45]

The opposition to Thaksin was centered in the Bangkok area and comprised many of the leadership elites from previous regimes as well as intellectuals and close advisers of King Bhumibol Adulyadej.[46] Although the opposition parties held only 24.6 percent of the seats in the Parliament, the opposition reflected the views of the core power holders of Thai politics—business leaders, the army, intellectuals, and upper echelons of the bureaucracy. In September 2005, public protests began in Bangkok over the issues of corruption and misuse of power by Thaksin. These demonstrations were organized by an anti-Thaksin coalition led by the People's Alliance for Democracy (PAD). Early in

2006, street protests in Bangkok gained mass support when the public discovered that controlling stock of Thailand's main television and telecommunications conglomerate—the Shin Corporation—was sold in a surprise deal to Singapore's government-owned investment company, Temasek Holdings, for the sum of US$1.87 billion. Prime Minister Thaksin and his family owned the Shin Corporation, and the sale had been facilitated by a recently passed amendment to Thai law permitting tax-free foreign investment in "strategic" Thai corporations. These amendments enabled Thaksin and members of his clan to reap phenomenal profits from that sale.[47]

With falling public support, Prime Minister Thaksin called a snap election for April 2, 2006, to reassert his claim to a national mandate. Recognizing their vulnerability, the opposition parties decided to boycott the election, which continued without their participation. In that election, Thaksin's Thai Rak Thai party won 16 million out of a total of 28 million votes, but in thirty-eight constituencies the unopposed TRT candidates failed to get the required minimum of 20 percent of the votes, making it difficult for Thaksin to form a new government. The opposition People's Alliance for Democracy called on the king to appoint a "royal prime minister," but the king declined because that would involve suspending the Constitution. Thailand's Constitutional Court eventually annulled the snap election of April 2006, and a new election date was set for October 15, 2006.[48]

One year earlier, in response to criticisms of his policies, Thaksin had agreed to create a National Reconciliation Commission (NRC) composed of forty-eight members under the leadership of Anand Panyarachun, a former prime minister. This body was charged with responsibility for advising the government on solutions to southern violence. One of the first actions of the NRC advised the government to revoke martial law. Thaksin ignored that recommendation.[49] In May 2006, during the interim period of crisis and stalemate, the NRC released its first report on violence in the southern provinces. That report provided a brief survey of the cycle of escalating violence and evaluated the costs of violence for all parties. In the last chapter, the commission outlined a set of proposals for promoting a reconciliation strategy. In October 2005, the NRC issued its final report, which proposed the creation of an unarmed Peace Unit called Shanti Sena, to include civilian experts on nonviolent methods and religious teachers, both Muslim and Buddhist, who are "well-versed in religion and culture." This body would promote reconciliation and "dialogue" with militant groups. Reconciliation was to be based on disclosing truth, promoting justice, accountability, forgiveness, nonviolence, remembering the past, and acceptance of risks. The report proposed Pattani Malay as "an additional working language." The report also proposed that Thai courts enforce some aspects of Sharia law for Thai Muslims. It made no recommendations relating to security strategy or issues of protecting vulnerable populations and physical infrastructure from terrorist attacks.[50] When the NRC released its final report, the Thaksin government ignored its proposals, but a pro-Thaksin TV talk show mounted a relentless criticism of its contents and NRC chairman, Anand Panyarachun. That TV show appealed to Buddhist chauvinism to oppose any concessions to Thai Muslims.[51]

Secret Peace Talks with Pattani Insurgents

Although Thaksin was often criticized for his ruthless anti-insurgency tactics, and for his unwillingness to pursue peace negotiations, it is not true that he never authorized negotiations with the insurgents. Instead, he was insistent that any such overtures should be conducted unofficially and with extreme secrecy. In July 2002 and in June 2004, Thaksin authorized secret talks with PULO and BRN, but they were canceled before they began. In August 2005, a representative of the Thai government engaged in four days of secret talks with representatives of PULO in Lausanne, Switzerland.[52] Earlier, in June 2005, Thai military officials and separatist insurgent leaders from PULO and Bersatu engaged in secret negotiations on the Malaysian resort island of Langkawi. Former Malaysian prime minister Mahathir acted as an intermediary to arrange these meetings. In October 2005, Mahathir visited Bangkok, and during an audience with Thailand's King Bhumibol, Mahathir received backing from the king for a peace initiative. Following Mahathir's visit, King Bhumibol and the Privy Council pressured Prime Minister Thaksin to reshuffle the army's high command. Thaksin agreed in October 2005 to appoint Sonthi Boonyaratglin commander-in-chief of the Royal Thai Army. General Sonthi became the first Muslim to head the Thai Army, and his knowledge of Muslim communities was expected to increase the effectiveness of the army and perhaps lead to a peace settlement with insurgents. At the time of his appointment, General Sonthi claimed that he would resolve the insurgency.

After General Sonthi became Thailand's Army commander-in-chief, he appointed Lieutenant General Vaipot Srinual to represent the army in secret discussions in Malaysia sponsored by Mahathir. The Thailand military delegation met with representatives from PULO, Bersatu, the BRN-Kongress, the Pattani Islamic Liberation Front, and GMIP. Mahathir advised the insurgent delegates to be realistic and not demand independence or even autonomy as a condition for peace. By December 2005, the discussions produced a peace plan entitled, "A Joint Peace and Development Programme for Southern Thailand." Its "points of agreement" included a program of economic development for the region, the restoration of the Southern Border Provinces Administrative Committee, recognition of Malay Muslims as a distinct ethnic community, and the use of Malay in schools and as an official language. Other demands, not accepted by army representatives, called for the creation of an independent tribunal to try government officers for human rights violations and a general amnesty extended to all insurgents. Insurgent groups represented at the negotiations did promise to end the violence.

Following those peace talks, insurgent attacks in southern Thailand intensified. During August of 2006, insurgents staged twenty-three simultaneous bombings of commercial banks. Following those attacks, General Sonthi publicly proposed to open direct negotiations with insurgents to seek a viable peace.[53] Prime Minister Thaksin did not endorse that proposal.

Coup Politics and the Southern Insurgency

On September 19, 2006, the Royal Thai Army staged a coup against Prime Minister Thaksin while he was in New York to address the UN. The coup-makers, calling themselves the Council of Democratic Reform, issued orders dissolving Parliament, the cabinet, and the Constitutional Court, and promised to draft a new democratic Constitution. As commander-in-chief of the Royal Thai Army, General Sonthi acted as leader and chief spokesman for the coup forces. On the day following the initial coup action, King Bhumibol gave his royal mandate to the new military regime under General Sonthi.[54]

Within one month, the coup leaders renamed the Council of Democratic Reform, calling it the Council on National Security (CNS). The latter body promulgated an interim Constitution that gave ultimate power to the CNS but also provided for a 242-member National Legislative Assembly (NLA) headed by a prime minister—all to be appointed by the coup group in the CNS. Retired Thai Army general Surayad Chulanont was appointed new interim prime minister. The CNS also appointed members of a Constitutional Drafting Assembly to create a new Constitution for Thailand for submission to a national referendum. If that draft did not receive majority approval in a national referendum, the CNS reserved the right to revise Thailand's previous Constitution and enforce it as Thailand's permanent Constitution. The CNS originally promised a return to democratic rule within one year, but later announced that civilian democratic rule would be reestablished by March 2008.[55]

In the aftermath of the Thai military coup, both General Sondhi and the new interim prime minister Surayud Chulanont toured the southern provinces, promising new policies to address grievances of Thailand's Muslims. During October, Prime Minister Surayud visited the southern provinces three times to make public apologies to the residents of the south for previous hard-line policies and mistakes by government authorities. He acknowledged that Muslims had legitimate grievances against the government for rights violations and other abuses of power that were blamed on the previous Thaksin administration. He announced that the Southern Border Provinces Administrative Center and the Combined 43rd Civilian-Police-Military Command would be reestablished to investigate complaints against government officials. He promised to abolish the blacklists and ordered the release of fifty-eight suspected militants detained in October 2004 at the Tak Bai protest incident. He also appointed Teera Mintrasak, a local Muslim, to be the new governor of Yala.[56]

The public was informed of the prior peace talks in Malaysia at Langkawi, including the draft agreement for a proposed peace settlement. After these discussions, the Thai Army called for insurgent leaders to demonstrate their control of militants in Thailand by enforcing a fourteen-day cease-fire and to indicate their willingness to enter substantive peace talks. However, the insurgent leaders at the Langkawi peace talks were unable to arrange a cease-fire with active insurgent forces on the ground in Thailand. Those peace talks had been with former leaders who no longer had any control over active insurgent forces in Thailand.[57]

Although General Sonthi and Prime Minister Surayud openly invited the insurgent leaders to engage in negotiations, the leaders of the insurgency in Thailand showed no interest in pursuing that option. Instead they mounted more frequent, more intense, and more deadly attacks after the Thai military coup. The number of violent incidents escalated to record highs, with insurgents detonating more than 500 bombs, with increasing power and technical capacity. Assassination attacks came with increased frequency, and in February, 29 bombs exploded in forty-five minutes across several southern provinces, targeting karaoke bars and restaurants. Between January 2004 and August 2006, insurgent attacks against civilians had killed 53 percent Muslims and 41 percent Buddhists.[58] Attacks on Buddhists in monasteries and mixed villages intensified, including beheading of civilians by hit-and-run death squads. Many Buddhists were forced to seek sanctuary at Buddhists temples and monasteries or to become refugees fleeing north. By September 2006, the attacks on Buddhist civilians had produced a mass exodus of an estimated 34,000 Buddhists from southern Thailand.[59] One year later, in September 2007, the estimated number of Buddhists fleeing from the south varied from 40,000 to 100,000.

The insurgents also intensified their attacks on state-operated secular schools and on government-funded Islamic schools. Insurgent leaflets called the Thai education system a "symbol of infidel occupation." A total of 194 schools were burned down, seventy-five teachers were killed, and ninety-one injured between January 2004 and June 2007. Muslims who were employed by the government or who were believed to have cooperated with officials in any form were accused of being kafirs and threatened by leaflets promising death, with Muslim parents subject to assault if they did not withdraw their children from government schools. Because of the continuing assaults on teachers and staff, combined with arson attacks by militants on government-operated schools, the Thai Teachers Federation decided, in November 2006, to close indefinitely all 944 government schools serving about 300,000 students in the three provinces of Pattani, Narathiwat, and Yala.[60] With increased military protection, some schools were later reopened, but about 700 schools remained closed.

The primary objective of these attacks by insurgent forces was to make the region ungovernable and to impose coercive control over Muslim communities.

Any criticism of their tactics or goals by Muslims was treated as an act of treason to be punished by death. While insurgents were organized into semi-autonomous cells, they operated with active participation of three main separate organizations, collaborating with common strategy and tactics. Thai authorities identified BRN-C, RKK, and GMIP as the prime organizers of the insurgency.[61] To stress their unified front, beginning about 2006, insurgents posted pronouncements and threats to the public in the name of Pejuan Kemerdekaan Pattani (Pattani Freedom Fighters). An insurgent commander, who claimed to control 250 fighters, stated to a foreign reporter: "Right now, we are winning. Why? Because the villagers support us." He explained, all suspected informers—men, women, teachers, even Muslim religious leaders—are legitimate targets. "If you spy on us, we'll take you out."[62]

During the first few months of the coup regime, government authorities seemed to be paralyzed by indecision and fear of generating protests mobilized by Muslim radicals. Bureaucratic rivalries, anticipation of peace talks, and fears of being blamed for earlier "failed policies" added to the ethos of indecision. Prime Minister Surayud's Reconciliation Policy with southern insurgents put a damper on security operations. Police investigations seldom were able to identify suspects after insurgent attacks, and when there were arrests, virtually none of those arrests led to conviction. The police had limited capacity to collect evidence, witnesses were fearful and unwilling to testify, and judges did not want to convict anyone accused without overwhelming evidence. Over a period of three years, only two people were tried and convicted in Thai courts for acts of violence committed in support of the insurgency.[63] After December 2006, militants mobilized numerous mass protests by women supporting the separatist cause. These protests frequently resulted in security forces releasing arrested suspects to avoid conflict incidents with protesters, with officials citing the "new reconciliation policy" to justify their actions.[64] The failure of the Thailand justice system to convict suspects for acts of violence provided an incentive for the Thai Army to once again rely on its Emergency Powers to imprison numerous insurgent suspects who were denied access to regular criminal proceedings.

In June 2007, Thailand's security forces, under the leadership of General Sonthi, initiated a new strategy of first blockading key insurgent villages, followed by large-force security sweeps through villages to detain suspects, collect evidence, and interrogate villagers. The blockade tactic was designed to prevent a rapid flight of suspects when security forces appeared. The first blockade and search operation began at the notorious insurgent stronghold of Bannang-Satta in Yala Province. The army later shifted its operations to other key insurgent villages in Narathiwat, and by the end of July, 1,930 insurgent suspects had been detained, including top-ranking members of RKK and seven suspected bombers. Among those arrested were 300 insurgent leaders who had supervised insurgent attacks. The police found stolen guns, bomb-making equipment, and key records of insurgent forces. They also reported that more Muslims than previously were cooperating with security forces because of their resentments over excessive intimidation by insurgents.[65]

The End of Military Rule

In Thailand, political pressure mounted against the coup regime, with new demands for a restoration of democracy and civilian rule. On August 19, 2007, the military regime submitted its draft of a revised Constitution to a national referendum. With a relatively small voter participation rate of 57.6 percent, the revised Constitution drafted by the coup military received the approval of 51.81 percent and rejections by 42.19 percent of votes in the referendum.[66] Shortly thereafter, the government announced that national elections would be held on December 23, 2007, to elect a new Parliament for a return to civilian rule. General Sonthi Boonyartglin, leader of the military coup group, announced his retirement as commander-in-chief of the Thai Army, amid speculation that he might seek a leading role in any new civilian government.[67]

During the coup regime, former prime minister Thaksin had been charged in court with corruption and electoral fraud, his Thai Rak Thai Party was banned, and 110 former TRT leaders were banned from politics for five years. When new parliamentary elections were announced, a new People's Power Party (PPP) was formed under the leadership of Samak Sundaravej, an old-style conservative politician. He openly announced that his PPP was a reincarnation of Thaksin's banned TRT and promised to continue Thaksin's populist agenda for Thailand's urban and rural poor. From exile in London and Hong Kong, Thaksin advised the PPP leaders and provided generous funds to bankroll the new party.[68]

During the coup regime, the prime support for the military intervention came from the Democratic Party (DP), which had earlier been endorsed by the military and by key members of the royal court. The new parliamentary elections that were held on December 23, 2007, involved the PPP versus the DP and a few minor parties. The People's Power Party won 233 seats in a 480-member legislature, and the Democratic Party won 165 seats. There were five smaller parties that won 37 or fewer seats each.[69] Because the Thai electoral law, drafted by the coup group, banned candidates from being reelected by proxy, Thaksin's opponents brought court action to disqualify PPP, but the Supreme Court ruled that it had no jurisdiction to take such action. This decision cleared the way for Samak Sundaravej, leader of the PPP, to form a six-party coalition with the smaller parties to secure a working majority of 310 seats for the new government sworn in on January 29, 2008.[70]

Most analysts viewed Thailand's new coalition government as having few proven politicians with experience, and Prime Minister Samak headed a fractious coalition.[71] The PPP campaign had promised that Thaksin would be granted an amnesty, and in February Thaksin returned to Thailand. Since Samak had campaigned as "Thaksin's nominee," Thaksin's presence in Thailand raised the issue of whether Samak was merely a stand-in for Thaksin. When the Thai economy took a downturn in mid-2008 due to rising oil prices and other causes, the People's Alliance for Democracy began month-long protests with up to 10,000 demonstrators in the streets demanding that Samak resign. While the Samak government was able to survive the vote in Parliament's lower house, political analysts predicted that Thailand's political crisis was likely to continue for months.[72] Confronted by political turmoil in Bangkok, Prime Minister Samak was unlikely to make any decisive moves for dealing with the southern insurgency.

Thailand's Counterinsurgency Dilemma

Political instability in Thailand will make it more difficult for Thai leaders to make substantive concessions to Thai Muslims. However, eventually significant concessions will need to be made, and that process is unlikely to begin without negotiations with Thai Muslim leaders who can command the respect and trust of the Thai Muslim population. If the insurgents are unwilling to negotiate, more Thai Muslims must become involved in all levels of government and public services. To be effective, Thai Muslim leaders must be given the authority to define and initiate policies to address the Muslim concerns and grievances. Some of the Langkawi Peace Plan proposals could be implemented as a first stage. To recruit Muslims into public services will be difficult because of the insurgent campaign to kill those deemed to be munafik. Therefore, effective security for Muslims in government must receive the highest priority.

If the southern conflict is to be resolved, permanent police and security forces will need to be established in key areas where insurgents operate. Because insurgents in 2008 controlled about 400 villages, police, backed by military units, will need to be permanently stationed in many of these villages. The police and security forces will then face the daunting task of building trust where hostility to Thailand has been cultivated for decades. Their most important task will be to provide security for those Muslims who support peace measures and are willing to cooperate with government authorities to address security issues, Muslim grievances, and the economic viability of each village.

While it will be advantageous to obtain the cooperation of Malaysia, that option will be insufficient to significantly limit foreign support for the insurgency. Malaysia is too cross-pressured by internal political divisions and with a public that has provided sympathetic support for the Pattani insurgency. Until there is a credible negotiation process between the government of Thailand and legitimate leaders of Thai Muslims, Malaysia is unlikely to risk becoming involved in promoting any solution to the Pattani insurgency. After a peace process gets well under way, it may be appropriate to initiate the "truth and reconciliation" process proposed by the National Reconciliation Commission. To begin that process too soon before the security situation improves and before moderate Muslims gain significant leadership roles in government and in public services would likely degenerate into a process of "accusation and retaliation" that would not build trust and empathy across the boundaries of religion and ethnicity. There is no one simple formula for success. Whatever develops, the peace process will be slow, costly, and punctuated with setbacks.

Notes

1. D. J. M Tate, *The Making of Modern South-East Asia,* Vol. 1, *The European Conquest,* rev. ed. (Kuala Lumpur: Oxford University Press, 1977), 483–487, 495–501. The Thai spelling of the southern province is "Pattani"; the Malaysian spelling is "Patani."

2. The British first pressured Siam to relinquish its tributary claims to Kelantan and Terengganu, which Siam agreed to by treaty in 1902. Later, in 1909, the division of sovereign authority between Britain and Siam was further clarified by the terms of the Anglo-Siamese Treaty, which provided for Siam to surrender all "sovereign rights" over Perlis, Kedah, and Terengganu to British authority. The state of Kedah was divided with one district of Kedah, known as Satun, ceded to Siam, with the remainder of Kedah ceded to British authority. In return, Siam was granted a loan of four million pounds sterling for Siamese railway construction, and Britain surrendered all claims to extraterritorial rights in Siam. Moshe Yegar, *Between Integration and Secession: Muslim Communities of the Southern Philippines, Southern Thailand, and Western Burma/Myanmar* (Lanham, MD: Lexington Books, 2002), 74–80; W. K. Che Man, *Muslim Separatism: The Moros of Southern Philippines and the Malays of Southern Thailand* (Singapore: Oxford University Press, 1990), 32–36; Clive J. Christie, *A Modern History of Southeast Asia: Decolonization, Nationalism and Separatism* (London: I. B. Tauris Publishers, 1996), 173–190.

3. Yegar, *Between Integration and Secession,* 76–88.

4. D. G. E. Hall, *A History of South-East Asia,* 3rd ed. (New York: St. Martin's Press, 1970), 804–814; Che Man, *Muslim Separatism,* 62–66; Yegar, *Between Integration and Secession,* 90–92.

5. To maintain their supply routes, the Japanese rapidly constructed the Bangkok to Kanburi "death railway" utilizing tens of thousands of prisoners of war and conscript labor from Malaya and Indonesia. The railway crossed the River Kwae and traversed Three Pagodas Pass. Japanese soldiers imposed harsh working conditions and inflicted extreme brutalities on the prisoners in order to accelerate the construction of the railway. The railway was completed in November 1943. During the construction of that rail line, 16,000 captured Allied troops and over 100,000 Asian conscript laborers died from maltreatment, starvation, and disease. See www.britain-at-war.com.uk.

6. Hall, *A History of South-East Asia,* 815–821.

7. Yegar, *Between Integration and Secession,* 93–96.

8. In letters seized by the Thai police, Haji Sulong asked Tunku Mayhiddin to take direct leadership of the separatist movement. Tunku Mayhiddin promoted the goal of restoring the Pattani Sultanate as an ultimate objective, but preferred to keep his role ambiguous because of the political implications in Malaya. Yegar, *Between Integration and Secession,* 101–108.

9. Che Man, *Muslim Separatism*, 98–113; Yegar, *Between Integration and Secession,* 141–149.

10. Zachary Abuza, "A Breakdown of Southern Thailand's Insurgent Groups," *Terrorism Monitor* 4, no. 17 (September 8, 2006), 1–4, www.jamestown.org/terrorism/news/article.php?articleid=2370121.

11. Yegar, *Between Integration and Secession,* 132–135; John F. Cady, *The History of Post-War Southeast Asia: Independence Problems* (Athens, OH: Ohio University Press, 1975), 419–448.

12. Abuza, "A Breakdown," 2, citing Reuters, May 7, 2004. For an analysis of the relative economic status and political subordination of Thai Muslims in south Thailand from 1960 to 2000, see Aurel Croissant, "Unrest in South Thailand: Contours, Causes, and Consequences Since 2001," *Strategic Insights* (Center for Contemporary Conflict, Naval Postgraduate School) 4, no. 2 (February 2005), 6–10, www.nps.edu.

13. Anthony L. Smith, "Trouble in Thailand's Muslim South: Separatism, Not Global Terrorism," *Asia-Pacific Security Studies* 3, no. 10 (December 2004), www.apcss.org; Dana Robert Dillon, "The Shape of Anti-Terrorist Coalitions in Southeast Asia," The Heritage Foundation, Lecture No. 773 (January 17, 2003), www.heitage.org/Research/AsiaandthePacific/hl773.cfm; Peter Chalk, "Commentary: Light Arms Trade in SE Asia," *Jane's Intelligence Review,* March 1, 2001, www.rand.org/commentary/030101JIR.html; Mark Barker, "Into the Heart of Darkness," *The Age* (Australia), November 16, 2002, www.theage.com.au. In 1997, the illegal economy of Thailand was estimated by a Chulalongkorn University study to be $9.4 billion, comprising mostly the underground sales of weapons and drugs. This is what was called the "black economy," which constituted an estimated 10 percent of the Thai economy in 1997. This black economy increased significantly up through 2003 and may have declined slightly thereafter. See Chalk, "Commentary," 8.

14. Abuza, "A Breakdown of Southern Thailand's Insurgent Groups," 1–4.

15. Smith, "Trouble in Thailand's Muslim South"; Joseph Liow, "Bangkok's Southern Discomfort: Violence and Response in Southern Thailand," *IDSS Commentaries,* No. 14 (May 2004), Institute of Defence and Strategic Studies, Nanyang Technological University, Singapore, www.idss.edu.sg; Stephen Brown, "Thailand's Rising Terrorism Problem," *Front Page Magazine*, July 17, 2003, www.frontpagemag.com/Articles/ReadArticle.asp?ID=8953; Alex, "Lessons to Learn from Southern Thailand Uprising," *Parti Islam Se Malaysia (PAS),* 2004, www.parti-pas.org; S. P. Harish, "Insurgency in Southern Thailand: Ethnic or Religious Conflict?" *IDSS Commentaries,* No. 17 (April 14, 2005), 1–3, www.idss.edu.sg.

16. Joseph Liow, "The Truth About Pondok Schools in Thailand," *Asia Times, Speaking Frankly,* www.atimes.com/atimes/Southeast_Asia/FI03Ae04.html; Kavi Chongkittavorn, "Thailand: International Terrorism and the Muslim South," in *Southeast Asian Affairs 2004* (Singapore: Institute of Southeast Asian Studies, 2004), 267–275.

17. John R. Bradley, "Waking Up to the Terror Threat in Southern Thailand," *The Straits Times,* May 27, 2004, yaleglobe.yale.edu/display.article?id=3985. The IIRO is affiliated with the Muslim World League, and after September 11, 2001, the US Treasury froze IIRO funds because of its alleged links to Al Qaeda.

18. "Crown Prince to Open Islamic Headquarters in Pattani," *The Nation* (Bangkok), March 6, 2004, www.nationmultimedia.com; John R. Bradley, "Islamist Schools Are Blamed for Bloody Uprising in Thailand," *The Independent,* May 15, 2004, www.selvesandothers.org/article 6523/html.

19. Frank Bures, "Muslim Unrest Flares in Thailand," *The Christian Science Monitor*, January 7, 2004, csmonitor.com/2004/0107/p06s01-wosc.html.

20. Bradley, "Waking Up to the Terror Threat in Southern Thailand"; Global Security.org, "Thailand Islamic Insurgency," April 27, 2005, 3–4, www.globalsecurity .org/military/world/war/thailand2.htm.

21. GlobalSecurity.org, "Thailand Islamic Insurgency"; Brown, "Thailand's Rising Terrorism Problem"; Alisa Tang, "Muslim Grievances May Lead to Connections with International Terrorism in Thailand's Troubled South," February 1, 2004, www .sfgate.com/cgi-bin/; John R. Bradley, "Waking Up"; Liow, "The Truth"; Andrew Perrin, "Thailand's Terror," *Time Asia,* November 25, 2002, www.time.com/time/ magazine/0,9263,7601021125,00.html?internalid=AC; Eric Teo Chu Cheow, "The Changing Face of Terrorism in Southeast Asia," *Pacific Forum,* No. 34 (August 14, 2003), The Center for Strategic and International Studies; Smith, "Trouble in Thailand's Muslim South."

22. Marc Erikson, "Osama bin Laden and al-Qaeda of Southeast Asia," *Asia Times*, February 6, 2002, www.atimes.com/se-asia/DB06Ae01.htm.

23. Jeremy Wagstaff, "Time to Get Tough," *Far Eastern Economic Review,* August 14, 2003, 12–16; Shawn W. Crispin and Jeremy Wagstaff, "The Terror War's Next Offensive," *Far Eastern Economic Review,* August 28, 2003, 12–16; Eric Koo, "Ba'asyir Trial and the Future of Jemaah Islamiah," *Asia Times,* November 3, 2004, www.atimes.com/atimes/Southeast_Asia/FK03Ae04.htm; Smith, "Trouble in Thailand's Muslim South"; Chongkittavorn, "Thailand: International Terrorism," 267–270; Ken Conboy, *The Second Front: Inside Asia's Most Dangerous Network* (Jakarta: Equinox Publishing, 2006), 147–164.

24. Center for Defense Information, "Thailand," August 25, 2004, www.cdi.org; Amnesty International, "If You Want Peace Work for Justice," January 2006, 21–22, www.amnestyusa.org/news/document.do?id=ENGASA390012006; Human Rights Watch, "Thailand: Blacklists Create a Climate of Fear," December 16, 2004, 1–3, hrw .org/english/docs/2005/12/16 /thaila12317_txt.htm; International Crisis Group, *Thailand's Emergency Decree: No Solution,* Asia Report, No. 105 (November 18, 2005), Jakarta, 7 8.

25. John R. Bradley, "Islamic Separatists Challenge Bangkok," *Washington Times,* May 15, 2004, 2, www.washtimes.com/world/20040515-111511-6564r.htm.

26. Joseph Chinyong Liow, "International Jihad and Muslim Radicalism in Thailand? Toward an Alternative Interpretation," *Asia Policy* 1, no. 2 (July 2006), The National Bureau of Asian Research, 89–108.

27. Denis D. Gray and Vijay Joshi, "Thailand Insurgency May Have Links to the Broader World of Radical Islam," *The Californian,* March 9, 2007, www.nctimes.com./ articles/2007/03/10/news /nation.

28. B. Raman, "Muslim Anger: The Thai Dilemma," *South Asia Analysis Group*, Paper No. 1156 (November 1, 2004), www.saag.org/papers12/paper1156.html. Indian intelligence sources identified students enrolled in radical Pakistani madrasahs by their country of origin during 2002. They included 167 from Malaysia, 149 from Thailand, and 84 from Indonesia. B. Raman, "Thailand & International Islamic Front," *South Asia Analysis Group*, Paper No. 890 (January 9, 2004), 1–9, www.saag.org/papers9/ paper890.html. In Bangladesh, forty militant Islamist groups operated fifty training camps by 2004. See the review by Bertil Lintner of the book by Hiranmay Karlekar, *Bangladesh: The New Afghanistan?* (Thousand Oaks, CA: Sage Publications, 2005) in *Far Eastern Economic Review* 168, no. 11 (December 2005), 62–64.

29. Andrew Holt, "Thailand's Troubled Border: Islamic Insurgency or Criminal Playground?" *Terrorism Monitor* 2, no. 10 (May 20, 2004), 1–4, www.jamestown.org/ publications_details .php?volume_id=400; John Pike, "Thailand Islamic Insurgency," www.globalsecurity.org/military/world/war/thailand2.htm.

30. Pike, "Thailand Islamic Insurgency," 5; Smith, "Trouble in Thailand's Muslim South," 3–4.

31. Bradley, "Islamic Separatists Challenge Bangkok"; Holt, "Thailand's Troubled Border," 1–4; B. Rahman, "Thailand: Dangers of Jihadi Reprisal," *South Asia Analysis Group,* Paper No. 989 (May 2, 2004), 1–4, www.saag.org; Mark Baker, "Global Terrorism Fears over Bloody Thailand Uprising," *Sydney Morning Herald*, May 6, 2004, www.smh.com.au/articles/2004/05/05/1083635207042,html.

32. Amnesty International, "If You Want Peace"; Asian Centre for Human Rights, "Mr. Shinawatra, Accountability Is the Issue," *ACHR Review,* April 27, 2005, 1–3, www.achrweb.org/Review/2005/70-05.htm.

33. "Thai Generals Removed from Posts," *BBC News*, March 7, 2005, news .bbc.co.uk/go/pr/fr/-/1/hi/world/asia-pacific/4326629.stm.

34. "Thai PM's Muslim Insurgency Blame Game a Blunder: Analysts," Channel NewsAsia, December 26, 2004, 1–4, www.channelnewsasia.com/stories/afp_asia pacific/view/124049/; B. Raman, "Muslim Anger: The Thai Dilemma," South Asia Analysis Group, Paper No. 1156 (November 1, 2004), 1–11, www.saag.org/papers12/ paper1156.html; Amnesty International, "If You Want Peace," 5–7.

35. Andreas Lorenz, "Post-Tsunami Politics: Thailand Incorporated," *Der Spiegel*, January 31, 2005, 1–3, service.spiegel.de/cache/international/spiegel/; Nick Cumming-Bruce, "For Thaksin, How Big a Victory?" *International Herald Tribune*, February 4, 2005, 1–3, www.iht.com/articles/2005/02/03/news/thailand.html; Muhammad Haniff Hassan, "Trouble in Thailand's Muslim South: What a Stronger Thaksin Can Do," *IDSS Commentaries* (2005), Institute of Defence and Strategic Studies, Singapore, 1–3, www.idss.edu.sg.

36. "Elections in Thailand," www.electionworld.org/thailand.htm; Colum Murphy, "'Thaksin, Get Out!': Why Thais Are Angry," *Far Eastern Economic Review* 169, no. 3 (April 2006), 8. Thaksin's Thai Rak Thai Party held 270 seats in the House of Representatives before the 2005 election.

37. "80-Day Plan to Form Pattani State," February 20, 2005, angkor.com/ 2bangkok/south3.shtml. This report may have been restricted to the Thai-language press to prevent tourists from becoming alarmed by the prospects of increasing terrorist threats. General Thammarak, Thai defense minister, reported an earlier version of this plan in January 2004 at a special live broadcast of a cabinet meeting. Ukrist Pathmanand, "Thaksin's Policies Go South," *Far Eastern Economic Review* 168, no. 7 (July/August 2005), 8–13.

38. "Thaksin Plan for South Criticized," *BBC News*, February 18, 2005, news.bbc.co.uk/go/pr/fr/-/1/hi/world/asia-pacific/4276279.stm; "South United: Zones Will Hurt," *The Nation* (Bangkok), February 28, 2005. By September 2005, in the province of Narathiwat, the army reported that 312 villages were classified in the red zone, 133 in the yellow zone, and 129 in the green zone. International Crisis Group, *Thailand's Emergency Decree,* 2–3, 7.

39. International Crisis Group, *Thailand's Emergency Decree,* 25–29.

40. Cited by Amnesty International, "If You Want Peace," 22–23.

41. Amnesty International, "If You Want Peace," 21–22; Human Rights Watch, "Thailand: Blacklists Create a Climate of Fear," December 16, 2005, hrw.org/english/ docs/2005/12/16/thaila12317.htm; International Crisis Group, *Southern Thailand: Insurgency, Not Jihad,* ICG Asia Report No. 98 (May 18, 2005), Jakarta/Brussels.

42. International Crisis Group, *Southern Thailand: The Problem with Paramilitaries,* Asia Report No. 140 (October 23, 2007), Jakarta/Brussels, 2, 15–19.

43. The number of violent incidents between militants and government troops averaged 30 to 35 per year from 1993 to 2003. During 2004, there were 900 incidents, and in

the first half of 2005 over 700 incidents were recorded. Marwaan Macan-Markar, "Fighting for Peace in Thailand," *Asia Times,* November 3, 2005, 1–3. Between January 4, 2004, and January 4, 2006, in the three states of Pattani, Yala, and Narathiwat, a total of 1,076 people were killed and 1,600 injured in attacks and combat operations. Police records for 2004 and 2005 record the assassination of nonsecurity personnel based on province and religion as follows: in Pattani, Muslim 330, Buddhist, 141; in Yala, Muslim 222, Buddhist 99; in Narathiwat, Muslim 1,406, Buddhist 237. Supalak Gunjanakhundee and Don Pathan, "New Face of Violénce in Southern Thailand," *The Nation*, January 9, 2006, 1–3, www.asianewsnet.net/print_template.php?news_id=50848&13sec=8.

44. Andrew Marshall, "The Troubled South," *Time Asia,* August 1, 2005, 1–5, www.time.com/time/asia/magazine/; Amnesty International, "If You Want Peace,'" 26–27, citing "Students Return to School but Teachers Are Fleeing in Droves," *The Nation,* November 1, 2005; Michael Kelly Connors, "Thailand: The Facts and F(r)ictions of Ruling," in Chin Kin Wah and Daljit Singh (eds.), *Southeast Asian Affairs 2005* (Singapore: Institute of Southeast Asian Studies, 2005), 365–384.

45. Pasuk Phongpaichit and Chris Baker, "Thaksin Dismantles the Opposition," *Far Eastern Economic Review* 168, no. 3 (March 2005), 25–29; Pathmanand, "Thaksin's Policies Go South," 8–13; "Thai PM Gets New Powers for South," BBC News, July 15, 2005, 1–3, news.bbc.co.uk/2/hi/asia-pacific/4684883.stm; Nick Comming-Bruce, "Emergency Declared in Thailand," *International Herald Tribune,* July 16, 2005, 1, www.iht.com /articles/2005/07/15/thai.php; "Thailand: Islamic Guerrillas and Thai Army Clash," *Asia News,* July 18, 2005, 1–2, www.asianews.it/view.php?l=en&art =3733; Thitinan Pongsudhirak, "Thaksin's Political Zenith and Nadir," in Daljit Singh and Lorraine Carlos Salazar (eds.), *Southeast Asian Affairs 2006* (Singapore: Institute of Southeast Asian Studies, 2006), 286–302.

46. For an account of the political role of Thailand's monarch, see Paul M. Handley, *The King Never Smiles: A Biography of Thailand's Bhumibol Adulyadej* (New Haven: Yale University Press, 2006).

47. Because the sale of Shin shares slightly exceeded the revised 49 percent maximum, the issue of its legality came before the Central Administrative Court. In May 2006, this court assessed a penalty of US$1.99 billion on the iTV branch of the Shin Corporation. Ukrist Pathmanand, "Thailand: iTV—Not Just a TV Station," *Asian Analysis,* August 2006, 11–12.

48. Simon Montlake, "Bangkok Rallies Raise Heat on Thaksin," *The Christian Science Monitor,* February 13, 2006, 7; Alex M. Mutebi, "Thailand's Independent Agencies Under Thaksin: Relentless Gridlock and Uncertainty," in Daljit Singh and Carlos Salazar (eds.), *Southeast Asian Affairs 2006* (Singapore: Institute of Southeast Asian Studies, 2006), 303–321; Murphy, "'Thaksin, Get Out!'" 7–13.

49. "Anand Promise: Peace Team Members to Be Selected This Month," *The Nation*, March 4, 2005.

50. Thailand, *Report of the National Reconciliation Commission* (Bangkok: The Secretariat of the Cabinet, 2006), 1–147.

51. "What Is Being Said on the Samak-Dusit Show?" *The Nation,* October 31, 2005, http://2bangkok.com/net/news05za.shtml.

52. Sebastien Berger, "Thailand 'in Secret Talks with Muslim Separatist Group,'" *Telegraph Group,* August 20, 2005, 1–2, news.telegraph.co.uk/news/main.jhtml?xml=/news/2005/08/29/; Stephen Ulph, "Thailand's Islamist Insurgency on the Brink," *Terrorism Focus* 2, no. 18 (October 4, 2005), 1, www.jamestown.org/terrorism/news/article.php?articleid=2369.

53. "Southern Violence: 23 Yala Banks Hit by Bomb Blasts," *The Nation,* August 31, 2006, 1–2, nationalmultimedia.com/2006/08/31/; Ron Corben, "Thai Army

Stymied in South, Seeks New Approach," *News VOA,* September 7, 2006, 1–3, www.voanews.com/english/2006-09-07-voa18.cfm; "Lifting the Lid on Thai Insurgents," *BBC News,* August 7, 2006, 1–4, news.bbc.co.uk/1/hi/world/asia-pacific/5252528.stm; "Thai Muslim Group Welcomes Army Talks Offer," *Reuters AlertNet,* September 3, 2006, 1, www.alertnet.org/thenews/newsdesk/BKK274512.htm; Duncan McCargo, "State of Denial: The Conflict in Thailand's South Reflects a Failure of Political Leadership," *Time Asia,* September 11, 2006, 2–3, www.time.com/time/asia/magazine/.

54. Pichit Likitkijsomboon, "Thais Pay the Price for Political Turmoil," *Far Eastern Economic Review* 169, no. 6 (July/August), 49–52; "Thai Leadership Uncertain After Coup," *CBS News,* September 19, 2006, 1–2, www.cbsnews.com/stories/2006/09/19/world/main2021898.shtml; Michael H. Nelson, "Bankok's Elitist Coup," *Far Eastern Economic Review* 169, no. 8 (October 2006), 27–30; Colum Murphy, "Putting Thailand Together Again," *Far Eastern Economic Review* 169, no. 8 (October 2006), 31–35; Ukrist Pathmanand, "How Long Before the Thai Junta Splinters?" *Far Eastern Economic Review* 169, no. 8 (October 2006), 36–38; "Profile: Thai Coup Leader," *BBC News,* September 19, 2006, 1–2, news.bbc.co.uk/2/hi/asia-pacific/5361932.stm; "Thai Military Coup," 1–8, [website of the Thai coup supporters] www.csmngt.com/coup.htm.

55. Shawn W. Crispin, "Thailand: All the King's Men," *Asia Times,* September 21, 2006, 1–4, www.atimes.com/atimes/Southeast_Asia/H121Ae02.html; Erik Martinez Kuhonta, "Constitution at the Heart of Thai Coup," *Asia Times,* Speaking Freely section, October 6, 2006, 1–4, www.atimes.com/atimes/Southeast_Asia/HJ06Ae02.html; John Funston, "Thailand: Wither Democracy?" *Asian Analysis,* November 2006, 10–14, asian-analysis@aseanfocus.com; Asian Human Rights Commission, "Thailand: Military Coup—Constitutional Fictions," *AHRC Statement,* October 9, 2006, 1–3, ahrc.hk.net. Various explanations for the Thai coup reveal a general consensus among political analysts that the opposition to Thaksin focused primarily on his domestic abuse of power and corruption. Criticisms of his handling of the southern insurgency appeared to be a secondary motivation for the coup.

56. Shawn Crispin, "No Peace in Sight for Southern Thailand," *Asia Times*, Asia Hand section, October 27, 2006, 1–4, www.atimes.com/atimes/Southeast_Asia/HJ27Ae01.html; "Thai PM 'to Reach Out to Muslims,'" *BBC News*, November 20, 2006, 1–2, newsvote.bbc.co.uk/mpapps/; Asian Centre for Human Rights, "Southern Thailand Seeks Justice, Not Apology," November 22, 2006, 1–4, www.achrweb.org/Review/2006/142-06.htm; Human Rights Watch, "Thailand: Insurgents Must Stop Targeting Civilians," *Human Rights News*, November 16, 2006, hrw.org/english/docs/2006/11/16/thaila14610.htm.

57. Don Pathan, "Mahathir Set Up Peace Talks," *The Nation,* October 6, 2006, 1–2, www.nationmultimedia.com/2006/10/06/headlines; Connie Levett, "King Backed Me, Mahathir Says," *Sydney Morning Herald,* October 9, 2006, 1–2, www.smh.com.au/news/world/; "Secret Peace Plan for Thailand's South," *Sydney Morning Herald,* October 7, 2006, newsstore.smh.com.au; Ismail Wolff and Daniel Ten Kate, "Peace Talks in Southern Thailand," *Asia Sentinel,* October 18, 2006, 1–6, www.asiasentinel.com/; "Malaysia Willing to Help If Thailand Seeks Support to Settle Southern Insurgency," *The Star,* October 16, 2006, 1–2, thestar.com.my/news/story.asp?file=/2006/10/16/nation/20061016; Connie Levett, "Thailand, Malaysia Consult on Rebels," *Sydney Morning Herald,* October 16, 2006, 1–2, www.smh.com.au/news/world/; "Malaysia's Mahathir Says Thai Separatists Shouldn't Demand Independent State, Autonomy," *International Herald Tribune,* January 8, 2007, 2–3, www.iht.com/articles/ap/2007/01/08/asia/AS-GEN-Malaysia-Thailand.

58. Human Rights Watch, "Thailand," 1–4; Denis D. Gray, "Muslim Insurgency Escalates in Thailand," *Boston Globe,* December 22, 2006, 1–3, www.boston.com/news/world/asia/articles/2006/12/22/; B. Raman, "The Raging Jihad—An Overview—International Terrorism Monitor," *South Asia Analysis Group,* Paper No. 162 (December 7, 2006), 6–8, www.saag.org/papers21/paper2054.html.

59. Human Rights Watch, "No One Is Safe: Insurgent Attacks on Civilians in Thailand's Southern Border Provinces," *Human Rights Watch Report* 19, no. 13C (August 2007), 47–94; Marshall, "The Troubled South," 5.

60. "Thailand to Close All 944 Schools in South," *China Post,* November 28, 2006, 1–2, www.chinapost.com.tw/asiapacific/detail.asp?ID=96278&GRP=C; "Southern Teachers to Discuss Unrest," *Bangkok Post,* November 29, 2006; Adrian Morgan, "Thailand: Schools Targeted in Muslim South," *Spero News,* November 27, 2006, 1–7, www:speroforum.com/site/article.asp?idarticle=6741; "Southern Teachers to Discuss Unrest," *Bangkok Post,* November 29, 2006, 1; Gray, "Muslim Insurgency Escalates," 1–3.

61. "Police Finds Al-Qaeda Videos in Muslim School in Southern Thailand," *AsiaNews,* January 27, 2006, 1, www.asianews.it/view.php?1=en&art=3349; "PRD Warns Local Security Units of Massive Insurgent Attacks," *Phujatkan,* December 2, 2006, www.2bangkok.com/06/south06dec.shtml.

62. "Authorities Fear New Year Attacks from Militants," *Sunday Herald* (Scotland), January 10, 2007, 1–2, www.sundayherald.com/international/shinternational/.

63. Zachary Abuza, "Three Years After the January 2004 Raids, the Insurgency in Southern Thailand Is Building Momentum," January 3, 2007, 1–11, zachary.abuza@gmail.com.

64. International Crisis Group, *Southern Thailand: The Impact of the Coup, Asia Report,* No. 129 (March 15, 2007), Jakarta/Brussels, 10–23.

65. Marc Askew, "Thailand: Thailand's Counter-Insurgency Operations in the Deep South," *Asian Analysis,* September 2007, article 6, www.aseanfocus.com/asiananalysis/; Ian Storey, "Thailand Cracks Down on Southern Militants," *Terrorism Monitor* (The Jamestown Foundation) 5, no. 17 (September 13, 2007), 1–3; Human Rights Watch, "No One Is Safe," 97–101; Croissant, "Unrest in South Thailand," 11–13.

66. Under the new Constitution, the lower House of Representatives was composed of 480 members, 400 of whom were directly elected in 140 multimember districts, while 80 members were elected by proportional representation from party lists in eight proportional representation districts. Bertil Lintner, *Asian Analysis,* September 2007, article 5, www.aseanfocus.com; Daniel Ten Kate, "Thailand's Political Flying Circus Is Back," *Asia Sentinel*, November 13, 2007, 1–3, www.asiasentinel.com.

67. "Thailand's Military Reshuffle Officially Announced," *Defense Post* (Thailand), September 7, 2007, 1–2, www.asiandefense.com/news/update/2007-09-20.html; "Thai Martial Law to Remain," *The Australian,* October 9, 2007, 1, www.theaustralian.news.com.au/.

68. Shawn W. Crispin, "Politics by Proxy in Thailand," *Asia Times,* Parts 1 and 2, August 10, 2007, 1–4, www.atimes.com/atimes/Southeast_Asia/IH10Ae01.html.

69. Marwaan Macan-Markar, "Challenges 2007–2008: Thailand Heading into a Political Storm," *Inter Press Service,* December 30, 2007, 1–2, ipsnews.net/news.asp?idnews=40639.

70. Oxford Analytica, "Challenges Ahead for Thailand's PPP," *Forbes,* December 31, 2007, 1–2, www.forbes.com/2007/12/31/; Marwaan Macan-Markar, "Court Clears Path for Pro-Thaksin Gov't," *Inter Press Service*, Politics-Thailand section, January 18, 2008, 1–2, ispnews.net/news.asp?idnews=40838; "Poised to Take Office in Thailand," *Economist Intelligence Unit,* January 22, 2008, 2–3, www.economist.com/display

Story.cfm?story_id=10557170; Debory Li, "Thailand: Newly-Elected Parliament Convenes," *Asia Media,* UCLA Asia Institute, January 25, 2008, 1–2, www.asiamedia.ucla.edu.

71. "Can the 'Ugly' Govt Deliver?" *The Nation*, February 8, 2008, 1, www.nationmultimedia.com/2008.02/08/.

72. Jonathan Head, "Unravelling Thailand's Political Turmoil," *BBC News,* June 24, 2008, 1–3, newsvote.bbc.co.uk/mpapps/; Sutin Wannabovorn, "Thai Prime Minister Headed for Victory," *AP News,* June 26, 2008, 2–4, www.pennlive.com/newsflash/index.ssf?/.

11

Aceh Separatism in Indonesia

Through the centuries, Aceh has a long history of political turmoil and revolutionary movements against incumbent rulers. This cycle of revolt, revolution, and recovery has been attributed to the proud traditions of independence of the Acehnese, their strong Islamic faith, and their distinctive identity making them unwilling to submit to external authority. Following Japan's defeat and the departure of its occupation forces, a Darul Islam movement rapidly emerged in Aceh. This movement gained momentum because of Aceh's isolation and because the fledgling Republic of Indonesia was preoccupied with its struggle to free Indonesia from Dutch rule. By 1946, virtual autonomy for Aceh had been achieved by an ulama-led revolution that defeated and eliminated Aceh's traditional uleebalang aristocracy and installed a government in Aceh headed by Daud Beureueh.

As described in Chapter 4, Aceh was nominally included within Indonesia according to the terms of the agreement with the Netherlands establishing Indonesian independence. However, six months later, when Sukarno unilaterally abolished the federal system that was based on that agreement, Daud Beureueh claimed de facto autonomy for Aceh derived from "primal sovereignty" and a commitment to the ideology of Darul Islam. In anticipation of Indonesian military action, he retreated with a supporting guerrilla force to Aceh's interior highlands to wage a six-year struggle. Over time, ruthless tactics by the Indonesian Army decimated the Darul Islam forces, isolating them in deep jungle hideouts. During that conflict, Jakarta formed its own Aceh government and then negotiated an agreement with that government providing for Aceh to have autonomy in religious affairs, in the administration of Sharia and Adat law, and in education. Eventually, with no hope of victory, the Darul Islam guerrillas signed a peace agreement with Indonesia in 1959 providing amnesty to their forces and gaining for Daud Beureueh a government pension as an ex-governor.[1] For many of Aceh's political activists, this 1959 agreement proved to be deceptively meaningless when Jakarta intervened in Aceh's politics and pressured Aceh to conform to the principles of Pancasila. Yet, despite the meager cultural and religious benefits derived from the "autonomy agreement," Aceh did gain substantial benefits from more than seventeen years of relative peace between 1959 and 1976.

The Free Aceh Movement

In 1953, when Daud Beureueh declared Aceh's independence from Jakarta, one of his political associates, Tengku Hasan M. di Tiro, was a member of the Indonesian Mission to the United Nations in New York. Tengku di Tiro resigned as a member of Indonesia's UN delegation and sought recognition as Aceh's ambassador to the UN. When that recognition failed, he lived in exile for twenty-five years at Riverdale, New York, engaging in various businesses. In 1976, he decided to return to Aceh to revive the independence movement. After secretly landing at a remote location in Aceh, he proceeded to an interior highland area where he made a formal declaration of Aceh's independence and announced the formation of the movement dedicated to that objective. That movement later became popularly known as Gerakan Aceh Merdeka (GAM, Free Aceh Movement).[2]

In his political manifesto, Hasan claimed to be the nephew of Tengku Chik Maat di Tiro, who was described as the last head of state of the Kingdom of Aceh. He also claimed for Aceh maximal boundaries based on Aceh's tributary system in the seventeenth century.[3] The manifesto stated that Aceh's war of national liberation was directed against the "Javanese Indonesian colonial occupation of Aceh." That manifesto made no mention of Islam and gave no hint of what kind of government would be formed if and when the insurgents came to power.[4] Considering Aceh's Islamic traditions as the "veranda of Mecca," this omission appeared to be a near revolutionary break with Aceh's past.

From 1976 to 1979, GAM began operations as a small cluster of about seventy ideologically driven members led by a few well-educated leaders. During its first few years of operations, Indonesian security forces pursued and killed many guerrillas, including some key leaders. By 1979, most of the remaining leaders of GAM fled to exile abroad. Hasan di Tiro and a few of his close associates obtained political asylum in Stockholm, Sweden, where they eventually acquired Swedish citizenship.[5] Refusing to abandon his cause, Hasan di Tiro approached Libya for an agreement to train GAM fighters to wage guerrilla warfare. Between 1986 and 1989, many recruits from Aceh came to Libya for military training and political indoctrination by Hasan di Tiro. Estimates on the number of Libyan-trained GAM recruits range from 600 to 5,000.[6] By 1989, these fighters returned to Aceh well-armed and ready to launch their campaign to "liberate" Aceh. Later, GAM established its own military training program in Aceh and also sent recruits to the MILF for training at Camp Abu Bakar in Mindanao.[7]

Indonesian authorities became alarmed by the escalating threat posed by GAM's new capabilities. To address that threat, in 1989 Suharto proclaimed Daerah Operasi Militer (DOM, Military Operation Zone), within which the Indonesian Army (TNI) was ordered to use extraordinary force to punish GAM's supporters and kill its fighters. The TNI employed terror tactics with the expectation that the local population would withhold support for GAM guerrillas. Villagers were forced to hunt for GAM members by sweeping an area in front of armed troops. If Indonesian troops came under fire, the nearby village was subjected to mass arbitrary arrests, and in one or two incidents, Indonesian security forces killed all the men in a suspect village. If villagers did not cooperate by providing valid intelligence, the village could be, and often was, burnt. Torture and targeted killings of civilians suspected of sympathy for GAM were part of the army's "shock therapy" strategy. In suspected areas of GAM support, security forces staged public events where forced oaths of loyalty to the Indonesian government became a standard operating practice. Public trials of GAM sympathizers ended with severe sentences, especially for teachers and intellectuals.

The Indonesian Army conducted anti-insurgency operations in collaboration with special combat forces and affiliated militias. Kopassus (Special Forces Command) staged covert "antisubversion" operations, including targeted killings of politically active citizens and those suspected of aiding GAM guerrillas. It also recruited, armed, and paid for militia units from among Javanese transmigrants who had settled in Central Aceh during the 1920s and 1930s. These irregular militia units were used to establish control over strategic territory and to establish surveillance of nearby Aceh villages believed to harbor GAM supporters. In addition, anti-insurgency operations were also conducted by the National Police Mobile Brigade, better known as Brimob. These paramilitary units were equipped with army weapons, but with different uniforms and lower pay. The Brimob forces engaged in gross violations of civil and human rights, while allowing the Indonesian Army to claim deniability for such atrocities. The Brimob conducted sweeps, made mass arrests, and specialized in counterterrorist tactics. Acehnese were most fearful of the Brimob because of their brutality and unpredictability.[8]

By 1998, the DOM operations of the Indonesian security forces had depleted GAM's fighting forces, but their brutal tactics had not reduced support for the insurgency. In 1989, GAM's guerrilla force was less than 500 fighters. By 1991, it had grown to an estimated 3,000 fighters, and GAM leaders claimed a supporting membership of 60,000.[9] The total number of the security forces stationed in Aceh in 2002 was reported to be 21,000 in the TNI, 12,000 in the police, and about 13,000 in Brimob units.[10]

During the DOM campaign, GAM fighters also employed brutal tactics against defectors or those who appeared not to be loyal to its cause, including targeted killings, brutal interrogations, bombings, kidnappings, and arson. GAM makes the claim that 30,000 lives were lost as a result of operations by the Indonesian armed forces from 1988 to 2001. Other sources estimate the number of killed at more than 10,000 and those persons displaced by military operations to be about 400,000. By 1998, the security situation appeared to be under control, and the dreaded DOM was lifted, but memories of terror and violations of human rights by combatants on both sides became an impediment to a peaceful resolution of the Aceh rebellion.[11]

During this nine-year campaign, the Indonesian government avoided any negotiations with rebels, although some junior Indonesian military commanders did make some unofficial contact with rebel leaders.[12] The Indonesian Army's anti-insurgency campaign had been quite successful from a military and security perspective, but those operations were a failure from a political and psychological perspective. The brutality of the tactics applied indiscriminately to the civilian population tended to confirm the image of GAM propaganda that the TNI was an army of conquest. GAM's leaders depicted the approximately 50,000 transmigrants from across Indonesia who came to Aceh's oil and gas fields as a horde of foreigners robbing Acehnese of their God-given birthright to Aceh's natural resources.

Oil and Politics

The vitality and persistence of the Free Aceh Movement cannot be attributed entirely to the draconian measures applied by the Indonesian Army during the DOM campaign. In 1971, well before the Free Aceh Movement had been formed, Mobil Oil discovered large oil and natural gas reserves along the northeast coast of Aceh. By 1978, Mobil Oil completed construction of a large liquefied natural gas (LNG) refinery near Arun to process LNG from what eventually became a total of more than fifty wells drilled at its Pase and Lhoksukon fields. Hasan di Tiro's Free Aceh Movement was formed after the news of the discovery of oil and gas deposits in Aceh had been well publicized and only a year before the Arun refinery started commercial production. In 1976, the Indonesian government created a special Lhokseumawe Industrial Development Zone (ZILS) that provided incentives for new industries to invest in the area and gave special authority to that agency for managing and promoting industrial development associated with gas and petroleum production. The primary contractor began as Mobil Oil, which was later reorganized in a 1998 merger as ExxonMobil. Pertamina, Indonesia's national oil company, became the Indonesian contract affiliate. The main customers for the LNG were Japan and South Korea, but a small fraction of the production was also diverted to domestic use, primarily to fertilizer plants that were constructed in the ZILS.

At full capacity, the Arun facility produced 12.3 million tonnes of LNG per annum. The entire petroleum industry in Aceh generated annually about US$2.6 billion of revenue for the central government. In 1990, the gross domestic product of Aceh constituted 3.6 percent of Indonesia's total GDP. Yet, despite the wealth from the petroleum sector, Aceh remained the second poorest province of Indonesia.[13]

The heavy investments and the economic inducements in the ZILS attracted a large influx of transmigrants from other parts of Indonesia. The population of North Aceh increased by 50 percent over eleven years and increased by 300 percent in the ZILS region. Very few workers in the petroleum sector and allied industries were Acehnese, partly because they did not have technical qualifications, but also because Pertamina officials from Jakarta managed local operations. The land and properties of local Acehnese were expropriated for satellite industries. Local peasants complained about serious pollution of rivers, fish ponds, and shrimp beds. They also experienced escalating costs of basic supplies while enjoying few benefits from an industry that generated billions of dollars for Indonesia's economy.

Among the new satellite industries were two fertilizer plants that used LNG production by-products to produce heavily subsidized fertilizer for Indonesia's rice farmers. A rattan furniture and handicraft production facility was also built, but that eventually failed.[14] The government of Aceh received some funds, but they were provided as a "donation" by the central government to the province, usually constituting about 8 to 11 percent of petroleum proceeds. In its political propaganda, GAM depicted the central government as a form of "Javanese colonialism" designed "to subjugate the Acehnese race for control of the latter's territory, homeland and natural resources."[15] GAM made comparisons between the poverty of Aceh and the exaggerated wealth of Brunei and Kuwait, with the argument that similar wealth and political power would accrue to the Acehnese when they finally achieved independence and gained full control of their natural resources.

The Resurgence of GAM

In 1998, the Indonesian economic crisis spiraled out of control, exposing the Suharto regime to a precipitous loss of public confidence. This drastic change of political fortunes had political consequences throughout Indonesia, especially where there were simmering conflicts with the national government. After Suharto resigned and B. J. Habibie was installed as president of Indonesia, the country entered a period of political instability, during which the Reformasi movement made its demands for democracy and political liberalization. Under both domestic and foreign pressure, President Habibie agreed to allow the East Timor conflict to be resolved by an internationally monitored referendum. Despite massive intimidation by the Indonesian military and their sponsored paramilitary formations, the East Timorese voted for independence in September 1999.

During this post-Suharto period of political instability, militant Islam began an open contest for power with nationalist factions, as well as with various reformist elements who claimed to be inspired by a popular democratic vision of politics. Their tactics were to trigger political instability, presumably to provide a justification for Suharto's return to power. This thinly disguised alliance between key elements of the pro-Suharto "green faction" in the Indonesian military and militant Islamist groups had a significant impact on political developments in Aceh. The concerns of Aceh political activists for a referendum made them natural political allies of the Reformasi movement, rather than with Islamist militants who were allied with their green faction military patrons. GAM had experienced the tactics of the army-supported Islamic-based militias and the Brimob force that used mass sweeps, brutal interrogations, mass killings, and terror tactics that were applied to both East Timor and Aceh. Whether these tactics were applied in the name of Islam or justified by nationalism, the end results were the same for the target population. Although the Acehnese have always been proud of their Islamic traditions, it is obvious that leaders of the Free Aceh Movement resented attempts by outsiders to use Islam to justify the brutal suppression of their political aspirations for an independent Aceh. These considerations probably were a factor when Osama bin Laden's top two lieutenants, al-Zawahiri and Mohammad Atef, were alleged to have come to Aceh in June 2000 to explore the possibility for a political and strategic alliance. Whatever may or may not have transpired, no political agreements were made between GAM and Al Qaeda.[16]

In the immediate aftermath of Suharto's departure, President B. J. Habibie was confronted with the issue of the future of East Timor. Of secondary importance was the situation in Aceh, which was viewed primarily as a security issue. In March 1999, President Habibie visited Aceh, and after granting amnesty and release to thirty-nine imprisoned GAM members, he promised that the military would not use force to resolve the issue of Aceh. He supported a Regional Autonomy Law that was later passed by Parliament (DPR) in 1999 during President Wahid's administration. This law provided for decentralization of powers to the provinces in the fields of religion, custom, and education.[17] The Indonesian Parliament also passed a Special Autonomy Law in August 1999, offering a special arrangement for Aceh. The name of the province was changed to Nanggroe Aceh Darussalam (NAD, The Province of Aceh an Abode of Peace), and that law also provided that 80 percent of petroleum and natural gas revenues were to be transferred to the province of Aceh. By contrast, other provinces (except Papua) were granted only 15 percent of petroleum revenue and 30 percent of natural gas from provincially derived production. This law also gave exclusive powers to Aceh to implement Islamic law and special powers over security matters.

Despite these concessions for increased autonomy, supporters of Aceh independence were encouraged by a changed political environment that gave new hope for their cause. In anticipation of greater leniency, some local NGOs and student groups in Aceh joined to organize public demonstrations for a referendum to express the "will of the people of Aceh." In November 1999, a public rally and strike was held in Banda Aceh calling for a referendum on Aceh's relationship with Indonesia and demanding an end to military violence. The organizers claimed that two million Acehnese participated in the rally, and that two-thirds of Aceh's population supported the strike.[18] This rally took place just after Abdurrahman Wahid became president of Indonesia. He was asked about the rally, and he made ambiguous comments that a referendum could be held in Aceh to end the conflict. Three weeks later, Wahid stated that a referendum for Aceh was "completely out of the question." To explain his abrupt shift, Wahid claimed that President Bill Clinton had intervened to rule out independence for Aceh as a viable option.[19] During the ensuing political controversy, Wahid renewed his commitment to find a peaceful settlement to the Aceh conflict.

Preliminary Peace Talks

After preliminary contacts, Indonesia's ambassador to the UN Hassan Wirajuda met GAM leader Hasan di Tiro in Geneva on January 27, 2000, at talks mediated by the Swiss-based Henry Dunant Center. During negotiations, a sharp debate took place in Jakarta concerning the tactics, benefits, and likely outcome of the talks. A more concealed debate also occurred among the top leadership of GAM. Eventually, the two parties agreed to a "Humanitarian Pause for Aceh" to go into effect from June 2 to September 2, 2000, and to establish an Independent Commission for the Investigation of Violence in Aceh.

During the first phase of the Humanitarian Pause, the level of violence remained high, with continuous violations on both sides. Despite the obvious failure of this first peace agreement, the two parties decided to extend the pause until January 15, 2001. During the second phase, conflicts between GAM and the TNI escalated even further. The talks in Switzerland continued, with GAM asserting that its demand for sovereignty was "non-negotiable" but expressing a willingness "to achieve their political objectives in a democratic way." Indonesia's representatives rejected full independence as totally unacceptable but were willing to discuss terms for autonomy and issues related to peace and order. With both sides operating with the "talk and fight" tactic, the level of conflict escalated. During this period, Libyan-trained guerrillas returning to Aceh enabled GAM to build up its forces and embark on a program of territorial expansion.[20] The Indonesian Army and Police engaged in forceful interrogation of civilians and mounted assaults on GAM bases, while GAM increased the areas under its control, extracted "taxes" from civilians, intimidated foreign aid workers, and mounted ambush attacks on military and police posts. GAM units also attacked workers at the ExxonMobil Arun gas field facilities, forcing suspension of LNG production for four months. After nearly a year of operation, the Independent Commission concluded that the Humanitarian Pause had failed. Civilian casualties remained high, while Indonesian Army and Police casualties also increased.

When the Humanitarian Pause expired in January 2001, President Abdurrahman Wahid was fighting for political survival with meager parliamentary support. His political vulnerability enabled the Indonesian Army to assume a more decisive role in Aceh. The army and police increased their forces in Aceh by 30,000 and opened a major military campaign in May 2001 to defeat GAM. That military offensive continued for over a year. By July 2002, the army commander in Aceh reported that 947 suspected GAM members had been killed while Indonesian troop casualties were reported to be 75 killed and 136 wounded.[21] With the renewal of an aggressive Indonesian military campaign, international pressure increased once again on both parties to resume peace negotiations. After much diplomatic sparring, new talks between Indonesia and GAM began in Geneva on February 2, 2002, with the Henry Durant Center again acting as moderator. Ten months later, at a conference in Tokyo attended by thirty-eight countries, GAM and Indonesia signed a Cessation of Hostilities Framework Agreement (CoHA) on December 9, 2002. GAM agreed to place its weapons in designated sites subject to inspection by international monitors, and the TNI was required to become a "defensive force" avoiding all offensive actions. Brimob units were to be confined to regular police activities. Substantive issues for a final peace settlement were to be addressed later.[22]

During the initial months of the CoHA, the number of fatalities decreased dramatically, but the provisions of the agreement did not lead to the disarmament of the guerrillas. The GAM fighters were suspicious of the intentions of the TNI and gave various reasons for failure to place their weapons in designated sites. The absence of military pressure from the TNI allowed GAM to recruit, train, and rearm its fighting force, which doubled in size during the CoHA cease-fire. By May 2003, GAM exercised control of about 70 to 80 percent of the province. To support its arms purchases, GAM engaged in various criminal activities, including extortion disguised as taxation on all persons within its region of control. It also skimmed an estimated 20 percent of foreign humanitarian aid funds that were part of the peace process agreement. In addition to these "taxation" activities, GAM forces continued with targeted assassinations, kidnapping for ransom, and trading in drugs, primarily marijuana. At the time, Aceh was estimated to produce about 30 percent of Southeast Asia's marijuana market. The conditions of the cease-fire enabled GAM to go on the offensive against Javanese transmigrants, some of whom had come to Aceh a century earlier to work at Dutch coffee plantations in Aceh's highlands. During the CoHA cease-fire, GAM also mounted operations against other non-Acehnese communities, and their attacks generated an estimated 50,000 refugees who abandoned their homes to flee the province.[23]

The political successes of GAM in extending its control over large segments of Aceh also came at a political price. The guerrilla structure of GAM made it very difficult for it to give the semblance of a stable system of government. GAM's decentralized structure allowed each guerrilla group to be self-financed by extortion, roadside levies, and criminal activities. At the time, the provincial government, nominally under the Indonesian flag, had low credibility and was widely viewed as corrupt. In these circumstances, the GAM forces were not competing against a credible political alternative.[24]

The strategy of the GAM representatives at peace negotiations reflected two primary concerns. First, they sought to secure cease-fire conditions enabling GAM activists in Aceh to recruit, regroup, and rearm. Second, but perhaps even more important, they devised their political strategy to internationalize the conflict in the expectation that international pressure on Indonesia would be the only way that their objective of independence could be attained. Much of the argument and the tactics were designed to secure favorable international press coverage depicting GAM as the popular expression of nationalist and democratic ideals. To improve this image, the exiled leadership in July 2002 drafted what was called the Stavanger Declaration, which enunciated democracy as the basis for the government of Aceh when it became independent. An elaborate description of offices and governmental powers was part of that declaration.[25] Missing from that document were provisions for a democratic process.

The concern of GAM's exiled leaders for an international audience also affected their approach to Islam. Hasan di Tiro claimed leadership and legitimacy through his claim of being the nephew of Tengku Chik Maat di Tiro, who was no sultan but was one of the last surviving holdouts of the ulama-led rebellion against the Dutch. With the long jihadi traditions of the di Tiro ulama behind him, it would be natural to assume that Hasan would utilize that Islamic tradition to claim independence for Aceh under his leadership. The issues addressed by GAM were difficult to articulate as a threat to Islam and a basis for jihad when prime issues in the dispute were over financial proceeds from petroleum revenues and the struggle for power and autonomy for Aceh.

As the strategy developed to internationalize the GAM cause and seek foreign support, the nationalist ideology provided GAM with a more receptive foreign audience. Islam was not rejected by GAM but also was not projected for external media exposure. Within Aceh, the Islamic legacy of the di Tiro ulama was proclaimed as a basis for legitimacy, and each of the GAM commanders were given the authority to enforce Sharia law and utilize Islam as the basis for GAM's claim to power. Peasants in Aceh were exposed to Islamist ideological perspectives, and Islam was not negated or diminished by the political rhetoric of ultranationalism.[26] Part of the success of the GAM leaders came from tailoring their messages to fit different audiences, both international and domestic.

GAM and LNG

The relationship of the Free Aceh Movement and the petroleum industry had always been ambiguous and problematical. On the one hand, the wealth generated by that industry energized the separatist movement. And yet, because that wealth was controlled from Jakarta and diverted to foreign contractors and to the Indonesian government, GAM engaged in guerrilla assaults to impede or halt petroleum operations. Before 1998, attacks by GAM on the LNG facilities and workforce were relatively few and largely the result of efforts to extract taxes from workers and management of enterprises in the ZILS district. When the Humanitarian Pause was coming to an end in January 2001, the Wahid government threatened an all-out campaign against GAM if progress was not made in the peace talks. GAM responded by making the petroleum industry a major target of GAM operations. The GAM commander, Abu Sofyan Daud, called on ExxonMobil to leave Aceh immediately "because we cannot guarantee their safety." The level of violence against the workers and facilities of ExxonMobil escalated rapidly, including shooting of workers, shooting at helicopters ferrying workers, and bombing of pipelines. In the United States, the International Labor Rights Fund filed a suit in a district court against Pertamina and ExxonMobil alleging that the defendants were responsible for "murder, rape, torture, and kidnapping" because they relied on Indonesian soldiers to protect the Arun facility, "thereby acknowledging and ratifying the Indonesian military's conduct." ExxonMobil categorically denied these charges. Even so, this case dragged on to involve damaging publicity and high costs of a legal defense.[27]

As the level of attacks and threats increased, ExxonMobil was forced to halt production of LNG at the Arun facility in March 2001. A majority of technical and management personnel were evacuated to the North Sumatra town of Medan, and ExxonMobil announced that it could no longer meet its contract obligations by declaring *force majeure*—the legal justification for contract nullification when unexpected events, such as insurgency, prevent meeting contract obligations. The US ambassador to Indonesia, Robert Gelbard, traveled to Banda Aceh to meet with GAM representatives and asked them to stop their threats and attacks against ExxonMobil, but no agreement or promises were forthcoming. By May 2001, peace talks began again between GAM representatives and the Indonesian government, but the attacks on ExxonMobil workers continued, this time with the abduction of a nine-man crew working at an offshore facility. Eventually the work crew was freed, probably with an unreported payment of a ransom. By July, the Arun gas processing plant started production once again, with increased security provided by a large increase in Indonesian troops and police. The loss of income for the LNG plant at Arun exceeded US$400 million.[28] Even though production resumed, later when peace talks stalled during 2002 and 2003, attacks on the petroleum facilities resumed.

When the CoHA cease-fire came into operation between December 2002 and May 2003, GAM expanded its financial collections from the petroleum industry. Attacks were usually not made directly on workers or against plant facilities, but through a system of taxes assessed on the wages and on proceeds of contracts. GAM collectors knew the precise wages of workers and the value of contracts. Contractors were assessed at about 10 to 12 percent of the contract value, while workers and staff were assessed at a slightly lower rate. Often assessment demands were made by mobile phone text messages. Failure to pay was enforced by threats of assassination or kidnapping for ransom. The Exxon-Mobil spokesman claimed the company "never knowingly paid money to GAM" but admitted that some workers "contributed" to the GAM cause.[29]

Peace by Exhaustion and Disaster?

The Cessation of Hostilities Framework Agreement that had been signed on December 9, 2002, had never been fully implemented. In March 2003, some peace monitors were threatened and organized mobs appeared, ordering the monitors to leave within one week. Under threats of physical violence, the monitors withdrew to their main offices in Banda Aceh.[30] Because of the stalemate, and alarmed by the expanding political presence of GAM on the ground in Aceh, the Jakarta establishment pressured President Megawati to resume police and army operations in order to reclaim control of Aceh. President Megawati's senior security minister, Susilo Bambang Yudhoyono, warned that the rebels must start disarming within two weeks or the Indonesian government would be forced to pull out from the peace deal.[31] Finally, on May 19, 2003, President Megawati imposed martial law for six months on Aceh and ordered a military offensive labeled Operasi Terpadu (Integrated Operation). TNI troop levels were increased to 35,000 and all Aceh residents were required to carry identification cards. All foreign NGOs were ordered to halt operations and depart the country. Severe restrictions were also placed on the local press and foreign correspondents. Indonesian policy toward Aceh returned once again to the military solution. Nearly all commentators predicted another bloodbath for the residents of Aceh.

The military and police in Aceh were placed under the overall authority of Senior Security Minister Yudhoyono and Armed Forces Commander General Endriatono Sutarto assumed operational command. General Sutarto announced that the objectives of Operasi Terpadu were to eliminate the GAM threat by intensified operations against the GAM leaders. Without access to Aceh by reputable international media, any human rights violations and atrocities that may have occurred during Operasi Terpadu were effectively concealed. Critics of the government's anti-insurgency operations alleged that the security forces engaged once again in grave human rights abuses, wanton killings, torture, and arbitrary detention. For one year, military operations in Aceh proceeded beyond the view of the international media. The tactics of GAM avoided direct engagement with the military, concentrating instead on sniping at security forces, destroying power lines, burning schools and government buildings, and engaging in kidnapping-for-ransom operations. By May 2004, large numbers of GAM guerrillas had been killed, captured, or surrendered, but most of the GAM leaders survived by retreating to the more remote interior locations of the province.

When national elections were held in 2004, the security situation in Aceh had become sufficiently stabilized to enable residents of Aceh to participate in those elections. The election results provide some indication of public attitudes toward Megawati's government as well as toward Yudhoyono, who had been security minister in charge of the anti-insurgency operations in Aceh, but also had become a candidate for president of Indonesia. In the first round of the presidential elections, 56 percent of Aceh voters supported Amien Rais of the National Mandate Party, 24 percent for Yudhoyono, and 5.6 percent for Megawati. Amien Rais's well-known identification with the Muhammadiyah movement made him a popular candidate for Acehnese voters. For the second round, held on September 20, 2004, Yudhoyono gained 80 percent of the vote in Aceh, while Megawati trailed with a meager 20 percent.[32]

At 7:58 A.M. on December 26, 2004, an earthquake with a magnitude of 9.3 on the Richter Scale ripped apart the seafloor 41 miles off the coast of northwest Sumatra. The ensuing tsunami killed a total of over 300,000 people in Sri Lanka, Thailand, India, the Maldives, Somalia, and Malaysia, with the largest damages and death toll in Indonesia, concentrated along the shores of Aceh. By the end of March, the death toll for Aceh was reported to be 126,000 confirmed dead and 93,000 missing. The homeless survivors of the tsunami in Aceh were estimated to be 800,000. The fatality rates in some parts of Aceh reached over 75 percent of the inhabitants. The hardest-hit areas of Aceh were at the northern tip extending south along the west coast. Most of the urban areas of Banda Aceh and Meulaboh were destroyed, and the small west coast town of Calang suffered a 90 percent death toll.[33] The magnitude of this disaster was captured on world television news, prompting an international effort to provide aid, medical relief, and reconstruction assistance to survivors in all countries affected. The previous Indonesian ban on foreign NGOs in Aceh was either immediately lifted or ignored. Within a few days, the Indonesian government revoked civil emergency powers as hundreds of NGOs began mobilizing their resources to address the gigantic tragedy that had struck Aceh.

Eventually, some 140 NGOs, including 30 major international organizations, with hundreds of staff and volunteers, arrived in Aceh to provide aid; administer the distribution of food, water, and temporary shelter; and prepare camps for the refugees. The removal of corpses; identification of the dead, when known; debris removal; sanitation; and protection against outbreaks of infectious diseases were all major issues that had to be addressed simultaneously. In less than a month, over 2,000 foreign nationals were delivering aid and services in Aceh. They were joined by many hundreds of Indonesians who came as volunteers or contract workers to help with the recovery process. To assist with the emergency relief effort, military personnel also came from the United States, Australia, Singapore, and Malaysia. The US government sent to Aceh a squadron of twenty-five ships, including the aircraft carrier USS *Abraham Lincoln* with ninety-four aircraft, to deliver supplies and provide emergency services. The first US supplies arrived via helicopter on January 2, 2005. A total of 15,000 US military personnel were involved in the relief effort, with only a few hundred at a time actually on the ground in Aceh.[34]

The tsunami disaster drastically altered the political environment but did little to change the political objectives of the two contending forces. Very few GAM guerrillas were killed by the tsunami because their main bases were in remote highland areas. Even so, many GAM fighters lost family members, since the west coast areas had been primary GAM recruiting areas. A GAM spokesman claimed that 1,777 GAM fighters detained in five government prisons in coastal areas were hit by the tsunami and presumed to be dead.[35] The day after the tsunami struck, GAM announced a unilateral cease-fire, but without terms or conditions specified. At the same time, the Indonesian government announced an "informal truce," also without terms and conditions. As humanitarian aid began to flow to the distressed areas, some armed GAM fighters commandeered relief supplies for their own needs, placing aid workers at risk between government security forces and the rebels. Within a short period, both sides had openly violated the informal truce. The Indonesian military continued its security operations and, by January 23, the army announced that it had killed 200 rebels during the preceding four weeks.[36]

To undermine GAM as a political force, Indonesian strategy involved building political support from Aceh's respected elites and civic leaders. The 2004 Indonesian parliamentary elections had produced a thirteen-member delegation that claimed to represent the people of Aceh. After the tsunami disaster, there was an increased realization among many Aceh elites that the ties between Indonesia and Aceh were essentially beneficial, provided that security, justice, and autonomy issues could be resolved. Like many other political disputes, good, fair, and efficient government was recognized to be an effective antidote to a separatist solution. For this reason, the Indonesian government gave greater stress to collaboration with local Acehnese by empowering new groups of people, organized at the district (*kabupaten*) and municipal levels where the issues of reconstruction and reconciliation needed to be addressed. These initiatives were also based on the assumption that the exiled leaders of GAM were becoming less salient for defining the political future of Aceh.[37]

Aceh Peace Negotiations

Before the tsunami devastated Aceh, Indonesia had requested that Sweden arrest GAM leaders living within its borders who had committed "crimes violating international law." Swedish police in June 2004 arrested three GAM leaders who were charged in court, but the Swedish court concluded that there was insufficient evidence and as Swedish citizens they could not be kept in custody. After the tsunami hit Aceh, Indonesia's Foreign Ministry asked once again for Sweden to arrest GAM members living in Sweden. In reply, Sweden's minister of foreign affairs, Laila Frievalds, announced that the government of Sweden "was prepared to help Indonesia resolve its standoff with the Free Aceh Movement." What assistance Sweden was willing to give Indonesia was never publicly revealed.[38]

When the massive international relief effort for Aceh began, Indonesia came under mounting international pressure to reopen peace negotiations with GAM leaders living in Sweden. Both GAM and Indonesia finally agreed to begin talks in Helsinki under the sponsorship of Finland's Crisis Management Initiative, headed by Finland's former president Martti Ahtisaari, as the mediator. The first round of talks took place in Finland from January 27 to 29, and discussed cease-fire agreements as well as issues related to international aid and reconstruction in the wake of the tsunami. The second round of talks discussed "a comprehensive solution within the framework of special autonomy for Aceh."[39] At those sessions, the Australian academic Damien Kingsbury joined the GAM delegation as an adviser. He reported that GAM leaders agreed to drop their demand for independence, and they were willing to discuss "self-government."

Prior to the third round of peace talks, Indonesia prepared a draft proposal offering to grant amnesty to all GAM prisoners except those involved in criminal cases. It also was willing to offer employment for demobilized GAM fighters at plantations and factories that had been closed because of insurgent activities.[40] Not surprisingly, the GAM delegation was more interested in political and economic concessions and a sustainable cease-fire system with international monitoring. One of the most sensitive issues for the Indonesians involved GAM's demand for trials against Indonesian security personnel for human rights abuses and atrocities committed from 1989 to the present. Both sides strenuously resisted any peace treaty provisions for trials against their own forces for earlier atrocities and civil rights abuses.[41] At the end of the third round of negotiations, both sides reached substantial agreement on future economic relations between Jakarta and Aceh, on taxation, and on the distribution of petroleum revenues.[42]

The GAM delegation placed a high priority on securing a lasting and enforceable cease-fire because Indonesia was utilizing the tactics of offering inducements to insurgent units to surrender while military operations were intensified against remaining GAM fighters. The extent of anti-insurgency operations was revealed when Brigadier General Suroyo Gino announced that 1,010 separatist rebels had been killed and 545 rebels had surrendered or been captured between November 17, 2004, and March 2005. He also reported that about 1,245 rebels remained as targets of the army's operations.[43] In Helsinki, the GAM negotiators must have realized that their forces were in jeopardy from aggressive operations by the Indonesian Army.

The Aceh Peace Agreement

From February through to August, the Indonesian delegation and the GAM delegation met at regular intervals in Helsinki and eventually agreed on terms for a peace treaty. On August 15, 2005, the two parties signed the Memorandum of Understanding (MoU) defining agreed terms for a peace treaty, which required further implementation through enabling legislation by the Indonesian Parliament, to be approved and passed by March 2006. The signing ceremony in Helsinki was televised and viewed in live transmission by an assembled crowd at the central Baiturahman Mosque in Banda Aceh.[44]

Under the terms of the agreement, 70 percent of revenues from natural resources are allocated to Aceh, including gas and petroleum production, forest products, and offshore fisheries. Aceh was given the right to set its own interest rates, to secure loans from abroad, and to invite foreign investments and promote tourism without approval from Jakarta. Article 1.2.3 provided for the direct election of the governor of Aceh beginning in April 2006 and for the election of a new Aceh legislature in 2009. Before the legislative elections were held, the Indonesian Parliament authorized "local political parties" to organize and to contest elections. This provision exempted Aceh from complying with Indonesia's previous election laws requiring political parties to demonstrate substantial support in many provinces in order to qualify for listing on election ballots. For the elections in 2009, GAM would have time to transform itself into a political party and to field a slate of candidates as a "local party" without disqualification. Article 1.1.2 acknowledges that Aceh will exercise its authority in conformity with the Constitution of Indonesia. That part of the agreement was interpreted to mean that the government of Aceh would not be allowed to hold any referendum on independence, since the Indonesian Constitution does not authorize such an action. Presumably, therefore, a newly formed GAM political party would also not be allowed to call for a referendum or a plebiscite for independence in any of its campaigning.

The security arrangements of the MoU provided for complete demobilization of all GAM forces and a substantial reduction of Indonesian forces, including the complete withdrawal of all "non-organic"[45] military and police personnel. GAM agreed to demobilize all its 3,000 troops and decommission

840 arms, while the Indonesian government agreed to reduce its forces in Aceh to 14,700 "organic military" and 9,100 "organic police." The demobilization, decommission, and departure operations were to be verified by foreign observers (the Aceh Monitoring Mission, AMM); these conditions were to be completed in four stages and were to be concluded by December 31, 2005.

"All persons who participated in GAM activities" were granted amnesty and all political prisoners and detainees were to be released unconditionally. Any GAM member who used weapons after the MoU was signed would be disqualified from amnesty.[46] The provisions for reintegration into society were both extensive and ambiguous. All "former combatants," "pardoned political prisoners," and citizens who suffered "demonstrable loss due to the conflict" were promised "suitable farming land, employment, or adequate social security." With no clear indication in the MoU of who is entitled to what degree of compensation, and who is obligated to provide such compensation, these provisions generated much concern among organizations already providing recovery assistance to Aceh's tsunami victims. Because the details of the military conflict compensation package were never worked out, these issues later generated many disputes among destitute competing claimants.[47]

To oversee this agreement, the MoU established the Aceh Monitoring Mission, composed of 230 unarmed personnel, with European Union states providing 130 members and Brunei, Malaysia, the Philippines, Singapore, and Thailand representing ASEAN states providing 100 members. Pieter Feith, from the EU Council General Secretariat, was appointed head of mission, and General Nipat Thonglek, from Thailand, became principal deputy. The AMM was made responsible for monitoring all provisions of the treaty, for resolving disputes, and for making rulings on its provisions that "will be binding on the parties." Before the peace treaty was signed, arrangements were made with contributing states to provide members for the AMM. Consequently, on August 15, 2005, when the peace agreement was signed, 82 AMM members were already deployed on site in Aceh.[48]

To facilitate its responsibilities, the AMM formed a Commission on Security Arrangements, under the chairmanship of Feith, with delegations representing the government of Indonesia, the Free Aceh Movement (GAM), and the province of Aceh. By maintaining cordial relations with all parties and by efficient planning of its operations, the AMM was able to oversee the main security and decommissioning provisions of the peace treaty according to schedule. By the end of the year, 25,000 Indonesian security forces had departed from Aceh, the required number of arms from GAM had been turned in and destroyed, and all GAM members in prison were released under amnesty. After consultations with the Aceh public, a new draft law on local government and elections was formulated and presented to the Indonesian Parliament for ratification. All these actions were monitored by the AMM, attesting that the terms of the treaty were being properly implemented.[49]

Unresolved Issues

The costs of the recovery from the tsunami, combined with the costs of demobilization and integration of GAM fighters into civilian life, put great strains on the financial and administrative capabilities of the Aceh government. The 70 percent of proceeds from natural resources were designed to provide a large increase in Aceh's budget. However, that source was considerably less than had been anticipated a few years earlier. In 2001, during the GAM campaign to force closure of the natural gas fields, ExxonMobil made seismic tests of the yield potential of those fields. Those tests revealed that the Aceh gas fields were approximately 80 percent depleted and that the output from those fields would rapidly diminish. In 1994, ExxonMobil's plant at Arun operated with six production lines, called trains, for conversion of raw natural gas into liquid natural gas. By 2004, only four trains operated, and in 2005 another train was mothballed. From 2006 to 2008, the company expected to operate two trains, and reduce production to one train from 2009 until 2014, when operations were expected to cease due to depletion of onshore Aceh gas fields.[50]

The Indonesian government wanted to guarantee a supply of LNG for two government-owned fertilizer plants in Aceh that produced subsidized fertilizer for Indonesia's farmers. Using its leverage over future oil explorations, Indonesia pressured ExxonMobil to supply LNG from Aceh to those fertilizer plants at a set price at about one-third of the market value for LNG. Because the offshore gas fields contain high levels of carbon dioxide, the contract producers were asking for 52 percent of revenues, in place of the previous 35 percent share allocated to producers.[51] Whatever agreements are made for future production of LNG, Aceh will receive substantially less revenue from its petroleum resources than its leaders had previously expected.

The Memorandum of Understanding peace agreement has a number of conditions that will have long-term consequences, not only for Aceh, but also for future relations between the central government and all of Indonesia's provinces. Under Article 1.1.2, a list of powers is reserved for the government of the Republic of Indonesia, while Aceh is accorded authority in all remaining "sectors of public affairs." International agreements that relate to the interests of Aceh "will be entered into in consultation and with the consent of the legislature of Aceh." Any decisions taken by the legislature of the Republic of Indonesia that relate to Aceh will require consultation and the consent of the legislature of Aceh. Administrative measures "with regard to Aceh" will require consultation and consent from "the head of the Aceh administration" (the governor of Aceh). Article 1.4.3 provides for the creation of an Aceh Court of Appeals in the Indonesian judicial system. What constitutes "consultation and consent" is left undefined. However, these provisions established the basic ingredients of "proto-federalism," with an allocation of powers between central and provincial levels of government, a court to exercise judicial review in matters of dispute between the provincial and central government, and a process of consultation and consent for intergovernmental affairs. In effect, the MoU acquires the status of a constitutional document by the terms of its definitions of powers and responsibilities for relations between the province of Aceh and the government of Indonesia.[52]

Another example of the constitutional character of the MoU concerns its provisions for the rule of law and for human rights. The agreement provides that the legislature of Aceh will redraft Aceh's legal code to comply with the UN International Covenant on Civil and Political Rights and the Covenant on Economic, Social, and Cultural Rights. It also states that the government of Indonesia will adhere to those two covenants, and that a Human Rights Court will be established for Aceh. The Covenant on Civil and Political Rights establishes guarantees for freedom of thought, freedom of expression, freedom to adopt a religion or belief of choice, freedom of association, "equality of rights and responsibilities of spouses as to marriage," and religious and linguistic rights for minorities.[53] The Covenant on Economic, Social, and Cultural Rights sets a number of goals for economic and social development but also calls for equal rights for men and women, including the principle of "equal pay for equal work." It also calls for equal opportunity for everyone to have employment and promotion "subject to no considerations other than those of seniority and competence."[54]

Since both Aceh and the government of Indonesia agreed to adhere to these covenants, both the province and the national government promised extensive revisions to their laws and administrative practices. To tackle these issues, proposed legislative enactments generated impassioned debate, especially from those committed to extending Sharia law to apply to all Muslims, as well as to non-Muslims for some crimes. Many non-Muslims were fearful that reference to international covenants would provoke militant Muslims to incite violence against liberal Muslims as well as non-Muslims. Despite these concerns, the MoU did increase political and legal pressures on Indonesia to give more attention to human rights issues as defined by international covenants and as legitimate goals for eventual emulation.[55]

Sharia Law in Aceh

The liberal and democratic principles that were incorporated into the Aceh peace settlement made no mention of Islam or Sharia law, but the agreement did provide that "Qanun Aceh" would be reestablished for Aceh based on "the historical traditions and customs of the people of Aceh."[56] In 1999, when the Indonesian Parliament passed the first Regional Autonomy Law No. 44, Aceh was given authority to introduce Sharia law, with cases to be tried in regular district courts. In 2001, another special autonomy law for Aceh provided for the creation of Sharia courts with jurisdiction that included family law, property law, and also criminal cases. By 2002, the government of Aceh was competing with GAM to establish its Islamic credentials. Consequently, a series of Qanuns were issued to expand the implementation of Sharia law to a wide range of topics. Administration of Sharia law was assigned to Dinas Sharia Islam (Department of Sharia Affairs), which controls Wilayatul Hisbah, otherwise known as "religious police" or "the vice and virtue patrol." The Aceh Ulama Assembly formulated the Qanuns that were subsequently endorsed by the Aceh legislature.

By 2004, prior to the peace agreement with GAM, the scope of Sharia law had been expanded to include education, zakat (alms tax), proper Muslim dress for men and women, criminal justice, economic transactions, mortgages, banking, religious donations, apostasy, deviant teachings and beliefs, failing to observe prayers, gambling, alcohol consumption, and khalwat (illicit sex relations). In addition, Islamic criminal punishments were prescribed, including three months' imprisonment, caning, and fines up to Rp5 million (about US$630). For Aceh, enforcement of the Qanun criminal offenses began in 2004. The first offenses to be subject to physical punishments were alcohol consumption (40 lashes with a rattan cane, or imprisonment from twenty to forty months); gambling (6 to 12 lashes for the gambler and a fine of Rp35 million [US$4,400] for those who allow gambling to take place on their premises); khalwat (3 to 9 lashes and/or a fine of Rp2.5 to 10 million [US$315 to US$1,260]); and failure to attend Friday prayers at the mosque (3 lashes). Sharia punishments were administered in public at the central mosque after Friday prayers.

Once these punishments were enforced, new proposals were made to extend the penalties and authority of the Wilayatul Hisbah. These proposed revisions included *zina* (adultery), with the penalty of death by stoning or 100 lashes, and the crimes of theft (amputation of a hand), murder, and possibly corruption, for which Sharia provides for a punishment of death.[57] Although the more severe punishments of Sharia were not enacted, these proposals created an escalating public controversy over their applicability to the Indonesian social and political setting. The Wilayatul Hisbah asked the public to make anonymous reports on the behavior of neighbors, friends, and relatives, which action generated many accusations. Fundamentalist ulama pointed to the discovery of thousands of bodies of naked women after the tsunami, and claimed that God had punished Aceh because of the immorality of Muslim women. This argument was used to justify the strict enforcement of "morality laws" on women. A disproportionate number of those who have been punished under Aceh's Sharia laws have been women from the lower classes, while higher-class residents have been largely exempted from investigations for potential Sharia-defined crimes and vices.[58]

Because the Indonesian Parliament defines criminal laws for all of Indonesia and the regular Indonesian courts enforce those laws, a clash between the two legal systems is inevitable. Within Aceh the leaders of GAM in the peace agreement opted for the more liberal principles of the UN International Covenants of Civil and Political Rights, but the Aceh Ulama Assembly became even more determined to enforce a draconian version of Sharia law. For Aceh, the conflicting assumptions of an Islamic theocratic state and a secular state became an issue in the first elections established under the Aceh peace agreement.

GAM Reorganized for Politics

The Helsinki MoU of 2005 initiated a complex process of multilevel consultations to monitor and enforce the peace agreement between Indonesia and GAM. Once the peace process began, local GAM commanders became parties to the process of implementation. That included liaison representation by GAM's fighting forces on AMM. To facilitate participation in an electoral political process, GAM was required to transform its military command structure into an institution that could make political decisions and mobilize political support from citizens on all sides of previous conflicts. In effect, the peace process shifted power from Aceh's older exiled symbolic leaders, to younger activists, and to GAM's military commanders who exercised leadership and control at the grassroots level.

To unify GAM and prepare for political activities, the exiled GAM prime minister Malik Mahmud returned to Aceh in 2005 and organized two new bodies: a Majelis Nasional (National Council) and a Komite Peralihan Aceh (Aceh Transition Committee, KPA). The former body was established to make political decisions and select party candidates, while the latter was given responsibility for demobilization of fighters, their return to civilian life, and the disbursement of "reintegration funds," as provided under the terms of the MoU. Later, in May 2006, GAM supporters throughout the world were invited to a two-day congress to formulate a strategy for GAM as a political party. That session, held at Syiah Kuala Universiti in Banda Aceh, attracted an attendance of 250 participants from eight countries, not including those delegates coming from Aceh and other provinces of Indonesia.[59]

Lack of consensus and competition for positions of leadership quickly revealed factional divisions within the ranks of GAM's supporters. The process of nominating candidates became so divisive that GAM's Majelis Nasional permitted any GAM member the right to stand as an independent, but also endorsed the candidacy of Humam Hamid as governor and Hasbi Abdullah as deputy governor. Humam had a Ph.D. in sociology and gained public recognition as a human rights activist, but he had never been a GAM member. His running mate, Hasbi, was the younger brother of Zaini Abdullah, GAM's exiled foreign minister in Sweden. Hasbi had been a GAM member but after his arrests and imprisonment for his support of GAM, he joined Partai Persatuan Pembangunan. These two men were nominated to head the GAM ticket with the expectation that Aceh's leading intellectual, combined with the organizational capacity of Indonesia's largest Islamic party, would produce a winning combination.

The leaders of GAM's active fighting force, now disarmed and represented by the Aceh Transition Committee, maintained close links with their rank-and-file members at the grassroots level. They were in no mood for complex coalition-building and ambiguous political compromises. With KPA support, a rival GAM slate was formed, composed of Irwandi Yusuf for governor and Muhammad Nazar as deputy governor. Yusuf had joined GAM after returning from the United States with a degree in veterinary science. He was arrested in 2003 and sentenced to nine years for rebellion but escaped from prison when the tsunami collapsed the prison walls where he was detained. After the initiation of the Aceh peace process, he became GAM's liaison with the AMM and from that position represented the ex-guerrillas. Muhammad Nazar made his reputation as organizer for the 1999 demonstrations for a referendum on Aceh independence.[60]

The Aceh election for governor and deputy governor and for *bupati* (district officers) to head the 19 kabupaten (regencies) of Aceh was held on December 11, 2006. Earlier polls had indicated that the Humam/Hasbi ticket was leading by a slim margin. However, when the vote was counted, Irwandi Yusuf and his deputy won with a plurality of 38.2 percent of the vote and the Humam/Hasbi duo came in second place with 16.62 percent of the vote. The combined vote for the two competing GAM tickets was 54.82 percent.[61] If GAM forces could reunite, this election provided a harbinger of future political successes for GAM operating as a political party.

The day after the election, Aceh's Wilayatul Hisbah published a draft of Sharia law Qanuns that would impose hand amputation on thieves if they stole property worth 3 ounces of gold or more. For theft of property worth less than 3 ounces of gold, the penalties ranged from a maximum of 60 strokes by cane flogging, and a fine of Rp60 million (US$7,560), and/or a maximum of ten years imprisonment. The minimum penalty for theft of property worth less than 3 ounces of gold was set at 2 strokes, Rp2 million (US$250) fine and/or four months imprisonment. As soon as these draft revisions to Sharia law were made public, Irwandi Yusuf promised that he would oppose any attempt to implement new Qanuns imposing hand-amputation and public-flogging penalties for theft.[62]

The timing of these proposed Sharia criminal penalties, on the day after the Aceh election, indicates that opponents of the new governor were issuing a challenge. Eight years earlier, President Habibie had sought the support of Aceh's influential ulama by giving them an enhanced stake in the provincial government supported by Jakarta. This action by the ulama revealed that they intended to remain a powerful force in the Aceh government. The Helsinki peace agreement only provided for the election of the governor and bupati, but not for local or provincial legislative assemblies. Irwandi Yusuf's election as governor gave him substantial authority over provincial administration, but that office had no power to veto legislation. Until the next provincial elections in 2009, he would be required to work with a legislative assembly that included a large contingent of ulama members. Proposals for implementing the extreme version of Sharia law were therefore designed to fracture Irwandi's electoral support and undermine his legitimacy as a Muslim leader.

Reintegration, Relief, and Regionalism

Before their installation on February 8, 2007, Irwandi Yusuf and Muhammad Nazar traveled to Jakarta to meet Indonesian president Susilo Bambang Yudhoyono. During the election campaign, Irwandi had stressed creating jobs, increasing investments, and accelerating reconstruction, but during that campaign, Irwandi had also promised to renegotiate the Law on Governing Aceh (LOGA), which included revenue-sharing of natural resources, the role of national police and military forces, and the implementation of Sharia law.[63] News reports on that meeting reported that President Yudhoyono had promised support to governor-elect Irwandi, but made only oblique mention of "conditions" that constrained that promise. In interviews following those discussions, Irwandi and Nazar stressed the issues of jobs, economic development, and reconstruction and reaffirmed Aceh's commitment to remain "within the fold of the Unitary State of the Republic of Indonesia." They also promised not to be partisan or discriminate against any community in Aceh and stated that there would be no "purges" of the existing bureaucracy.[64]

As Irwandi began his five-year term as governor of Aceh, he commanded significant executive powers but faced much larger problems than those powers could solve. Aceh was receiving in 2007 total disbursements of about US$1.8 billion per year. From the natural resource revenue-sharing agreement Aceh received about US$1.25 billion per year, but that sum was dependent on petroleum prices and any decline in LNG production. Oil and gas revenues derived from the production-sharing agreements went to the government of Aceh and were therefore subject to the budget controlled by the Aceh legislative assembly. A Special Autonomy Fund established by the government of Indonesia allocated US$1.4 billion per year for relief and rehabilitation in Aceh. Together these sources provided revenues that were six times greater than Aceh had available in 1999. However, most of those funds were controlled and monitored by the Indonesian government's Bureau for Reconstruction and Relief for Aceh and Nias (BRR), or directly administered by various UN agencies or NGOs. Therefore, relatively few funds that were being disbursed in Aceh were available to and under the direct control of the governor.[65]

The challenges and issues facing the new administration were gargantuan. Toward the end of 2006, the unemployment rate was more than 12 percent, and 28.5 percent of the population lived below the poverty line of US$14 per capita per month. Construction had been completed for 58,269 new houses, but the estimated need for new housing called for the construction of 130,000 more houses and the repairing of 75,000 damaged houses. Families displaced by the conflict were significantly worse off than those displaced by the tsunami. Among the demobilized GAM fighters, the unemployment rate was over 75 percent.[66] Because of rapid depletion of gas reserves, the manufacturing sector of the economy was declining, but overall, the economy was improving, largely because of foreign and Indonesian disaster relief. By September 2007, foreign donors had pledged US$673 million of relief, and Aceh received US$3 billion annual disbursements from oil and gas revenues. Because so many Acehnese had become dependent on these relief programs, dependency on handouts created serious economic problems. Aceh's economy suffered from rampant inflation, peaking at 41 percent in December 2005, and subsiding to 10 percent in 2007. A shortage of skilled workers combined with tight credit and a lack of private investments impeded efforts to revive the domestic economy. Even so, there was a general optimism that Aceh would gradually overcome its disaster mode and was finally on the road to recovery.[67]

The new administration of Irwandi Yusuf faced a daunting task of addressing these and other problems. The Aceh legislature had no members with GAM affiliation, and that body was led by ulama who were opposed to the secular political ideology of Governor Irwandi. To address immediate issues, cooperation from the legislature was essential for budget issues and for passing any reforms. Aceh's bureaucracy had the reputation of having the highest level of corruption of any province of Indonesia. Anticorruption reforms would be extremely difficult to implement without legislative support. Governor Irwandi's support base was from the KPA, led by demobilized GAM commanders, who had few administrative and political skills and were not noted for their commitment to the rule of law. Fortunately, most sectors of Aceh society had come to the realization that peace with political controversy was far preferable to the previous state of war, rebellion, and deadly violence.

In February 2008, Indonesia's technology and research agency reported that a German research vessel had recently completed a two-dimensional seismic survey of the offshore ocean basin near Simeulue Island. That survey revealed evidence of a massive hydrocarbon deposit that could hold between 107 billion and 320 billion barrels of oil equivalent. This survey site had been the epicenter that triggered the 2004 Indian Ocean tsunami. If that hydrocarbon survey data proves accurate, Indonesia could surpass Saudi Arabia as the world's largest oil producer. Saudi Arabia has the world's biggest hydrocarbon reserves of 264.21 billion barrels of proven oil reserves, while Indonesia has 8.6 billion barrels of proven oil reserves and 185.8 trillion cubic feet of proven gas reserves. The head of the Indonesian research team stated that further three-dimensional seismic data would be collected to confirm these new offshore findings.[68] In response, independent oil analysts cautioned that seismic data can only suggest where oil might be found and that confirmation of proven oil reserves requires test drilling. Furthermore, to drill where the earth's crust has been fractured by earthquake and volcanic activity can be extremely hazardous and costly. Drilling through heavily fractured strata can result in dangerous oil spills, and earthquakes give no advance warning. Even if new massive oil deposits are confirmed off Aceh's west coast, the critical issues will be how much of the oil is recoverable, what new technology will be required, and what will be the costs to extract the oil. It will take a few years of research and test drilling to answer these questions.

If large-scale oil production does begin off Aceh's western shores, its economy will be transformed and its politics will become much more contentious. If oil deposits are not confirmed or are not recoverable, Aceh's recovery from disaster and rebellion will be slow, costly, and difficult. Either way, the challenges ahead for Aceh's leaders will be enormous. For Aceh, there are too many "ifs" in alternate scenarios to make credible predictions about the future.

Notes

1. Earlier, in 1950, the Indonesian government reconstituted the prewar Dutch province of North Sumatra to include Aceh as a subdivision. In December 1956, while the Darul Islam rebellion in Aceh was displaying its strength, Sukarno gave approval for the creation of a separate province of Aceh. Ali Hasjmy, a former PUSA leader, was appointed to be governor of Aceh. This concession paved the way for the treaty in May 1959 that granted Aceh limited autonomy related to Islam, Adat law, and education. Daud Beureueh did not surrender with his guerrilla forces until May 8, 1962. Nazaruddin Sjamsuddin, *The Republican Revolt: A Study of the Acehnese Rebellion* (Singapore: Institute of Southeast Asian Studies, 1985), 34–47, 159–310.

2. Tim Kell, *The Roots of Acehnese Rebellion* (Ithaca, NY: Cornell Modern Indonesia Program, 1995), 61; Tengku Hasan di Tiro, *The Price of Freedom: The Unfinished Diary* (Markam, Canada: Open Press Holdings, 1984), excerpts reproduced at "Free Aceh (ASNLF)," acehnet.tripod.com. Initially the organization was called National Liberation Front of Aceh-Sumatra. Later, the name changed to Aceh-Sumatra National Liberation Front. About 1989, the organization adopted as its popular name Free Aceh Movement (Gerakan Aceh Merdeka, GAM), while retaining ASNLF as its formal title.

3. Di Tiro, *The Price of Freedom,* 2. Hasan di Tiro claimed to be the last surviving heir to the royal line of Aceh sultans. The hero of the ulama-led struggle against the Dutch was Tengku Chik di Tiro, who was killed in January 1891. Chik di Tiro was never sultan of Aceh, but he was one of the di Tiro ulama who opposed the Dutch for over three decades until 1913. The last sultan of Aceh was Tuanku Muhammad Daud Shah, who ruled from 1874 to 1903. Sultan Daud surrendered to the Dutch in 1903 and shortly thereafter was deposed. When Daud continued to undermine Dutch authority, he was exiled in 1906 to Batavia and later to Ambon. Kell, *The Roots of Acehnese Rebellion*, 61; Anthony Reid, *The Contest for North Sumatra: Atjeh, the Netherlands and Britain 1858–1898* (Kuala Lumpur: Oxford University Press, 1969), 204, 252–256, 275–283. By Hasan's definition, Aceh's borders included the Batak and Minangkabau

regions of Sumatra as well as Deli Serdang, Asahan, and Siak extending south to the towns of Indrapiri on the east coast and Indrapura on the west coast of Sumatra.

4. Edward Aspinall, "Modernity, History and Ethnicity: Indonesian and Acehnese Nationalism in Conflict," *Review of Indonesian and Malaysian Affairs* 36, no. 1 (2002), 3–33; Edward Aspinall, "Sovereignty, the Successor State, and Universal Human Rights: History and the International Struggle of Acehnese Nationalism," *Indonesia* 73 (2002), 1–24.

5. Kirsten E. Schulze, *The Free Aceh Movement (GAM): Anatomy of a Separatist Organization* (Washington, DC: East-West Center Washington, 2004), 14; Kell, *The Roots of Acehnese Rebellion,* 65–66.

6. Kell, *The Roots of Acehnese Rebellion,* 14, 30–33. Hasan di Tiro claimed that about 5,000 guerrillas had trained in Libya, while Indonesian military intelligence placed the number at 583, and others estimated the figure at between 700 and 800. These trained fighters made a significant impact on the security situation in Aceh when they returned to do battle with the Indonesian Army.

7. Schulze, *The Free Aceh Movement*, 23.

8. Damien Kingsbury, *Power Politics and the Indonesian Military* (London: RoutledgeCurzon, 2003), 92–96, 106–107, 135–136.

9. Minority Rights Group, *Aceh Briefing,* 1–4, extracted from Mieke Kooistra, *Indonesia: Regional Conflicts and State Terror* (London: Minority Rights Group International, 2001), www. minorityrights.org; Kell, *The Roots of Acehnese Rebellion*, 74–75.

10. Rizal Sukma, *Security Operations in Aceh: Goals, Consequences and Lessons* (Washington, DC: East-West Center Washington, 2004), 16.

11. Ibid., 66–79; Minority Rights Group, *Aceh Briefing,* 1–4; Michael L. Ross, "Resources and Rebellion in Aceh, Indonesia," Paper prepared for the Yale–World Bank project "The Economics of Political Violence," June 5, 2003, 1–8, mlross@polisci.ucla.edu; Sukma, *Security Operations in Aceh,* 3–12.

12. Kell, *The Roots of Acehnese Rebellion,* 61–69.

13. Sukma, *Security Operations in Aceh,* 3 and 30; Ross, "Resources and Rebellion," 9–16.

14. Kell, *The Roots of Acehnese Rebellion,* 13–28.

15. Ibid., 64, citing Aceh/Sumatra National Liberation Front, "A Black Paper Documenting Javanese/Indonesian Crime of Genocide Against the People of Aceh/Sumatra 1990" (Norsborg, Sweden: ASNLF Information Department, November 1990), 1.

16. A report from CNN on July 9, 2002, stated that Umar Faruk (acting as an Al Qaeda liaison agent responsible for contacts with local radical Islamist groups) visited Aceh in June 2000 accompanied by the top two officers from Al Qaeda, Ayman al-Zawahiri and Mohammed Atef. These three were also reported to have traveled on to Maluku to make a political assessment of that area. An account of these meetings is included in the article by Andrew Tan, "The Acehnese Conflict: Transnational Linkages, Responses and Implications," *IDSS Commentaries,* 25/2003 (July 2003), Institute of Defence and Strategic Studies (Singapore: Nanyang Technological University), 1–4, www.idss.edu.sg. Later, Umar Faruq was arrested on June 4, 2002, by Indonesian intelligence officers and transferred to US custody at Bagram airbase in Afghanistan. Under interrogation, Faruq gave an account of his activities and admitted that he had traveled to Aceh with Syawal in mid-December 1999 to attend meetings with the small Aceh rebel faction called Front Mujahidin Islam Aceh. When questioned about the visits, he denied ever meeting al-Zawahiri or Atef in Aceh or Maluku. Ken Conboy, *The Second Front: Inside Asia's Most Dangerous Terrorist Network* (Jakarta: Equinox Publishing, 2006), 101–105, including 101n, 173–175.

17. Rizal Sukma, "The Acehnese Rebellion: Secessionist Movement in Post-Suharto Indonesia," in Andrew T. H. Tan and J. D. Kenneth Boutin (eds.), *Non-Traditional Security Issues in Southeast Asia* (Singapore: Select Publishing, 2001), 389; Kevin O'Rourke, *Reformasi: The Struggle for Power in Post-Soeharto Indonesia* (Crows Nest, Australia: Allen & Unwin, 2002), 333; Edward Aspinall and Harold Crouch, *The Aceh Peace Process: Why It Failed* (Washington, DC: East-West Center Washington, 2003), 8.

18. Aspinall and Crouch, *The Aceh Peace Process*, 7–8, 24–26.

19. O'Rourke, *Reformasi,* 333–334; Minority Rights Group International, *Aceh Briefing,* 2; Sukma, "The Acehnese Rebellion," 390–392.

20. Aspinall and Crouch, *The Aceh Peace Process,* 11–15; Sukma, "The Acehnese Rebellion," 396–400; Konrad Huber, *The HDC in Aceh: Promises and Pitfalls of NGO Mediation and Implementation* (Washington, DC: East-West Center, 2004), 13–76.

21. Aspinall and Crouch, *The Aceh Peace Process,* 15–24.

22. Ibid., 30–34; Rodd McGibbon, *Secessionist Challenges in Aceh and Papua: Is Special Autonomy the Solution?* (Washington, DC: East-West Center Washington, 2004), 46–48; Department of Politics and Social Change, Centre for Strategic and International Studies, "The Bali Inferno and the Settlement of Aceh Conflict," *Indonesian Quarterly* 30, no. 4 (2002), 385–386.

23. Schulze, *The Free Aceh Movement*, 17, 24–27, 34–35, 39; Sukma, *Security Operations in Aceh,* 20–21; International Crisis Group, *Aceh: A Fragile Peace,* Asia Report No. 47 (February 27, 2003), Jakarta/Brussels, 1–3, www.crisisweb.org; Lesley McCulloch, *Aceh: Then and Now* (London: Minority Rights Group, 2005), 21–23.

24. International Crisis Group, *Aceh: Slim Chance for Peace,* Asia Briefing No. 14 (March 27, 2002), Jakarta/Brussels, 1; International Crisis Group, *Aceh: A Fragile Peace*, 1–3.

25. Schulze, *The Free Aceh Movement*, 10–14; ASNLF, "The Stavanger Declaration," July 21, 2002, www.acheh-eye.org.

26. Schulze, *The Free Aceh Movement*, 7–8, 51–56.

27. "Mobil Caught in Sumatra Crossfire," *Upstream,* August 21, 1999, 1–2; "ExxonMobil Hit with Abuse Suit," *Upstream,* June 21, 2001, 1–2; "ExxonMobil Will Appeal Aceh Case," *Upstream,* March 21, 2006, 1–2; "More Force Majeure in Aceh, Indonesian Crisis Rolls On," *Upstream,* March 23, 2001, 1–2; www.upstreamonline.com.

28. "Bottom-Line Blues for ARUN," *Upstream,* July 17, 2001, www.upstreamonline.com.

29. Schulze, *The Free Aceh Movement*, 25–27; Ross, "Resources and Rebellion," 25–26.

30. Later evidence revealed that these attacks on the peacekeeping monitors were organized by army-supported militia proxies in Aceh. Edward Aspinall, "Aceh/Indonesia: Conflict Analysis and Options for Systemic Conflict Transformation" (Berghof Foundation for Peace Support, August 2005), 11, www.berghof-peacesupport.org/publications/Aceh_final%20version.pdf.

31. BBC News: "Violence Threatens Aceh Deal," April 4, 2003; "Aceh Peace Monitors Besieged," April 7, 2003; "Concern over Aceh Peace Deal," April 10, 2003; "Aceh Peace Talks Cancelled," April 24, 2003, news.bbc.co.uk/2/hi/asia-pacific/.

32. "Yudhoyono Under Pressure to End Aceh War," *Discover Indonesia Online,* November 15, 2004, 1–2, indahnesia.com/DB/Story/item.php?code=20041115.

33. Mark Honigsbaum and Richard Jinnan, "First Earthquake Claimed Almost 300,000 Lives," *The Guardian,* March 29, 2005, 1–2, www.guardian.co.uk/international/

story/0,1447263,00.html; "Tsunami Aid in Aceh Is Hampered by Rains," *Bloomberg,* www.bloomberg.com/apps/news?pid=71000001; Adam Jay, "Tsunami Death Toll Rises to 225,000," *The Guardian Unlimited,* January 19, 2005, 1–3, www.guardian.co.uk/indonesia/Story/0,27631394002,00.html.

34. C. S. Kuppuswamy, "Indonesia: Aceh's Future." *South Asia Analysis Group,* Paper 1236 (January 28, 2005), 1–8, www.saag.org/%5Cpapers13%5Cpaper1236.html; Cheryl Pellerin, et al., "The U.S. Tsunami Relief Effort 2005: Going the Distance," US Department of State, International Information, April 10, 2005, 2–4, usinfo.state.gov/products/pubs/tsunami.

35. Tom McCawley, "Separatist Conflict Poses Risk to Relief Effort in Aceh," *The Christian Science Monitor,* January 11, 2005, 2–4, www.csmonitor.com/2005/0111/p07s01-woap.html. Later information revealed that many of the imprisoned GAM members escaped when the tsunami collapsed the external walls of one of the main prisons.

36. "Indonesia to Hold Cease-Fire Talks," *MSNBC News,* January 24, 2005, 1–4, www.msnbc.msn.com/id/6754820.

37. USINDO–East-West Center Washington Joint Forum, "National Integration in Indonesia: The Cases of Aceh and Papua," with Sastrohandoyo Wiryono, Rizal Sukma, Samsu Rizal Panggabean, and John Rumbiak, October 1, 2002, Washington, DC, www.unindo.org/Briefs; USINDO–East-West Center Washington Joint Program, "National Integration in Indonesia: The Cases of Aceh and Papua," with Sastrohandoyo Wiryono, Edward Aspinall, Larry Niksch, and Muthiah Alagappa, March 1, 2004, Washington, DC, www.usindo.org/Briefs/2004; USINDO Open Forum, "Aceh: The Political Picture," with David DiGiovanna, January 18, 2005, Washington, DC, www.usindo.org/Briefs/2005; USINDO Brief, "Indonesia Under SBY: Consolidating Democracy," Douglas E. Ramage, March 8, 2005, Washington, DC, www.usindo.org/Briefs/2005.

38. "Profile: Aceh's Gam Separatists," *BBC News,* January 24, 2005, news.bbc.co.uk/go/pr/fr/-/2/hi/asia-pacific/3039243.stm. The detained GAM leaders and their claimed titles were: Hasan di Tiro, founder and supreme leader; Malik Mahmud, prime minister; Zaini Abdullah, foreign minister. In an interview, Malik Mahmud revealed that GAM leaders in Sweden communicated with field commanders in Aceh by cell phone text messages. Richard C. Paddock, "In Sweden, a Sultan of Rebellion," *The Los Angeles Times,* June 30, 2003, 1–7, www.vanzorgreport.com/news/popup/index.cfm; Adianto P. Simamora, "Swedish Government Vows to Help Indonesia on GAM Issue," *The Jakarta Post,* March 12, 2005, www.thejakartapost.com/misc/PrinterFriendly.asp.

39. At the second-round talks, GAM accused Finnish president Ahtisaari and the Crisis Management Initiative of being biased in favor of the Indonesians. For that reason, the CMI report on the second-round sessions was removed from the CMI web page "due to unintentional misunderstandings." Crisis Management Initiative, press release, April 8, 2005, www.cmi.fi/?content=press&id=50.

40. Christine T. Tjandraningsih, "Indonesia to Offer Concessions to Aceh Rebels in Helsinki Talks," *Antara News,* April 11, 2005, 1–2, www.antara.co.id/en/seenws/index.php?id=2618.

41. Rizal Sukma, "Secessionist Challenge in Aceh: Problems and Prospects," in Hadi Soesastro, Anthony L. Smith, and Han Mui Ling (eds.), *Governance in Indonesia: Challenges Facing the Megawati Presidency* (Singapore: Institute of Southeast Asian Studies, 2003), 175–181.

42. Raj Rajendran and Brett Young, "Aceh Peace Talks End Early, Real Progress Made," *Reuters,* April 16, 2005, 1–2, www.reuters.com/newsArticle.jhtml?type=worldNews.

43. "More Than 1,000 Aceh Rebels Have Been Killed Since Mid-November," *West Papua News*, March 14, 2005, 1–2, www.westpapuanews.com/articles/publish/article_2072.shtml.

44. *Memorandum of Understanding Between the Government of the Republic of Indonesia and the Free Aceh Movement,* August 15, 2005, Crisis Management Initiative, Helsinki, Finland, www.cmi.fi/?content=aceh_project.

45. In Indonesia the term *organic* is applied to persons who are indigenous to or legal residents of a province.

46. *Memorandum of Understanding,* Article 3.1.

47. Council of Foreign Relations, "Interview with Sidney Jones on Aceh Peace Agreement," August 30, 2005, 2, www.cfr.org/publications/8790.

48. "Aceh Monitoring Mission: A New Challenge for ESDP," *European Security Review* 27 (October 2005), 1–5, www.isis-europe.org/ftp/Download/ARTICLE%22.pdf; Amnesty International, "Indonesia: A Briefing for EU and ASEAN Countries Concerning the Deployment of the Aceh Monitoring Mission to Nanggroe Aceh Darussalam Province," September 9, 2005, 1–4, web.amnesty.org/library/Index/.

49. International Crisis Group, "Aceh: So Far, So Good," Asia Briefing No. 44 (December 13, 2005), www.crisisgroup.org/home/index.cfm?id=3831; Ayi Jufridar, "Indonesian Soldiers Leave Aceh Province," *CNN News,* December 29, 2005, 1–2, channels.netscape.com/news/story.jsp?floc=FF-APO-1104&idq; "Tsunami—One Year After—EU Supports Aceh Peace Process," TV Link, February 26, 2006, 1–3, www.tvlink.org/vnr.cfm?vidID=161; "Aceh Rebels' Move into Politics," *Tempo,* January 10, 2006, 1–2, BBC Worldwide monitoring supplied to Asia-Pacific Daily News Review, January 11, 2006.

50. "Whispers of Aceh Tests," *Upstream,* May 2, 2001; "Aceh Unrest and Declining Output Prompts Rethink," *Upstream,* April 30, 2004; "Arun Plant on Road to Retirement," *Upstream,* June 2, 2004; www.upstreamonline.com.

51. "Indonesia: Troubles in Indonesia's LNG Industry," US Embassy, Economic Section, 2005; "Indonesia to Sweeten Terms," *Upstream,* August 10, 2006, www.upstreamonline.com.

52. The provisions of the MoU are likely to influence relations between the central government and other provinces. The Aceh Agreement could also provide a template for resolving the long-simmering separatist movement in Irian Jaya, where about 100,000 people have died as a result of military operations against separatist guerrillas.

53. *The United Nations International Covenant on Civil and Political Rights,* Articles 18, 19, 22, 23, 27, www.hrweb.org/legal/cpr/.html.

54. *International Covenant on Economic, Social and Cultural Rights,* Articles 3 and 7, www. unhchr.ch/html/menu3/b/a_cescr.htm.

55. For an evaluation of the MoU and the competing interests of the key stakeholders, see Aspinall, "Aceh/Indonesia," 2–28.

56. Since Qanun are administrative edicts related to administration of Sharia law, this provision provided the legal basis for expanding the enforcement of existing provisions of Sharia law as previously authorized and adopted by Aceh. *Memorandum of Understanding,* Article 1.1.6.

57. "Aceh Introduces Islamic Law," *CNN,* January 2, 2002, 2–3, edition.cnn.com/2002/WORLD/asiapcf/southeast/01/02/aceh.sharia; International Crisis Group, *Islamic Law and Criminal Justice in Aceh,* ICG Asia Report No. 117 (July 31, 2006) Jakarta/Brussels, 1–14. Zina and theft were not included in the 2004 set of Qanuns defining Sharia-enforced criminal penalties.

58. *ABC Online,* "PM—Conflict over Sharia Law in Aceh," September 1, 2006, 1–3, www.abc.net.au/pm/content/2006/s1731262.htm; Natasha Fatah, "Religion and

Natural Disasters Shouldn't Mix," *CBC News,* February 22, 2008, 1–2, www.cbc.ca/news/viewpoint/vp_fatah/200880222.html.

59. International Crisis Group, *Aceh's Local Elections: The Role of the Free Aceh Movement (GAM),* Asia Briefing No. 57 (November 29, 2006), Jakarta/Brussels, 1–5.

60. Ibid., 6–14.

61. "Aceh's Election: The Alternative to War," *The Economist,* December 13, 2006, 2–3, www.economist.com/world/asia/displaystory.cfm?story_id=8413207; "Former Rebel Wins in Aceh's First Elections in Indonesia," *HULIQ,* December 13, 2006, 2–3, www.huliq.com/3795. The rules provided for election by plurality unless no candidate gains at least 25 percent of the vote, in which case a run-off election would be held. Sixteen bupati were elected in the first round, and GAM candidates won in eight of those contests. In three kabupaten no candidate gathered 25 percent and run-off elections were scheduled for February 11, 2007. "Some Aceh Races Get Second Round," *Jakarta Post,* December 21, 2006, 1, www.fkmcpr.nl/?page=6036; International Crisis Group, *Indonesia: How GAM Won in Aceh,* Asia Briefing No. 61 (March 22, 2007), Jakarta/Brussels, 1–24.

62. Ridwan Max Sijabat and Nani Afrida, "Amputation Bill Riles Acehnese," *The Jakarta Post,* December 17, 2006, 1–2, www.thejakartapost.com/misc/PrinterFriendly.asp; "Draft Law Calls for Amputation of Thieves' Hands in Indonesia's Aceh," *International Herald Tribune,* December 12, 2006, www.iht.com/articles/ap/2006/12/12/asia; "Aceh: A Struggle Commences over Sharia," John Mark Ministries, 1–2, jmm.aaa.net.au/articles/18831.htm; "Aceh's Sharia Bylaws 'Hurting the Needy and Protecting the Wicked,'" *Jakarta Punya Berita,* January 14, 2007, 1–3, www.jaknews.com/2006/english/des/22122006-1100jak09.htm.

63. The LOGA statute passed by Indonesia's Parliament modified the MoU agreement terms by limiting Aceh's rights to manage its natural resources and to secure direct foreign investments. LOGA also altered the MoU Article 1.1.2b,c&d providing that "consent" from Aceh would be required for international agreements and parliamentary decisions affecting "matters of special interest to Aceh." Instead, the LOGA only provided for "consultation" on such matters. Large protests of about 10,000 people formed in Banda Aceh on August 15, 2006, to object to these modifications to the terms of the MoU agreed to at Helsinki. "Thousands in Aceh Accuse Gov't of Failing on Peace Deal," Associated Press, August 15, 2006, 1–2, www.kabar-irian.com/pipermail/kabar-indonesia/2006-August/15.

64. Ben Hillman, "Aceh's Rebels Turn to Ruling," *Far Eastern Economic Review* 170, no. 1 (January/February 2007), 50–52; Antara News Agency, "SBY Asks Aceh's Governor, Vice Governor–Elect Not to Be Partisan," January 21, 2007, 1, www.acheh-eye.org.

65. The combined funds allocated for reconstruction and rehabilitation for Aceh and Nias as promised by the government of Indonesia, NGOs, and international donors had reached a total of US$5.8 billion by the end of October 2006. At that date, only 38 percent of those funds had been disbursed for relief projects, and the per-year disbursement rate for 2007 was expected to be about US$1.8 billion per year. World Bank, "The World Bank Support for Post-Tsunami Reconstruction in Aceh and Nias, Indonesia, Reconstruction Progress, Disbursements and Physical Outputs," November 2006, 1–3, web.worldbank.org/id; International Crisis Group, *Aceh: Post Conflict Complications,* Asia Report No. 139 (October 4, 2007), Jakarta/Brussels, 1–25.

66. Mark Forbes, "Democracy Calling," *The Age,* December 11, 2006, 1–4, www.theage.com.au/news/in-depth/democracy-calling/2006/12/11; "Aceh Today: A Post-Election Spat," *Tempo Magazine,* January 6, 2007, 2–3, www.acheh-eye.org; World Bank, "The Aceh Peace Agreements: How Far Have We Come," December 2006, 1–5,

www.worldbank.org/id; Sidney Jones, "Indonesia Outlook 2007—Political Priorities for a GAM-Led Government in Aceh," *The Jakarta Post,* January 15, 2007, 1–3, www.thejakartapost.com/Outlook/pol09b.asp.

67. The World Bank, Indonesia, "Brief: Reconstruction Progress, Disbursements and Physical Outputs," 2007, 1–2; World Bank, Indonesia, "Brief: Housing Financing and Progress Report," 2007, 1–4; World Bank, "Aceh Economic Update," April 2007, 1–4, www.worldbank.org; Fabio Scarpello, "Diplomacy Key for Former Rebel Turned Governor in Indonesia's Aceh," *World Politics Review,* February 2007, 1–4, www.worldpoliticsreview.com/article.aspx?=523; Oakley Brooks, "The Rebirth of Aceh," *Far Eastern Economic Review* 170, no. 9 (November 2007), 30–33.

68. "Survey Data Raises Hopes for Aceh Play," *Upstream,* February 14, 2008, 3–4, www.upstreamonline.com.

PART 5

Facing Hard Choices

12

Democracy and Islam in Indonesia

The two themes of democracy and political Islam are inexorably interlinked, especially in those Southeast Asian countries where Muslims constitute an overwhelming majority of the population. For comparison and contrast, this chapter is one of two chapters exploring the processes of democratic transition and Islamic-based politics in Indonesia and Malaysia. The final chapter assesses the long-term trajectory of political Islam as a political force within an evolving and rapidly changing Southeast Asian political environment.

The Collapse of Legitimacy

The end of the Suharto regime was not quite a revolution, but it was a time of severe political trauma. Suharto's downfall came as much from the failure of his system of governance to manage the economy as it did from an upsurge of revolutionary fervor from disaffected sectors of society. A regime heavily dependent on patronage has a difficult time during an economic downturn to restrict the benefits of government largesse and impose the economic discipline required during a tight market economy. The overextension of credit and the high national debt load had been sanctioned for political reasons, rather than as a strategy for prudent management of the national economy. Failed economic policies led to the collapse of government legitimacy.

In this setting, the Reformasi movement emerged as a symptom of national distress. It grew nearly spontaneously, without a coherent political agenda except to dislodge Suharto from power and to blame him, his supporters, and his "cronies" for the economic and political trauma facing the country. Even though the Reformasi movement had an incoherent political agenda, it did stress democracy as a process for overcoming past injustices and creating policies to address the nation's multidimensional crisis. After decades of Sukarno's Guided Democracy and Suharto's New Order patrimonial authoritarianism, the common political mantra became "democracy." What variety of democracy was suitable for Indonesia? That was the challenge facing governments formed in the wake of Suharto's departure.

The Presidency of B. J. Habibie

B. J. Habibie assumed the office of president when Suharto resigned on May 21, 1998, when the Indonesian Parliament voted to end his term of office. The period of Habibie's presidency was characterized by the fragmentation of political power, with many contending factions competing against each other. Habibie attempted to create a supporting coalition consisting of elements of Golkar, conservative and radical Muslim groups, and key leaders of the Indonesian military high command. In effect, he attempted to reconstruct the New Order system of Suharto, but without the extensive patronage and system of political controls that had been perfected during the Suharto era. His opposition came from leaders of the three largest mass parties, who campaigned for Reformasi but were united largely by their desire to make Habibie's presidency transitional and short-term. The three contending opposition leaders and their parties were as follows: Megawati Sukarnoputri, who headed the Indonesian Democratic Party of Struggle (PDI-P); Amien Rais, who headed the Muhammadiyah and later founded and led the National Mandate Party (PAN); and Abdurrahman Wahid, who headed Nahdlatul Ulama and later founded and led the National Awakening Party (PKB).

During this period of transition under the presidency of Habibie, mass violence erupted in East Timor involving army operations and army-backed militia units mounting operations to crush the East Timor independence movement led by the Fretlin movement. In Ambon, Muslim and Christian communities became entangled in open conflicts in November 1998 that became more deadly when some police and army units joined with Muslim militia forces to attack Christian communities and their militia forces in Maluku and Poso.[1] President Habibie was attempting to forge ahead with democratic political reforms in competition with his political critics. He called for a special session of the People's Consultative Assembly (MPR), apparently with the objective of confirming his authority as president. To protect the session, regular troops were mobilized and aided by autonomous private militia units identified as "self-made security forces." The latter included progovernment youths, hired preman, and radical Muslim paramilitary units linked to the Indonesian Army, including the radical Islamist organizations Indonesian Committee for Islamic Solidarity (KISDI), the Islamic Defense Front (FPI), and Laskar Jihad. For the Reformasi movement, this action by Habibie appeared as overt intimidation designed to influence the MPR as it was being convened to consider what measures were appropriate to address the political and economic crisis facing Indonesia. In response to these moves, students and the reform faction political alliance also mobilized and became involved in street skirmishes with pro-Habibie militia groups and with the army even before the MPR sessions began.

In this highly charged political atmosphere, the four most prominent reform leaders met to draft a manifesto for an agreed program of political reform. The signatories of what came to be known as the Ciganjur Declaration were Abdurrahman Wahid, Megawati Sukarnoputri, Amien Rais, and Sultan Hamengkubuwono X. The declaration stated four main demands: free and fair general elections; the end of the army's representation in Parliament; the end of corruption; and the dissolution of all "self-made security forces" guarding and threatening the Parliament.[2] The Ciganjur Declaration made clear to Habibie that the Special Session of the MPR should not be stage-managed by the president's supporters, and that the coalition of Reformasi supporters placed political reforms high on the political agenda for the MPR session.

President Habibie realized that his administration could not survive after the next election with Golkar as its only source of support. Only a multiparty coalition could sustain a government in the post-Suharto era. Consequently, he determined to craft his own package of democratic reforms. A selected "Team of Seven," under the leadership of Syarwan Hamid, minister of home affairs, met to prepare a draft of electoral reforms. The proposals were presented to the cabinet, with Habibie having final approval. The approved proposals were submitted to the MPR when it met in Jakarta in November. During these deliberations Parliament was surrounded by an estimated 30,000 paramilitary (including the fearsome Laskar Jihad) that had been recruited and moved into Jakarta by Indonesian security forces. Large numbers of Reformasi supporters were confronted by progovernment paramilitary contingents triggering frequent clashes that escalated into rioting and arson. The worst incident occurred at Semanggi in Jakarta, where 16 persons were shot dead and 200 injured. While violence and street battles raged in Jakarta, Parliament debated the reform proposals submitted by the Habibie administration. These reforms were being considered by a Parliament that had been elected and appointed under Suharto's authoritarian political system that assured government majorities through the large number of appointed seats, combined with the controlled system of managed elections.[3] When the MPR considered reform proposals to its own structure, it eventually passed legislation to begin the process of democratization of Indonesia's political institutions.

As passed by the MPR, the new electoral reforms allowed parties to form freely and their platforms did not need to subscribe to the Pancasila ideology. To be eligible for election, parties had to establish electoral support and administrative presence in more than half of the provinces. The reform legislation gave the lower-chamber People's Representative Council (DPR) greater powers, including the power to investigate government agencies and to require reports from government officers, including the president. In the reformed

DPR (legislative assembly) the total number of seats remained at 500, with 462 seats to be filled by contested election. A total of 84 percent of the seats were to be elected by direct popular voting, and 16 percent were to be elected by a complicated system of proportional representation that favored smaller underrepresented political parties. The geographic allocation of elected seats gave Java 234 seats and the Outer Islands 228 seats. The nonelected appointed seats, allocated to the military, were reduced by half to 38 appointed seats. The reform package provided that the larger MPR, which included the entire DPR membership, also included 200 additional seats composed of 135 regional representatives, selected by provincial-level legislatures, and 65 functional representatives appointed by the national government. The MPR had unique powers to elect the president and to amend the Constitution.[4] With these reforms, the government still retained substantial powers over the legislative process, but the balance of power had been tipped to a significant degree so that further reforms could be passed by legislative initiative. At the time, the Reformasi supporters viewed these reforms as a capitulation to the previous New Order regime, and their disappointments were expressed by massive protest demonstrations. Because their ultimatum demands had not been met, many university students who advocated more drastic reforms and an open democratic system felt betrayed.[5] In the passions of the moment, few could foresee that the process of democratization had only just begun, but that the most formidable obstacles to further reforms had been surmounted.

With the passage of election and political reforms, the next election was set for June 7, 1999. A total of 145 parties were formed, but only 48 were able to meet the criteria for contesting the election. The campaigning was vigorous, vicious, and occasionally violent, with several mysterious bombings that appeared designed to provoke communal violence. The campaign revealed a general three-way cleavage in political support between the incumbent Golkar coalition, parties that stressed secularism, and parties that were avowedly Islamist.[6] Eventually, this three-way division of political support would determine who was elected as the next president of Indonesia.

On election day, some 103 million Indonesian voters went to the polls to participate in the most fair and open election that had ever been held in Indonesia. From 1971 to 1997, Golkar had gained voting majorities of 62.1 percent to 74.3 percent. For the 1999 election, Golkar's political support plummeted to less than one-third of its former levels. The remainder of the parties all campaigned in opposition to the government, but they were also so highly fragmented that no sustainable opposition coalition emerged. Because no single party could command a majority, Golkar, while weakened, remained a significant force in Indonesian politics. One of the more surprising results from the election involved the electoral performance of parties identified as "Islamic" that also promised an Islamic form of government and the implementation of Sharia law. The two Islamic parties with the largest voter support were PKB and PAN. Abdurrahman Wahid, who had gained political prominence as leader of Nadhlatul Ulama, led PKB. Amien Rais, who gained his political following as leader of Muhammadiyah, led PAN. Both these leaders identified their parties as Islamic but also endorsed the secularist ideology of Pancasila in order to attract a wider constituency of support. On this basis, these two largest Islamic parties can be classified as "secularist Muslim." From the election results, all parties that claimed to be Muslim, including both "secularist Muslim" and "Islamist," gained a combined vote of 37.5 percent of the total votes cast. However, if the two "secularist Muslim" parties are excluded, the "Islamist" category gained only 17.8 percent of the total votes cast.[7] Considering that Muslims constitute about 85 percent of the population of Indonesia, it becomes apparent that other issues than Islam motivated most voters, and that political support for a radical Islamist ideology was much narrower than had been predicted.[8] (See Table 12.1 for election results.)

These election results gave some indication of who would become leading candidates in the vote cast by the entire MPR membership to elect the president of Indonesia. President Habibie was the incumbent who headed the Golkar bloc and was expected to gain additional support from the selection of regional representatives and military delegates.[9] The PDI-P had campaigned on the themes of the Reformasi movement and was able to win the most votes and the largest number of DPR seats. As leader of that party, Megawati was clearly the front-runner candidate who appeared to have sufficient political momentum to defeat Habibie in a runoff election. There were a few lesser contenders who were assumed to be entering the contest for president largely as a gambit to extract political concessions and to secure a presence in any future coalition government. In this latter category was Abdurrahman Wahid, who headed PKB, which had won only 12.7 percent of the vote and a meager 51 seats in the 200-seat MPR. Because Wahid had suffered two strokes and had diabetes that had left him frail and virtually blind, most observers assumed that he was not a viable candidate for president.

Table 12.1 Indonesia 1999 Elections to DPR

Party	Percentage of Votes	Number of Seats
PDI-P	33.73	153
Golkar	22.46	120
PKB	12.66	51
PPP	10.72	58
PAN	7.12	34
PBB	1.94	13
Other forty-two parties	11.37	33
Total	100.00	462

Source: Leo Suryadinata, *Elections and Politics in Indonesia* (Singapore: Institute of Southeast Asian Studies, 2002), Appendix I, 218–223.

By the time the new MPR convened on October 2, 2000, there had been much behind-the-scenes political maneuvering to build stronger political coalitions, but no majority-controlling coalition had yet emerged. There were three main coalitions, each commanding from 25 percent to 30 percent of the vote, plus a smaller floating group of military delegates who combined with an anti-Habibie minority faction of Golkar that was led by Akbar Tanjung.[10] The three main coalitions were: (1) Habibie's loyalist Golkar group; (2) Megawati's PDI-P, supplemented by a few non-Islamist minority parties; and (3) what came to be called *poros tengah* (Central Axis), led by Amien Rais and composed of Muslim parties, both secular and Islamist. At each stage of the process, each party sought to become part of a winning coalition but also gave even higher priority to blocking or vetoing any candidate of a more-feared opponent coalition.

Nine days after the election of the Speaker, on October 14, President Habibie delivered his "speech of accountability" to the MPR. Outside of Parliament there were thousands of protesters confronting lines of troops. Habibie reviewed the accomplishments of his regime, stressing economic stability, a liberalized press, and completion of successful free elections. He also touched on the East Timor issue and admitted that there had been human rights violations, for which he asked for forgiveness from the victims' relatives. Immediately following Habibie's speech, the MPR took no action, but five days later, after all coalitions had been canvassed, a vote was called. Parliament rejected Habibie's "accountability speech" by a vote of 355 against to 322 in favor.[11] Although the vote was not technically a vote of confidence, and Habibie could have remained a presidential candidate, he concluded that he could not win the contest for president and decided to withdraw as an active candidate. By this move, he freed Golkar loyalists to support an alternative candidate, which action decisively tipped the political balance.

During the early stages of the Reformasi protests against Suharto, Abdurrahman Wahid had offered to forge a coalition with Megawati Sukarnoputri. This coalition appeared to be intact through the early stages of the parliamentary election campaign, but after various coalition-building moves, Wahid and his PKB shifted to an anti-Megawati stance. At the same time, Amien Rais, who led the Central Axis coalition, began promoting Wahid as a viable presidential candidate. Even though the PKB held only fifty-one seats in the MPR, the support of poros tengah elevated Wahid to a credible contender. When Habibie released the Golkar votes, Golkar members realized that they could deny Megawati the presidency by casting their vote for Wahid. When the vote was called, Wahid gained 373 votes to Megawati's 313 votes. From the dynamics of the process, it became apparent that many delegates had voted for their "least worst candidate." Megawati was crestfallen and angry about the surprising turn of events and what she referred to as "the betrayal of her close friend." In some cities, Megawati supporters expressed their anger over the presidential election results by triggering riots and bomb explosions.[12]

After some hesitation, Wahid decided to offer Megawati the position of vice president. She at first refused the offer, but her aides persuaded her to stand as a candidate after they determined that she could win. When the vote for vice president was called, Megawati won by a vote of 396 votes to 284 votes for Hamzah Haz, the leader of PPP, the Islamist party with the un-Islamic title: United Development Party.

The Presidency of Abdurrahman Wahid

Affectionately known as "Gus Dur," President Wahid began his term in office with significant support, combined with a general anxiety over the question of whether he had the capacity to address the many serious issues facing the nation. He was known for preaching doctrines of tolerance and the necessity to deal with the problems of corruption and misgovernment, but he had no prior experience in government office. He came from the center of the political spectrum between the secularists and the Islamists, which was why he was elected president, even though his party was relatively small, ranking fourth largest in number of seats. He had not been elected by a well-constructed political coalition but rather by an ephemeral configuration of shifting vote blocs representing diverse political factions.

In recognition of the weak support base for his government, President Wahid began by assembling a thirty-five-member "rainbow" cabinet based on proportionate power sharing among all the major parties. Very shortly, he learned that this diverse cabinet was incapable of addressing any controversial issues without becoming hopelessly deadlocked. The high ideals of Wahid's rhetoric had to confront the political reality of multiple unresolved conflicts. The failure of the cabinet to achieve consensus on policy issues, combined with President Wahid's limited support base, generated stalemate and escalating conflicts. Wahid expected to utilize the prerogative powers of the president to break any deadlock in order to further his own agenda of reform.

The political dilemmas of President Wahid exposed flaws and ambiguities in Indonesia's political institutions. The 1945 Constitution was short, vague, and somewhat contradictory. It had borrowed from both presidential and parliamentary models of governmental organization. During the regime of both Sukarno and Suharto, the Constitution was turned into a legal fiction so that its institutional coherence was never tested and no binding precedents were established. Furthermore, there was no authoritative process for constitutional interpretation such as a constitutional court or a system of judicial review. The constitutional reforms of 1999, which provided for free elections to Parliament and for "presidential accountability" to Parliament had not resolved other constitutional ambiguities. Could the president exercise autonomous presidential powers without reference to Parliament, or did the president hold office only so long as he obtained majority support from the DPR? With this question unanswered, nearly every contentious substantive issue rapidly became a matter of legal and constitutional dispute, with no authoritative resolution mechanism available.[13]

His physical limitations and behavioral traits compounded Wahid's political dilemma. His near blindness and frail physique meant that he relied on oral communications from close aides. He gave no formal television reports to the nation but did make short impromptu speeches at public gatherings. With his high self-confidence, he had a tendency to respond to policy questions with quick and ill-considered pronouncements before the issues had been discussed within the cabinet among coalition partners. When the ruling coalition was formed, he had not established a clear process of collegial decisionmaking. Consequently, his unilateral actions and impromptu statements on important policy issues created dissension within the ruling coalition. His critics viewed Wahid as unpredictable, vacillating, and inconsistent.[14]

Wahid's very personal, haphazard style of decisionmaking and administrative management was ill suited to the accumulation of problems and issues confronting Indonesia after the events of the previous three years. Among many difficult issues, corruption was the most contentious. Nearly all parties claimed to support measures to uncover and punish KKN (*korupsi, kolusi, nepotisme*). Furthermore, when Wahid became president, he faced intense international pressure for investigation of human rights violations, especially in East Timor. Nearly every time Wahid authorized an investigation of an important political or military figure, the investigation stalled or was hampered by court proceedings, and the ensuing political controversies produced a significant shift of political support to the opposition. Among the more important figures Wahid authorized to be investigated or accused of corruption included former president Suharto and his son, Tommy Suharto.[15]

Political deadlock became more severe with Wahid's authorized corruption investigations of cabinet members. Wahid asked five cabinet members to resign as a result of corruption investigations. Among the accused were General Wiranto, Hamza Haz, Laksamana Sukardi, and Yusuf Kalla.[16] Each of these individuals was able to defend himself with both a legal and a political defense. Wahid's critics accused him of using the anti-KKN campaign to enhance his powers and replace his coalition partners with compliant supporters.

The case against General Wiranto was both more significant and much more fraught with risk than the other corruption and human rights cases. Wiranto had served as commander-in-chief of the armed forces during the last year of Suharto's regime and continued in command of the army through Habibie's interregnum. These were the years when the Indonesian Army had been frequently confronting the Reformasi protesters, including the incident involving the deadly Trisakti shootings. Later, the army, under General Wiranto, waged a proxy war by supporting preman militias against the East Timor independence movement. After the 2000 election, when Wahid solicited support for his presidential bid, he needed the votes of the military delegates to the MPR. To secure their support, he promised General Wiranto the portfolio of minister for politics and security. Upon his election, Wahid fulfilled that promise.

In January 2000, before Wahid's installation as president, the National Commission on Human Rights (Komnas HAM) issued a report on human rights violations in East Timor that implicated Wiranto as a potential defendant in "crimes against humanity committed in East Timor." With the support of President Wahid, the DPR approved the establishment of such a court in March 2001, but with the stipulation that the court could only hear evidence of crimes committed after August 30, 1999, the date of the East Timor referendum.[17] With the Komnas report already made public, Wahid decided to allow an investigation of Wiranto's complicity in East Timor crimes to proceed. After a number of political moves to limit Wiranto's options, President Wahid was finally able to obtain Wiranto's resignation. The issue of civilian political supremacy over the military had been effectively confirmed without triggering a military coup, but Wiranto left office without being subjected to proceedings by the human rights court. This victory for President Wahid came at the price of further weakening his support in Parliament.[18]

By June 2000, opponents of President Wahid began to consider impeachment proceedings to remove the president. When Wahid's critics learned that Wahid had received a donation from the sultan of Brunei of US$2 million and that US$3.5 million was missing from the accounts of the National Food Logistics Agency (Bulog), they were quick to "reverse" the charges of corruption. The DPR authorized an inquiry into these transactions that became known in the press as "Buloggate" and "Bruncigate." The investigation revealed that the president's masseur had embezzled money from Bulog and that the donation from the sultan of Brunei was not illegal but should have been disclosed as a financial contribution. Both cases against Wahid were dropped, but the DPR passed a vote of condemnation further undermining his support.

Facing a growing threat to his presidency, Wahid reshuffled his cabinet several times and then made a power-sharing proposal to Vice President Megawati. She replied with skepticism and with an unstated awareness that she would become president if Wahid were impeached. After a number of other desperate moves, Wahid threatened to declare a state of emergency and dissolve Parliament if he were threatened with impeachment. The MPR Speaker, Amien Rais, stated that such an action would be met immediately by a special session of the MPR to impeach President Wahid. Members of his cabinet and high-ranking military officers warned Wahid not to invoke an emergency decree. Despite this advice, President Wahid suddenly declared a state of emergency in the early hours of July 23, 2001. The presidential decree dissolved Parliament and the Golkar Party and called for new elections within a year. Later, the MPR, meeting in emergency session boycotted by the PKB, voted unanimously (591 in favor) to impeach President Abdurrahman Wahid.

He claimed that the impeachment proceedings were unconstitutional and warned that 400,000 of his supporters would stage a national rebellion if he were removed from office. Yet, during the crisis he remained in the President's Palace surrounded by his supporters. By his actions, he calmed the crowd, and after a long standoff, he eventually agreed to depart for the United States for a "medical check-up."[19]

The Presidency of Megawati Sukarnoputri

Megawati Sukarnoputri became Indonesia's fifth president, not by a vote of the MPR, but rather by her accession from the office of vice president when President Abdurrahman Wahid was impeached by the MPR. Immediately following that action, the MPR proceeded to the election of a new vice president. A number of candidates contested and on the third round of voting, Hamzah Haz was elected with Megawati's support and endorsement by a vote of 340 to 237. She realized the strategic importance of the poros tengah coalition that Hamzah Haz headed. By joining Megawati's government, Hamzah provided an Islamic counterbalance to Reformasi with its secular nationalist ideology that was part of Megawati's political legacy. Hamzah Haz's earlier statement that "no woman was fit to lead a Muslim nation" was quickly forgotten when he gained Megawati's endorsement for vice president of Indonesia.[20]

During Megawati's term as vice president, she witnessed firsthand the collapse of political support for Wahid, and that experience colored her perspective on the role of the president. She had gained her charisma as the fearless champion of Reformasi without articulating a precise political agenda and without making political deals to build a wider coalition of support. She capitalized on her status as the daughter of Indonesia's founding president Sukarno, but even among her ardent supporters she was a political enigma. Once in office as president, she had to chart a political course to address a maze of accumulated problems that remained from Wahid's failed presidency.

Despite the high expectations and the backlog of issues, President Megawati moved slowly and deliberately. Her cabinet was composed of about the same range of parties that had been within the Wahid cabinet, and included many of the same faces. Borrowing a slogan from the Sukarno era, Megawati called it Kabinet Gotong Royong (Mutual Assistance Cabinet). Perhaps out of concern that the political balance of her support base could be undermined by decisive action on controversial issues, she developed a very conservative and deliberate style of leadership that appeared to be overly cautious. The strident demands of the Reformasi movement for reform and justice were quickly forgotten as Megawati opted for a low-key leadership style that she seemed to assume would preserve political stability without generating turmoil and controversy by assertive action or a reform agenda. She avoided interviews with the press. She gave very few speeches. She avoided controversial political issues.[21] However, eventually unforeseen public events thrust her back into the political limelight.

The events of September 11, 2001, in New York and Washington, DC, had a far more important impact on Indonesia than was apparent to Indonesian leaders at the time. In Chapter 8, we recounted how President Megawati was the first Southeast Asian leader to visit Washington in the post-9/11 era and how she gained a substantial aid package for Indonesia with an agreement to support the US-led campaign against terrorism. However, when she returned to Jakarta she confronted domestic attitudes of disbelief that Indonesia had any links with the 9/11 attackers. The Indonesian public tended to assume that the United States was at least partly responsible for becoming a target for terrorism due to its policies in the Middle East. Megawati realized that there were no members of her cabinet willing to support a strong stance against terrorism, and she assumed that strong measures against local Muslim militants would upset Indonesia's fragile political balance.

Megawati's low-key approach to radical Muslim groups created political space for their activities and allowed their defenders to define a political agenda critical of the "war on terror" by minimizing security threats to Indonesia. Indonesia's Vice President Hamzah Haz stepped forward as the most vocal critic and leader of the opposition to Megawati's agreement with the United States to support the war on terror. In the main Jakarta mosque, Hamzah Haz stated that the 9/11 attacks were justified and seemed pleased with the impact of the attack. When the United States began operations against the Taliban regime in Afghanistan, Megawati gave a speech at the Jakarta mosque condemning that action and stating that no country had the right to attack another because of the actions of individuals. The Indonesian Council of Ulamas (MUI) issued a fatwa calling for jihad against the United States, and the radical Islamic Defense Front threatened to start "sweep" operations against US and British citizens in Indonesia. The Indonesian Association of Muslim Intellectuals issued a fatwa stating that all Muslims were obliged to join a jihad against the United States if the United States attacked Afghanistan's Islamic government. With an upsurge of anti-American sentiments being recorded in opinion surveys, Megawati remained silent and allowed Islamic radicals to dominate the news and define the political discourse. Eventually, the radical tone of the public rhetoric alarmed moderate Muslim leaders and prompted Nadhlatul Ulama and Muhammadiyah to assert a more cautionary perspective. In December 2001, leaders from these two organizations held meetings to forge a joint statement pledging their organizations to fight "extremism" in order to change the image of Islam from hatred, violence, and terrorism to one of promoting peace and tolerance.[22]

What had been largely a war of words became more ominous when Singapore and Malaysia arrested twenty-eight suspected terrorists from Singapore, Malaysia, and Indonesia who were preparing to bomb targets in Singapore. After interrogation, Singapore authorities determined that most of those arrested were both members of Jemaah Islamiyah and graduates of the pesantren operated by Abu Bakar Ba'asyir. He was a well-known political activist and founder of the Al Mukmin Pesantren boarding school at Ngruki in Central Java, and was a founding member of the Mujahideen Council of Indonesia (MMI). The interrogations also revealed that Ba'asyir was the emir of Jemaah Islamiyah. The Singapore police interrogations did not obtain evidence that Ba'asyir had personally ordered the foiled Singapore bombing attacks. When Singapore and Malaysia requested Indonesia to arrest Abu Bakar Ba'asyir, Indonesian authorities replied that they had received no evidence any crime had been committed.[23] Until 2002, Indonesia declined to examine bank accounts linked to terrorist groups and chose to deport terrorist suspects identified by foreign intelligence, rather than investigate them for possible criminal activities.

Indonesia's passive policy toward militant Islamist terrorist activities generated increasing pressure and criticism from the United States. Finally, in early May 2002, Indonesian authorities arrested Jafar Umar Thalib, the leader of Laskar Jihad, and charged him with inciting a massacre of Christian villagers in Maluku in April 2001.[24] Vice President Hamzah Haz immediately visited Jafar in jail and announced that "there are no terrorists in Indonesia." On June 6, Indonesia arrested Omar al-Faruq on the basis of evidence obtained by interrogations of Abu Zubaydah, the highest-level Al Qaeda official then in US custody. Three days later al-Faruq was deported to Afghanistan where he was placed in detention and interrogated by CIA investigators. For three months al-Faruq was a noncooperative prisoner, but on September 9, he finally confessed that he was Al Qaeda's senior official in Southeast Asia and he provided information on Al Qaeda agents, funding sources, past operations, and future plans for bombings and terror attacks. Among his many revelations were reports of two failed operations to assassinate Megawati Sukarnoputri. He also revealed how Abu Bakar Ba'asyir and Riduan Isamuddin, better known as Hambali, were actively involved in Al Qaeda operations.[25]

With this information from al-Faruq's interrogation, President Bush asked President Megawati to extradite Abu Bakar Ba'asyir to the United States. Megawati refused to have Ba'asyir arrested because he was prominent politically and she believed that his arrest would create political instability in Indonesia.[26] The earlier actions of Vice President Hamzah Haz, who endorsed and supported both Ba'asyir and Jafar Umar Thalib against accusations and criminal charges, had mobilized public support for Ba'asyir. Both Vice President Hamzah Haz and Din Syamsuddin (leader of Muhammadiyah) played active roles in escalating anti-US sentiments in the aftermath of 9/11. Both men had given notice that the poros tengah parties would undermine Megawati's government if she openly collaborated with President Bush's war on terror.[27] Under these circumstances, Megawati concluded that no rigorous police investigations of Jemaah Islamiyah suspects could be undertaken at that time.

Megawati's strategy of low-key politics could not easily accommodate both international pressures for action against terrorists and Indonesian domestic sensitivities opposed to arrests of radical Islamists. The political mood in Indonesia supported those who openly voiced anti-US sentiments. Megawati's dilemma suddenly ended on October 12, 2002, when two large bombs exploded nearly simultaneously in a crowded tourist resort area of Bali. The bombing in Bali killed 202 people, 88 of whom were Australian tourists, and 352 others were injured. An opinion poll of 14,000 Indonesians taken shortly after the Bali blast revealed that 82 percent of Indonesian respondents attributed the Bali bombings to the CIA.[28] Many Indonesians preferred to believe rumors that shifted attention away from domestic suspects.

Responsibility for the investigation of the bombing was assigned to Police General I Made Mangku Pastika, a Balinese who had some international police training and experience. Altogether, ten nations provided police and forensic experts and other assistance. Within a relatively short period of time, the police made forty arrests, including the two prime suspects, Amrozi bin Nurhasyim and Imam Samudra. The televised confessions of these two and other key suspects provided ample evidence to the public that the guilty had been apprehended. Most of the arrested suspects were either confirmed members of JI or were former students at Ba'asyir's Al Mukmin Pesantren. The police also discovered a book, written in Arabic, giving the organization and operating procedures of Jemaah Islamiyah and identifying Ba'asyir as its emir. Whether Ba'asyir ordered, sanctioned, or had prior knowledge of the Bali bombing remained unclear and unproven.

Three days after the Bali bombing, Laskar Jihad announced that it had disbanded. A few days later, Abu Bakar Ba'asyir was arrested and charged with plotting to overthrow the Indonesian government and organizing the church bombings in Indonesia the previous year. Habib Rizieq Shihab, chairman of the Islamic Defense Front, was also arrested and charged with inciting his followers to conduct raids against dance halls and entertainment centers in Jakarta. Two days after his arrest, Shihab announced that the FPI had been "frozen," apparently in anticipation of the new antiterrorist regulations that were being drafted by the government.[29]

The day after the Bali bombing, President Megawati visited the site, and one week later, under emergency decree, the Indonesian government issued two antiterrorism regulations, largely based on Canada's antiterrorist legislation. These regulations were later incorporated into an antiterrorism bill that was passed by the DPR on March 6, 2003.[30] The bill defines terrorism as "any violent act that could create terror or insecurity among the public or cause destruction of vital facilities." The legislation provided for all suspects to be tried in regular civilian courts, with maximum punishment of death and the minimum set at three years' imprisonment. Intelligence reports, electronic communication, wiretaps, and bank accounts were authorized as legal evidence. Suspects could be detained for up to six months for questioning. These new regulations also provided that antiterrorist regulations could be implemented retroactively. This latter provision created an unresolved legal issue. Indonesia's Constitution in Article 28 stipulates that the right of citizens not to be prosecuted retroactively is a basic human right that shall not be diminished under any circumstances.[31] The conflict between the new regulations and the Constitution over retroactive legislation later became a critical issue in the legal proceedings of many key defendants arrested in the aftermath of the Bali bombing.

Between October 2002 and January 2004, the five principal suspects in the Bali bombing were tried in court and four were convicted. Three of the accused received death sentences, one received a life sentence, and the fifth defendant was acquitted of involvement with the first Bali bombing, but sentenced to life imprisonment for planning the 2003 Marriott bombing. Abu Bakar Ba'asyir, who had been identified as the leader of Jemaah Islamiyah, was charged with subversion and the attempted assassination of Megawati. After the initial trial, Ba'asyir was convicted, but on an appeal to the Jakarta District Court, the subversion and assassination charges were dismissed, due to lack of evidence, and only a minor immigration offense and forgery charge were upheld. On those charges, he received a sentence of four years. After further appeals to the Supreme Court, he was acquitted for involvement in the Bali bombing, but charged and convicted for his involvement in the Marriott hotel bombing in 2003. In March 2005, Ba'asyir was sentenced to thirty months imprisonment, but after an Independence Day remission of four-and-a-half months, he served only twenty-six months and was released on June 14, 2006, returning to his pesantren at Ngruki near Solo.[32]

On July 28, 2004, Indonesia's newly established Constitutional Court ruled, by a narrow 5 to 4 vote, that the antiterrorism law could not be used to convict the Bali bombers because the provisions of that law sanctioning retroactive application were unconstitutional and therefore void.[33] This decision put into question all the earlier convictions of the Bali bombing suspects and convictions from any terrorist acts committed prior to October 18, 2002. It also meant that new trials and charges had to be laid against the accused based on the previously existing laws in effect at the time of the Bali bombing. All suspects tried under the new antiterrorism laws would either need to be released or tried again based on revised charges. In comparison to the antiterrorism law, the earlier criminal laws were much more lax with regard to penalties and more stringent with regard to acceptable evidence. The Constitutional Court's decision did not answer the question of whether the earlier convictions under the antiterrorist laws were "mistrials." If they were, the accused could be tried again for the same offenses but under preexisting laws. If they were not "mistrials," all the earlier conviction verdicts were invalidated, and therefore the accused could not be retried, even with earlier laws, because of the "double jeopardy" guarantee against an accused defendant being tried twice for the same crime. The ensuing legal confusion affected some twenty-seven suspects who had either been convicted or were facing trial for involvement in prior terrorist activities.[34]

During Megawati's watch as president of Indonesia, her administration shifted from a policy of relaxed toleration of militant insurrectionary activities, which were cloaked under the banner of Islam, to a policy that efficiently pursued the perpetrators of terrorist acts through effective police investigation. The process of enforcement and conviction then floundered through a combination of inadequate criminal prosecution of the terrorist cases, and the contradictory chaotic nature of the Indonesian legal system. Under Suharto, the Indonesian judiciary had a reputation of being politically controlled and easily corrupted, but now the courts operated with a high degree of autonomy and unpredictability. Whether the judiciary, in these cases, responded to the shifting moods of Indonesian politics or responded to open threats of violence issued by the supporters of militant defendants became the subject of much speculation without conclusive evidence.[35]

In the aftermath of the Bali bombing, other terrorist acts and incidents occurred, some of them in apparent protest response to the trials against the previously detained suspects. The targets chosen for attack by radical Islamists were considered to be symbols of foreign presence in Indonesia. On August 5, 2003, while the trials of the Bali bombers were in progress, the J. W. Marriott Hotel in Jakarta was car-bombed by a suicide bomber, resulting in the death of 12 persons, nearly all of whom were Indonesians, and more than 150 persons wounded.[36] Within three weeks the police arrested nine suspects and traced the payment of US$45,000 to the bombers from Hambali, the operational commander of Jemaah Islamiyah, who was hiding in Thailand. This payment was made to fund the bombing operation. The Indonesian police also determined that the bomb-makers were Malaysians who had designed and helped to construct the Bali bombs. They were the British-educated Azahari Husin and his assistant, Noordin Mohammed Top. During Megawati's tenure as president, the police were not able to apprehend either of these two primary suspects.[37]

Just over one year after the Marriott bombing, on September 9, 2004, a suicide bomber detonated about 200 kilograms of high explosives in a car-bomb in front of the Australian Embassy in Jakarta. That blast made an impact hole 9 feet deep and blew out most of the windows in the heavily fortified embassy as well as creating extensive damage to other large multistory office buildings in the area. Ten Indonesian bystanders plus the suicide bomber died in the blast and 182 people were injured. About 45 minutes before the blast, someone transmitted a cell-phone text message to Indonesian police stating that Jemaah Islamiyah was planning to bomb Western interests if Indonesian authorities did not immediately release Abu Bakar Ba'asyir from detention. Within ten weeks after this attack on the Australian Embassy, the Indonesian police arrested four suspects who were accused of organizing the bombing, but the two key suspected Malaysian bomb-makers continued to elude an intensive police manhunt.[38] The arrested suspects in both the Marriott and the embassy bombings were now clearly subject to the more stringent antiterrorist laws because their criminal actions postdated those laws. The prospects of their acquittal or conviction with very light sentences were greatly reduced from what had been the outcome of the Bali bomber trials.

Democratic Reforms: Electing a President

Although Megawati's administration had acted with debilitating confusion and divided purpose in matters of domestic terrorism, it made significant progress on issues of democratic reforms. A series of amendments to the Constitution were passed, both during Wahid's tenure and under the administration of Megawati, which transformed Parliament by making the primary legislative body—the DPR—entirely elected through a complicated electoral system that combined a proportional representation system with voting for individual candidates. The membership of the DPR was increased to 550 members, with all candidates selected on party tickets. All parties were encouraged to nominate women for at least 30 percent of their candidates, but there were no penalties imposed for failure to do so.

The most significant reform involved a new system for the selection of the president. For the first time in Indonesian history, the president was to be selected by direct popular election. The election law provided that candidates for president and vice president must be nominated by one of the larger parties in the DPR, and that the election would be held in three stages. The first stage involved elections to the DPR. The second stage involved direct popular elections for nominated presidential tickets. The third stage involved a direct popular runoff election between the two leading presidential tickets. The election was scheduled to begin on April 5, 2004, and would finally terminate half a year later on October 20 with the inauguration of the next president and vice president.[39]

In the campaign, Megawati Sukarnoputri began as the frontrunner for president who expected to gain a second term by utilizing the powers of the presidency and the legacy of her father as Indonesia's founding president. The primary challenger to her reelection in the early stages of the campaign appeared to be the continuing political power exhibited by Golkar, representing the legacy and the institutional edifice of Suharto. When Megawati first formed her cabinet, she appointed Susilo Bambang Yudhoyono as security minister. He was a retired army general who acquired a public reputation as a "middle-road" reformer committed to preserving the unity of Indonesia. In his official capacity, he gained public recognition through his effective campaign to uncover and detain terrorists. He had been given responsibility for devising policies to address the separatist challenges of Aceh and Papua, and he devised new anti-insurgency tactics that combined political dialogue and gave more attention to human rights issues and a more restrained role for the military. Even if his policies did not live up to the public image, his political stock quickly escalated, especially in comparison with Megawati's lackluster public demeanor. In 2002, Yudhoyono, while remaining a cabinet minister, assumed a leading role in the formation of a new political party called the Democrat Party (DP). From its label it appeared to be an offshoot of Megawati's PDI-P (Indonesian Democratic Party–Struggle), but the DP was formed independently from the ground up, and by 2004 it had qualified for contesting the 2004 national legislative elections.[40]

On April 5, 2004, about 124.4 million Indonesian voters went to the polls to vote for members to the House of Representatives (DPR), the House of Regional Representatives (DPD), and for provincial legislative bodies. This election was one of the most complicated elections held in any country and it was conducted without significant violence. It was also closely monitored by thousands of election monitors to assure its fairness and accuracy. At the national level, twenty-four parties contested for support. After the votes were cast, it took almost three weeks before results were counted and certified. For the DPR, no party gained a commanding plurality. Megawati's PDI-P suffered the greatest loss of support, falling from its 1999 election, when it gained 153 seats in a 462-member DPR, to winning only 109 seats in 2004 for a 550-member DPR. (See Table 12.2.) These results reflected public disillusionment with the performance and policies of Megawati's government. Even so, her party came in second behind Golkar. Of the 550 seats in the new DPR, 400 members were elected for the first time, creating a large influx of inexperienced members just when the DPR's role was being greatly enhanced.

Table 12.2 Dewan Perwakilan Rakyat (DPR) Elections, 2004

Party	Percentage of Votes	Percentage of Members	Number of Members
Golkar	21.58	23.00	127
PDIP	18.53	19.82	109
PKB	10.57	9.45	52
PPP	8.15	10.35	58
PD	7.45	10.18	56
PKS	7.34	8.18	45
PAN	6.44	9.63	53
Combined total for seventeen other minor parties	19.94	9.39	50
Total	100.00	100.00	550

Source: Jakarta Post, citing General Elections Commission, "Final Results of April 5 Legislative Election," www.thejakartapost.com/Pres_Leg_Tally.htm.

As soon as the new DPR convened, the second election campaign began with intensity and much political maneuvering. Parties that won at least 3 percent of the seats or 5 percent of the votes were permitted to sponsor a presidential ticket. This system not only favored major parties, but also encouraged coalition-building since the winning ticket would need to gain over 50 percent of the votes in either the first primary election or the second runoff election. Out of this process emerged five presidential tickets linking at least two or more parties into electoral coalitions. General Wiranto selected Solahuddin Wahid, the brother of Abdurrahman Wahid, as his vice presidential running mate. Megawati chose the chairman of Nadhlutal Ulama, Hasyim Muzadi, as her vice presidential running mate. Amien Rais created a coalition of six minor Islamic and middle-road parties, and S. B. Yudhoyono created a coalition of smaller reform-minded and Islamic parties. For his running mate, Yudhoyono selected M. Jusuf Kalla, a well-known businessman who had previously been affiliated with Golkar. This choice reflected his campaign strategy designed to bridge the Islamic-nationalist divide. This strategy proved to be remarkably successful in the first round of the presidential elections, when Yudhoyono's coalition of parties headed by the Democrat Party gained a plurality, but remained vulnerable to a possible majority coalition in the runoff against Megawati.[41] (See Table 12.3.)

The final election on September 20, 2004, tended to focus on Megawati's performance as president over the previous three years. S. B. Yudhoyono stressed four main issues in his campaigning, promising to stimulate the economy, to curb separatism, to fight corruption, and to counter terrorism. The slow recovery of the Indonesian economy, the high level of corruption, and the high unemployment rate were liabilities that detracted from Megawati's support and were issues that were readily exploited by Yudhoyono. Both candidates avoided the key issues that had previously energized Islamic politics, such as the status of Sharia law and the extent of public support for Islamic in-

Table 12.3 First-Round Presidential Election, July 5, 2004

For President	Party	For Vice President	Party	Percentage of Votes
Wiranto	Golkar	Solahuddin Wahid	PKB	22.15
Megawati Sukarnoputri	PDI-P	Hasyim Muzadi	NU	26.61
Amien Rais	PAN	Siswono Yudo Husodo	PBR	14.66
S. B. Yudhoyono	DP	M. Jusuf Kalla	Golkar	33.57
Hamzah Haz	PPP	Agum Gumelar		3.01

Sources: François Raillon, "Islam and Democracy: Indonesia's 2004 Election and Beyond," (Brussels, CNRS, May 6, 2004), 1–11, www.eias.org/specialbriefing/islam0605/raillon.pdf; Netherlands Institute for Multiparty Democracy, "Indonesian Election Monitor #9," June 9, 2004, www.nimd.org; *The Jakarta Post,* "The Final Results of July 5 Presidential Election," citing General Elections Commission, www.thejakartapost.com/Pres_Leg_Tally.htm.

stitutions. When the votes were finally tabulated, Yudhoyono gained 60.6 percent to Megawati's 39.4 percent of the total vote. Megawati was so distraught by the tenor of the campaign and her dismal support that she declined to meet with him to arrange for a smooth transition. On October 20, 2004, Yudhoyono and his running mate Jusuf Kalla were installed as president and vice president in an inauguration that Megawati chose not to attend.[42]

The Presidency of Susilo Bambang Yudhoyono

Yudhoyono was the first president of Indonesia to enter office by the direct popular vote of the electorate. Although he gained a decisive mandate, he then faced the problem of having only minority support in Parliament. His Democrat Party held only 56 seats in the 550-seat DPR, winning only 7.45 percent of the votes in the April 2004 national elections. To provide support for his administration, President Yudhoyono formed a coalition with the United Development Party (PPP), the National Mandate Party (PAN), the Prosperous Justice Party (PKS), and various smaller parties already grouped together as Democratic Pioneer Star (BPD). This enlarged coalition relied heavily on Islamic-based parties that avoided raising sensitive Islamic issues. Adopting the name "People's Coalition," it secured support of 233 seats in the DPR. The first plenary sessions of the DPR revealed that President Yudhoyono headed a minority government, since the president failed to get approval for his nominees for the chairmanships of the eleven powerful DPR commissions that controlled the legislative agenda of Parliament.

The effective majority in the DPR was led by Megawati Sukarnoputri, who formed what was called the "Nationhood Coalition," composed of her Indonesian Democratic Party–Struggle (PDI-P), Golkar, the Reform Star Party (PBR), and the Prosperous Peace Party (PDS). This coalition also gained unpledged support from the National Awakening Party (PKB) to give it approximately 300 seats and thus a clear majority in the DPR. With a deadlock between the president and the DPR from its very first sessions, it became apparent that some form of power-sharing would have to be negotiated if the Indonesian government was not to become paralyzed in an extended power struggle.[43] After a period of boycotts and threats of political stalemate, agreements were worked out to allocate commission chairmanships proportionately and President Yudhoyono formed a "rainbow cabinet" comprised of representatives from all the major parties in the DPR. In effect, these agreements established rather narrow political parameters within which the new administration could operate.

The looming threat to President Yudhoyono's presidency became much less formidable one month after the new administration took office. Vice President Jusuf Kalla decided to contest for the leadership of his party and won the election in October as chairman of Golkar. With this victory, Kalla shifted

Golkar's bloc of 127 seats to the government side. This action also gave him the support of a larger bloc of votes in parliament than the president controlled through his Democrat Party. With this shift in power, the new administration increased its support within the DPR from 42 percent, to a majority of 66 percent. After Kalla gained the leadership of Golkar, the opposition Nationhood Coalition dissolved as an entity, but the political fragmentation of power remained a salient feature of the political landscape.[44]

Barely two months after Yudhoyono assumed office, an earthquake-induced tsunami ravaged Aceh and the western shores of North Sumatra. The enormity of this natural disaster presented the Yudhoyono administration with its biggest test. Could it deliver emergency assistance and disaster relief to the half million homeless survivors as well as handling the enormous influx of international aid workers and the massive stream of supplies donated from around the world? Most news reports on the aid operations gave the new Indonesian administration high marks for its efforts to address this cataclysmic emergency. However, as the aid effort evolved through various stages of relief and infrastructure reconstruction, it became apparent that Indonesian authorities were divided over policies and often worked at cross-purposes with each other. As explained in Chapter 11, Yudhoyono had enunciated a strategy of seeking a political solution to the Aceh conflict, at the same time that steady pressure was mounted on the insurgents by the security forces. He expected to secure the cooperation of moderate the Aceh elites who were to be offered favorable inducements to support a peace process. Following the tsunami, Yudhoyono supported peace talks with the GAM leaders, but Vice President Kalla argued for intense pursuit of the GAM forces and their leaders. On January 12, 2005, Kalla announced that the thirty countries engaged in relief work in Aceh would have to leave by March 26, and foreign troops must leave even sooner. Of the 35,000 Indonesian troops in Aceh, 15,000 were supporting relief efforts, while 20,000 were assigned to security operations against GAM. Yudhoyono later modified Kalla's hard line against foreign relief workers and downplayed reports that Kalla was "running the show." Even so, serious policy differences within the cabinet could not be concealed.[45]

During the first half year of his administration, President Yudhoyono gave high priority to establishing contacts with foreign governments. He made official visits to Egypt, Singapore, the United States, Australia, and China. These actions revealed that President Yudhoyono was charting a course to reintegrate Indonesia into the global political and economic system, while also stressing Indonesia's Islamic identity and cultural heritage.[46] He was implicitly promising the international community, foreign investors, and the world's tourists that the Indonesian government would play an important role in defining Islam as a religion that stresses democracy, tolerance, a modern productive workforce, and peaceful resolution of domestic conflicts. Such conditions would be essential to revive a market-oriented economy and restore international confidence that Indonesia was a safe and productive partner for investment and a hospitable site for its previously lucrative tourist trade. What remained ambiguous was how Yudhoyono proposed to promote this vision of a modernist, democratic, tolerant, and peaceful Islam, and what actions would be taken to restrain or convert those Indonesians committed to radical revolutionary Islam.

Islamist Resurgence and "Direct Action" Politics

At the time of Yudhoyono's inauguration as president in October 2004, the issue of Sharia reform came to Indonesia's Parliament for consideration. Prior to the election, the Religious Affairs Ministry had selected a team to examine existing Islamic laws and to propose revisions. The leader of the revision team explained that some existing Islamic laws failed to meet universal principles of Islam, "such as equality, brotherhood and justice, basic principles of civil society including pluralism, gender equality, human rights and democracy."[47] The most far-reaching revisions proposed in the draft report, entitled "Compilation of Islamic Law," provided for the legalization of interfaith marriages, the prohibition of polygamy, and the promotion of gender equality regarding marriage, divorce settlements, and inheritance. This report was praised by the Islamic Liberal Network but was severely condemned by a leader of the Indonesian Mujahideen Council, who referred to the draft proposals as the "Compilation of the Devil's Law" and asserted, "If we follow this, we can become apostates."[48] Prosperous Justice Party, Crescent and Star Party, and United Development Party vigorously opposed the proposed changes to existing Sharia laws, while Nahdlatul Ulama and Muhammadiyah were less critical but unwilling to support the proposals.

Several weeks before the Sharia reform report was released to the public, Nadhlatul Ulama and Muhammadiyah agreed on a model of Sharia reform called "deformalisation." Abdul Mukti, chairman of Muhammadiyah's youth wing explained: "The overemphasis on formality and symbolism has drained Islam of its ethical and humane dimension. . . . The first mission of deformalisation is to recover this missing dimension." The second mission is "to separate the sharia from political realms."[49] The practical effect of the "deformalisation" agreement enabled Sharia reform to die in committee without a public vote.

The political regime of President Yudhoyono projected the image of a cautious but progressive leader supported by a reform-minded, but divided, coalition. The Islamists remained a visible but powerful minority waiting for an opportunity to reassert their presence on the Indonesian political scene. In June 2005, without warning, a crowd appeared at the Ahmadiyah headquarters and educational center in Bogor, West Java, known as Mubarak Campus. The crowd hurled stones, broke windows, and destroyed property before dispersing. A month later, on July 15, a larger crowd of 10,000 appeared at the same site, armed with staves and clubs. The attackers claimed to be enforcing the fatwa issued by the Indonesian Ulama Council twenty-one years earlier that had banned Ahmadiyah teachings as heretical.[50] The government had never endorsed that fatwa, but the hostile attackers demanded that Ahmadiyah facilities be closed immediately. Without provocation, the assembled crowd damaged buildings, burned library books, and set fire to the women's dormitory. More than 390 police officers were present at the campus but the police never intervened to deter or arrest attackers. Instead, they detained about 500 of the defending Ahmadis and after the attackers finally left the scene, the police closed the damaged Ahmadiyah facilities. The next day, Indonesia's director general of Islamic affairs, A. Qadir Basalamah, stated that the teachings of Ahmadiyah are against Islam and that Ahmadiyah followers were banned "from propagating the teachings, as it may create conflict." The local Bogor Regency authorities ordered a halt to all Ahmadiyah activities, and the Bogor Police enforced that order.[51]

This assault on the Ahmadiyah headquarters and educational facilities coincided with the annual meetings of the Indonesian Ulama Council (MUI). That body, representing Indonesia's ulama, convened under the leadership of Maruf Amin as chairman, and with Din Syamsuddin, recently elected chairman of Muhammadiyah, as the secretary-general of MUI. President Yudhoyono attended the opening session of the MUI, and his presence gave added prestige and public attention to the sessions. During the final sessions of the MUI congress, a series of eleven proposed fatwas were read to the 300 participants and approved without debate or opposition. On the issue of the Ahmadiyah community, the earlier fatwa from 1984 that had condemned the Ahmadiyah as murtad (heresy) was reaffirmed and its scope was expanded to ban the Ahmadiyah organization and freeze all its activities and assets. Another fatwa stated that "liberalism, secularism and pluralism contradict Islamic teachings." On the subject of marriage, a fatwa defended polygamy as permitted in Islam and condemned those wanting to change its provisions. One fatwa declared that interfaith marriages were haram and were prohibited for all Muslims. Another fatwa forbade interfaith prayers unless led by a Muslim, and women were banned from leading prayers whenever Muslim men were present.[52]

After these new fatwas were announced, the MUI chairman Maruf Amin explained that the fatwa declaring liberalism, secularism, and pluralism to be forbidden under Islam, had been issued in response to the doctrines and activities of the Liberal Islam Network (JIL) and the Muhammadiyah Youth Intellectuals Network (JIMM).[53] Din Syamsuddin explained that the MUI was not against social and political pluralism—just religious pluralism: "If you look at what the idea of religious pluralism is, it's the idea that you embrace all religions as the same. It says there's no absolute truth in one religion. The ulama in the MUI see this as a contradiction to Islam, which is the absolute truth."[54]

The assault on the Ahmadiyah compound, followed by the fatwas of the Indonesian Ulama Council, set off a sharp public debate over human rights and religious freedoms versus the claims of fundamentalist Muslims that public authorities must defend the primacy of Islam as defined by the MUI. The counterclaims of other religions or the criticisms of "deviant and heretical Muslims" would not be tolerated. Azyumardi Azra, rector of the Islamic State University in Jakarta, and former president Abdurrahman Wahid headed a long list of Indonesian leaders and intellectuals who protested the actions of the MUI and the failure of the Bogor Police to protect citizens against civil rights violators. The International Crisis Group identified the Dewan Dakwah Islamiyah Indonesia, the Indonesian Committee for Islamic Solidarity, and the Islamic Defense Front as clandestine organizers of the assault on the Ahmadiyah complex.[55]

In the aftermath of the attack on Mubarak Campus, President Yudhoyono appeared to have capitulated to Islamist demands. After discussions with the president, the minister of religion Mahtuh Basyuni announced that "the teaching of Ahmadiyah is against Islam and therefore we forbid the propagation of this misleading faith."[56] However, as the political debate raged, the government decided that it would not dissolve the Indonesian Ahmadiyah Congregation (JAI) and it would not ban its teachings. Instead, government authorities suggested that the MUI should take the matter to court.[57] Since fatwas in Indonesia have no legal status unless the government endorses them, that left the issue open for court resolution.[58] Ahmadiyah leaders also considered legal action but came to the conclusion that Indonesian courts would provide no remedy.[59] Indonesia's regular courts, public prosecutors, and the police do not have a positive record of defending minority communities from actions of human rights violators. Behind the scenes, the issue of the status of Ahmadiyah festered without resolution. The MUI continued to accuse Ahmadis of heresy and blasphemy. Ahmadiyah communities were subject to periodic attacks by the FPI and other vigilante groups that destroyed Ahmadiyah mosques. Thousands of Ahmadis had their homes and villages torched and were forced to live in temporary shelters in abject poverty while concealing their religious convictions and their identity.

In January 2008, the attorney general's office finally decided not to outlaw Ahmadiyah, citing a "12 point explanation" submitted by Ahmadiyah leaders of their beliefs. The Islamic Community Forum (FUI) and the FPI condemned the decision of the attorney general's office and promised to organize "mass actions" to force Ahmadiyah followers to repent. They demanded that Ahmadis renounce their beliefs, destroy their holy book, and submit to the Indonesian Ulama Council for guidance and return to the right path.[60]

Perhaps in response to these attacks, one group of Ahmadis formed an offshoot sect, calling themselves al-Qiyadah al-Islamiyah. Under their leader, Ahmad Mushaddeq, that sect began gathering a following of about 41,000 members in Bogor, Jakarta, Yogjakarta, Padang, and Batam. The FPI and the Muslim Youth Front declared this sect to be propagating "false teachings" that were heretical. They accused al-Qiyadah members of failing to pray five times a day and not being required to take the haj pilgrimage. Its leader was accused of proclaiming himself as the next prophet, thereby denying that Muhammad was the "last and final prophet" of Allah. With this "evidence," the MUI issued a fatwa declaring al-Qiyadah to be a deviant heresy and charged its members with blasphemy against Islam. The Muslim Youth Front staged a rally in West Java demanding that Ahmad Mushaddeq be sentenced to death. The FPI announced that it would launch raids against al-Qiyadah communes if government authorities failed to act.[61]

After the MUI issued the fatwa banning al-Qiyadah, Indonesia's attorney general announced that the government would soon confirm that ban and would prohibit its teachings. Ahmad Mushaddeq surrendered to the Jakarta Police and admitted that he had been "misguided." Even so, he was charged with blasphemy, and national police chief General Sutanto issued an order to arrest all other leaders of al-Qiyadah, who could face a penalty of 10 years for "insulting Islam." He explained that his order had two objectives: to prevent false teachings, and to prevent potential violence against those accused of "false teachings," who would be imprisoned both for their beliefs and for their safety.[62]

In November 2007, Indonesia's Supreme Court sentenced another religious leader, who claimed to be a reincarnation of the Prophet Muhammad, to three years imprisonment for blasphemy. Based on that precedent, the attorney general's office announced that it would pursue blasphemy charges against Ahmad Mushaddeq despite his earlier admission that his teachings were "misguided."[63] Religious freedom was trapped between conflicting legal principles, inadequate public protection of minority rights, and vigilante terrorism.

A coalition of Islamist groups, including the FPI and Abu Bakar Ba'asyir's Majelis Mujahidin Indonesia, organized massive street demonstrations culminating in a march of 10,000 on the presidential palace, demanding that Ahmadiyah be dissolved. On June 9, 2008, the day of that Islamist demonstration, the Religious Affairs Ministry resealed a decree that allowed Ahmadiyah to continue to worship provided it did not attract any other worshipers. Later, the ministry spokesman stated that the public could monitor the implementation of the report on Ahmadiyah and the earlier MUI report on "deviant sects." In effect, this was an open invitation for vigilante action against minority Muslim sects, and by implication against any "unregistered" minority religious groups, such as Christian "home churches."[64]

The Breeding Ground of Radicalism

When President Yudhoyono assumed office in October 2004, he enjoyed a commanding mandate with 62 percent support of voters and a favorable international environment of high world economic growth, record-high energy prices, and very low world interest rates. The Indonesian economy had never fully recovered from the economic crisis of 1998 and was plagued by low economic growth of around 4.5 percent, high inflation, very high unemployment, and a negative flow of direct foreign investment. Indonesia had major economic and social problems, and Yudhoyoyo promised to address those problems with reforms and decisive pragmatic actions. Because of his decision to form a rainbow cabinet with members from nine political parties, the process of decisionmaking became partially paralyzed with many ministers being appointed for political reasons rather than being qualified for their assigned responsibilities.[65]

During the first year of his administration, President Yudhoyono made a serious effort to deal with the problem of corruption through the establishment of the Corruption Eradication Commission, the Financial Transactions Report Analysis Center, and the Anticorruption Court. A number of prominent officials and public figures were brought to trial, but the issue of corruption was so widespread and was so much a part of the culture of public services that these bodies made only a slight impact on established and well-concealed practices. When cases of corruption were brought to trial, the judiciary gave most accused suspended sentences. The issues of the efficiency of the public services and the low pay of civil servants were not addressed, and apart from a few convictions, the anticorruption campaign did little to prevent the civil servants collecting "administrative charges" for their services.[66]

By the end of the first year in office, public confidence in Yudhoyono began to wane. While democratic reforms had been consolidated, the pace of decisions for reform of the economy and of social services had lagged. Between February 2005 and March 2006, the numbers of Indonesians living below the poverty line (US$1 per day) had increased by 3.95 million people to reach a total of almost 40 million, representing 17.75 percent of the population. About 12 million people were unemployed and when the unemployed were combined with the underemployed, the total comprised 40 percent of a total workforce of 105 million. President Yudhoyono had promised to halve unemployment by 2009, but in early 2006 that figure was instead increasing at an alarming rate.[67]

The challenge of low economic growth and massive poverty could not be addressed by piecemeal policies. For Yudhoyono, the solution lay in the revival of export-oriented industries that had generated Indonesia's spectacular economic growth during the 1980s and 1990s. That strategy required prudent fiscal policies, ending massive investment in state subsidies for favored industries, and initiating reforms in secular education. Reforms were also needed for the judiciary, for labor laws, for increasing the efficiency of government, to attract foreign investment, and to eliminate the lingering threats of terrorist attacks against Western targets and personnel. In short, Indonesia needed to compete on world markets with the more dynamic economies of China, India, South Korea, Japan, Taiwan, Malaysia, and Thailand. This multidimensional strategy involved participation in the economic dynamism of globalization.

These were not policies that Islamists could support. Islamist parties gained much of their support from those who had attended Indonesia's 38,500 madrasahs. Indonesia's workforce in 2006 ranked lowest in education in comparison to its neighbors. Only 0.03 percent of the Indonesian workforce had a university degree, and only 39 percent of the primary school–age population advanced to secondary school. About 21 percent of students at the junior-secondary level were enrolled in Islamic schools that provided few employable skills but instead propagated a mix of radical Islamic doctrines that frequently depicted non-Muslims and "foreign influences" as mortal enemies.[68] In effect, the Islamists represented those sectors of Indonesian society most affected by chronic unemployment and poverty, yet their political leaders were unable or unwilling to devise coherent economic and social programs to address the enormous cluster of problems generated by poverty, unemployment, and low productivity. Islamist politicians defended policies of government assistance and subsidies to the poor, but were unwilling to support Indonesia's active participation in a globalized economy in order to create jobs for those trapped in poverty.

Although only about 16 percent of Indonesian voters supported hard-line Islamist parties in 1999, the elections of 2004 gave Islamists an enhanced stake in political affairs. In 2004, the Islamist vote increased to 21 percent. In 1999, the Prosperous Justice Party gained less than 1.5 percent of the vote. By 2004, in the elections to Parliament, PKS had increased its vote to 7.5 percent and gained forty-five seats in Parliament. That party modeled its ideology on the works of Hasan al-Banna and Sayyid Qutb of the Muslim Brotherhood but suspended their antidemocracy and antitolerance ideology to maximize their role in a multiparty coalition. Their leaders called for the creation of an Islamic caliphate but, in the 2004 election, focused on the primary theme of eliminating corruption. The PKS was one of nine parties in the "rainbow coalition" formed by President Yudhoyono.[69]

With a politically divided cabinet and a relatively weak party base from his own Democrat Party, President Yudhoyono became overly cautious, tending to make no decisions that created controversy, avoiding many of the difficult issues of administrative and judicial reforms, and postponing long-term economic recovery strategies. A combination of factors kept foreign investments at a low level. An unfavorable taxation system, a corrupt and inefficient bureaucracy, weak law enforcement, and poor infrastructure all contributed to low investor confidence in Indonesia. But, perhaps the two most important detriments for foreign investors were the unpredictable and politically tainted judicial system and the lack of credible security against terrorist acts and threats from antiforeign vigilante actions. Indonesia was ranked as one of the worst countries in the world for enforcement of contracts—ranked at 145 out of 155.[70] Its judicial system, including public prosecutors, responded to shifting public sentiments, coercive threats, and political favoritism to create legal ambiguity and a low respect for the law.[71]

Rule of Law Compromised

A few examples of court decisions will provide a glimpse into the problem of judicial reform. On June 14, 2006, Abu Bakar Ba'asyir was released from prison. The Indonesian court took a very restrictive view of what evidence would be allowed in his trial, and the prosecution made a dismal presentation of what evidence was permitted. Although arrested terrorists in Singapore gave detailed accounts of how Ba'asyir provided ideological directives for terrorist attacks, including the Bali bombings, the Indonesian court refused to accept their evidence. The Indonesian police arrested more than 200 Jemaah Islamiyah militants who cited Ba'asyir as their inspirational and ideological leader, but all charges linking him to the Bali and Marriott bombings and other terrorist attacks were eventually dropped. Instead, he was convicted on minor charges of immigration violations and sentenced to four years in prison. With remission, he served a sentence of only twenty-five-and-a-half months. During his confinement, prison authorities allowed him to be served by seven acolytes who acted as his bodyguards and who enabled him to preach his version of radical Islam by tape recordings and by cell phone. Upon his release, Ba'asyir reiterated his claim that "Jemaah Islamiyah does not exist," and he resumed his call for jihad against the United States and Australia, whom he called "the real terrorists."[72] When he was released from prison, many observers believed that the police would closely watch him and that his rhetoric would have little impact on Indonesian politics. However, after his release, Ba'asyir was able to reenergize the clandestine network of supporters who were lying low and avoiding detection by security authorities.[73]

Earlier reference was made to the trial of President Suharto's son, popularly known as "Tommy" Suharto. He had been convicted of first-degree murder by hiring two gunmen to kill a Supreme Court justice, Syafiuddin Kartasasmita, who had previously sentenced Tommy Suharto to eighteen months in prison for corruption in a multimillion-dollar real estate scam and for fleeing from justice. Following his conviction for murder, he was sentenced to only fifteen years in jail. During his incarceration, he was housed in special luxury accommodations and was regularly allowed out of jail to visit Jakarta for about a month at a time. In 2005, the Supreme Court cut five years off his original light sentence, and with other remissions, he was released after having served only four years in prison for crimes that provided for a maximum penalty of death.[74]

An earlier account made reference to the violent attacks by radical Muslim militias on Christian communities in Ambon, Maluku, and Central Sulawesi. In the area of Poso, over 1,000 people died in Muslim-Christian conflicts from 1999 to 2002. In August 2001, Laskar Jihad and Laskar Jundullah sent their forces to Poso to escalate that conflict, killing Christians, burning their villages, and forcing many Poso Christians to take refuge in the predominantly Christian lake-side town of Tentena. In response to these attacks against Christian communities, three Catholics from Flores—Fabianus Tibo, Dominggus da Silva, and Marius Riwu—arrived in Poso in May 2000 to help with the rescue of Christians from villages being attacked and burned by radical Islamic militias. They also volunteered for the local Christian defense militia and gained mid-level leadership roles in the local Christian defense force. By May and June 2000, the Christian militia mounted counterattacks against Islamic militants at the Walisongo Pesantren, where about 100 Muslims were killed.

In April 2001, Tibo, da Silva, and Riwu were tried for the massacres of Muslims in the Poso conflict. Because no witnesses could confirm their direct participation in murders, the case rested on a charge that the defendants had incited other people to murder, based on their alleged leadership positions in the Christian militia. Their trial was conducted during mass demonstrations of Muslims demanding the death penalty. All three defendants were sentenced to death and they remained in prison pending various appeals.[75]

Meanwhile, the police and provincial authorities attempted to prosecute those who were determined to continue their revenge killings and terror tactics. Laskar Jihad had spearheaded attacks against Christian communities for more than two years in Maluku and Central Sulawesi, during which more than 9,000 people were killed, a substantial majority of whom were Christians. The leader of Laskar Jihad, Jafar Umar Thalib, was finally brought to trial and accused of incitement to violence in April 2002, with the charge based on his speech imploring Muslims "to prepare our bombs, and ready our guns" to wage jihad against Christians. The charges alleged that his "hate speech" led two days later to a massacre of twelve Christians and the torching of thirty homes at the village of Soya near Ambon by the Laskar Jihad militia that Thalib commanded. That trial ended on January 30, 2002, with Thalib's acquittal on all charges.[76] His close affiliation with politicians and high-level Indonesian Army officers may have protected him from punishment for the many atrocities carried out by his militia units. Two days prior to Thalib's acquittal, a Christian leader, Alex Manuputty, was sentenced to three years in prison, not for killing anyone, but for "promoting separatism." During the period from 1998 until 2006, over 150 people, both Muslims and Christians, were put on trial in Sulawesi for murder, arson, and other crimes of violence. Most of those who were convicted received sentences of five years or less, with the maximum sentence of fifteen years imprisonment, except for the three Catholic militia members who were sentenced to death.

Camouflaged Jemaah Islamiyah Revived

In 2005, President Yudhoyono acknowledged that the threat of terrorism remained a continuing concern for security services. In an address at the Asia-Europe Editors Forum in Jakarta, he stated, "We know that the terrorist cells are still active. They are still hiding, recruiting, networking, trying to find new funding sources, and even planning."[77]

One month after President Yudhoyono's ominous warning, three suicide bombers entered a crowded and popular restaurant in Bali on October 1, 2005, and detonated their vest bombs in near simultaneous explosions. The location was not far from the nightclub destroyed in the first Bali bombing of October 2002. This second Bali bombing killed 22 people and wounded 104 others.[78] Identified in the local press as "Bali II," this blast appeared to be designed as a reminder to the Indonesian public that Jemaah Islamiyah was still active and that its political activities depended on inspiring new supporters and recruits for its radical Islamist cause. The Indonesian police identified Azahari bin Husein and Noordin Top as the two prime suspects who had been bomb-makers for the Bali I, Marriott, and Australian Embassy bombings. They had successfully eluded capture by moving to "safe houses" maintained by jihadi sympathizers.[79]

After police gained vital information from the arrest of a subordinate of Azahari, they mounted a predawn raid on November 9, 2005, at a safe house on the outskirts of Semarang. As police approached the compound, one occupant set off a bomb, blowing the roof off the house. Azahari appeared suddenly and was killed by police before he could trigger the vest-bomb he was wearing. At the safe house, police discovered a cache of thirty bombs ready for use and primed to explode. Noordin Top was not present when the police made their raid and remained beyond detection and apprehension. A few days later, the police recovered a stash of weapons and bombs from two storage dumps near Ponogoro, in East Java.[80]

For two years, the Indonesian police unsuccessfully pursued Noordin Top as their most important terrorist suspect. Later, he announced the formation of a new group called Tandzim Qaedat al Jihad dedicated to continuing an anti-Western bombing campaign. By early 2007, Indonesian intelligence officials concluded that Noordin Top had probably fled to the southern Philippines to seek refuge with radical Islamist groups there. Although there were no further bombings in Java or Bali, there was plenty of evidence that Jemaah Islamiyah was being revived, and militants were preparing for renewed campaigns of violence and terror. By 2005, they began to focus once again on Sulawesi as a prime base for their next campaign against infidels.

Jihad in Poso

Within a few years after the founding of Jemaah Islamiyah, Central Sulawesi became a critical link in an international web for the propagation of an Islamist revolution in Southeast Asia. Earlier chapters traced the religious conflicts that were exploited by aspiring power seekers to make Sulawesi Muslims especially receptive to Islamist radicalism. Even more important, the small Central Sulawesi port of Poso provided a ready link with Malaysia and the southern

Philippines via native sail craft and high-speed boats used by smugglers and illegal immigrants to cross porous international borders. For Jemaah Islamiyah, Poso became a key hub for the transportation of mujahideen, munitions, and money to and from training bases in Mindanao and to operational locations elsewhere in Southeast Asia.

In 2002, the International Crisis Group identified three militia networks in the Poso area, all utilizing the name Laskar Jundullah—meaning "Army of Allah." Added to this mix of militias was Mujahideen KOMPAK, sponsored by the Islam Propagation Council of Indonesia and allied with Jemaah Islamiyah. Together this web of Islamist paramilitary forces operated guerrilla-training camps in Mindanao in collaboration with the Moro Islamic Liberation Front.[81]

In Central Sulawesi, violence between Christian and Muslim militias subsided after the signing of the Malino Accord in February 2002 between thirty-five Christian and thirty-five Muslim leaders from the Palu-Poso area. As part of that agreement, local Christian and Muslim militias agreed to surrender their arms, and Laskar Jihad returned most of its forces to Java. However, in effect, the Christian communities became more vulnerable, because the local Laskar Jundullah contingents remained in the area and were able to renew their supply of arms. During Abu Bakar Ba'asyir's initial trial for complicity with the Bali bombings, he claimed that Jemaah Islamiyah did not exist. Active members of Jemaah Islamiyah received the clear message that they avoid any knowledge of that network. The multinetwork links between militias and Jemaah Islamiyah remained, but the Jemaah Islamiyah name vanished.[82]

In the years following the Malino Accord, periodic attacks continued to be mounted against Christian communities in Central Sulawesi. These attacks were launched by militants affiliated with a local radical Islamic pesantren that had been loosely allied with Jemaah Islamiyah and with Pondok Ngruki in Java, founded and led by Abu Bakar Ba'asyir. In Sulawesi, the center of the complex of jihadi attackers was at the Ulil Aldab Pesantren for girls in Poso and the al-Amanah Pesantren for boys located in Landangan, about 9 kilometers from Poso. Both schools were under the leadership of Adnan Arsal, who commanded a Laskar Jundullah militia unit. When local police attempted to identify suspects of violence that were believed to be hiding at the pesantren, the students and staff would raise an alarm and mount demonstrations that effectively protected suspects from arrest or interrogation.[83]

In August 2006, Adnan Arsal organized mass demonstrations to demand that the three Christian militia members who had been sentenced to death be promptly executed. The three condemned men appealed to President Yudhoyono for clemency in April 2005, but that appeal was denied. The Indonesian court ruled that they were to be executed on August 12, 2006, but when European leaders, including Pope Benedict XVI, appealed for leniency, the executions were postponed to September 20. On that date, Tibo, Riwu, and da Silva were taken to the Palu airfield and executed by firing squad. Their bodies were not delivered to their next of kin, but buried secretly. In retaliation, two Muslim fish traders were killed while driving through a Christian village, but most Christians in Central Sulawesi remained subdued because of a large police presence and an awareness of the risks of sectarian conflict. The largest protests against the executions were on Flores Island where the three executed men had family and their homes.[84]

The release from prison of Abu Bakar Ba'asyir, the execution of the three Christian militia leaders, and the overall increase in the imprint of radical Islam appeared to have changed the political landscape. Some of the more radical Islamist leaders may have assumed that they enjoyed impunity from the law and that jihadi politics could claim center stage in Indonesian politics. Indonesian police and intelligence gained information that Jemaah Islamiyah had received instructions to implement the strategy of "targeting Western interests" and "fomenting sectarian conflicts." For Indonesia, JI operatives concluded that large industries and plants were too well guarded, but that "sectarian conflicts" could be more easily rekindled.[85]

In Central Sulawesi, sectarian conflict was already being waged. The Ulil Aldab Pesantren located in a shantytown subdivision of Poso provided an ideal center of operations. Located amidst the rubble of a landslide wasteland area called Tanah Runtuh (fallen earth), the school operated by Adnan Arsal was surrounded by a cluster of houses providing sanctuary for scores of mujahideen fighters and recruits. In 2002, a Jemaah Islamiyah operative named Hasanuddin arrived at Tanah Runtuh to organize a more efficient and well-trained fighting force. He was a graduate of the Moro Islamic Liberation Front's Camp Abu Bakar, and after his arrival, he married Adnan Arsal's daughter, Aminah. Under his leadership, the pace of attacks on Christians increased in number and intensity.

The attacks included the beheading of a village headman, bombings in the central markets of Poso and Tentena, and in October 2005, Hasanuddin and two other mujahideen from Tanah Runtuh attacked four Christian schoolgirls with machetes. One girl escaped after being slashed, and the other three were killed and beheaded. Later, the three heads were delivered to a Christian community with a written message that they were an 'Id al-Fitr gift. In October 2006, the leader of the Central Sulawesi Protestant Church, Reverend Irianto Kongoli, was killed by a sharpshooter who fled on a motorcycle. The local police identified potential suspects but may not have collected sufficient evidence to make arrests. The police were also fearful of triggering a violent reaction from the local Muslim community at Tanah Runtuh.

Based on information obtained from police raids in Java, the local police arrested Hasuniddin on May 9, 2006, and within a few days arrested three others who confessed to taking part in the beheadings of the three Christian schoolgirls. After the assassination of Reverend Kongoli, President Yudhoyono ordered top police officials and a Brimob contingent of 700 men to Poso to investigate that murder. On October 22, a combined police and Brimob force approached Tanah Runtuh but were repelled by a hail of bullets from local defenders. A week later, police arrested fifteen suspects with twenty-nine additional suspects undetected and in hiding.[86] After that incident, Adnan Arsal flew to Jakarta, where he called for Muslim militias to join a new jihad campaign in Poso.

Following the failed Brimob raid, police attempted to secure the voluntary surrender of the twenty-nine hiding suspects. Adnan Arsal announced that their surrender would come only if Christians responsible for past violence were prosecuted. Finally, President Yudhoyono intervened by ordering two anti-terrorist Densus 88 rapid-reaction units to Poso to back the Brimob contingent sent earlier. On January 11, 2007, a combined contingent of police, Brimob, and Densus 88 units mounted a raid on Tanah Runtuh, resulting in eighteen militants arrested, nine militants killed, and a large cache of weapons, bombs, and explosives seized. On January 22, police staged a second raid on Tanah Runtuh, during which one officer and thirteen militants were killed, and twenty suspects were arrested.[87]

In response to these events, Adnan Arsal issued a call to arms from supporters, and in Java, Abu Bakar Ba'asyir pronounced jihad against what he referred to as the "*thoghut* [anti-Islamic] government of Indonesia." In Java, the Laskar Jihad militia that had been officially disbanded in 2002 was reactivated and prepared to travel to Poso. The police in Central Sulawesi warned that security forces would interdict any nonlocal militia forces attempting to land in Sulawesi.[88]

Evidence from the Tanah Runtuh raid revealed that Abu Dujana became military commander of Jemaah Islamiyah following the death of Azahari Husin in 2005. Following those leads, a Densus 88 squad mounted a series of raids near Surabaya to arrest seven men, including Abu Dujana, and in December, he was charged in court for involvement with the 2002 Bali bombing, the Marriott Hotel bombing in 2003, and the 2004 Australian Embassy bombing. He was also charged with harboring Noordin Top and Azahari Husin. In an interview with reporters, Abu Dujana confirmed that Abu Bakar Ba'asyir remained as spiritual leader of Jemaah Islamiyah.[89]

Indonesia's Evolving Counterterror Strategies

With the intervention of federal police and security forces in October 2006, Vice President Jusuf Kalla played a leading role in devising a strategy to check hostilities and restore amicable relations between Muslim and Christian communities in Sulawesi. In 2001, he had facilitated the signing of the first Malino Declaration, whereby Muslim and Christian leaders agreed to end three years of deadly conflicts. With the obvious failure of that agreement, Kalla secured the approval of President Yudhoyono in late 2006 to devise new programs and policies designed to resolve interreligious conflicts in Sulawesi. Vice President Kalla was known as a hard-line defender of Islamic interests, having actively supported the call to jihad against Christian militias in 2000 and a year later sponsored the Malino Declaration that was expected to bring peace but also left the Christian communities largely defenseless. Now, following the escalating attacks on Christian settlements in 2005, new policy initiatives were needed and Kalla's role in policymaking was largely concealed from public view.[90]

As a first priority, Kalla insisted on execution for the three Christian militia members who had been convicted of participation in two massacres at Muslim settlements. Two months after those executions, trials began in Jakarta during November 2006 for thirteen of the arrested Muslim suspects from Poso and Palu who were accused of killing Christians. Those trials finally concluded in December 2007. During the trials, many of the relatives of the victims expressed a willingness to forgive their assailants, and most of the accused expressed regret for their actions, promising not to repeat their attacks. The thirteen accused Muslim assailants were charged with killing forty-six Christian victims, including the leader of Sulawesi Christians and the three beheaded schoolgirls. Their trial ended with guilty convictions for all the accused Muslims, who were sentenced to from ten to twenty years' imprisonment. During those trials, another larger group of seventeen accused Christians were tried for killing two Muslims, and their trial also ended with a guilty verdict for all the accused, who were sentenced to from eight to fourteen years in prison.[91]

After the terrorist trials concluded in Jakarta, the government initiated a set of reconciliation measures for Central Sulawesi. At first, government officials considered closing Adnan Arsal's two pesantren schools at Tanah Runtuh and Landangan that had been the centers for Muslim militants. Although Adnan Arsal had been the putative head of Jemaah Islamiyah, he had never been convicted of any terrorist activities and he enjoyed wide popular support in Sulawesi. Therefore, it was politically difficult to close those two radical pesantren. Under Vice President Kalla's leadership, the government decided instead to build a new, "modern" pesantren called Ittihadul Ummah (Unity of the Ummah) that would be sponsored by Muhammadiyah to compete with Adnan Arsal's radical pesantren. By 2008, construction for this new pesantren was well underway at Tokorondo, about 8 kilometers from Poso. The government allocated US$1.7 million for this new facility, twenty-two buildings with accommodations for 480 students. Therefore, Poso Muslims will now be able to choose for their education between Muhammadiyah orthodoxy and Jemaah Islamiyah radicalism.

To address the issues of fairness, the government also allocated US$700,000 to upgrade the Protestant theological school in Tentena to convert it into the Christian University of Tentena (Universitas Kristen Tentena), which was expected to eventually have facilities for close to 400 students. Because of limited space at the existing theological school, the new university will need to construct facilities at a new campus site. To address the problems of ex-prisoners returning to civilian life, the government allocated US$5.8 million to provide cash grants of about $1,000 to Muslims returning from prison to the Poso District. A similar program was extended to Christians returning from prison after conviction for participation in militia-induced violence. Cash grants were also offered to ex-prisoners who joined together to form cooperative enterprises, involving such activities as fish-raising and auto repair.[92] Whether these measures would lead to reconciliation between Muslim and Christian communities was uncertain. By March 2008, Central Sulawesi had experienced no major violent incidents for over one year, but on May 2, 2008, a Muslim mob burnt the Christian village of Horale on Seram Island in Maluku. The village, housing 2,300 residents, was completely burned and twenty fishing boats were destroyed. Four Christians were killed and 56 were wounded. A police contingent arrived to protect the survivors, but there were no reports that any attackers had been arrested.[93]

The Jakarta trials of the thirteen Islamic militants from Poso and the reconciliation policies for Poso may have been effective in reducing local conflicts between Muslim and Christian communities in Sulawesi, but these actions had very little effect on the overall threats from militant groups throughout Indonesia. During 2007, the International Crisis Group made a survey of the capabilities of Jemaah Islamiyah following police raids against JI cells in Central and East Java. Based on police reports and documentary evidence, this report concluded that JI retained the capacity to reconstitute its ranks and that it had operational cells in most regions of Indonesia with a total of more than 900 active members. Within the organization, there were disputes about tactics, but these differences did not diminish their determination to continue with jihadi attacks that would be religiously justified to inspire and attract new recruits.[94] The existence of other radical militia groups, such as the Majelis Mujahidin Indonesia, KOMPAK, Front Pembala Islam, Laskar Jundullah, Laskar Mujahidin, and Laskar Jihad, provided ample opportunities for collaboration between militant paramilitary groups.

In 2003, Indonesia adopted antiterrorism laws relating to defined acts of terrorism, but Jemaah Islamiyah and other terrorist groups in Indonesia were not banned. In 1996, the UN Security Council 1267 Committee placed Abu Bakar Ba'asyir and Jemaah Islamiyah on the global terrorist list.[95] The Indonesian government promised to abide by Resolution 1267, but Indonesian officials argued that the government lacked the power to ban Jemaah Islamiyah because "it is not a formal organization." Yet, a total of 250 Islamic sects that are peaceful but are viewed as nonorthodox or "deviant" by the Majelis Ulama Indonesia have been banned and their leaders subject to criminal prosecution.

By contrast, JI and other radical groups have been allowed to engage in recruitment, propagation (dakwah), and fundraising, so long as overt terrorist acts are not committed. Indonesian authorities assume that it is better for Islamic radicals to become involved in nonviolent activities than to force them into hiding.[96]

A 2005 study of Indonesian book publishers revealed that about 10,000 books are produced each year in Indonesia and close to one-third of them are on Islam. Usually a book on Islam starts with a print run of about 3,000 copies, with some books selling over 100,000 copies. The International Crisis Group identified thirteen publishing conglomerates having links to Jemaah Islamiyah. These publishers are usually unregistered and headed by individuals who have been members of JI or are identified with the Indonesian Islamic Propagation Council (DDII). Their books are published with high-quality paper and graphics and sell for about US$2 a copy, which indicates that production costs are subsidized. About 400 to 500 titles are printed, mostly in Indonesian language, by these JI-linked publishing conglomerates, and their list of authors reads like a "Who's Who of Jihadis." These books openly disseminate salafiya jihadi ideology espousing and glorifying bombings and terror attacks against "kafir interests." These publications attract significant numbers of readers, generating new recruits and stimulating funding for radical Islamist groups. It is uncertain whether Indonesian authorities subject these publishing firms to any form of monitoring of their funding and of the activities of their financial supporters.[97]

Against the vast panorama of Indonesian politics, these events were but a small skirmish in an extended battle for the future of Islam. Yet, these events could also be viewed as a turning point in how that contest would unfold. The capacity of the Indonesian police to track down active terrorist cells had been proven effective ever since the first Bali bombing. Whether justice was served depended on the capabilities of judicial administration and on courts that were independent but not always professional and impartial. For President Yudhoyono, the main issue was how Islamic-inspired violence could be prevented and prosecuted without alienating the support of large numbers of Indonesian Muslims. He had gained large majorities from Muslim constituencies, and the Indonesian lower classes were desperately needing a government that could establish order and revive an economy that had been seriously damaged by more than eight years of violence, political chaos, and economic mismanagement. The militants have been very effective in waging a political battle for public support and were quick to dismiss as irrelevant and un-Islamic the esoteric doctrines of "impartial justice" and theories of "rule of law" as applied by a secular government.

The task ahead for President Yudhoyono's government was to generate wide public support for a system that protected the rights, liberties, and security of all citizens, as well as foreign visitors, regardless of religious affiliations and sectarian divisions. Those were issues that had been largely ignored by previous presidents of Indonesia. Because of divisions within his ruling coalition, President Yudhoyono approached those issues with timidity and without sufficient commitment and affirmative support from Indonesia's moderate Muslims who constitute a virtually silent majority.

Notes

1. International Crisis Group, *Indonesia: Overcoming Murder and Chaos in Maluku,* ICG Asia Report No. 10 (December 2000), Jakarta/Brussels.

2. Leo Suryadinata, *Elections and Politics in Indonesia* (Singapore: Institute of Southeast Asian Studies, 2002), 56–59; Kevin O'Rourke, *Reformasi: The Struggle for Power in Post-Soeharto Indonesia* (Crows Nest, Australia: Allen & Unwin, 2002), 174–178.

3. O'Rourke, *Reformasi,* 178–188. Suharto's most loyal henchmen managed the heavy infusion of paramilitary forces into Jakarta at the time of the MPR sessions. They attempted to create civil strife to undermine Habibie and pave the way for Suharto's return as a "strong man."

4. Dwight Y. King, *Half-Hearted Reform: Electoral Institutions and the Struggle for Democracy in Indonesia* (Westport, CT: Praeger, 2003), 47–74.

5. Ibid., 198–203; David Bourchier, "Habibie's Interregnum: *Reformasi*, Elections, Regionalism and the Struggle for Power," in Chris Manning and Peter Van Diermen (eds.), *Indonesia in Transition: Social Aspects of Reformasi and Crisis* (London: Zed Books, 2000), 16–19; Suryadinata, *Elections and Politics,* 85–101; National Democratic Institute, *The New Legal Framework for Elections in Indonesia: A Report of an NDI Assessment Team* (Washington, DC: National Democratic Institute for International Affairs, 1999).

6. O'Rourke, *Reformasi.* 203–243; Suryadinata, *Elections and Politics*, 92–101; King, *Half-Hearted Reform*, 75–104; Keith B. Richburg, "Indonesia Holds Its First Free Elections in 44 Years," *Washington Post,* June 8, 1999, A12.

7. Suryadinata, *Elections and Politics,* 105–109.

8. King, *Half-Hearted Reform,* 141–165.

9. When the regional representatives were finally chosen, Golkar gained sixty-two additional seats and PDI-P gained forty additional seats in the full MPR. O'Rourke, *Reformasi,* 297, citing "Kartu Golkar di Tangan Akbar," *Tajuk,* October 21, 1999.

10. Akbar Tanjung had been a cabinet minister from 1988 to 1999 and was elected chairman of Golkar in 1998. He was known as a reformist and also for being very politically astute. He displayed his Islamic credentials but was also open in his support for Pancasila.

11. O'Rourke, *Reformasi,* 307–312; Marcus Mietzner, "The 1999 General Session: Wahid, Megawati and the Fight for the Presidency," in Manning and Van Diermen, *Indonesia in Transition,* 39–57.

12. O'Rourke, *Reformasi,* 298–317; Suryadinata, *Elections and Politics,* 140–160; Angela Rabasa and Peter Chalk, *Indonesia's Transformation and the Stability of Southeast Asia* (Santa Monica, CA: Rand Corporation, 2001), 9–16.

13. Paulo Gorjão, "Abdurrahman Wahid's Presidency: What Went Wrong?" in Hadi Soesastro, Anthony L. Smith, and Han Mui Ling (eds.), *Governance in Indonesia: Challenges Facing the Megawati Presidency* (Singapore: Institute of Southeast Asian Studies, 2003), 13–15; Stephen Sherlock, *Struggling to Change: The Indonesian Parliament in an Era of Reformasi: A Report on the Structure and Operation of the*

Dewan Perwakilan Rakyat (DPR) (Canberra: Centre for Democratic Institutions, Australian National University, January 2003).

14. Spokespersons for Indonesia's major parties candidly expressed their views of Wahid's leadership at a forum held in Singapore on May 4, 2001. Overall their evaluations are remarkably consistent. Ade Komarudin et al., *Trends in Indonesia: Visions for Indonesia's Future* (Singapore: Institute of Southeast Asian Studies, 2001), 1–47.

15. Former president Suharto was able to avoid prosecution for a corruption case involving US$570 million when the South Jakarta District Court ruled that Suharto's health made him physically and mentally unfit to stand trial. In October 2000, Tommy Suharto was convicted by the Supreme Court of corruption in a multimillion-dollar real estate scam and was sentenced to eighteen months in prison. Tommy Suharto asked President Wahid for clemency, but Wahid rejected his appeal. Following this verdict, Tommy Suharto did not surrender to the court, but went into hiding and remained a fugitive from justice for over a year before he finally surrendered. One Supreme Court judge, Syafiuddin Kartasasmita, who heard the case, was assassinated just four days after President Wahid was impeached. After extensive investigation, Tommy was convicted of ordering and paying two assassins for the murder of the judge. The case went to the Supreme Court in July 2002. In that murder trial, Tommy Suharto was judged guilty and given a sentence of fifteen years in jail, for a crime that in Indonesia carries a maximum sentence of death. A UN investigator described the trial as "one of the worst he has ever seen," because the prosecutors had only asked for a maximum sentence of fifteen years when the nature of the crime was so severe. "No pardon for Tommy Suharto," *CNN News,* October 4, 2000, news.bbc.co.uk/1/hi/world/asia-pacific/955578.htm; CNN.com, "Tommy Suharto Jailed for Murder," July 26, 2002, cnn.worldnews; O'Rourke, *Reformasi,* 409–410, 413.

16. Hamzah Haz was leader of PPP, the largest party in the Central Axis coalition and a long-time political opponent of Wahid. Hamzah Haz held the position of coordinating minister of people's welfare and poverty eradication. Wahid persuaded Haz to resign after suggesting to him that evidence was present to justify a corruption investigation against him. With similar accusations of corruption, Wahid forced both Laksamana Sukardi and Yusuf Kalla to resign their cabinet positions. Sukardi was a member of the PDI-P, a key adviser to Megawati, and was state minister of investment and enterprise development. Kalla was a member of Golkar and minister of industry and trade.

17. Kumiko Mizuno, " Indonesian Politics and the Issue of Justice in East Timor," in Soesastro, Smith, and Ling, *Governance in Indonesia,* 114–164.

18. Gorjão, "Abdurrahman Wahid's Presidency," 13–43; Komarudin, et al., *Trends in Indonesia,* 1–47; Irman G. Lanti, "Lessons from Gus Dur's Failed Presidency," in *Archived Perspectives* (Singapore: Institute of Defence and Strategic Studies, Nanyang Technological University, 2001), www.idss.edu.sg.

19. Irman G. Lanti, "Indonesia: The Year of Continuing Turbulence," in *Southeast Asian Affairs 2002* (Singapore: Institute of Southeast Asian Studies, 2002), 111–117; Gorjão, "Abdurrahman Wahid's Presidency," 30–43.

20. "Profile: Hamzah Haz," *BBC News,* July 26, 2001, news.bbc.co.uk/1/hi/world/asia-pacific/1457865.stm.

21. Hadi Soesastro, "Indonesia Under Megawati," in Soesastro, Smith, and Ling, *Governance in Indonesia,* 1–12; Lanti, "Indonesia," 111–120.

22. Leonard C. Sebastian, "Indonesian State Responses to September 11, the Bali Bombings and the War in Iraq: Sowing the Seeds for an Accommodationist Islamic Framework?" *Cambridge Review of International Affairs* 16, no. 3 (October 2003), 434–438; Richard Langit, "Indonesian Militants a Law unto Themselves," *Asia Times,*

January 19, 2002, www.atimes.com/se-asia/DA19Ae01.html. Nadhlatul Ulama claimed a membership of 40 million while Muhammadiyah claimed a membership of 25 million members.

23. "Unusual Suspects," *Far Eastern Economic Review,* January 17, 2002, 11; Sheldon W. Simon, "Southeast Asia and the U.S. War on Terrorism," *NBR Analysis* 13, no. 4 (July 2002), 28–32; Angel M. Rabasa, "Moderates Against Extremists," *International Herald Tribune,* October 31, 2002, www.rand.org/commentary/103102IHT.html.

24. For a profile of Jafar Umar Thalib based on a personal interview and an analysis of his ideology in comparison with other leaders of Islamic militant groups, see Jessica Stern, *Terror in the Name of God: Why Religious Militants Kill* (New York: HarperCollins, 2003), 63–84.

25. "Confessions of an al-Qaeda Terrorist," *Time Magazine,* September 15, 2002, 1–5, www.time.com/time/world/0,8816,351169,00.html; Dan Murphy, "How Al Qaeda Lit the Bali Fuse: Part One," *The Christian Science Monitor,* June 17, 2003, 1–4, www.csmonitor.com/2003/0617/p01s04-woap.htm. Omar Al-Faruq was held at the Bagram Airbase in Afghanistan until July 2005 when he escaped with four other prisoners and later made a video aired on the Al Arabiya network, during which he explained how the escape had been arranged with the assistance of the Taliban. On September 25, 2006, British forces in southern Iraq shot and killed a hostile attacker who was later confirmed by DNA tests to be Omar al-Faruq. Dan Murphy, "Escape Spotlights Troubled US Detention Efforts," *Christian Science Monitor,* November 7, 2005, 4.

26. The information about the request by President Bush to President Megawati for the transfer of Abu Bakar Ba'asyir to US custody was revealed by Fred Burks, a State Department interpreter, who translated at the meeting between Bush's special assistant and Megawati. Burks later testified for the defense in Indonesia's criminal trial against Abu Bakar Ba'asyir. Elinor Hall, "Bashir Trial Reveals Alleged US Arrest Plot," Australian Broadcasting Corporation, January 14, 2005, www.abc.net.au/am/content/2005/s1282108.htm.

27. Moch. Nur Ichwan, "Megawati and Radical Islam," paper presented to Third International Convention of Asia Scholars, August 19–22, 2003, Raffles City Convention Centre, Singapore, 1–6, www.berubah.org/MegawatiandIslamism.pdf.

28. Theodore Friend, *Indonesian Destinies* (Cambridge, MA: The Belknap Press of Harvard University Press, 2003), 522.

29. International Crisis Group, *How the Jemaah Islamiyah Terrorist Network Operates,* ICG Asia Report 43 (December 11, 2002), Brussels, 5; "Impact of the Bali Bombings, Report of a Conference," *USINDO Report,* November 26, 2002, 1–9; Theodore Friend, *Indonesian Destinies,* 522–524; Tatik S. Hafidz, "Assessing Indonesia's Vulnerability in the Wake of the American-Led Attack on Iraq," in Kumar Ramakrishna and See Seng Tan (eds.), *After Bali: The Threat of Terrorism in Southeast Asia* (Singapore: Institute of Defence and Strategic Studies, 2003), 388–393; Ken Conboy, *The Second Front: Inside Asia's Most Dangerous Terrorist Network* (Jakarta: Equinox Publishing, 2006), 164–184; Greg Barton, *Indonesia's Struggle: Jemaah Islamiyah and the Soul of Islam* (Sydney: University of New South Wales Press, 2004), 7–24, 44–89; William M. Wise, *Indonesia's War on Terror* (Washington, DC: USINDO, August 2005), 3–23.

30. Indonesia, Law No. 15/2003, for the Eradication of Acts of Terrorism. The Constitutional Court's decision of July 28, 2004, invalidated the provisions of "retrospective prosecution," but sustained the validity of the remainder of the Law for the Eradication of Acts of Terrorism. Petra Stockmann, "Indonesia Six Years After the Fall of Suharto—Proceeding Democratically Back to the New Order?" paper presented at Hong Kong Baptist University, Department of Government and International Studies, December 4, 2003, 1–9, home.snafu.de/watchin/petra23.04.04.htm.

31. Staff, Department of Politics and Social Change, "The Bali Inferno and the Settlement of Aceh Conflict," *The Indonesian Quarterly* 30, no. 4 (2002), 375–383; Leonard C. Sebastian, "Indonesia's New Anti-Terrorism Regulations," *IDSS Commentaries,* 25/2002, Institute of Defence and Strategic Studies (Singapore: Nanyang Technological University, October 2002), 1–4, www.idss.edu.sg/Perspective/Research_050225.htm; "Death Row Bomber Plotted New Attack on Smuggled Laptop," *The Times,* August 24, 2006, 1–3, www.timesonline.co.uk/news/asia/article617892.ece.

32. Hadi Soesastro, "Global Terrorism: Implications for State and Human Security," in Uwe Johannen, Alan Smith, and James Gomez (eds.), *September 11 & Political Freedom: Asian Perspectives* (Singapore: Select Publishing, 2003), 72–83; Angel Rabasa, *Political Islam in Southeast Asia: Moderates, Radicals and Terrorists* (Singapore and New York: Oxford University Press, 2003), 32–35; Sebastian, "Indonesian State Responses to September 11," 431–448; Zachary Abuza, "The Trial of Abu Bakar Ba'asyir: A Test for Indonesia," The Jamestown Foundation, June 24, 2005, www.jamestown.org/; Rohaiza Binte Ahmad Asi, "Ba'asyir Release: Implications for Islamist Militancy in Indonesia," *IDSS Commentaries,* 51/2006 (June 13, 2006), 1–3; "Abu Bakar Ba'asyir Free to Fight for Sharia," *Asia News*, June 14, 2006, 1, www.asianews.it/view_p.php?1=en&art=6438.

33. "Timeline: Bali Bomb Trials," *BBC News,* August 24, 2004, 1–5, news.bbc.co.uk/1/hi/world/asia-pacific/3126241.stn; P. S. Suryanarayana, "A Drive Against Terrorism," *Frontline* 20, no. 20 (September 27–October 10, 2003), 1–7, www.frontlineonnet.com/fl2020/stories/20031010000706200.htm.

34. Kathy Marks, "Bali Bombers May Be Freed After Court Rules Against Terror Laws," *The Independent,* July 24, 2004, 1–2, www.christusrex.org/www/news/indep-7-24-04b.html; Tim Lindsey and Ross Clarke, "Will Amrozi Walk Free?: Indonesia's Jemaah Islamiyah Trials," Asian Law Centre, Asian Institute Seminars, University of Melbourne, n.d. [September 2003], 1–10, www.griffith.edu.au/centre/asiainstitute/seminars_lectures; Tim Lindsey and Simon Butt, "Indonesian Judiciary in Constitutional Crisis," *Jakarta Post,* August 7, 2004, 1–3, www.geocities.com/urimesing/jp090804.htm?20051; Roslina Johari, "Constitutional Court Ruling on Bali Trials: Indonesia on Road to Country of Law?" *IDSS Commentaries,* September 9, 2004, 1–3, www.idss.edu.sg; Leonard C. Sebastian, "The Indonesian Dilemma: How to Participate in the War on Terror Without Becoming a National Security State," in Ramakrishna and Tan, *After Bali,* 357–381.

35. Bill Guerin, "Indonesia's Trial by Terror," *Asia Times,* March 12, 2005, 1–6, www.atimes.com/Southeast_Asia/GC12Ae06.html. The earlier assassination of Supreme Court judge Syafiuddin Kartasasmita in July 2001 had been a powerful reminder that defendants protected by militant vigilante groups could extract lethal revenge for any punitive judicial actions by members of the judiciary.

36. Kumar Ramakrishna and See Seng Tan, "Is Southeast Asia a 'Terrorist Haven'?" in Ramakrishna and Tan, *After Bali,* 1–2; John McBeth, "Weak Link in the Terror Chain," *Far Eastern Economic Review,* October 24, 2002, 12, 14–18.

37. Matthew Moore, "Police Hint at Bali-Marriott Bomb Link," *The Age,* August 13, 2003, www.theage.com.au/articles/2003/08/12/10605883091413.html; CNN, "Marriott Blast Suspects Named," August 19, 2003, 1–2, cnn.worldnews.printthis.clickability.com/pt.

38. Simon Elegant, "The Fire This Time: A Suicide Bombing in Jakarta Shows How Vulnerable Indonesia Remains to Terrorism," *Time Asia,* September 13, 2004, 1–5, www.time.com/time/asia/magazine/printout,0,13675,50104092; CNN, "Text 'Warned of Jakarta Bomb,'" 1–3, edition.cnn.com/2004/WORLD/asiapcf/09/10/indonesia.blast; PWHCE, "Asia Pacific Report 62, Jakarta Embassy Bombing," September 17, 2004,

1–3, www.pwhce.org/apr62.html; Matthew Moore, "Four Bombers Captured," *The Age,* November 25, 2004, 1–2, www.theage.com.au/news/War-on-Terror/Four-bombers-captured.

39. The Regional Representatives Council (Dewan Perwakilan Rakyat Daerah, DPRD) was created by Law No. 22/1999. See Minh Nauven, "Indonesia: The Political and Human Rights Situation," *View on Asia Briefing Series* (Kings Cross, Australia: Uniya, 2004), 4–5, www.uniya.org; Stephen Sherlock, "The 2004 Indonesian Elections: How the System Works and What the Parties Stand For" (Canberra: Australian National University, Centre for Democratic Institutions, February 2004), 4–17; Andrew Ellis, "Countdown to 2004: Indonesia's New General Election Law," *USINDO Brief,* July 16, 2003, 1–7, www.usindo.org/Briefs/2003/Andrew%Ellis%2007-16-03.htm. Indonesian election laws from www.ifes.org.

40. Partai Demokrat (Democrat Party) was founded on September 9, 2001, by S. Budhisantoso. Susilo Bambang Yudhoyono became formally associated with DP in March 2004 after he resigned from the cabinet. C. S. Kuppuswamy, "Indonesia: Votes for Change," *South Asia Analysis Group,* Paper No. 1124 (September 27, 2004), www.saag.org/papers12/paper1124.html.

41. Stephen Sherlock, *Consolidation and Change: The Indonesian Parliament After the 2004 Elections* (Canberra: Australian National University, Centre for Democratic Institutions, June 2004), 4–13; South Asia Analysis Group, "Indonesia: Change of Guards," Paper No. 1152 (October 28, 2004), 1–5, www.saag.org/papers12/paper 1152.html.

42. Gary LaMoshi, "Indonesia's Transition: The Good, the Bad, the Ugly," *Asia Times,* October 20, 2004, www.atimes.com/atimes/Southeast_Asia/FJ20Ae01.html.

43. "Indonesia's Parliament Deadlocked: Signs of Troubles Ahead for Yudhoyono," Associated Press, November 2, 2004; Ridwan Max Sijabat and Meidyatama Surodiningrat, "House in War for Political Supremacy," *The Jakarta Post,* November 3, 2004; Devi Asmarani, "Yudhoyono Faces Trial of Strength with Lawmakers," *The Straits Times,* November 3, 2004; "Irresponsible Politicians," *The Jakarta Post,* Editorial, November 3, 2004; Mochtar Buchori, "Deadlock in the House: Where Will It Lead Us To?" *The Jakarta Post,* November 3, 2004; "Our Public Representatives in the House Need to Grow Up," *The Jakarta Post,* November 3, 2004; "Rival Coalitions Disagree on How to End Deadlock," *The Jakarta Post,* November 4, 2004; all the above reports available from www.infid.be/dpr_in_war.htm.

44. Jusuf Wanandi, "Indonesia Outlook 2005—Political: Turning over a New Leaf in RI Politics," *The Jakarta Post,* June 25, 2005, 1–4, www.thejakartapost.com/outlook/pol01b.asp; Endy M. Bayuni, "Indonesia Outlook 2005—Political: Power Sharing—Who Is Really in Charge?" June 25, 2005, 1–6, www.thejakartapost.com/outlook/pol02b.asp.

45. Michael Vatikiotis, "Yudhoyono, Indonesia's Man in Charge," *International Herald Tribune,* February 17, 2005, 1–3, www.iht.com/articles/2005/02/16/opinion.edvati.html; John Roberts, "Sharp Divisions in Jakarta over Foreign Presence in Aceh," World Socialist Web Site, January 26, 2005, 1–4, citing *Borneo Bulletin* website, www.wsws.org/articles/2005/jan2005/aceh-j26.shtml; Eric Teo Chu Cheow, "The Tsunami and Political Islam and Nationalism in Indonesia," Singapore Institute of International Affairs, March 2, 2005, 1–3, www.siiaonline.org/et_030305.

46. Anthony L. Smith, "Indonesia and the United States 2004–2005: New President, New Needs, Same Old Relations," *Asia-Pacific Center for Security Studies,* February 2005, 1–8, www.apcss.org; Tony Agus Ardie, "Revisiting Indonesia–United States Relations," *The Jakarta Post,* July 3, 2005, 1–5, www.thejakartapost.com/special/gpb07_2.asp; Rand Research Brief, "Indonesia's Future: Challenges and Implications

for Regional Stability," 1–4, www.rand.org/publications/RB/RB70; Mike Nathan, "Strengthening Ties Between Australia and Indonesia," *Institute of Public Affairs,* 1–2, www.ipa.org.au/files/news_946.html.

47. Muninggar Sri Saraswati, "Govt Initiates 'Revolution' in Islamic Law," *The Jakarta Post,* October 5, 2004, 1, www.infid.be/islam_law.htm.

48. Sukino Harisumarto, "Indonesia Draft Sharia Law Triggers Controversy," United Press International, October 22, 2004, 1–4, washingtontimes.com/upi-breaking/20041022-101916-3985r.htm.

49. Zainuddin Sardar, "Can Islam Change?" *New Statesman,* September 13, 2004, 4, www.newstatesman.com/200409130016.

50. The Department of Religion never endorsed that fatwa from 1984 and therefore it had no legal standing, but it remained on the records of the Indonesian Ulama Council. For a detailed account of the 1984 fatwa pronounced by the MUI against Ahmadiyah, see M. B. Hooker, *Indonesian Islam: Social Change Through Contemporary Fatawa* (Crows Nest, Australia: Allen & Unwin, and Honolulu: University of Hawaii Press, 2003), 70–71.

51. *AsiaNews,* "Indonesia: Thousands of Islamic Extremists Against the Ahmadis," July 16, 2005, 1–2, www.asianews.it/view.php?1=en&art=3742; "Thousands Besiege Ahmadiyah Complex," *The Jakarta Post,* July 16, 2005, 1–2, www.thepersecution.org/world/indonesia/05/jp_1607.html; "Govt Bans Ahmadiyah Teachings in Indonesia, Minister Says," *Antara News,* July 20, 2005, 1, news.antara.co.id/en/seenws/?id=5260; Theresia Sufa and Wahyoe Boediwardhana, "Scholars Urge MUI to Lift Ahmadiyah Ban," *Jakarta Post,* July 22, 2005, 1–3, www.thepersecution.org/world/indonesia/05jp_2207.html. News reports generally give 200,000 as the number of Ahmadiyah in Indonesia, but the leaders of the community claim to have a membership of 250,000 within Indonesia.

52. "Fatwa Feud," *The Guardian Unlimited,* August 2, 2005, 1–4, www.guardian.co.uk/; Eric Unmacht, "A Muslim Schism," *Newsweek, International Edition,* August 15, 2005, 1–3, www.msnbc,msn.com/id/8825859/; David Kootnikoff, "Indonesia Struggles with Extremism," *OhMyNews,* August 15, 2005, 1–3, english.ohmynews.com/. "MUI Issues 11 Fatwa," *The Jakarta Post,* August 15, 2005, 1–2, www.thejakartapost.com.

53. For statements of Jaringan Islam Liberal, see islamlib.com. The fatwa condemning "liberalism, secularism and pluralism" reveals political divisions within Muhammadiyah, since Din Syamsuddin was secretary-general of the MUI that passed the fatwa condemning the actions of a Muhammadiyah-affiliated organization that he headed as chairman.

54. Eric Unmacht, "A Muslim Schism," *Newsweek International,* August 15, 2005, part 2, 1, www.msnbc.msn.com/; Hera Diani and Siamet Susanto, "MUI Slammed over Controversial Fatwas," *The Jakarta Post,* August 2, 2005, 1–2, www.thepersecution.org/world/indonesia/05/jp_0208.html; "Gus Dur: Government Must Follow Constitution, Not MUI Fatwa," www.gusdur.net; John Aglionby, "Fatwa Feud," *The Guardian Unlimited,* August 2, 2005, 1–4, www.guardian.co.uk/.

55. Unmacht, "A Muslim Schism," 1; "Ahmadiyah Prepares Legal Action Against MUI," *The Jakarta Post,* July 19, 2005, 1–2, www.thepersecution.org/world/indonesia/05/jp_1907b.html; Sadanand Dhume, "Radicals March on Indonesia's Future," *Far Eastern Economic Review* 168, no. 5 (May 2005), 11–19; International Crisis Group, *Indonesia: Implications of the Ahmadiyah Decree,* Asia Briefing No. 78 (July 7, 2008), Jakarta/Brussels, 11–14.

56. "Govt Bans Ahmadiyah Teachings in Indonesia, Minister Says," *Antara News,* July 20, 2005, 1–2, news.antara.co.id/en/seenws/?id=5260.

57. "Indonesia: Government Rejects Integralists' Request to Ban Ahmadis," *Asia News,* August 12, 2005, 1–2, www.asianews.it/view.php?1=en&art=3907.

58. Most fatwas banning organizations and ideas have a common characteristic. They are nearly always drafted as "bills of attainder." The bans and penalties are applied directly to persons or organizations to have the immediate consequence of conviction without the intervening process of trial, examination of evidence, and regular judicial procedures, with the rights of defendants unprotected by due process of law. In the legal systems of most democratic countries, bills of attainder are unconstitutional and recognized as a violation of basic principles of the rule of law.

59. "RI Carrying Burdens over Unresolved Human Rights Cases: President," *Judicial System Monitoring Programme,* August 16, 2005, www.jsmp.minihub.org/News/.

60. "FPI Protests Against Decision on Ahmadiyah," *The Jakarta Post,* January 8, 2008, 1, www.thejakartapost.com; "FUI to Conduct 3-Month Campaign for Ahmadiyah Ban," *Antara News*, January 19, 2008, 1, www.antara.co.id/en/arc/2008/1/19/; Asian Legal Resource Centre, "Indonesia: Religious Intolerance and Discrimination an Ongoing Concern," February 21, 2008, 1–2, www.thepersecution.org/world/indonesia/08/02/alrc21.html; M. Dawam Rahardjo, "Terror upon Ahmadiyya and Freedom of Religion," *Jaringan Islam Liberal,* March 9, 2008, 1–3, www.islamlib.com/en.

61. Kenneth Conboy, "Indonesian Sect Comes Under Fire," *CounterTerrorism Blog,* October 31, 2007, 1–2, counterterrorismblog.org/2007/10/; "Who's Playing God?" *The Jakarta Post,* October 31, 2007, 1–2, www.asia-pacific-action.org/news/; Syofiardi Bachyul, "Indonesia: Sect Crackdown Criticized," *The Jakarta Post,* October 10, 2007, 1–2, www.thejakartapost.com.

62. "Police Order Sweep of Sect Leaders," *The Jakarta Post,* October 30, 2007, 1–2, www.asia-pacific-action.org/news/; "Islamic Sect Leader Repents, Says Al-Qiyadah Was Misguided," *The Jakarta Post,* November 11, 2007, 1–2, www.thejakartapost.com.

63. Peter Gelling, "Unorthodox Sects Face Prosecution in Indonesia," *International Herald Tribune,* November 15, 2007, 1–3, www.iht.com/bin/printfriendly.php?id=8349165.

64. International Crisis Group, *Indonesia: Implications of the Ahmadiyah Decree,* 1–17.

65. Hal Hill, "Yudhoyono's Six Challenges to Get Indonesia Growing," *Far Eastern Economic Review* 168, no. 1 (December 2004), 55–58; Chris Manning, "Indonesia: The First Year of the Yudhoyono-Kalla Government," *Asian Analysis* (November 2005), 6–9.

66. Dwi Atmanta, "Pseudo-checks and Balances at Play," *The Jakarta Post,* October 19, 2006, 3–10; Ati Nurbaiti, "Onward Antigraft Soldiers—But to Where?" *The Jakarta Post,* October 20, 2006, 1–2, www.thejakartapost.com.

67. Michael Vatikiotis, "Need for Speed in Indonesia," *Asia Times,* September 16, 2006, 1–3, atimes.com/atimes/Southeast_Asia/HI19Ae01.html; Jusuf Wanandi, "Two Years of the Yudhoyono Presidency," *The Jakarta Post,* September 20, 2006, 2–5, www.thejakartapost.com/; Chris Manning, "Indonesia: Indonesia Promotes Economic Reform: What Results So Far?" *Asian Analysis* (October 2006), 5–6.

68. Bill Guerin, "Indonesia Behind the Learning Curve," *Asia Times,* August 31, 2006, 1–5, www.atimes.com/atimes/Southeast_Asia/HH31Ae01.html.

69. For the view supporting a gradual moderation of Islamic politics due to democratic processes, see Greg Fealy, "In Fear of Radical Islam in Indonesia: A Critical Look at the Evidence," USINDO Brief (August 18, 2005), 1–4, www.usindo.org/Briefs/2005/. For the view that Indonesia was entering a cycle of radicalization, see Dhume, "Radicals March on Indonesia's Future," 11–19; Muhammad Nafik, "Review

2005 National: Radicalism Extends Its Roots, Becoming Institutionalized," *The Jakarta Post,* September 24, 2005, 1–3, www.thejakartapost.com/review/nat01.asp; Zachary Abuza, "Out of the Woodwork: Islamist Militants in Aceh," *Terrorism Monitor* 3, no. 2 (January 2005), 1–4.

70. John McBeth, "Evolving Democratic Trends in Indonesia," speech at Asian New Zealand Foundation, 2006, 1–4, www.asianz.org.nz/business/issues-speeches/.

71. Charmain Mohamed, "Justice in Jakarta," *Human Rights Watch,* November 20, 2006, 1–2, hrw.org/english/docs/2006/11/20/indone14645.htm.

72. For a detailed account of Ba'asyir's founding of Jemaah Islamiyah and of its front organization, Majelis Mujahidin Indonesia, see International Crisis Group, *How the Jemaah Islamiyah Terrorist Network Operates,* ICG Asia Report No. 43 (December 11, 2002), Jakarta/Brussels, 4–5, 8. For Ba'asyir's pronouncements on Islamic governance and on the obligations of Muslims to support jihad, see Scott Atran, "The Emir: An Interview with Abu Bakar Ba'asyir," *Spotlight on Terror* 3, no. 9 (September 15, 2005), 1–11, jamestown.org/terrorism/news/article.php?articleid=2369782.

73. Lee Hudson Teslik, "Profile: Abu Bakar Bashir," Council on Foreign Relations Backgrounder, June 14, 2006, 1–3, www.cfr.org/publications/10219/; "Bali Terror Cleric Freed from Jail," CNN.com, June 14, 2006, 1–3, www.cnn.com/2006/WORLD/asiapcf/06/13/bakar.release/; Bill Guerin, "Indonesia's Fizzling Terrorist Threat," *Asia Times,* June 22, 2006, 1–5, www.atimes.com/atimes/Southeast_Asia/HF22Ae01.html; Rohaiza Binte Ahmad Asi, "Ba'asyir Release: Implications for Islamist Militancy in Indonesia," *IDSS Commentaries,* June 13, 2006, 1–3, www.idss.edu.sg.

74. "Tommy Suharto Jailed for Murder," *CNN World News,* July 26, 2002, 1–2, cnn.worldnews; "Tommy's Special Treatment, A Sick Joke," *Laksamana*, August 19, 2005, http://laksamana.net/read.php?gid=62; "Tommy Suharto Freed from Prison," *BBC News,* October 30, 2006, 1–2, news.bbc.co.uk/go/pr/fr/-/2/hi/asia-pacific/6098010.stm.

75. David McRae, "Executing Tibo Solves Nothing," *The Jakarta Post,* September 20, 2006, 2–7, www.infid.be/poso_amnesty_dismay.htm; Philip S. Golingai, "Coming Through Slaughter," *Southeast Asian Press Alliance,* n.d. [2006], 1–5, www.seapabkk.org/newdesign/fellowsipsdetail.php?No=528.

76. "Profile: Jafar Umar Thalib," *BBC News,* January 30, 2003, 1–3, news.bbc.co.uk/2/hi/asia-pacific/1975345.stm.

77. "Indonesia Heightens Vigilance Against Terrorist Attacks," *The Jakarta Post,* August 31, 2005, 1–2, www.thejakartapost.com/; Matthew Moore, "Four Bombers Captured," *The Age,* November 25, 2004, 1–2, www.theage.com.au/news/.

78. Tom McCawley and Dan Murphy, "Bombs in Bali, Despite Crackdown," *The Christian Science Monitor,* October 3, 2005, 1 and 10; "Bali Police Seek Bomb Clues," *CBSNews*, October 4, 2005.

79. David Leppard, "Blast Suspect Trained with Bin Laden," *The Sunday Times—Britain*, October 2, 2005, 1–2, www.timesonline.co.uk/article/0,,2087-1807284,00.html; Shawn Donnan, "Bali Bombing Suspect Eludes Police," *Financial Times,* October 7, 2005, 1, us.ft.com/; International Crisis Group, *Terrorism in Indonesia: Noordin's Networks,* Asia Report No. 114 (May 5, 2006), Jakarta/Brussels, 11–19.

80. Margie Mason, "Indonesia: Bin Husin Shot Going for Bomb," *Guardian Unlimited*, November 10, 2005, 1–3, www.guardian.co.uk/worldlatest/story/0,1280,-5405809,00.html; "Weapons Storage of Azahari Network Uncovered," *The Jakarta Post,* November 13, 2005, 1–2, www.thejakartapost.com/; International Crisis Group, *Terrorism in Indonesia,* 1–19.

81. International Crisis Group, *How the Jemaah Islamiyah Terrorist Network Operates,* 17–19; Barton, *Indonesia's Struggle,* 17–19; International Crisis Group, *Indonesia*

Backgrounder: Jihad in Central Sulawesi, ICG Asia Report No. 74 (February 3, 2004) Jakarta/ Brussels, 4–12.

82. Bill Guerin, "Added Spice to Indonesia's Terror," *Asia Times,* May 13, 2005, 1–5, www.atimes.com/atimes/Southeast_Asia/GE13Ae01.html; Adrian Morgan, "Indonesia: The Roots of Muslim Christian Conflict," *Spero,* October 25, 2006, 1–10, www.speroforum.com/site/print.asp?idarticle=6285.

83. International Crisis Group, *How the Jemaah Islamiyah Terrorist Network Operates,* 17–19; Greg Barton, *Indonesia's Struggle,* 17–19; International Crisis Group, *Indonesia Backgrounder,* 16–25; International Crisis Group, *Jihadism in Indonesia: Poso on the Edge,* Asia Report No. 127 (January 24, 2007), Jakarta/Brussels, 1–8. Adnan Arsal was one of the signers of the Malino Accord representing Muslims of Central Sulawesi. The ICG reports provide details of seventy-five incidents of violence in Poso from December 31, 2001, to December 4, 2003, mostly perpetrated against Christians. These attacks on the Christian community continued at about the same pace during 2004 and up through January 2007.

84. Australian Broadcasting Corporation, "Christians Executed in Indonesia," September 22, 2006, 1–3, www.abc.net.au/pm/content/2006/s1746918.htm; Adrian Morgan, "Indonesia: The Roots of Muslim Christian Conflict," *Spero News*, October 25, 2006, 1–10, www.speroforum.com/site/print.asp?idarticle=6285.

85. Zachary Abuza, "JI's Two-Pronged Strategy in Indonesia," *Terrorism Focus* 3, no. 16 (April 25, 2006), 1–3, www.jamestown.org/terrorism/news/. The strategy may have been based on the audiotape by Ayman al-Zawahiri and broadcast on al-Jazeera television on October 1, 2004.

86. Indonesia Matters, "Tanah Runtuh Marches," October 31, 2006, 1–4, www.indonesiamatters.com/789/tanah-runtuh-marches; International Crisis Group, *Jihadism in Indonesia,* 1–27.

87. Indonesia Matters, Poso News, June 16, 2006, 1–3, www.indonesiamatters.com/355/poso-news/; Adrian Morgan, "Indonesia: Islamist Insurgency on Poso Erupts Again," *Spero News,* January 23, 2007, 2–5, www.speroforum.com/site/article.asp?idarticle=7593; Jonathan Lyons, "Poso Violence Could Strengthen Indonesian Militants," *Reuters AlertNet,* January 29, 2007, 1–2, www.alternet.org/thenews/newsdesk/SP16582.htm; International Crisis Group, *Jihadism in Indonesia,* 9–14; Ruslan Sangadji, "Police Arrest Two Highest-Ranked Suspects in Poso," *The Jakarta Post,* February 2, 2007, 1–2, www.thejakartapost.com; Fabio Scarpello, "Poso: Indonesia's Latest Front in the War on Terror," *Foreign Politics Watch,* February 19, 2007, 1–3, www.worldpoliticswatch.com/article.aspx?id=559; Alvin Darlanika Soedarjo, "Poso Surrenders to Army Seen as 'Face-Saving,'" *The Jakarta Post,* February 26, 2007, 1–2, www.thejakartapost.com/yesterdaydetail.asp?field=20070226.A07; International Crisis Group, *Jihadism in Indonesia,* 15–19; International Crisis Group, *Indonesia: Tackling Radicalism in Poso,* ICG Policy Briefing, No. 75 (January 22, 2008), Jakarta/Brussels, 1–3.

88. "Indonesia: Poso Residents Fear Alleged Arrival of Militants," *AdnKronos International News,* February 4, 2007, 1–2, www.adnki.com/; Sidney Jones, "Countering Terror in Poso," *Van Zorge Report,* February 20, 2007, 7–11.

89. Pankaj Kumar Jha, "The Implications of Abu Dujana's Arrest," Institute of Peace and Conflict Studies, Article 2316 (June 21, 2007), New Delhi, 1–4; www.ipcs.org; Indonesia Matters, "Abu Dujana," March 21, 2007, 1–5, www.indonesiamatters.com/1175/abu_dujana; Lindsay Murdoch, "Terrorist Leader Warns of More Bali Bombings," *Sydney Morning Herald*, December 22, 2007, 1–2, www.smh.com.au/news/world/.

90. Jusuf Kalla was born in South Sulawesi and over the years he cultivated his political base, eventually becoming chairman of the South Sulawesi Golkar branch during the Suharto regime. He also became a very successful businessman owning a large portfolio of investments operated by the Kalla Group, including a hydroelectric power plant located on the river that runs through Poso. In 2007, *Forbes* listed his net worth at US$230 million; www.forbes.com/lists/2007/.

91. US Department of State, "Indonesia: Country Reports on Human Rights Practices, 2007," 1–4, www.state.gov/g/drl/rls/hrrpt/2007; Indonesia Matters, "Beheadings Trial," March 21, 2007, 1–15, www.indonesiamatters.com/804/beheadings-trial; Benteng Reges, "Light Sentence for Terrorists Who Beheaded Three Christians," *Asia News,* December 4, 2007, 1, www.asianews.it/view4print.php?1=en&art=10953; International Crisis Group, *Jihadism in Indonesia,* 1–12.

92. International Crisis Group, *Indonesia: Tackling Radicalism in Poso,* 1–11.

93. "Maluku Clash Kills 3," *The Jakarta Post,* May 3, 2008, 1, www.thejakarta post.com/news/2008/05/08/malaku-clash-kills-3.html; "Indonesian Christian Village Burnt to Ground by Neighboring Muslims," Barnabas Fund, May 21, 2008, www .barnabasfund.org/news/archives/text.php?ID_news_items=411.

94. International Crisis Group, *Indonesia: Jemaah Islamiyah's Current Status,* Update Briefing No. 63 (May 3, 2007), Jakarta/Brussels, 1–15.

95. UN Consolidated List maintained by the 1267 Committee, www.un.org/sc/ committees/1267/consolist.shtml.

96. Zachary Abuza, "The State of Jemaah Islamiyah: Terrorism and Insurgency in Southeast Asia Five Years After Bali," The Fletcher School, The Jebsen Center for Counter-Terrorism Studies, Research Briefing Series 2, no. 1 (November 2007), Medford, MA, 1–7; Pankaj Kumar Jha, "Indonesia's Move Against Terrorism," *Peace and Conflict Monitor,* February 15, 2006, 1–7, www.monitor.upeace.org/archive.cfm?id_ article=344; Peter Gelling, "Unorthodox Sects Face Prosecution in Indonesia," *International Herald Tribune,* November 15, 2007, 2–3, www.iht.com.bin/printfriendly .php?id=3849165.

97. International Crisis Group, *Indonesia: Jemaah Islamiyah's Publishing Industry,* Asia Report, No. 147 (February 28, 2008), Jakarta/Brussels, 1–16.

13

Ethnicity and Islam in Malaysia

In the post-Mahathir era, Malaysia faced many of the same issues of democratic transition, political reform, and the role of Islam in politics that also energized and confounded Indonesian politics. A significant difference can be attributed to the fact that, for Malaysia, its political institutions remained more stable while these contentious issues were being addressed. Prime Minister Mahathir's decision to retire at a time of his own choosing and by naming his own successor had enabled a smooth transition of power without public controversy or political competition over the choice of his successor. Mahathir is reported to have stated, perhaps in jest, that he would like his successor to be his clone. If such a candidate had been available, that potential successor would, no doubt, have clashed with Mahathir several years earlier and thereby would have lost any possible endorsement as Mahathir's successor. The person Mahathir eventually selected to succeed himself, in matters of political style and temperament, was far from being a clone of Mahathir.[1]

Abdullah Ahmad Badawi had earned the reputation of being an able and articulate, if somewhat pedantic bureaucrat, and had been a second-level UMNO politician over a number of years. After some stormy political episodes in the 1980s and 1990s, he gradually worked his way into the upper echelons of the government.[2] Within UMNO, he was viewed as a consensus builder and as a basically honorable politician whose political style avoided bombast or displays of charismatic fervor. Before his retirement, Mahathir gave his supporters assurances that he was confident that his legacy and the basic policies that he had championed would be continued without major alteration when Badawi assumed the office of prime minister. Although Badawi became prime minister with a status quo image, there was both public expectation and trepidation over what would change when a bureaucratic and less dynamic leader replaced a charismatic and forceful prime minister.

Abdullah Ahmad Badawi was inaugurated as Malaysia's fifth prime minister on October 31, 2003. As his first priority, he was determined to reduce the high levels of deficit spending that had accumulated over the previous five years and risen even more during Mahathir's last days in office. Among the mega-projects canceled or postponed were the planned US$3.8 billion high-speed rail system designed to extend from Singapore through Malaysia to China and the proposed mega-bridge to link Johor with Singapore. Purchases of advanced military aircraft for the Malaysian Air Force were also postponed. While keeping a fairly low public profile, Badawi promised a campaign against graft and corruption. A Royal Commission was also created to examine police operations and to propose reforms.[3] In his public statements, Prime Minister Badawi projected a populist image of a thoughtful, consensual, concerned, hard-working, and cautious leader.

The primary opposition to the new government came from Partai Islam, which held twenty-seven seats in Parliament and had led the Barisan Alternatif in the 1999 elections. Badawi had earned a bachelor's degree in Islamic studies from the University of Malaya and could read Arabic, so his Islamic credentials enabled him to speak with more authority on issues related to Islam than had been the case with Mahathir. Government programs for promoting and administering Islam remained as before, but Badawi made the case for a "tolerant, inclusive, moderate and modern Islam." To identify his vision of what Islam should be, he coined the term "Islam Hadhari" (defined as "Islamic Management" or "Civilizational Islam").[4] He made no specific proposals for policy changes but rather called for increased sensitivities toward Malaysia's non-Muslim minorities, at the same time he promised increased emphasis on Islamic principles as the foundation for a new tolerant and modern Malaysia.

Without a personal electoral mandate, Badawi's legitimacy could easily be challenged, and there was much speculation on whether he was an interim prime minister or had the capacity to provide long-term leadership for the party and the nation. The next parliamentary elections were due by November 2004, but sooner elections were anticipated in order to confirm the selection and the legitimacy of Abdullah Badawi and his new administrative team. As a first step, in January 2004, Badawi appointed Najib Tun Razak as deputy prime minister. On March 4, Badawi dissolved Parliament and called for new elections that were scheduled for March 21. The previously formed opposition coalition of Barisan Alternatif had collapsed in 1999, and it was apparent that a new opposition coalition was unlikely to be formed.[5]

The legal campaign period for the 2004 election was reduced to eight days. A constituency redistricting scheme created twenty-six new parliamentary seats and sixty-three new state assembly seats in states controlled by the Barisan Nasional, but no new additions were provided for states controlled by Partai Islam. As usual, the press and the visual media were under the complete control of the government through ownership, licensing, censorship, and their news coverage that gave favorable reports and space to the Barisan Nasional message and its candidates.

The 2004 election results reveal that UMNO had regained majority support from the Malay voters that had been lost to the BA in the 1999 election. Under Abdullah Badawi's leadership, the Barisan Nasional gained 63.9 percent of the vote, while the Barisan Alternatif—now reduced to only two parties, Partai Islam and Keadilan—gained only 24.1 percent of the total vote. Part of the increase in support for the government can be attributed to conflicts and disarray within the opposition. Partai Islam in 2004 campaigned on a more openly Islamist agenda, unrestrained by a coalition with the Chinese-based Democratic Action Party that was not allied with any other opposition party. Even so, voter support for Partai Islam's candidates remained remarkably stable at 15.0 percent in 1999 and 15.2 percent in 2004. In the previous bitter and contentious election of 1999, the Barisan Nasional gained a slim majority of only 56.53 percent of the vote, while Barisan Alternatif, symbolically led by the imprisoned Anwar Ibrahim, gained support from 40.21 percent of the electorate. The big difference in the number of seats for Partai Islam between the two elections can be attributed to the disintegration of the smaller coalition party—Keadilan—in the latter election. The election statistics for Partai Islam provide evidence of the political support for a fundamentalist version of Islam. Many other issues, apart from Islam, could generate support for a multiethnic opposition coalition that could eventually combine with this core Islamist opposition to challenge the government's hold on power. In 2004, such a coalition never formed, partly because the overall levels of public discontent and distrust of the government had been greatly reduced under the low-key and nonflamboyant leadership of Prime Minister Abdullah Badawi.

Anwar Ibrahim's "Renaissance"

During the 2004 election, the putative leader of the Barisan Alternatif continued to be Anwar Ibrahim, who remained in jail serving a combined sentence of fifteen years' imprisonment following two trials, one for corruption and the other for sodomy and sexual misconduct. In the intervening period, Anwar's lawyers had filed a number of briefs to overturn his sentence and reduce his penalties. Malaysian courts had rejected all these appeals. However, various international human rights organizations and some foreign governments, including the United States, openly criticized the trials of Anwar as well as the severe penalties imposed upon him. Anwar Ibrahim's continued presence in prison created a negative image, especially abroad, for the new prime minister, who cherished his image as a noncontentious leader. For Prime Minister Badawi to commute the sentence or pardon Anwar would have soured relations with Mahathir and with the vast majority of Badawi's political supporters. However, for the court to soften its earlier interpretations of law and fact would remove from Badawi's public image in foreign perceptions a stain that was rapidly becoming indelible.

In September 2004, the Malaysian Supreme Court reviewed another appeal from Anwar's lawyers. This time, in a surprise move, the court ruled that the main witness testifying on the sodomy charges was unreliable, and therefore it reversed the earlier conviction related to sodomy. The other conviction on charges of corruption remained in force, but since his sentence on that charge had been for six years, and he had already served six years in prison, he was released from prison. Because of his conviction on corruption charges, he continued to be banned from contesting for political office for five more years, and the court declined to overturn that condition, which prevented him from standing for election until after April 2008.[6]

Shortly after his release from prison, Anwar left for Germany where he received medical attention for his back. Then he proceeded to Saudi Arabia where he was feted and provided with a private jet. When Oxford University offered him a fellowship, he accepted and announced that he hoped to become a mediator to bridge the divisions that had developed between the United States and the Muslim world.[7] At Oxford University, he gave talks and seminars on the topics of "Democracy, Islam, and Terrorism" and used his time to renew political contacts with prominent British and US leaders, including former vice president Al Gore. In April 2005, he was invited by Johns Hopkins University to be a distinguished senior fellow at their School for Advanced International Studies. While in Washington, DC, he was awarded the honor "The Democrat of the Year" by the Center for the Study of Islam and Democracy.[8] In all his activities, Anwar gave every indication that he would return to the Malaysian political scene, despite the legal impediments imposed by Malaysia's criminal justice system.

In June 2005, Anwar returned to Malaysia, where he attracted a crowd of 10,000 in Penang and an even larger crowd in Kedah. His activities were not reported in the Malaysian press and television news because editors and directors were warned that their licenses might be withdrawn if they covered his political activities. Most commentators believed that it would be extremely difficult for Anwar Ibrahim to return as a major political player in Malaysian politics. Even so, his presence on the Malaysian scene generated both excitement and high levels of political anxiety within UMNO and the ruling Barisan Nasional coalition.[9] Whatever might happen in the future, Malaysian politics was not likely to become dull and prescripted from the centers of political power. The big question was how he would script his return.

In July 2006, Anwar made dramatic revelations accusing Mahathir and other UMNO politicians of complicity in the RM30 billion (US$11.6 billion) loss of government funds by speculations on the foreign exchange markets between 1992 and 1994.[10] He also launched a RM100 million (US$39.2 million) "defamation and conspiracy" suit against the retired but still powerful former prime minister Mahathir. In March 2007, he announced that he would be a candidate for prime minister of Malaysia in the next elections, anticipated to be held in 2007 or 2008. Because his earlier court convictions had banned him from holding political office until after April 2008, his announcement indicated that he intended to challenge or defy that ban.[11] Meanwhile, Malaysian politics had generated new issues and accumulated a backlog of unresolved problems.

Malaysian Democracy Under Pressure

Prime Minister Abdullah Badawi inherited a system of power that had been built up by his predecessor, and although Badawi gained a commanding mandate in the 2004 election, he was constrained by the nature of his office and shaped by past policies and practices. Within the prime minister's office a large bureaucracy was committed to defining, propagating, and enforcing Islam and Sharia law. Prime Minister Badawi's political support came from the United Malays National Organization, which had been built up into a vast patronage network designed to lift the Malays from poverty and redistribute wealth across the ethnic and religious divide that defined Malaysian politics. Both the nature of his office and the configuration of vested interests reflected in existing political alignments began to undermine Badawi's stated intentions to promote a moderate and an efficient modern economy that would improve the standard of living for all Malaysians. The rhetoric was moderate, liberal, and tolerant, but a strategy for achieving those goals had not been subject to Malaysia's political reality test.

Over the years, the politics of UMNO had been based on the rewards of patronage and the allocation of benefits derived from the segmented distribution of derivative political powers. The large number of UMNO-owned corporations and an even larger number of government-linked corporations (GLCs) provided both jobs and investment opportunities for Malays, most of whom were UMNO party members who were expected to give appropriate political support to party and national leaders. In August 2005, the GLCs controlled 36 percent of Malaysia's total market capitalization with a total value of RM260 billion (US$100.4 billion).[12] The close linkage between corporate wealth and political power made it virtually impossible to determine when political decisions were made for public purposes or for private benefits. With few boundaries to define conflicts of interest between economic and political structures of power, the distinction between legitimate political representation and "graft" was severely obscured.

Because Prime Minister Badawi did not come to power with a broad political support base of his own, those who had been beneficiaries of the previous patronage system began to complain about the loss of state contracts and easy credit. In response to these criticisms, he became more cautious and his reforms were watered down. His actions shifted from enforcement and prosecution of abuses, to exhortation for GLCs to raise their performance and profitability.

Because he could not reform the system of privilege, he had to reward his own supporters and did so by creating an alternative structure of patronage. At the apex of the new patronage system were his Oxford-educated son-in-law Khairy Jamaluddin and his son Kamaluddin Abdullah. Khairy Jamaluddin was made deputy chief of staff, but because of public criticism of nepotism, he resigned in 2003. However, Khairy retained a key advisory role in government policy-making and was a top executive for Khazanah Holdings that operated as a state-run investment GLC managing and distributing RM25 billion (US$9.66 billion) worth of government funds. Kamaluddin Abdullah became a leading investor in the local oil and gas company known as the Scomi Group. By March 2007, that company had secured an estimated RM1 billion (US$367 million) of government contracts during Abdullah Badawi's tenure in office. Linked to these two key patrons was a new coterie of younger client operators who held key administrative positions within the political circle headed by the prime minister. Some Malaysians expressed concern over the rapid development of a new family business empire headed by the prime minister, while others expressed the cynical view that "this is the way to do business in UMNO if you want to stay in power." The time-honored patterns of politics known as "consociational democracy" facilitated party elites within the Barisan Nasional to trade political support for economic concessions that provided advantageous benefits for their politically linked economic enterprises, and did so without being exposed to much public scrutiny. The constitutionally defined doctrines of Malay "special rights" and doctrines of Muslim primacy within the political order provided convenient justifications for these extraordinary transactions.[13]

When Abdullah Badawi first became prime minister in 2003, he gave high priority to human resource development and made fewer investments in construction and physical infrastructure investments. After his commanding election victory in the 2004 election, he made further shifts in public policies that reflected his newly won electoral mandate. By 2005, many of the projects and initiatives that Prime Minister Mahathir had previously sponsored and had expected to be his legacy had been abandoned or scaled down. In 2005, Badawi signed a free trade agreement with Japan that ended tariffs on knocked-down auto parts for Japanese carmakers. Under the terms of that agreement, tariffs on Japanese finished cars were to be eliminated by 2015. That agreement also promised Japanese assistance to the Malaysian auto industry to increase its competitiveness.[14] Because Malaysia's auto industry had been founded with Mahathir's assistance and sponsorship, the Proton automobile had become a symbol of Mahathir's commitment to industrialization and a modernized lifestyle for all Malaysians. The auto industry had been built in Malaysia with government funding and very high tariff protection. To threaten the future of that industry appeared to Mahathir as a rejection of his far-sighted leadership to create a self-reliant Islamic society. Perhaps, for Mahathir, the ultimate insult to his legacy came later when the government announced that construction would be halted on the partially built new national capital at Putrajaya, about 25 miles south of Kuala Lumpur.

After making a number of barbed comments about his successor, Mahathir called a news conference in June 2006 to launch a full-scale assault on Badawi's leadership. Mahathir accused Badawi of breaking his promise to continue the policies of his regime and argued that the Malaysian government had plenty of money to invest in capital infrastructure projects. Mahathir said that he regretted choosing Badawi to be prime minister and accused him of betraying his trust and showing no gratitude to him for all of his support. He was particularly upset over the new National Automobile Policy that exposed the Proton automobile to global competition from foreign producers. Over the next year, Mahathir launched a series of vicious personal attacks on Prime Minister Badawi, but the latter refused to answer these attacks directly. Instead, responses came from members of the government team, who argued that Badawi answered to the Malaysian public during the last election when he received a stronger mandate than any previous Malaysian prime minister. Commentators noted that this dispute involved a contest between two competing patron-client networks for contracts, jobs, and economic clout. The powers of incumbency were manifest, but uncertainty remained over how this contest would impact the unity of the United Malays National Organization.[15]

Murtad in Malaysia

Prime Minister Badawi's proposal to promote Islam Hadhari as a "tolerant, inclusive, moderate, and modern Islam" began to be tested by events and by conflicts that were beyond the control of federal authorities. The issues of religious freedom and tolerance for religious diversity raised by the Ahmadiyah case in Indonesia were also raised in Malaysia at about the same time but with a different religious group. One of the first tests of religious tolerance did not involve conflicts between major established religions, but with a minor sect led by a charismatic religious leader who attracted a small band of devoted followers. A Malay Muslim named Arrifin Mohamad began about 1975 attracting a following as a spiritual leader. He changed his name to Ayah Pin (Father Pin) and formed a sect called Sky Kingdom, which he claimed to be a synthesis of all religious faiths, including Muslim, Christian, Hindu, Buddhist, and others. He engaged in faith healing and claimed to be sent by God to teach religious tolerance.

By 1994, Ayah Pin's followers were living together in a community at Kemaman in Terengganu. Through community efforts by devotees, they constructed a worship site that had as its primary symbols a large concrete teapot and an umbrella. The Terengganu state religious authorities became concerned that Muslims were being attracted to this new sect and issued a fatwa in 1997 prohibiting Muslims from any association with Ayah Pin. When four of his followers publicly renounced Islam in 1998, they were charged with murtad, and after trial in a Sharia court, the four were jailed. Religious authorities then attempted to close the commune for its violation of land-use laws, but those charges were not upheld in court. Finally, Ayah Pin was arrested in 2001 by state religious authorities, brought to trial in a kathi court, and convicted of murtad with a sentence of eleven months imprisonment. He served this sentence and, when released, he returned to the Sky Kingdom complex to resume his leadership of the faith community that had continued to thrive. By 2005, he claimed to have 1,000 followers in Malaysia and another 10,000 abroad.

On July 18, 2005, a vigilante mob of thirty masked men arrived at the Sky Kingdom complex and proceeded to set fire to buildings and vehicles with petrol bombs and to destroy other properties of the sect. Ayah Pin escaped the mob and went into hiding. When the police arrived on the scene two days later, they made no arrests of any of the attackers, but they did arrest fifty-eight sect members for violating the fatwa prohibiting any Muslim from associating with Ayah Pin and his Sky Kingdom movement. On August 1, state religious officials arrived with bulldozers to demolish the remains of the Sky Kingdom complex, and in doing so, ignored a court order that had reversed their decision to demolish that facility. In previous apostasy trials, when Muslim defendants cited Malaysia's Federal Constitution, which in Article 11 confers freedom of religion to "every person," the Federal Courts avoided the issue by upholding the jurisdiction of the Sharia courts and thus indirectly leaving unchallenged any decisions concerning freedom of religion that Islamic courts made regarding murtad cases. This time, however, two of the fifty-eight arrested sect members filed habeas corpus petitions challenging the murtad criminal punishments for Muslims. Malaysia's National Human Rights Commission (Suhakam) decided to support the case of the defendants and also filed a formal complaint with the United Nations Human Rights Commission regarding the case against Ayah Pin.

At issue in these cases was the question of whether the constitutional rights of religious liberty were only available to non-Muslim citizens. Or could Muslims invoke constitutional rights of religious liberty when they renounced Islam or if they failed to comply with Sharia law and fatwas regarding religious beliefs and obligations? Although not directly involved, Prime Minister Badawi was placed in an awkward political position. Liberal Muslim organizations were defending more religious freedom for Muslims, while more conservative Muslims were unyielding in their demands for murtad convictions against "deviant" Muslims.[16]

Revisions to Islamic Family Law

Another test of tolerance within Islam arose over issues of reform to Islamic family law. Under the Malaysian Constitution, Islam falls within the jurisdiction of the states. However, because of differences between state laws, beginning in 2003 federal authorities directed the states to adopt a standardized Islamic Family Law drafted by the Department for the Advancement of Islam. By 2005, most states had adopted the draft law without opposition, and in December 2005 the draft legislation was submitted to Parliament for application to the three federal territories of Kuala Lumpur, Labuan, and Putrajaya. When that legislation came to the attention of a liberal women's advocacy group called Sisters in Islam, that organization mounted a campaign to amend the draft law submitted to Parliament. Sisters in Islam argued that the legislation substantially diminished rights for women in marriage and enhanced the capacity of men to enter into polygamous marriages without reference to obligations made to the first wife and with diminished responsibility for their children. Under the new draft, a Muslim husband could prevent his wife from accessing her bank account or other assets and could claim a share of her property, including the matrimonial home, when he contracts a polygamous marriage. In effect, the husband could use the assets of the first wife to support his new lifestyle with another wife. Under existing Islamic law, the husband could obtain a divorce by pronouncing its dissolution (*talak*) three times to his wife. By contrast, if the husband does not assent to a divorce, the wife seeking a divorce must prove her case through costly legal action in a Sharia court. These unequal provisions concerning divorce, child custody, and matrimonial assets were continued or enhanced in the new draft legislation.

When the Islamic Family Law Bill was introduced to Parliament, a coalition called the Joint Action Group on Gender Equality organized public protests concerning gender inequality in the proposed legislation. Sisters in Islam joined with various other women's organizations to protest the legislation. A memorandum of opposition was sent to all members of Parliament, and a publicity campaign exposed the injustice to Muslim women. By the time the campaign became organized, the Islamic Family Law Bill had already passed the lower house (Dewan Rakyat), but when it came to the Senate (Dewan Negara), the bill met determined opposition, including a contingent of Barisan Nasional senators. To secure passage, Prime Minister Badawi invoked severe party disciplinary penalties if BN members failed to vote for the bill. To address their concerns, Badawi promised that the attorney general would not gazette the new law until after it had been reviewed in consultation with women's groups, raising expectations that concessions would be forthcoming to address issues of gender equality. Yet, after the Islamic Family Law passed Parliament, no changes were made to that legislation.[17]

Universal Rights vs. Sharia Obligations

The escalating issues related to enforcement of Sharia obligations created a heightened sense of hostility and suspicion across religious boundaries. Many non-Muslims became concerned that the strictures of Islam were impinging on their religious freedoms. At the same time, more strident and conservative Muslims became increasingly fearful that too often secular Muslims were seeking to abandon their faith and were attracted to overt or covert murtad. The issues of apostasy and proselytizing across religious boundaries became, for many Muslims, a matter of intense passion and anger.

The relationship between Article 11 of Malaysia's Federal Constitution and Sharia law became much more complicated after 1988. Article 11 (1) states: "Every person has the right to profess and practice his religion and, subject to Clause (4) to propagate it." In 1988, Parliament passed a constitutional amendment for Article 121 (1A) that states: High Courts of the judiciary "shall have no jurisdiction in respect of any matter within the jurisdiction of Syariah courts."[18] In effect, this amendment exempted Sharia courts from judicial review by Malaysia's regular secular courts. Since the jurisdiction of Sharia courts extends to Islam and Islamic law, this amendment was interpreted to mean that any Muslim who wished to renounce Islam or claim the rights of religious liberty promised in Article 11, must first secure the approval of a Sharia court. Sharia law, however, defines apostasy as a serious crime that cannot be sanctioned. This constitutional amendment also gave Sharia law and Sharia courts exclusive jurisdiction over domestic and inheritance civil cases when one of the litigants is a Muslim and the other is non-Muslim. In practice this has meant that the Muslim litigant gains preemptive rights over the non-Muslim litigant in both domestic and inheritance cases. For example, a new convert to Islam married to a non-Muslim could claim a divorce and full custody of all children and deem those children to be Muslim, without the permission of a now-divorced non-Muslim spouse.

During 2006, apostasy issues became a subject of much dispute, in part through newspaper reports covering the court appeals of Azhar Mansor and Lina Joy, who attempted to secure legal approval for the renunciation of their status as Muslims.[19] Azlina Jailani was a Malay who converted to Christianity in 1980 and changed her name to Lina Joy. She applied first to the National Registration Department and then to the Federal High Court to have her religious identity changed. After appeals through three courts, the Federal Court ruled by a 2 to 1 majority that the jurisdiction rested with the Sharia court. Because her status as a Muslim could not be renounced, her only option, if she wished to profess Christianity, was to leave the country. The Muslim establishment praised this verdict as "protecting Islam." Some alarmist Muslim activists made the accusation that as many as 250,000 Muslims were prepared to renounce their religion. Others, who consulted Sharia court records, reported that the number of apostates among Muslims was less than 300, and only a few recent converts to Islam had been given permission to renounce Islam to recover their previous status.[20]

Because primary jurisdiction for administration of Islam is assigned to the states, several states passed laws providing for "rehabilitation" of "deviant"

Muslims. Such "faith restoration" laws were passed in Sabah, Perak, Kelantan, Terengganu, and Perlis. A number of other states established similar "rehabilitation" programs through statutes defining Sharia criminal law. Any Muslim who was deemed to be "deviant" or who applied to change his/her status from "Muslim" to "non-Muslim" could be sentenced by the Sharia court to a "faith restoration center" to undergo reeducation by an imam authorized to preach approved Islamic doctrines. The time in detention usually ended when the detainee acknowledged the validity of "true Islam." The periods of enforced detention ranged from a few months up to three years.

In 2000, the federal government drafted a Federal Territory Restoration of Faith Bill providing for detention of up to one year to check incidences of apostasy and deviant Islamic teachings among Muslims. Construction of a "federal faith restoration center" had already begun when twenty-nine lawyers and human rights activists petitioned the Human Rights Commission of Malaysia (Suhakam), charging that the bill violated Article 11 of the Federal Constitution.[21] Because of these protests, the government withdrew the Restoration of Faith Bill, but existing state laws providing for "rehabilitation" of wayward Muslims remained in force.

Because of the intensifying Islamization process that began to challenge the validity of constitutional guarantees of religious liberty, women's rights groups and liberal Muslim intellectuals formed a statutory body called the Inter Faith Council (IFC), which met for the first time in April 2005. Members of the IFC included human rights advocates, lawyers, and social activists. Mainline Islamic groups refused to participate in IFC sessions and instead organized large demonstrations to disrupt and close IFC forums whenever they met. At the center of the anti-IFC coalition was an organization called the Allied Coordinating Committee of Islamic NGOs (ACCIN). They accused the IFC of attempting to usurp the powers of state Islamic religious bodies and of infringing on the rights of Muslims to practice Islam. The ACCIN also accused the IFC of being an anti-Muslim body sponsored by the Malaysian Council of Buddhism, Christianity, Hinduism, Sikhism, and Taoism.[22] In response to the heightened religious tensions, the Malaysian government ordered the IFC to disband.

Shortly thereafter, a new coalition of liberal Muslims and non-Muslim activists founded a new body called Article 11 that sponsored forums to discuss constitutional rights of citizens. It circulated a petition sent to the government asking for religious freedom for Muslims and greater judicial equity for non-Muslims. That petition gained 20,000 signatures, but its objectives were vigorously opposed by a larger coalition organized by ACCIN. When Article 11 forums were held in Penang and Johor Baru, ACCIN staged mass protests that the police used as a justification for closing the forums, claiming that protesters could not be controlled. On July 24, 2006, the ACCIN organized a mass demonstration of 10,000 at the Federal Mosque to demand that the prime minister ban the Article 11 coalition. Prime Minister Badawi responded by banning all Article 11 forums and any public discussions of interfaith issues.[23]

The ban on public discourse did not apply to public meetings to demand more stringent laws to enforce Islamic obligations and to protect against "deviant doctrines." In November, the International Islamic University sponsored a conference on apostasy featuring spokesmen from Malaysia's religious establishment and various defenders of the Sharia judiciary. The participants argued for more severe penalties for Muslims guilty of apostasy, and one panelist argued that Muslim apostates should be imprisoned without trial under provisions of the Internal Security Act.[24] The hard-line Islamists who wanted to assert the absolute supremacy of Sharia law and reject the applicability of Article 11 for all Muslims were particularly contemptuous of those Muslims who favored freedom of and from religion, as promised by that article. For the Islamists, concepts of universal human rights posed what they described as a "clear and present danger" to the supremacy of Islam in Malaysia. Progressive, modernist, and liberal Muslims in Malaysia were stigmatized as heretical, disloyal, and kafir. Instead of the earlier slogans of "Malay supremacy," which had motivated UMNO since its founding, the newer slogans and ideology stressed "Islamic supremacy." A number of political analysts referred to these activists as the "New Islamists" and their political goal as "desecularisation."[25] To many Malaysian Muslims, this dispute appeared to be a decisive moment in Malaysia's political evolution when the options were posed as a stark choice between a "desecularized" orthodox Islam and a "secular" political order.

"Special Rights" and Education

The strident debates over Islamic apostasy and freedom of religion had the effect of opening the parameters of public dialogue to include other sensitive political issues. Another "red flag" issue that was kept brewing at a low simmer for a number of years concerned the way education was made the key component of the system of Malay "special privileges." Over the period of five decades, government policies radically transformed the earlier colonial system of education.[26] These policies were designed to raise the educational level of the Malays and prepare them for assuming a dominant role in the economic and cultural life of the country. Systematically applied, these policies produced a dramatic transformation in the political landscape by generating a tremendous increase in the educational levels of the Malays and by promoting Malays into the upper ranks of the economy, as well as reinforcing their preeminent power within the political system. Even so, by the time Prime Minister Badawi assumed leadership of the country, new and recurring issues prompted a reexamination of old assumptions.

Primary and secondary education in National Schools was infused with a curriculum stressing Malay culture with an increasing infusion of Islamic content. Many Malay leaders expected that the independent Chinese schools would be phased out and all Malaysians would gain their primary and secondary education in a single system of National Schools, where the primacy of Malay culture and political power would be appropriately preserved and celebrated. This vast experiment in social engineering did not take into account how non-Malays would respond to the elaborate system of privileges, preferential treatments, and subsidies for Malays.

Many leaders of the Chinese community had been products of English-media schools of the colonial era. When the Chinese vernacular schools seemed to be under threat, the Chinese community as a whole mobilized a mass campaign to save independent Chinese schools. Eventually, a compromise was reached with the government in 1966 whereby Chinese "national-type" schools continued to operate independently, but Malay was adopted as the medium of instruction. A few Chinese schools remained independent, but the "national-type" schools became the bastion of those seeking to preserve both Chinese culture and Malaysia's multicultural panorama. There were also a few Tamil "national-type" schools. By private donations and the collection of school fees, the quality of these schools and their enrollments steadily increased. The non-Malays, especially the Chinese, campaigned tenaciously for their independent schools. Essentially, the government reluctantly recognized these other three educational streams, but attempted to impede their progress by a deliberate policy restricting funding. By 2004, only 2 percent of Chinese students attended government-operated National Schools, while enrollment in Chinese "national-type" schools increased to about 640,000 students, of which 65,000 were non-Chinese, including within that number about 35,000 Malays.[27]

Under the New Economic Policy and its successor policies, the government used tertiary education as a prime instrument for the restructuring of Malaysian society and its economy. Universities acted both as "gatekeepers" to control access to valued jobs and professions and also to generate a new entrepreneurial and professional workforce staffed by a preponderant majority of Malays. Malay youth, supported by generous government bursaries, flooded into the rapidly expanding system of universities and technical colleges. In addition, tens of thousands of Malays were sent abroad for study at prestigious universities primarily in the United States, the United Kingdom, Australia, and Canada. Nearly all Malays who met required academic qualifications received full Malaysian government scholarships in a massive investment in human resources to redress the educational imbalance between Malays and non-Malays.

To facilitate this educational and cultural transformation, non-Malays faced restrictive admission quotas to Malaysian universities. At the tertiary level, Malaysia created eleven universities and numerous technical colleges supported by the state. Admission to those institutions of higher education was on a quota system that gave overwhelming allocations to Malay students as part of the system of Malay "special rights." The quotas varied slightly from institution to institution, with one university restricting its enrollment exclusively to Bumiputra (which category embraced all Malays and a very few "indigenous peoples"). The system of severely restricted quotas for the admission of non-Malays to Malaysian institutions of higher learning generated heightened competition for few available admissions. Non-Malays approached their studies with greater commitment to high academic achievement. When they were denied entrance to Malaysian universities, many non-Malays chose to continue their studies abroad, either through self-financing or through foreign scholarship support. In each year, the number of non-Malays gaining advanced degrees abroad usually surpassed the number of Malays who went abroad for education on fully funded government scholarships. Although fewer in number, non-Malays acquired as many foreign degrees from quality institutions and generally with higher levels of achievement than those Malays who took advantage of the generous scholarships provided by the Malaysian government.

The quota system also applied to university faculty, with Malay graduates being recruited in preponderant numbers to fill faculty positions. After recruitment, Malay faculty rose rapidly through the ranks, while non-Malay faculty were usually restricted to the lower ranks. For most government-funded universities, Malays monopolized most administrative staff positions and all vice chancellor positions. Because of the limited admission quotas for non-Malay students, those few students who were admitted did so with high qualifications, and they later made above-average grades. To avoid the appearance of discrimination against the less-qualified Malay students, universities established a grade review process that equalized grade averages between Malay students and non-Malay students. This semisecret process had the effect of inflating grades of Malay students to make their average grades equal to the grade averages earned by non-Malay students. Over time, these differential evaluations became reflected in the postgraduation performances of both Malays and non-Malays.

To address the escalating demand for greater access to university-level education for non-Malays, the government in 1996 permitted the formation of a private university called Universiti Tun Abdul Razak, which had strong political links with UMNO. Five years later, another private university was authorized, called Universiti Tunku Abdul Rahman, with strong political links to the Malayan Chinese Association. Since then, a number of other private universities have been formed, with some of them having "twinning" links with foreign universities. While these private universities have relieved some of the pressure by non-Malays for access to higher education, their academic quality has been mixed and their fees are high because no government funds subsidize these private sector institutions.[28]

Malaysia's public universities, which continue to admit a preponderant proportion of Malay students, are funded at very high levels in comparison to GDP per capita spent by Singapore and Thailand. Even so, the quality of these institutions has eroded through resignation of highly productive faculty to foreign universities and institutes. These public universities have operated with bloated and inefficient bureaucracies, and too often members of senior teaching staff have mediocre research and publication records. For example, the University of Malaya was ranked at 89 on the Times Higher Education Supplement survey of world universities in 2004, was ranked at 169 in 2005, and fell to 192 in 2006. The Universiti Sains Malaysia was ranked at 111 in 2004 but failed to make the list the next year. The Universiti Kebangsaan Malaysia was ranked at 185 in 2006.[29] The overall impact of religious-ethnic quotas for student admissions and faculty recruitment was extracting a very high cost, both in the efficient allocation of public funding and in the investment in national human resources.

Revisiting the New Economic Policy

Following the deadly racial riots of May 13, 1969, the Malaysian government had gradually formulated in 1971 a comprehensive recovery strategy that included as one component what came to be called the New Economic Policy. Two economic goals were established: "to reduce and eventually eradicate poverty for all Malaysians" and "to eventually eliminate race with economic function." Over the years, the first goal was pursued with fluctuating commitments and ineffectual policies. The second goal became the cornerstone of government economic policies, seeking to "restructure society" by giving the Malays a major stake in the economy and promoting Malay ownership and participation in all sectors of the economy. At the time that the NEP was initiated, the government announced a goal of achieving 30 percent of Malay ownership of all industrial and commercial activities by 1990. The instruments to achieve this goal involved expanding Malay rights and privileges, utilizing quotas in the public and private sector to improve employment opportunities for Malays. In addition, massive government funds were allocated for Bumiputra trust agencies to generate a vast array of enterprises that were to be transferred to Malay ownership and that would provide employment and on-the-job training for Malays in commercial and industrial enterprises. These NEP policies were initially viewed as "affirmative action" policies that presumably would end when the announced target goal had been achieved.[30]

Two years before the 1990 NEP target date, the government formed a special body called the National Economic Consultative Council to advise on future policy regarding poverty reduction and "ethnic restructuring." After much debate and political maneuvering, the NECC determined that the NEP goal had not been met and proposed that the government continue with intensified programs designed to enhance the economic wealth and power of the Malays.

The nonethnic poverty alleviation programs were endorsed but given a lower priority.[31] The new program was called the National Development Program, which continued from 1990 to 2000. When that program expired, again a reassessment generated what was called the National Vision Policy (NVP), which was designed to continue to 2020. Under this NVP mandate, the basic NEP programs of "ethnic restructuring" were continued but with more flexible ethnic quotas.

At each juncture in the planning cycle, the issue of "ethnic-restructuring" target objectives was addressed. In 1989, opposition politicians argued that the Malays had achieved the target of 30 percent of the economy by 1983. Critics made similar arguments with each new planning cycle. According to official government calculations, Bumiputra equity ownership was 2.4 percent in 1970, 19.3 percent in 1990, 18.7 percent in 2004, and 19.9 percent in 2005. These official statistics ignored Malay participation and ownership of Bumiputra trust agencies and in GLCs that were formed with government funds and then privatized at artificially low prices to Malays for their employment and ownership. Similarly, Malays were able to purchase lucrative real estate properties at mandated discounts, but their extensive ownership in the properties market was also ignored in government statistics. Because Malays were able to buy shares on the Malaysian stock market at government-mandated reduced values, many stock shares were purchased by Malays and quickly resold at market value for quick risk-free profits. Therefore, Malay equity tended to be channeled into economic ventures that received special advantages for Bumiputra as mandated by government policies.

In November 2005, Prime Minister Abdullah Badawi introduced the 9th Malaysia Plan that endorsed the NEP-type policies, which were projected to continue up through 2020. In response to that policy initiative, the private "think tank" Asian Strategic Leadership Institute (ASLI), affiliated with the Centre for Public Policy Studies in Kuala Lumpur, examined the issues of corporate equity trends in 2006. Previously, in 2002, a University of Malaya team had also studied this issue. The results of these three studies came to rather different conclusions, partly as a function of utilizing different data sources and operating from different assumptions.

The Centre for Public Policy Studies released the report of the ASLI just prior to the November general assembly sessions of UMNO. It created a storm of controversy by stating that the 30 percent Bumiputra corporate equity goal had been substantially surpassed, and it implied, but did not state, that the racial preference policies of the NEP and its successor plans should either be abolished or be reformed. Mirzan Mahathir, son of former prime minister Mahathir, was president of the ASLI center, and when the report on Bumiputra equity was first released, he announced that the study was based on flawed assumptions. Consequently, Mirzan withdrew the report from public circulation without an explanation of what were the "flawed assumptions." Prime Minister Badawi also announced that the government's data were correct, and because the issue was "sensitive" there should be no further discussion of the

ASLI report's findings. The principal investigator for the report was the renowned economist Lim Teck Ghee, who defended his study based on careful and comprehensive research of relevant data. To defend the integrity of his report, Lim resigned as director of the Centre for Public Policy Studies.[32] (See Table 13.1.)

In November, the United Malays National Organization held its week-long annual meeting. During those sessions, one delegate from Melaka brandished a Malay short sword called a *keris* and issued an ominous warning: "UMNO is willing to risk lives and bathe in blood to defend the race and religion. Don't play with fire. If the [other races] mess with our rights, we will mess with theirs." After issuing his threat, he kissed his keris and called on UMNO Youth chief Hishammudin Hussein to "unsheath his keris."[33]

In January 2007, the chairman of the ASLI Centre for Public Policy Studies, Tan Sri Ramon Navaratnam, gave a speech at the 9th Malaysia Strategic Outlook Conference in which he outlined a set of objectives for a "New National Agenda." He discussed a number of issue areas in need of reform but gave particular emphasis to four main topics that required reform and a shift of priorities. First, he called for poverty eradication without reference to race. Second, he proposed to utilize "balanced quotas" based on Malaysia's ethnic population distributions for admissions and staffing at government-supported higher education institutions as well as for recruitment into the civil service, the army, and the police. Third, he called for a completely independent Anti-Corruption Agency to prosecute white-collar crime at the highest levels. Fourth, he called for cross-cultural exchanges and the promotion of tolerance among all sectors of Malaysia's multicultural society. Navaratnam made no

Table 13.1 Comparison of Three Studies on Bumiputra Equity Ownership

Government Economic Planning Unit (2005)	Asian Strategic Leadership Institute (2006)	University of Malaya Study (2002)
Bumiputra own 18.9% in 2005	Bumiputra own 45.4% in 2005	Bumiputra own 33.7% in 1997
Study involves 600,000 companies registered in Malaysia	Study involves top 1,000 listed companies on the Bursa Malaysia stock market	Study involves public listed companies on Kuala Lumpur Stock Exchange
Calculation based on par value of shares	Calculation based on market value of shares	Calculations based on par values of shares
Government-linked corporations (GLCs) not included as Bumiputra ownership	70% of GLC shares classified as Bumiputra	GLCs not included as Bumiputra ownership

Sources: Maznah Mohamad, "Malaysia in 2006: The Enemies Within," research paper (2007), 1–15, www.iseas.edu/sg/rof07mm.pdf; Beh Li Yi, "Bumi Equity Hit NEP Targets 10 Years Ago," Malaysiakini.com (November 1, 2006); Centre for Public Policy Studies, "Corporate Equity Distribution: Past Trends and Future Policy," CPPS (2006), Kuala Lumpur, 1–40.

mention of the earlier controversy over the ASLI report on Bumiputra corporate equity. Instead, he articulated a set of proposals that he believed would appeal to all Malaysians, both Malay and non-Malay. He proposed that those who are committed to reform the economy should support a more equitable economic and political system by the gradual elimination of ethnic preference policies that date back to the era of the British colonial administration.[34]

An Opposition Coalition Revived

In April 2007, the death of a Selangor state assemblyman forced a by-election in the district of Ijok, a semirural constituency consisting mostly of palm oil farmers, factory workers, and civil servants. Although this was a politically insignificant seat, the election became a test of political support for both the Barisan Nasional and Partai Keadilan Rakyat (PKR). The government allocated US$10 million to persuade 12,000 voters to support the BN. Roads were repaved, a new mosque and a Chinese high school were built, and 200 free sewing machines were distributed.

Anwar Ibrahim entered the Ijok campaign as the star attraction, distributing an election manifesto entitled "A Malaysian Economic Agenda,"[35] which blamed Malaysia's economic decline on inefficiency, corruption, waste of resources, and a failure to fully invest in human resources caused by ethnic preference policies. The message was a mix of populist rhetoric about the failure of ordinary Malays to benefit from "special rights," while politically favored Malays monopolized the benefits. Anwar combined that message with the promise that Malaysia could compete in the global economy if Malaysians were treated with equality and gained the capacity to tolerate and appreciate their cultural differences. In the election on April 28, the BN candidate won with 5,884 votes to the PKR candidate's 4,034 votes. Prime Minister Abdullah Badawi praised the BN victory, claiming that it was a decisive rejection of the leadership of Anwar Ibrahim.[36] The Ijok by-election was significant, not in its electoral outcome, but because that campaign raised many "sensitive issues" that were being openly debated for the first time in an election.[37]

Because of concerns over government manipulation of elections, a coalition of opposition parties formed a committee to demand electoral reforms. Adopting the acronym Bersih, meaning "clean" in Malay, its demands included providing free candidate access to state-owned media, a clean-up of registered voter rolls, use of indelible ink to mark those who vote to prevent voter fraud, and abolition of postal votes. To promote their cause, Bersih leaders announced a public rally for November 10 to deliver a memorandum for electoral reform to the Paramount Ruler, Sultan Azlan Shah, who had a thirty-year career in the Malaysian judiciary and had acquired a reputation as an advocate for reforms. The government warned citizens not to join the rally because an application for a public gathering had been denied. Police roadblocks were set up around Kuala Lumpur to prevent protesters from approaching the Istana Negara (National Palace). Large contingents of riot police were stationed at key locations to block the movement of protesters, who were assaulted with chemically laced water cannon and tear gas, resulting in injuries and many arrests. Eventually, some marchers arrived at the palace to deliver their petition to the ruler's secretary. The international press reported that protesters numbered 40,000, while the government-controlled press reported a figure of only 4,000 participants.[38]

Two weeks after the Bersih rally, another large protest was mounted, this time sponsored by Hindraf (Hindu Rights Action Force) representing Malaysian Indians. Since 1980, about 300,000 Indian plantation workers lost their jobs as a result of the purchase of privately owned plantations by government-linked corporations or by sale of plantation lands for township development schemes. These workers not only lost their jobs but also their housing, their vegetable plots, their cattle, and their Hindu temples, which were systematically demolished by action of state authorities. These displaced workers moved into urban slums where they competed for the lowest-paid menial jobs and encountered high unemployment and discrimination from local authorities. The "affirmative action" policies of Malay "special rights" represented an added form of discrimination against Indians relating to jobs, education admissions, business licenses, and access to public services. During 2006 and 2007, eighteen Hindu temples were demolished by Malaysian authorities, including a 107-year-old temple at Shah Alam.[39]

To draw attention to the plight of poverty-stricken Indians, Hindraf called for a mass rally on November 25 to deliver a memorandum to Queen Elizabeth II. The petition accused the British government of exploiting Indian indentured laborers for 150 years and of failing to protect their rights when independence was granted to the Federation of Malaya. Queen Elizabeth was requested to appoint a Queen's Counsel to argue their case in British courts, seeking about US$1 million in damages for every resident Malaysian Indian. On the day of the rally, between 20,000 and 30,000 protesters assembled in central Kuala Lumpur and were assaulted by tear gas and chemical-laced water cannon by police in riot gear. About 400 people were arrested and over 100 detained. The protesters were blocked from approaching the British High Commission, but a copy of their memo was sent to the commissioner via fax.[40]

Prior to the rally, the government arrested three top leaders of Hindraf, charging them with sedition. At their trial, the court acquitted the accused due to lack of evidence. The next day, on December 12, Prime Minister Badawi invoked the Internal Security Act (ISA) to arrest again and imprison the three top leaders of Hindraf for an indefinite sentence, not subject to review by the courts. Five Hindraf lawyers were also arrested for "spreading allegations against the government" and given indefinite sentences under the ISA by order of Prime Minister Badawi.[41]

Malaysia's 2008 Elections

Because of government concern over the role of Anwar Ibrahim in mobilizing political opposition to the incumbent Barisan Nasional government led by Prime Minister Ahmad Badawi, most political observers assumed that new parliamentary elections would probably be called before April 14, 2008. By the terms of Anwar Ibrahim's previous criminal convictions, he was prevented from contesting any elective office until after that date. As expected, Parliament was dissolved on February 13, and elections were set for March 8, 2008. All licensed newspapers supported the BN, giving it overwhelming coverage, and virtually ignored the opposition. Five parties—Democratic Action Party (DAP), Party Keadilan (PKR), Partai Aislam Sa-Malaysia (PAS), Socialist Party of Malaysia (PSM), and People's Party of Malaysia—formed an opposition coalition initially called Barisan Rakyat (People's Front) and later renamed Pakatan Rakyat (People's Consensus). Anwar Ibrahim became the key leader in forging the opposition coalition, acting as an intermediary, especially between the DAP and PAS, over issues relating to the role of Islam and Malay "special rights." The leader of PAS agreed to downplay its commitment to Sharia law and focus instead on health care, economic issues, "equal justice to all, justice in economic opportunities, and freedom of religion."[42] The opposition campaign focused on the abuse of power, corruption, the lack of democracy, arbitrary arrests and detention without trial of critics under the Internal Security Act, the increasing poverty gap between the rich and the poor, and economic mismanagement of the economy. The Barisan Nasional campaign referred once again to Anwar's sodomy conviction and warned Malay voters that the opposition would "end Malay special rights." Anwar threatened suit against those who accused him of moral turpitude. He proposed to end the New Economic Policy because it undermined productivity and the benefits of the New Economic Policy were only going to rich and politically connected Malays.

On election day, 8 million Malaysians cast votes that resulted in the Barisan Nasional suffering the worst electoral performance of any ruling coalition since independence in 1957. (See Table 13.2.) The BN gained 50.27 percent of the total vote, while the opposition Barisan Rakyat gained 46.75 percent of the vote. In Parliament, the BN retained 140 seats, while the BR gained 82 seats. Election results revealed that ethnic Chinese support for the Barisan Nasional shifted from 63 percent in the previous election to 35 percent in 2008. Support from the Indian community plunged from 82 percent to 47 percent. And support from Malays slipped from 63 percent to 58 percent.[43] In five states, the opposition BR gained a majority control of the state legislature. In Kedah, the margin of seats for Barisan Rakyat was 21 to 14; in Kelantan it was 39 to 6; in Penang it was 29 to 11; in Perak it was 31 to 28; and in Selangor it was 36 to 20. In all these states, the BR appointed a multiracial cabinet and their coalition leaders promised to represent all races. Acting as the head

Table 13.2 Malaysia: Elected Seats in Dewan Rakyat, 2008, 2004, and 1999

Parties	2008 Federal	2008 States	2004 Federal	2004 States	1999 Federal
Barisan Nasional					
UMNO	79	239	109	302	72
MCA	15	32	31	76	29
MIC	3	7	9	19	7
Other BN	43	29	49	56	40
BN total	140	307	198	453	148
	(63.0%)	(60.7%)	(90.4%)	(89.7%)	(76.7%)
Barisan Rakyat					
PAS	23	83	7	36	27
DAP	28	73	12	15	10
PKN/PKR	31	40	1	—	5
Other	—	—	—	—	3
BR total	82	196	20	51	45
	(36.9%)	(38.8%)	(9.1%)	(10.1%)	(23.3%)
Independent	—	—	1	1	—

Sources: The Star, "Election 2004" and "Election 1999," thestar.com.my/election2004/results 1999/results.html and thestar.com.my/election2004/results/results.htm; *The Star,* "Malaysia Decides 2008," elections2.thestar.com.my/results/results.html.

of the Barisan Rakyat, Anwar Ibrahim stated "that if there was no fraud in the election, we would have won. If we had two percent more votes we would have formed the new government."[44]

Among the BR victors were Anwar's wife, Wan Azizah Wan Ismail, who was reelected to Parliament, and his daughter, Nurul Izzah Anwar, who defeated a cabinet minister to gain a seat in Parliament. A Hindraf lawyer, Manoharan Malayalam, jailed under the ISA, contested as a DAP candidate and won a state seat while remaining incarcerated. Most commentators assumed that an elected PKR member of Parliament would probably resign after April 14 to force a by-election to allow Anwar Ibrahim to contest for a seat in Parliament. His leadership of the Barisan Rakyat coalition was essential to generate unified policy positions for its reform agenda. At network blog sites and in election commentaries, there was much speculation about whether Malaysia was entering a new period of two-coalition competitive politics that would effectively challenge the ethnic-based elite "consociational" power-broker system operated by the earlier alliance and Barisan Nasional. Anwar Ibrahim promised to move Malaysian politics toward a nonethnically based political system that would reexamine previous communal policies and establish a more open democratic system based on merit, equality, human rights, fairness, and multicultural tolerance.[45]

Whether the Malaysian public was prepared to support that political agenda was the prime topic of most political commentaries. Most observers of Malaysian politics seemed to assume that the 2008 election would be followed by a period of political turmoil with various maneuvers to restructure political coalitions. Could the Barisan Nasional recover its support base to return to its dominant role in Malaysian politics? Could the Barisan Rakyat win majority support by recruiting defectors from the ruling coalition? Would the leaders of UMNO offer to restore Anwar's membership in that party and support him for prime minister as a tactic to dismantle the Barisan Rakyat? Would Malaysia experience four years of continuing political stalemate that would only be resolved by the next election? In the immediate aftermath of the 2008 elections, the spirit of Reformasi that appeared to have withered and died after the 1999 election had once again been revived with renewed energy and enthusiasm.

Notes

1. M. Bakri Musa, "Post-Mahathir Malaysia: Coasting Along," in Amy McCreedy (ed.), *Passing the Mantle: A New Leadership for Malaysia,* Asia Program Special Report No. 116 (September 2003), Washington, DC, Woodrow Wilson International Center, 13–18.

2. In 1987, Badawi was allied with Tengku Razaleigh's "Team B" challenge to gain control of UMNO and displace Mahathir as prime minister. In the aftermath of that dispute, Badawi attempted to mediate between the Team B UMNO "dissidents" and the winning faction led by Prime Minister Mahathir. When that effort failed, Badawi, who had been elected UMNO vice president, gradually became rehabilitated into the UMNO power structure under Mahathir's leadership. In 1990, Badawi was appointed head of the National Economic Consultative Council (NECC), and in 1991, he was appointed minister of foreign affairs. In February 1999, he became deputy prime minister and minister of home affairs. Gordon P. Means, *Malaysian Politics: The Second Generation* (Singapore: Oxford University Press, 1991), 174–175, 204–268 passim.

3. Bridget Welsh, "Malaysia's Transition: Elite Contestation, Political Dilemmas and Incremental Change," in McCreedy, *Passing the Mantle*, 4–12; Bridget Welsh, "Tears and Fears: Tun Mahathir's Last Hurrah," in *Southeast Asian Affairs 2004* (Singapore: Institute of Southeast Asian Studies, 2004), 151–152; Mushahid Ali and Joseph Liow, "Malaysia: PM Abdullah Badawi's Performance and Prospects," *IDSS Commentaries*, No. 04/2004, (Singapore: Institute of Defence and Strategic Studies, 2004), 1–3.

4. Later, the Department for the Advancement of Islam in the Prime Minister's Department issued an official explanation of Islam Hadhari. From that document, the government promised to infuse Islamic content and principles into nearly all social and educational services provided to Muslims. As the proposals became more specific, the reactions and controversies from the public also increased. See Sekretariat Islam Hadhari, "The Concept of Islam Hadhari," July 12, 2005, 1–3, www.islam.gov.my/islamhadhari/concept.html; Audrey Dermawan, "Islam Hadhari the Way Forward," July 9, 2005, 1–3, www.nst.com.my/Current_News/NST/Saturday/National/20050709.

5. Khoo Boo Teik, "Malaysian Politics in 2004: Transitions and Elections," *Trends in Southeast Asia* 7 (2004), 6–18; Mushahid Ali and Joseph Liow, "Malaysia: PM Abdullah Badawi's Performance and Prospects," *IDSS Commentaries,* 04/2004, February 25, 2004, 1–3, www.idss.edu.sg.

6. Lena Kay, "Malaysia: Anwar Is Not the Answer," Asia Report No. 83, Pacific Forum CSIS (September 24, 2004), 1–3, www.glocom.org/special_topics/asia_rep/20040924_asia_s83/.

7. Simon Montlake, "Malaysian Dissident Now Eyes World Stage," *Christian Science Monitor,* November 23, 2004, 8.

8. When Anwar Ibrahim was presented with the "Democrat of the Year" award, he gave a keynote address entitled "Islam and Democratization—The Winds of Change," available at www.islam-democracy.org/6th_Annual_Conference_papers.asp.

9. M. G. G. Pillai, "Anwar Ibrahim at Oxford Menaces UMNO," MGG Commentary, January 29, 2005, 1–4, www.mggpillai.com/article.php3?sid=2067; Marzuki Mohamad, "Post-Prison Anwar Politics—National Reconciliation or Continuing Tensions?" *Asian Analysis* (October 2004), 5–7, www.aseanfocus.com/asiananalysis/article.cfm?articleID=784; M. G. G. Pillai, "The Tortoise and the Hare," *Sajakkini,* May 18, 2005, 1–7, sajakkini.blogsome.com/2005/05/18/the-tortoise-and-the-hare/; Baradan Kuppusamy, "Politics-Malaysia: Anwar Who?" Inter Press Service News Agency, June 6, 2005, 1–3, www.ipsnews.net/africa/interna.asp?idnews=28955; Simon Tisdall, "Anwar Returns to Malaysian Politics," *The Hindu International*, June 10, 2005, 1, www.hindu.com/2005/06/01/stories/2005060103451600.htm.

10. Arfa'eza A. Aziz, "Forex Loss: Anwar Names Those Responsible," *Malaysiakini,* July 19, 2006, 1–2, www.malaysia-today.net/; Phar Kim Beng, "Malaysia: The Politics of Compliance, Conviction and Convenience: A Rudimentary Analysis of Anwar Ibrahim," *Asian Analysis* (February 2006), 5–6.

11. Khoo Boo Teik, "Wake Me Up at Half Past Six," *Aliran,* September 14, 2006, 1–6, www.aliran.com/; Tom Burgis, "Malaysia's Anwar Seeks Return to Power," *Financial Times,* March 15, 2007, 1, www.ft.com/cms/s/05cbac4-d2e7-11db-829f-00b5df10621.html.

12. "Corporate Equity Distribution: Past Trends and Future Policy," Centre for Public Policy Studies (2006), Kuala Lumpur, 10–11.

13. Ioannis Gatsiounis, "Anti graft War Backfires in Malaysia," *Asia Times,* March 21, 2007, 1–6, www.atimes.com/atimes/Southeast_Asia/IC21Ae01.html; Phar Kim Beng, "Malaysia: Assessing Pak Lah," *Asian Analysis* (May 2006), 6–7; William F. Case, "Malaysia: Abdullah in the Middle," *Asian Analysis* (June 2006), 7–8; Phar Kim Beng, "Malaysia: The 'Missing' Prime Minister?" *Asian Analysis* (August 2006), 6–8.

14. Channel NewsAsia, "Japan, Malaysia Agree on FTA to Open Up Malaysian Auto Sector," May 25, 2005, 1–2, www.bilaterals.org/article.php3?id_article=1954.

15. Brendan Pereira, "Mahathir Hits Out," *Business Times,* June 8, 2006, 1–3, www.btimes.com.my; Joceline Tan, "Has Dr. M Gone Too Far This Time?" *The Star,* June 9, 2006, thestar.com.my/news/; "Mahathir-Badawi Spat," *Asian Pacific Post,* June 28, 2006, 1–3, www.asianpacificpost.com/; James Chin, "Malaysia: Mahathir's Internet Politics," *Asian Analysis* (September 2006), 6–7; Phar Kim Beng, "Malaysia: Dr. Mahathir and His Unrelentless Criticism of the Malaysian Government," *Asian Analysis* (December 2006), 7–9; Michael Vatikiotis, "Mahathir's Long, Dark Shadow," *Asia Times,* November 7, 2006, 1–3, www.mggpillai.com/print.php3?artid=15450.

16. "Mob Attack on Commune a Black Incident," *Malaysiakini,* July 19, 2005; "Sky Kingdom Raid: Vigilante Violence Shameful," *Malaysiakini,* July 22, 2005; "Ayah Pin Issue Not About Freedom of Faith," *Malaysiakini,* July 28, 2005; all available at www.malaysiakini.com/letters.

17. Joint Action Group on Gender Equality, "Memorandum to Ahli Dewan Negara to Review the Islamic Family Law (Federal Territories) (Amendment) Bill 2005," memo dated December 8, 2005, 1–3, sistersinislam@pd.jaring.my; Jane Perlez, "Within Islam's Embrace, a Voice for Malaysia's Women," *New York Times,* February 19, 2006, 1–3, www.nytimes.com/2006/02/19/international/asia/19malaysia.htlm; Nik Noriani Nik Badlishah, "Islamic Family Law Bill Fundamentally Unjust," *Malaysiakini,* February 24, 2006, 1–4, www.malaysiakini.com/letters/47433; Rose Ismail, "The Modern Malay Women's Dilemma," *Far Eastern Economic Review* 169, no. 2 (March 2006), 49–52.

18. *Laws of Malaysia, Federal Constitution* (Kuala Lumpur: Percetakan Nasional Malaysia, Bhd, 2002), 21, 104–105.

19. Formerly known as Azlina Jailani, Lina Joy became a Christian in 1980 and was baptized in 1998. Sarah Page, "Malaysian Court Considers Conversion Issue," *Human Rights Watch,* May 4, 2005, 4–5, www.hrwf.net/html/2005PDF/Malaysia_2005.pdf; "Malaysian Woman Not Allowed to Abandon Islam," June 27, 2006, 3, www.hrwf.net/html2006PDF/Malaysia_2006.pdf; Timo Kortteinen, "Ethnicization of the State and Islamic Resurgence in Malaysia—The Case of Lina Joy," paper presented at EuroSEAS Conference, Naples, Italy (September 12–14, 2007).

20. "Apostasy@Murtad Is the Hottest Word in Malaysia Nowadays!" n.d., 1–6, mahaguru58.blogspot.com/2006/11/apostasy-of-malaysia-muslims-study.html.

21. "Petition to the Human Rights Commission of Malaysia, Re: Restoration of Faith Bill," September 25, 2000, 1–4, www.accin-badailies.org/G29%20Memo%20to%Suhakam.htm; Salbiah Ahmad, "Islam in Malaysia, Constitutional and Human Rights Perspectives," *Muslim World Journal of Human Rights* 2, no. 1, article 7 (2005), 1–57, www.bepress.com/mwjhr/vol2 /iss1/art7; Leong Kar Yen, "'Apostasy' Bill Contravenes Constitution, Says Group," *Malaysiakini,* January 20, 2006, 1–2, www.malaysiakini.com/news.

22. Malik Imtiaz Sarwar, "A Response to Criticism of the Interfaith Commission Initiative," *Aliran* 25, no. 6 (2005), 1–9, www.aliran.com/oldsite/monthly/2005a/6g.html. After the ACCIN was formed, UMNO deputy president Najib Tun Razak acknowledged that UMNO had taken an active role in the founding of ACCIN, despite its being self-identified as an NGO.

23. Ioannis Gatsiounis, "In Malaysia, 'Too Sensitive' for Debate," *Malaysia Today,* August 4, 2006, 1–6, www.malaysia-today.net/Blog-e/2006/08/; "The Coalition Called Article 11: Myths and Facts," *Aliran,* March 27, 2007, 1–5, www.aliran.com/; Maznah Mohamad, "Malaysia in 2006: The Enemies Within," research paper, Institute of Southeast Asian Studies, 2007, 1–16, www.iseas.edu/sg/rof07mm.pdf.

24. Fauwaz Abdul Aziz, "Apostasy: Tighten Law Says Negri Sembilan Mufti," *Malaysiakini.com,* November 29, 2006, as cited by Mohamad, "Malaysia in 2006," 4. The Ministry of Education approved a syllabus for Islamic education in public schools, which stated under the heading "Ways of Dealing with Apostates": "1. Advise and persuade the offender to repent and return to Islam. 2. To impose the death sentence." See "Malaysia—Nurturing a Nation of Jihadists," May 26, 2006, 1–5, www.danielpipes.org/comments/46488.

25. Clive S. Kessler, "Malaysia: The Long March Toward Desecularisation," *Asian Analysis* (October 2006), 8–11; Farish A. Noor, "Rev Up the Hate Machine," paper, May 30, 2005, 1–3, www.malaysia.net/trackback/2025.

26. During the colonial period, four separate school systems operated within the country, including three vernacular school systems with instruction in Malay, Chinese, and Tamil. The Malay schools were totally government supported but only operated at the primary level. The Chinese schools were privately supported and taught in Mandarin at both the primary and secondary level. The Tamil schools were government assisted and taught in Tamil only at the primary level. In addition, there were government-aided schools operated by Methodists and Catholics that taught in English and prepared students for admission to British universities. The English-language schools provided the elite education for all communities that facilitated the later development of "consociational democracy" based on interethnic bargaining by elites who had common experiences and friendships across ethnic boundaries in the English-language schools. Prime Minister Badawi was a product of that system, having attended the Penang Methodist Boys School in his youth.

27. Tan Liok Ee, "Keeping the Dream Alive," *AsiaWeek,* www.asiaweek.com/asia week/98/0904/feat_5_books.html; "Asians Get Serious About Mandarin," *Asia News Network,* April 5, 2005, www.asiannewsnet.net/; Yang Pei Keng, "National Education After 44 Years," Parts I and II, *Johore Bar,* April 28, 2003, 1–20, www.johorebar.org .my/content/view/102/27/2003.

28. Francis Loh, "Crisis in Malaysia's Public Universities?" *Aliran Monthly* 25, no. 10 (2005), 1–12, www.aliran.com.

29. Frederik Holst, "Malaysia: To Think or Not to Think—Malaysia's University Dilemma," *Asian Analysis* (December 2005), 6–7. For an assessment of the long-term impact of racial-religious quotas and special rights on tertiary education in Malaysia, see Centre for Public Policy Studies, "Achieving Higher Performance in Tertiary Education," CPPS (2006), Kuala Lumpur, 1–19.

30. Means, *Malaysian Politics: The Second Generation,* 23–27.

31. Ibid., 265–270; R. S. Milne and Diane K. Mauzy, *Malaysian Politics Under Mahathir* (London: Routledge,1999), 72–74.

32. "Bumiputera Equity Controversy: Asli Man Quits in Protest," *New Straits Times,* October 12, 2006, 1; Francis Loh, "A Season of Odd and Silly Events," *Aliran,* January 23, 2007, 1–6, www.aliran.com/cotent/view/183/10.

33. Ioannis Gatsiounis, "Racial Divide Widens in Malaysia," *Asia Times,* November 23, 2006, 1–3, www.atimes.com/atimes/Southeast_Asia/HK23Ae01.html.

34. Ramon Navaratnam, "Malaysian Strategic Challenges in 2007 and Beyond: Towards a New National Agenda," speech at 9th Malaysia Strategic Outlook Conference 2007, January 29, 2007, 1–9, www.asli.com.my/Documents/Tan_Sri_Navaratnam_ Speech.doc.

35. Anwar Ibrahim, "A Malaysian Economic Agenda," election manifesto, Keadilan, April 2007, 1–8. For a more comprehensive account of his strategy, see Andrew Sia, "Anwar's 'New' Agenda," *The Star,* April 8, 2007, 1–9, thestar.com.my/news.

36. Jonathan Kent, "Anwar Shakes Up Malaysia Politics," *BBC News,* May 1, 2007, 1–3, newsvote.bbc.co.uk/; "Probe into Swing Against BN in Ijok By-Elections," *The Star,* May 1, 2007, 1–2, thestar.com.my; "Ijok By-Election: Real Losers and Winners," *Politics 101 Malaysia,* April 30, 2007, 1–9, politics101malaysia.blogsome.com/ 2007/04/30.

37. The Sedition Act creates criminal penalties for anyone who questions or criticizes in public any matter, right, or privilege related to Malay special rights, the status of Malay rulers, the status of Islam, and the status of Malay as the sole national language. Means, *Malaysian Politics: The Second Generation,* 10–16.

38. "Police Disperse Illegal Assembly," *The Star,* November 10, 2007, 1, thestar .com.my/; Danny Lim, "Rallying for Rights in Malaysia," *Far Eastern Economic Review* 170, no. 10 (December 2007), 40–42; Lim Teck Ghee, "Malaysia's Prospects: Rising to or in Denial on Challenges?" in *Regional Outlook Forum 2008* (Singapore: Institute of Southeast Asian Studies, January 7–8. 2008), 1–11.

39. "Tempers Flare After Malaysia Demolishes Hindu Temple," Reuters, November 5, 2007, 1, in.reuters.com/articlePrint?articleId=INIndia-30342020071105; "Destruction of Ethnic Minorities in Malaysia," August 22, 2007, 1–8, www.danielpipes org/comments/106706; Lim Teck Ghee, "Malaysia's Prospects," 1–7.

40. "30,000 Hindraf Protesters Rally in KL Streets," *Malaysiakini,* November 25, 2007, 1–2, www.malaysiakini.com/news/75250; Simon Montlake, "Race Politics Hobbles Malaysia," *Far Eastern Economic Review* 171, no. 2 (March 2008), 36–39.

41. "Opposition Plans to File Application for Two Lawyers Under ISA Detention," *The Star,* December 14, 2007, 1–2, thestar.com.my/news/.

42. Patrick Goodenough, "Islamist Party Downplays Shari'a Ahead of Malaysia Election," *CNS News,* February 26, 2008, 1–4, www.cnsnews.com; Mohamed Nawab Mohamed Osman, "Reforming PAS: From Islamism to Post-Islamism," *The Jakarta Post,* March 26, 2008, 1–2, www.thejakartapost.com/news/2008/03/16.

43. "Malaysia Polls Shatter Race-Based Politics," *MSN News,* March 10, 2008, 1–2, news.my.msn.com/regional/article.aspx?cp-documentid=1283777.

44. "Malaysia's Anwar Says Moving Toward Forming New Govt," *MSN News,* March 19, 2008, 1–2, news.my.msn.com/regional/article.aspx?cp-documentid=1297912.

45. "Making Sense of the 2008 General Election Results," *Malaysia Votes,* March 9, 2008, 1–7, malaysiavotes.wordpress.com/2008/03/08; Chandra Muzaffar, "The 2008 Malysian Election—and the BN Debacle," JUST, n.d., 1–4, www.just-international.org/article_print.cfm?newsID=20002680; Wing Thye Woo, "Malaysian Elections: Rejection of the Usual Politics," Brookings, March 25, 2008, 1–5, www.brookings.edu/opinions/2008/0310_malaysia_woo.aspx?p=1.

14

Southeast Asian Islam in Transition

Islam is a product of human endeavor that has produced varied interpretations of its doctrines and diverse cultural manifestations of its practices over the past fourteen centuries. It began with the divine revelation that Muhammad received as recorded in the Quran, which has continued to inspire an increasing number of people throughout the ages to make its precepts the basis for their faith and their beliefs and to define the basis for their social, economic, and political systems. The collective interpretations and understanding of Islam by Muslims have evolved through the ages, depending on their diverse cultures, their differential knowledge, and the unique consequences of political conflicts that have shaped their life experiences. That evolutionary process has continued unabated in the past and will continue to do so into the indefinite future.

Earlier chapters have traced how Muslims in the early centuries of Islam's history adapted the ideals of Islam to the practical necessities of governance and social organization. In the medieval period, the ruling caliphs developed the techniques for managing and controlling the political dimensions of Islam to create a medieval synthesis. In the thirteenth century, when Islam came to Southeast Asia, the native rulers who converted to Islam learned how Islam could enhance their authority, and they developed the strategies to accomplish that objective. The Southeast Asian converts adapted their newly professed religion to the mores and assumptions of their culture and way of life to create a Southeast Asian synthesis. In the colonial era, non-Muslim colonial authorities experimented with various strategies to counter, manipulate, or neutralize Islam as a political force. And in the postcolonial era, Islam competed with the ideologies of nationalism and communism to shape the politics of decolonization. With the defeat of communism in Indonesia in 1965 and in Malaysia in the late 1980s, the Muslim-majority areas of Southeast Asia became embroiled in a low-level contest between "secular" nationalism and an increasingly strident and orthodox version of Islam. This was also a period during which political leaders manipulated electoral systems to sustain the rituals of democracy while operating with semiauthoritarian structures of authority.

By the 1980s, the dakwah movement spread through Muslim areas of Southeast Asia, heavily influenced by political events and ideologies from the Middle East. Through all these historical periods, there have been contests over the control of Islam because rulers and aspiring power seekers realized that Islam established a basis for political power. The prevalent doctrine of Islam that it is a "total way of life"—*al-deen*—embracing the entire gamut of personal, community, and political life provides the justification and the impetus for "political Islam." The traditions and institutions of these earlier periods were essentially authoritarian, and incumbent rulers learned how to utilize and manage Islam to legitimize their authority. Islam was not the cause of authoritarian principles of rule, but Islam, like most other major religions, acquired the precedents, institutions, and legal principles of authoritarianism that were prevalent throughout the world before the nineteenth century. By the end of the twentieth century, one of the most important changes involved increasing public demands for democratic reforms.

Islamic Politics in a Crisis Environment

The two largest Muslim-majority states in Southeast Asia each experienced similar challenges during the seven- to eight-year cycle that followed the Asian financial crisis of 1997–1998. That crisis triggered political instability, because the economic foundations of the state were undermined and the legitimacy of the political and social order was seriously challenged by newly energized opposition movements claiming to champion reforms of one variety or another. In both Indonesia and Malaysia, the process of recovery involved a fairly similar reexamination of the political order, but that process also produced rather different outcomes in each state.

In Indonesia, under the stress of crisis, the political activism of Islamic-based parties and groups intensified and Islam's political roles also changed. In the precrisis period in Indonesia, the government contained and neutralized Islamic politics by forcing the key Islamic organizations to combine into a government-sanctioned party, which was supervised and indirectly managed by imposed political controls. The natural divisions within Indonesian Islam over cultural and doctrinal differences, combined with a managed and rubber-stamp legislative process, effectively neutralized nearly all political activities related to an Islamic political agenda. Only after the Suharto regime began to lose public support did it change tactics regarding the role of Islam in politics. Rather than encapsulate and sideline parties that espoused an Islamic agenda, the Suharto regime attempted to recruit Muslim activists to shore up its already crumbling support base. This effort came too little, too late and appeared to be too insincere to attract a sufficient number of new supporters to rescue the discredited old regime. Instead, popular support shifted to the Reformasi movement, being energized by students and inspired and led by Megawati Sukarnoputri. This movement was moving Indonesia in a different and essentially secular direction.

The period of maximum political turmoil in Indonesia enabled a variety of Muslim political groups to form and flourish by forming militia units and engaging in vigilante-style politics. Some of the Islamic-based militias were surreptitiously supported and armed by elements of the Indonesian Army that were affiliated with an imperiled and beleaguered Suharto. These vigilante groups, such as Laskar Jihad, the Islamic Defense Front, and KISDI, were able to gain political leverage and public support by triggering ethnic and religious conflicts that were depicted in their propaganda as direct threats to Indonesia's Islamic identity. Although the mainstream Muslim parties of Indonesia avoided direct involvement with these vigilante operations of radical Islamist groups, there were very few Muslim leaders who were willing to condemn such operations during the most deadly cycles of mass killings. Only much later, after the Al Qaeda–supported Jemaah Islamiyah staged the Bali bombing in October 2002, did most of the mainstream Muslim parties and their leaders take more public stands against the wanton violence and terror that was the inevitable byproduct of vigilante-based politics.

In Malaysia, public policies toward Islam followed a much different pattern than those of Indonesia. The earlier precolonial and colonial system conferred on each Malay ruler, within the boundaries of his state, jurisdiction over Islam as the supreme leader of the Muslim community. That system of state sponsorship and control of Islam was continued and incorporated into the constitutional arrangements of postcolonial Malaysia. Whereas Indonesia had a nominally secular government ruling an overwhelmingly Muslim society, Malaysia established Islam as the state religion with a nominally Islamic government that ruled a society comprising a slim majority of Muslims and large numbers of non-Muslims in a diverse multiethnic society. Rather than sideline and isolate the political expression of Islam, the institutional structures of Islam were supported by the state, which also defined "true Islam" and protected that version of Islam from the actions and doctrines of "deviant sects." Whenever deviant sects were detected or peasant grievances led to political disturbances, the federal authorities were quick to act with decisive force backed by the extraordinary legal powers of the Internal Security Act. With this combination of surveillance and arbitrary powers, Malaysian authorities were able to detect and detain both Islamic radicals and "deviationists" before they gained a sustaining constituency of supporters.

A central theme of Malay politics has been to secure Malay political supremacy. To achieve that objective, Islam acquired a critical political role to assure that supremacy in perpetuity. The Constitution established an elaborate system of Malay "special rights and privileges" and then tied those special rights to Islam through the legal definition of who qualifies as a "Malay" for those constitutionally awarded benefits. With this elaborate legal and constitutional linkage, Islam, as a community, acquired a bundle of rights and privileges that were vigorously protected and exploited by Malay political leaders to assure the dominant political position of the Malays within Malaysia. These provisions gave Islam a political salience that was unmatched in Indonesia.

While the government of Malaysia was established with an Islamic base, its primary opposition came from Partai Islam, which sought to intensify the political commitment to Islam. These competitive pressures made the Malaysian government ever more Islamic in its symbolism and progressively more responsive to its Malay/Muslim constituents. One byproduct of this competition involved an expansion of the Islamic administrative structure serving Malay communities. As the Islamic administrative structure expanded, it also acquired more effective oversight mechanisms to keep the authorities informed of political and religious developments at the "grassroots" level.

When the Asian financial crisis triggered the destabilization of Malaysia's political system, the challenge to the government came not through an Islamist-inspired insurgency, but through a fracture in the Malay electoral support base previously firmly committed to UMNO. During the 1999 election, Partai Islam provided the core support for the opposition coalition of Barisan Alternatif that included non-Muslim parties. An Islamic political agenda never became part of the Barisan Alternatif campaign manifesto. Both the incumbent Barisan Nasional and the opposition Barisan Alternatif considered Islam to be a critical component of politics, but to maintain their multiethnic coalitions, neither side made Islam a central issue of that election. Instead, that campaign degenerated into mutual accusations against the two contending political leaders of personal moral turpitude, corruption, favoritism, and abuse of office. The results gave Barisan Alternatif a substantial representation in Parliament, but it never came close to gaining power at the national level. And shortly after the election, the Barisan Alternatif collapsed as a coherent political entity. In contrast to Indonesia, the political crisis that began with the Asian monetary crisis was effectively resolved through the ballot box and never undermined the legitimacy and the capabilities of the Malaysian government to maintain order and provide services. When the retiring Mahathir chose a new leader, public pressure for democratic reforms and greater protection for civil liberties remained at low levels. The new prime minister Abdullah Badawi promised to maintain the same course heading set by Mahathir, with only slight adjustments as appropriate.

The new political regimes in both Malaysia and Indonesia came to office in 2004 with high hopes and a long agenda of unresolved issues and unfulfilled promises. While Islam was not at the top of their agenda, Islam had to be included in the calculations of costs and risks and an evaluation of its likely political trajectory. In both countries, very few policies can avoid being subjected to the calculus of religion and of ethnicity. The learning experience of past politics and changes in economic roles and opportunities can have a slowly transforming effect on patterns of politics that eventually become reflected in policy outcomes.

Malaysia: New Questions for Old Answers

Just over one year before Prime Minister Mahathir retired and transferred power to his successor, he gave a speech to the Harvard Club of Malaysia in which he expressed his own distress over failure to achieve all his previously stated goals. As stated in his earlier book, *The Malay Dilemma* (written in 1960 but published in 1970),[1] Mahathir characterized the Malays as poorly educated peasants with low aspirations and motivations based on cultural traits that were inappropriate for an advanced industrial society. To overcome this deficit, he set out goals of transforming Malays into highly trained, motivated, and productive citizens, who would become leaders in all sectors of a modern industrial-based economy and in government service with incomes and wealth proportionate to those of non-Malays. This book became the ideological and political justification for Malaysia's New Economic Policy. The Malays were expected to use their superior control over political power to attain economic power. Malay "special rights and privileges" and employment quotas[2] had been the central keystone in the elaborate bureaucratic edifice designed by Mahathir to address the "Malay Dilemma." After twenty-two years of pursuing this grand design, with much despair and pathos, Mahathir gave a bleak assessment of what had been accomplished.

He explained that he had thought that, by giving the Malays government-funded opportunities for higher education and access to jobs and business positions, they would soon attain the target of 30 percent equity ownership in the economy. He explained that Malays "are laid-back and prone to take the easy way out. And the easy way out is to sell off whatever they get and ask for more. This is their culture." He continued:

> To succeed the Malays must change their culture. They must look towards work as a reward in itself. . . . They must have proper work ethics which involve taking pride in the result of their work rather than the monetary reward alone. . . . Today they can lean on the crutches of Malay privileges to protect them. . . . The new dilemma is whether they should or should not do away with the crutches that they have gotten used to, which in fact they have become proud of.[3]

Mahathir accused Partai Islam of contributing to the problem of Malay attitudes and motivation by generating ingratitude among the Malays for what they received from the government. "The emergence of the Islamic Party has resulted in the struggle to build the resilience of the Malays being deflected by the religious imperatives invented by political Islam."[4] From this assessment, Mahathir concluded that Malay "special rights and privileges" had not aided the Malays as much as he had expected. At the end of this speech, he raised the question whether the system should now be gradually dismantled, but failed to give a definitive answer to that question. With Mahathir's impending retirement, he was passing a burning torch to his successor with an awareness that this issue was too hot to handle.

Three years later in 2005 at the same locale, Prime Minister Badawi addressed virtually the same audience at the Harvard Club of Malaysia Dinner. In that speech, he argued that the country needed to shift its priorities from infrastructure and capital investments to human capital—knowledge, skills, and values. Education must be enhanced. The judiciary and Parliament must be strengthened. "Civil society must be given space to engage with Government and express their views constructively and responsibly." He went on to identify "three addictions" that Malaysians had acquired: First, addiction to cheap foreign labor, rather than adopting labor-efficient high technology; second, an addiction to subsidies; third, addiction to rent-seeking. On this third addiction he observed, "we would rather go for 'know-who' than 'know-how.' Rather than investing to become better than our competitors or to add value in our products and services, we . . . seek leverage on our sense of privilege and entitlement. . . . We seem to think: surely someone else, at the very least, the Government, owes us a living."

Rather than address the issue raised in Mahathir's earlier speech of the long-term impact of Malay "special rights and privileges" Badawi suggested that Islam could provide the answer for some of the "addictions" that he had identified. He continued, "In this and other matters, we must go back to basics, and we must go back to the primacy of values and principles. This is my stand, as can be seen for example in the approach of 'Islam Hadhari' that I have espoused."[5] On that note, his speech ended.

If one reads between the lines of these two speeches by Malaysia's two most recent prime ministers, Malaysian policymakers at high levels were seeking to energize and recast the national psyche, especially for Malays. The objective was to produce a core ethos within Malaysian society that would generate high achievement motivations, work ethic, and skills that would sustain a dynamic economy and create a modern tolerant civil society for the country. Behind the scenes in Islamic circles, there had been some discussion of the possibilities of an Islamic Reformation that would parallel the Protestant Reformation in Europe. Many Muslim students studying abroad had been exposed to the theories of Max Weber, who had identified the Protestant Reformation as providing the ideological foundations for the rise of capitalism and the development of the industrial revolution in Europe and North America. Weber's theory was that Protestantism, especially in its Calvinist form, led to "this-worldly" activism, individual achievement motivation, and an intensified work ethic on the assumption by those committed to these new doctrines that they were "chosen by God" and must show their devotion to God by doing his work. Whether the theories of Max Weber and T. H. Tawney are valid is a matter of some dispute among contemporary social scientists. What is not in dispute is that these changes in religious belief and in social-economic relations in the European context were not generated by government institutions. To initiate an Islamic Reformation by an agency within the Prime Minister's Department would be a radically different source for the transformation of a religio-political culture.[6] While discussing policy issues with a sophisticated audience, both leaders were able to consider options with a cost-benefit analysis and examine more than raw economic statistics. However, in office, both leaders became captive to the demands of their supporters—those who were the prime beneficiaries of these partially "failed policies."

The complex interlinking of politics, patronage, and ethnic preference (based on Islam) created a large sector of Malaysia's economic infrastructure that was not prepared for and probably not capable of competing in the global economy without some forms of direct or indirect government assistance. These patronage benefits to the politically linked Bumiputra corporate sector were what Mahathir referred to as "crutches" that he had so readily dispensed over the years, but which he finally acknowledged had generated unintended side-effects. The new Bumiputra business class had come to depend on subsidies, untendered contracts, tariff protections, and government bailout rescues from bankruptcy. In the rough and tumble of real politics in an environment of competition for political support, the "rational calculus" models of analysis were quickly displaced by the "patron-client calculus," where deference and political support were traded for easily identified material benefits. The most militant defenders of the NEP and Malay "special rights" were those in UMNO Youth, anticipating future rewards. Established Malay business tycoons were also strong supporters of those policies, but some of them who had become relatively successful were able to contemplate the possibility that those special benefits need not be projected into the indefinite future. Over time, some Malay professionals had become more secure, and with that confidence, they were willing to forgo some or all of the advantages of "special rights."[7] For most critics of special rights, the issue was not whether those rights should be abruptly terminated, but whether that system should be gradually adjusted and eventually eliminated as Malays acquired economic parity with non-Malays. While the system of Malay special rights achieved many of its intended goals, it had done so with enormous costs and an increase in ethnic and religious polarization.

Although both Prime Minister Mahathir and Prime Minister Badawi were willing to identify flaws and ancillary costs in the political economy that had been built up to assure Malay supremacy and guarantee stable political support from Malaysia's largest religio-ethnic community, neither of these two leaders was prepared to propose significant reforms to that structure of authority, perhaps because they were products of that system. After the ruling elite split into two contending factions, the challenging faction was expelled from power, and its leader was imprisoned for corruption and moral turpitude but also gained the freedom to openly criticize the basis of established authority. What had been defined as "sensitive issues" legally removed from public debate, later became the key topics of political contestation. By 2008, with the return of Anwar Ibrahim to the Malaysian political scene, a new configuration of politics was beginning to be formed. What had been a dominant coalition of ethnic parties was now being challenged by an opposition coalition that claimed to be more inclusive, demanding democratic reforms and a greater emphasis on individual rights and freedoms. The unknown ultimate outcome of that contest would shape the future of Malaysian politics for a generation or more.

Indonesia: New Institutions for Unanswered Questions

Over the period of five years, from 1999 to 2004, Indonesia acquired a radically reformed constitutional system based on direct free and open elections for legislators as well as for a president. More that 80 percent of registered voters participated in the election for legislative members, and five months later almost 80 percent elected the new president—Susilo Bambang Yudhoyono. What was surprising was the fact that these democratic reforms were approved and implemented by a Parliament elected under the old authoritarian system. By 2004, the long struggles and debates over political reforms had finally been largely resolved, but in the process of gaining agreement for reforms, many other high-priority issues accumulated. During the election, the debate shifted from institutional reforms to substantive policy issues related to the economy, the implementation of decentralization, corruption, legal reform, patronage, bringing the army under civil control, ethnic conflicts, and the threats posed by terrorism.

President Yudhoyono's first task was to forge a political coalition that could support his administration. When his vice president, Yusuf Kalla, contested and won the election as chairman of Golkar, what had been a minority coalition turned into a workable majority coalition. However, the inclusion of Golkar within the government raised serious concerns. Would the party founded by Suharto, and now led by Yusuf Kalla, support needed reforms relating to the economy, democracy, and the role of the army? Would the cluster of Islamic parties in the government coalition exercise an Islamic veto or pursue an Islamic agenda as a priority for government policies? The Islamic parties in Yudhoyono's ruling coalition were identified by the media as "modern," "moderate," or supporters of "liberal Islam" partly because they had not campaigned for the implementation of Sharia law or for an "Islamic agenda" that would give Muslims a distinctive or privileged status in Indonesia. Instead, both National Mandate Party (PAN) and Prosperous Justice Party (PKS) had placed "corruption" as a top issue, although PKS had campaigned in 1999 when it was Partai Keadilan on a rather elaborate Islamist agenda.[8] In a national survey conducted in February 2005, Indonesians had identified economic problems as their greatest concern, with corruption as their next most serious concern.[9] President Yudhoyono's priorities reflected these concerns, which also had the politically favorable effect of avoiding some of the more contentious issues of an Islamic agenda.

Indonesia has long been known as one of the most corrupt countries in the world. With government officials underpaid, it developed a culture of "fee for service" with the "fees" determined by the financial resources and ethnic origin of the beneficiaries. This system was perfected to such a degree that most customers of public services were unable to determine whether they were paying "regular fees" or "bribes." The system also involved transaction fees within the public service so that public funds transferred from one agency to another were "skimmed" at various levels. Some of the skimmed money went for the support of intermediate administration and some went directly into the pockets of government officials. With no adequate conflict of interest laws, inadequate accounting, a flawed system of prosecution, and a politically controlled judicial system, corruption in Indonesia became rampant but was usually justified as "the Indonesian way of conducting government business."[10]

Before Yudhoyono became president, Parliament passed a number of anti-corruption laws, but they had not been effectively administered and produced very few convictions.[11] In 2004, Indonesia's attorney general estimated that US$2.35 billion of public funds had been lost to corruption over the previous two years. This issue became even more urgent after the tsunami hit Aceh, since there were credible allegations from foreign donors that millions of dollars in aid funds were being "skimmed" by local officials, police and military, and private contractors.[12] Once in office, Yudhoyono gave a special presidential instruction to the entire executive branch to speed up measures to eliminate corruption. The most prominent case involved the governor of Aceh, Abdullah Puteh, who was arrested in December 2004 and tried and sentenced to ten years in prison in April 2005 for embezzling many millions of dollars from state purchases.[13]

When Yudhoyono assumed office, he had the advantage of assuming responsibility for an economy making a slow recovery from the turmoil of the 1999 crisis. Most key indicators of economic health were slowly improving as a result of prudent economic management and improving political stability since the turbulent days of 1998 and 1999. One of the more glaring exceptions to economic recovery was the low level of foreign direct investment (FDI). Corruption, red tape, political instability, foreign competition from China and India, and finally terrorism had all taken their toll on Indonesia's FDI statistics.

The Bali bombing was estimated to have cost the Indonesian economy US$10 billion in lost revenues from tourism during the year following that blast. The Indonesian tourist industry was almost eliminated and began recovering very slowly. The images of the Bali, Marriott, and Australian Embassy blasts also had a depressing effect on FDI for several years thereafter. With Indonesian public opinion polls in 2005 showing that voters ranked the economy as their highest concern, Yudhoyono placed that issue at the top of his agenda.

Early in his administration, Yudhoyono improved relations with the United States and Australia. With President Yudhoyono's encouragement, a new era of collaboration began among Indonesia, international donors, and NGOs operating in Indonesia.[14] Perhaps this collaboration was prompted in part by the tsunami disaster that hit Aceh only a few weeks before the meetings of the Consultative Group on Indonesia on January 19, 2005. The World Bank produced a report entitled *Indonesia: New Directions,* which outlined in general terms a development and reform strategy covering critical issues facing Indonesia. In the aftermath of that conference, the World Bank and the Asian Development Bank (ADB) produced twenty policy briefs under the general title of "Ideas for the Future," designed as "an invaluable resource for policy analysts and policymakers, academics, NGOs and Civil Society."[15]

Within the policy proposals generated by the World Bank and in the political agenda of President Yudhoyono's government, there was virtually no mention of policy initiatives regarding Islam or Islamic institutions. The unstated assumption appeared to be that good governance, participatory democracy, and addressing pressing social and economic issues with a pragmatic agenda of "results-based management programs" would diminish the appeal of radical Islamist ideology. Yet, behind the scenes, there were efforts to promote more liberal forms of Islamic religious beliefs and practices.

Liberal Islam

Both Indonesia and Malaysia have been exposed to "liberal Islam" for many decades. During the colonial era, many Muslim elites sent their children to schools operated by Christian missions that taught in English or Dutch with a secular nonproselytizing curriculum. These Muslim students retained their Islamic identity while exercising freedoms of belief and behavior that most students from other faith communities also enjoyed. When the dakwah movement began to impose severe social pressure and public condemnation on "lax and wayward" Muslims, many of these "secular Muslims" continued to value and practice the same freedoms as before but within the restricted space of government-defined Islam. For many moderate Muslims, their religious liberties depend on their judicious silence and nonchalance.

The mobilization of political Islam, combined with growing demands to enforce Sharia law for more than family and inheritance issues, provided a powerful motivation for reform-minded Muslims to form political associations to defend individual rights and freedoms on religious and political issues. To claim the rights of individual interpretation of Islamic texts and to exercise individual freedom of conscience without deference to the pronouncements of the existing hierarchy of Islamic authority may eventually become the Muslim equivalent of the Protestant Reformation, but that process has only just begun.

In Indonesia, Jaringan Islam Liberal (JIL, Liberal Islam Network) began as informal meetings of intellectuals who applied for legal status in 2001 as an educational and political action group. By 2005, it had only about 150 core members, but a much larger regular listening audience that came from JIL's sponsorship of news and talk shows that were broadcast over forty radio stations in Indonesia. It also organized discussion groups on Islam and published books and pamphlets on liberal Islam, pluralism, multiculturalism, and human rights. The organization was funded by private contributions from Indonesian Muslims, as well as receiving some support from the Asia Foundation, the Ford Foundation, and from various Australian sources.[16]

Although JIL has had an extremely small core of active members, it received high visibility because of virulent attacks on it from militant Islamists. The fatwas issued by the Indonesian Ulama Council (MUI) condemning "liberal Islam, pluralism, and secularism" as being forbidden under Islam provided the justification for white-robed vigilantes from the Islamic Defenders Front, armed with samurai swords, to attempt enforcement of that fatwa. Beginning in July 2005, various Islamist vigilante groups formed an association called the Anti-Apostasy Movement (AAM), and together they campaigned with threats and displays of violence to eject JIL from their headquarters in Jakarta's Utan Kayu complex. In addition, the AAM engaged in a direct action campaign to close Christian churches and informal prayer groups meeting in homes and shops. By October 2005, they had forced the closure of twenty-three churches and prayer groups "because they did not have permits."[17] With more-effective police protection in the area of its headquarters, JIL continued operations despite the harassment and threats from the Anti-Apostasy Movement.

In Malaysia, the perspectives of liberal Islam have been most effectively promoted through the activities of Muslim professional women. In 1983, the Malaysian government's dakwah organization sponsored an international conference on the topic "Muslim Women in Development." Altogether, 260 delegates from twenty-six countries attended the six-day conference held at the Haj Complex near the airport serving Kuala Lumpur. Many of the delegates were professional women who were dedicated to reforming the practices of Muslim societies toward women. Among the topics discussed were "equality of women," "family planning," "marriage obligations in a patriarchal system," "polygamy," "child marriage," and "religious mixed marriages." On these issues, it was apparent that there were considerable differences of opinion between the views of the delegates and the formal speeches given by politicians and local ulama. In the report of that conference, papers calling for reform and challenging existing practices were not published but instead were summarized and "sanitized" to avoid raising sensitive and contentious issues that were discussed with such passion by delegates attending the conference.[18]

In Malaysia five years later, in 1988, the Association of Women Lawyers began exploring how Islamic family law was being implemented in the Sharia court system. A small group of Muslim women lawyers met regularly to read the Quran, to examine the administration of Sharia law, and to collect data on cases of injustice to Muslim women. They concluded that the Quran promotes equality, justice, freedom, and dignity, but that these values were not being upheld and defended by Islamic family law in Malaysia.[19] Amina Wahud was one of the women involved with this effort. She had been recruited by the International Islamic University to teach Islamic studies and had acquired a reputation as a reformer. Together this small group became dedicated to combining scholarship with political activism.

In 1990, Sisters in Islam (SIS) became a registered organization. Their first public statement addressed the issue of polygamy, based on the verse in the Quran that states: "And if you fear that you cannot do justice, marry only one, that would be best for you." When that policy statement appeared in the local papers, Sisters in Islam attracted both positive and hostile reactions. Among the members who joined Sisters in Islam were Marina Mahathir, daughter of former prime minister Mahathir, and Nori Abdullah, daughter of Prime Minister Abdullah Badawi. Over the years, SIS produced a series of policy papers on the hudud laws, freedom of religion, dress codes, domestic violence, human rights, polygamy, and apostasy laws. On all these issues, SIS objected to the coercive aspects of Islamic laws, especially for Muslim women. They opposed infringements of individual freedoms for both Muslims and non-Muslims.[20] The arguments of SIS are based on the assumption that the revelations of the Quran are divine and unchallenged, but that the Sharia was created several centuries later by fallible humans from incomplete and suspect sources. They argued that what was created by fallible and self-serving humans must be subjected to critical public scrutiny, open debate, and the processes of democracy. To make that process reflect a public consensus and meet the needs of the contemporary Muslim society, Islam must uphold the principles of justice, freedom, equality, and human dignity.[21] From these convictions, Sisters in Islam became an effective and powerful voice for a liberal version of Islam.

One Islam, Many Voices

On theological and doctrinal issues, Muslims will often assert the precept that "there is only one Islam." Yet, Muslims have a great diversity of beliefs about that "one Islam." This diversity of belief is vigorously contested because of the common assumption that Islam must ultimately be unified, while "deviant beliefs" and heresies must be expunged. Who is a "true Muslim" and who is a "deviant Muslim" becomes a matter of determining social and political inclusion or being subjected to social ostracism, even if the more severe Sharia punishments for apostasy and heresy are not applied. The debate is thus not about abstract issues of theology, but about the allocation of real power and status within the political order of Islamic society.

The doctrinal and ideological diversity in the Muslim world has been "mapped" in an analytical study with an ordinal scale placing "radical fundamentalists" on one end of the scale and "radical secularists" on the other end of the scale.[22] Each of these categories on the scale have their unique interpretations of Islamic doctrine, views on appropriate political order, human rights, marriage relations, role of women, criminal law, appropriate dress, status of minorities, and the role of the state in enforcing Islamic beliefs and norms. In both Indonesia and Malaysia, Muslim opinion and beliefs can be identified and ranked along points on this scale. Since there has been no comprehensive survey of religious opinion and beliefs utilizing this scale for any population set in Southeast Asia, we can only guess about the distribution within Southeast Asian Islam. Individual Muslims may hold noncongruent beliefs or migrate from one position to another. Even without application of random sample survey data, the scale is useful because it provides a guide to the diversity of beliefs and attitudes that exists within contemporary Islamic societies. It is possible to use its "mapped" belief categories to assess how various political groups can be ranked along this "orthodoxy to liberalism" scale.

In 2003 the Pew Research Center conducted a multistate survey that included Indonesia as a research site. Among a variety of issues covered were the opinions of Muslim respondents on government and social issues in comparison with Muslims in other countries. Indonesian Muslim respondents were fairly moderate in their attitudes toward social issues and gender relations, but also expressed more solidarity with Muslims in other countries and were moderately higher than other Muslims in their perceptions of potential threats to Islam. In the aggregate, Indonesian Muslims appeared to be slightly more liberal than Muslims in other states that were surveyed. Indonesian Muslims viewed Islam to be more salient for their personal life and were more supportive of democracy and individual freedoms than most other Muslims.[23] Because Malaysia was not included in this survey, comparisons between Indonesian and Malaysian Muslims cannot be made based on this data set.

The Continuing Appeal of Sharia Law

For pious Muslims, the demand for the implementation of Sharia law has become a symbolic issue used as a measure of commitment to Islam. Because it is supposedly based on the Quran and the Hadith, Sharia law is assumed to be the ultimate rules for individual behavior and belief and the prescription for a proper and just Muslim political and social order. Because Sharia law has many variants and has almost never been fully implemented, the public demand for its implementation becomes a political weapon of a minority used to undermine the legitimacy of an established regime that claims an Islamic basis for its authority. The Quran is fixed in content, but subject to many alternative interpretations. The Hadith is far more flexible because of its reliance on oral reports on the Prophet Muhammad's actions and sayings and the difficulties of determining *ahadith* from Hadith—invalid from valid sources. Likewise, many issues arise from the determination of which Hadiths are appropriate for creating the specific legal prescriptions of Sharia law.[24] Differences within Islam on a wide range of topics, doctrines, and beliefs involve citing obscure medieval sources and making quasilegal arguments that have been called the "Hadith Wars."

The wide political support among Muslims for Sharia law is based on a number of interlinked factors. Most ulama preach and support the doctrine that Sharia law is the ultimate ideal that should be emulated, but not changed or criticized. The Islamic notion of "political correctness" do s not sanction a free discussion of the practicality or the ethical foundations for the provisions of Sharia law. Laws based on "God's commands" are to be obeyed, not challenged, debated, or ignored.

Many Muslims assert that the social evils of modern society will be solved if Sharia law is fully implemented and enforced, especially regarding personal morals and criminal acts. The draconian punishments combined with public and community involvement in punishment of wrongdoers is assumed to be the most effective way to rid society of the evils of prostitution, homosexual and lesbian sex, robbery, theft, alcoholism, drugs, teenage pregnancies, and the breakdown of family authority. The slogan "Islam is the answer" is widely repeated by Muslims in contemporary Southeast Asia, but without an explanation or discussion of how it might work and whether Sharia has all the answers for the afflictions of modern society.[25]

Two other characteristics of the Sharia appeal to many Muslims because of their political implications. Moderate Muslims who favor a modern, tolerant civil society with democracy and rights for non-Muslims will sometimes cite the original agreement made between the Prophet Muhammad and the Jews and other non-Muslim citizens of Yathrib (later renamed Medina). Usually known as the "Treaty of Medina" or the "Constitution of Medina," this agreement provided for freedom of religion for the God-fearing (Jews, Christians, and other monotheists) who remained under Islamic rule and pledged to abide by the rules of citizenship under Muhammad's political leadership. These non-Muslims put themselves under the "protection" of Islam and were treated as part of the community.[26] While the Treaty of Medina provided the basis for a civil society and interfaith dialogue, non-Muslims are often disturbed by the implications of the rights afforded to non-Muslims in that document. They are offered protection and freedom of their religion, provided that they acknowledge the hegemony of Muhammad's rule. Their status was that of *dhimma*—under the "protection of Islam." In Muhammad's time, no citizen had a right of political participation. When this precedent is cited in the contemporary political context, it appears to justify exclusive political rule by Muslims, leaving non-Muslims with the status of "protected" and limited freedom to practice their religion. This status is known as "dhimmitude" and, if instituted completely, would result in the denial of political and civil rights for all non-Muslims. What is viewed as the denial of basic rights for non-Muslims can just as easily be viewed by orthodox Muslims as one of the primary advantages that can accrue from the full implementation of Sharia law and the establishment of a genuine Islamic State according to the doctrines of radical Islamists.[27]

The coercive aspects of Islamic law limit critical evaluation of the Quran, the Hadith, and the basis of Sharia law. Apostasy laws, fatwa edicts, and the legal criminal powers of the Muslim State inhibit open debate on many of the most critical issues of public policy. Muslim intellectuals are constrained by their human environment, the political environment, and by the enormous powers of the state. Until very recently they have not been able to count on a minimal consensus from other intellectuals to rise to their defense if they come into the spotlight for public scorn and legal sanctions regarding religious thought, belief, or doctrine. That lack of capacity of intellectuals to participate in open free debate on sensitive subjects may be changing, partly due to the influence of Internet communication and access to "blog" websites.

Civil Islam in a Democratic Setting

During the authoritarian rule of Suharto, Islamic teachers and activists began to question the relevance of the literalist interpretations of the Quran and the Sunna that were being propagated by most dakwah groups. At the State Institute for Islamic Studies (IAIN) in Yogyakarta a forum known as the Limited Group invited Islamic thinkers and scholars for free discussion of religious and theological issues.[28] Among the participants was Nurcholish Madjid, who challenged the traditional literalist theology as being incompatible with science and the social issues of the modern era. Grand pronouncements about the Unity of God and the Universality of Islam were at such a high level of abstraction that it became difficult for Muslims to translate these principles into pragmatic guidance and instead led so often to endless pedantic definitional disputes. Madjid observed that if everything was attributed to an Absolute transcendental divine source, then it becomes impossible to distinguish between transcendental values and those that are temporal. Without such a distinction, a hierarchy of values is virtually impossible to determine. Starting with the Islamic concept of tauhid (Unity of God), Madjid argued that Muslims must distinguish between Islamic values of divine origin and those derived from merely human origins. In this way, tawhid justifies clearly identifying the secular, which derives from man, and the Absolute Truth of Revelation derived from God. Mankind must be concerned primarily with temporal affairs. The commitment of humans to science, reason, and knowledge can be understood as an act of devotion to God the Creator, whose Truth can also be revealed through discovery of the natural laws of the world. "Thus modernity resides in a process of discovery of which truths are relative, leading to the discovery of that Truth Which Is Absolute, that is Allah."[29] Only Allah possesses Absolute Truth, and that Truth is beyond human comprehension. For Madjid, the limited capacity of man to comprehend truth leads to the "poly-interpretability of Islam," and this in turn creates the imperative for tolerance of religious diversity, both within Islam and between Islam and all other religions.

This theological argument enunciated by Madjid desacralized much of traditional Islamic doctrine concerning the relationship between Islam and the state, producing for Islam a near-equivalent to Christian doctrines that distinguish between the sacred and the secular. While he defended the view that "Westernized secularism" is rejected in Islam, his categorization of God's plan and intention increased the scope of man's responsibility and diminished the rigid reliance on the Sharia to answer nearly all issues related to the state, politics, and public policy. From this stance, Madjid and his associates concluded that Islam does not call for the formation of an Islamic State. Indeed, he argued, the term *state* (*dawlah*) does not even appear in the Quran. This argument, denying the validity of an Islamic State, was later expanded by other like-minded intellectuals who argued that Muslims needed to focus on the core values and objectives of Islam, rather than on the formalistic and rigid legalisms of an earlier age. Following this line of thought, some participants in the debates concluded that the eternal core principles of Islam included justice, consultation, participation, and egalitarianism. From this, they concluded that Muslims needed state guarantees of political rights and freedoms, including religious freedom.

In combination with other like-minded "new intellectuals," these revised interpretations of Islamic doctrine, briefly summarized above, produced the basis for an emerging dynamic, liberal, and democratic form of Islamic discourse that Robert Hefner calls "Civil Islam." Among the list of its contributors and advocates, in addition to Nurcholish Madjid, were the following: Ahmad Syafii Maarif, Abdurrahman Wahid, Djohan Effendi, Amien Rais, Utomo Dananjaya, Harun Nasution, Munawar Syadzali, Dawam Rahardjo, and a host of others.[30]

Did this "Civil Islam" movement have an impact on Indonesian politics? That is a difficult question to answer since the evidence is so ephemeral and interpretation depends on intuitive impressions. The number of Indonesians committed to these new doctrines was very minuscule, and the belief systems of most Muslims probably did not change regarding Islamic doctrine. There is no evidence that ideas were systematically propagated to mass public audiences for their enlightenment and debate. Three of the participants at the Limited Group became major political leaders of Indonesia. Abdurrahman Wahid became leader of Nahdlatul Ulama, the largest Islamic party in Indonesia, and later became president of Indonesia.[31] Amien Rais was selected in 1995 as the leader of Muhammadiyah, the second largest Islamic political organization in Indonesia. Nurcholish Madjid became a founding member of the ICMI and quickly assumed the leadership of its "neomodernist" faction.[32] While their ideology and theological perspectives were probably genuine, when confronted with the politics of power and competition with political rivals, it became difficult for these elites to collaborate and form mutually supportive coalitions, especially when those in power played the game of pitting one faction against another. An ideology of "Civil Islam" was never a dominant theme at the popular and grassroots level in Indonesia, and when political crisis increased domestic tensions, that ideology did not prevent some very "uncivil" rhetoric and behavior of leaders claiming to be motivated by those ideals.

For many decades, an increasing number of Muslim scholars and political activists have made the argument that Islam authorizes and sanctions democratic processes for an Islamic political order. These arguments were made while most Muslims lived in countries ruled under authoritarian and autocratic systems, often under military-backed regimes exercising draconian powers. Malaysia and Indonesia provide examples of two Muslim-majority states that have made significant democratic reforms and have become committed to making democracy work in combination with what is called "Civil Islam." The issue of whether Islam sanctions democracy was never subject to open public debate in either of these two states. Instead, an overwhelming proportion of the general public merely assumed that Islam and democracy were indeed compatible. The Reformasi movements in both countries focused on the authoritarian characteristics of their incumbent regime and made demands for democratic participatory reforms. Whether democracy could deliver the reforms that they sought was not asked or addressed. For these reformers, Islam was no impediment to democracy. Since crisis and grievances have generated the pressures for democracy, not theological debate, the more significant public policy question is not whether Islam sanctions democracy. Rather it becomes: How does Islam adapt and respond to democratic institutions and a democratic political culture once those institutions become viable?

In the current literature on the political and social transformation in Southeast Asia following the Asian financial crisis and 9/11, there have been two common themes explored: first, to study the processes of democratic transformation, and second, to examine the continuing threats of violence from Islamist-inspired clandestine terrorist organizations. These contrasting themes are especially noticeable in contemporary works on Indonesia, while similar studies examining developments in Malaysia tend to stress a slow but incremental democratic transition and a lesser threat of violence from clandestine radical Islamist groups. A brief summary of some of these somewhat conflicting interpretations of contemporary events will reveal how informed specialists differ in their views about the challenges of the future.

Some studies on the political and institutional transformations within Muslim societies in Southeast Asia make the claim that these societies are moving inexorably toward a genuine "civil society" model that tolerates diversity, gives space for individual freedom, promotes pluralism, and respects civil decency. The attitudinal and behavioral characteristics of a civil society are claimed to be the essential qualities for democratization or are deemed to be necessary precursors for future democratization. Some of these studies were concluded before 9/11, while other studies covered the period up to the installation of President Yudhoyono of Indonesia and Prime Minister Badawi of Malaysia.[33]

Nearly all these cited works utilize the same definition of "civil society" as consisting of citizens participating in voluntary associations where they learn habits of participation, collaboration through compromise, and acquire a tolerance for political and social diversity. The evidence for the expansion of voluntary associations formed to address a host of social and political objectives is impressive. If NGO formation and voluntary citizen participation in political organizations is the sufficient condition for the formation of civil society, then the emergence of viable democracies in Southeast Asia appears to be very promising. Whether democratic values of tolerance, mutual respect, and the recognition of individual human rights and liberties have become thoroughly accepted as part of those core beliefs of the citizenry is left unanswered without adequate research. Some political organizations that have supported jihadi vigilantism and that do not favor equal participation of all citizens in the political process also claim to be "civil society" organizations. What kind of democracy will they support?

What these studies do reveal is the ferment and turmoil within Muslim communities about the content of their religion, its relevance to politics, and the necessity of fundamental reforms to address the challenges of the contemporary world. While these issues have not been resolved within Islamic society, there has been a substantial mobilization of activists to defend traditional precepts or promote significant reforms and modifications to the existing canon. The increase in voluntary associations pursuing a political agenda has not only included those dedicated to democracy, human rights, and pluralism. It has also included volunteers for radical antidemocratic groups dedicated to terrorism against real and imagined enemies and determined to capture power through jihadi politics. Some of these studies have either given no attention to radical or terrorist groups within Islam, or they have attributed outbreaks of domestic political violence to the crass manipulations of failed authoritarian leaders. What these Islamic civil society studies have documented very well is that some power seekers have used Islam very effectively to defend democracy, while others have sought to use Islam to defeat democracy by vote or violence.[34] What remains unclear is which form of Islamic "civil society" associations will ultimately prevail in Southeast Asia to shape the governments and politics of the future.

The Costs of Violence and Terrorism

Another set of studies has concentrated on political violence and terrorism in Southeast Asia.[35] Some of that violence is attributed to radical Islamic groups, ethnic conflicts, regional disputes, economic grievances, and long-standing cultural attributes. Although political violence has multiple causes, these works devote primary attention to the continued threat in Southeast Asia posed by a web of international terrorist organizations. Such organizations have gained support from those Muslims who are attracted to the doctrines of radical Islamists and those that constitute a support base and recruit pool for clandestine terrorist groups. Many studies of Islamic-based revolutionary terror groups are based largely on police-collected evidence, on interrogations of arrested terrorists, and on their intercepted communications. Data from these sources exposed the continued existence of a number of interlinked terrorist organizations, including Jemaah Islamiyah and Abu Sayyaf, which have been linked with Al Qaeda.

In various publications, Zachary Abuza argues that Islamist parties in Indonesia have adapted to democratic institutions as a temporary strategy but have not modified their political objective of establishing an Islamic State with Sharia law as its core agenda. Although Islamist parties gained only 14 percent of the vote in the 2004 parliamentary elections, they gained 20 percent of the seats. When Yudhoyono formed his coalition, two Islamist parties were included in the government—the PKS and the Crescent Moon and Star Party (PBB). While these parties did not campaign with an Islamist manifesto, Abuza argues that their political support is rising, and when the time is appropriate they will unveil their core Islamist agenda. Among moderate and secular leaders, there is a reticence to criticize those who support Islamist doctrines and who defend their causes. Abuza sees radical Islam as making headway as an increasing political force that could well continue to increase due to poor economic performance, unemployment, and the fear of globalization. With these "realities," he sees the "pond" for recruiting young people into radical groups becoming both "wider and deeper." If this trend continues, he suggests there may be a serious challenge to democracy and its capacity to sustain a viable pluralistic society. He does not quite make a prediction of what will transpire, but he does issue a warning of potential trouble ahead for Indonesian democracy.[36]

In a collaborative study done by the Rand Corporation entitled *The Muslim World After 9/11*, the sources of Islamic radicalism are attributed to formative conditions, sustaining processes, and what were called "catalytic events." Economic and political failure combined with "structural anti-Westernism" and the centralization of religious authority provide the ideal conditions for the spawning of radical Islam. The processes that sustain and accelerate Islamic radicalism are: Islamic resurgence, the spread of Arabization of the non-Arab Muslim world, foreign funding links from oil-rich Muslim sources to radical Islamic groups, the growth of radical Islamic networks and mass media, and the impact on the Muslim world of other Muslims in conflict situations—Palestine, Kashmir, Kosovo, and others. The catalytic events include: the Iranian revolution, the Afghan War, the Gulf War of 1991, September 11, the global war on terrorism, and finally the Iraq War. From this overall analytical perspective, this study made an evaluation of the overall political and strategic situation in each region of the world.

For Southeast Asia, the Rand report on *The Muslim World After 9/11* concluded that the preexisting moderate traditions of Islam are being challenged by Islamic radicalism that has acquired a significant foothold in the region but remains a relatively small minority among the mass-based traditional and modernist Islamic groups and institutions of Southeast Asia. The diversity of opinion and belief among Muslims was analyzed by ranking Islamic organizations on their commitment to democracy and their attraction to violence as a political and ideological tactic. According to their analysis, democracy receives overwhelming support among Southeast Asian Muslims, with a fairly low level of support for jihadi violence as a tactic, especially after the Bali bombings. At the same time, survey data reveal that there remained quite strong support for some Islamist doctrines, especially regarding the implementation of Sharia law. The mixed patterns and somewhat contradictory evidence led the authors to suggest that there will be continued ideological and political contestation for the foreseeable future, with moderates and pragmatic secularists gradually gaining increased popular support, provided that governments remain effective in addressing social and economic issues.[37]

The policy recommendations of *The Muslim World After 9/11* are addressed to US policymakers. The authors note that the United States does not have sufficient credibility with Muslims to counter the inroads of radical political Islam. Only moderate Muslims have the ability to check the political and ideological appeal of the radicals. Therefore, they proposed that Western states and institutions should forge links with "civil Islam" to assist in the promotion of democratic ideals and to strengthen the capacity of existing political systems and governments to address substantive policy issues. The report stressed that economic recovery, combined with domestic peace and security, will greatly reduce the threats from terrorism.[38]

Analysts and actors outside the region produced these assessments of domestic support for Islamist causes and the continuing threats of terrorism in Southeast Asia summarized above. Within the region, officials and political leaders have been more hesitant to publicize security concerns or issue dire warnings because of their potential detrimental economic impact and their aversion to critical responses from domestic constituents having sympathetic affiliation with radical Islamist groups. The Australian government issued a white paper in 2004 entitled *Transnational Terrorism: The Threat to Australia.* That publication warned that terrorism in Southeast Asia posed a continuing threat despite the arrests of hundreds of Jemaah Islamiyah operatives by the governments of that region. Every year, the US State Department issued "Country Reports on Terrorism" that provided an assessment on the terrorist threats in East Asia and the Pacific. The report for 2007 warned that there were serious threats to Western and regional interests, especially in Indonesia and the southern Philippines. Terrorist attacks also continued in southern Thailand, but those attacks had not specifically targeted US citizens or interests. This report assessed the terrorist threat level for the Asia Pacific region as continuing, but at a decreased level from previous years.[39]

The outbreak of violent attacks by militant Islamists against Christian communities in Sulawesi in 2006 and 2007 revealed that Jemaah Islamiyah continued to survive. It did so through decentralized regeneration and active recruitment of new members from an expanding pool of disaffected Muslims, primarily youth, many of whom have been radicalized at pesantren where Islamist doctrines are propagated. The Indonesian police identified active JI cells operating in Java, Sumatra, Sulawesi, and West Nusa Tenggara. Their strength in 2007 was estimated to be 900, and some of their best recruiters were released JI prisoners who had been sentenced for earlier involvement with terrorist operations. Other militant terrorist groups have also survived, and together these organizations that follow the Al Qaeda line retain links with the MILF in the Philippines and with small radical cells in Malaysia.[40]

The political ideology and worldview of the Islamists may not be the primary cause of most violence in the region, but it becomes the primary motivational appeal to recruit converts for Islamist-inspired jihadi operations from a pool of alienated youth. The propagation of radical Islamist doctrines helps to create support constituencies for clandestine terrorist groups, and these doctrines become the common element that cannot be ignored or dismissed as only marginally relevant in checking the threat from terrorism.

The two prevailing perspectives on Southeast Asian political affairs may seem to be in conflict—an emerging "civil society" or the "uncivil" politics of violence and terror. The one vision of the future heralds the dawn of a new era of democratic institutions and freedoms. The other warns of the chaos and loss of legitimacy that derives from persistent terrorism and organized domestic violence. Yet, these two apparently alternative scenarios need not be mutually exclusive. The "civil society" accounts do take cognizance of the legal and institutionalized forms of politics that have recently emerged, while the "terrorism threat" accounts report on the underground and illegal politics of highly motivated but numerically minuscule minorities. The key issue is not which perspective is valid, but what are the consequences when both perspectives attract supporters and activists. There are very few historical examples of terrorist and underground guerrilla movements that have flourished and eventually been defeated without having incumbent authorities impose draconian measures undermining democratic principles and substituting some form of authoritarian rule. To avoid this scenario, competent and efficient police work must combine with an independent and incorruptible judiciary to become the front line for the prosecution of violent acts of domestic terrorism.

The nature of the terrorist threat in Southeast Asia has evolved since 9/11, in part because of the effective interdiction and arrest of key leaders and operatives within organizations dedicated to the Al Qaeda version of global jihad. The organizational structures of Jemaah Islamiyah and Abu Sayyaf and other aspiring terrorist groups have been seriously disrupted and weakened, but key members of their leadership circles remain at large. Moreover, these terrorist organizations retain a capacity for active recruitment and regeneration. Links with other radical groups within the Muslim world, including Al Qaeda, have been strengthened at the same time that each cell and faction becomes more autonomous and self-sufficient. What has emerged is an amorphous global movement, motivated more by a core ideology than a system of hierarchical command and control. The "no name" autonomy of these cells makes them much more difficult to track and interdict. Bomb-making technology is easily acquired; bomb ingredients are readily available and relatively easy to transport; the cost of staging bombings, kidnappings, and assassinations is relatively negligible. Therefore, the post-9/11 financial controls over terrorist financial transactions have had a diminishing impact because Al Qaeda affiliates need much less money to operate than previously.[41]

Public opinion in the region cannot be neatly divided between those who support democracy and those who support the stated objectives and the leadership of terrorist groups. Large proportions of Muslims in the region do not believe that democracy and terrorism are mutually incompatible and antithetical. There are so many cross-pressures of competing values and so much uncertainty about the consequences of political and ideological choices that the public attitudes can become contradictory and somewhat incoherent. For example, in a global comparative survey in 2003, 53 percent of Indonesian Muslim respondents reported that "democracy is a Western way of doing things that would not work here," and only 41 percent believed that "democracy can work here."[42] Yet, within two years after that survey, major democratic reforms had been passed and Indonesia held the most open democratic elections for Parliament and for president, with the largest voter turnout, of any Muslim country in the world. On another issue, in a national opinion survey in 2002, 27 percent of Muslim respondents in Indonesia answered that "violence against civilians is sometimes or often justified in defense of Islam." A repeat survey in 2005 asked the same question with only 15 percent of Muslims answering that "violence is justified against civilians." Yet, in 2003, 58 percent of Indonesian Muslims reported that they had "confidence in bin Laden as a world leader," and in the 2005 survey, 35 percent of Indonesian Muslims reported "confidence in bin Laden."[43] Support for "violence against civilians in defense of Islam" was decreasing, and so were the numbers of Muslims expressing "confidence in bin Laden." Even so, the percentage of Osama bin Laden supporters and admirers identified in the poll results gives some idea of the potential support base for radical Islamist organizations dedicated to violent and revolutionary tactics. These same people very likely actively participated in democratic elections and in "civil society" organizations, but also did not see any contradiction in playing a double role as democrats and as radical Islamists. Not all of those people admiring bin Laden would support an Islamist revolution. Yet, even a very small proportion would be sufficient to support a clandestine terrorist organization that would have the capacity to represent a clear and present danger to the economy and to the stability of the political system. The number of people who are attracted to this apocalyptic vision is relatively small, but their intensity and commitment can be boundless.

The Pew Global Attitudes Project did not survey other predominantly Muslim states and regions of Southeast Asia. Residual support for Osama bin Laden is very likely to be substantial, both because of the levels of political conflict and also because other surveyed Muslim states reveal such a pattern. In the same 2005 survey cycle, support for bin Laden was 60 percent in Jordan, 51 percent in Pakistan, 26 percent in Morocco, 7 percent in Turkey, and 2 percent in Lebanon.[44] Impressionistic accounts from local sources suggest that Muslims in Malaysia were somewhat less likely than their Indonesian counterparts to express admiration for Osama bin Laden, but the percentage who would do so is likely to be fairly substantial.

This very limited evidence of public attitudes does not mean that Islamist revolutionary groups are about to stage dramatic new deadly attacks in any of these Southeast Asian areas. But some attacks or other acts of violence remain within the capability of clandestine Islamist networks. Such attacks are far more likely to continue where separatist movements continue to fester. Political leaders in Southeast Asia need to secure regional cooperation to resolve the separatist movements in southern Thailand and the southern Philippines. The leaders of Malaysia are in a strategic location where their roles will be especially important. In other areas, the risks and prospects for violence continue, but at a lower level than in the immediate aftermath of 9/11. What remains is a continued low-level threat of violence that will need to be addressed by effective police work and successful prosecution, combined with programs to bring the disaffected into the mainstream of civil discourse. Effective government, reforms in education, and an expanding economy to reduce unemployment will erode the support base for Islamist radicalism. However, that version of radical Islamist fundamentalism will continue to attract the interest and loyalty of a small minority, including some from among the ranks of the elite and the well educated. These will be the persistent political and economic challenges confronting governments in the region for decades into the foreseeable future.

Southeast Asian Islam in a Globalized World

Islam is a religion of many faces. The historical progression of Islam in a span of fourteen centuries produced an accumulated evolution of diverse principles, doctrines, and practices that were expressed with divergent cultural enhancements. The geographic progression of Islam increased that diversity when Islam expanded to the non-Arab world of alien religions, cultures, and systems of political and social order. Southeast Asian Islam is the product of greater historical evolution and geographic distance from Islam's epicenter than other regions of the Muslim world. That rich diversity within Southeast Asian Islam was preserved and increased during the colonial era, when each colonial power pursued somewhat different policies for the administration of Muslim affairs and the management of public order.

One of the prime consequences of the colonial experience involved the diffusion of cultures and the stimulation and promotion of population mobility and immigration across state borders. This combination of new peoples and new cultures migrating into moderately stable societies created the conditions for intensified religio-ethnic conflicts and increased cultural diversity. Colonial powers tended to view religion as a stabilizing force within the societies that they ruled. In both the British and Dutch colonies, colonial authorities established a system of "indirect rule," which involved support for native rulers who collaborated with the colonial system. This policy involved recognition and support for Islam where Muslim states had been established. Islamic laws and practices were codified and incorporated into the system of colonial authority. What had been an evolving religious and social system was made part of a colonial structure of authority. As a concession to native practices and to Muslim rulers, a medieval version of Islam was encased and preserved by colonial powers, and for many regions, especially in South and Southeast Asia, Muslims became politically aligned with colonial authorities that were especially sensitive to Muslim interests and sensitivities. Without intention or assessment of long-term consequences, this political strategy of colonial authorities tended to relegate the majority of Muslims to remain as peasant agriculturalists. Led by ulamas, Muslim peasants lived with the preserved local-based institutions of medieval Islam that provided protection against the pressures and challenges of the industrial revolution and an increasingly globalized world.

For Islam, the colonial era represented a period of arrested development, during which colonial authorities supported policies that inhibited the natural processes of religious adaptation to the economic, educational, technological, and cultural changes that were taking place in the world at large. The gradual recognition of Muslims that their societies and their faith had become somewhat anachronistic came only after the Muslim-majority colonies gained independence and were able to assess the role of Islam in defining their political and cultural life. The dakwah movement was part of that reassessment. The pace of change within the umma was suddenly accelerated with the expectation that medieval Islam could be converted into "modernist" Islam in the course of one or two decades. Their goal has been to create an Islam that was tolerant, equalitarian, democratic, peace loving, and supportive of civil society. For those who look for historical precedents, Christianity took over three centuries to confront its authoritarian traditions, its institutionalized intolerance, and its draconian punishments meted out to heretics, apostates, and "free thinkers," before doctrines of tolerance, democracy, equality, and civil society began to take root. And, even after that long interlude, some of the assumptions of medieval Christianity survive to the present as "fundamentalist" minority denominations within the broad Christian tradition. If this historical analogy can be taken as a rough guide of long-term processes, Muslims will be involved for a very long time in the reevaluation and reinterpretation of their faith and their religious traditions. The process may not take three centuries, but it will probably extend over a century or more. It will also be a time of much conflict and debate between Muslims as to what their faith demands and what interpretations of Islamic doctrines are appropriate and relevant to the rapidly changing conditions of the contemporary world.

For Islam, this crisis of adaptation has been prolonged and contentious. In part, a major obstacle to reform has been the view of so many Muslims that Islam's initial founding society must become the model for a new universal Islamic world order. In its extreme Islamist form, this backward-oriented vision of an eschatological utopia is justified by declaratory assertions of "revealed truth." What is divine cannot be answered or challenged by rational arguments, because absolute and "eternal truth" cannot be compromised by accommodations to cultural diversity or shifting societal norms. If Islam is to be defined exclusively by ulama and those in the established bureaucracy of Islam, then the processes of change and reformation will be exceedingly slow. If change comes from Muslim intellectuals not linked to the Islamic bureaucracy, then that process of reform and regeneration will become accelerated and self-generating. The central issue that is being addressed, but not yet resolved, is whether Islam is locked in an epic battle with modernity and with the non-Muslim world. Or, does Islam have the capacity to make a congruent adaptation to the social and cultural changes generated by processes of modernization, democracy, and globalization? This is the cultural predicament of contemporary Islam.[45]

The answer to this predicament cannot be found by listening to the strident voices of the ulama or the hectoring polemics of those who seek political power through manipulation of Islamic symbols of divine sanction derived from the sovereignty of God. Instead, in the long run, the answer to this unresolved Islamic predicament will gradually evolve by how ordinary Muslims combine the basic values and assumptions of their faith with the realities of their everyday lives. That resolution will evolve quicker and with less domestic strife if democracy prevails and if individual freedoms of speech, religion, and the press are preserved to permit individual Muslims to make those decisions and choices for their own lives and for the selection of their leaders. Because the Islamic-majority states of Southeast Asia appear to have acquired a greater commitment to democracy and to the expansion of individual freedoms, perhaps these states may eventually also become exemplars for the rest of the Muslim world for how that basic cultural predicament can and should be resolved.

Notes

1. Mahathir bin Mohamad, *The Malay Dilemma* (Singapore: Asia Pacific Press, 1970). Also see the summary and analysis of arguments and themes of *The Malay Dilemma* in Khoo Boo Teik, *Paradoxes of Mahathirism: An Intellectual Biography of Mahathir Mohamad* (Singapore: Oxford University Press, 1995), 24–34.

2. Gordon P. Means, "'Special Rights' as a Strategy for Development," *Comparative Politics* 5, no. 1 (October 1972), 29–61; Gordon P. Means, "Ethnic Preference Policies in Malaysia," Neil Nevitte and Charles H. Kennedy (eds.), *Ethnic Preference and Public Policy in Developing States* (Boulder, CO: Lynne Rienner Publishers, 1986), 95–118.

3. Mahathir Mohamad, "The New Malay Dilemma," speech to the Harvard Club of Malaysia, July 29, 2002, Kuala Lumpur, "Archives," 1–8, www.pmo.gov.my. Also see Maznah Mohamad, "Malaysia in 2002: Bracing for a Post-Mahathir Future," in *Southeast Asian Affairs 2003* (Singapore: Institute of Southeast Asian Affairs, 2003), 154–157. For an account of Mahathir's views concerning the "Second Malay Dilemma," see Khoo Boo Teik, *Beyond Mahathir: Malaysian Politics and Its Discontents* (London: Zed Books, 2003), 188–199.

4. Mahathir, "The New Malay Dilemma," 6.

5. Speech by Abdullah bin Ahmad Badawi, Prime Minister of Malaysia, to Harvard Club of Malaysia, May 5, 2005, Kuala Lumpur, 1–5, www.pmo.gov.my.

6. For an introductory exposure to these theories, see Max Weber, *The Protestant Ethic and the Spirit of Capitalism,* trans. by Talcott Parsons (Los Angeles: Roxbury, 1996); R. H. Tawney, *Religion and the Rise of Capitalism* (New York: Harcourt, Brace and Co., 1926); and S. N. Eisenstadt (ed.), *The Protestant Ethic and Modernization: A Comparative View* (New York: Basic Books, 1968). For comparison with developments in Islam, see Dale F. Eickelman, "Who Speaks for Islam? Inside the Islamic Reformation," in Michaelle Browers and Charles Kurzman (eds.), *An Islamic Reformation?* (Lanham, MD: Lexington Books, 2004), 18–27.

7. For example, see Edmund Terence Gomez, "The Perils of Pro-Malay Policies," *Far Eastern Economic Review* 168, no. 8 (September 2005), 36–39; Anonymous, "Apartheid State," *Asian Analysis,* The Australian National University, ASEAN Focus Group, January 2002, 1–2, www.aseanfocus.com/asiananalysis/article.cfm?articleID=462; anonymous Malaysian scholar, "Saying 'No' to Singapore," Jeff Ooi's Screenshots, May 31, 2005, 1–3, www.littlespeck.com/region/CForeign-My-050531.htm; Ramon Navaratnam, "The Malaysian Dilemma," Monash Ideas Forum, July 7, 2000, 1–4, www.monash.edu.au/alumni/events/malaysia/malaysian_dilemma.

8. Djisman S. Simandjuntak, "Walking the Walk on Reform in a New Era," *The Jakarta Post,* July 21, 2005, 1–2, www.thejakartapost.com/outlook/eco01b.asp; Kahlil Rowter, "RI's New Gov't: A Diagnosis and a Prognosis," *The Jakarta Post,* July 21, 2005, 1–3, www.thejakartapost.com/outlook/eco03b.asp. For an account of Partai Keadilan's fifty-page Islamist manifesto for the 1999 election, see Francois Raillon, "Islam and Democracy: Indonesia's 2004 Election and Beyond," www.eias.org/special briefing/islam0605/raillon.pdf, citing Mathias Diederich, "A Closer Look at Dakwah and Politics in Indonesia," *Archipel* (Paris) 64 (2002).

9. International Foundation for Election Systems, *Public Opinion Survey Indonesia—2005* (Jakarta: IFES, 2005), 24–26.

10. In 2001, 79 percent of businesses in Indonesia reported that they had to pay "extra cost" when dealing with bureaucracy. The actual figure was probably much higher, since this response was a tacit admission that their business was a party to corruption. M. Chatib Basri, Institute for Economic and Social Research, University of Indonesia, in a 2004 speech at Institute of Southeast Asian Studies, 2004.

11. The anticorruption laws included Law No. 29/1999, Law No. 31/1999, Law No. 20/2001, and Law No. 30/2002. An Anti-Corruption Court was also established to try cases under these laws. Saldi Isra, "Getting Rid of Corruption in Indonesia: The Future," *The Jakarta Post,* August 8, 2005, 1–4, www.thejakartapost.com/outlook/eco08b.asp.

12. Rachel Harvey, "Corruption Costs Indonesia $2bn," *BBC News,* June 18, 2004, newsvote.bbc.uk/mpapps/; Rachel Harvey, "Corruption Challenge for Aceh Aid," *BBC News,* May 31, 2005, 1–4, newswww.bbc.net.uk/2/hi/asia-pacific/4583557.stm.

13. "Aceh Governor Arrested as Corruption Suspect," *Laksamana,* December 7, 2004, www.indonesia-house.org/focus/aceh,2004/12/120704Aceh_gov; "Aceh Governor Gets Fired & 10 Years for Graft," *Laksamana*, April 11, 2005, 1–3, www.infid.be/aceh_puteh.htm.

14. The Consultative Group on Indonesia (CGI) was a planning forum attended by donor countries and international organizations providing foreign aid and social services in Indonesia. The meetings were held annually to discuss economic development and assistance issues among nineteen participants, including the United States, Australia, the Netherlands, Japan, Great Britain, and Canada, plus thirteen international institutions, including the IMF, the Asian Development Bank, United Nations Children's Fund, and the United Nations Development Programme. The CGI was the successor organization to the earlier Inter-Governmental Group on Indonesia (IGGI), which had been formed in 1967, but had been dissolved when President Suharto opposed its activities.

15. All these World Bank and ADB policy reports and briefs on Indonesia are available from web.worldbank.org or www.adb.org. For a summary of the *Indonesian Development Plan, 2005–2009*: Asian Development Bank, *Country Strategy Update—Indonesia 2005*, www.adb.org.

16. "Jaringan Islam Liberal," *The Pluralism Project,* updated February 1, 2006, 1, www.pluralism.org/research/profiles/display.php?profile=74164.

17. Ahmad Najib Burhani, "Indonesia Outlook 2006—Political: Competition Between Liberal and Conservative Groups," *The Jakarta Post,* March 8, 2006, 1–3, www.thejakartapost.com/Outlook2006/pol08b.asp; Tom McCawley, "In Indonesia, the Struggle Within Islam," *The Christian Science Monitor,* October 5, 2005, 1 and 10.

18. *Muslim Women in Development: Final Report of the First Regional Conference for South East Asia and Pacific* (Subang, Malaysia: Kompleks Jemaah Haji, 1982). For an account of that conference, see Gordon P. Means, "Women's Rights and Public Policy in Islam, Report of a Conference," *Asian Survey* 27, no. 3 (March 1987), 340–352.

19. Maznah Mohamad, "Democratization and Islamic Family Law Reforms in Malaysia," paper presented at the Second Malaysian Studies Conference of the Malaysian Social Science Association, Kuala Lumpur, August 2, 1999, 1–14; Maila Stivens, "(Re)Framing Women's Rights Claims in Malaysia," in Virginia Hooker and Norani Othman (eds.), *Malaysia: Islam, Society and Politics* (Singapore: Institute of Southeast Asian Studies, 2003), 126–146.

20. Jacqueline Ann Surin, "Sisterhood in Islam: Conversations with Zainah Anwar," *The Sun,* July 17, 2004, 1–11, www.sun2surf.com/article.cfm?id=4081; Nora Murat, "Sisters in Islam: Advocacy for Change Within the Religious Framework," and Sisters in Islam, "Challenging Fundamentalisms," November 2003, 1–2, both papers available at www.sistersinislam.org.my; Simon Tisdall, "Sisters Take on Scholars in Battle for Islam," *The Guardian Unlimited,* June 1, 2005, 1–3, www.guardian.co.uk/international /0,1496273,00.html.

21. For a survey of the ideological and theological doctrines of liberal Islam, see Charles Kurzman, "Liberal Islam: Prospects and Challenges," 1–9, liberalinstitute.com/LiberalIslam.html. For an articulate exposition of liberal Islam, see Salbiah Ahmad, *Critical Thoughts on Islam, Rights and Freedom in Malaysia* (Petaling Jaya, Malaysia: Strategic Information and Research Development Centre, 2007), 1–405.

22. Cheryl Benard, *Civil Democratic Islam: Partners, Resources and Strategies* (Santa Monica, CA: Rand Corporation, 2003), 1–24. The analytical categories are as follows: Radical Fundamentalists, Scriptural Fundamentalists, Conservative Traditionalists, Reformist Traditionalists, Modernists, Mainstream Secularists, and Radical Secularists. The dominant attitudes and beliefs for each category are summarized for the following subjects: democracy, human rights and individual liberties, polygamy, Islamic criminal law, Hijab, beating of wives, status of minorities, Islamic state, public participation of women, jihad as personal betterment or as an obligation to wage holy war, and the sources utilized to support their doctrines. The attitudes and beliefs on these issues are directly correlated to topical categories to provide a system of ranking that measures ideological diversity within Islam.

23. The Global Attitudes Project, *Views of a Changing World* (Washington, DC: The Pew Research Center for the People and the Press, June 2003), 33–46.

24. G. A. Parwez, *The Status of Hadith,* trans. by Aboo B. Rana, Chapter 1, 1–8, www.toluislam.com/pub_online/position/hadith1.htm.

25. Elizabeth Fuller Collins, "'Islam Is the Solution': Dakwah and Democracy in Indonesia," academic paper, Ohio University, June 20, 2004.

26. For example, see Nurcholish Madjid, "Potential Islamic Doctrinal Resources of the Establishment and Appreciation of the Modern Concept of Civil Society," in Nakamuro Mitsuo, Sharon Siddique, and Omar Farouk Majunid (eds.), *Islam and Civil Society in Southeast Asia* (Singapore: Institute of Southeast Asian Studies, 2001), 149–163. This paper by Madjid has an English translation of the Treaty of Medina as an appendix.

27. For an exploration of this issue see Bat Ye'or, *Islam and Dhimmitude: Where Civilizations Collide,* trans. from French by Miriam Kochan and David Littman (Madison, NJ: Fairleigh Dickinson University Press, 2002).

28. Under the direction of A. Mukti Ali, this forum operated from 1967 to 1971, exploring, debating, and challenging the prevailing dakwah dogma. Nurcholish Madjid became one of the earliest proponents of revitalization of Islam through scholarly reexamination of established canon. He had served two times as leader of the Himpunan Mahasiswa Islam (HMI) and had graduated from IAIN. His initial ideas were presented in 1970 in a speech to four Islamic organizations on the topic of "Renewal of Islamic Thought." Later, from 1978 to 1984 he went for a graduate degree in Islamic Studies at the University of Chicago, during which he explored more aspects of his theological interpretations of Islam. Robert Hefner refers to this new version of Islamic thought as part of "Civil Islam," while Bahtiar Effendy gives it the label "New Islamic Intellectualism." See Bahtiar Effendy, *Islam and the State in Indonesia* (Singapore: Institute of Southeast Asian Studies, 2003), 66–72.

29. Robert W. Hefner, *Civil Islam: Muslims and Democratization in Indonesia* (Princeton, NJ: Princeton University Press, 2000), 117, quoting Nurcholish Madjid, "Modernisasi Ialah Rasionalisasi Bukan Westernisasi," 174.

30. Bahtiar Effendy, *Islam and the State,* 102–123 .

31. Hefner, *Civil Islam,* 129–129, 162–163. For a biography of Wahid and an account of his leadership of Nahdlatul Ulama, see Douglas Ramage, *Democracy, Islam and the Ideology of Tolerance* (London: Routledge, 1995), 49–53; Greg Barton, *Abdurrahman Wahid: Muslim, Democrat, Indonesian President* (Honolulu: University of Hawaii Press, 2002); Paridah Abd. Samad, *Gus Dur: A Peculiar Leader in Indonesia's Political Agony* (Ampang Selangor, Malaysia: Penerbit Salafi, 2001).

32. Hefner, *Civil Islam,* 143–144; Adam Schwarz, *A Nation in Waiting: Indonesia's Search for Stability* (Boulder, CO: Westview Press, 2000), 180.

33. The works that explore "civil society" in Southeast Asian Islam include: Hefner, *Civil Islam*; Mitsuo, Siddique, and Bajunid, *Islam and Civil Society in Southeast Asia*; Michael G. Peletz, *Islamic Modern: Religious Courts and Cultural Politics in Malaysia* (Princeton, NJ: Princeton University Press, 2002); Effendy, *Islam and the State*; Hooker and Othman, *Malaysia: Islam, Society and Politics*; Robert W. Hefner (ed.), *Remaking Muslim Politics: Pluralism, Contestation, Democratization* (Princeton, NJ: Princeton University Press, 2005); Robin Bush, "Islam and Civil Society in Indonesia," *Journal of the International Center for Islam and Pluralism* 2, no. 3 (June 2005).

34. On the contest between "Islamic Democracy" and "Islamic Terrorism" see Jean-François Revel, *Democracy Against Itself: The Future of the Democratic Impulse* (New York: The Free Press, 1993), 199–221.

35. Ingrid Wessel and Georgia Wimhöfer (eds.), *Violence in Indonesia* (Hamburg: Abera Verlag Markus Voss, 2001); Kim Cragin and Peter Chalk, *Terrorism and Development: Using Social and Economic Development to Inhibit a Resurgence of Terrorism* (Santa Monica, CA: Rand, 2003); Zachary Abuza, *Militant Islam in Southeast Asia: Crucible of Terror* (Boulder, CO: Lynne Reinner, 2003); Zachary Abuza, "Muslims, Politics, and Violence in Indonesia: An Emerging Jihadist-Islamist Nexus?" *NBR Analysis* 15, no. 3 (September 2004), 5–55; Zachary Abuza, "The State of Jemaah Islamiyah: Terrorism and Insurgency in Southeast Asia Five Years After Bali," The Fletcher School, The Jebsen Center for Counter-Terrorism Studies, Research Briefing Series 2, no. 1 (November 2007), Medford, MA; Rohan Gunaratna, *The Changing Face of Terrorism* (Singapore: Eastern Universities Press, 2004); Greg Barton, *Indone-*

sia's Struggle: Jemaah Islamiyah and the Soul of Islam (Sydney: University of New South Wales Press, 2004); Australian Government, *Transnational Terrorism: The Threat to Australia* (Canberra: Department of Communications. 2004).

36. Abuza, "Muslims, Politics." For a very similar argument presented in a report on the increasing political clout of radical Islamists in Indonesia, see Sadanand Dhume, "Radicals March on Indonesia's Future," *Far Eastern Economic Review* 168, no. 5 (May 2005), 11–19.

37. Angel M. Rabasa, Cheryl Bernard, Peter Chalk, C. Christine Fair, Theodore Karasik, Rollie Lal, Ian Lesser, and David Thaler, *The Muslim World After 9/11* (Santa Monica, CA: Rand Corporation, 2004).

38. Ibid., 367–412.

39. The Australian Government, *Transnational Terrorism,* 1–130; US State Department, "East Asia and Pacific Overview," *Country Reports on Terrorism* (April 30, 2007), 2–11, www.state.gov/s/ct/rls/crt/2006/82731.htm.

40. In Indonesia there are over 14,000 pesantren, out of which only five pesantren were identified in 2005 as recruiting centers for Jemaah Islamiyah. Sharif Shuja, "Gauging Jemaah Islamiyah's Threat in Southeast Asia," *Terrorism Monitor* 3, no. 8 (April 21, 2005), 1, jamestown.org/terrorism/news/article.php?articleid=2369632. By 2007, the Indonesian police had identified at least twenty pesantren across Indonesia where Jemaah Islamiyah gained supporters and established operational cells. Indonesian officials estimated in 1999 that JI had inducted about 2,000 active members and had a support base of about 5,000. In 2007, its active members were estimated to number 900. International Crisis Group, *Indonesia: Jemaah Islamiyah's Current Status,* Asia Briefing No. 63 (May 3, 2007), Jakarta/Brussels, 1–16; International Crisis Group, *Jihadism in Indonesia: Poso on the Edge,* Asia Report No. 127 (January 24, 2007), Jakarta/Brussels.

41. Bruce Hoffman, "Global Trends and Patterns in International Terrorism," in *Regional Outlook Forum 2005, Terrorism: International and Regional Dimensions* [Trends in Southeast Asia Series, 3 (2005)] (Singapore: Institute of Southeast Asian Studies, 2005), 1–11.

42. The Pew Global Attitudes Project, *Views of a Changing World* (Washington, DC: The Pew Research Center, June 2003), 33–34.

43. The Pew Global Attitudes Project, *Islamic Extremism: Common Concern for Muslim and Western Publics* (Washington, DC: The Pew Research Center, July 14, 2005), 27–29.

44. Ibid., 29.

45. For commentary on the contemporary predicament of Islam, see Bassam Tibi, *The Challenge of Fundamentalism: Political Islam and the New World Disorder* (Berkeley: University of California Press, 1998), 63–72; Bassam Tibi, *Islam Between Culture and Politics* (New York: Palgrave, 2001), 24–52, 87–115, 210–230; Abdullahi Ahmed An-Na'im, *Islam and the Secular Sate: Negotiating the Future of Shari'a* (Cambridge, MA: Harvard University Press, 2008); Emmanuel Sivan, *Radical Islam: Medieval Theology and Modern Politics*, enl. ed. (New Haven, CT: Yale University Press, 1990), 1–15, 83–129.

Glossary and Acronyms

abangan	nonreligious, unbelieving people
ABIM	Angkatan Belia Islam Malaysia, Islamic Youth League of Malaysia
ABRI	Angkatan Bersenjata Republik Indonesia, Indonesian Armed Forces (after 1999 the army was named TNI, Tentara Nasional Indonesia, Indonesian National Military)
ACCIN	Allied Coordinating Committee of Islamic NGOs, a Malaysian organization opposing Liberal Islam and against religious liberties for Muslims
Adat	Malay/Indonesian customary law
akidah	religious faith, Islamic doctrine based on "revealed truth," religious belief, faithful commitment to genuine Islam
al-deen	the doctrine that Islam is a "total way of life"
Al Haramain	Al Haramain Islamic Foundation, a charity based in Saudi Arabia, alleged to be an Al Qaeda front and designated as a "terrorist organization" by the US Treasury Department
alim	someone who is learned in Islamic law and doctrine; plural: ulama
Al Qaeda	literally, "The Base"; the political organization headed by Osama bin Laden that has waged jihad against all Western interests, especially the United States
AMM	Aceh Monitoring Mission
Ansor	the "Companions of the Prophet," the name of Nahdlatul Ulama's paramilitary youth organization
ARMM	Autonomous Region of Muslim Mindanao
ASEAN	Association of Southeast Asian Nations
ASG	Abu Sayyaf Group, an Islamist terrorist group in the Philippines
BA	Barisan Alternatif, Alternative Front, the opposition coalition formed for the 2004 Malaysia elections, later reformed in 2008 as Barisan Rakyat (BR)
bay'a	a contract of loyalty or oath of allegiance recognizing the absolute authority of the caliph or of a Muslim ruler
bayt al-mal	the treasury in an Islamic state

BBMP	Barisan Bersatu Mujahideen Patani, United Front of Pattani Fighters
BIAF	Bangsamoro Islamic Armed Forces, the military wing of the MILF
bilal	the Muslim functionary who makes the call to prayer
BJE	Bangsamoro Juridical Entity, the proposed region for Muslim autonomy as part of a potential peace treaty with the MILF
BMA	Bangsa Moro Army, the military wing of the MNLF
BNPP	Barisan Nasional Pembebasan Patani, National Front for the Liberation of Pattani
bomoh	a shaman, spirit manipulator, or medicine-man who practices occult rituals to effect cures
BPD	Democratic Pioneer Star, a political coalition in 2005 of smaller Indonesian parties
BR	Barisan Rakyat, People's Front, the opposition coalition formed for the 2008 Malaysia elections
BRN	Barisan Revolusi Nasional, National Revolutionary Front
BTI	Barisan Tani Indonesia, Indonesian Peasant Front
Bumiputra	a legally defined category for Malaysia that includes about 90 percent Malays and 10 percent non-Muslim indigenous peoples, mostly from Sarawak and Sabah
burka	Arab-style black flowing robes, totally covering the body; *jilbab*
CAFGU	Civilian Armed Forces Geographical Units, paramilitary units formed under the authority of ARMM
caliph	for Sunni Muslims, the successor to Muhammad and the political and spiritual leader of Islam
CGI	Consultative Group on Indonesia, a planning forum for donor countries and organizations to Indonesia
CPP	Communist Party of the Philippines
dakwah	missionary activity that energizes lapsed Muslims to the faith or makes new converts for Islam
DAP	Democratic Action Party (Malaysia)
Darul Arqam	a Muslim movement in Malaysia that was banned for being "deviant"
darul-harb	"the abode of war"; hostile territory where non-Muslims rule
darul-Islam	"the abode of peace"; the dominion of Islam, where Muslims rule and Islamic law is enforced
dato/datuk	a Malay chief, a title of high rank
daulat	the Malay concept of divine sovereignty
DDII	Dewan Dakwah Islamiyah Indonesia, Indonesian Council for Islamic Preaching
derhaka	disloyal, traitorous, treason, rebellion, revolution
dhimmi	people who follow "revealed religions" to whom hospitality and protection are provided by a Muslim state under Sharia law, provided that superior Muslim authority is acknowledged
DPR	Dewan Perwakilan Rakyat, People's Representative Assembly (Indonesia)
fatwa	an opinion on Islamic law or an enforcement order given by a mufti or by a duly authorized committee of ulama interpreting Islamic law

fiqh	Islamic jurisprudence, technical rules of Sharia law
fitnah	slander, libel, uttering a malicious falsehood designed to damage a person's or a ruler's character and moral standing, undermining authority
FKM	Front Kedaulatan Maluku, Moluccas Sovereignty Front
FPI	Front Pembala Islam, Islamic Defense Front, or Islamic Defenders Front, founded in 1998, an Islamist paramilitary force
FY	fiscal year
GAM	Gerakan Aceh Merdeka, Free Aceh Movement
GAMPAR	Gabungan Melayu Pattani Raya, Association of the Malays of Greater Pattani
Gerakan	Gerakan Rakyat Malaysia, Malaysian People's Movement, a multiethnic Malaysian political party with strong support in Penang
Gestapu	an Indonesian acronym meaning "September 30th Movement," referring to the failed coup of 1965 that was attributed to the Communist Party of Indonesia
Golkar	Golongan Karya, the government-sponsored party during the New Order period in Indonesia, which later continued as an autonomous political party
GMIP	Gerakan Mujahideen Islam Pattani, Islamic Mujahideen Movement of Pattani
GPII	Gerakan Pemuda Islam Indonesia, Indonesian Islamic Students Movement
GRP	government of the Republic of the Philippines
guru	a teacher
hadd	serious crimes
Hadith	a report of the Prophet Muhammad's deeds and sayings that are a source for defining Muslim belief and practice
haj	the pilgrimage to Mecca, required of all Muslims at least once
haji	a title conferred upon males who have completed the haj pilgrimage to Mecca
halal	permissible according to the standards of Islam, especially relating to food
Hanafiah	the largest of four schools of jurisprudence, considered to be "orthodox" in Egypt, Sudan, Syria, Iraq, and Central Asia
haram	forbidden or prohibited for Muslims, especially involving food
Hijrah	Muhammad's flight from Mecca to Medina in 622 A.D.
HMI	Himpunan Mahasiswa Islam, Islamic University Students Association, Indonesia
hudud	physical punishments of Sharia criminal law, including amputation, stoning, caning, execution by sword, and crucifixion
HUJI	Harkat-ul-Jihad-al-Islami, a radical political group in Pakistan and Bangladesh that trained jihadi recruits for Southeast Asia
IAIN	Institut Agama Islam Negri, State Institute for Islamic Studies, in Yogyakarta
ICMI	Ikatan Cendekiawan Muslim Indonesia, Indonesian Association of Muslim Intellectuals
'Id al-Fitr	the Muslim festival when the fast of Ramadan is broken
IDF	Islamic Defense Front; see FPI

ijtihad	reinterpreting the faith and laws of Islam according to the needs of contemporary society; the right of individual interpretation of the Quran, Hadith, and Sunna.
ikhtilaf	public interest, a justification for deviation from strict Sharia principles
ikhwan	a brotherhood of Muslim believers
'ilmu	knowledge
'ilmu agama	theology; literally "knowledge of religion" as applied to Islam, rather than other religions
imam	a mosque official; for Shia Islam, a successor to the Prophet Muhammad, descended from Ali, who governs by divine authority
Imam Mahdi	the leader who will come as a savior for Muslims before doomsday
IMF	International Monetary Fund
inqilab	revolution, to rebel against political authorities who ignore God's commandments
intifada	literally "shaking off," referring to the Palestinian campaign to end Israel's occupation of Palestine
irtidad	apostasy, abandoning or rejecting the beliefs and way of life of Islam
ISI	Inter-Services Intelligence Directorate (Pakistan)
Islam Hadhari	defined by Prime Minister Badawi as "Islam that is tolerant, inclusive, moderate and modern," also called "civilizational Islam"
jahiliyya	the pre-Islamic age when unbelief, "heedlessness," ignorance, and savagery prevailed, also used by radical Islamists to describe contemporary regimes in Muslim-majority states that share power with non-Muslims and do not enforce Sharia law
JAI	Jama'ah Ahmadiyah Indonesia, Indonesian Ahmadiyah Congregation
JAKIM	Jabatan Kemajuan Agama Islam Malaysia, Department for the Advancement of Islam, which operates under the authority of the Prime Minister's Department in Malaysia
Jemaah Islamiyah	literally "Islamic Congregation," a radical revolutionary Islamist organization that became linked to Al Qaeda
jihad	striving for religious perfection, a holy war of Muslims against infidels
JIL	Liberal Islam Network
JIMM	Jaringan Islam Muda Muhammadiyah, Muhammadiyah Youth Intellectuals Network, a liberal faction in Muhammadiyah
jizya	the poll tax levied on non-Muslims in a Muslim-ruled society
kabupaten	a district, the largest subdivision of a province in Indonesia
kafir	an unbeliever in Islam, one who is ungrateful to God for his gifts and mercy, an infidel, a non-Muslim, a pagan, a heretic; *mengkafir* heresy, the boundary of Islam where disbelief and paganism flourish, principles that violate Islam
kafir harbi	belligerent infidels who threaten or victimize Muslims, which threat justifies jihad to kill and expel all kafir; this doctrine is invoked to justify genocide and ethnic cleansing against "threatening" non-Muslims
kanun	state-promulgated regulations or codes of law that preempt Sharia law
kathi	a judge in an Islamic court

ketuanan Melayu	Malay dominance, the concept of inherent rights of Malay supremacy in Malaysia and the necessity for "Malay unity" to enforce that claim through political power
khalwat	the Sharia law governing relations between a man and a woman who are not close blood relatives, who are not married to each other, and who are found together in "suspicious proximity"
khatib	one who reads the sermon at Friday prayers in a mosque
kiai	a Javanese title given to Islamic religious teachers
KISDI	Komite Indonesia untuk Solidaritas dengan Dunia Islam, Indonesian Committee for Solidarity with the Muslim World
KOMPAK	Komite Penanggulangan Krisis, Action Committee for Crisis Response, founded in 2000 by Agus Dwikarna, Laskar Jundullah's leader, to recruit volunteers to fight Christians in Sulawesi and Ambon; also known as Mujahideen KOMPAK
Kostrad	The Strateic Army Reserve in the Indonesian Armed Forces
KPSI	Komite Penegakan Syariat Islam, Committee for the Enforcement of Islamic Law, a radical Islamic group that formed in South Sulawesi in the late 1990s
Laskar Jihad	"Holy Warriors," a militant Islamic paramilitary force in Indonesia, allied with KISDI and secretly supported by Kostrad in 1998 and 1999
Lebaran	the celebration at the end of the fasting month, marking the beginning of the New Year in the Muslim calendar
LNG	liquefied natural gas
LPI	Laskar Pembala Islam, Army of the Defenders of Islam
madrasah	a secondary-level Islamic religious school
mafkura	ideology, the core belief system of Islam
Mahdi	see Imam Mahdi
MaK	Maktab al Khidmat lil-Mujahidin al-Arab, also known as the Arab Bureau or the Afghan Service Bureau
maslaha	divergence of opinion (on law and theology)
maumin	a true believer, a genuine Muslim
MCA	Malaysian Chinese Association
MIC	Malaysian Indian Congress
MILF	Moro Islamic Liberation Front
MIM	Mindanao Independence Movement
MMI	Majelis Mujahidin Indonesia, Council of Indonesian Mujahideen, a council of Islamist organizations founded by Abu Bakar Ba'asyir in 2000
MNLF	Moro National Liberation Front
MoU	Memorandum of Understanding, the peace treaty signed by Indonesia and GAM on August 15, 2005
MPAJA	Malayan Peoples Anti-Japanese Army, a guerrilla group operating during World War II in Malaya that was led by the Communist Party of Malaya
MPR	Majelis Permusyawaratan Rakyat, People's Consultative Assembly (Indonesia)
mu'alaf	a new convert to Islam
MUI	Majelis Ulama Indonesia, Ulama Council of Indonesia, a council created by the government in 1975 to provide authoritative interpretations of Islam

mujahideen	an Islamic fighting force; *mujahid,* a Muslim warrior who fights for his religion
munafik	hypocrite, those whose fidelity and zeal for Islam is suspect or insincere
murtad	apostasy, an apostate, one who abandons the true faith of Islam; considered a serious crime under Sharia law, which provides for a penalty of death
musjawarat dan mufakat	literally "deliberation and consensus"—an ideology to suppress dissent based on the argument that political contestation violated Indonesian norms of polite and civilized behavior; this became a theme of both Suharto's Guided Democracy as well as Suharto's New Order
muttawwiun	religious police, Islamic morality enforcement officers
muzakarah	consultation, a public forum
NAD	Nanggroe Aceh Darussalam, The Province of Aceh an Abode of Peace
NC	Nationhood Coalition, the opposition coalition formed by Megawati Sukarnoputri to oppose President Yudhoyono
NDF	National Democratic Front, the political party that was sponsored by the Communist Party of the Philippines
NEP	New Economic Policy (Malaysia)
NGO	nongovernmental organization
NLFP	Barisan Nasional Pembabasan Petani, National Liberation Front of Patani
NOC	National Operations Council (Malaysia)
NPA	New People's Army, the armed wing of the Communist Party of the Philippines
NU	Nahdlatul Ulama, The Awakening of Islamic Scholars
OIC	Organization of the Islamic Conference, an international grouping of Islamic states
OPEC	Organization of Petroleum Exporting Countries
Operasi Terpadu	Integrated Operation, a military-police campaign in Aceh against GAM from May 2003 to May 2004
PAN	Partai Amanat Nasional, National Mandate Party
PAP	People's Action Party, Singapore's governing party
PAS	Partai Aislam sa-Malaysia, the Pan-Malaysian Islamic Party, Partai Islam (all these titles have been used to identify the party, with the initials PAS being most common); before the formation of Malaysia, its formal name was Partai Aislam Se-Malaya
PBB	Partai Bulan Bintan, Crescent and Star Party, an Indonesian party espousing strident Islamist doctrines
PBR	Partai Bulan Reformasi, Reform Star Party
PDI	Partai Demokrasi Indonesia
PDI-P	Partai Demokrasi Indonesia Perjuangan, Indonesian Democratic Party of Struggle; this party was formed by Megawati Sukarnoputri after she and her supporters were expelled from PDI by the actions of Suharto in 1996
PERKIM	Pertubuhan Kebajikan Am, Muslim Welfare Society (Malaysia)
pesantren	a primary-level Islamic boarding school in Indonesia, often linked to the political organization Nahdlatul Ulama
PKI	Partai Komunis Indonesia, Indonesian Communist Party

PKB	Partai Kebangkitan Bangsa, National Awakening Party
PKN	Parti Keadilan Nasional, National Justice Party (Malaysia), reorganized as PKR in 2007
PKP	the first and original Philippine Communist Party, founded in 1930 and later reorganized as the CPP
PKPIM	Persatuan Kebangsaan Pelajar Islam Malaysia, National Muslim Students Association of Malaysia
PKR	Parti Keadilan Rakyat, People's Justice Party (Malaysia)
PKS	Partai Keadilan Sejahtera, Justice and Welfare Party, formerly Justice Party (PK), an Islamist party that joined the ruling coalition under President Yudhoyono
PNI	Indonesia Nationalist Party
pondok	a small "hut" school where Islamic instruction is provided, usually to rural students
PPP	Partai Persatuan Pembangunan, United Development Party (Indonesia)
PPP	People's Power Party (Thailand)
preman	young males organized into strong-armed groups that engage in profit-oriented criminal activities
priyayi	a traditional official, part of the Javanese court circle of officials
PSM	Parti Sosialis Malaysia, Socialist Party of Malaysia
PULO	Pertubohan Persatuan Pembibasan Pattani, Pattani United Liberation Organization
PUSA	Persatuan Ulama Seluruh Aceh, All-Aceh Ulama Association
Qanun	an edict issued by Islamic authorities for the administration of Sharia law
qibla	the direction toward the Kaabah at Mecca, which Muslims face when performing prayers
qisas	criminal punishments in Sharia law based on the principle "an eye for an eye and a tooth for a tooth"
Ramadan	the ninth month of the Muslim lunar calendar, which is the fasting month for Muslims
riba	interest derived from money-lending or investments with fixed rates of return; usury, which is prohibited in Islam
RSM	Raja Solaiman Movement, a radical Islamic movement mostly composed of Filipinos who worked in the Middle East and who became Muslim through conversion
salafiya	"return to the ancestors" movement, an attempt to redress the backwardness of the Muslim world by a restoration of the ideals and practices of the first Muslim community that existed under Muhammad's rule; derived from the doctrines of Muhammad 'Abduh and the Muslim Brothers of Egypt, it developed into a radical and revolutionary version of Islam that became the basis for the doctrines of Osama bin Laden
salat	obligatory Muslim prayers five times each day
Santri	Indonesian orthodox Muslims
Saudara Bahru	literally "new friends," referring to recent converts to Islam
saum	obligatory fasting during daylight hours in the month of Ramadan
semburit	sodomy, homosexual sex between men
shura	an advisory council to a Muslim ruler, a council established by a Muslim ruler to choose his successor

SOBSI	Sentral Organisasi Buruh Seluruh Indonesia, Central Organization of Workers in All-Indonesia, a mass organization sponsored by the PKI
Sunna	the accounts of the practices and decisions of the Prophet Muhammad in the first Islamic community under his rule, which becomes for Sunni Muslims an authoritative guide of how Muslims should live and how the ideal society should be governed; "the trodden path"
syirk	polytheism, associating other beings with God or with God's divine powers, the ultimate blasphemy against Allah
takfir	to declare someone an unbeliever, a form of excommunication from the umma
taqlid	"imitation," following the example of pious men for the development of Sharia law, the equivalent of precedent for Islamic law
tanzimat	"reorganization," the rationalization of Sharia in Turkey to make it into a modern legal structure based on concepts derived from European legal systems
tarikat	a doctrine of Sufi mystics that the path to truth can be experienced through physical action and combat
tawazun	equilibrium, a principle of balance in public policy and in principles of justice
tawhid	the "oneness of God," the assertion of monotheism, complete submission to God, devotion to duty, the basis for political legitimacy
TNI	Tentera Nasional Indonesia, National Army of Indonesia; see ABRI
ulama	Islamic religious scholar, those learned in the Quran, plural of *alim*
uleebalang	in Aceh, a district chief
umma	the community of Islam, the community of true believers
UMNO	United Malays National Organization
usuliyya	fundamentalism, belief in the Quran as the inerrant word of God, radical political Islam under Sharia law
ustaz	an Islamic religious teacher
VOC	United East India Company or Dutch East India Company (Vereenigde Oostindische Compagnie)
Wilayatul Hisbah	Islamic religious police, the "vice and virtue patrol"
yayasan	an Islamic humanitarian organization that is exempt from taxes in Indonesia
zakat	annual alms tax of about 2.5 percent, calculated on agricultural harvest, livestock, and monetary wealth
ZILS	Zona Industri Lhok Seumawe, Lhokseumawe Industrial Zone in Aceh
zina	adultery, sexual relations between a man and a woman outside the bonds of marriage

Bibliography

Abdullah, Kamarulnizam. *The Politics of Islam in Contemporary Malaysia.* Bangi: Penerbit Universiti Kebangsaan Malaysia, 2003.

Abdullah, Taufik, and Sharon Siddique (eds.). *Islam and Society in Southeast Asia.* Singapore: Institute of Southeast Asian Studies, 1986.

'Abdur Rahman I. Doi, *Shari'ah: The Islamic Law.* Kuala Lumpur: A. S. Noordeen, reprint of 1984, 1990.

Abuza, Zachary. "A Breakdown of Southern Thailand's Insurgent Groups." *Terrorism Monitor* 4, no. 17 (September 8, 2006), 1–4.

———. "Funding Terrorism in Southeast Asia: The Financial Network of Al Qaeda and Jemaah Islamiya." *Contemporary Southeast Asia* 25, no. 2 (August 2003), 169–199.

———. "Funding Terrorism in Southeast Asia: The Financial Network of Al Qaeda and Jemaah Islamiyah." *NBR Analysis* 14, no. 5 (December 2003), 1–68.

———. "MILF's Stalled Peace Process and Its Impact on Terrorism in Southeast Asia." *Terrorism Monitor* 4, no. 4 (July 13, 2006), 1–3.

———. *Militant Islam in Southeast Asia: Crucible of Terror.* Boulder, CO: Lynne Rienner, 2003.

———. "Muslims, Politics, and Violence in Indonesia: An Emerging Jihadist-Islamist Nexus?" *NBR Analysis* 15, no. 3 (September 2004), 5–55.

———. "Out of the Woodwork: Islamist Militants in Aceh." *Terrorism Monitor* 3, no. 2 (January 27, 2005).

———."Peace Talks Resume as Cease-Fire Comes Under Strain in the Philippines." *Terrorism Focus* 3, no. 34 (September 6, 2006), 1–2.

———. "The State of Jemaah Islamiyah: Terrorism and Insurgency in Southeast Asia Five Years After Bali." The Fletcher School, The Jebsen Center for Counter-Terrorism Studies, Research Briefing Series 2, no. 1 (November 2007), Medford, MA, 1–7.

———. "Tentacles of Terror: Al Qaeda's Southeast Asian Network." *Contemporary Southeast Asia* 24 (2002).

Acharya, Arbinda. "Training in Terror." *IDSS Commentaries,* 17/2003. Singapore: Nanyang Technological University, 2003.

Ahmad, Bishiruddin Mahmud. *The Life of Muhammad.* Rabwah, Pakistan: Tahrik-i-Jadid [1950].

Ahmad, Salbiah. *Critical Thoughts on Islam, Rights and Freedom in Malaysia.* Petaling Jaya, Malaysia: Strategic Information and Research Development Centre, 2007.

———. "Islam in Malaysia, Constitutional and Human Rights Perspectives." *Muslim World Journal of Human Rights* 2, no. 1 (article 7, 2005), 1–57. www.bepress.com/mwjhr/vol2/iss1/art7.

Ahmad, Zakaria Haji, "The 1999 General Elections: A Preliminary Overview." *Trends in Southeast Asia* 1 (2000), 1–11.

Al-Attas, Sayed Muhammad Al-Naguib. *Islam and Secularism.* Kuala Lumpur: ISTAC, 1993.

———. *Sufism Among the Malays of Malaysia.* Singapore: Malaysian Sociological Research Institute, 1963.

———. *Islam, Secularism and the Philosophy of the Future.* London: Mansell Publishing, 1985.

Alhabshi, Syed Othman. *An Inspiration for the Future of Islam: A Brief History of the Institute of Islamic Understanding Malaysia.* Kuala Lumpur: IKIM, 1994.

'Ali, Muhammad. *The Religion of Islam: A Comprehensive Discussion of Its Sources, Principles and Practices.* Lahore, Pakistan: The Ahmadiyyah Anjuman Isha'at Islam, 1950.

Aliran. *Issues of the Mahathir Years.* Penang, Malaysia: Aliran, 1988.

Alisjahbana, S. Takdir. *Indonesia: Social and Cultural Revolution.* Kuala Lumpur: Oxford University Press, 1966.

Allen, James de V. *The Malayan Union.* New Haven: Yale University Press, 1967.

Amnesty International. *Indonesia and East Timor.* London: Amnesty International Publications, 2000. www.amnesty.org.

———. *Thailand: "If You Want Peace Work for Justice."* London: Amnesty International Publications, 2006. www.amnestyusa.org/news/document.do?id=ENGASA390012006.

Andaya, Barbara Watson, and Leonard Y. Andaya. *A History of Malaysia,* 2nd ed. Honolulu: University of Hawaii Press, 2001.

Anderson, Benedict (ed.). *Violence and the State in Suharto's Indonesia.* Ithaca, NY: Cornell University, Southeast Asia Program Publications, 2001.

Anderson, Benedict, and Ruth McVey. *A Preliminary Analysis of the October 1, 1965 Coup in Indonesia.* Ithaca, NY: Cornell Modern Indonesia Project, 1971.

An-Na'im, Abdullahi Ahmad. *Toward an Islamic Reformation: Civil Liberties, Human Rights, and International Law.* Syracuse, NY: Syracuse University Press, 1990.

———. *Islam and the Secular State: Negotiating the Future of Shari'a.* Cambridge: Harvard University Press, 2008.

Anshari, E. Saifuddin. *The Jakarta Charter 1945: The Struggle for an Islamic Constitution in Indonesia.* Kuala Lumpur: Muslim Youth Movement of Malaysia, 1979.

Anwar Ibrahim. *The Asian Renaissance.* Singapore: Times Books International, 1996.

Anwar, Zainah. "The Fundamentalist Challenge in Malaysia." *Trends in Southeast Asia* 4 (2003), 1–8.

———. *Islamic Revivalism in Malaysia: Dakwah Among the Students.* Petaling Jaya, Malaysia: Pelanduk Publications, 1987.

Archer, Raymond Leroy. "Muhammadan Mysticism in Sumatra." *Journal of the Royal Asiatic Society, Malay Branch* 15 (1937), Part 2, 1–126.

Armstrong, Karen. *Islam: A Short History.* London: Phoenix Press, 2001.

Arndt, H. W., and Hal Hill (eds.). *Southeast Asia's Economic Crisis: Origins, Lessons and the Way Forward.* Singapore: Institute of Southeast Asian Studies, 1999.

Asi, Rohaiza Binte Ahmad, "Ba'asyir Release: Implications for Islamist Militancy in Indonesia." *IDDS Commentaries* 51/2006 (June 13, 2006), Institute of Defence and Strategic Studies. Singapore: Nanyang Technological University, 1–3.

Aslam Syed (ed.). *Islam: Enduring Myths and Changing Realities.* Thousand Oaks, CA: Sage Publications, 2003 [published as *The Annals of the American Academy of Political and Social Science* 588 (July 2003)].

Aspinall, Edward, "Aceh/Indonesia: Conflict Analysis and Options for Systematic Conflict Transformation." Berghof Foundation for Peace Support, August 2005.

———. "Modernity, History and Ethnicity: Indonesian and Acehnese Nationalism in Conflict." *Review of Indonesian and Malaysian Affairs* 36, no. 1 (2002), 3–33.

———. *Opposing Suharto: Compromise, Resistance, and Regime Change.* Stanford, CA: Stanford University Press, 2005.

Aspinall, Edward, and Harold Crouch. *The Aceh Peace Process: Why It Failed.* Washington, DC: The East-West Center Washington, 2003.

Atran, Scott. "The Emir: An Interview with Abu Bakar Ba'asyir." *Spotlight on Terror* 3, no. 9 (September 15, 2005), 1–11.

Australian Government. *Transnational Terrorism: The Threat to Australia.* Canberra: Department of Communications, 2004.

Ayoob, Mohammed (ed.). *The Politics of Islamic Reassertion.* London: Croom Helm, 1981.

Bacani, Benedicto. *The Mindanao Peace Talks: Another Opportunity to Resolve the Moro Conflict in the Philippines,* Special Report. Washington, DC: United States Institute of Peace, January 2005.

Baker, Raymond William. *Islam Without Fear: Islam and the New Islamists.* Cambridge, MA: Harvard University Press, 2003.

Baker, Richard W., et al. (eds.). *Indonesia: The Challenge of Change.* Singapore: Institute of Southeast Asian Studies, 1999.

Bakhash, Shaul. *The Reign of the Ayatollahs: Iran and the Islamic Revolution.* New York: Basic Books, 1984.

Baljon, J. M. S. *Modern Muslim Koran Interpretation.* Leiden: E. J. Brill, 1961.

Barton, Greg. *Abdurrahman Wahid: Muslim, Democrat, Indonesian President.* Honolulu: University of Hawaii Press, 2002.

———. *Indonesia's Struggle: Jemaah Islamiyah and the Soul of Islam.* Sydney: University of New South Wales Press, 2004.

Barton, Greg, and Greg Fealy (eds.). *Nahdlatul Ulama: Traditional Islam and Modernity in Indonesia.* Melbourne: Monash Asia Institute, 1996.

Bat Ye'or. *Islam and Dhimmitude: Where Civilizations Collide,* trans. from French by Miriam Kochan and David Littman. Madison, NJ: Fairleigh Dickinson University Press, 2002.

Benard, Cheryl. *Civil Democratic Islam: Partners, Resources and Strategies.* Santa Monica, CA: Rand, 2003.

Benda, Harry J. "The Beginnings of the Japanese Occupation of Java," in Harry J. Benda, *Continuity and Change in Southeast Asia.* New Haven: Yale University Southeast Asia Studies, 1972.

———. *The Crescent and the Rising Sun: Indonesian Islam Under the Japanese Occupation, 1942–1945.* The Hague and Bandung: W. van Hoeve, 1958.

Berg, Herbert. *Method and Theory in the Study of Islamic Origins.* Leiden: Brill, 2003.

Bergen, Peter L. *Holy War, Inc.: Inside the Secret World of Osama bin Laden.* New York: The Free Press, 2001.

Berkey, Jonathan P. *The Formation of Islam: Religion and Society in the Near East, 600–1800.* Cambridge: Cambridge University Press, 2003.

Bertrand, Jacques. *Nationalism and Ethnic Conflict in Indonesia.* Cambridge: Cambridge University Press, 2004.

Bickerton, Ian J., and Carla L. Klausner. *A Concise History of the Arab-Israeli Conflict.* Englewood Cliffs, NJ: Prentice Hall, 1991.

Bjornlund, Erik. *Indonesia's Road to Constitutional Reform: The 2000 MPR Annual Session.* Washington, DC: National Democratic Institute for International Affairs, 2001.

Blitz, Amy. *The Contested State: American Foreign Policy and Regime Change in the Philippines.* Lanham, MD: Rowman & Littlefield Publishers, 2000.

Boland, B. J. *The Struggle of Islam in Modern Indonesia.* The Hague: Martinus Nijhoff, 1971.

Bourchier, David, and Vedi R. Hadiz (eds.). *Indonesian Politics and Society.* London: RoutledgeCurzon, 2003.

Brackman, Arnold C. *The Communist Collapse in Indonesia.* New York: W. W. Norton, 1969.

Brands, H. W. *Bound to Empire: The United States and the Philippines.* New York: Oxford University Press, 1992.

Brockelmann, Carl. *History of the Islamic Peoples*, trans. by Joel Carmichael and Moshe Perlmann. London: Routledge & Kegan Paul, 1948.

Brooks, Oakley. "The Rebirth of Aceh." *Far Eastern Economic Review* 170, no. 9 (November 2007), 30–33.

Browers, Michaelle, and Charles Kurzman (eds.). *An Islamic Reformation?* Lanham, MD: Lexington Books, 2004.

Bruinessen, Martin van. "Genealogies of Islamic Radicalism in Post-Suharto Indonesia." *Southeast Asia Research* 10, no. 2 (2002), 117–154.

———. "Indonesia's Ulama and Politics: Caught Between Legitimizing the Status Quo and Searching for Alternatives." *Prisma—The Indonesian Indicator* (Jakarta) 49 (1990), 52–69.

Buckley, Charles Burton. *An Anecdotal History of Old Times in Singapore.* Singapore: Fraser & Neave, 1902, reprinted Kuala Lumpur: University of Malaya Press, 1965.

Budiman, Arief (ed.). *State and Civil Society in Indonesia.* Monash Papers on Southeast Asia, No. 22, Clayton, UK, 1990.

Budiman, Arief, B. Hatley, and Damien Kingsbury (eds.). *Reformasi: Crisis and Change in Indonesia.* Melbourne: Monash Asia Institute, 1999.

Buendia, Rizal G. "The GRP-MILF Peace Talks: Quo Vadis?" in *Southeast Asian Affairs 2004* (Singapore: Institute of Southeast Asian Studies, 2004).

Bunge, Frederica M. *Indonesia: A Country Study.* Washington, DC: American University Foreign Area Studies, 1983.

Burgat, François. *Face to Face with Political Islam.* New York: I. B. Tauris, 2003.

Burke, Jason. *Al-Qaeda: Casting a Shadow of Terror.* London: I. B. Tauris, 2003.

Bush, Robin. "Islam and Civil Society in Indonesia." *Journal of the International Center for Islam and Pluralism* 2, no. 3 (June 2005).

Caballero-Anthony, Mely. "The Winds of Change in the Philippines: Wither the Strong Republic?" in *Southeast Asian Affairs 2003.* Singapore: Institute of Southeast Asian Studies, 2003.

Cady, John F. *The History of Post-War Southeast Asia.* Athens: Ohio University Press, 1974.

———. *Southeast Asia: Its Historical Development.* New York: McGraw-Hill, 1964.

Caldarola, Carlo (ed.). *Religion and Societies: Asia and the Middle East.* Berlin: Mouton Publishers, 1982.

Callard, Keith. *Pakistan: A Political Study.* London: George Allen & Unwin, 1958.
Camroux, D. "State Responses to Islamic Resurgence in Malaysia: Accommodation, Cooption and Confrontation." *Asian Survey* 36, no. 9 (September 1996), 852–868.
Centre for Public Policy Studies. "Corporate Equity Distribution: Past Trends and Future Policy," Kuala Lumpur, 2006, 1–40. www.cpps.org.my.
Chai Hon-Chan. *The Development of British Malaya, 1896–1909,* 2nd ed. Kuala Lumpur: Oxford University Press, 1967.
Chaffee, Frederic H. *Area Handbook for the Philippines.* Washington, DC: US Government Printing Office, 1969.
Chanda, Nayan. "Managing Globalization." *Far Eastern Economic Review* 165, no. 12 (December 26, 2002–January 2, 2003), 25.
Chandler, Michael, and Rohan Gunaratna. *Countering Terrorism: Can We Meet the Threat of Global Terrorism?* London: Reaktion, 2007.
Che Man, W. K. *Muslim Separatism: The Moros of Southern Philippines and the Malays of Southern Thailand.* Singapore: Oxford University Press, 1990.
Chin, James. "Malaysian Chinese Politics in the 21st Century: Fear, Service and Marginalisation." *Asian Journal of Political Science* 9, no. 2 (December 2001), 78–94.
Chin Kee Onn. *Malaya Upside Down,* 3rd ed. Singapore: Federal Publications, 1976.
Chongkittavorn, Kavi. "Thailand: International Terrorism and the Muslim South," in *Southeast Asian Affairs 2004.* Singapore: Institute of Southeast Asian Studies, 2004.
Christian Federation of Malaysia. *Malaysia as an Islamic State: An Analysis.* CFM, January 2002.
Christie, Clive J. *A Modern History of Southeast Asia: Decolonization, Nationalism and Separatism.* London: I. B. Tauris Publishers, 1996.
Cole, Juan. "The Baha'is of Iran." *History Today* 40, no. 3 (March 1990), 24–29.
Collins, Elizabeth Fuller. "Islam and the Habits of Democracy: Islamic Organizations in Post–New Order South Sumatra." Paper for USINDO—Asia Foundation Conference, Washington, DC, February 7, 2002.
———. "'Islam Is the Solution'. Dakwah and Democracy in Indonesia." Conference paper, Ohio University, June 20, 2004.
Colombijn, Freek, and J. Thomas Lindblad (eds.). *Roots of Violence in Indonesia.* Singapore: Institute of Southeast Asian Studies, 2002.
Conboy, Ken. *The Second Front: Inside Asia's Most Dangerous Terrorist Network.* Jakarta: Equinox Publishing, 2006.
Cone, Patricia. *God's Rule: Government and Islam.* New York: Columbia University Press, 2004.
Cragin, Kim, and Peter Chalk. *Terrorism and Development: Using Social and Economic Development to Inhibit a Resurgence of Terrorism.* Santa Monica, CA: Rand, 2003.
Cribb, R. (ed.). *The Indonesian Killings of 1965–66: Studies from Java and Bali.* Monash Papers on Southeast Asia No. 21. Melbourne: Monash University Center of Southeast Asian Studies, 1990.
Cristalis, Irene. *Bitter Dawn: East Timor, a People's Story.* London: Zed Books, 2002.
Croissant, Aurel. "Unrest in South Thailand: Contours, Causes, and Consequences Since 2001." *Strategic Insights* (Center for Contemporary Conflict, Naval Postgraduate School) 4, no. 2 (February 2005), 1–17.
Crone, Patricia. *God's Rule: Government and Islam.* New York: Columbia University Press, 2003.
Crone, Patricia, and Michael Cook. *Hagarism: The Making of the Islamic World.* Cambridge: Cambridge University Press, 1977.

Crouch, Harold A. *The Army and Politics in Indonesia*, rev. ed. Ithaca, NY: Cornell University Press, 1988.

———. *Government and Society in Malaysia*. Ithaca, NY: Cornell University Press, 1996.

———. *Malaysia's 1982 General Elections*. Singapore: Institute of Southeast Asian Studies, 1982.

Crouch, Harold A., Ahmad Fauzi Abdul Hamid, Carmen A. Abubakar, and Yang Razali Kassim. "Islam in Southeast Asia: Analysing Recent Developments." *Trends in Southeast Asia* (January 2002).

Cutler, Abigail, and Saleem Ali. "*Madrassah* Reform Is Key to Terror War." *Christian Science Monitor* (June 27, 2005), 9.

Dahm, Bernard. *History of Indonesia in the Twentieth Century*. New York: Praeger, 1971.

———. *Sukarno and the Struggle for Independence*, translated from German by Mary Somers Heidhues. Ithaca, NY: Cornell University Press, 1969.

Davidson, Jamie S. "The Politics of Violence on an Indonesian Periphery." *South East Asia Research* 11, no. 1 (March 2003), 59–89.

Davis, Michael. "Laskar Jihad and the Political Position of Conservative Islam in Indonesia." *Contemporary Southeast Asia* 24, no. 1 (April 2002), 12–32.

Davis, Paul K., and Brian Michael Jenkins. *Deterrence and Influence in Counterterrorism: A Component in the War on al Qaeda*. Santa Monica, CA: Rand National Defense Research Institute, 2002.

Day, Clive. *The Policy and Administration of the Dutch in Java*. London: Macmillan, 1904; Kuala Lumpur: Oxford University Press reprint, 1966.

Desker, Barry. "Islam and Society in Southeast Asia After 9-11." *IDSS Commentaries*, 14/2002, Institute of Defence and Strategic Studies. Singapore: Nanyang Technological University, 2002, 1–4. www.idss.edu.sg/Perspectives/research.

———. "The Jemaah Islamiyah (JI) Phenomenon in Singapore." *Contemporary Southeast Asia* 25, no. 3 (December 2003), 489–507.

Dhume, Sadanand. "Indonesia: The New Mainstream." *Far Eastern Economic Review* (January 9, 2003), 46–49.

———. "Indonesia: Terror's Web." *Far Eastern Economic Review* (December 19, 2002), 20.

———. "Indonesia: Opportunity Knocks." *Far Eastern Economic Review* (December 19, 2002), 21–22.

———. "Four Takes on the Forces Behind Indonesia's Islamism." *Far Eastern Economic Review* 168, no. 4 (April 2005), 552–555.

———. "Radicals March on Indonesia's Future." *Far Eastern Economic Review* 168, no. 5 (May 2005), 11–19.

Diamond, Larry, and Marc F. Plattner (eds.). *Democracy in East Asia*. Baltimore: Johns Hopkins University Press, 1998.

Diermen, Peter Van, and Chris Manning (eds.). *Indonesia in Transition: Social Aspects of Reformasi and Crisis*. Singapore: Institute of Southeast Asian Studies, 1999.

Djalal, Dini. "Forced to Serve." *Far Eastern Economic Review* 165, no. 4 (April 4, 2002), 50–52.

———. "Indonesia: Burden of Truth." *Far Eastern Economic Review* 165, no. 11 (November 21, 2002), 24–25.

———. "Indonesia: A New Crusade." *Far Eastern Economic Review* 165, no. 6 (June 13, 2002), 54–57.

Doi, 'Abdur Rahman I. *Shari'ah: The Islamic Law*. Kuala Lumpur: A. S. Nordeen, 1990 (reprint from 1984).

Donnan, Hastings, ed. *Interpreting Islam.* London: Sage Publications, 2002.
Dunn, James. *Timor; A People Betrayed.* Sydney: ABC Books, 1996.
Dupree, Louis. *Afghanistan.* Princeton, NJ: Princeton University Press, 1980.
Dutton, Y. *The Origins of Islamic Law.* Richmond, UK: Curzon Press, 1999.
Effendy, Bahtiar. *Islam and the State in Indonesia.* Singapore: Institute for Southeast Asian Studies, 2003.
Eklöf, Stefan. *Indonesian Politics in Crisis: The Long Fall of Suharto, 1996–98.* Copenhagen: Nordic Institute of Asian Studies, 1999.
Eliraz, Giora. *Islam in Indonesia: Modernism, Radicalism, and the Middle East Dimension.* Sussex, UK: Sussex Academic Press, 2004.
Elson, R. E. *Suharto: A Political Biography.* New York: Cambridge University Press, 2002.
Embong, Abdul Rahman, and Jürgen Rudolph (eds.). *Southeast Asia into the Twenty-First Century: Crisis and Beyond.* Bangi, Selangor: Penerbit Universiti Kebangsaan Malaysia, 2000.
Emerson, Rupert. *Malaysia: A Study in Direct and Indirect Rule.* New York: Macmillan, 1937.
Endicott, Kirk Michael. *An Analysis of Malay Magic.* Oxford: Clarendon Press, 1970.
Ernst, Carl W. *Following Muhammad: Rethinking Islam in the Contemporary World.* Chapel Hill: University of North Carolina Press, 2003.
Esposito, John L. *Islam: The Straight Path.* Oxford: Oxford University Press, 1988.
——— (ed.). *Political Islam: Revolution, Radicalism, or Reform?* Boulder, CO: Lynne Rienner Publishers, 1997.
———. *Unholy War: Terror in the Name of Islam.* New York: Oxford University Press, 2002.
Faruqi, Ismail Raji al-. *Divine Transcendence and Its Expression.* Kuala Lumpur: Muslim Youth Movement of Malaysia (ABIM), 1983.
Fatimi, S. Q. *Islam Comes to Malaysia.* Singapore: Malaysian Sociological Research Institute, 1963.
Federspiel, Howard M. *Islam and Ideology in the Emerging Indonesian State: The Persatuan Islam (PERSIS), 1923 to 1957.* Leiden: Brill, 2001.
———. *Persatuan Islam: Islamic Reform in Twentieth Century Indonesia.* Ithaca, NY: Cornell University Press, 1970.
———. "Modernist Islam in Southeast Asia: A New Examination of 20th Century Modernist Activity in Malaya, Singapore, Southern Thailand and Indonesia." *The Muslim World* 92, nos. 3 and 4 (Fall 2002), 371–386.
Feith, Herbert. *Decline of Constitutional Democracy in Indonesia.* Ithaca, NY: Cornell University Press, 1964.
Fisher, Sydney Nettleton, and William Ochsenwald. *The Middle East: A History.* New York: McGraw-Hill, 1990.
Forrester, Geoff (ed.). *Post-Soeharto Indonesia: Renewal or Chaos.* Bathurst, Australia: Crawford House Publishing, 1999.
Forte, David F. *Studies in Islamic Law: Classical and Contemporary Application.* Lanham, MD: Austin & Winfield, 1999.
Foster, William. *England's Quest for Eastern Trade.* London: Hakluyt Society, 1933.
Friedmann, Yohanan. *Islam in Asia.* Jerusalem: Magnes Press 1984.
———. *Tolerance and Coercion in Islam: Interfaith Relations in the Muslim Tradition.* Cambridge: Cambridge University Press, 2003.
Friend, Theodore. *Indonesian Destinies.* Cambridge, MA: The Belknap Press of Harvard University Press, 2003.

Fritz, Nicole, and Martin Flaherty. *Unjust Order: Malaysia's Internal Security Act.* New York: The Joseph R. Crowley Program in International Human Rights, Fordham Law School, 2003.

Fuller, Graham E. *The Future of Political Islam.* London: Palgrave Macmillan, 2003.

Funston, John. "Malaysia's Tenth Elections: Status Quo, Reformasi or Islamization?" *Contemporary Southeast Asia* 22, no. 1 (April 2000), 23–59.

———. "Malaysia's Election: Malay Winds of Change?" *Trends in Southeast Asia* 1 (2000), 49–56.

———. *Malay Politics in Malaysia: A Study of the United Malays National Organisation and Party Islam.* Kuala Lumpur: Heinemann Educational Books, 1980.

———. *Political Careers of Mahathir Mohamad and Anwar Ibrahim: Parallel, Intersecting and Conflicting Lives.* Bangi, Malaysia: Institute of Malaysian and International Studies, Universiti Kebangsaan Malaysia, 1998.

Furber, Holden. *Rival Empires of Trade in the Orient, 1600–1800.* Minneapolis: University of Minnesota Press, 1976.

Gale, Bruce. *Musa Hitam: A Political Biography.* Petaling Jaya, Malaysia: Eastern Universities Press, 1982.

———. *Politics & Business: A Study of Multi-Purpose Holdings Berhad.* Singapore: Eastern Universities Press, 1985.

———. *Politics and Public Enterprise in Malaysia.* Singapore: Eastern Universities Press, 1981.

———. *Readings in Malaysian Politics.* Petaling Jaya: Pelanduk Publications, 1986.

Geertz, Clifford. *Islam Observed: Religious Development in Morocco and Indonesia.* Chicago: University of Chicago Press, 1968.

———. *The Religion of Java.* New York: The Free Press of Glencoe, 1964.

George, T. J. S. *Revolt in Mindanao: The Rise of Islam in Philippine Politics.* Kuala Lumpur: Oxford University Press, 1980.

Ghani, Mohamad Nor Abdul, et al. (eds.). *Malaysia Incorporated and Privatization: Towards National Unity.* Petaling Jaya, Malaysia: Pelanduk Publications, 1984.

Ghoshal, Baladas. "Radical Islam and Terrorism in Indonesia." Typescript abstract of a paper presented at Universiti Utara Malaya, n.d. [2003].

Gill, Ranjit. *Anwar Ibrahim: Mahathir's Dilemma.* Singapore: Epic Management Services, 1998.

The Global Attitudes Project. *Views of a Changing World.* Washington, DC: The Pew Research Center for the People & the Press, June 2003.

Goh Cheng Teik. *The May Thirteenth Incident and Democracy in Malaysia.* Kuala Lumpur: Oxford University Press, 1971.

Gomez, Edmund Terence. *Money Politics in the Barisan Nasional.* Kuala Lumpur: Forum, 1991.

———. "The Perils of Pro-Malay Policies." *Far Eastern Economic Review* 168, no. 8 (September 2005), 36–39.

———. *Political Business: Corporate Involvement of Malaysian Political Parties.* Townsville, Australia: James Cook University of North Queensland, 1994.

———. *Politics in Malaysia: The Malay Dimension.* London: Routledge, 2007.

——— (ed.). *The State of Malaysia: Ethnicity, Equity and Reform.* London: Routledge Curzon, 2004.

Gomez, Edmund Terence, and K. S. Jomo (eds.). *Malaysia's Political Economy: Politics, Patronage and Profits.* Cambridge: Cambridge University Press, 1997.

Gordon, Alijah (ed.). *The Propagation of Islam in the Indonesian-Malay Archipelago.* Kuala Lumpur: Malaysian Sociological Research Institute, 2001.

Government of Malaysia. *The Memali Incident.* Parliamentary Paper, No. 21 of 1986. Kuala Lumpur: Jabatan Percetakan Negara, 1986.

———. *Rukunegara.* Kuala Lumpur: Jabatan Chetak Kerajaan, 1970.

———. *The Second Malaysia Plan. 1971–1975.* Kuala Lumpur: Jabatan Chetak Kerajaan, 1971.

———. *Towards National Harmony.* Kuala Lumpur: Jabatan Chetak Kerajaan, 1971.

Gowing, Peter Gordon. *Muslim Filipinos: Heritage and Horizon.* Quezon City: New Day Publishers, 1979.

———. *Understanding Islam and Muslims in the Philippines.* Quezon City: New Day, 1988.

Gowing, Peter Gordon, and Robert McAmis (eds.). *The Muslim Filipinos.* Manila: Solidaridad Publishing House, 1974.

Gregorian, Vartan. *Islam: A Mosaic, Not a Monolith.* New York: The Carnegie Corporation, 2002.

Grunebaum, Gustave E. von. *Medieval Islam,* 2nd ed. Chicago: University of Chicago Press, 1961.

———. *Islam: Essays in the Nature and Growth of a Cultural Tradition*, 2nd ed. London: Routledge & Kegan Paul, 1961.

——— (ed.). *Unity and Variety in Muslim Civilization.* Chicago: University of Chicago Press, 1955.

Gunaratna, Rohan K. "Al-Qaeda's Trajectory in 2003." *IDSS Working Paper*, 03/2003. Singapore: Nanyang Technological University, 2003, 1–6.

———. *The Changing Face of Terrorism.* Singapore: Eastern Universities Press, 2004.

———. *Inside Al Qaeda: Global Network of Terror.* New York: Columbia University Press, 2002.

———. "The Method, the Means and the Will: The Hallmarks of Al-Qaida." *IDSS Commentaries,* 34/2002, Institute of Defence and Strategic Studies. Singapore: Nanyang Technological University, 2003, 1–5.

———. "Terrorism in Southeast Asia: What to Expect." *Trends in Southeast Asia* 3 (2003), 1–10.

Gunaratna, Rohan K., Arabinda Acharya, and Sabrina Chua. *Conflict and Terrorism in Southern Thailand.* Singapore: Marshall Cavendish, 2006.

Gullick, John M. *Malay Society in the Late Nineteenth Century.* New York: Oxford University Press, 1987.

Haar, Bernard ter. *Adat Law in Indonesia,* trans. by E. A. Hoebel and A. A. Schiller. New York: Institute of Pacific Relations, 1948.

Hall, D. G. E. *A History of South-East Asia*, 3rd ed. New York: St. Martin's Press, 1970.

Hameedullah Khan, Mohammad. *The Schools of Islamic Jurisprudence: A Comparative Study.* New Delhi: Kitab Bhavan, 1991.

Hamid, Ahmad Fauzi Abdul. "Political Dimensions of Religious Conflict in Malaysia: State Responses to an Islamic Movement." *Indonesia and the Malay World* 28, no. 80 (2000), 32–65.

Hamka [Abdulmalik bin Abdulkarim bin Rullah]. "Developments in Islam," in Bruce Ross-Larson (ed.), *Malaysia 2001: A Preliminary Inquiry.* Kuala Lumpur: Syed Kechik Foundation, 1978.

Handley, Paul M. *The King Never Smiles: A Biography of Thailand's Bhumibol Adulyadej.* New Haven: Yale University Press, 2006.

Haneef, Suzanne. *What Everyone Should Know About Islam and Muslims,* 14th ed. Chicago: Kazi Publications, 1996.

Hanna, Don. "Poor Policy, Not Oil, Saps Faith in Jakarta." *Far Eastern Economic Review* 168, no. 8 (September 2005), 57–59.

Haque, M. Shamsul. "The Role of the State in Managing Ethnic Tensions in Malaysia." *American Behavioral Scientist* 47, no. 3 (November 2003), 240–266.

Harish, S. P. "Changing Conflict Identities: The Case of Southern Thailand." *IDSS Commentaries*, No. 107. Singapore: Nanyang Technological University, February 2006, 1–32.

Hassan, M. Kamal. "The Influence of Mawdudi's Thought on Muslims in Southeast Asia: A Brief Survey." *The Muslim World* 93, nos. 3 and 4 (July/October 2003), 429–464.

Hefner, Robert W. *Civil Islam: Muslims and Democratization in Indonesia*. Princeton: Princeton University Press, 2000.

——— (ed.). *Remaking Muslim Politics: Pluralism, Contestation, Democratization.* Princeton, NJ: Princeton University Press, 2005.

Henderson, John W., et al. (eds.). *Area Handbook for Indonesia.* Washington, DC: American University, Foreign Area Studies, 1970.

Heryanto, Ariel. *State Terrorism and Political Identity in Indonesia: Fatally Belonging.* London: Routledge, 2006.

Heryanto, Ariel, and Sumit K. Mandal (eds.). *Challenging Authoritarianism in Southeast Asia: Comparing Indonesia and Malaysia.* London: RoutledgeCurzon, 2003.

Heufers, Rainer. "The Politics of Democracy in Malaysia." *Asien* 85 (October 2002): 39–60.

Heussler, Robert. *British Rule in Malaya: 1942–1957.* Singapore: Heinemann Asia, 1985.

Hewson, Kevin, Richard Robinson, and Garry Rodan (eds.). *Southeast Asia in the 1990s: Authoritarianism, Democracy and Capitalism.* St. Leonards, Australia: Allen & Unwin, 1993.

Hill, Hal. "Four Men Who Changed Indonesia." *Far Eastern Economic Review* 168, no. 10 (November 2005), 41–44.

———. *The Indonesian Economy in Crisis: Causes, Consequences and Lessons.* Singapore: Institute of Southeast Asian Studies, 1999.

——— (ed.). *Indonesia's New Order: The Dynamics of Socio-economic Transformation.* Honolulu: University of Hawaii Press, 1994.

———. "Yudhoyono's Six Challenges to Get Indonesia Growing." *Far Eastern Economic Review* 168, no. 1 (December 2004), 55–58.

Hill, Hal, and Joao M. Saldanha (eds.). *East Timor: Development Challenge for the World's Newest Nation.* Singapore: Institute of Southeast Asian Studies, 2001.

Hilley, John. *Malaysia: Mahathirism, Hegemony and the New Opposition.* London: Zed Books, 2001.

Hillman, Ben. "Aceh's Rebels Turn to Ruling." *Far Eastern Economic Review* 170, no. 1 (January 2007), 49–52.

———. "New Elections, Old Politics." *Far Eastern Economic Review* 169, no. 1 (January/February 2006), 26–29.

Hiro, Dilip. *War Without End: The Rise of Islamist Terrorism and the Global Response,* rev. ed. London: Routledge, 2002.

Hitam, Musa. "Islam and State in Malaysia." *Trends in Southeast Asia* (September 2001).

Hodgson, Marshall G. S. *The Venture of Islam.* Chicago: University of Chicago Press, 1974.

Hoffman, Bruce, Rohan K. Gunaratna, and Sidney Jones. *Regional Outlook Forum 2005, Terrorism: International and Regional Dimensions.* Singapore: Institute of Southeast Asian Studies, 2005.

Holt, Andrew. "Thailand's Troubled Border: Islamic Insurgency or Criminal Playground?" *Terrorism Monitor* 2, no. 10 (May 20, 2004), 1–3.

Hooker, M. B. *Adat Laws in Modern Malaya*. Kuala Lumpur: Oxford University Press, 1972.

———. *Indonesian Islam: Social Change Through Contemporary Fatawa*. Honolulu: University of Hawaii Press, 2003.

———. *The Personal Laws of Malaysia: An Introduction*. Kuala Lumpur: Oxford University Press, 1976.

Hooker, Virginia, and Norani Othman (eds.). *Malaysia: Islam, Society and Politics*. Singapore: Institute of Southeast Asian Studies, 2003.

Hooker, Virginia, and Amin Saikal (eds.). *Islamic Perspectives on the New Millennium*. Singapore: Institute of Southeast Asian Studies, 2004.

Hughes, John. *The End of Sukarno*. London: Angus & Robertson, 1968.

———. *Indonesian Upheaval*. New York: David McKay, 1967.

Human Rights Watch Asia. "Indonesia Breakdown: Four Years of Communal Violence in Central Sulawesi." *A Human Rights Watch Report* 14, no. 9 (December 2002).

———. "No One Is Safe: Insurgent Attacks on Civilians in Thailand's Southern Border Provinces." *A Human Rights Watch Report* 19, no. 13(C) (August 2007).

———. "The Violence in Ambon." *A Human Rights Watch Report* 11, no. 1 (March 1999).

Hunter, Thomas B. "Terror in the Philippines." *Journal of Counterterrorism & Security* 9, no. 4 (June 2001).

Huntington, Samuel P. "The Clash of Civilizations?" *Foreign Affairs* 72 (Summer 1993), 22–49.

Hussin Mutalib. *Islam in Malaysia: From Revivalism to Islamic State*. Singapore: Singapore University Press, 1993.

———. "Islamic Revivalism in ASEAN States: Political Implications." *Asian Survey* 30, no. 9 (September 1990).

Hwang, In-Won. *Personalized Politics: The Malaysian State Under Mahathir*. Singapore: Institute of Southeast Asian Studies, 2003.

Ibrahim, Ahmad. *Islamic Law in Malaya*. Singapore: Malaysian Sociological Research Institute, 1965.

International Bar Association. *Justice in Jeopardy: Malaysia 2000*. London: International Bar Association, 2000. www.ibanet.org/general/FindDocuments.asp.

International Crisis Group. *Aceh: Can Autonomy Stem the Conflict?* Brussels: International Crisis Group, n.d. [2001].

———. *Aceh: A Fragile Peace*. Asia Report, No. 47, February 27, 2003.

———. *Aceh: Post Conflict Complications*. Asia Report, No. 139, October 4, 2007.

———. *Aceh's Local Elections: The Role of the Free Aceh Movement (GAM)*. Asia Briefing, No. 57, November 29, 2006.

———. *Aceh: Slim Chance for Peace*. Asia Briefing, No. 14, March 27, 2002.

———. *How the Jemaah Islamiyah Terrorist Network Operates*. Asia Report, No. 43, December 11, 2002.

———. *Indonesia Backgrounder: Jihad in Central Sulawesi*. Asia Report, No. 74, February 3, 2004.

———. *Indonesia: How GAM Won in Aceh*. Asia Briefing, No. 61, March 22, 2007.

———. *Indonesia: Implications of the Ahmadiyah Decree*. Asia Briefing, No. 78, July 7, 2008.

———. *Indonesia: Jemaah Islamiyah's Current Status*. Asia Briefing, No. 63, May 3, 2007.

———. *Indonesia: Jemaah Islamiyah's Publishing Industry*. Asia Report, No. 147, February 28, 2008.

———. *Indonesia: Overcoming Murder and Chaos in Maluku.* Asia Report, No. 10, December 2000.

———. *Indonesia: Rethinking Internal Security Strategy.* Asia Report, No. 90, December 20, 2004.

———. *Indonesia: Tackling Radicalism in Poso.* ICG Policy Briefing, No. 75, January 22, 2008.

———. *Islamic Law and Criminal Justice in Aceh.* Asia Report, No. 117, July 31, 2006.

———. *Jemaah Islamiyah in South East Asia: Damaged but Still Dangerous.* Asia Report, No. 63, August 26, 2003.

———. *Jihadism in Indonesia: Poso on the Edge.* Asia Report, No. 127, January 24, 2007.

———. *The Philippines: Counter-Insurgency vs. Counter-Terrorism in Mindanao.* Asia Report, No. 152, May 14, 2008, 1–26.

———. *Philippines Terrorism: The Role of Militant Islamic Converts.* Asia Report, No. 110, December 19, 2005.

———. *Recycling Militants in Indonesia: Darul Islam and the Australian Embassy Bombing.* Asia Report, No. 92, February 22, 2005.

———. *Southern Philippines Backgrounder: Terrorism and the Peace Process.* Asia Report, No. 80, July 13, 2004.

———. *Southern Thailand: The Impact of the Coup.* Asia Report, No. 129, March 15, 2007.

———. *Southern Thailand: Insurgency, Not Jihad.* Asia Report, No. 98, May 18, 2005.

———. *Southern Thailand: The Problem with Paramilitaries.* Asia Report, No. 140, October 23, 2007.

———. *Terrorism in Indonesia: Noordin's Networks.* Asia Report, No. 114, May 5, 2006.

———. *Thailand's Emergency Decree: No Solution.* Asia Report, No. 105, November 18, 2005.

———. *Weakening Indonesia's Mujahidin Networks: Lessons from Maluku and Poso.* Asia Report, No. 103, October 13, 2005.

Iqbal, Muzaffar. "Challenges to Islam and Muslims: What Is to Be Done?" *Islamic Studies* 42, no. 4 (2003), 595–637.

Isaacson, Jason F., and Colin Rubenstein (eds.). *Islam in Asia: Changing Political Realities.* New Brunswick, NJ: Transaction Press, 2002.

Ismail, Rose. *Hudud in Malaysia: The Issues at Stake.* Kuala Lumpur: SIS Forum, 1995.

———. "The Modern Malay Woman's Dilemma." *Far Eastern Economic Review* 169, no. 2 (March 2006), 49–52.

Israeli, Raphael, and Anthony H. Johns (eds.). *Islam in Asia*, vol. 2, *Southeast and East Asia.* Jerusalem: Magnes Press, Hebrew University; Boulder, CO: Westview Press, 1984.

Jacq-Hergoualc'h, Michel. *The Malay Peninsula: Crossroads of the Maritime Silk Road*, trans. by Victoria Hobson. Leiden: Brill, 2002.

Jacquard, Roland. *In the Name of Osama Bin Laden: Global Terrorism & the Bin Laden Brotherhood.* Durham, NC: Duke University Press, 2002.

Jay, R. R. *Religion and Politics in Rural Central Java.* New Haven, CT: Yale University, Southeast Asia Studies, 1963.

Jayasankaaran, S. "Malaysia: A Plan to End Extremism." *Far Eastern Economic Review* 165, no. 51 (December 26, 2002–January 2, 2003), 12–16.

Jenkins, Brian Michael. *Countering al Qaeda: An Appreciation of the Situation and Suggestions for Strategy*. Santa Monica, CA: Rand Corporation, 2002.

Jenkins, D. *Soeharto and His Generals: Indonesian Military Politics 1975–1983.* Ithaca, NY: Cornell University Press, 1984.

Johannen, Uwe, and James Gomez. *Democratic Transitions in Asia.* Singapore: Select Books, 2001.

Johannen, Uwe, Alan Smith, and James Gomez (eds.). *September 11 & Political Freedom: Asian Perspectives.* Singapore: Select Publishing, 2003.

Jomo Kwame Sundaram. *A Question of Class: Capital, the State and Uneven Development in Malaya.* Singapore: Oxford University Press, 1986.

———. *Mahathir's Economic Policies,* 2nd ed. Kuala Lumpur: Insan, 1989.

——— (ed.). *Malaysian Eclipse: Economic Crisis and Recovery.* London: Zed Books, 2001.

——— (ed.). *Southeast Asian Paper Tigers? From Miracle to Debacle and Beyond.* London: RoutledgeCurzon, 2003.

Jomo Kwame Sundaram and Ahmed Shabery Cheek. "The Politics of Malaysia's Islamic Resurgence." *Third World Quarterly* 10, no. 2 (April 1988).

Jones, Sidney R. "Countering Terror in Poso." *Van Zorge Report,* February 20, 2007, 7–11.

———. "'It Can't Happen Here': A Post-Khomeini Look at Indonesian Islam." *Asian Survey* 20, no. 3 (March 1980), 311–323.

Jonge, Huub de, and Nico Kaptein (eds.). *Arabs, Politics, Trade and Islam in Southeast Asia.* Leiden, Netherlands: KITLV Press, 2002.

Jubair, Salah. *Bangsamoro: A Nation Under Endless Tyranny.* Mansoorah, Pakistan: Islamic Research Academy, 1984.

Juergensmeyer, M. *Terror in the Mind of God: The Global Rise of Religious Violence.* Berkeley: University of California Press, 2001.

Kahin, George McTurnin. *Nationalism and Revolution in Indonesia.* Ithaca: Cornell University Press, 1952.

Kamarudin, Raja Petra. *The Reformasi Trial.* [Shah Alam, Malaysia]: Raja Petra Kamarudin, 2001.

Kat Angelino, A. D. A. de. *Colonial Policy; Abridged Trans. of Staatskundig Beleid en Bestuurszorg in Ned. Indie by G. J. Reinier,* 2 vols. The Hague: 1931.

Kell, Tim. *The Roots of Acehnese Rebellion.* Ithaca, NY: Cornell Modern Indonesia Project, 1995.

Kennedy, Malcolm. *A History of Communism in East Asia.* New York: Frederick A. Praeger, 1956.

Kepel, Gilles. *Bad Moon Rising.* London: Saqi, 2003.

———. *Jihad: The Trail of Political Islam,* trans. by Anthony F. Roberts. Cambridge, MA: Harvard University Press, 2002.

———. *The War for Muslim Minds: Islam and the West.* Cambridge, MA: Harvard University Press, 2004.

Kerkvliet, Benedict. *The Huk Rebellion: A Study of Peasant Revolt in the Philippines.* Berkeley: University of California Press, 1977.

Khan, Amjad Mahmood. "Persecution of the Ahmadiyya Community in Pakistan: An Analysis Under International Law." *Harvard Human Rights Journal* 16 (Spring 2003), 217–245.

Khare, R. S. *Perspectives on Islamic Law, Justice, and Society*. Lanham, MD: Rowman & Littlefield Publishers, 1999.

Khoo Boo Teik. *Beyond Mahathir: Malaysian Politics and Its Discontents.* London: Zed Books, 2003.

———. *Paradoxes of Mahathirism—An Intellectual Biography of Mahathir Mohamad.* Kuala Lumpur: Oxford University Press, 1995.

Khoo Kay Kim. *Malay Society: Transformation and Democratisation.* Petaling Jaya, Malaysia: Pelanduk Publications, 1991.

King, Dwight Y. *Half-Hearted Reform: Electoral Institutions and the Struggle for Democracy in Indonesia.* Westport, CT: Praeger, 2003.

Kingsbury, Damien. "Analysis: Aceh's Non-Federation with Indonesia." *Federations* 5, no. 2 (March/April 2006), 25–26.

———. *The Politics of Indonesia,* 3rd ed. South Melbourne, Australia: Oxford University Press, 2005.

———. *Power Politics and the Indonesian Military.* London: RoutledgeCurzon, 2003.

———. *Violence in Between: Conflict and Security in Archipelagic Southeast Asia.* Singapore: Institute of Southeast Asian Studies and Monash University Press, 2006.

Kingsbury, Damien, and Budiman Arief (eds.). *Indonesia: The Uncertain Transition.* Bathurst, Australia: Crawford House Publishing, 2001.

Klaveren, J. J. Van. *The Dutch Colonial System.* Rotterdam: Drukkerij Benedictus, 1953.

Klerck, Eduard Servaas de. *History of the Netherlands East Indies.* 2 vols. Rotterdam, Netherlands: W. L. and J. Brusse, 1938.

Kling, Zainal. "Magical Practices in a Rural Malay Community in Sarawak," in H. M. Dahlan (ed.), *The Nascent Malaysian Society: Developments, Trends and Problems,* 71–97. Kuala Lumpur: Jabatan Antropologi dan Sociologi, Universiti Kebangsaan Malaysia, 1976.

Kooistra, Mieke. *Indonesia: Regional Conflicts and State Terror.* London: Minority Rights Group International, 2001.

Kramer, Gudrun. "Islamist Notions of Democracy," in Joel Beinin and Joe Stork (eds.), *Political Islam: Essays from Middle East Report,* 71–82. London: I. B. Tauris Publishers, 1997.

Kratoska, Paul H. *Malaya and Singapore During the Japanese Occupation.* Singapore: Singapore University Press, 1995.

Kreuzer, Peter. *Political Clans and Violence in the Southern Philippines.* Frankfurt: Peace Research Institute Frankfurt, Report No. 71, 2005.

Kristiansen, Stein. "Violent Youth Groups in Indonesia: The Cases of Yogyakarta and Nusa Tenggara Barat." *Journal of Social Issues in Southeast Asia* 18, no. 1 (April 2003), 110–138.

Kroef, Justus M. van der. *The Communist Party of Indonesia.* Vancouver: University of British Columbia Press, 1965.

———. *Indonesia After Sukarno.* Vancouver: University of British Columbia Press, 1971.

Kuppuswamy, C. S. "Indonesia: Aceh's Future." *South Asia Analysis Group,* Paper 1236 (January 28, 2005)

Lachica, Eduardo. *The Huks: Philippine Agrarian Society in Revolt.* New York: Praeger, 1971.

Laffan, Michael Francis. *Islamic Nationhood and Colonial Indonesia: The Umma Below the Winds.* London: RoutledgeCurzon, 2003.

Lanti, Irman G. "Islamic Revival in Indonesia and Its Political Consequences." *IDSS Working Paper,* Institute of Defence and Strategic Studies. Singapore: Nanyang Technological University, 2002, 1–4.

Lapidus, Ira M. *A History of Islamic Societies.* Cambridge: Cambridge University Press, 1988.

Laqueur, Walter. *No End to War: Terrorism in the Twenty-First Century.* New York: Continuum, 2003.
Lau, Albert. *The Malayan Union Controversy, 1942–1948.* Singapore: Oxford University Press, 1991.
———. *A Moment of Anguish: Singapore in Malaysia and the Politics of Disengagement.* Singapore: Times Academic Press, 1998.
"Laws of Malaysia, Federal Constitution (Reprint), Incorporating All Amendments up to 31 January 2002," *Malayan Law Journal* (2002), 130–133.
Lee Hock Guan (ed.). *Civil Society in Southeast Asia.* Singapore: Institute of Southeast Asian Studies, 2004.
———. "Malay Dominance and Opposition Politics in Malaysia," in *Southeast Asian Affairs 2002.* Singapore: Institute of Southeast Asian Studies, 2002, 177–195.
Lee, Oey Hong. "Sukarno and the Pseudo Coup of 1965." *Journal of Southeast Asian Studies* 7, no. 1 (March 1976).
Lee, Raymond. "The State, Religious Nationalism, and Ethnic Rationalizations in Malaysia." *Ethnic and Racial Studies* 13, no. 4 (October 1990), 482–502.
Lee Ting Hui. "Singapore Under the Japanese." *Journal of the South Seas Society* 16, no. 1 (1961), 31–69.
Leirvik, Oddbjørn (ed.). *Report of the Oslo Coalition Working Group on Indonesia: Freedom of Religion or Belief.* Oslo: Oslo Coalition, 2002.
Lenczowski, George. *The Middle East in World Affairs*, 2nd ed. Ithaca: Cornell University Press, 1957.
Leong, Ho Khai, and James Chin (eds.). *Mahathir's Administration: Performance and Crisis in Governance.* Singapore: Times Editions, 2003.
Levy, Reuben. *The Social Structure of Islam.* Cambridge: Cambridge University Press, 1957; reprinted 1962.
Lewis, Bernard. *The Crisis of Islam: Holy War and Unholy Terror.* London: Weidenfeld and Nicolson, 2003.
———. *From Babel to Dragomans: Interpreting the Middle East.* New York: Oxford University Press, 2004.
Liddle, R. William. "Indonesia's Threefold Crisis." *Journal of Democracy* 3 (October 1992), 60–74.
———. "The Islamic Turn in Indonesia: A Political Explanation." *Journal of Asian Studies* 55 (August 1996).
———. "Soeharto's Indonesia: Personal Rule and Political Institutions." *Pacific Affairs* 58, no. 1 (Spring 1985), 69–90.
Likitkijsomboon, Pichit. "Thais Pay the Price for Political Turmoil." *Far Eastern Economic Review* 169, no. 6 (July/August 2006), 49–52.
Lim, Danny. "Rallying for Rights in Malaysia." *Far Eastern Economic Review* 170, no. 10 (December 2007), 40–42.
Lim Kit Siang. *Human Rights in Malaysia.* Petaling Jaya, Malaysia: DAP Human Rights Committee, n.d. [1986].
Lintner, Bertil. "A Cocoon of Terror." *Far Eastern Economic Review* (April 4, 2002), 14–17.
Liow, Joseph Chinyong. "The 49th PAS Congress: Politics Behind the Rhetoric." *IDSS Working Paper,* 34/2003. Singapore: Nanyang Technological University, 2003.
———. "Crisis of Chinese Politics in Malaysia's Ruling Coalition." *IDSS Commentaries,* 06/2003, Institute of Defence and Strategic Studies. Singapore: Nanyang Technological University, 2003.
———. "International Jihad and Muslim Radicalism in Thailand? Toward an Alternative Interpretation." *Asia Policy* 1, no. 2 (July 2006), 89–108.

Lloyd, Grayson J., and Shannon L. Smith (eds.). *Indonesia Today: Challenges of History*. Singapore: Institute of Southeast Asian Studies, 2001.

Loeb, Edwin M. *Sumatra—Its History and People*. Vienna: Verlag des Institutes fur Volkerkunde der Universitat, 1935 (reprinted Kuala Lumpur: Oxford University Press, 1972).

Loh Kok Wah, Francis, and Khoo Boo Teik (eds.). *Democracy in Malaysia: Discourses and Practices*. Richmond, UK: Curzon Press, 2002.

Loh Kok Wah, Francis, and Johan Saravanamuttu (eds.). *New Politics in Malaysia*. Singapore: Institute of Southeast Asian Studies, 2003.

Loo Lai Mee, et al. (eds.). *The Anwar Judgment*. Kuala Lumpur: Malayan Law Journal, 1999.

Lukens-Bull, Ronald. *A Peaceful Jihad: Negotiating Identity and Modernity in Muslim Java*. New York: Palgrave Macmillan, 2005.

Lyons, M. L. "The Dakwah Movement in Malaysia." *Review of Indonesian and Malaysian Affairs* 13 (1979), 34–45.

Magdalena, Fererico V. "The Peace Process in Mindanao: Problems and Prospects," in *Southeast Asian Affairs 1997*. Singapore: Institute of Southeast Asian Studies, 1997.

Mahajani, Usha. *The Role of Indian Minorities in Burma and Malaya*. Bombay: Vora, 1960.

Mahathir bin Mohamad. *The Challenge*. Petaling Jaya, Malaysia: Pelanduk Publications, 1987.

———.*Globalisation and the New Realities*, ed. by Hashim Makaruddin. Subang Jaya, Malaysia: Pelanduk Publications, 2002.

———. *The Malay Dilemma*. Singapore: Asia Pacific Press, 1970.

———. *Terrorism and the Real Issues*. Subang Jaya, Malaysia: Pelanduk Publications, 2003.

———. *Vision 2020*. Kuala Lumpur: Institute of Strategic and International Studies, 1991.

———. *The Way Forward*. London: Weidefeld and Nicolson, 1998.

Majul, Cesar Adib. *The Contemporary Muslim Movement in the Philippines*. Berkeley, CA: Mizan Press, 1985.

———. *Muslims in the Philippines*. Quezon City: University of the Philippines Press for the Asian Center, 1973.

Majumdar, R. C., H. C. Raychaudhuri, and Kalikinkar Datta. *An Advanced History of India*, 2nd ed. London: Macmillan, 1953.

Mandaville, Peter. *Political Islam, Global Politics: The International Relations of the Muslim World*. London: Routledge, 2004.

Manning, Chris, and Peter van Diermen (eds.). *Indonesia in Transition: Social Aspects of Reformasi and Crisis*. London: Zed Books, 2000.

Marshall, Paul (ed.). *Radical Islam's Rules: The Worldwide Spread of Extreme Shari'a Law*. Lanham, MD: Rowman & Littlefield Publishers, 2005.

Marr, David G., and A. C. Milner (eds.). *Southeast Asia in the 9th to 14th Centuries*. Singapore: Institute of Southeast Asian Studies, 1986.

Marrison, G. E. "The Coming of Islam to the East Indies." *Journal of the Royal Asiatic Society, Malay Branch* 24, part 1 (1951), 28–37.

Martinez, Patricia A. "The Islamic State or the State of Islam in Malaysia." *Contemporary Southeast Asia* 23, no. 3 (December 2001), 474–503.

Mauzy, Diane K. *Barisan Nasional: Coalition Government in Malaysia*. Kuala Lumpur: Marican & Sons, 1983.

———. "The Human Rights and 'Asian Values' Debate in Southeast Asia: Trying to Clarify the Issues." *The Pacific Review* 10, no. 2 (1997), 210–236.

Maxwell, Bruce (ed.). *Terrorism: A Documentary History.* Washington, DC: CQ Press, 2003.

Maxwell, William George, and W. S. Gibson (eds.). *Treaties and Engagements Affecting the Malay States and Borneo*. London: J. Truscott & Son, 1924.

May, Brian. *The Indonesian Tragedy*. London: Routledge and Kegan Paul, 1978.

McAmis, Robert Day. *Malay Muslims: The History and Challenge of Resurgent Islam.* Grand Rapids, MI: Eerdmans Publications, 2002.

McBeth, John. "Indonesia: The Army's Dirty Business." *Far Eastern Economic Review* (November 7, 2002), 20–21.

———. "Terrorism: In Search of Justice." *Far Eastern Economic Review* (October 31, 2002), 20–22.

———. "Weak Link in the Terror Chain." *Far Eastern Economic Review,* October 24, 2002, 12, 14–18.

McCargo, Duncan, and Ukrist Pathmanand. *The Thaksinization of Thailand.* Copenhagen: Nordic Institute of Asian Studies, 2005.

McCarthy, Edward J. *Spanish Beginnings in the Philippines.* Washington, DC: The Catholic University of America Press, 1943.

McCawley, Tom. "Indonesia's Stature Rises." *The Christian Science Monitor* (January 17, 2006), 6.

McCoy, Alfred W. (ed.). *Southeast Asia Under Japanese Occupation.* New Haven, CT: Yale University Southeast Asian Studies, 1980.

McCreedy, Amy (ed.). *Passing the Mantle: A New Leadership for Malaysia.* Asia Program Special Report, No. 116, Washington, DC, Woodrow Wilson International Center, September 2003.

——— (ed.). *Piety and Pragmatism: Trends in Indonesian Islamic Politics.* Asia Program Special Report, No. 110, Washington, DC, Woodrow Wilson Center, April 2003.

McCulloch, Lesley. *Aceh: Then and Now.* London: Minority Rights Group International, 2005.

McGibbon, Rodd. *Secessionist Challenges in Aceh and Papua: Is Special Autonomy the Solution?* Washington, DC: East-West Center Washington, 2004.

McGraw Donner, Fred. *The Early Islamic Conquests.* Princeton, NJ: Princeton University Press, 1981.

McIntyre, Angus. *The Indonesian Presidency: The Shift from Personal Toward Constitutional Rule.* Lanham, MD: Rowman and Littlefield, 2005.

Means, Gordon P. "The Democratic-Authoritarian Blend in the Political Traditions of Malaysia and Singapore," in Marc Plattner and Larry Diamond (eds.), *Democracy in East Asia*, 96–110. Washington, DC: Johns Hopkins University Press and the National Endowment for Democracy, 1998.

———. "Ethnic Preference Policies in Malaysia," in Neil Nevitte and Charles H. Kennedy (eds.), *Ethnic Preference and Public Policy in Developing States*, 95–118. Nova Scotia: Lancelot Press for Acadia University, 1985.

———. "Exploring Individual Modernity in Sumatra." *Sojourn* 4, no. 2 (August 1989), 157–189.

———. "Malaysia in 1989: Forging a Plan for the Future," in *Southeast Asian Affairs, 1990*, 181–203. Singapore: Institute of Southeast Asian Studies, 1990.

———. "Malaysia: Islam in a Pluralistic Society," in Carlo Caldarola (ed.), *Religion and Societies: Asia and the Middle East*, 445–496. Berlin: Mouton, 1982.

———. *Malaysian Politics*, 2nd rev. ed. London: Hodder and Stoughton, 1976.

———. *Malaysian Politics: The Second Generation.* Singapore: Oxford University Press, 1991.

———. "Public Policy Toward Religion in Malaysia." *Pacific Affairs* 51, no. 3 (Fall 1978), 384–405.

———. "The Role of Religion in the Political Development of Malaysia." *Comparative Politics* 1 (January 1969), 264–284.

———. *The Rural Sector and Human Resource Development in Indonesia.* Joint Centre on Modern East Asia, Canada and the Pacific Working Paper, No. 39, Toronto, 1985.

———. "Soft Authoritarianism in Malaysia and Singapore," in Larry Diamond and Marc F. Plattner (eds.), *Democracy in East Asia.* Baltimore: Johns Hopkins University Press, 1998, 96–110.

———."'Special Rights' as a Strategy for Development." *Comparative Politics,* 5, no. 1 (October 1972), 29–61.

———. "Women's Rights and Public Policy in Islam." *Asian Survey* 27, no. 3 (March 1987), 340–354.

Mehden, Fred R. Von der. *Two Worlds of Islam: Interaction Between Southeast Asia and the Middle East.* Gainesville: University Press of Florida, 1993.

Mehmet, Ozay. *Islamic Identity and Development.* London: Routledge, 1990.

Mernissi, Fatima. *Islam and the Fear of Democracy.* London: Virago Press, 1993.

Meuleman, Johan (ed.). *Islam in the Era of Globalization: Muslim Attitudes Towards Modernity and Identity.* London: RoutledgeCurzon, 2002.

Miichi, Ken. "Islamic Youth Movements in Indonesia." *IIAS Newsletter* 32 (November 2003), 22.

Milne, R. S., and Diane K. Mauzy. *Government and Politics in Malaysia.* Vancouver: University of British Columbia Press, 1978.

———. *Malaysian Politics Under Mahathir.* London: Routledge, 1999.

———. *Malaysia: Tradition, Modernity and Islam.* Boulder, CO: Westview Press, 1986.

Mitsuo, Nakamura, Sharon Siddique, and Omar Farouk Majunid (eds.). *Islam and Civil Society in Southeast Asia.* Singapore: Institute of Southeast Asian Studies, 2001.

Mohaddessin, Mohammad. *Islamic Fundamentalism: The New Global Threat.* Washington, DC: Seven Locks Press, 2nd ed. 2001.

Mohamad, Maznah. *Ethnicity and Inequality in Malaysia: A Retrospect and a Rethinking.* Working Paper, No. 9, Oxford University, Queen Elizabeth House, February 2005.

———. "Malaysia in 2002: Bracing for a Post-Mahathir Future," in *Southeast Asian Affairs 2003.* Singapore: Institute of Southeast Asian Studies, 2003.

———. "Malaysia in 2006: The Enemies Within," research paper (2007), 1–15, www.iseas.edu/sg/rof07mm.pdf.

Mohamed Abu Bakar. "Islamic Revivalism and the Political Process in Malaysia." *Asian Survey* 21 (1981), 1040–1059.

Mohamed Azam Mohamed Adil. "Restrictions in Freedom of Religion in Malaysia: A Conceptual Analysis with Special Reference to the Law of Apostasy." *Muslim World Journal of Human Rights* 4, no. 2 (2007). www.bepress.com/mwjhr/vol4/iss2/art1.

Mohammadi, Ali (ed.). *Islam Encountering Globalization.* London: RoutledgeCurzon, 2002.

Mohammed Ariff (ed.). *Islamic Banking in Southeast Asia.* Singapore: Institute of Southeast Asian Studies, 1988.

Montlake, Simon. "Malaysian Dissident Now Eyes World Stage." *Christian Science Monitor* (November 23, 2004), 8.

———. "Race Politics Hobbles Malaysia." *Far Eastern Economic Review* 171, no. 2 (March 2008), 36–39.

———. "Thailand's Exposed Southern Flank." *Far Eastern Economic Review* 170, no. 4 (May 2007), 35–38.

Morais, J. Victor. *Anwar Ibrahim: Resolute in Leadership.* Kuala Lumpur: Arenabuku, 1983.

Morgan, Adrian. "Indonesia: The Roots of Muslim Christian Conflict." *Spero News* (October 25, 2006), 1–10. www.speroforum.com/site/print.asp?idarticle=6285.

Moussalli, Ahmad S. *The Islamic Quest for Democracy, Pluralism, and Human Rights.* Gainesville: University of Florida Press, 2001.

Mujani, Saiful, and William Liddle. "Indonesia's Approaching Elections: Politics, Islam and Public Opinion." *Journal of Democracy* (January 2004).

Murphy, Colum. "Abdullah's Imperfect Plan." *Far Eastern Economic Review* 169, no. 6 (July/August 2006), 19–23.

———. "Friction on the Thai-Malay Fault Line." *Far Eastern Economic Review* 168, no. 10 (November 2005), 21–25.

———. "'Thaksin, Get Out!': Why Thais Are Angry." *Far Eastern Economic Review* 169, no. 3 (April 2006), 7–13.

———. "A Tug of War for Thailand's Soul." *Far Eastern Economic Review* 169, no. 7 (September 2006), 23–28.

Murphy, Dan. "Al Qaeda's Asian 'Quartermaster.'" *The Christian Science Monitor* (February 12, 2002), 6.

———. "Al Qaeda's New Frontier: Indonesia." *The Christian Science Monitor* (May 1, 2002), 1 and 10.

———. "Filipino Police Uncover 1995 Leads to Sept. 11 Plot." *The Christian Science Monitor* (February 14, 2002), 7.

———. "Indonesian Cleric Fights for a Muslim State." *The Christian Science Monitor* (May 2, 2002), 7.

———. "Southeast Asia Easy Source of Al Qaeda Recruits." *The Christian Science Monitor* (October 9, 2002), 7.

———. "US Troops Rile Filipino Separatists." *The Christian Science Monitor* (February 20, 2002), 6.

Mutalib, Hussein. *Islam in Malaysia: From Revivalism to Islamic State?* Singapore: Singapore University Press, 1993.

Mutebi, Alex M. "Thailand's Independent Agencies Under Thaksin: Relentless Gridlock and Uncertainty," in Daljit Singh and Carlos Salazar (eds.), *Southeast Asian Affairs 2006*, 303–321. Singapore: Institute of Southeast Asian Studies, 2006.

Muzaffar, Chandra. *Islamic Resurgence in Malaysia.* Petaling Jaya, Malaysia: Penerbit Fajar Bakti, 1987.

———. "Malaysian Politics: The Emerging Scenario Under Abdullah Badawi." *Trends in Southeast Asia* 15 (2003).

———. *Muslims, Dialogue, Terror.* Petaling Jaya, Malaysia: International Movement for a Just World, 2003.

———. *Rights, Religion and Reform.* London: RoutledgeCurzon, 2002.

Mydans, Seth. "Warnings of Terrorism Along a Porous Border in Southern Thailand." *New York Times* (November 16, 2002), sect. A, 11.

Nagata, Judith. *The Reflowering of Malaysian Islam: Modern Religious Radicals and Their Roots.* Vancouver: University of British Columbia Press, 1984.

———. "Religious Ideology and Social Change: The Islamic Revival in Malaysia." *Pacific Affairs* 53 (1980), 405–439.

Nakamura, M., S. Siddique, and B. Omar Farouk (eds.). *Islam and Civil Society in Southeast Asia.* Singapore: Institute of Southeast Asian Studies, 2001.

Nakamura, Rie. "The Coming of Islam to Champa." *Journal of the Malaysian Branch of the Royal Asiatic Society* 73, no. 1 (2000), 55–66.

Napoleoni, Loretta. *Modern Jihad: Tracing the Dollars Behind the Terror Networks.* London: Pluto Press, 2003.

Nathan, K. S. "Malaysia: 11 September and the Politics of Incumbency," in *Southeast Asian Affairs 2002.* Singapore: Institute of Southeast Asian Studies, 2002.

Neill, Wilfred T. *Twentieth Century Indonesia.* New York: Columbia University Press, 1973.

Nevitte, Neil, and Charles H. Kennedy (eds.). *Ethnic Preference and Public Policy in Developing States.* Boulder, CO: Lynne Rienner Publishers, 1986.

Nevo, Yehuda D., and Judith Koren. *Crossroads to Islam: The Origins of the Arab Religion and the Arab State.* Amherst, NY: Prometheus Books, 2003.

Nguyen, Thang D., and Frank-Jürgen Richter (eds.). *Indonesia Matters: Diversity, Unity and Stability in Fragile Times.* Singapore: Times Editions, 2003.

Nieuwenhuijze, C.A.O. van. *Aspects of Islam in Post-Colonial Indonesia.* The Hague and Bandung: W. van Hoeve, 1958.

Noble, Lela G. "The Moro National Liberation Front in the Philippines." *Pacific Affairs* 49 (Fall 1976), 405–424.

Noer, Deliar. *Administration of Islam in Indonesia.* Ithaca, NY: Cornell University Modern Indonesia Project, Monograph No. 58, 1978.

Noor, Farish A. "Blood, Sweat and *Jihad*: The Radicalization of the Political Discourse of the Pan-Malaysian Islamic Party (PAS) from 1982 Onwards." *Contemporary Southeast Asia* 25, no. 2 (August 2003), 200–232.

Noor, Ismail, and Muhammad Azaham. *The Malays Par Excellence . . . Warts and All, An Introspection.* Subang Jaya, Malaysia: Pelanduk Publications, 2000.

Ongkili, James P. *Nation-Building in Malaysia, 1946–1974.* Singapore: Oxford University Press, 1985.

Onn, Chin Kee. *Malaya Upside Down,* 3rd ed. Singapore: Federal Publications, 1976.

O'Rourke, Kevin. *Reformasi: The Struggle for Power in Post-Soeharto Indonesia.* Crows Nest, Australia: Allen & Unwin, 2002.

Othman, Norani. "Shari'a and the Citizenship Rights of Women in a Modern Nation-State." IKMAS Working Paper, Universiti Kebangsaan Malaysia, Bangi, 1997.

Palmier, Leslie. *Communists in Indonesia.* London: Weidenfeld & Nicolson, 1973.

Parkinson, C. Northcote. *British Intervention in Malaya, 1867–1877.* Singapore: University of Malaya Press, 1960.

Pathmanand, Ukrist. "Thaksin's Policies Go South." *Far Eastern Economic Review* 168, no. 7 (July/August 2005), 8–13.

Paul H. Nitze School of Advanced International Studies. *Political Islam in Southeast Asia.* Conference Report. Washington, DC: Johns Hopkins University, March 25, 2003, 1–22.

Peletz, Michael G. *Islamic Modern: Religious Courts and Cultural Politics in Malaysia.* Princeton: Princeton Studies in Muslim Politics, 2002.

Peng, Chin. *My Side of the Story.* Singapore: Media Masters, 2003.

Peretz, Don. *The Middle East Today*, 4th ed. New York: Praeger Publishers, 1983.

Perlez, Jane. "U.S. Labels Indonesian Faction as Terrorist." *New York Times* (October 24, 2002), sect. A, 15.

———. "Within Islam's Embrace, a Voice for Malaysia's Women." *New York Times* (February 19, 2006), 1–3. www.nytimes.com/2006/02/19/international/asia/19malaysia .htlm.

The Pew Global Attitudes Project. *Islamic Extremism: Common Concern for Muslim and Western Publics.* Washington, DC: The Pew Research Center, July 14, 2005.

Phongpaichit, Pasuk. *Thaksin: The Business of Politics in Thailand.* Chiang Mai, Thailand: Silkworm Books, 2004.

Phongpaichit, Pasuk, and Chris Baker. "Thaksin Dismantles the Opposition." *Far Eastern Economic Review* 168, no. 3 (March 2005), 25–29.

Pipes, Daniel. *In the Path of God: Islam and Political Power.* New York: Basic Books, 1983.

Pitney Lamb, Beatrice. *India: A World in Transition.* New York: Frederick A. Praeger, 1963.

Pluvier, J. M. *South-East Asia from Colonialism to Independence.* Kuala Lumpur: Oxford University Press, 1974.

Pongsudhirak, Thitinan. "Thaksin's Political Zenith and Nadir," in Daljit Singh and Lorraine Carlos Salazar (eds.), *Southeast Asian Affairs 2006*, 285–302. Singapore: Institute of Southeast Asian Studies, 2006.

Post, Peter, and Elly Touwen-Bouwsma (eds.). *Japan, Indonesia and the War: Myths and Realities.* Leiden: LITLV Press, 1997.

Rabasa, Angel. *Political Islam in Southeast Asia—Moderates, Radicals and Terrorists.* Singapore and New York: Oxford University Press for The International Institute for Strategic Studies, 2003.

Rabasa, Angel, and Peter Chalk. *Indonesia's Transformation and the Stability of Southeast Asia.* Santa Monica, CA: Rand Corporation, 2001.

Rabasa, Angel, and John Haseman. *The Military and Democracy in Indonesia: Challenges, Politics and Power.* Santa Monica, CA: Rand Corporation, 2002.

Rabasa, Angel, Cheryl Bernard, Peter Chalk, C. Christine Fair, Theodore Karasik, Rollie Lal, Ian Lesser, and David E. Thaler. *The Muslim World After 9/11.* Santa Monica, CA: Rand Corporation, 2004.

Rahman, Afzalur. *Islam: Ideology and Way of Life.* Singapore: Pustaka Nasional, 1980.

Rahman, Fazlur. *Islam and Modernity: The Transformation of an Intellectual Tradition.* Chicago: Chicago University Press, 1982.

Rahman, Tunku Abdul. *Contemporary Issues in Malaysian Politics.* Petaling Jaya, Malaysia: Pelanduk Publications, 1984.

Ramadan, Said. *Islamic Law,* 2nd ed. London: Macmillan, 1961.

Ramage, Douglas E. *Democracy, Islam and the Ideology of Tolerance.* London: Routledge, 1995.

———. *Politics in Indonesia: Democracy, Islam and the Ideology of Tolerance.* London: Routledge, 1995.

Ramakrishna, Kumar. "Jemaah Islamiah: Aims, Motivations and Possible Counter-Strategies." *IDSS Working Paper.* Singapore: Nanyang Technological University, 2003.

Ramakrishna, Kumar, and See Seng Tan (eds.). *After Bali: The Threat of Terrorism in Southeast Asia.* Singapore: Institute of Defence and Strategic Studies, 2003.

Rashid, Rehman. "Destinies Delayed (But Not Denied): Reflections on the Transition of Malaysian Administrations." *Trends in Southeast Asia* 8 (2003), 1–10.

Reid, Anthony. *The Blood of the People: Revolution and the End of Traditional Rule in North Sumatra.* Kuala Lumpur: Oxford University Press, 1979.

———. *Charting the Shape of Early Modern Southeast Asia.* Cheng Mai, Thailand: Silkworm Books, 1999.

———. *The Contest for North Sumatra: Atjeh, the Netherlands and Britain 1858–1898.* Kuala Lumpur: Oxford University Press, 1969.

———. *An Indonesian Frontier: Acehnese and Other Histories of Sumatra.* Singapore: Singapore University Press, 2005.

———. *Indonesian National Revolution, 1945–50.* Hawthorn, Vic., Australia: Longman, 1974.

——— (ed.). *The Making of an Islamic Political Discourse in Southeast Asia.* Melbourne: Monash University Press, 1993.

———. "Nineteenth Century Pan-Islam in Indonesia and Malaysia." *Journal of Asian Studies* 26, no. 2 (1967), 267–283.

———. *Southeast Asia in the Age of Commerce, 1450–1680.* New Haven, CT: Yale University Press, 1988.

——— (ed.). *Southeast Asia in the Early Modern Era: Trade, Power and Belief.* Ithaca, NY: Cornell University Press, 1993.

Rejwan, Nissim. *The Many Faces of Islam: Perspectives on a Resurgent Civilization.* Gainesville: University Press of Florida, 2000.

Ressa, Maria. *An Eyewitness Account of Al Qaeda's Newest Center of Operations in Southeast Asia.* New York: The Free Press, 2003.

Revel, Jean François. *Democracy Against Itself: The Future of the Democratic Impulse.* New York: The Free Press, 1993.

Rich, Paul B., and Richard Stubbs (eds.). *The Counter-Insurgent State: Guerrilla Warfare and State Building in the Twentieth Century.* New York: St. Martin's Press, 1997.

Ricklefs, Merle C. *A History of Modern Indonesia Since c. 1200,* 3rd ed. Stanford: Stanford University Press, 2001.

Riddell, Peter G. *Islam and the Malay-Indonesian World: Transmission and Responses.* Honolulu: University of Hawaii Press, 2001.

Ringuet, Daniel Joseph. "The Continuation of Civil Unrest and Poverty in Mindanao." *Contemporary Southeast Asia* 24, no. 1 (April 2002), 33–49.

Roberson, B. A. (ed.). *Shaping the Current Islamic Reformation.* London: Frank Cass, 2003.

Robinson, Chase F. *Islamic Historiography.* Cambridge: Cambridge University Press, 2003.

Robinson, Kathryn, and Sharon Bessell (eds.). *Women in Indonesia: Gender, Equality, and Development.* Singapore: Institute of Southeast Asian Studies, 2002.

Robinson, Richard. *Indonesia: The Rise of Capital.* Sydney: Allen & Unwin, 1986.

———. *Pathways to Asia: The Politics of Engagement.* St. Leonards, Australia: Allen and Unwin, 1996.

Rodan, Garry, Kevin Hewison, and Richard Robinson (eds.). *The Political Economy of South-East Asia: Conflicts, Crisis, and Change,* 2nd ed. Melbourne: Oxford University Press, 2001.

Rodell, Paul A. "The Philippines: Gloria *in Excelsis*," in *Southeast Asian Affairs 2002.* Singapore: Institute of Southeast Asian Studies, 2002.

———. "The Philippines: Playing Out Long Conflicts," in *Southeast Asian Affairs 2004.* Singapore: Institute of Southeast Asian Studies, 2004.

Rodinson, Maxime. *Islam and Capitalism.* London: Penguin, 1973.

Roff, William R. (ed.). *Islam and the Political Economy of Meaning: Comparative Studies of Muslim Discourse.* Sydney: Croom Helm, 1987.

———. (ed.). *Kelantan: Religion, Society and Politics in a Malay State.* Kuala Lumpur: Oxford University Press, 1974.

———. "The Malayo-Muslim World of Singapore at the Close of the Nineteenth Century." *Journal of Asian Studies* 24, no. 1 (1964), 75–90.

———. *The Origins of Malay Nationalism*. New Haven: Yale University Press, 1967.

Rosenthal, E. I. J. *Islam in the Modern National State*. Cambridge: Cambridge University Press, 1965.

———. *Political Thought in Medieval Islam*. Cambridge: Cambridge University Press, 1958.

Rosenthal, Justin A. "Southeast Asia: Archipelago of Afghanistans?" *Orbis: A Journal of World Affairs* 47, no. 3 (Summer 2002), 470–493.

Ross, Michael L. "Resources and Rebellion in Aceh, Indonesia." Paper prepared for Yale–World Bank project on "The Economics of Political Violence," June 5, 2003, typescript from e-mail.

Ross-Larson, Bruce (ed.). *Malaysia 2001: A Preliminary Inquiry*. Kuala Lumpur: Syed Kechik Foundation, 1978.

———. *The Politics of Federalism: Syed Kechik in East Malaysia*. Singapore: Times Printers, 1976.

Roy, Chandra K., Victoria Tauli-Corpuz, and Amanda Romero-Medina (eds.). *Beyond the Silencing of the Guns*. Bagio City, Philippines: Tebtebba Foundation, 2004.

Roy, Oliver. *The Failure of Political Islam*. Cambridge, MA: Harvard University Press, 1994.

———. *Globalized Islam: The Search for the New Ummah*. New York: Columbia University Press, 2004.

Sabri Zain. *Face Off: A Malaysian Reformasi Diary (1998–1999)*. Singapore: BigO Books, 2000.

Sachedina, Abdulaziz. *The Islamic Roots of Democratic Pluralism*. Oxford: Oxford University Press, 2001.

Safa, Reza F. *Inside Islam: Exposing and Reaching the World of Islam*. Washington, DC: Strang Communications, 1997.

Safi, Omid (ed.). *Progressive Muslims on Justice, Gender, and Pluralism*. Oxford: Oneworld, 2003.

Saikal, Amin. *Islam and the West: Conflict or Cooperation*. Houndmills, UK: Palgrave Macmillan, 2003.

Salamé, Ghassan (ed.). *Democracy Without Democrats? The Renewal of Politics in the Muslim World*. London: I. B. Tauris, 1996.

Salim, Arskal, and Azyumardi Azra (eds.). *Shari'a and Politics in Modern Indonesia*. Singapore: Institute of Southeast Asian Studies, 2003.

Samad, Paridah Abd. *Gus Dur: A Peculiar Leader in Indonesia's Political Agony*. Ampang Selangor, Malaysia: Penerbit Salafi, 2001.

Samson, A. A. "Religious Belief and Political Action in Indonesian Islamic Modernism," in R. William Liddle (ed.), *Political Participation in Modern Indonesia*, 116–142. New Haven, CT: Yale University Press, 1973.

Sardar, Ziauddin. *The Future of Muslim Civilization*. London: Mansell Publishing, 1987.

———. *Introducing Chaos*. New York: Totem Books, 1998.

———. *Islamic Futures: The Shape of Ideas to Come*. Petaling Jaya, Malaysia: Pelanduk Publications, 1988.

Schacht, Joseph. *An Introduction to Islamic Law*. Oxford, UK: Clarendon Press, 1964.

———. *The Origins of Muhammadan Jurisprudence*. London: Oxford University Press, 1959.

Schevill, Ferdinand. *A History of Europe from the Reformation to the Present Day*, rev. ed. New York: Harcourt, Brace, 1947.

Schulze, Kirsten E. *The Free Aceh Movement (GAM): Anatomy of a Separatist Organization*. Washington, DC: East-West Center Washington, 2004.

Schwarz, Adam. *A Nation in Waiting: Indonesia's Search for Stability,* 2nd ed. St. Leonards, NSW, Australia: Allen & Unwin, 2002.

Scott, James C. *Weapons of the Weak: Everyday Forms of Peasant Resistance*. New Haven, CT: Yale University Press, 1985.

Sebastian, Leonard C. "Indonesia's New Anti-Terrorism Regulations." *IDSS Commentaries,* 25/2002. Singapore: Nanyang Technological University, 2002.

———. "Getting to the Root of Islamic Radicalism in Indonesia." *IDSS Working Paper*. Singapore: Nanyang Technological University, 2003.

———. "Indonesian State Responses to September 11, the Bali Bombings and the War in Iraq: Sowing the Seeds for an Accommodationist Islamic Framework?" *Cambridge Review of International Affairs* 16, no. 3 (October 2003), 431–448.

Shadid, Anthony. *Legacy of the Prophet: Despots, Democrats and the New Politics of Islam.* Boulder, CO: Westview Press, 2001.

Shalom, Stephen Rosskamm. *The United States and the Philippines: A Study of Neocolonialism.* Philadelphia: Institute for the Study of Human Issues, 1981.

Shamsul, A. B. "Malaysia's International Role Post–September 11." *IDSS Commentaries,* 31/2002, Institute of Defence and Strategic Studies. Singapore: Nanyang Technological University, 2003.

Shaw, William. *Tun Razak: His Life and Times.* Kuala Lumpur: Longman Malaysia, 1976.

Sherlock, Steven. *Consolidation and Change: The Indonesian Parliament After the 2004 Elections.* Canberra: Australian National University, Centre for Democratic Institutions, June 2004.

———. *Struggling to Change: The Indonesian Parliament in an Era of Reformasi. A Report on the Structure and Operation of the Dewan Perwakilan Rakyat (DPR).* Canberra: Australian National University, Centre for Democratic Institutions, January 2003.

Short, Anthony. *The Communist Insurrection in Malaya, 1948–1960.* New York: Crane Russak, 1975.

Siegel, James T. *The Rope of God.* Berkeley: California University Press, 1969.

———. *A New Criminal Type in Jakarta: Counter Revolution Today.* Durham, NC: Duke University Press, 1998.

Simon, Sheldon W. "Managing Security Challenges in Southeast Asia." *NBR Analysis* 13, no. 4 (July 2002). www.nbr.org.

———. "Philippines Withdraws from Iraq and JI Strikes Again." *Comparative Connections*, 3rd Quarter 2004, Pacific Forum CSIS, 1–9. csis.org/pacfor/cc/0403 Qus_asean.htm.

———. "Southeast Asia and the U.S. War on Terrorism," *NBR Analysis* 13, no. 4 (July 2002), 25–37.

Simons, Thomas W. *Islam in a Globalized World.* Stanford, CA: Stanford University Press, 2003.

Singapore Ministry of Home Affairs. *The Jemaah Islamiyah Arrests and the Threat of Terrorism*, January 2003.

Singh, Bilveer. *Succession Politics in Indonesia.* London: Macmillan Press, 2000.

Sison, Jose Maria. *US Terrorism and War in the Philippines.* Breda, Netherlands: Uitgeverij Papieren Tijger, 2003.

Sivan, Emmanuel. *Radical Islam: Medieval Theology and Modern Politics*, enl. ed. New Haven, CT: Yale University Press, 1990.

Sjamsuddin, Nazaruddin. *The Republican Revolt: A Study of the Acehnese Rebellion.* Singapore: Institute of Southeast Asian Studies, 1985.

Skeat, Walter William. *Malay Magic: An Introduction to the Folklore and Popular Religion of the Malay Peninsula.* London: Macmillan, 1900.

Slimming, John. *Malaysia: Death of a Democracy.* London: John Murray, 1969.

Smith, Anthony L. "The Role of the United Nations in East Timor's Path to Independence." *Asian Journal of Political Science* 9, no. 2 (December 2001), 25–53.

———. "Trouble in Thailand's Muslim South: Separatism, Not Global Terrorism." *Asia-Pacific Security Studies* 3, no. 10 (December 2004), 1–4.

Smith, Goldwin. *A History of England.* Chicago: Charles Scribner's Sons, 1949.

Smith, Paul J. *Terrorism and Violence in Southeast Asia: Transnational Challenges to States and Regional Stability.* Armonk, NY: M. E. Sharp, 2005.

Smith, Vincent A. *The Oxford History of India*, 3rd ed. Oxford: Clarendon Press, 1961.

Sodhy, Pamela. "U.S.-Malaysian Relations During the Bush Administration: The Political, Economic and Security Aspects." *Contemporary Southeast Asia* 25, no. 3 (December 2003), 363–386.

Soenarno, Radin. "Malay Nationalism, 1900–1945." *Journal of Southeast Asian History* 1, no. 1 (March 1960), 9–15.

Soesastro, Hadi, Anthony L. Smith, and Han Mui Ling (eds.). *Governance in Indonesia: Challenges Facing the Megawati Presidency*. Singapore: Institute of Southeast Asian Studies, 2003.

Spear, Percival. *India: A Modern History*. Ann Arbor: University of Michigan Press, 1961.

Stark, Jan. "The Islamic Debate in Malaysia: The Unfinished Project." *South East Asia Research* 11, no. 2 (July 2003), 173–201.

Stauth, Georg. *Politics and Cultures of Islamization in Southeast Asia: Indonesia and Malaysia in the Nineteen-Nineties.* New Brunswick, NJ: Transaction Publishers, 2002.

Steinberg, David Joel (ed.). *In Search of Southeast Asia*, rev. ed. Honolulu: University of Hawaii Press, 1987.

Stern, Jessica. *Terror in the Name of God: Why Religious Militants Kill.* New York: HarperCollins, 2003.

Stewart, Ian. *The Mahathir Legacy: A Nation Divided, A Region at Risk.* Singapore: Talisman , 2004.

Storey, Ian. "Malaysia's Role in Thailand's Southern Insurgency." *Terrorism Monitor* (The Jamestown Foundation) 5, no. 5 (March 15, 2007): 1–4.

———."Thailand Cracks Down on Southern Militants." *Terrorism Monitor* (The Jamestown Foundation) 5, no. 17 (September 13, 2007), 1–3.

Stubbs, Richard. *Hearts and Minds in Guerrilla Warfare: The Malayan Emergency, 1948–1960.* Singapore: Oxford University Press, 1989.

Sukma, Rizal. *Security Operations in Aceh: Goals, Consequences, and Lessons.* Washington, DC: East-West Center Washington, 2004.

Suryadinata, Leo. *Elections and Politics in Indonesia*. Singapore: Institute of Southeast Asian Studies, 2002.

Sutherland, Heather. *The Making of a Bureaucratic Elite: The Colonial Transformation of the Javanese Priyayi.* Singapore: Heinemann Educational Books, 1979.

Swettenham, Frank. *British Malaya*, 3rd rev. ed. London: George Allen & Unwin, 1948.

Syukri, Ibrahim. *History of the Malay Kingdom of Patani*, trans. by Conner Bailey and John N. Miksic. Ohio University Southeast Asia Series, No. 68, 1985.

Tamney, Joseph B., and John G. Condran. "The Decline of Religious Homogeneity: The Indonesian Situation." *Journal for the Scientific Study of Religion* 19, no. 3 (September 1980), 267–280.

Tan, Andrew T. H. "The Acehnese Conflict: Transnational Linkages, Responses and Implications." *IDSS Commentaries,* 25/2003, Institute of Defence and Strategic Studies. Singapore: Nanyang Technological University, 2003.

Tan, Andrew T. H., and J. D. Kenneth Boutin (eds.). *Non-Traditional Security Issues in Southeast Asia.* Singapore: Select Publishing, 2001.

Tan, Andrew T. H., and Kumar Ramakrishna (eds.). *The New Terrorism: Anatomy, Trends and Counter-Strategies.* Singapore: Eastern Universities Press, 2002.

Tan, Gerald. *ASEAN Economic Development and Cooperation,* 2nd ed., Singapore: Times Academic Press, 2000.

Tan Kong Yam, Toh Mun Heng, and Linda Low. "ASEAN and Pacific Economic Co-operation." *ASEAN Economic Bulletin* 8, no. 3 (1992), 317–319.

Tan, Samuel K. *The Filipino Muslim Armed Struggle, 1900–1972.* Manila: Filipinas Foundation, 1977.

Tantor, Richard, Mark Sheldon, and Stephen R. Shalom (eds.). *Bitter Sweet Flowers: East Timor, Indonesia, and the World Community.* Lanham, MD: Rowman & Littlefield Publishers, 2001.

Tarling, Nicholas. *A Concise History of Southeast Asia.* New York: Frederick A. Praeger, 1996.

———. *Piracy and Politics in the Malay World.* Singapore: Donald Moore, 1963.

———. *Southeast Asia: A Modern History.* South Melbourne: Oxford University Press, 2001.

Tas, S. *Indonesia: The Underdeveloped Freedom.* Indianapolis, IN: Pegasus, 1974.

Tate, D. J. M. *The Making of Modern South-East Asia,* Vol. 1, *The European Conquest,* rev. ed. Kuala Lumpur: Oxford University Press, 1977.

———. *The Making of Modern South-East Asia,* Vol. 2, *The Western Impact, Economic and Social Change.* Kuala Lumpur: Oxford University Press, 1979.

Taylor, John G. *Indonesia's Forgotten War: The Hidden History of East Timor.* London: Zed Books, 1991.

———. *East Timor: The Price of Freedom.* London: Zed Books, 1999.

Tellis, Ashley J., and Michael Wills (eds.). *Strategic Asia 2004–05: Confronting Terrorism in the Pursuit of Power.* Seattle: The National Bureau of Asian Research, 2004.

Thaib, Lukman. *Acheh's Case: A Historical Study of the National Movement for the Independence of Acheh-Sumatra.* Kuala Lumpur: University of Malaya Press, 2002.

Thailand National Reconciliation Commission. *Overcoming Violence Through the Power of Reconciliation.* Bangkok: Secretariat to the NRC, May 16, 2006.

Tham Seong Chee. *Malays and Modernization: A Sociological Interpretation.* Singapore: Singapore University Press, 1977.

Thayer, Carlyle A. "Political Terrorism and Militant Islam in Southeast Asia." *Trends in Southeast Asia* 7 (2003), 11–30.

Tibi, Bassam. *The Challenge of Fundamentalism: Political Islam and the New World Disorder.* Berkeley: University of California Press, 1998.

———. *Islam and the Cultural Accommodation of Social Change.* Boulder, CO: Westview Press, 1990.

———. *Islam Between Culture and Politics.* New York: Macmillan, 2005.

Turner, Mark, A. J. May, and Respall Lalu Turner (eds.). *Mindanao: Land of Unfulfilled Promise.* Quezon City, Philippines: New Day Publishers, 1992.

Turner, Mark. "Terrorism and Secession in the Southern Philippines: The Rise of the Abu Sayyaf." *Contemporary Southeast Asia* 17, no. 1 (1995).

Uhlin, Anders. *Indonesia and the "Third Wave of Democratization": The Pro-Democracy Movement in a Changing World.* New York: St. Martin's Press, 1997.

Ulil Abshar-Abdalla. "Islam: The Challenge from Extremist Interpretations." *Trends in Southeast Asia* 4 (2003), 11–21.

UN Development Programme. *Human Development Report, 1991.* New York: Oxford University Press, 1991.

US Department of State. *Indonesia: International Religious Freedom Report 2004.* Washington, DC: Bureau of Democracy, Human Rights and Labor, 2004.

———. *Thailand: International Religious Freedom Report 2000.* Washington, DC: Bureau of Democracy, Human Rights and Labor, 2000.

———. *Malaysia: International Religious Freedom Report 2004.* Washington, DC: Bureau of Democracy, Human Rights and Labor, 2004.

US Institute of Peace. *The Mindanao Peace Talks: Another Opportunity to Resolve the Moro Conflict in the Philippines.* Washington, DC: Special Report 131, January 2005.

Van Dijk, C. *Rebellion Under the Banner of Islam: The Darul Islam in Indonesia* [Verhandelingen, Van Het Koninklijk Instituut Voor Taal-, Land- en Volkenkunde, Vol. 94]. The Hague: Martinus Nijhoff, 1981.

Van Dijk, Kees. *A Country in Despair: Indonesia Between 1997 and 2000.* Leiden: KITLV Press, 2001.

Vatikiotis, Michael R. J. *Indonesian Politics Under Suharto: The Rise and Fall of the New Order,* 3rd ed. London: Routledge, 1998.

———. "One Angry Man." *Far Eastern Economic Review* (October 30, 2003), 18–22.

———. *Political Change in Southeast Asia: Trimming the Banyan Tree.* London: Routledge, 1996.

———. "Indonesia's Elections: Political and Business Implications." *Singapore Institute of International Affairs Reader* 4, no. 1 (January 2004), 57–62.

Vatikiotis, P. J. *Islam and the State.* London: Routledge, 1987.

Verma, Vidhu. *Malaysia: State and Civil Society in Transition.* Boulder, CO: Lynne Rienner Publishers, 2002 and Petaling Jaya, Malaysia: Strategic Information Research Development, 2004.

Vitug, Marites Dañguilan, and Glenda M. Gloria. *Under the Crescent Moon: Rebellion in Mindanao.* Quezon City, Philippines: Ateneo Center for Social Policy and Public Affairs, 2000.

Vlekke, Bernard H. M. *Nusantara: A History of Indonesia,* rev. ed. The Hague and Bandung: W. van Hoeve, 1959.

Vorys, Karl von. *Democracy Without Consensus: Communalism and Political Stability in Malaysia.* Princeton, NJ: Princeton University Press, 1975.

Wah, Chin Kin, and Daljit Singh (eds.). *Southeast Asian Affairs 2005.* Singapore: Institute of Southeast Asian Studies, 2005.

Wali Ullah, Mir. *Muslim Jurisprudence and the Quranic Law of Crimes*, 2nd rev. ed. Lahore, Pakistan: Islamic Book Service, 1982.

Warr, Peter. *Thailand Beyond the Crisis.* London: RoutledgeCurzon, 2005.

Warraq, Ibn (ed.). *The Quest for the Historical Muhammad.* Amherst, NY: Prometheus Books, 2000.

Weiss, Bernard G. *The Spirit of Islamic Law.* Athens: University of Georgia Press, 1998.

Welsh, Bridget. "Attitudes Toward Democracy in Malaysia: Challenges to the Regime?" *Asian Survey* 36, no. 9 (September 1996), 882–903.

——— (ed.). *Reflections: The Mahathir Years.* Baltimore: Southeast Asia Studies Program, Johns Hopkins University, 2004.

Wertheim, W. F. *Indonesian Society in Transition: A Study of Social Change*, 2nd rev. ed. The Hague: W. van Hoeve, 1959.

Wessel, Ingrid, and Georgia Wimhöfer (eds.). *Violence in Indonesia.* Hamburg: Abera-Verlag Voss, 2001.

Wheeler, Richard S. *The Politics of Pakistan: A Constitutional Quest.* Ithaca: Cornell University Press, 1970.

Whiting, Amanda. "Situating Suhakam: Human Rights Debates and Malaysia's National Human Rights Commission." *Stanford Journal of International Law* 39, no. 1 (Winter 2003), 59–98.

Wilkinson, R. J. *Malay Beliefs*. London: Luzak, 1906.

Winstedt, R. O. *A History of Malaya.* London: Luzak, 1935.

———. *Malaya and Its History,* 3rd ed. London: Hutchinson's University Library, 1953.

———. *The Malay Magician: Being Shaman, Saiva and Sufi*. London: Routledge and Kegan Paul, 1961.

———. *The Malays: A Cultural History*. London: Routledge and Kegan Paul, 1961.

———. *Shaman, Saiva and Sufi: A Study of the Evolution of Malay Magic.* London: Constable, 1925.

Winters, Jeffrey. *Power in Motion: Capital Mobility and the Indonesian State.* Ithaca, NY: Cornell University Press, 1996.

Winzeler, Robert L. (ed.). *Indigenous Peoples and the State: Politics, Land, and Ethnicity in the Malayan Peninsula and Borneo.* New Haven, CT: Yale Southeast Asia Studies, Monograph 46, 1997.

Wise, William M. *Indonesia's War on Terror.* Washington, DC: USINDO, August 2005.

Wolpert, Stanley. *A New History of India.* New York: Oxford University Press, 1993.

Wong, James Wing-On. "Malaysia in Transition: The Battle for the Malay Mind." *Trends in Southeast Asia* 8 (2003), 13–20.

Woodward, Mark R. *Islam in Java: Normative Piety and Mysticism in the Sultanate of Yogyakarta*. Tucson: University of Arizona Press, 1989.

World Bank. *World Development Report,* 7 vols. New York: Oxford University Press, 1990–1997.

Wright, Robin. *Sacred Rage: The Wrath of Militant Islam*, rev. ed. New York: Simon & Shuster, 2001.

Wurfel, David. *Filipino Politics: Development and Decay*. Ithaca: Cornell University Press, 1988.

Yale, William. *The Near East: A Modern History.* Ann Arbor: University of Michigan Press, 1958.

Yamamoto, Tadashi (ed.). *Emerging Civil Society in the Asia Pacific Region.* Singapore: Institute of Southeast Asian Studies, 1995.

Yau Souchou. "After *The Malay Dilemma*: The Modern Malay Subject and Cultural Logics of 'National Cosmopolitanism.'" *Sojourn: Journal of Social Issues in Southeast Asia* 18, no. 2 (October 2003), 201–229.

Yegar, Moshe. *Islam and Islamic Institutions in British Malaya: Policies and Implementation.* Jerusalem: The Magnes Press, Hebrew University, 1979.

———. *Between Integration and Secession: The Muslim Communities of Southern Philippines, Southern Thailand, and Western Burma/Myanmar.* Lanham, MD: Lexington Books, 2002.

Yeo Weimeng. "The JI Spectre Is Still Here." *IDSS Working Paper*, 13/2003, Institute of Defence and Strategic Studies. Singapore: Nanyang Technological University, 2003.

Young Hum Kim. *East Asia's Turbulent Century.* New York: Appleton-Century-Crofts, 1966.

Zakaria, Fareed. *The Future of Freedom: Illiberal Democracy at Home and Abroad.* New York: W. W. Norton, 2003.

Zakaria, Rafiq. *The Struggle Within Islam: The Conflict Between Religion and Politics.* London: Penguin Books, 1989.

Index

About the Book

Gordon Means traces the evolution of Islamic politics in Southeast Asia, ranging from the early arrival of Islam in the region to the challenges it generates, and faces, today.

The analysis presented by Means encompasses both the events and actions shaping Islamic politics and the impact of Islamic politics on government and public policy outcomes. It also offers insightful answers to such questions as: How was the Islam that first came to Southeast Asia shaped by four centuries of colonial rule? Are democracy and political Islam compatible? Is Islamic radicalism gaining ground in the region, and what are its prospects for establishing a system of Islamic governance? Is there open opposition to radical Islam?

A fundamental issue raised in the book is whether contemporary regimes in the region have the capacity to address the demands of political Islam and also provide economic and social equity for all citizens, not only to meet basic needs, but also to compete effectively in a globalized world economy.

Gordon Means is professor emeritus of political science at McMaster University. His publications include *Malaysian Politics: The Second Generation* and *The Past in Southeast Asia's Present*, as well as the coedited *Temiar-English, English-Temiar Dictionary* and *Sengoi-English, English-Sengoi Dictionary.*